Issues for Debate in
American Public Policy

Issues for Debate in
American Public Policy

Third Edition

Selections from *The CQ Researcher*

CQ PRESS

A Division of Congressional Quarterly Inc.
Washington, D.C.

CQ Press
1255 22nd Street, N.W., Suite 400
Washington, D.C. 20037

(202) 729-1900; toll-free, 1-866-4CQ-PRESS (1-866-427-7737)

www.cqpress.com

⊚ The paper used in this publication meets the minimum requirements of the American
National Standard for Information Sciences—Permanence of Paper for Printed Library Materials,
ANSI Z39.48-1992.

Printed and bound in the United States of America

06 05 04 03 02   5 4 3 2 1

A CQ Press College Division Publication

Director	Brenda Carter
Acquisitions editor	Charisse Kiino
Marketing manager	Rita Matyi
Managing editor	Ann Davies
Production editors	Precious Sherry and Belinda Josey
Cover designer	Dennis Anderson
Composition	Paul Cederborg
Print buyer	Liza Sanchez
Sales manager	James Headley

Library of Congress Cataloging-in-Publication Data

In process

ISBN: 1-56802-756-7

Photo credits: 21, 24, 41, 61, 93, 94, 101, 108, 112, 132, 134, 138, 157, 160, 162, 164, 167, 168, 170,
177, 189, 197, 200, 217, 219, 222, 228, 232, 240, 268, 275, 280, 281, 283, 291, 301, 304, 307, 311, 314,
AP; 218, 227, 237, 310, Reuters.

Contents

Annotated Table of Contents   ix
Preface   xiii
Contributors   xv

EDUCATION

1 School Vouchers Showdown   1
  Do school voucher plans improve students'
    educational performance?   2
  Do voucher plans hurt public schools?   3
  Do school voucher plans unconstitutionally
    subsidize religious schools?   5
  Background   6
    Common Schools   6
    School Choice   7
    Voucher Experiments   8
  Current Situation   11
    Monitoring Programs   11
    Aiding Religion?   14
  Outlook: Waiting for the Court   16
  Notes   17
  Bibliography   19

2 Testing in Schools   21
  Should standardized tests be used to measure
    school performance?   23
  Do schools do too much to prepare students
    for standardized testing?   24
  Should federal aid be cut for "failing" schools? 26
  Background   28
    Rise of Testing   28
    Raising Alarms   31
    Setting Standards   32
    Campaigning for Tests   33
  Current Situation   34
    Testing in Congress   34
    Testing in the States   36
  Outlook: Testing Results   37
  Notes   38
  Bibliography   39

HEALTH CARE

3 Mental Health Insurance   41
  Would expanded mental health parity force
    employers and workers to drop health
    insurance?   44
  Should mental health parity only apply to
    severe disorders?   46
  Is quality treatment available under managed
    benefits?   48
  Background   51
    Rise of Federal Programs   51
    Push for State Parity   52
    Raising the Profile   53
    New Medications   54
  Current Situation   54
    New Push   54
    Court Breaches Wall   54
  Outlook: Band-Aid Approach?   56
  Notes   57
  Bibliography   59

4 Rating Doctors   61
  Do doctors treat patients based on scientific
    findings?   62
  Have "best-practice" guidelines made medical
    care more effective?   65
  Would public report cards rating doctors
    and hospitals improve care?   67
  Background   68
    Questionable Variations   68
    Rise of Guidelines   72
  Current Situation   72
    Guidelines Controversy   72
    Rating Health Plans   74
    Rewarding Quality   74
  Outlook   76
    High-Tech Solutions   76
    Helping Consumers   76
  Notes   77
  Bibliography   79

SOCIAL POLICY

5 Affordable Housing   **81**
    Is there a housing crisis?   83
    Is prosperity bad for housing?   84
    Is enough being done to solve the affordable-
        housing problem?   85
    Background   88
    U.S. Gets Involved   88
    Congress Acts   90
    Nixon's Legacy   90
    HUD's New Approach   90
    Current Situation   92
    Martinez to Head HUD   92
    Public-Private Efforts   96
    Corporate Initiatives   96
    Predatory Lending   97
    Outlook: President Bush's Focus   97
    Notes   98
    Bibliography   99

6 Welfare Reform   **101**
    Did welfare reform move recipients off the
        welfare rolls and into employment?   104
    Are welfare recipients and their children
        better off after they leave the rolls?   106
    Background   112
    Widows' Relief   112
    Welfare Reform   113
    The Working Poor   115
    Current Situation   116
    Reauthorizing TANF   116
    Work Requirements   116
    Unwed Mothers   119
    Outlook   121
    Decline Tapering Off?   121
    Political Consensus?   121
    Notes   122
    Bibliography   125

7 Affirmative Action   **127**
    Should colleges use race-based admissions
        policies to remedy discrimination against
        minorities?   128
    Should colleges use race-based admissions
        policies to promote diversity in their student
        populations?   130
    Should colleges adopt other policies to try to
        increase minority enrollment?   131
    Background   133
    Unequal Opportunity   133
    Affirmative Action   133
    Negative Reaction   134
    Legal Battles   137
    Current Situation   139
    Legal Confusion   139
    Legal Appeals   140

    Outlook: Ideals and Reality   142
    Notes   142
    Bibliography   144

ENVIRONMENT

8 Nuclear Waste   **145**
    Is Yucca Mountain a safe repository?   146
    Should the U.S. invest in transmutation to
        solve its nuclear waste disposal problem?   147
    Background   148
    The Arms Race   148
    Congress Acts   149
    Current Situation   150
    Opposition in Nevada   150
    Utah Indians' Deal   150
    More Waste?   152
    Outlook: The Jeffords Factor   152
    Notes   154
    Bibliography   155

9 Energy Security   **157**
    Can nuclear power plants be made safe from
        terrorist attack?   159
    Would drilling for oil in the Arctic National
        Wildlife Refuge enhance energy security?   160
    Should conservation play a more prominent
        role in energy policy?   161
    Background   164
    Oil Shocks   164
    Jimmy Carter's Plan   166
    Domestic Risks   167
    Energy Use   168
    Current Situation   169
    Competing Energy Plans   169
    Increasing Security   170
    Outlook: Changing Alliances   172
    Notes   173
    Bibliography   175

CIVIL LIBERTIES, CIVIL RIGHTS AND JUSTICE

10 Civil Liberties in Wartime   **177**
    Should the Justice Department monitor
        conversations between lawyers and
        defendants in the interest of preventing
        further terrorist attacks?   179
    Is the detention of hundreds of terrorism
        suspects an overreaction to the events of
        Sept. 11?   180
    Should the federal government try suspected
        terrorists in a military court?   183
    Has the press bowed to patriotic fervor and
        not reported critically on U.S. efforts to fight
        terrorism?   184

Background 186
Lincoln's Action 186
Attacks on Labor 188
The Palmer Raids 188
Japanese Internment 189
Cold War McCarthyism 189
Current Situation 192
USA Patriot Act 192
Outlook: Back to Normal Soon? 193
Notes 194
Bibliography 195

11 Cyber-Crimes **197**
Is it safe for consumers and merchants to
do business online? 200
Should computer network security problems
be publicly disclosed? 202
Should software companies be liable for
Internet security breaches? 203
Background 204
Early Hackers 204
Phone "Phreaks" 208
Hacking with PCs 208
Anti-Hacking Law 208
Current Situation 210
Cyber-Crime and FOIA 210
Tougher Sentences 212
Outlook: Losing Battle? 213
Notes 213
Bibliography 215

12 Reparations Movement **217**
Should the United States pay reparations to
African-American descendents of slaves? 220
Have efforts to collect reparations for
Holocaust victims gone too far? 221
Does putting a price tag on suffering
diminish that suffering? 223
Background 224
Ancient Notion 224
Native Americans 226
Japanese-Americans 227
The Holocaust 228
Current Situation 230
Reparations for Slavery 230
Outlook: Starting a Dialogue 233
Notes 233
Bibliography 235

BUSINESS AND THE ECONOMY

13 Future Job Market **237**
Are young people out of touch with
job-market realities? 240
Will many of today's young people end
up in "bad" jobs? 242

Will future employees and companies be
loyal to each other? 244
Background 246
The Bad Old Days 246
The IBM Model 246
Downsizing Dinosaurs 248
Current Situation 248
Waiting Out a Recession 248
Bright Spots 249
Lifelong Training 249
Unprepared Graduates 252
Outlook: Labor Shortage 253
Notes 253
Bibliography 255

14 Regulating the New Economy **257**
Should the government be granted
expanded surveillance powers over
the Internet? 259
Should the government lift some regulations
to narrow the "digital divide"? 261
Should states be allowed to collect taxes on
Internet sales? 263
Background 267
To Regulate or Not 267
Action in Congress 268
Current Situation 270
Overhauling the FCC 270
Outlook: Protecting U.S. Security 271
Notes 271
Bibliography 273

FOREIGN POLICY

15 War on Terrorism **275**
Should the U.S. topple foreign governments
that harbor or support terrorists? 278
Will tougher wiretapping and immigration
laws help fight terrorism without unduly
infringing on civil liberties? 279
Will the new Office of Homeland Security
have the authority it needs to protect the
country from terrorists? 282
Background 283
Ages of Terrorism 283
"Blessed" Missions 284
Rule of Law? 287
America Attacked 288
Current Situation 290
Forging a Coalition 290
Military Options 291
Tangled Trails 297
Outlook: More to Come? 298
Notes 298
Bibliography 300

16 Globalization Backlash **301**
    Does globalization hurt people in developing
      countries? 303
    Should the anti-globalization movement
      revise its tactics? 304
    Are police overreacting to the anti-globalization
      movement? 305
  Background 308
  Rise of IMF, World Bank 308
  Zapatistas vs. NAFTA 310

  Current Situation 312
    New Demands 312
    Protests in Colombia 314
    China to Enter WTO 315
  Outlook: New Strategy 315
  Notes 316
  Bibliography 319

Annotated Table of Contents

The 16 *CQ Researcher* articles reprinted in this book have been reproduced essentially as they appeared when first published. In a few cases in which important new developments have occurred since an article came out, these developments are mentioned in the following overviews, which highlight the principle issues examined.

EDUCATION

School Vouchers Showdown

After raging for more than a decade, the school vouchers debate was the subject of a constitutional showdown. On June 27, 2002, the U.S. Supreme Court upheld the constitutionality of a program in Cleveland that provides public funds for tuition at religious and other private schools. A federal appeals court had previously ruled the program improperly subsidized religious schools. Voucher supporters hope the ruling will eliminate constitutional doubts over vouchers, which they say improve educational opportunities and spur educational reform. Opponents say that despite the ruling, they will continue to resist vouchers because they divert money and attention from public schools — the schools attended by 90 percent of U.S. children.

Testing in Schools

President Bush wants to require public schools to test all students in grades 3–8 in reading and math every year. Bush says testing will help teachers to improve student achievement and allow parents and public officials to hold schools and school districts accountable for their performance. The proposal has bipartisan support in Congress and seemingly broad approval from the public. But many educators say the emphasis on testing forces them to spend too much time on test preparation at the expense of more important learning. Some advocacy groups also say that standardized testing has a built-in bias against minority youngsters. And Democratic lawmakers oppose Bush's voucher-type plan to allow students at "failing schools" to use federal aid to attend private schools.

HEALTH CARE

Mental Health Insurance

More than 30 million Americans suffer from schizophrenia, severe depression and other mental disorders. Several years ago, Tipper Gore revealed her struggles with depression. Now, recent events such as the murder trial of Andrea Yates, who drowned her five children, and the Oscar-winning movie "A Beautiful Mind" are again raising the public's awareness of mental illness. Historically, employers' insurance has paid much lower treatment benefits for mental problems than for medical illness. Congress is considering broadening the federal law requiring equal treatment — or "parity" — in health insurance. But conservative lawmakers and business lobbies claim the cost of parity is too high.

Rating Doctors

Recent publicity over medical mistakes has revived a longstanding critique of the quality of American medicine. Just as harmful to patients as outright errors, experts warn, is the profession's reluctance to adopt proven treatments. Hundreds of government and professional guidelines aimed at bringing doctors up to date have gathered dust on physicians' shelves. Doctors have traditionally resisted public disclosure of their failure rates, but some states are already publishing such information. And several big employers are rewarding consumers that use highly rated hospitals. Unless consumers have a reliable way to distinguish good doctors from bad, medical quality will never improve, consumer advocates contend. An Internet-savvy public may soon demand the right to know more.

SOCIAL POLICY

Affordable Housing

The long U.S. economic expansion has been a boon for housing. Prosperity has driven the homeownership rate to a record 67.7 percent, putting two-thirds of the country's households into their own homes. By all measures, Americans are better housed than at any time in the country's history. Yet, there's a black lining to this silver cloud: For millions of Americans — many of them middle-class families — it is impossible to find decent, affordable shelter. The stock of existing low-cost housing is shrinking rapidly, while production of modestly priced housing is stalled. Meanwhile, wages at the bottom quarter of the earnings scale haven't kept pace with housing inflation. An economic slowdown isn't expected to drastically ease what some call an affordability crisis.

Welfare Reform

The destitution among children and single mothers that liberals predicted when welfare was overhauled in 1996 has not come to pass. Conservatives credit the sweeping welfare reforms with a historic rise in employment among former welfare mothers. But many remain in poverty. With welfare reform up for reauthorization in Congress in 2002, Republicans will argue for trimming funding, since half as many people are on welfare. But Democrats will argue for generous funding to help those still unable to work and to assist new workers with child care and other work expenses. More aid may be forthcoming, now that welfare mothers have become the "working poor" — a group the American public is far more willing to help.

Affirmative Action

A major battle over the use of race in college admissions may be headed for the U.S. Supreme Court. Unsuccessful white applicants to the University of Michigan's undergraduate college and law school are challenging policies that give an advantage to minority applicants. The university says the policies are needed to ensure racial and ethnic diversity on campus. A federal judge approved the current undergraduate admissions policy, but another judge struck down the law school's system. A federal appeals court heard the two cases in December 2001; a ruling is still outstanding. Both sides say the cases may reach the Supreme Court, which has not examined the issue since the famous Bakke decision in 1978 barred racial quotas but allowed colleges to consider race as one factor in admissions.

ENVIRONMENT

Nuclear Waste

Tens of thousands of tons of potentially deadly radioactive waste are being temporarily stored at sites around the United States. The Department of Energy is studying the suitability of storing the waste — which is generated by nuclear power plants and nuclear weapons manufacturing — in tunnels deep under Nevada's Yucca Mountain. But scientists, politicians and community activists disagree over whether the site is leakproof, and whether shipping the wastes to the site by rail or truck will endanger communities in the 43 states along the route. Meanwhile, with President Bush calling for the construction of more nuclear power plants to combat what he calls a national "energy crisis," the need for permanent storage could become more acute.

Energy Security

The nation's dependence on foreign oil has troubled energy experts since the Arab oil embargo in 1973. Policies calling for more reliable sources of oil, curbs on energy consumption and the development of alternative fuels have reduced the dependence, but U.S. use of foreign oil still has continued to grow. Now the Sept. 11 terrorist attacks have intensified energy concerns. Some observers say the use of airliners as weapons places the entire domestic energy system at risk, including nuclear power plants and oil pipelines. But most experts agree that the biggest threat to U.S. energy security remains dependence on foreign oil. To reduce the risk, the Bush administration proposes more domestic production — including drilling in the Arctic National Wildlife Refuge — while Democrats favor conservation measures and increased use of renewable fuels.

CIVIL LIBERTIES, CIVIL RIGHTS, AND JUSTICE

Civil Liberties in Wartime

Following the Sept. 11 terrorist attacks on the World Trade Center and the Pentagon, the Bush administration and Congress acted forcefully to deter future incidents. A new law was passed giving the government more authority to conduct surveillance and track Internet communications. The administration also detained more than 600 possible suspects and announced it might use military tribunals to try alleged foreign terrorists. Civil libertarians say the tough, new procedures abridge fundamental constitutional rights like due process and the attorney-client privilege. Some media-watchers, meanwhile, contend that journalists are not aggressively reporting on the war in Afghanistan and the crackdown on terrorism out of fear of seeming unpatriotic during wartime.

Cyber-Crimes

Cyber-crime has reached epidemic proportions. More than 90 percent of the corporations and government agencies responding to a recent survey reported computer-security breaches in 2001. Disgruntled employees and hackers commit many cyber-crimes, and others are committed by con artists using the Web to perpetrate auction fraud, identity theft and other scams. Credit-card users are liable only for the first $50 of fraudulent charges, but financial institutions get hit hard. Identity thefts cost them $2.4 billion in losses and expenses in 2000. Some policymakers, wary of Internet-facilitated terrorist attacks, call for tough, new laws to prevent computer crimes. Others fear that such initiatives will trample civil liberties. Still others want legislation to make Microsoft and other computer-software companies liable for damages caused by their software-security failures.

Reparations Movement

After the Civil War, efforts to compensate former slaves were blocked. Now calls are getting louder for payments to the ancestors of slaves to help the nation come to terms with a gross historical injustice. Opponents worry that reparations would only widen the divide between the races. Meanwhile, survivors of the Nazi Holocaust have had considerable success in obtaining restitution from governments and corporations linked to Hitler's "final solution." Seeking reparations is not about money, they say, but about winning justice for the victims. But some Jewish Americans argue that the reparations movement has turned a historical tragedy into a quest for money. Other mistreated groups recently have picked up the call for reparations, including World War II "comfort women" and Australian Aborigines.

BUSINESS AND THE ECONOMY

Future Job Market

Labor experts predict a shortage of workers over the next two decades. The good news: The best jobs will pay well, even though they will require more education. The bad news: The continuing shift to a service and retail economy means more jobs — such as cashiers and clerks — with low pay, few benefits and limited upward mobility. Yet, the middle ground is not barren. Many high-demand jobs will require modest education or training and still pay fairly well. Jobs in nursing, computer support and dental hygiene require only associate's degrees; desktop publishers and

tractor-trailer truck drivers need only on-the-job training and a vocational certificate. To succeed in the workplace, experts say tomorrow's workers must continually update their skills. They also warn job seekers to be realistic: High aspirations are fine, but there are only so many good jobs to go around.

Regulating the New Economy

The Sept. 11 terrorist attacks on New York and Washington and the subsequent economic downturn have shifted the political landscape for regulating the digital economy. Many observers believe the Internet and other telecommunications systems constitute critical infrastructure in a time of national emergency and contend the government should adopt an industry-friendly approach that is free of onerous regulations. However, important policy debates continue to rage over such issues as the digital divide, Internet taxation and government surveillance of electronic communications. Policymakers will have to factor these issues into broader deliberations over the U.S. economy and national security if they want to develop a coherent framework for governing the technology sector in the face of new terrorist threats.

FOREIGN POLICY

War on Terrorism

The United States attacked Afghanistan in response to the horrific Sept. 11 terrorist attacks on the World Trade Center and the Pentagon that killed more than 3,000 people. Supported by a broad international coalition, President Bush intended to eliminate terrorist leader Osama bin Laden and his global Al Qaeda network, as well as the Taliban government that harbors the Saudi exile. While some analysts say states that support terrorists must be targeted, others caution that toppling governments risks enraging many in the Islamic world and creating legions of new terrorists. Meanwhile, to protect Americans at home, Bush set up a new Office of Homeland Security and asked Congress for sweeping new law enforcement powers. But civil libertarians warn that new police powers might endanger Americans' long-cherished constitutional freedoms.

Globalization Backlash

Last July, 150,000 protesters besieged the world economic summit in Genoa, Italy. The protesters contended that the free trade promoted by globalization is engendering poverty, inequality and environmental degradation on a global scale. Moreover, they said the wealth and prosperity generated by the World Bank and similar institutions mainly benefit multinational corporations, private-sector financiers and corrupt officials. Business leaders and free-trade advocates say that the protesters don't understand the complexities of globalization, and that nations that embrace open trade and investment policies have seen income rise and poverty decrease. Meanwhile, First Amendment advocates warn that tough law-enforcement responses to anti-globalization demonstrations trample protesters' civil liberties.

Preface

Instructors are continually in search of material that will spark intelligent and lively debate in the classroom. And questions about current and controversial public policy issues certainly get students thinking and talking. Do school voucher plans unconstitutionally subsidize religious schools? Should states be allowed to collect taxes on Internet sales? Does globalization hurt people in developing countries? As the world becomes more and more complex, we rely on government to solve a greater range of difficult public problems. To add color and insight to a theoretical understanding of how public policy works, provocative, real-world examples are needed to give students a deeper appreciation of the various ways that government responds to different issues. Presenting an up-to-date collection of recent articles from *The CQ Researcher,* the third edition of *Issues for Debate in American Public Policy* illustrates just how broadly contentious policy issues impact citizens and affect government.

This reader is a compilation of sixteen recent articles from *The CQ Researcher,* a weekly policy brief that offers in-depth looks at complicated issues on the public agenda. *The CQ Researcher* brings often complex issues down to earth. Difficult concepts are not oversimplified, but they are explained in plain English. Offering thorough, objective and forward-looking reporting on a specific topic, each article chronicles and analyzes past legislative and judicial action as well as current and possible future political maneuvering, whether at the local, state or federal level. *Issues for Debate* is designed to encourage discussion, to help readers think critically and actively about these vital issues and to facilitate further research.

The collection is organized into seven subject areas that span a range of important public policy concerns. The pieces were chosen to expose students to a wide range of subjects, from civil rights to foreign policy. We are gratified to know that *Issues for Debate* is appealing to several audiences. It is being used as a supplement in both introductory public policy and American government courses, and interested citizens, journalists and business and government leaders are turning to it to familiarize themselves with key issues, actors and policy positions.

The CQ Researcher

The CQ Researcher was founded in 1923 under a different name: *Editorial Research Reports.* ERR was sold primarily to newspapers, which used it as a research tool. The magazine was given its current name and a design overhaul in 1991. Today, *The CQ Researcher* is still sold to many newspapers, some of which reprint all or part of each issue. But the audience for the magazine has shifted significantly over the years, and today many libraries subscribe. Students, not journalists, are now the primary audience for *The CQ Researcher.*

People who write *Researcher*s often compare the experience with that of drafting a college term paper. Indeed, there are many similarities. Each article is as long as many term papers—about 11,000 words—and is written by one person, without any significant outside help.

Like students, staff writers begin the creative process by choosing a topic. Working with the publication's editors, the writer tries to come up with a subject that has public policy implications and for which there is at least some existing controversy. After a topic is set, the writer embarks on a week or two of intense research. Articles are clipped, books ordered and information gathered from a variety of sources, including interest groups, universities and the government. Once a writer feels well informed about the subject, he or she begins a series of interviews with experts—academics, officials, lobbyists and people working in the field. Each piece usually requires a minimum of ten to fifteen interviews. Some especially complicated subjects call for more. After much reading and interviewing, the writer begins to put the article together.

Chapter Format

Each issue of the *Researcher,* and therefore each selection in this book, is structured in the same way, beginning with an introductory overview of the topic. This first section briefly touches on the areas that will be explored in greater detail in the rest of the chapter.

Following the introduction is a section that chronicles the important debates currently going on in the field. The section is structured around a number of questions known as "Issue Questions," such as "Should standardized tests be used to measure school performance?" or "Does globalization hurt people in developing countries?" This section is the core of each chapter: the questions raised are often highly controversial and usually the object of much argument among those who work in and think about the field. Hence, the answers provided by the writer are never conclusive. Instead, each answer details the range of opinion within the field.

Following these questions and answers is the "Background" section, which provides a history of the issue being examined. This look back includes important legislative and executive actions and court decisions from the past. Readers will be able to see how the current policy evolved.

An examination of existing policy follows the background section. Each "Current Situation" provides an overview of important developments that were occurring when the article was originally published. Finally, each selection ends with an "Outlook" section, which gives a sense of what might happen in the near future. This part looks at whether there might be new regulation afoot, anticipates court rulings and considers possible initiatives from the White House or Capitol Hill.

Each selection contains other regular features that augment the main text. Each selection has two or three sidebars that examine issues related to the topic. An "At Issue" page provides opposing answers to a relevant question, from two outside experts. Also included are a chronology, which cites important dates and events, and an annotated bibliography detailing some of the sources used by the writer of the article.

Acknowledgments

We wish to thank many people for helping to make this collection a reality. Tom Colin, managing editor of *The CQ Researcher,* gave us his enthusiastic support and cooperation as we developed this third edition. He and his talented staff of editors and writers have amassed a first-class library of *Researcher* articles, and we are privileged to have access to that rich cache. We also thankfully acknowledge the advice and feedback from current readers. We are gratified by their success with the book. Several scholars commented on our plans for this revision and helped us keep the volume up to date with articles that seemed especially suited to the classroom. In particular, we thank Richard Barke at Georgia Tech, David M. Brodsky at the University of Tennessee at Chattanooga, Michael Coulter at Grove City College, Kay Hofer at Southwest Texas State University, John Robey at the University of Texas at Brownsville and Pamela Stricker at California State University–San Marcos.

Some readers of this collection may be learning about *The CQ Researcher* for the first time. We expect that many readers will want regular access to this excellent weekly research tool. Anyone interested in subscription information or a no-obligation free trial of the *Researcher* can contact CQ Press at *www.cqpress.com* or 1-866-4CQ-PRESS (1-866-427-7737, toll-free).

We hope that you will be pleased by the third edition of *Issues for Debate in American Public Policy.* We welcome your feedback and suggestions for future editions. Please direct comments to Charisse Kiino, CQ Press, 1255 22nd Street, N.W., Suite 400, Washington, D.C. 20037; or send e-mail to *ckiino@cqpress.com.*

—*The Editors of CQ Press*

Contributors

Thomas J. Colin, managing editor, has been a magazine and newspaper journalist for more than 25 years. Before joining Congressional Quarterly in 1991, he was a reporter and editor at the *Miami Herald* and National Geographic and editor in chief of *Historic Preservation* magazine. He has degrees from the College of William and Mary (English) and the University of Missouri (journalism).

Adriel Bettelheim covers science and technology for the *CQ Weekly.* He is the author of *Aging in America A to Z* (CQ Press, 2001) and was a member of the *CQ Researcher* team that won the 1999 Society of Professional Journalists Award for Excellence for a 10-part series on health care. He has a bachelor's degree in chemistry from Case Western Reserve University.

Mary H. Cooper specializes in environmental, energy and defense issues. Before joining *The CQ Researcher* as a staff writer in 1983, she was a reporter and Washington correspondent for the Rome daily newspaper *l'Unità.* She is the author of *The Business of Drugs* (CQ Press, 1990). She also is a contract translator-interpreter for the U.S. State Department. Cooper graduated from Hollins College in English.

Sarah Glazer specializes in health, education and social policy issues. Her articles have appeared in the *Washington Post, Glamour, The Public Interest* and *Gender and Work,* a book of essays. Glazer covered energy legislation for the Environmental and Energy Study Conference and reported for United Press International. She holds a B.A. in American history from the University of Chicago.

Brian Hansen specializes in environmental issues. He previously reported for the *Colorado Daily* in Boulder and Environment News Service. His awards include the Scripps Howard Foundation award for public service reporting and the Education Writers Association award for investigative reporting. He holds a B.A. in political science and an M.A. in education from the University of Colorado.

Kenneth Jost has covered legal affairs since 1970 and has written for *The CQ Researcher* since 1991. Jost is a graduate of Harvard College and Georgetown University Law Center, a member of the District of Columbia Bar and an adjunct law professor at Georgetown. He is the author of *The Supreme Court Yearbook* (CQ Press) and contributes to the *American Bar Association Journal* and other publications. He was chief legislative assistant to Rep. Al Gore from 1977 to 1980.

Patrick Marshall is a freelance writer in Bainbridge Island, Wash., who specializes in technology, trade and defense issues. He is a former *CQ Researcher* staff writer, reviews editor for *Federal Computer Week,* technology columnist for the *Seattle Times,* and former associate editorial page editor of the *Oakland Tribune.*

David Masci specializes in social policy, religion and foreign affairs. Before joining *The CQ Researcher* as a staff writer in 1996, he was a reporter at CQ's *Daily Monitor* and *CQ Weekly.* He holds a B.A. in medieval history from Syracuse University and a law degree from George Washington University.

Jane Tanner is a freelancer in Charlotte, N.C., who writes for the *New York Times* and other publications. She earned her B.A. (social policy) and M.A. (journalism) degrees from Northwestern University. Her recent *CQ Researcher* reports include "Women in Sports" and "Future Job Market."

1 School Vouchers Showdown

KENNETH JOST

Christine Suma has lived in Cleveland all her life. But no one in her family has ever attended a Cleveland public school — neither she, her husband nor any of their 12 children.

"The public schools don't have the best record in Cleveland," Suma explains. "I don't want my children where they may get an education and they may not. I don't want them where they might be safe or not. I don't want to take a risk with my children. I want a sure bet."

Like their parents, the Suma children have all gone to parochial schools in Cleveland. Up until 1996, the Sumas had to pay the tuition out of their own pockets. Today, however, the family receives about $1,500 in taxpayer funds for each of the children under a controversial school voucher program that faced a constitutional showdown before the Supreme Court. On June 27, 2002, the court upheld the constitutionality of the Cleveland voucher program, although the debate continues between voucher supporters and opponents.

Suma, who intervened in the case to urge the high court to uphold the program, says the vouchers provide the kind of school choices for her children already enjoyed by higher-income families. "I want my education tax dollars put where I want them to go," Suma says. "This voucher system is giving us opportunities."

Doris Simmons-Harris — a single mother of three children who have gone to Cleveland's public schools — has her complaints about the system

From *The CQ Researcher*,
February 15, 2002
(Revised July 2002).

Christine Suma receives $1,500 a year in taxpayer funds per child for her children's Catholic school tuition in Cleveland. The controversial school voucher program faced a constitutional showdown before the U.S. Supreme Court.

Courtesy Institute for Justice

too. But she believes vouchers can only exacerbate the Cleveland schools' major problem: lack of money.

"Our quality went down since I went to school," Simmons-Harris says. "They cut out art classes and after-school activities because of money. My child's in a class in which every child doesn't have a book."

Two of Simmons-Harris' children have graduated from Cleveland schools; her younger son — who has a behavioral disability — is in high school now. She lent her name to the legal challenge against the voucher program in part because she believes the plan would ignore special-needs students like her son.

"He could never go to a private school because of his handicap," Simmons-Harris says. "The public schools take children with a handicap, but a private school would not."

The school vouchers debate has raged for more than a decade over an array of educational policy issues.[1] Advocates of "school choice" — largely, but not exclusively, political conservatives — say families deserve the chance to use public funds at whatever school, public or private, best serves their children's needs. And a voucher system, they say, will create competition that will force stultified public school systems to take needed steps to improve.

Opponents — including teachers' unions and school administrators as well as civil liberties and civil rights groups — argue that vouchers will benefit at most only a few students while diverting resources from the public schools that will continue to educate the vast majority of American youngsters.* In addition, they say neither of the two major public voucher programs operating today — in Cleveland and Milwaukee — has actually produced significant academic gains for the students using the vouchers to attend private schools. A third program, in Florida, has only 44 voucher students. (*See chart, p. 4.*)

So far, the Cleveland and Milwaukee programs both are also attracting fewer students than the number of vouchers that could be awarded. The Wisconsin legislature capped Milwaukee's program at 15 percent of the system's current enrollment; that would

---

* An estimated 47.2 million youngsters attended public schools and 5.9 million were in private schools in fall 2001, according to the National Center on Education Statistics. Catholic schools enroll close to 50 percent of private school students, other religious schools about 35 percent and nonsectarian schools about 15 percent.

allow slightly more than 15,000 students, but only 10,882 are currently receiving vouchers. In Cleveland the number of voucher students is theoretically limited by the size of the state appropriation for the program. But over the past three years the program has not spent some 37 percent of the $33.8 million allocated.

The issue has split racial and ethnic minorities, who constitute the major populations served by the big-city systems most often depicted by critics as "failing schools." School choice advocates have gained allies among African-Americans and Latinos by touting vouchers as an immediate option for minority youngsters to escape low-performing schools.

"For right now, vouchers are the only means to provide parents with the opportunity to select a school environment from a menu of schools that's best for their children," says Kaleem Caire, president of the two-year-old Black Alliance for Educational Options (BAEO).

Traditional civil rights groups, however, insist that vouchers will end up hurting most minority youngsters. "Vouchers might be good for the few poor kids who can take advantage of them," says Theodore Shaw, associate director of the NAACP Legal Defense and Educational Fund. "But systemically, they are going to further undercut public education, where the vast majority of African-American, Latino and poor children are going to remain."

Despite the broad-ranging debate, the issue facing the Supreme Court when it heard arguments Feb. 20 on the constitutionality of the Cleveland voucher program was a narrow one. The justices were asked to decide whether the program — now in its sixth year — aids religious schools in violation of the Establishment Clause, the Bill of Rights provision that bars any law "respecting the establishment of religion." The court eventually ruled that the program is not an unconstitutional endorsement of religion.

Opponents — who filed a federal court challenge to the plan after the Ohio Supreme Court gave its blessing to the program — emphasize that virtually all of the 4,456 students currently receiving vouchers are attending religious schools.

"This is nothing but a direct subsidy of the educational mission of religious denominations," says Barry Lynn, executive director of Americans United for Separation of Church and State. "And in the same way that one should not expect taxpayers to support churches, they should not be expected to support church-related educational facilities either."

Supporters counter that both the Cleveland and Milwaukee systems leave it up to parents to decide where to use the tax-paid stipends.

"The scholarship program is neutral on its face," says Clint Bolick, litigation director of the Institute for Justice, the Washington-based libertarian law firm that has spearheaded the voucher movement. "Funds are directed to religious schools only through the true private choices of individual parents, therefore satisfying Establishment Clause requirements."

The case — formally called *Zelman v. Simmons-Harris*, after Ohio's superintendent of public instruction, Susan Tave Zelman — reached the Supreme Court after a series of recent decisions that somewhat loosened the restrictions on government programs that benefit religious schools. In the most recent of those decisions, the court in *Mitchell v. Helms* in 2000 approved a federally funded program for lending computers and other equipment to parochial schools. [2]

Supporters and opponents of vouchers vow to continue their fight in state legislatures around the country, despite the court's decision.

Voucher proponents say they have the momentum on the issue. "The movement is progressing extremely well," says Bolick, "and I think it will

continue to produce educational opportunities for children regardless of what happens in the Supreme Court."

But opponents point out that legislatures in only three states — Wisconsin, Ohio, and, most recently, Florida — have approved voucher plans, while voters have rejected voucher or tuition tax-credit ballot proposals in five states since 1990. (*See chart, p. 8*.)

"It's very hard to believe that they have momentum, since every single ballot initiative has been defeated," says Robert Chanin, general counsel of the National Education Association (NEA), the country's largest teachers' union. "Everybody keeps proposing [voucher statutes], and nobody passes them."

Pollsters get somewhat different results on school vouchers depending on the phrasing of the question, but the most recent polls indicate that a majority of Americans oppose the idea, and that support has declined since the late 1990s. In the most favorable result for voucher advocates, 44 percent of respondents said last year that they would favor a proposal that would allow parents to send their children to any school of their choice with the government paying all or part of private school tuition; 54 percent of the respondents said they would oppose such a proposal. [3]

As the voucher debate continues, here are some of the major questions that divide supporters and opponents:

Do school voucher plans improve students' educational performance?

Six years into the Cleveland voucher program, student test scores have risen enough to encourage supporters, but not enough to impress or win over opponents. The results in other programs are similarly murky, though researchers generally appear to agree that African-American students in privately funded voucher schemes are making distinctive gains.

Researchers at Indiana University's Indiana Center for Evaluation have officially evaluated Cleveland's program each year since its inception. [4] They found no significant differences in academic progress between voucher students and comparable public school students after the first year. In the next two evaluations, they measured distinctive gains in language and science, but not in reading, mathematics or social studies.

In the most recent of the Indiana evaluations — published in September 2001 — researchers found that students who entered the voucher program as kindergartners had higher test scores as first-graders than other students, but by the end of third grade the gap had narrowed.

"Vouchers make at least a small but statistically significant difference," says Kim Metcalf, the center's director and an associate professor in the department of curriculum and instruction at the university's School of Education.

In Milwaukee's voucher program, scant information exists about students' academic performance, partly because test scores have not been collected since the 1994–95 school year, when the program was limited to secular schools and had few participants. The legislature dropped testing and evaluation requirements when it expanded the program. The official evaluator — John Witte, director of the University of Wisconsin's La Follette School of Public Affairs in Madison — reported no significant academic gains for voucher students compared to others, though research teams from Harvard and Princeton did find some distinctive gains for voucher students in some areas. [5]

Voucher supporters acknowledge that the evidence of academic gains is spotty at best. "The findings range from mildly positive to strongly positive," Bolick says. But, he adds, "I am unaware of any study that does not find at least mildly positive results from school choice in terms of academic performance. I expect those findings will grow stronger when later studies are done in terms of graduation rates."

"The impacts are not detectable for any groups other than African-Americans," says Paul E. Peterson, a prominent voucher advocate and director of the Program on Education Policy and Governance at Harvard's Kennedy School of Government in Cambridge, Mass.

Voucher opponents say studies show the programs do not produce the academic gains supporters predict. "There is almost nothing in the research literature that suggests vouchers succeed as an academic intervention," says Alex Molnar, a confirmed voucher opponent who taught at the University of Wisconsin in Milwaukee before moving to Arizona State University at Tempe last August. "There is no clear benefit one way or another with respect to the academic performance of students."

"When you get behind the hired guns or the committed proponents and look at the more objective [studies] — those written by researchers retained by a specific state — at best it's a wash," says Chanin, the NEA lawyer.

The evidence of gains among African-American students comes from three privately funded scholarship programs in Dayton, Ohio; New York City and Washington, D.C. A study by Peterson's group at Harvard released in September 2000 found that African-American students scored 6 percentiles higher in overall test performance than control-group students. But no statistically significant effects, positive or negative, were found among other ethnic groups. [6]

Peterson calls the gains for black students "fairly sizable" — comparable, he says, to the gains found in a recent class-size reduction experiment in Tennessee. "If you got that kind of impact in subsequent years, you could talk about reducing the test-score gap between blacks and whites," he says.

Indiana University's Metcalf acknowledges the gains but questions whether they can be attributed to vouchers. "We don't know how that effect was produced," he says. "One pos-

sible reason is that [scholarship students] have been put in classrooms with higher-achieving classmates whose families are more supportive of education. It may be a peer effect, not related to the productivity of the school itself."

Overall, two disinterested research organizations — the U.S. General Accounting Office and the Rand Corporation, the respected private research organization — find that the evidence of academic gains among voucher students is inconclusive so far. "Long-term effects on academic skills and attainment are as yet unexamined," Rand researchers write in a book-length study published last summer. [7] The GAO says "little or no" evidence of academic gains has been found in official evaluations in Milwaukee and Cleveland. [8]

For his part, Metcalf agrees that the evidence is inconclusive, but he sees a trend in favor of vouchers. "It isn't clear yet whether it's a good thing or a bad thing, but the data have not been negative about vouchers," Metcalf concludes.

Do voucher plans hurt public schools?

With no recent test scores, Milwaukee's voucher program offers no good opportunity to examine its effect on students receiving the stipends. But one prominent researcher says the decade-long experiment does provide useful — and encouraging — information about the effects on the overall performance of the city's public schools.

To test the hypothesis that vouchers will encourage public schools to change because of increased competition, Harvard economics Professor Caroline Hoxby studied academic performance in Milwaukee public schools since the start of the experiment. She found above-average gains in many of the schools — and particularly high gains in schools in low-income neighborhoods that she said faced the greatest "competition" from vouchers.

"Overall, . . . public schools made a

The Nation's Three Public Voucher Programs

Milwaukee's Parental Choice Program is the oldest and largest of the nation's three publicly funded voucher programs. Florida's "A-Plus" program is the newest, and the only statewide program. The Supreme Court ruled June 27, 2002, whether the Cleveland program violates the U.S. Constitution.

Program (Date Established)	Number of students receiving vouchers	Amount of voucher	Eligibility Requirements	Percentage of voucher students attending religious schools
Milwaukee Parental Choice Program (1990)	10,882	$5,553 (max.) (based on tuition)	Parents' income 175% of poverty level ($30,000 for household of four); child attended public school (any grade) or private school (K-3), enrolled in Choice program prior year.	70% (est.)
Cleveland Pilot Scholarship and Tutoring Program (1995)	4,456	$2,250 (max.; varies with income) (Parent pays min. 10% of tuition)	Parents' income up to 200% of federal poverty level ($35,000) for maximum amount; others receive $1,875; schools limited to $2,500 tuition.	96-99% *
Florida "A-Plus" Accountability and School Choice Program (1999)	44	$3,700 (max.)	Child attended Florida public school graded "F" in 2 out of 4 previous years (two schools so far); no income eligibility.	90.9%

* Lower figure for 1999-2000 school year, from Ohio Dept. of Education; higher figure for 2001-2002 school year from the education newsletter Catalyst-Cleveland.

Sources: Wisconsin Dept. of Public Instruction; Ohio Dept. of Education; Florida Dept. of Education

strong push to improve achievement in the face of competition from vouchers," Hoxby writes in an academic paper on her study. [9] In an interview, she is more direct: "They improved a lot for three years in a row at an absolutely unprecedented rate. As an educational researcher, I've never seen improvement like that."

Rand researcher Brian Gill finds Hoxby's study provocative. "I don't think that's a definitive result, but it's certainly very promising," he says. But two other experts familiar with the Milwaukee program — with opposite viewpoints on vouchers — dismiss the report.

"I don't think there's any evidence" for Hoxby's conclusion, says Witte, who supports vouchers targeted at low-income students and is the official

evaluator of the Wisconsin project. "Test scores did go up, but they've now flattened out. I think they went up because there was an enormous push to get them up" — not because of the voucher program.

Voucher opponent Molnar also finds Hoxby's study unpersuasive. He says the test scores she used are "incomplete" and "not comparable" between different schools. More broadly, he says, Hoxby's conclusion requires "a series of [unrealistic] assumptions" about the reasons for the changes in reported test scores. "It's silly," Molnar says. "Schools and schooling are complex. [Hoxby's conclusion] flies in the face of all the things that we know about human beings and human nature."

A similar debate is raging over the effects of Florida's "A-Plus Accountability

and School Choice Program," which provides vouchers to students attending public schools that fail to improve performance one year after receiving an "F" grade in a state evaluation. Jay P. Greene, a research associate at Harvard's Program on Education Policy and Governance, found evidence that schools that received a failing grade in 1999 — and thus faced the threat of vouchers — achieved test-score gains more than twice those recorded at other schools in Florida. But Gregory Camilli, a professor of education at Rutgers Graduate School of Education, concludes that Greene "vastly overestimated" the test score gains and contends that other aspects of Florida's program besides the threat of vouchers may be responsible for any improvements. [10]

Critics of vouchers say that far from

helping, the stipends will actually hurt public schools — first, by providing incentives for better students to leave the public education system, and, second, by diverting money and other resources from already struggling public schools.

The evidence on the so-called cream-skimming issue is sketchy and inconclusive. Official evaluators Witte in Milwaukee and Metcalf in Cleveland say students entering the two voucher programs had achievement levels and demographic characteristics similar to other low-income public school students. On the other hand, the parents of voucher students — predominantly, single mothers — had slightly higher education levels and appeared more strongly motivated than parents of other students.

As for the fiscal impact, critics say the methods of funding both the Cleveland and Milwaukee programs take money from the public school systems. Supporters counter that both school systems continue to receive more per capita state aid than the cost of the vouchers, and that in any event the schools save money by having fewer students to educate.

Most broadly, voucher opponents contend that vouchers divert energy and attention, as well as money, from more productive education reforms.

"You've got powerful long-term studies that demonstrate the impact of early childhood education on the later educational success of children who participate in those programs," Molnar says. "Would I choose vouchers over that? No.

"What about reducing classroom size? The evidence suggests that that is a powerful intervention. What about providing high-quality educational opportunities for poor children over the summer? Research suggests that poor kids 'fall behind' because of what happens over the summer. Would I choose vouchers over any of those? No."

But Bolick of the Institute for Justice insists that the Cleveland and Milwau-

kee programs — as well as the newer, more limited program in Florida — have pressured the school systems to change because of the fear of losing voucher students to private schools.

"The Cleveland system was one of the absolute worst in the country," Bolick says. "Two years ago, it failed every one of 28 of the state's criteria. This year, it passed three. These were the first stirrings of signs of life in an extremely troubled system."

Competition, Bolick says, is the key: "The rules of economics are not suspended at the schoolhouse door."

Do school voucher plans unconstitutionally subsidize religious schools?

When Milwaukee began its voucher program in 1990, the rules effectively limited participation to a handful of secular private schools established to serve low-income, minority students. Five years later, after lobbying by the Roman Catholic archdiocese and the business community, the Republican-controlled legislature expanded the program to include parochial schools.

"Catholic schools were the moving force on the 1995 legislation," Witte says. "The archdiocese was heavily involved."

The change — signed into law by then-Gov. Tommy Thompson, now President Bush's secretary of Health and Human Services — was immediately challenged in court as an unconstitutional subsidy for religious schools. But the Wisconsin Supreme Court rejected the challenge in 1998 — allowing the program to more than triple its enrollment at the beginning of the 1998-1999 school year.

Parochial-school advocates have battled over public-funding issues since the mid-1800s. In a series of decisions since 1948, the U.S. Supreme Court has approved some programs that provided aid to parochial-school students but barred more direct subsidies. The court's most recent decisions have loosened, but not eliminated, restrictions

on the use of public funds at church-affiliated schools.

Church-state separationists argue that the use of vouchers at parochial schools violates the Constitution's prohibition against government establishment of religion. "The one central message [in the First Amendment] is that government is not intended to directly support religion — not one particular religion or religion in general," says Lynn of Americans United for Separation of Church and State.

But parochial-school advocates argue that both the Cleveland and Milwaukee programs meet the Supreme Court's guidelines on aid to religious schools. Scholarships are constitutional, says Mark Chopko, general counsel of the U.S. Conference of Catholic Bishops, if they are awarded "based on neutral, non-religious criteria that do not create incentives for choosing to attend religious schools."

Chopko acknowledges the financial problems facing parochial schools. "They're running at the line or below the line constantly," he says. But he forcefully denies that either of the programs in Cleveland or Milwaukee is a "bailout" for the parochial systems. "Absolutely not," he says.

Instead, Chopko views the programs as supporting Catholic schools' updated mission of providing education for mostly non-Catholic, mostly minority students in inner cities. "The participation of religious schools in these programs has been to qualify as providers of the assistance," Chopko continues. "The beneficiaries are really the children in these school districts."

Lynn, however, says Catholic schools — as well as schools operated by Christians, Jews, Muslims or other faiths — serve primarily religious purposes.

"Religious schools exist to promote faith," says Lynn, a United Church of Christ minister. "It doesn't just happen in a religion class. Religion imbues the curriculum in a Catholic school or a Muslim school from the time the bell

Vouchers in Cleveland

March 3, 1995 *Federal judge, ruling in school desegregation case, orders state takeover of Cleveland public school system.*

June 28, 1995 *Ohio General Assembly approves Pilot Scholarship Program aimed at providing vouchers for low-income families in Cleveland; signed by Gov. George Voinovich on June 30.*

January 1996 *Challenge to voucher program filed in state court.*

July 31, 1996 *State court judge rules program constitutional.*

September 1996 *Program takes effect for 1996-97 school year.*

May 27, 1999 *Ohio Supreme Court rules program unconstitutional but says program does not improperly aid religious schools.*

June 29, 1999 *Gov. Bob Taft signs bill re-enacting program.*

July 20, 1999 *New challenge filed in federal court.*

Aug. 24, 1999 *Federal Judge Solomon Oliver issues preliminary injunction against program.*

Nov. 5, 1999 *Supreme Court, by 5-4 vote, stays injunction, allowing program to continue, pending further proceedings.*

Dec. 20, 1999 *Judge Oliver rules program unconstitutional.*

Dec. 11, 2000 *Federal appeals court in Cincinnati affirms lower court decision, 2-1.*

Sept. 25, 2001 *Supreme Court agrees to hear appeal by state, private schools and pro-voucher parents.*

Feb. 20, 2002 *U.S. Supreme Court hears arguments.*

June 27, 2002 *U.S. Supreme Court upholds constitutionality of the Ohio school voucher program.*

rings in the morning until the children are dismissed in the afternoon."

Opponents of the Cleveland program are basing their legal challenge on the evidence that the vast majority of the schools participating in the program are church-affiliated and enroll all but a small number of the voucher students. Of the 50 schools currently participating, only four are secular; the others include 37 Catholic schools, seven affiliated with other Christian denominations and two Islamic academies.

The opponents contend that the program inevitably channels students to parochial schools because of the relatively low limit on tuition — $2,500 — that participating schools can charge. Catholic schools — subsidized by church funds — typically have lower tuition than secular private schools.

"When the government sets up a program and says you can spend this money only in the limited universe of schools — the vast majority of which are religious — that's not a free and independent choice by the parents," says the NEA's Chanin. "It's a choice dictated by the government."

Bolick says he expects more non-religious schools to participate in the programs over time. In any event, he says, the predominant role of parochial schools in the programs today is no grounds for throwing them out.

"The question is whether the fact that only a few non-religious schools elected to throw an educational life preserver should mean that the whole voucher program should be invalidated," Bolick says. "In my view, to ask the question is to answer it."

Legal advocates and experts have differing views about how the court is likely to rule on the constitutional issues. Apart from that, however, Rand researcher Gill sees "no good reason" to exclude Catholic schools from voucher programs.

"There is some research indicating that they may have unique benefits" for at-risk students, especially African-Americans, Gill says. Another reason "is the common-sense notion that to exclude the largest number of private schools seems counterproductive." ■

BACKGROUND

Common Schools

Public and private education have co-existed throughout American history. [11] Church-affiliated schools dominated in Colonial times, but so-called common schools — tax-supported, secular public schools with compulsory, universal attendance — began to take shape in the 1800s and gained nearly complete acceptance by the start of the 20th century. Private and religious schools remained an important feature of U.S. education, but received only limited government assistance.

Thomas Jefferson advocated free, universal public education as early as 1779, but the creation of the common school is normally attributed to an education reform movement of the 1830s and '40s. [12] The most prominent of the reformers was Horace Mann, who — as secretary of the board of education in Massachusetts from 1837 to 1849 — supervised the establishment of the country's first statewide educational system. Mann strongly believed in the value of education in promoting character and citizenship but disapproved of teaching what he called "doctrinal religion" — favoring one particular sect or denomination over another. [13]

The church-affiliated schools of Colonial times were — like the colonists themselves — predominantly Protestant. By the 1830s, however, Catholic immigration to the United States was increasing rapidly — first from Ireland and later in the century from Southern and Eastern Europe. The influx of Catholics engendered nativist intolerance among many Protestant Americans. For their part, Catholics, accustomed to religious schools in their native lands and resentful of the dominant Protestantism of American public schools, wanted their own schools.

The issue of public funding for religious schools flared as early as the 1820s, fueled both by the incipient common school movement and by anti-Catholic sentiment. [14] The Free School Society of New York City — forerunner of the public school system — successfully moved in 1822 to block church-affiliated schools from receiving grants from the city's school fund. Two decades later, New York Gov. William Seward called for public funding for parochial schools in order to ensure the education of the newly arriving Catholic immigrants. The legislature approved instead a bill barring public funds for any school that taught "any religious sectarian doctrine or tenet." The law left funding issues to local districts; New York City continued to bar funds for most parochial schools.

Divisions between public and parochial school advocates intensified after the Civil War. President Ulysses Grant recommended legislation in 1875 to prohibit the use of public funds "for the benefit of . . . any religious sect or denomination." As later introduced by Sen. James Blaine, R-Maine, the proposal called for barring funds to schools teaching "sectarian" tenets. The Blaine amendment became a partisan issue between Republicans and Democrats, who cultivated the Catholic vote in the North and Midwest. Although the amendment failed, Congress later required newly admitted states to establish public schools "free from sectarian controls." [15]

By the early 1900s, the public school system had taken shape with tax-supported education and compulsory-attendance laws in all states. Some public school advocates even tried to prohibit private and religious education. Oregon enacted such a law — with evident anti-Catholic motivation. In a landmark decision, the U.S. Supreme Court ruled it unconstitutional. Parents have a constitutional right to choose how to educate their children, the court ruled unanimously. [16]

Despite the constitutional protection, Catholic schools have had a hard time in the 20th century. Enrollment declined from 19th-century levels because of the increased availability of public schooling and — especially after World War II — because of growing assimilationist tendencies among Catholic families. Parochial schools received some government assistance, but over time financial aid was limited. The Supreme Court approved textbook loans and transportation for parochial-school students but eventually banned direct government funding in order to enforce separation of church and state. By the 1970s, many Catholic educators were openly asking whether Catholic schools could survive.

School Choice

The current school voucher movement originated not among parochial-school advocates but with a seminal academic article written in the mid-1950s by the libertarian economist Milton Friedman. [17] Support for the idea was originally limited to conservatives, but popular discontent with public education fed its growth, along with the conservative resurgence during Ronald Reagan's presidency in the 1980s. Then in the 1990s school choice supporters broadened their constituencies by successfully persuading many African-Americans that vouchers offered a way for black youngsters to escape inadequate, inner-city schools.

Friedman's 23-page article — simply entitled "The Role of Government in Education" — accepted the goal of compulsory universal education. [18] But he contended that government could accomplish that goal more effectively by giving families fixed amounts of money — vouchers — for them to use to enroll their children at schools, publicly or privately operated, that met certain standards of curriculum and instruction. The "denationalization of education," he said, would "widen the range of choice available to parents" by bringing about "a healthy increase in the variety of educational institutions available and in competition among them."

The article drew sufficient attention to prompt Virgil Blum, a Jesuit priest and political scientist at Marquette University, to found in 1957 a still-extant advocacy group, Citizens for Educational Freedom, to lobby for vouchers. A decade later, the liberal Harvard University sociologist Christopher Jencks endorsed a more regulated voucher system, with individual amounts adjusted to give greater benefits to low-income families. [19] Jencks' article in the journal *Public Interest* — "Are Public Schools Obsolete?" — prompted the Office of Economic Opportunity to offer grants to test the voucher concept in a few cities. One test — from 1972 to 1976 in a suburb of San Jose, Calif. — produced limited results and drew lukewarm reactions.

Voters in Eight States Reject Vouchers

Voters overwhelmingly rejected providing parents with vouchers and tuition tax credits in the eight states that have voted on proposals. Since 1972, the votes against vouchers have been 60 percent or more.

Voucher Referenda, 1970-2000

State	Year	Election Result	
		Vote Against	Vote For
Michigan, Proposal C *	1970	43.2%	56.8%
Maryland, Question #18, General Election	1972	55.0	45.0
Michigan, Proposal H	1978	74.0	26.0
Colorado, Amendment 7	1992	66.8	33.2
California, Proposition 174	1993	70.0	30.0
Washington state, Initiative 173	1996	64.5	35.5
Michigan, Proposal 1	2000	69.0	31.0
California, Proposition 38	2000	70.7	29.3

Tuition Tax-Credit Referenda 1981-1998

State	Year	Vote Against	Vote For
Washington, D.C., Initiative 7	1981	89.0	11.0
Utah, Initiative C	1988	70.0	30.0
Oregon, Measure 11	1990	67.0	33.0
Colorado, Amendment 17	1998	60.3	39.7

* Proposal C amended the Michigan Constitution to prohibit any direct and indirect public funding to aid non-public elementary or secondary schools — thus the vote for the proposal was a vote against vouchers.

Source: People for the American Way Foundation, February 2002

Interest in vouchers remained low through the 1970s, but President Reagan gave the movement a major boost in the 1980s by endorsing a different school choice mechanism: tuition tax credits for private schools. The Reagan administration also boosted the voucher movement by the 1983 publication of the famous — some would say infamous — critique of the American education system, *A Nation at Risk.* Public school critics acclaimed the report — depicting U.S. students as falling behind students from other countries in such areas as science and math — as a needed wake-up call,

but public school advocates denounced it as alarmist and thinly documented.

The new attention produced no concrete results, however. Congress spurned Reagan's tuition tax-credit proposal; and the vast majority of school officials, education advocacy groups and education policy experts continued to oppose vouchers through the 1980s.

Then at the end of the decade, two academics — Brookings Institution senior fellow John Chubb and Stanford University political scientist Terry Moe — breathed new life into the movement with their book, *Politics, Markets and America's Schools.* [20] They

called for creation of a voucher-driven, competitive marketplace for education among public and private schools, including religious schools. Public-school bureaucracies would be replaced with "choice offices" and "parent information centers." Schools themselves would be minimally regulated and would be free to set their own admission policies subject only to non-discrimination requirements.

Chubb and Moe called the concerns about failing schools especially "grave" in inner cities and proposed higher stipends for students with "very special educational needs — arising from economic deprivation, physical handicaps, language difficulties, emotional problems and other disadvantages." [21] Apart from that proviso, however, Chubb and Moe presented their proposal as a universal reform, not one targeted at disadvantaged youngsters. But in the 1990s, school choice advocates discovered that targeting voucher proposals at low-income students was an effective strategy for moving the idea out of academic discussion and into the real world.

Voucher Experiments

Voucher proponents finally got a chance to test their theories in the 1990s in the two closely watched, sharply contested programs in Milwaukee and Cleveland. Both programs drew support from conservatives broadly critical of public education and African-Americans specifically disenchanted with inner-city public schools. Teachers' unions, civil rights groups and church-state separationists opposed both programs before they were established and — in court — afterward. Both sides looked to the Supreme Court for some word on the constitutional issues while girding for continuing fights regardless of how the court rules.

The prime mover for the Milwaukee

Chronology

Before 1950

"Common schools" become dominant pattern in U.S. education; private schools given constitutional protection but religiously affiliated systems struggle financially.

1884
U.S. Conference of Catholic Bishops calls for parochial schools in every parish, triggering unsuccessful congressional effort to bar government funds for religious schools.

1925
Supreme Court upholds parents' right to send children to private schools.

1950s–1970s

First stirrings of school voucher proposals, with limited effect; Catholic schools seek government funds as enrollment falls, but Supreme Court limits assistance by barring direct subsidies.

1955
Economist Milton Friedman publishes article calling for universal system of vouchers for parents to use to pay for children's education in public or private schools of their choice, but it has little immediate impact.

1973
Supreme Court bars direct government subsidies of parochial schools or tuition reimbursement or tax credits for parents of parochial-school students.

1980s *School choice movement gains strength.*

1983
U.S. Department of Education report, *A Nation at Risk*, damns public schools for "mediocre" education; public school advocates call report alarmist, undocumented.

1990s *Voucher programs established in Milwaukee, Cleveland; challenged in court with mixed results. Voters reject vouchers in several states.*

1990
Wisconsin legislature approves program to provide vouchers to low-income students in Milwaukee for use at non-religious schools; scholars John E. Chubb and Terry M. Moe detail proposal for universal voucher system in their book, *Politics, Markets and America's Schools.*

1995
Wisconsin legislature expands Milwaukee voucher program to allow parochial schools to participate; move brings court challenge based on separation of church and state.

1997
Supreme Court rules, 5-4, that school systems can provide federally funded remedial and enrichment services on the grounds of parochial schools.

1998
Wisconsin Supreme Court upholds constitutionality of Milwaukee voucher program in June; U.S. Supreme Court declines in November to review decision.

1999
Florida approves first statewide voucher program, providing stipends for students at schools that receive "failing" grade and do not improve performance after one year; Illinois approves tax credits for families for private-school tuition; Maine and Vermont supreme courts uphold exclusion of religious schools from public "tuitioning" programs; Cleveland federal judge rules voucher program unconstitutional, but Supreme Court allows program to continue, pending appeal.

2000s *Legal challenges to voucher programs continue; voters reject voucher proposals.*

June 28, 2000
U.S. Supreme Court upholds, 6-3, federally funded program to lend computers and other equipment to parochial schools; school choice advocates say opinions support constitutionality of vouchers.

Nov. 7, 2000
Voters in California, Michigan reject voucher proposals by 2-1 margins.

Dec. 11, 2000
Cleveland voucher program ruled unconstitutional by federal appeals court in Cincinnati by 2–1 vote.

Sept. 25, 2001
U.S. Supreme Court agrees to hear Cleveland voucher case; arguments heard Feb. 20, 2002.

June 27, 2002
U.S. Supreme Court upholds constitutionality of Ohio school voucher program.

Parochial Schools on the Move

New Catholic schools are going up in fast-growing suburbs and exurbs around the country, where they are attracting growing numbers of non-Catholic students. But total enrollment in Catholic schools has risen only slightly over the past decade, and Roman Catholic archdioceses are shuttering schools in many big cities that form their traditional base.

The modest growth over the past decade reverses a 40-year-long decline that saw Catholic school enrollment fall by half. The total number of schools has continued to decrease, however, and many of the remaining schools are struggling financially — often raising tuitions to come closer to covering their real costs. [1]

Despite the financial problems, Catholic educators present an upbeat picture of their system — which last year enrolled about 2.6 million students. Enrollment is increasing, they say, because Catholic schools offer a safe, quality education for inner-city families and a values-rich education for urban and suburban families alike.

"The state of many inner-city schools leads parents to want something a little more secure for their children," says Sister Glenn Anne McPhee, secretary for education of the U.S. Conference of Catholic Bishops in Washington.

Catholic schools are growing in the suburbs even though public school systems there are often regarded as providing a good education. "In suburban areas, parents are looking for more in the spiritual dimension of their children's education," says Sister Dale McDonald, director of public policy and research at the National Catholic Educational Association.

The parochial school system of today traces back to the decision by the bishops' conference in 1884 to call on every Catholic parish to establish a school. "Popular education has always been a chief object of the Church's care," the bishops declared in a pastoral letter. [2] In contrast to other Western countries, however, the United States has generally not provided direct funding for Catholic schools.

Despite the limited governmental support, Catholic school enrollment grew to more than 5 million by 1950. But a combination of factors caused enrollment to shrink drastically over the next 40 years. Catholics formed part of the population shift from city to suburb. Church attendance declined. And the number of nuns — who traditionally held most of the teaching positions — declined as fewer women entered religious orders.

By 1990, enrollment stood at around 2.5 million students. The number has increased about 2.7 percent since then, to 2,647,301 — including 2,004,037 elementary or middle-school students and 643,264 high school students. The figure includes about 358,000 non-Catholics, or nearly 14 percent of the total.

Hispanics comprise 11 percent of the total, and African-Americans about 8 percent; total minority enrollment is 26 percent.

With the nation's population shifts, new Catholic schools are going up in the suburbs and in the South and West: Some 54 new facilities were built last year. Out of 8,146 Catholic schools, nearly half — 44 percent — have waiting lists for admissions. But schools in inner cities are being closed or consolidated — 61 last year — usually because they are under capacity.

Catholic educators tout the academic benefits of parochial schools. John Witte, director of the University of Wisconsin's La Follette School of Public Affairs and formerly the official evaluator for Milwaukee's school voucher program, says research studies do document favorable results for Catholic schools.

For example, Catholic school students are less likely to drop out and more likely to go on to college and stay in college, Witte says. He also says that "the majority of studies" indicate some "achievement effects" in terms of higher test scores. But he adds that experts disagree whether those studies "have adequately controlled for selection into and expulsion from Catholic schools." [3]

Whatever the academic benefits, Catholic educators stress that religion is an integral part of the curriculum. "Our schools are still thoroughly Catholic," McPhee says. "Catholic values permeate all curriculum areas." McDonald, however, adds that the increased number of non-Catholics has made the schools "more inclusive."

Voucher proposals like those enacted in Milwaukee and Cleveland offer one source of financial support for Catholic schools, Catholic educators and officials acknowledge. But they insist that the church is committed to providing education in the inner city with or without vouchers.

"If there were no voucher program, we would continue to try to educate children in the same way," says Mark Chopko, general counsel of the bishops' conference. McPhee agrees: "The Catholic Church has made a commitment to remain in the inner city as a beacon of hope for many inner-city parents who want something that's not only safe but also very community-minded."

---

[1] See *United States Catholic Elementary and Secondary School Statistics, 2000-2001* (2001), www.ncea.org.

[2] Cited in Mark E. Chopko, "American and Catholic: Reflections on the Last Century in Catholic Church-State Relations." The paper will appear as a chapter in a forthcoming book on church-state relations being prepared by the DePaul University Center for Church/State Studies to be published by Carolina Academic Press in 2002.

[3] For background, see Anthony S. Bryk, Valerie E. Lee, and Peter B. Holland, *Catholic Schools and the Common Good* (1993).

---

voucher program was Polly Williams, a black Democratic state senator who began pushing the idea in the late 1980s to give black youngsters alternatives to the city's public schools. As approved by the Wisconsin legislature in 1990, the program provided vouchers up to $2,500 to a maximum of 950 low-income families to be used only at non-religious schools. Since then, the legislature has increased both the amount of the voucher and the number of participants, and opened the program in 1995 to participation by parochial schools. Today, voucher advocate Moe says the Milwaukee program was the first to show that vouchers could be "politically potent" when targeted solely at kids who need help the most." [22]

In Cleveland, the impetus for the voucher program came from a federal judge's March 1995 ruling in a school-desegregation suit, in which he ordered that the state take over the troubled city school system. The Ohio General Assembly responded in June by establishing a pilot voucher program in any school district subject to such a takeover order — effectively, only for Cleveland. The program provided up to 2,000 elementary-age students with vouchers worth up to $2,250 annually to attend any participating school. The schools had to limit their tuition for those students to $2,500. Low-income families had priority. Higher-income families were eligible for any unused vouchers, limited to $1,875, but with no cap on the participating schools' tuition.

Both programs drew swift legal challenges. In Milwaukee's case, a state trial court judge ruled in January 1997 that the expansion of the program to include parochial schools was unconstitutional. But the Wisconsin Supreme Court reversed that decision in June 1998, holding that the program did not violate church-state restrictions in either the state or U.S. constitutions. [23] Advocates on both sides of the issue looked to the U.S. Supreme Court to hear the opponents' appeal, but the justices in November 1998 declined to review the decision.

Opponents of the Cleveland program also filed their initial challenge in state court. A lower court judge found the program unconstitutional in July 1996. The Ohio Supreme Court gave opponents a temporary victory in May 1999 by ruling that the legislature had violated the state constitution's "single-subject" rule by including the program in an unrelated bill. [24] The legislature quickly fixed the problem, however. The Ohio justices also said that the program did not violate either the state or

federal constitutions on religious grounds.

By the late 1990s, school choice advocates from coast to coast were pushing proposals for vouchers, tuition tax credits and privately run public schools known as charter schools. [25] Florida in 1999 became the first state to approve a statewide voucher program, but it was limited to students from schools that failed to meet state performance standards and then failed to improve a year afterward. It also provided vouchers for students with disabilities to attend a school of their choice.

In the same year, Illinois became the first state to give parents a direct tax credit for private-school tuition expenses. Two other states have tax-credit provisions for donations to groups providing scholarships to private schools: an individual tax credit in Arizona and a corporate credit in Pennsylvania.

On the other hand, school choice advocates failed in their efforts to get so-called tuitioning programs in Maine and Vermont opened up to participation by religious schools. Those programs give students in towns without a public high school vouchers to use at public or private schools elsewhere. The supreme courts in both states ruled in 1999 that religious schools could be excluded without improperly limiting parents' right to choose how to educate their children. [26] In addition, voters in six states defeated ballot initiatives to establish voucher programs — most notably in California, where voters in November 2000 defeated a proposal for universal $4,000 school vouchers by more than a 2-to-1 margin.

With the Supreme Court's refusal to consider the Milwaukee case, opposing camps looked to the Cleveland case as the most likely vehicle for settling the constitutionality question. Opponents moved into federal court following the Ohio Supreme Court's decision. In August 1999 — on the eve of a new school year — U.S. District Court Judge Solomon Oliver tentatively sustained the opponents' legal

challenge and issued a preliminary injunction against the program. School officials scurried to get a modification to allow students already receiving vouchers to continue at participating schools. Then in November the Supreme Court — dividing 5-4 along conservative-liberal lines — stayed the injunction, thus allowing the program to continue pending further legal proceedings.

A month later, Judge Oliver issued his final ruling, again holding that the program provided unconstitutional aid to religious schools. The federal appeals court agreed, in a 2-1 decision in December 2000. [27] While acknowledging that the program was neutral on its face, the appeals court majority said that in operation it promoted religion, primarily because the low tuitions that were permitted limited participation to Catholic schools.

In dissent, Judge James Ryan said the program passed constitutional muster. "Whether public funds find their way to a religious school is of no constitutional consequence," Ryan wrote, "if they get there as a result of genuinely private choice." ∎

CURRENT SITUATION

Monitoring Programs

Ohio legislators established the Cleveland voucher program to give low-income students an alternative to what was seen as the city's failing public school system. But recent studies indicate that most of the 4,456 students currently using the vouchers have never attended Cleveland public schools.

In addition, the studies — by both a liberal-leaning research institute and

Supreme Court Takes Zig-Zag Course

Supreme Court decisions since 1930 have upheld some government programs providing aid to students attending religiously affiliated schools, but until recently the justices barred programs giving parochial schools direct subsidies. School choice advocates say the court's most recent decisions appear to support private-school vouchers, but opponents disagree.

Case	How the Court Voted
Cochran v. Louisiana Board of Education, 281 U.S. 370 (1930) *Upholds providing textbooks to students at parochial and other schools.*	**9-0**
Everson v. Board of Education of Ewing, 330 U.S. 1 (1947) *Upholds New Jersey law providing reimbursement to parents for the cost of public transportation for students attending parochial and other non-public schools.*	**5-4**
Board of Education of Central School District No. 1 v. Allen, 392 U.S. 236 (1968) *Upholds New York state textbook-loan program for parochial and other non-public schools.*	**6-3**
Lemon v. Kurtzman, 403 U.S. 602 (1971) *Invalidates two "direct aid" statutes: Rhode Island law supplementing teacher salaries at non-public schools and Pennsylvania law reimbursing non-public schools for teacher salaries, textbooks and instructional materials. "Lemon test" bars aid to religious institutions unless it has a secular purpose, does not advance or inhibit religion and does not result in excessive governmental entanglement with religion.*	**9-0**
Tilton v. Richardson, 403 U.S. 672 (1971) *Upholds federal construction grants to church-affiliated colleges.*	**5-4**
Levitt v. Committee for Public Education and Religious Liberty, 413 U.S. 472 (1973) *Nullifies New York law providing per-capita payments to non-public schools for state-mandated testing and record keeping.*	**8-1**
Hunt v. McNair, 413 U.S. 734 (1973) *Upholds South Carolina law authorizing bonds for construction of secular facilities at church-affiliated or nonsectarian colleges and universities.*	**6-3**
Committee for Public Education and Religious Liberty v. Nyquist, 413 U.S. 756 (1973) *Invalidates New York "parochaid" statute providing maintenance and repair grants to non-public schools (9-0) and tuition reimbursement or tax credits for parents of students at non-public schools (7-2).*	**9-0, 7-2**
Meek v. Pittinger, 421 U.S. 349 (1975) *Upholds, 6-3, Pennsylvania law authorizing textbook loans for non-public schools, but strikes, by different 6-3 vote, loans of instructional materials and equipment.*	**6-3, 6-3**

a reform-minded education newsletter — show that African-Americans are underrepresented among the participants, compared with their enrollment in the city's school system, and that a whopping 99.4 percent of the voucher students are attending religious schools. Only 25 Cleveland voucher recipients attend secular schools.

Critics say the newest information shows that the program has failed to meet the goals established by supporters to sell the idea to Ohio legislators. "If the goal of the program was to get students to leave the failing Cleveland public schools, the program has not achieved any of its aims," says Michael Charney, professional-issues director of the Cleveland Teachers Union. "And if the goal was to create competition and to give parents real

Case	How the Court Voted
Roemer v. Maryland Board of Public Works, 426 U.S. 736 (1976) *Upholds program of general annual grants to private colleges, including church-related schools.*	**5-4**
Wolman v. Walter, 433 U.S. 229 (1977) *Upholds, 6-3, Ohio law providing non-public schools with textbooks and standardized testing and scoring, but strikes, 5-4, aid for instructional material, equipment and field trips.*	**6-3, 5-4**
Committee for Public Education and Religious Liberty v. Regan, 444 U.S. 646 (1980) *Upholds New York law reimbursing non-public schools for cost of administering, grading and reporting results of standardized tests.*	**5-4**
Mueller v. Allen, 463 U.S. 388 (1983) *Upholds Minnesota tax deduction for parents of children in public or private schools for tuition, textbooks or transportation.*	**5-4**
School District of Grand Rapids v. Ball, 473 U.S. 373 (1985) *Bars Grand Rapids, Mich., program reimbursing parochial schools for remedial and enrichment classes during school day (7-2) or after hours (5-4).*	**7-2, 5-4**
Aguilar v. Felton, 473 U.S. 402 (1985) *Bars New York City system from providing remedial and counseling services to disadvantaged students in non-public schools.*	**5-4**
Witters v. Washington Dept. of Services for the Blind, 474 U.S. 481 (1986) *Allows use of federal funds to aid blind seminary student.*	**9-0**
Zobrest v. Catalina Foothills School District, 509 U.S. 1 (1993) *Allows government to pay for sign-language interpreter to accompany deaf student to parochial school.*	**5-4**
Agostini v. Felton, 521 U.S. 203 (1997) *Allows New York City to use federal funds to provide remedial services to disadvantaged children on site at non-public schools; overrules* Aguilar v. Felton.	**5-4**
Mitchell v. Helms, 530 U.S. 793 (2000) *Upholds federally funded program lending computers and other instructional equipment to religious and other private schools. Four justices vote to uphold any neutral, secular aid program; Justices O'Connor and Breyer concur on narrower ground.*	**6-3**
Zelman v. Simmons-Harris, - U.S. - (2002) *Upholds constitutionality of Ohio law providing tuition vouchers for parents of students in Cleveland school system to use at participating schools.*	**5-4**

Sources: Joan Biskupic and Elder Witt, Guide to the U.S. Supreme Court (3d. ed.), 1997, pp. 490-498; Kenneth Jost, Supreme Court Yearbook 1996-1997, 1997, pp. 54-57; Supreme Court Yearbook, 1999-2000, 2000, pp. 63-66.

choice, then the program has failed, because it doesn't include any of the elite private schools, [even as] it transfers $6 million to $8 million per year [away from] disadvantaged students in the Cleveland public school system."

However, Charney notes wryly, "If the goal of the program was to subsidize an economically failing parochial-school system, then it's succeeding."

Supporters, however, see it differently. "I think it's working wonderfully," says Rosa-Linda Demore-Brown, executive director of Cleveland Parents for School Choice. "The proof is in the testing, the parent level of satisfaction and the children. The children are very happy, doing very well."

Demore-Brown — mother of two grown children who attended both public and private schools — interprets test scores to show that voucher students are progressing academically and matching comparable public-school students. She blames the high proportion of students attending religious schools on the failure of elite private schools or suburban public schools to participate. "It's not that parents are looking to send their children to a religious school," she says.

A bare majority of Cleveland's voucher students — 53 percent — are African-American, according to a recent analysis by the education newsletter *Catalyst*. By comparison, African-Americans comprised 71 percent of the Cleveland public-school system's students. [28] But Demore-Brown, who is African-American, discounted the significance of the gap. "There are still more African-American children [than whites] receiving vouchers," she says.

Information about the percentage of voucher students who previously attended public schools comes from a report published in September by the liberal-leaning research institute Policy Matters Ohio. It shows that 21 percent of current voucher students previously attended Cleveland public schools while 33 percent had gone to private schools in the city. Most of the remaining 46 percent were entering kindergarten, but 6 percent of those had been attending preschool programs at private schools. [29]

Zach Schiller, the senior researcher who wrote the report, says it shows the voucher program "hasn't done what its proponents claimed." The program "has served students already going to private schools more than those who were attending public schools," he says. The organization also published the study in January showing the continuing rise in the percentage of voucher students attending religious schools. [30]

A separate analysis by *Catalyst* shows that the 10 Cleveland public schools that lost 17 or more students to vouchers over the last five years have test scores somewhat higher than the dis-

trict's overall average. In addition, 24 percent of the students at the 10 schools passed the Ohio Proficiency Test, compared with 16 percent for the district overall. [31]

Information about the Milwaukee program is less definitive because of the Wisconsin legislature's decision in 1995 to drop reporting and testing requirements for participating schools. The Roman Catholic archdiocese favored lifting the requirements, ostensibly to avoid government entanglement. But the University of Wisconsin's Witte believes voucher supporters wanted to reduce accountability. "I think the pro-voucher people didn't want anything that looked negative," he says.

In its latest report on the program, the legislature's auditing arm — the Wisconsin Legislative Audit Bureau — estimated that 70 percent of the voucher students were attending religious schools. About 62 percent of the voucher students were African-Americans, compared with 61 percent of the overall Milwaukee public school enrollment. [32]

The audit bureau's report notes that the so-called choice schools are not required to administer standardized tests. Nine of the 86 schools participating in the 1998–99 school year lacked accreditation and administered no standardized tests, the bureau found. It also noted that the state's Department of Public Instruction was investigating a complaint that 17 schools had violated program requirements, including rules requiring random admissions, prohibiting fees and requiring schools to allow pupils to opt out of religious activities. The complaint — filed by People for the American Way and the NAACP — is now in mediation.

"No one knows how [the Milwaukee program] is working because for the last six years there has been no data collected on the students participating in the voucher program," says Barbara Miner, managing editor of an education reform newsletter, *Rethinking Schools*. "It's incredibly significant

that we have no clue about how these kids in the voucher programs are performing academically." [33]

Aiding Religion?

Regardless of students' test scores, Cleveland's voucher program was decided in the Supreme Court over a different question: whether it impermissibly supported religious education. Opponents found the program so "heavily skewed toward religion" that it violated the Establishment Clause, while Ohio state officials and pro-voucher allies insisted the program was "religiously neutral."

Opponents said the relatively small size of the voucher — a maximum $2,250 — inevitably steered students to religious education because only low-tuition parochial schools were willing to participate. "The great majority of voucher program parents must send their children to sectarian private schools providing a religious education in order to obtain the benefits that the program offers," NEA lawyer Chanin wrote in his brief to the Supreme Court.

To the contrary, the Ohio attorney general's office argued, "[N]o social coercion or financial incentives influence parents toward selection of religious, as opposed to secular, schooling." Indeed, the state lawyers noted, voucher parents must pay at least 10 percent of the cost of any private education — creating a disincentive to leave the public schools. In his brief, the Institute for Justice's Bolick — representing Suma and other families receiving vouchers — argued that more secular schools will participate eventually, once legal challenges are resolved.

The law allows Cleveland students to use the vouchers at public schools outside the city, but none of the adjoining, suburban districts has ever agreed to participate. The size of the voucher is cited as one deterrent to

At Issue:

Will school vouchers help students from low-income families?

BOYCE W. SLAYMAN
VICE PRESIDENT
BLACK ALLIANCE FOR EDUCATIONAL OPTIONS

WRITTEN FOR THE CQ RESEARCHER, FEBRUARY 2002

*t*hinking people cannot ignore the mounting evidence that our knowledge-based economy is at long-term risk because of chronic shortages of high-skilled workers. Enlightened thinkers should also appreciate that our society cannot remain vibrantly democratic without effective education of the general population.

How will we ensure that our children receive the quality K-12 education that is critically necessary to reach a middle-class standard of living and otherwise thrive in the 21st century?

Given the continued failure of many urban public school systems to deliver quality education, parents want alternatives. Those with means can find them by moving or putting their children in private school. Those without means are trapped unless they can access resources to do the same.

Educational "choice" is about equalizing the playing field for low-income families. And the choices should include vouchers.

The Black Alliance for Educational Options actively supports parental choice to empower families and increase educational options for black children. We support choice because we see far too many low-income black children failing to realize their or their parents' aspirations for them within the current system. We believe that keeping the promise of educational opportunity for all requires turning away from 18th-century educational models and toward solutions that will work in a global, knowledge-based economy.

The debate about the desirability of school vouchers is over. Study after study — including both liberal and conservative research — shows that the majority of Americans support school vouchers and that African-American support is stronger than that of all other demographics. This is no accident of demography; it is a reality of geography. These are the parents of students trapped in largely urban and failing public school systems. They want better educational outcomes. They need choices.

No other domestic issue provokes such strong emotional responses, or is as important to the future of the republic, or creates such weird politics as educational choice. Yet, school choice, vouchers included, should not be viewed as a "left vs. right" issue. At its core, educational choice is a social- and economic-justice issue that is caught up in a very unproductive political maelstrom.

Without a strong education, our children will not have a real chance to engage in the practice of freedom and the process of transforming their world.

THEODORE M. SHAW
ASSOCIATE DIRECTOR-COUNSEL
NAACP LEGAL DEFENSE AND EDUCATIONAL FUND

WRITTEN FOR THE CQ RESEARCHER, FEBRUARY 2002

*f*rustrated with the failure of public school systems nationwide to provide quality education, some African-Americans have joined the voucher movement in seeking public subsidies for private-school tuition. The voucher movement is traditionally the terrain of white conservatives, including those who have abandoned public schools to escape racial desegregation and those who advocate public support for religiously sectarian education.

The U.S. Supreme Court currently is considering a Cleveland case in which two lower courts invalidated Ohio's voucher program. In that case, *Zelman v. Simmons-Harris*, the Institute for Justice, a conservative legal organization that cut its teeth opposing school desegregation and affirmative action, represents a group of black parents who support vouchers. Their brief asserts that voucher programs are necessary to fulfill *Brown v. Board of Education's* promise of "equal educational opportunity for all."

Putting aside the cynical manipulation of black parents' frustration with the failures of public schools, the voucher issue taps deep sensitivities. *Brown* held out the promise of equal educational opportunity. However, it was primarily about school desegregation and addressed quality education only to the extent that it was denied as a consequence of segregation. Almost 50 years after *Brown*, vast numbers of African-American children are still trapped in racially isolated and educationally failing schools.

The appeal of vouchers is understandable. All responsible parents do what they can to provide their children the best possible education. On a systemic level, however, vouchers are a disaster. Voucher programs signal the further abandonment of public schools; more practically, they skim badly needed financial resources and the most motivated and able students. Vouchers will further exacerbate the differences between private and public schools, which will continue to enroll the overwhelming majority of African-American students.

As the Cleveland case demonstrates, voucher programs usually serve white students — many of whom are already enrolled in private schools — in greater proportion than black students. Most voucher programs do not provide enough money to pay private-school tuition. Thus, their promise as a solution for the problems of black children is illusory.

Nothing short of a massive commitment to public schools by legislatures and policy-makers, reflected in money and reform, will produce equal educational opportunity for all.

the suburban districts, but Bolick sees another motive. "Suburban schools do not want inner-city kids coming out to their schools," he says. "I don't think that's a noble explanation, but it's the world where we operate, sadly."

In their briefs, the opposing lawyers tried to fit the facts of the Cleveland case into differing Supreme Court precedents. Opponents relied principally on a 1973 decision, *Committee for Public Education and Religious Liberty v. Nyquist*, which struck down a New York "parochaid" law providing direct grants to religious schools. They said the voucher funds received by parochial schools in Cleveland amount to "direct unrestricted government payments" akin to those ruled unconstitutional in *Nyquist*.

Voucher supporters cited more recent Supreme Court decisions that uphold general government programs that provide assistance to students in religious or secular private schools. In 1993, for example, the court upheld the use of taxpayer funds to pay for an interpreter for a deaf student attending a religious high school. Most recently, the court in 1997 and 2000 upheld federally funded programs that provide remedial or enrichment services for disadvantaged students attending secular or religious private schools or allow local school districts to lend private schools computers and other equipment. As in those programs, voucher supporters argued, religious and secular schools are eligible for the Cleveland program because the funds go to religious schools only after "true, independent choice" by parents, not the government.

The case attracted an unusually large number of friend-of-the-court briefs on both sides. Lawyers representing the plaintiffs included attorneys from the NEA, the American Civil Liberties Union, People for the American Way and Americans United for Separation of Church and State. The dozen or so friend-of-the-court briefs on their side

came from education groups, such as the National School Boards Association, the NAACP Legal Defense Fund and the American Jewish Committee.

Voucher supporters drew more than 30 briefs from organizations or individuals, including conservative advocacy groups such as the American Center for Law and Justice, religious organizations such as the U.S. Conference of Catholic Bishops, and the Black Alliance for Educational Options. A group of 30, mostly conservative, constitutional law professors also urged the court to uphold the program.

The Bush administration weighed in, arguing to uphold the voucher program. In a brief filed by Solicitor General Theodore Olson, the government said the program "fits comfortably within [the] framework" of Supreme Court decisions allowing aid that benefits religious schools if it results from "genuinely independent and private choices of aid recipients."

O'Connor Seen as Key Vote

In recent cases, the court has been divided roughly along conservative-liberal lines on church-state separation issues. Chief Justice William Rehnquist and three fellow conservatives — Justices Antonin Scalia, Anthony Kennedy and Clarence Thomas — argued in the most recent case, *Mitchell v. Helms*, that any general government aid program operated on religiously neutral principles could pass constitutional muster under the Establishment Clause. Three liberal justices — John Paul Stevens, David Souter and Ruth Bader Ginsburg — said they would have ruled the computer loan program in question unconstitutional.

In the pivotal opinion, the centrist conservative Justice Sandra Day O'Connor voted to uphold the computer loan program but declined to join Thomas' broader opinion. O'Connor said the program did not have "the impermissible effect of advancing" or endorsing religion, but she said "neutrality" was not

a sufficient criterion for upholding the program. In rejecting any impermissible endorsement of religion, O'Connor said there was "significant" difference between a per-capita student aid program and "a true private-choice program." Justice Stephen Breyer, who usually votes with the liberals on church-state issues, joined O'Connor's opinion.

Lawyers on both sides agreed that O'Connor held the key to the Cleveland case. "There is no question that on Establishment Clause issues O'Connor has been the key vote," Bolick says. In their briefs, supporters of the Cleveland vouchers argued that it fits O'Connor's definition of a "true private-choice program."

Voucher opponents insisted, however, that the Cleveland program was more like the direct-aid programs prohibited under older Supreme Court decisions. "If the court rules consistently with the past, it will be unconstitutional," said Ralph Neas, president of People for the American Way, before the ruling. "But this is a very closely divided court right now." ∎

OUTLOOK

Waiting for the Court

Five decades after his groundbreaking proposal for school vouchers, economist Friedman takes only scant satisfaction from the limited voucher programs enacted so far. "I have been much more optimistic than has been justified," Friedman told *Education Week* late last year. [34]

Friedman, now 89, contrasts his call for a universal system of vouchers to the programs enacted so far, which are targeted to low-income families. "A program for the poor will be a poor program," he said. "All parents should have the same choice."

Voucher proponents say the limited scope of the existing programs is a calculated strategy that bows to political realities. "It is very, very difficult for us to defeat the parade of hypotheticals that are raised against school choice programs," the Institute for Justice's Bolick says, referring to the string of unsuccessful school choice ballot measures. "It's better to get small programs started either through the legislatures or through private philanthropy and grow them through there."

However, opponents say voucher programs are small and few in number because the public does not really support them. "The public has spoken forcefully against vouchers in general," says Sandra Feldman, president of the American Federation of Teachers. Polls "make clear their preference for investing in public schools" rather than instituting vouchers, she says.

Voucher opponents think the Supreme Court decision to strike down the Cleveland program will be a decisive setback for supporters of the idea. "There will be no large-scale programs because you can't have a large program without sectarian schools," NEA lawyer Chanin says. However, since the court upheld the program, opponents will continue to fight them politically. "It won't change how the public feels," he says.

For their part, voucher supporters were confident of victory. "We designed a program to survive Supreme Court scrutiny," Bolick says. A ruling to uphold the program would "create tremendous momentum" for similar programs, he says. "School choice is one of the issues in which constitutional objections are often raised in the legislative process. A positive decision would remove a major obstacle."

Bolick says more voucher programs would promote the goal of equalizing educational opportunities regardless of income or race. "It would help vindicate the promise of *Brown v. Board of Education*," he says, referring to the Supreme Court's landmark 1954 decision outlawing racial segregation.

Arizona State University's Molnar disagrees. Expanded voucher programs, he says, will result in "a further exacerbation of the inequities that already exist in state-run educational systems."

Voucher opponents also say the programs will hamper other, more productive efforts to improve U.S. schools. "We do that by investing in schools, not by abandoning them," Feldman says.

But Hoxby, the Harvard economist, says voucher programs will stimulate needed changes. "If you really want public schools to be good, you want to have some forces that put some pressure on them to be good," she says.

In Cleveland, opponents concede that they cannot defeat the program except in court. "It's not a major issue in Cleveland," Charney of the local teachers' union says.

But Simmons-Harris, the parent plaintiff, still insists the program is bad for the schools. "Vouchers will take away from public schools," she says. "You're taking away from the masses for just the few."

School choice advocate Demore-Brown counters that voucher programs can be good for all students. "This is a win-win for everyone if they would just look at the total big picture," she says. "The bottom line is that these children we are educating today will run the country tomorrow. Everyone should be saying, 'Let's get these children educated and get this done right.' " ■

Notes

[1] For background, see Kathy Koch, "School Vouchers," *The CQ Researcher*, April 9, 1999, pp. 281-304; David Masci, "School Choice Debate," *The CQ Researcher*, July 18, 1997, pp. 625-648.

[2] See Kenneth Jost, *Supreme Court Yearbook, 1999-2000* (2000), pp. 61-66. For background, see Patrick Marshall, "Religion in Schools," *The CQ Researcher*, Jan. 12, 2001, pp. 1-24.

[3] "The 33rd Annual Phi Delta Kappa/Gallup Poll of the Public's Attitudes Toward the Public Schools," Phi Delta Kappan (September 2001), pp. 44-45, http://www.pdkintl.org/kappan/kimages/kpoll83.pdf. The telephone sample of 1,108 adults was conducted May 23-June 6, 2001.

[4] The annual evaluations are at www.indiana.edu/~iuice.

[5] See John F. Witte, *The Market Approach to Education: An Analysis of America's First Voucher Program* (2000), pp. 119-143; Jay P. Greene, Paul E. Peterson, and Jiangtao Du, "Effectiveness of School Choice: The Milwaukee Experiment," Program in Education Policy and Governance, John F. Kennedy School of Government, Harvard University (March 1997), www.ksg.harvard.edu/pepg; Cecilia Elena Rouse, "Schools and Student Achievement: More Evidence from the Milwaukee Parental Choice Program," Industrial Relations Section, Princeton University (January 1998); "Private School Vouchers and Student Achievement: An Evaluation of the Milwaukee Parental Choice Program," Princeton University (December 1996), www.irs.princeton.edu/pubs.

[6] William G. Howell, Patrick J. Wolf, Paul E. Peterson and David E. Campbell, "Test-Score Effects of School Vouchers in Dayton, Ohio, New York City, and Washington, D.C.: Evidence from Randomized Field Trials," Program on Education Policy and Governance, John F. Kennedy School of Government, Harvard University (August 2000), http://data.fas.harvard.edu/pepg.

[7] Brian P. Gill *et al.*, *Rhetoric Versus Reality: What We Know and What We Need to Know About Vouchers and Charter Schools* (2001), p. xvi.

[8] General Accounting Office, "School Vouchers: Publicly Funded Programs in Cleveland and Milwaukee" (August 2001), pp. 27-31.

[9] Caroline M. Hoxby, "How School Choice Affects the Achievement of Public School Students," paper presented at Hoover Institution, Stanford, Calif., Sept. 20-21, 2001 (http://post.economics.harvard.edu/faculty/hoxby/papers.html).

[10] See Jay P. Greene, "An Evaluation of the Florida A-Plus Accountability and School Choice Program," Manhattan Institute (2001), www.manhattan-institute.org; Gregory Camilli and Katrina Bulkley, "Critique of 'An Evaluation of the Florida A-Plus Accountability and School Choice Program,' " Education Policy Analysis Archives (March 4, 2001), www.epaa.asu.edu.

[11] Some background drawn from "Public Education in the United States" and "Private Education in the United States," Encarta (http://En-

carta.msn.com) (visited January 2002).

[12] For background, see Lawrence A. Cremin, *The American Common School: An Historic Conception* (1951).

[13] *Ibid.*, pp. 191-203.

[14] Richard J. Gabel, *Public Funds for Church and Private Schools* (1937), pp. 351-361.

[15] *Ibid.*, pp. 523-525.

[16] The case is *Pierce v. Society of Sisters*, 268 U.S. 510 (1925).

[17] Some background drawn from Charles S. Clark, "Friends and Foes of Vouchers Envision Salvation for Poor and Tax Breaks for Rich," *The CQ Researcher*, July 26, 1996, pp. 662-663.

[18] Milton Friedman, "The Role of Government in Education," in Robert A. Solo (ed.), *Economics and the Public Interest* (1955), pp. 123-145.

[19] Christopher Jencks, "Is the Public School Obsolete?" *The Public Interest* (winter 1966), pp. 18-27.

[20] John E. Chubb and Terry M. Moe, *Politics, Markets, and America's Schools* (1990). See Richard L. Worsnop, "Brookings Book Sparks Debate Over Choice Plans," *The CQ Researcher*, May 10, 1991, p. 265.

[21] Chubb & Moe, *op. cit.*, p. 220.

[22] Terry M. Moe, *Schools, Vouchers, and the American Public* (2001), pp. 371-372.

[23] *Jackson v. Benson*, 578 N.W.2d 602 (Wis. 1998).

[24] For detailed state-by-state information from a pro-school choice organization, see Robert E. Moffit *et al.*, "School Choice 2001: What's Happening in the States," Heritage Foundation, 2001 (www.heritage.org/school).

[25] *Simmons-Harris v. Goff*, 711 N.E.2d 203 (Ohio 1999).

[26] The cases are *Bagley v. Raymond School Department*, Maine Supreme Court, April 23, 1999; *Chittenden Town School District v. Vermont Department of Education*, Vermont Supreme Court, June 11, 1999.

[27] *Simmons-Harris v. Zelman*, 234 F.3d 945 (CA6 2000)

[28] Piet van Lier and Caitlin Scott, "Fewer choices, longer commutes for black vouch-

FOR MORE INFORMATION

American Federation of Teachers, 555 New Jersey Ave., N.W., Washington, D.C. 2001; (202) 879-4400; www.aft.org. The country's second-largest teachers' union and its local affiliate, the Cleveland Teachers' Union, have both strongly opposed the Cleveland voucher plan.

Americans United for Separation of Church and State, 518 C St., N.E., Washington, D.C. 20002; (202) 466-3234; www.au.org. The church-state separationist group is part of the coalition legally challenging the Cleveland voucher program.

Black Alliance for Educational Options, 501 C St., N.E., Suite 3, Washington, D.C. 20002; (202) 544-9870; www.baeo.org. The two-year-old organization supports school vouchers.

Institute for Justice, 1717 Pennsylvania Ave., N.W., Suite 200, Washington, D.C. 20006; (202) 955-1300; www.ij.org. The libertarian public interest law firm has taken the lead role in the school choice movement, including lobbying and litigation on behalf of vouchers.

NAACP Legal Defense and Educational Fund, 99 Hudson St., Suite 1600, New York, N.Y. 10013; (212) 965-2200; and 1444 I St., N.W., Washington, D.C. 20005; (202) 682-1300; www.naacpldf.org. The longtime civil rights organization opposes vouchers.

National Education Association, 1201 16th St., N.W., Washington, D.C. 20036; (202) 833-4000; www.nea.org. The country's largest teachers' union has strongly opposed school vouchers and is part of the coalition that brought the challenge to the Cleveland program.

U.S. Conference of Catholic Bishops, 32114th St., N.E., Washington, D.C. 20017; (202) 541-3300; www.nccbuscc.org. The conference supports school vouchers; it also superintends the Catholic school system in the United States.

er students," *Catalyst* (December 2001/January 2002) www.catalyst-cleveland.org. The newsletter, published six times a year, was founded in 1999; funders include the Cleveland Foundation, the George Gund Foundation and the Joyce Foundation.

[29] Zach Schiller, "Cleveland School Vouchers: Where the Students Come From," Policy Matters Ohio (September 2001), www.policymattersohio.org.

[30] Amy Hanauer, "Cleveland School Vouchers: Where the Students Go," *Policy Matters Ohio* (January 2002), *Ibid.* The study was based on an earlier figure for the total num-

ber of voucher students: 4,202.

[31] Caitlin Scott, "Better district schools lose students to vouchers," *Catalyst* (December 2001/January 2002), www.catalyst-cleveland.org.

[32] "Milwaukee Parental Choice Program," Wisconsin Legislative Audit Bureau (February 2000), www.legis.state.wi.us.

[33] See www.rethinkingschool.org. The newsletter, now published on line, was founded by Milwaukee-area teachers in 1986.

[34] Mark Walsh, "Friedman Disappointed That Voucher Plans Aren't Bolder," *Education Week*, Dec. 12, 2001 (www.edweek.org).

Bibliography
Selected Sources

Books

Byrk, Anthony S., Valerie E. Lee and Peter B. Holland, *Catholic Schools and the Common Good*, Harvard University Press, 1993.

The authors trace the history of Catholic schools in the United States and detail largely positive research findings about their impact on student academic achievement and other outcomes. The book includes detailed source notes and a 14-page list of references. Byrk is a professor at the University of Chicago, Lee at the University of Michigan in Ann Arbor; Holland is superintendent of schools, Lexington, Mass.

Fuller, Bruce, and Richard F. Elmore, with Gary Orfield (eds.), *Who Chooses? Who Loses? Culture, Institutions, and the Unequal Effects of School Choice*, Teachers College Press, 1996.

The nine essays in this collection are by educational-policy experts representing a range of views on school choice. In their conclusion, co-editors Fuller and Elmore say school choice "may produce useful innovations in previously unresponsive systems" but also "seems to increase the social disparities between those who choose and those who do not." Fuller is a professor at the University of California-Berkeley School of Education and a coauthor of a more recent, critical paper, "School Choice: Abundant Hopes, Scarce Evidence of Results" (Policy Analysis for California Education, 1999); Elmore is a professor at Harvard's School of Education.

Moe, Terry M., *Schools, Vouchers, and the American Public*, Brookings, 2001.

The book, based in part on a national opinion survey, views vouchers as a growing — and increasingly popular — challenge to the traditional U.S. system of education. Includes extensive statistics, reference notes. Moe, a professor at Stanford University and fellow at the Hoover Institution, was coauthor with John E. Chubb of Politics, Markets and America's Schools (Brookings, 1990).

Peterson, Paul E., and Bryan C. Hassel (eds.), *Learning From School Choice*, Brookings, 1998.

Sixteen papers by pro-school choice authors cover voucher, charter school and public school choice programs. Includes tabular material, chapter notes. Peterson is director of Harvard's Program on Education Policy and Governance; Hassel is an education and policy consultant in Charlotte, N.C.

Viteritti, Joseph P., *Choosing Equality: School Choice, the Constitution, and Civil Society*, Brookings, 1999.

A professor at New York University argues that school choice can be a tool for promoting equal educational opportunity. Includes extensive chapter notes.

Witte, John F., *The Market Approach to Education: An Analysis of America's First Voucher Program*, Princeton University Press, 2000.

Witte examines Milwaukee's voucher program during its first five years — before the program was expanded to allow religious schools to participate. Witte, director of the La Follette School of Public Affairs at the University of Wisconsin-Madison, was the official evaluator of the voucher program during the period. Includes extensive tabular material and an eight-page list of references.

Reports and Studies

Gill, Brian P., P. Michael Timpane, Karen E. Ross and Dominic J. Brewer, *Rhetoric vs. Reality: What We Know and What We Need to Know About Vouchers and Charter Schools*, Rand 2001 (www.rand.org/publications).

The book-length study reviews the theoretical foundations for school vouchers and charter schools and the empirical evidence for their effectiveness. Includes source notes, 32-page list of references. Gill is a researcher in the Rand Corporation's Pittsburgh office.

Moffit, Robert E., Jennifer J. Garrett and Janice A. Smith, *School Choice 2001: What's Happening in the States*, Heritage Foundation, 2001 (www.heritage.org/schools).

The pro-choice think tank provides detailed information on public and private school choice programs in each of the 50 states, the District of Columbia and Puerto Rico. Includes appendix with list of national pro-choice organizations.

"The 33rd Annual Phi Delta Kappa/Gallup Poll of the Public's Attitudes Toward the Public Schools," *Phi Delta Kappan* (September 2001), pp. 41-58, http://www.pdkintl.org/kappan/kimages/kpoll83.pdf.

The telephone sample of 1,108 adults was conducted May 23-June 6, 2001. The 18-page report by the international education fraternity and the well-known polling organization covers public opinion on a range of education issues, including school vouchers and charter schools

U.S. General Accounting Office, "School Vouchers: Publicly Funded Programs in Cleveland and Milwaukee," August 2001 (GAO 01-914; www.gao.gov).

The 50-page report provides an objective overview of the operation of the Cleveland and Milwaukee voucher programs and the various studies of the programs' effectiveness. Includes three-page listing of studies.

2 Testing in Schools

KENNETH JOST

Back in 1987, Ohio Education Superintendent Franklin Walter helped create a proficiency test that every Ohio public school student had to pass to graduate.

Now Ohio school kids are hit with tests just about every year. For fourth- and eighth-graders, there's a week of proficiency tests in five areas; other grades get standardized tests every year.

"That's entirely too much testing," says Walter, now a professor of educational administration at Ohio State University. "When you combine standardized tests with the amount of tests that teachers give, it becomes too much testing. It takes too much time away from instruction."

Many Ohio parents and teachers agree. "It's testing gone insane," says Mary O'Brien, a member of the grassroots group Parents Against Unfair Proficiency Testing, whose five children have all attended Ohio public schools.

"People are not happy with the tests," says John Grossman, president of the Columbus Education Association, a teachers' union. "There's too much pressure on the young people, and they don't see any point."

If President Bush has his way, however, youngsters in most states will be seeing more tests than they already face in public schools. Bush is proposing to require annual testing for all students in reading and math from third through eighth grade.

Test results, Bush says, will help parents, students, teachers and administrators measure the performance of individual students, schools and school

From *The CQ Researcher*, April 20, 2001.

Students at Vail Middle School in Middletown, Ohio, prepare for the state's standardized tests. President Bush proposes requiring annual reading and math tests for all public school students in grades 3-8.

AP Photo/Al Behrman

districts. And he wants to use the scores to designate "failing schools" that would face the possibility of reduced federal aid if they do not improve performance within three years.

"Without yearly testing, we don't know who is falling behind and who needs help," Bush said in announcing his plan on Jan. 23, during his first week in office. "Without yearly testing, too often we don't find failure until it is too late to fix."

Bush's proposal is moving forward in Congress with bipartisan support. House and Senate bills both include annual testing requirements, though in different forms. But Democratic lawmakers strongly oppose Bush's voucher-type plan to allow students in failing schools to use public funds to attend private schools.

Whatever happens to Bush's bill, the push for greater use of testing is likely to remain strong. "Testing is more and more popular in the United States as a means of providing accountability for the schools and for evaluating the progress of students relative to state and local standards," says Ray Fenton, supervisor of assessment evaluation for the Anchorage, Alaska, public schools and past

president of the National Association of Test Directors.

"Tests in education are like tests in medicine," says Chester Finn, an assistant secretary of Education under President Ronald Reagan and now president of the conservative Thomas B. Fordham Foundation. "They help you find out what's actually going on, what problems are present, what treatments are and are not working and what the patient's prognosis is."

Testing advocates are facing an array of skeptics, critics and outright opponents. They contend that most standardized tests do not accurately measure student or school performance, that testing hurts rather than helps classroom instruction and that the emphasis on testing distracts policy-makers and the public from the real problems of American education.

"The Bush plan is an unnecessary and unhelpful federal mandate that will have the effect of putting the weight of the federal government behind the overuse and misuse of standardized tests, with educationally harmful results," says FairTest, an advocacy group that considers standardized tests discriminatory.

African-American and Hispanic advocacy groups criticize standardized tests as racially and culturally biased and oppose the use of scores as the sole basis for promotion decisions. More recently, parents in predominantly white, well-to-do suburbs have joined the opposition to standardized tests — partly in response to the move in some states to establish uniform tests as a requirement for graduation from high school.

"Upper-middle-class communities are generally satisfied with their schools," says John Jennings, a longtime Democratic aide to the House Education Committee and now presi-

Testing in the States

Only 15 states and the District of Columbia require annual, standardized math and reading tests for all public school students in grades 3-8. Under President Bush's proposal, all students in those grades would be tested.

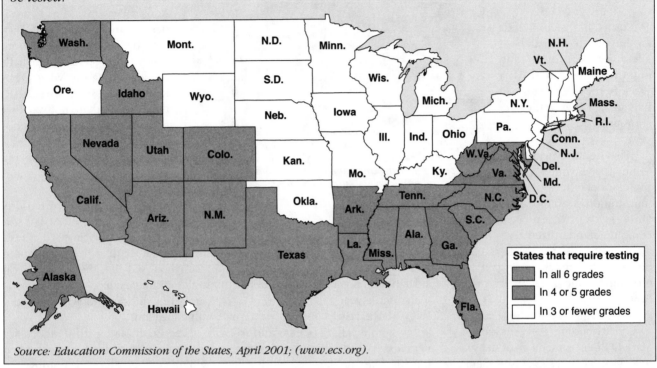

States that require testing

- In all 6 grades
- In 4 or 5 grades
- In 3 or fewer grades

Source: Education Commission of the States, April 2001; (www.ecs.org).

dent of the Center on Education Policy. "Their kids are going to college. They feel they control their schools. And they don't want high school exit exams interrupting their kids' path to college."

Teachers form part of the resistance to tests used to determine promotion for students or funding levels for schools or school districts — called high-stakes testing. "We have absolutely no problem with the appropriate and proper role of testing," says Bob Chase, president of the National Education Association (NEA), the nation's biggest teachers union. "Our concern more is with the overuse or abuse of tests and the unintended consequences if they are used as a single measure of how schools are doing and how kids are doing."

The testing issue emerged in a separate forum in February when the president of the University of California called for dropping the most

widely used college entrance examination — the SAT — as a requirement for admission. The proposal by Richard Atkinson — which would require approval by the university's Academic Senate and the state's Board of Regents — renewed a perennial debate over the prominence of SAT scores in determining admission to selective colleges and the effect on educational opportunities for students from disadvantaged backgrounds, particularly African-American and Hispanic youngsters. (*See story, p. 26.*)

In Ohio, the backlash against testing focused on a rule that would have required fourth-graders to pass a reading proficiency test before promotion. About 58 percent of fourth-graders passed the test in spring 2000. Had the rule been in effect, 42 percent of the state's

128,000 fourth-graders — 53,000 children — would have been held back. [1]

"That's been dropped," says Robert Bowers, the top testing administrator in the Ohio Department of Education. Under a bill moving through the Ohio legislature, the reading test would be given in the third grade beginning in 2003 and tied to giving remedial assistance rather than denying promotion.

Despite the controversy over the reading test, Bowers insists most Ohioans support testing. And the testing legislation — endorsed by Republican Gov. Bob Taft and already approved by the GOP-controlled Senate — essentially preserves the requirement of annual tests while working to better align testing with the state's curricular standards.

Testing opponents have mixed

views of the legislation. "We view the action of the Senate as being very positive," says teachers' union leader Grossman. But activist O'Brien says the bill makes the situation worse. The bill "will alter and drastically increase testing here in Ohio," she says.

As the debate over educational testing continues in Washington and in state capitals and local communities throughout the country, here are some of the major questions being considered:

Should standardized tests be used to measure school performance?

Baltimore's city schools have their share of the kinds of problems that affect large urban school systems throughout the country. When the state of Maryland moved last year to take over three troubled elementary schools, however, officials cited one reason above all others for the move: the schools' failure to meet the state's standards for student performance on proficiency tests. [2]

Proponents of high-stakes standardized testing see the connection between test scores and school performance as elementary. "Testing is to schools what profit-and-loss statements are to a business," says Bush education adviser Sandy Kress. "It shows you — not perfectly, but reasonably well — how the enterprise is working."

Critics, however, say standardized tests were never intended to measure schools' overall performance and are not an accurate way to tell how well schools are doing.

"If the tests are one part of a richer accountability mix and the tests are well designed and not used themselves for high stakes, then fine," says Monty Neill, executive director of FairTest. "But they are not well designed, and they only measure a limited slice of what kids should learn."

"These tests were not designed for

Math Test Scores Improved

Students' scores improved significantly on the math part of the National Assessment of Educational Progress (NAEP) over the past 30 years. Scores rose slightly in reading. The tests, which generate what has been called the "nation's report card," are administered every few years to a nationally representative sample of students.

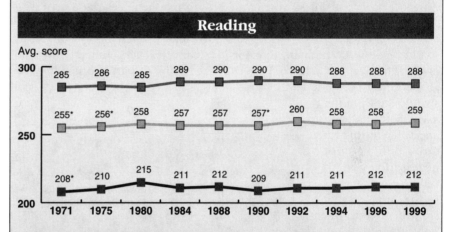

Reading

Avg. score

	1971	1975	1980	1984	1988	1990	1992	1994	1996	1999
Age 17	285	286	285	289	290	290	290	288	288	288
Age 13	255*	256*	258	257	257	257*	260	258	258	259
Age 9	208*	210	215	211	212	209	211	211	212	212

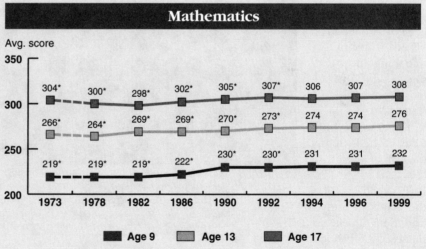

Mathematics

Avg. score

	1973	1978	1982	1986	1990	1992	1994	1996	1999
Age 17	304*	300*	298*	302*	305*	307*	306	307	308
Age 13	266*	264*	269*	269*	270*	273*	274	274	276
Age 9	219*	219*	219*	222*	230*	230*	231	231	232

■ Age 9   ☐ Age 13   ■ Age 17

* Indicates statistically significant changes from this point to 1999; the tests will be given again in 2003

Note: Dashes represent extrapolated data

Source: National Center for Education Statistics, National Assessment of Educational Progress, "1999 Long-Term Trend Assessment"

this purpose," says Vincent Ferrandino, executive director of the National Association of Elementary School Principals. "They have taken on a life of their own. They've been a scorecard for public consumption."

The Bush blueprint says that "annual academic assessments" will give parents "the information they need to know how well their child is doing in school, and how well the school is educating their child." In addition, the document reads, "annual data is a vital diagnostic tool for schools to achieve continuous improvement."

Supporters of Bush's plan see annual testing as essential. "Only with annual testing do you see the most important thing about schools, which is the value-added measure," Finn says. "Where is [a student] this year as compared to last year? There's no way to know that unless you measure him twice. The same thing is true for schools."

But Andrew Rotherham, director of the 21st Century Schools Project at the centrist Democratic Progressive Policy Institute, says that imposing an annual testing requirement is not necessarily beneficial.

"It's not enough simply to tell the states to test every year in grades 4 to 8," Rotherham says. "That's a recipe for one thing: more testing. It's not a recipe for more effective testing."

Experts on both sides of the issue say the actual design of the tests is critical. Bush would leave it to the states to "select and design assessments of their choosing." Rotherham says he fears that many states "will simply go to the lowest denominator test" — purchasing the "least expensive but not necessarily the best or most reliable test."

Jennifer Vranek, an expert with the test advocacy group Achieve, founded in 1996 with support from businesses and state governors, also voices concerns about states buying commercially available tests.

"Fifteen to 20 states are still looking at off-the-shelf tests: multiple choice, low-level, hard-to-teach-to tests that tend mostly to reflect students' socioeconomic backgrounds," Vranek says. "I can see how it would be frustrating to have your school judged on those kinds of tests."

On the other hand, Vranek says, "If a state sets out academic standards and then uses rigorous tests to test those standards, we think they are valid and reliable."

Many teachers and parents criticize testing in part because they see no connection between tests and

President Bush outlines his education-reform plans on Jan. 23, 2001, with Education Secretary-designate Rod Paige. Bush's proposal for annual testing is getting bipartisan support in Congress, but Democrats oppose Bush's plan to allow students in failing schools to use public funds to attend private schools.

classroom instruction. Jennings of the Center on Education Policy echoes the concern.

"You have to have testing for accountability, but what's sorely needed is testing for diagnosis, so that a teacher early in the school year knows where each kid stands and what each kid needs," Jennings says. "The politicians keep mixing those things up."

For his part, FairTest's Neill says any valid assessment of school performance needs to use more infor-

mation than test scores. "Looking at the actual work that kids do in school ought to be the central part of an accountability measure," he says.

Whatever the advantages and disadvantages of testing, Robert L. Linn, a professor of education at the University of Colorado at Boulder and an expert on testing, says there may not be any alternatives for enhancing schools' accountability. "The perfect system is hard to identify," Linn says. "But people want to know [how schools are doing], and it's widely accepted, and it has some positive aspects. It lets you focus — as in Texas — on whether poor and African-American kids are making gains on closing the gap. It also makes it clear that you have common expectations for students who come from different backgrounds, and that's also good."

Do schools do too much to prepare students for standardized testing?

An *Education Week* survey of teachers about standards and testing late last year found that most believed stronger academic standards had helped to make schools' curriculums more demanding and to raise expectations of students' performance. But most of the teachers also registered unfavorable opinions about the impact of testing on their classroom instruction.

Nearly seven in 10 teachers said that instruction stresses state tests "far" or "somewhat" too much, while 66 percent said tests were forcing them to concentrate on things covered in the tests to the detriment of other important topics. The responses, the weekly concluded, "suggest state tests may be looming too large in classrooms and encouraging undesirable practices." [3]

Concern about teachers' "teaching to the test" recurs frequently in the debate over testing. Critics see it as a danger. "It's a matter of making sure that tests don't drive curriculum," says NEA President Chase.

Supporters of annual testing, however, either discount the fear or directly challenge the underlying premise. "If they're good tests, and if they're secure tests, then teaching to the test is a virtue not a vice," says the Fordham Foundation's Finn. "It's teaching the things that you want kids to know."

"Is it possible for folks concerned with the short term rather than the long term to spend too much time teaching to the test?" Bush adviser Kress asks rhetorically. "You bet. But typically that doesn't work for long; that's not the best way to teach. And those practices are typically exposed and usually modified."

The Bush blueprint gives little guidance on the question of how — or whether — to "align" school curriculums with testing. It merely says that states must have "clear, measurable goals focused on basic skills and essential knowledge." Annual assessments in math and reading for grades 3–8, the blueprint continues, "will ensure that the goals are being met for every child, every year."

So far, states vary in shaping their assessment tools to the recent rounds of standard-setting. "Every state has developed its own assessment systems," says Fenton of the National Association of Test Directors. "Some of the national reviews have raised questions about the extent to which people are teaching to the test in the wrong way — narrowing the curriculum and trying to outguess the tests."

But Achieve's Vranek says states are moving away from what she calls

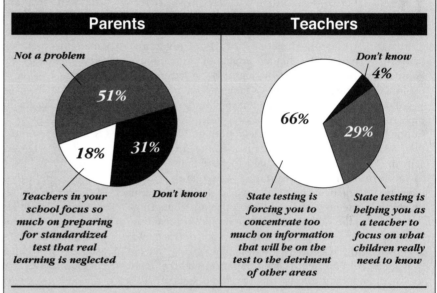

Is There Too Much Testing?

Parents and teachers disagree about whether state testing negatively affects student learning.

Parents

Not a problem — 51%
Teachers in your school focus so much on preparing for standardized test that real learning is neglected — 18%
Don't know — 31%

Teachers

Don't know — 4%
State testing is forcing you to concentrate too much on information that will be on the test to the detriment of other areas — 66%
State testing is helping you as a teacher to focus on what children really need to know — 29%

Note: Percentages may not add up to 100 because of rounding.

Sources: Public Agenda, "National Poll of Parents of Public School Students," 2000 (left); Education Week, "National Survey of Public School Teachers," 2000 (right).

the "old fill-in-the-bubble" multiple-choice tests. "Because states are setting more challenging standards, they have to come up with new ways to test," Vranek says. Some 30 states, she says, now use longer-answer formats for at least part of their tests.

Critics have cited the emphasis on high-stakes testing as a factor in an apparent increase in cheating on tests by students and, in a few well-publicized instances, teachers or principals. [4] Even in the absence of scandal, anti-testing advocate Neill says schools are bound to spend too much time preparing students for tests as testing assumes a greater role in assessing student and school performance.

"The schools will end up turning themselves into test-coaching programs," Neill says. "The kids will get a bad education, and we'll end up wasting years going down this road that does not lead to educational improvement."

Ferrandino of the elementary school principals' group agrees. "You're going to end up with kids who are very good test-takers, to the exclusion of a great many other things that need to be taught in schools," he says.

Testing expert Linn acknowledges the likelihood that teachers will shape their instruction with tests in mind, but says better testing will minimize the problem. "Teachers and principals are human beings," Linn says. "There will be teaching to the test. But if you have more ambitious tests, it's less of a concern to me."

"If it's a solid test," says Heritage Foundation education policy expert Krista Kafer, "it's going to give teachers the direction they need."

In Jennings' view, testing can benefit classroom instruction only if teachers are given more information about the results than raw scores. "They need

"Dump the SAT" Trend . . .

High school students who live in dread of standardized college entrance examinations have a high-powered new ally.

Richard Atkinson, president of the University of California, startled the higher education community in February by proposing that his highly regarded university no longer require applicants to take the exam.

"America's overemphasis on the SAT is compromising our educational system," Atkinson told the American Council on Education in a widely publicized speech on Feb. 18. Atkinson, an expert on memory and learning, said the test is widely perceived to be unfair, especially to minority and disadvantaged youngsters; distorts educational practices; and can have "a devastating impact on the self-esteem and aspirations of many youngsters." [1]

Officials at the College Board, the nonprofit organization that owns the test, quickly rallied to its defense. While acknowledging "a tendency to overemphasize" the SAT, College Board President Gaston Caperton said that the test "plays an important role in truly fair admissions processes" and also "supports the goals" of the current standards movement to improve school curriculums. [2]

Atkinson's proposal — which would need approval from the university's Academic Senate and Board of Regents — renewed a debate that has raged periodically over the reliability and fairness of the SAT for several decades. Some 2 million students took the test last year — about 44 percent of high school seniors.

Supporters contend the test provides a good measure of a student's mathematical and verbal abilities and — when used in conjunction with high school grades — somewhat accurately predicts future college performance.

"The SAT can be a device that sorts people in terms of the likelihood of success," says David Murray, director of research at the private Statistical Assessment Service in Washington, D.C. "It gives them a message about what next step will be most productive for their education."

Critics say that the test's predictive value is overstated

and that racial and ethnic disparities in test scores operate to limit educational opportunities for African-American and Hispanic students. "When you use the SAT, those inequities get perpetuated at the higher-education level," says Christina Perez, a testing-reform advocate at the advocacy group FairTest, based in Cambridge, Mass. "Students from economically disadvantaged backgrounds are once again locked out of learning opportunities."

The SAT — known for most of its history as the Scholastic Aptitude Test but reduced to an acronym a few years ago — grew out of the intelligence-testing movement of the 1920s. The test was first administered to some 8,000 college applicants in 1926, according to journalist Nicholas Lemann in his recent book *The Big Test*. [3]

According to Lemann, Harvard University President James Bryant Conant began using the test in the 1930s to identify gifted students from outside Harvard's traditional feeder schools in New England. As university enrollments grew beginning in the 1950s, more and more colleges required the test as part of the application process.

In its current form, SAT I is divided into two parts — mathematical and verbal — with scores from 200 to 800. Over time, the College Board added achievement tests in science, history and foreign languages. Today, those tests are called SAT II and are optional at some schools and mandatory at others, including the University of California. Many students will take a battery of three tests, including the widely administered writing exam.

In proposing to scrap the SAT I requirement, Atkinson disclaimed any broad attack on standardized tests. In fact, he said that for the time being he would continue requiring UC applicants to take the SAT II because it measures "actual achievement" on courses included in the student's high school curriculum. In the longer term, Atkinson called for developing standardized tests "directly tied to the college preparatory courses" required of UC applicants.

College Board officials concur with critics' view that some colleges overemphasize SAT scores in admissions

training in how to use tests so that they can understand what tests mean, so that they can diagnose kids, instead of just getting a pile of computer data from a company," he says.

Should federal aid be cut for "failing" schools?

Conservative education reformers have been promoting school vouchers for years as a way to hold low-performing schools accountable by

reducing the tax dollars they receive if their students choose to go elsewhere. [5] President Bush's proposal adopts this philosophy in limited form by providing that federal aid would be reduced to individual schools and to school districts and states on account of poor performance as measured by test scores.

Bush's proposal heartens advocates of vouchers, though they say it does not go far enough. Critics — including

Democratic lawmakers and both major teachers' unions, the NEA and the American Federation of Teachers (AFT) — say it goes too far by allowing students who quit public schools to take their federal aid dollars with them to private or parochial schools.

Supporters of Bush's plan say the penalty provisions are essential to turning around so-called failing schools. "If there are no consequences, there will be no change in

... Slowly Gaining Support

decisions and that people should not use the scores to compare universities with each other.

"People tend to think of it as a very, very important factor in admissions and in how universities rank, which is totally wrong," says Amy Schmidt, director of higher education evaluation and research at the College Board.

They also acknowledge that high school grades taken alone are a slightly better predictor of first-year college grades than SAT I scores taken alone. But they say that the use of SAT scores along with high school grades gives a measurably better prediction about an applicant's performance than either one used alone.

Critics discount the marginal improvement in predicting first-year grades and minimize the scores' value in forecasting an applicant's later college performance. "As time goes on, those scores mean less and less," Perez says. In any event, she says too many colleges — especially public universities — adopt a "rigid formula of test scores and grades" that operates as "a barrier to opportunities" for many students, especially minority youngsters.

Critics say that the advantages enjoyed by well-to-do students include the opportunity for private coaching for the SAT. Perez says some of the SAT preparation courses can cost up to $800 or more and can raise scores by 100 points. In his speech, Atkinson cited figures showing that 150,000 students spent more than $100 million with private coaching companies last year. But he stopped short of claiming that the coaching raises scores, saying only that it contributes to a perception of unfairness among minority communities.

College Board officials say that systematic research does not support the anecdotal information that coaching can raise SAT scores. Schmidt says the most recent study — by a statistician with no connection to the testing or the coaching industry — concluded that coaching raises SAT scores by "a rather small amount" — about 14–15 points on the math section and 6–8 points on the verbal. [4]

As for the disparities in SAT scores — white and Asian-American students have higher average scores than black or Hispanic youngsters — College Board officials insist that critics are "scapegoating" the SAT for inequities in public education generally.

"The same racial and ethnic gap exists in grades and class rank," Schmidt says. "Getting rid of the SAT is not getting rid of the underlying problem."

Unlike many other educational-policy issues, the SAT debate does not break down neatly along ideological lines. The criticism from liberal and minority groups is echoed by some conservative experts. "SATs are the most abused test of all," says Chester Finn, assistant secretary of Education under President Ronald Reagan and now president of the conservative Thomas B. Fordham Foundation.

Instead, the defense of the SAT is voiced most strongly from college and university officials who insist that the test scores help make better admissions decisions Nonetheless, a slowly growing minority of colleges and universities — now numbering around 380 — have dropped the SAT requirement, according to FairTest. [5]

Schmidt describes the reaction to Atkinson's proposal as "mixed." "Some people are applauding," she acknowledges. For her part, she says the effect of the speech has been healthy. "When someone of President Atkinson's stature raises questions, it causes the whole community to reflect on our practices," Schmidt says. "And that's a really good thing."

---

[1] Atkinson's speech can be found on the President's Home Page on the University of California's Web site (www.ucop.edu). For op-ed articles by Atkinson, see *Sacramento Bee*, Feb. 21, 2001; *San Jose Mercury News*, Feb. 23, 2001.

[2] Caperton's reply, dated Feb. 27, can be found at www.collegeboard.org/press.

[3] Nicholas Lemann, *The Big Test: The Secret History of America's Meritocracy* (1999). For an adaptation, see *Newsweek*, Sept. 26, 1999, pp. 52-57.

[4] Derek C. Briggs, "The Effect of Admissions Test Preparation," *Chance*, Vol. 14, No. 1 (2001), pp. 10-21. Briggs is a professor at the Graduate School of Education at the University of California at Berkeley; *Chance* is the magazine of the American Statistical Association.

[5] For a complete list and commentary, see www.fairtest.org.

---

behavior," Finn says. "If the results don't matter, if they don't bring either intervention or reward or punishment, then nothing will happen."

Opponents counter by criticizing the reliance on test scores to trigger the potential reduction in financial aid. "You're going to have a very high error rate," Neill says. "Schools are going to be unfairly penalized."

In addition, the opponents challenge the underlying premise that reducing aid to low-performing schools will help them improve. "I've never seen any evidence that that's true, "Neill says, "and it contravenes common sense."

Bush's plan uses a carrot-and-stick approach to low-performing schools and school districts. Any school or district that fails to make "adequate yearly progress" for one academic year is to be identified by the state and provided assistance to improve academic performance. But if a school fails to make adequate progress for a second year, the district must implement "corrective action" and allow all students at the school the option of attending a different public school.

If a school fails to make adequate progress for a third year, any disadvantaged student would be allowed to use federal funds to transfer to a higher-performing public or private school or receive educational services from some other provider. Students exercising that option could attend the new school for the same period of time they would have attended the failing school.

Bush's plan also calls for reducing administrative funds to a state education agency if the state fails to make adequate yearly progress for disadvantaged students.

Jennings of the Center on Education Policy says the "carrot" in Bush's proposal is inadequate. "He doesn't offer much help to states," Jennings says. "He does not offer much remedial assistance through Title I or other programs."

Bush adviser Kress acknowledges the criticism, but insists the proposal moves in the right direction. "Some people say it's not enough, but I think it's going to be significant," he says. "Is it enough? We could always do more, but it's a good first step."

Kress resists calling the "stick" part of Bush's plan a penalty or sanction. He calls the corrective measures "responses or consequences for performance that does not work for children." Whatever term is used, educators are strongly opposed.

"It would be wrongheaded to take resources away from those that are most in need," Fenton says.

NEA President Chase also says troubled schools need more help, not less. "No one wants to see a low-performing school — certainly not teachers, and certainly not the NEA," he says. "If you put forth the effort to turn those schools around, they will."

Rotherham of the 21st Century Schools Project agrees on the need for corrective action for low-performing schools, but he faults Bush's proposal as off target. "There should be action with regard to schools that aren't doing well, because the people who are being penalized are the students," he says. "It's unconscionable

to stand by and make excuses."

But Rotherham says vouchers alone will not solve the problem. He calls for expanding public school choice provisions, forcing states to get more involved with low-performing schools and making greater use of charter schools "to increase the supply of high-quality options." Without such action, he says, "you're simply rearranging the deck chairs on the *Titanic* in too many communities." ■

BACKGROUND

Rise of Testing

Standardized testing has played an important role in U.S. education from the debut of "intelligence tests" in the 1920s through the development of aggregated data on student achievement beginning in the late 1960s. With each expansion, standardized testing has drawn criticism about the reliability of the information and its use or potential misuse.

Two French psychologists — Alfred Binet and his student Theodore Simon — developed the first intelligence test in 1905. [6] A decade later, Stanford University psychologist Lewis Terman revised the IQ test for use in the United States. The Army used the tests for evaluating recruits and assigning jobs during World War I. With the war over, school reformers championed IQ testing as a way to individualize education for children of different abilities.

The influential columnist Walter Lippman launched the first popular attack on the use of IQ tests in 1922. He contended that the tests were unreliable and that their use would

lead to a "caste system." Terman, who viewed intelligence as hereditary and largely immutable, derided his critics as sentimentalists. The controversy proved to have little effect. By the end of the decade, Terman's test was selling 2 million copies a year.

Over the next several decades, intelligence testing became routine practice in U.S. schools. Their use surged in the late 1950s after the Soviet Union's launch of the satellite *Sputnik* raised alarms about American math and science education. Educators used the tests primarily for "tracking" — placing pupils in an academic or in a non-academic ("general" or "vocational") curriculum. As Diane Ravitch, a historian and former assistant secretary of Education, points out, the tests had few critics. Today, however, Ravitch, a professor at New York University, reflects the widely held view that by restricting educational opportunities for many students, IQ testing was "more negative than positive." [7]

The *Sputnik* scare spurred Congress in 1958 to approve the National Defense Education Act, a modest bill providing loans for college students in science and math and a small sum for testing and counseling in elementary or secondary education. Over the next several years, liberals and conservatives joined battle over proposals for broader federal aid to grades K-12. Liberals finally won the battle, at the height of President Lyndon B. Johnson's "Great Society" program, with the enactment of the Elementary and Secondary Education Act in 1965. The centerpiece of the law — now known as Title I — earmarked extra funds for schools with high concentrations of low-income or "disadvantaged" children.

Education Commissioner Francis Keppel was calling at the time for a federal testing program to make sure federal dollars were producing re-

Chronology

Before 1900

Public high schools exist in few communities.

— • —

1901–1960

IQ tests developed and widely used for pupil assignment.

1920s
IQ tests introduced into U.S. public schools; their use expands despite criticism.

1926
Scholastic Aptitude Test (SAT) administered as college entrance examination for first time.

1933
University of Iowa launches Iowa Test of Basic Skills.

1950s
Cold War and civil rights revolution prepare ground for federal role in improving public education.

— • —

1960s–1970s

Federal program to aid disadvantaged students established; states adopt minimum-competency tests.

1965
Congress passes Elementary and Secondary Education Act (ESEA), providing funds under Title I to aid schools with disadvantaged students.

1969
National Assessment of Educational Progress (NAEP) inaugurated to give national measure of student achievement.

Mid-to-late 1970s
Many states establish "minimum competency tests" for high school students.

— • —

1980s

Public schools criticized for lagging scores on standardized tests.

1983
A Nation at Risk report claims declining test scores indicate "rising tide of mediocrity" in U.S. schools; SAT scores are only data specifically cited.

1989
President George Bush convenes academic summit of nation's governors, lays out six national goals for education.

— • —

1990s

Standards movement aims to improve school curriculums; states add testing, but national test is opposed.

1991
President Bush proposes education bill for national goals, standards and tests, but legislation dies in Congress.

1994
ESEA reauthorization includes requirement that states receiving Title I funds adopt standards and accompanying tests by 2000-2001 academic year.

1997
President Bill Clinton's call for voluntary national tests meets strong opposition from both liberal and conservative lawmakers. Congress bans any moves toward national testing in 1998, reinforces prohibition in 1999.

— • —

2000s

President George W. Bush proposes annual state testing for grades 3-8 in reading and math.

August 2000
Student achievement continues to rise slowly, according to "nation's report card," but gap between white and minority students persists.

Fall 2000
Bush and Vice President Al Gore offer rival plans for educational reform in down-to-the-wire presidential campaign; after winning narrow Electoral College victory, Bush vows to make education top priority.

January 2001
Bush pushes education reform in inaugural address; releases outline of reform plan three days later. Plan lets states design own tests; would use NAEP scores to "verify" results. Proposal would let students at "failing schools" use federal funds for private schools or tutoring.

March 2001
Senate Education Committee approves annual state testing plan as part of reform bill, but defers debate on Bush's voucher plan to Senate floor; comparable bill introduced in House.

A Closer Look at the "Texas Miracle"

During the presidential campaign, George W. Bush often referred to the "Texas miracle." But the rising scores claimed on student achievement tests in Texas have been questioned as possibly inflated.

Ironically, the same checking procedure that President Bush wants to adopt to validate all the states' academic assessments was used in Texas.

In his testing proposal now pending in Congress, Bush calls for states to design their own annual tests for students in grades 3–8. To confirm those results, he also proposes using scores from the National Assessment of Educational Progress (NAEP).

Researchers from the Rand Corporation published a report last fall that adopted that very procedure: They compared the scores on the Texas Assessment of Academic Skills (TAAS) with the scores from Texas students on the NAEP. Their conclusion: The "serious discrepancies" between the two sets of figures raised "serious questions" about the validity of the substantial gains reported in reading and math on Texas's test.

The Rand report — "What Do Test Scores in Texas Tell Us?" — stirred partisan debate when it was released on Oct. 24, two weeks before the presidential election. [1] Vice President Al Gore and other Democrats cited the report in questioning Bush's credit-taking for improvements in Texas's educational record. Bush and other Republicans criticized the report and the timing of its release as politically motivated.

The researchers compared TAAS and NAEP scores for fourth-graders in reading and mathematics and for eighth-graders in math. [2] Texas students improved in all three NAEP scores over a four-year period (1994 to 1998 for fourth-grade reading, 1992 to 1996 for the others). But, the researchers continued, "the average test score gains on the NAEP in Texas exceeded those of the nation in only one of the three comparisons, namely: fourth-grade math."

For the same time periods, Texas was reporting substantially larger gains on all three measures. In addition, scores on the TAAS showed a narrowing gap between white students and African-American and Latino students. By contrast, the researchers said analysis of the NAEP data showed a slight increase in the gap between white and minority youngsters.

"The large discrepancies between TAAS and NAEP results

raise serious questions about the validity of the TAAS scores," the researchers concluded. While they said they did not know the source of the differences, they suggested test preparation as "one plausible explanation."

"Many schools are devoting a great deal of class time to highly specific TAAS preparation," they wrote. "It is also plausible that the schools with relatively large percentages of minority and poor students may be doing this more than other schools."

The researchers also cited two other factors that may have "somewhat inflated" the gains in Texas's NAEP scores compared to the nationwide average: increases in Texas in the exclusion of students with disabilities and in the number of students dropping out or being held back. Both factors, they said, "would have the effect of producing a gain in average test scores that overestimates actual changes in student performance."

Texas Education Commissioner Jim Nelson criticized the Rand report when it was released. He called the research "shoddy" and claimed that it contradicted an earlier, "more thoroughly researched" report by different Rand researchers released in August. That report concluded that Texas's gains on NAEP tests were among the highest in the nation — second highest to North Carolina among the states. [3]

Rand President James Thomson, however, saw no contradiction between the two reports. He said the later report differed "in scope," "in methodology" and "most of all in focus."

"The new report suggests a less positive picture of Texas education than the earlier effort," Thomson said in a written statement. "But I do not believe that these efforts are in sharp conflict. Together, in fact, they provide a more comprehensive picture of key education issues."

---

[1] Stephen P. Klein et al., "What Do Test Scores in Texas Tell Us?" RAND Corporation, Oct. 24, 2000 (www.rand.org/publications). For news coverage, see Debra Viadero, "Candidates Spar Over Test Gains in Texas," Education Week, Nov. 1, 2000 (www.edweek.org).

[2] The TAAS tests are mandatory for all public school students in Texas in grades 3-8; NAEP tests are given every two years to a representative sampling of students across the country in grades 4, 8 and 12. Because of the schedule, the researchers had no NAEP scores for eighth-graders in reading.

[3] David Grissmer et al., "Improving Student Achievement: What State NAEP Test Scores Tell Us," RAND Corporation, July 2000 (www.rand.org/publications).

sults. But Congress rejected the idea after education groups warned that it could lead to federal control of schools and a national curriculum. As an alternative, Keppel developed a plan for a limited testing program

based on a test to be administered to nationally representative samples of students. Congress approved funding for the plan, which debuted in 1969 as the National Assessment of Educational Progress, or NAEP.

Initially, NAEP had "no impact," according to Lawrence Feinberg, a spokesman for the National Assessment Governing Board, which now oversees the program. The test scores announced were only for individual questions. "There was no overall scale, nothing called math in general," Feinberg recalls. In addition, no scores were given for individual schools or school districts or even for individual states.

The test drew more attention beginning in the 1980s when the private Educational Testing Service (ETS) was awarded the contract to administer the tests. As part of the takeover, ETS rescored the previous tests to generate uniform overall results over time. Today, NAEP's 30-year trend line shows a slight increase in math scores and steady scores in reading. "If you were to describe it in one word, the best word would be flat," says testing expert Linn. (See graphs, p. 23.)

Raising Alarms

T est scores became a major focus of public concern in the 1970s and '80s. Critics of public education claimed that a decline in student achievement scores demonstrated that schools were failing to serve vast numbers of students and failing to meet the demands of the U.S. economy. But supporters of public education argued that test scores — far from demonstrating schools' shortcomings — actually showed that most school systems were performing well while educating a growing and diversifying student population.

The public alarm about the quality of schools resulted in a nationwide push in the 1970s to set minimum academic standards in the form of "competency tests." [8] By the end of the decade, more than two-thirds of the states established programs requiring some minimal competency tests. NAEP helped fuel the movement with a report in 1977 based on reading test scores through the de-

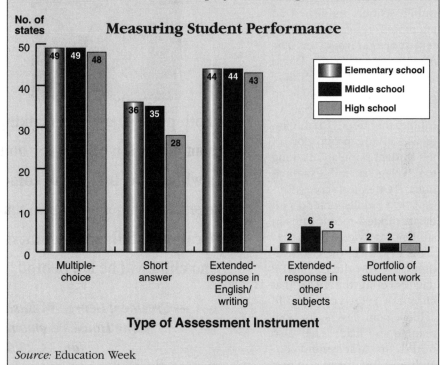

Multiple-Choice Tests Widely Used

Almost all the states assess students' knowledge with multiple-choice tests. While short-answer test items and extended-response questions for writing are used by many states, far fewer use extended-response items in other subjects. Only Kentucky and Vermont use portfolios of students' work to measure their performance against state standards.

Measuring Student Performance

No. of states

- Elementary school
- Middle school
- High school

Type of Assessment Instrument	Elementary	Middle	High
Multiple-choice	49	49	48
Short answer	36	35	28
Extended-response in English/writing	44	44	43
Extended-response in other subjects	2	6	5
Portfolio of student work	2	2	2

Source: Education Week

cade. The report estimated 13 percent of the nation's 17-year-old high school students were "functionally illiterate."

The perception of deteriorating academic standards in public schools hardened in the 1980s after the release of an alarmist report by an 18-member commission appointed by Education Secretary Terrel Bell. The report, titled *A Nation at Risk* and released in 1983, decried what it called "a rising tide of mediocrity" in public education that was threatening the U.S. position in the global economy.

Test scores were cited as the main evidence for the indictment, but with flimsy documentation. [9] The report cited the functional illiteracy estimate

from the earlier NAEP report and also appeared to be citing NAEP for evidence of declining student achievement in science through the 1970s. It also claimed — without attribution — that average achievement of high school students on "most standardized tests" was lower than at the time of *Sputnik's* launch. But the only statistics specifically included in the report were scores on the Scholastic Aptitude Test (SAT), which the commission said, "demonstrate a virtually unbroken decline from 1963 to 1980."

President Ronald Reagan responded to the report by calling for dismantling the U.S. Department of Education and ending "federal intrusion" in local public schools. For its part, the NEA accepted the panel's recommendations for more rigorous academic standards but said the proposals would require "additional billions of dollars — and a big boost from the federal government."

More than a decade later, two academics sympathetic to public schools published an attempted refutation of the test-score alarms. In *The Manufactured Crisis*, David Berliner and Bruce Biddle acknowledge the decline in average SAT scores but attribute the trend to the increase in the proportion of the student population taking the college-bound examinations. [10] Other test scores, Berliner and Biddle contend, "indicate modest recent gains in student knowledge."

As evidence, the two academics reproduced NAEP data covering the 1970s that showed relatively stable achievement levels in both reading and math. They also noted an assessment co-authored by testing expert Linn in 1990 that showed average scores had increased on all five of the most commonly used commercial achievement tests — including the oldest of the five, the Iowa Test of Basic Skills. But the gains were concealed, Berliner and Biddle explain, because the "norm-referenced" tests are recalibrated each year so that the "average" student scores at the 50th percentile.

Today, even critics of public education acknowledge some of this rebuttal. Finn, for example, acknowledges that SAT scores should not be used to evaluate the overall quality of public education, while the Heritage Foundation's Kafer describes the NAEP scores as "stagnant" but not in decline. As for the practical impact of *A Nation at Risk*, public education supporters say that

"Both parties have been talking about education reform for quite a while now. It's time to come together and get it done so that we can truthfully say, in America no child will be left behind."

— *President George W. Bush*
White House ceremony
Jan. 23, 2001

federal aid to education declined both under Reagan and under his successor, President George Bush.

Setting Standards

Bipartisan agreement emerged in the 1990s around two education policies: setting higher-than-minimum academic standards for students to master and holding schools and school systems more accountable for students' performance. Standard-setting initially stalled because of fierce disagreements over curricular issues and then advanced slowly at the state

but not the national level. Meanwhile, testing proposals aimed at enhancing school system accountability were initially deferred and then also became mired in curricular and jurisdictional disputes. [11]

President George Bush moved quickly in 1989 to make good on his campaign pledge to be an "education president" first by offering a modest education bill in April and then convening an "education summit" of the nation's governors in the fall in Charlottesville, Va. There, he teamed with the then-president of the National Governors' Association — Arkansas Gov. Bill Clinton — to lay out six educational goals for the nation to achieve by 2000. But the Bush legislation stalled in an end-of-session filibuster in 1990 by conservative Republicans opposed to greater federal involvement in education.

The next year, two conservative groups — one a presidential advisory committee of business leaders and educators, the other an education group — laid out plans, respectively, for national testing of elementary and secondary students and of graduating high school seniors. Bush included national goals, standards and tests in new legislation proposed in 1991, but again Congress failed to act. In the meantime, though, Bush's Education Department provided funding for national education groups to develop voluntary curriculum standards.

The standard-writing effort bore fruit not during Bush's presidency but Clinton's — and it proved to be a debacle, at least nationally. Conservatives viewed the proposals that emerged not as tough, "back-to-basics" guidelines but as trendy academic revisionism with a liberal bent. Proposed standards for teaching U.S. history became a major political issue; opposition led by social conservatives resulted in a 99–1 Senate vote against the standards in January 1995 and their later disavowal by Education Secretary Richard W. Riley. [12] Standards for English and math similarly provoked sharp attacks.

States, meanwhile, were making greater progress in putting curricular standards on paper. Many states had begun writing standards before Clinton took office in January 1993. Clinton and the Democratic-controlled Congress spurred the movement by including in the reauthorization of the Elementary and Secondary Education Act in 1994 a requirement that schools receiving Title I funds adopt standards and accompanying tests by 2000–2001. By decade's end, all states except Iowa were working on developing new academic standards.

The results, however, were mixed. "Most of the standards don't cut the mustard," Chester Finn wrote in an opinion article in *Education Week* in November 1998. He and his Fordham Foundation colleagues complained that many state standards were "extremely vague," "hostile to knowledge," or "entranced by relevance." [13] In its most recent annual survey, *Education Week's* reporters and editors similarly say many standards are too vague. Overall, though, the newspaper credits the more hopeful view that the movement has resulted in a more demanding curriculum and higher expectations in many classrooms. [14]

As for testing, the issue fell victim to politicization at the national level. Clinton in 1997 proposed voluntary national tests for fourth-graders in reading and eighth-graders in math. After a bitter debate, the Republican-controlled Congress banned even limited field-testing in fiscal 1998. It followed the next year by including in a budget measure a permanent ban on national tests unless explicitly authorized by Congress.

For their part, states were revamping their own testing programs, but again with mixed results. Many teachers complained that they were being pressured to put too much emphasis on tests, while outside experts worried that many states were using "off-the-shelf" commercial tests and failing to align testing with emerging new standards. Meanwhile, parental opposition surfaced with news that many students and schools were failing the new tests.

Campaigning for Tests

Education became a major issue in the 2000 presidential campaign between George W. Bush, then serving his second four-year term as governor of Texas, and Vice President Al Gore, the Democratic standard-bearer. Bush made annual testing the keystone of a plan to increase schools' accountability and overall quality. Once in the White House, Bush made his testing proposal the central part of an education reform plan he submitted to Congress in his first full week as president.

Bush and Gore emphasized education as a campaign issue despite the federal government's relatively limited role in financing or overseeing secondary and elementary schools. [15] Bush emphasized his plan — including testing, vouchers, charter schools, and new initiatives for recruiting teachers and teaching readers to young students — from the beginning of the primary season through the end of the fall campaign. The plan represented a shift for the Republican Party, which in the past had generally opposed federal intrusion into local control of schools.

For his part, Gore emphasized school accountability by proposing to require states and districts to publish school report cards annually. He called for more aggressive steps to turn around poor-performing schools, including reorganizing schools that fail to improve after two years. He also supported creating more charter schools, but criticized Bush on school vouchers.

The two candidates clashed sharply on education in the final weeks of the campaign. Bush fired the first volley in early October by citing what he described as the NAEP's declining or stagnant achievement scores as evidence that the country was in an "education recession." Democrats, including Education Secretary Riley, countered by saying that SAT and NAEP scores had actually increased during Clinton's eight years in office. [16] The exchange served as a backdrop for the two candidates' recitation of their opposing education plans in the first of three presidential campaign debates on Oct. 3.

In a sharper exchange with the election less than two weeks away, Gore seized on a newly released report by the Rand Corporation to dispute Bush's depiction of Texas' "education miracle" during his governorship. [17] Gore said the researchers' conclusion showed that test-score gains repeatedly claimed by Bush during his campaign were "illusory." Bush campaign officials insisted other studies supported Bush's claims. "Texas is a national leader in student achievement," a campaign spokesman said.

Bush used his inaugural address on Jan. 20 to repeat his vow to "reclaim America's schools." In a heavily publicized White House ceremony three days later, he released the outlines of his education plan in a 28-page blueprint entitled "No Child Left Behind." With Education Secretary Rod Paige at his side, Bush emphasized that he hoped lawmakers from both parties would unite behind his proposal.

"Both parties have been talking about education reform for quite a while now," Bush said. "It's time to come together and get it done so that we can truthfully say, in America no child will be left behind."

Some Democratic lawmakers did voice qualified support for Bush's initiative. Sen. Joseph I. Lieberman, D-Conn., said he would reintroduce a proposal by centrist Democrats with many features similar to Bush's proposal. But Democrats criticized the voucher component of Bush's plan, as did the NEA. "This voucher proposal is sure to divide us," NEA President Chase told *Education Week*. [18]

The testing proposal raised many questions among state officials about the impact of the new requirement on classroom instruction and on state and local budgets. The proposal also gave critics of testing an opportunity to renew the debate over the reliability of tests and the role of test preparation in the schools.

"Bush is asking for so much testing that he's forcing people to think about the proper use of tests," Jennings of the Center on Education Policy commented to *Education Week*. "So we could have a good debate, I hope, on how these tests are used, and that would be the best thing." ■

CURRENT SITUATION

Testing in Congress

President Bush's proposal for annual testing in public schools is drawing support from members of Congress in both parties with only scattered questions or dissent. While other details of Bush's education reform plan are still being debated — including the controversial

voucher plan — the testing requirement is viewed as all but certain to be included in legislation that could clear Congress by the summer recess in August.

Senators meeting with administration officials on the legislative vehicle for Bush's plan — the reauthorization of the 1965 Elementary and Secondary Education Act (ESEA) — completed negotiations on a bipartisan compromise just before starting a two-week recess on April 6. [19] The plan would allow students in failing schools to switch to other public schools and to receive federal funds for private tutoring, but would not provide vouchers for private schools as Bush favors. Instead, the private-school voucher issue will be debated as an amendment after the bill is brought to the Senate floor during the week of April 23.

Despite the partial setback, Bush education adviser Kress pronounced himself satisfied with the course of negotiations. "Both sides are trying in a genuine way to address each other's concerns," Kress said.

Senate Republicans also said they were pleased. "We've done a good job of getting what the president wants," Sen. Judd Gregg of New Hampshire said. Gregg, who plans to introduce the voucher amendment on the floor, was the administration's principal advocate during the Education Committee's markup of the bill the week of March 5. Committee Chairman James Jeffords, R-Vt., opposed including the most controversial parts of Bush's proposal in the bill at the committee stage.

Democratic senators also called the negotiations productive. "We're within reach of an overall agreement on a joint amendment that will have the support of Republicans and Democrats," Sen. Lieberman said. But some Democrats voiced concern that the funding levels for the Title I program to aid schools serving disadvantaged populations would not

be adequate. "If we don't get a significant ESEA increase in funding, all of this can be off," Sen. Edward M. Kennedy of Massachusetts said.

Democrats are asking for $32.8 billion in funding for programs under the ESEA for fiscal 2002, an increase of nearly $15 billion over fiscal 2001. Bush is proposing a $1.6 billion increase for ESEA programs.

Sen. Paul Wellstone, D-Minn., was the only senator to publicly challenge the testing provisions during the committee's deliberations. He sponsored legislation to prohibit using performance on a standardized test as the single determinant for a decision on promotion, tracking or graduation. Bush's plan is "overly reliant on standardized tests that fail to assess more than a narrow slice of student learning," Wellstone wrote in an op-ed article published in *The New York Times* after the Senate committee markup. [20]

Wellstone declined to sign on to the compromise package agreed to earlier this month and predicted "strong opposition" from Senate Democrats without what he called "an iron-clad commitment" on funding. "Because if you don't do that, and you have this testing every year, you set everybody up for failure," he told *The New York Times*.

Senators were also working on a compromise to allow a pilot program for Bush's "charter states" plan, which would let some states use federal funds for virtually any educational purpose as long as academic results improved. And the agreement included a third major component of Bush's plan to give states much greater flexibility in using federal Title I funds.

In the House, the bill introduced by Education Committee Chairman John A. Boehner, R-Ohio, differs from Bush's plan in one significant respect. The Senate bill includes Bush's proposal to require states to give the NAEP — the voluntary, sampling test used to generate the "nation's report card" — to validate the state's own

At Issue:

Should Congress pass President Bush's proposal for annual testing of students in grades 3–8?

REP. JOHN A. BOEHNER, R-OHIO
CHAIRMAN, HOUSE COMMITTEE ON EDUCATION AND THE WORKFORCE

WRITTEN FOR THE CQ RESEARCHER, APRIL 2001

*p*resident Bush has pledged to "leave no child behind" when it comes to reforming our nation's education system. Measuring student achievement is a critical part of the president's plan and must be included in any legislation that passes Congress. We can close the achievement gap between the most disadvantaged students and other children through tough accountability standards — which include annual assessments, as well as more flexibility for schools and giving parents more choice about where to educate their children.

We recently introduced President Bush's plan as H.R. 1, the No Child Left Behind Act. The bill demands accountability by asking states and local schools to perform annual testing of student progress in reading and math for every student in grades three through eight. Assessments will provide parents with much needed information about how their children are performing and how well schools are teaching them.

H.R. 1 gives states flexibility to build on their current assessment systems while still ensuring that every child learns and succeeds. States may select and design assessments of their choosing, but the results must be comparable from year to year. Federal funds are provided for states to design the tests.

Annual assessments are the best way to provide timely information on students' academic progress. Testing less frequently than every year does not provide enough information to make useful changes or for schools to make adjustments to meet their children's educational needs.

Annual assessments do not constitute a national test. In fact, H.R. 1 explicitly prohibits the adoption of a national test. States will choose a test that best suits their needs, and the federal government will provide funding for states that do not have annual assessments to develop them.

Using state assessments, schools that fail after one year would qualify for emergency help. Schools that continue to fail after three years would face sanctions, while parents would gain new options.

A state's improvement in academic achievement also would be measured by its annual assessments. A valid sample such as the National Assessment of Educational Progress (NAEP) or another comparable assessment would be used as a "snapshot" to confirm the results of the state tests for the purpose of rewards and sanctions. States that show significant progress in closing achievement gaps would be rewarded.

H.R. 1 will give students a chance, parents a choice and schools a charge to be the best in the world.

REP. ROBERT C. SCOTT, D-VA.
MEMBER, HOUSE COMMITTEE ON EDUCATION AND THE WORKFORCE

WRITTEN FOR THE CQ RESEARCHER, APRIL 2001

*t*ests, when validated and used appropriately, can serve as powerful diagnostic tools to expose shortcomings in our educational system and help individual students. Regretfully, President Bush's proposal to increase the number of tests for children in grades 3 through 8 fails to adequately address what to do after the tests are given.

In the absence of such a plan, test results may be used merely to punish students and schools rather than to help them achieve.

Any educational test must comply with the standards for testing outlined by the National Academy of Sciences and other scientific groups. These standards require that educational tests must be reliable and valid for the purposes for which they are being used; aligned with the curriculum that students are being taught; and given only after children have had the opportunity to learn the material being tested.

Furthermore, these standards prohibit "high-stakes" tests — tests that serve as the single determinant for tracking, promotion or graduation of individual students, without consideration of other factors, such as grades, classroom performance or other tests.

The development of new, valid tests will not be easy. Present law already requires testing in grades 3, 5 and 8. After approximately six years since enactment, and after spending $400 million this year alone, most states have yet to comply with the law.

Notwithstanding the issues of quality and quantity in testing, the real challenge for educational reform comes after the test. Schools already engage in testing, and the results are in. Students fail when they sit in crumbling and over-crowded schools, are taught by unprepared and overburdened teachers and receive generally inadequate resources.

It is doubtful that more tests will give us any new information in this regard. Simply measuring student performance will not change student performance. Remember the old farmer's adage, "You don't fatten the pig by weighing the pig."

The president's plan inadequately addresses how to use test results to help individual students and schools. While a major element of the plan is "choice," allowing only a privileged few to leave, the school does not improve educational opportunities for the overwhelming majority of children who will be left behind in the failing school. It makes more sense to invest new resources in proven strategies to improve student achievement, rather than simply giving more tests.

test. Boehner's bill allows each state to select the test used to corroborate its own assessment.

"That knocks the stuffing out of Bush's proposal because there's no independent check on how the states are doing," Jennings of the Center on Education Policy says. "A state will go out and shop for tests that show they're doing a good job based on their test."

As in the Senate, the testing provision has drawn little criticism so far in the House. Boehner and the committee's ranking Democrat, Rep. George Miller of California, both support annual testing. And Rep. Tim Roemer, D-Ind., is sponsoring a bill backed by other "New Democrats" that couples the accountability features Bush is requesting with higher funding. The only vocal criticism of testing has come from Rep. Robert C. Scott, D-Va., who has worked with civil rights groups to criticize standardized testing as biased against African-Americans and Hispanics.

The House bill includes Bush's voucher proposal, which Republicans label a "safety mechanism." Republicans have a narrow majority in the House — compared with the 50–50 split in the Senate — and pro-voucher conservatives hold considerable sway within the GOP caucus. But Democrats are warning that including the voucher proposal will force a fight when the bill reaches the House floor.

"You're not going to have a bipartisan bill with vouchers," Miller says. The House committee is expected to start work on the bill in mid-May.

Testing in the States

P resident Bush's testing proposal would lead to more tests for students and teachers and higher costs and new financial risks for administrators and local and state education agencies. Educators and local and

state education policy-makers have voiced concern about the changes, but so far they have not materially slowed the progress of the proposal in Congress.

"We are moving quickly without any attempt to integrate this federal mandate with what states are currently doing," says David Griffith, director of governmental relations for the National Association of State Boards of Education. "They're moving so quickly that it's frustrating."

Currently, every state but Iowa requires some form of statewide assessment, but only 15 states plus the District of Columbia test all public school students in reading and math in grades 3–8 as the Bush proposal would require. [21] Even most of those states would face changes. Only seven use a so-called criterion-referenced test based on state standards, as Bush proposes, according to *Education Week*. Six of the others rely primarily on norm-referenced, off-the-shelf exams, while the remaining two use a combination. [22]

States currently spend about $422 million a year on testing, according to an estimate compiled by the on-line state news service stateline.org. [23] The cost is certain to rise if Bush's proposal is enacted into law. In addition to the new tests themselves, the Bush plan imposes new requirements for handling the scores — for example, computer storage of results.

Both the Senate and the House bills seek to offset the costs somewhat. The Senate bill provides $400 million to help states pay for development of new tests, the House bill $320 million. The Senate bill also provides that the federal government will pay for half the cost of administering the new tests; the House bill has no comparable provision.

Both bills give the states a few years to put the new requirements into effect. The House bill would require states to have the new tests ready for school year 2004–2005; the

Senate bill would kick in in 2005–2006. Either deadline would be difficult to meet, Griffith says. He notes that a few states are not yet in compliance with a narrower assessment requirement included in the 1994 ESEA reauthorization.

Commercial test publishers themselves would have problems keeping up with the demand for new testing instruments, according to industry officials. "There's one heck of a capacity problem," H. D. Hoover, incoming president of the National Council on Measurement in Education and senior author of the Iowa Test of Basic Skills (ITBS), told *The Washington Post* earlier this year. [24]

The industry is dominated by just three test publishers that make their money off relatively low-cost standardized tests used widely across the country. Tests individually tailored to meet separate state standards are more expensive — $20 to $30 per student compared to $6 to $12 per student for generic tests — because they cannot be used widely and because they use more open-ended questions.

Bush's plan to change the use of the NAEP by comparing a state's results on that test with scores on its own assessments is also creating concerns among the states and from some education experts. In Congress, some Republican lawmakers fear that Bush's plan would turn the NAEP into a de facto national test, which they view as a step toward a national curriculum.

State officials fear that inconsistent results — for example, higher scores on their own tests than on the NAEP — would prompt questions about the validity of the state's assessments. "This whole notion that NAEP will be used to confirm or validate state assessments is wrong," Griffith says.

Some educators fear, however, that using NAEP to check states' progress would reduce its value as an independent measure of student achievement. "It works as a barometer because there isn't any invitation to teach to it in a direct way," said Lauren Resnick, director of the Learning Research and Development Center at the University of Pittsburgh. [25]

Meanwhile, a branch of the National Academy of Sciences is recommending a "major program of research" to design new tests to yield fairer and more accurate information about students. The report by a 17-member committee appointed by the National Research Council says existing tests reveal little about a student's academic strengths and do little to help teachers improve classroom instruction despite major advances in knowledge about how students learn. "A vision for the future is that assessments at all levels — from classrooms to state — will work together in a system that is comprehensive, coherent and continuous," the report says. [26]

OUTLOOK

Testing Results

A cting under a state mandate to show improvement in test-passing rates, the Columbus, Ohio, public school system experimented with three new elementary-school reading programs at the start of the 1999–2000 school year. When fourth-grade pupils took the state's reading test seven months later, in March 2000, the results were neither consistent nor impressive. [27]

One of the programs called for a daily 90-minute block of structured reading activities. Out of 22 schools that used that program, 17 recorded lower passing rates on the test. Three schools that used a second program — a form of scripted rote learning — varied from modest gains at two schools to a 10-percentage-point drop at the third.

Most of the schools — 63 — used a program called "comprehensive literacy" that gave teachers greater flexibility. Their results were better, with more than half showing gains ranging up to 31 percent. Overall, though, the net gain averaged only 1 percent.

Columbus' effort to raise reading scores illustrates that testing by itself does not improve students' education. Nationally, the NAEP results given in the "nation's report card" yield a similar caution. The most recent figures, released April 6, show only modest gains in reading over the past decade, for example. Less than one-third of fourth-graders — 32 percent — scored "proficient" or "advanced" on the reading test in 2000, compared to 28 percent in 1992, while the number who scored below proficient showed a negligible drop, from 38 percent to 37 percent.

In announcing the figures, Education Secretary Paige said they showed that previous reform efforts have been inadequate. "After decades of business-as-usual school reform, too many of our nation's children still cannot read," Paige told reporters.

Democrats, however, continue to fault Bush on education funding. "He will not be able to turn around failing schools with his anemic education budget," Rep. Miller commented after the president's budget was released on April 9. The budget proposes $44.5 billion in federal spending on education for fiscal 2002. The administration says the figure is an 11.5 percent increase over fiscal 2001; but Democrats say that after taking a late appropriation into account the administration's figure raises education spending by only 5.7 percent over the current year.

Supporters of Bush's proposal are confident that the additional testing will help bring about improved education for students. "We've got evidence that the more you know, the better you do — the more accurate your interventions, and the better your reforms and changes," Finn says. Testing "gives you better information that makes it more likely that you'll make wise and appropriate policy changes because you'll know more."

Testing officials also voice confidence in the effects of better assessments but have mixed views on the details of Bush's plan.

"There's good evidence that having high-quality feedback systems on the performance of individual students is useful for improving the performance of individual students in schools," says Fenton of the National Association of Test Directors. As for Bush's proposal, "We're going to need to look at the details before making a judgment about whether it will support the efforts that are going on around the country."

Democrats are less certain of the power of testing to lift student achievement. "I just hope that after you go through the evolution from standards to tests and accountability, we get to the real help stage, where we help teachers get trained on what they're supposed to teach and where we provide some extra assistance to students who don't pass the test," says the Center on Education Policy's Jennings. "It's a three-step program: You establish standards, you measure results with tests and hold them accountable and then you provide some real assistance. Bush's plan is very light on the third step."

For their part, educators are also cautioning that the testing should be viewed as nothing more than one step toward Bush's professed goal to "leave no child behind."

"We have no problem with the accountability aspect of this, but we also recognize that it is only one piece of it," says Ferrandino of the elementary school principals' group. "That alone is not going to be the solution to the problems in our educational system." ∎

Notes

[1] See *Columbus Dispatch*, Nov. 26, 2000.

[2] See *Baltimore Sun*, Feb. 2, 2000; Feb. 3, 2000; *Education Week*, Feb. 9, 2000.

[3] "Quality Counts 2001: A Better Balance: Standards, Tests, and the Tools to Succeed," *Education Week*, Jan. 11, 2001, p. 8.

[4] See Kathy Koch, "Cheating in Schools," *The CQ Researcher*, Sept. 22, 2000, pp. 745-768.

[5] For background, see Kathy Koch, "School Vouchers," *The CQ Researcher*, April 9, 1999, pp. 281-304.

[6] For background, see Sarah Glazer, "Intelligence Testing," *The CQ Researcher*, July 30, 1993, pp. 649-672; Diane Ravitch, *Left Back: A Century of Failed School Reforms* (2000), pp. 130-161.

[7] *Ibid.*, p. 160.

[8] For background, see Marc Leepson, "Competency Tests," *Editorial Research Reports*, Aug. 18, 1978, pp. 601-620.

[9] See National Commission on Excellence in Education, *A Nation at Risk* (1983), pp. 8-11.

[10] David C. Berliner and Bruce J. Biddle, *The Manufactured Crisis: Myths, Frauds, and the Attack on America's Public Schools* (1995). Berliner is dean of the College of Education, Arizona State University; Biddle is a professor emeritus of psychology and sociology at the University of Missouri.

[11] For background, see Kathy Koch, "National Education Standards," *The CQ Researcher*, May 14, 1999, pp. 401-424.

[12] For background, see Kenneth Jost, "Teaching History," *The CQ Researcher*, Sept. 29, 1995, pp. 849-872.

[13] Chester E. Finn Jr. *et al.*, "The State of State Standards: Four Reasons Why Most 'Don't Cut the Mustard'," *Education Week*, Nov. 11, 1998; the article is on the Fordham Foundation Web site, www.edexcellence.org.

[14] "Quality Counts 2001," *Education Week*, pp. 12-22.

[15] See "Bush vs. Gore: The Candidates on Education, Issue by Issue," *Education Week*, Sept. 6, 2000.

FOR MORE INFORMATION

Achieve, Inc., 8 Story St., Suite 1, Cambridge, Mass. 02138; (617) 496-6300; www.achieve.org. The independent, bipartisan organization was founded in 1996 by governors and corporate CEOs to promote higher academic standards and "demanding tests" to enhance school accountability.

FairTest (National Center for Open and Fair Testing), 342 Broadway, Cambridge, Mass. 02139; (617) 864-4810; www.fairtest.org. The organization seeks to end what it calls "the abuses, misuses and flaws of standardized testing" and to eliminate "racial, class, gender and cultural barriers to equal opportunity posed by standardized testing."

Heritage Foundation, 214 Massachusetts Ave., N.E., Washington, D.C. 20002; (202) 546-4400; www.heritage.org. The conservative think tank has generally supported use of standardized tests to promote academic standards and school accountability.

National Association of State Boards of Education, 277 South Washington St., Suite 100, Alexandria, Va. 22314; (703) 684-4000; www.nasbe.org. The organization calls annual testing a "costly and inefficient way to evaluate schools and districts."

National Association of Test Directors, c/o Mary Yakimowski-Srebnick (president), Hampton City Schools, 144 Research Dr., Hampton, Va. 23666; (757) 896-8314; www.natd.org. The association represents local and state officials and professionals responsible for administering assessment programs in public schools K-12.

National Education Association, 1201 16th St., N.W., Washington, D.C. 20036; (202) 833-4000; www.nea.org. The nation's largest teachers union has questioned the use of "high-stakes" tests to penalize underperforming schools or school districts.

[16] *Education Week*, Oct. 4, 2000.

[17] *Education Week*, Nov. 1, 2000.

[18] *Education Week*, Jan 23, 2001.

[19] Coverage drawn from *CQ Weekly*, April 7, 2001, p. 783; *The New York Times*, April 8, 2001, p. A20; *The Washington Post*, April 6, 20001, p. A8.

[20] Paul Wellstone and Jonathan Kozol, "What Tests Can't Fix," *The New York Times*, March 13, 2001, p. A25. Kozol is an author and liberal advocate on educational policy.

[21] Nearly all Iowa public school districts voluntarily participate in the student achievement testing offered through the Iowa Testing Programs at the University of Iowa.

[22] *Education Week*, Jan. 31, 2001.

[23] See www.stateline.org. For news coverage, see *Education Week*, March 14, 2001, p. 18.

[24] *The Washington Post*, Feb. 10, 2001, p. A3.

[25] *Education Week*, March 14, 2001, p. 1.

[26] "Knowing What Students Know: The Science and Design of Educational Assessment," National Research Council, April 2001. See *Education Week*, April 11, 2001.

[27] See *Columbus Dispatch*, Oct. 17, 2000.

Bibliography

Selected Sources Used

Books

Berliner, David C., and Bruce J. Biddle, *The Manufactured Crisis: Myths, Frauds and the Attack on America's Public Schools*, Perseus, 1996.

The two academics strongly argue that the critique of U.S. public education is based on myths, including spurious claims about declining scores by U.S. students on standardized tests. Berliner is dean of the College of Education, Arizona State University; Biddle is a professor emeritus of psychology and sociology at the University of Missouri.

Jennings, John F., *Why National Standards and Tests? Politics and the Quest for Better Schools*, SAGE, 1998.

Jennings, a longtime Democratic aide with the House Education and Labor Committee, chronicles the standards movement from its birth in the late 1980s through the controversies of the early and mid-'90s. The book also provides a detailed account of Congress' reauthorization of the Elementary and Secondary Education Act (ESEA) in 1994 and the education policy debates of the 1992 and '96 presidential campaigns. The book includes 12 pages of references. Jennings is director of the Center on Education Policy.

Kohn, Alfie, *The Schools Our Children Deserve: Moving Beyond Traditional Classrooms* and "Tougher Standards," Houghton Mifflin, 1999.

Kohn, a leading critic of standardized tests, argues that the standards movement with its reliance on high-stakes testing hurts rather than helps education. The book includes detailed notes and a 30-page list of references.

Lemann, Nicholas, *The Big Test: The Secret History of the American Meritocracy*, Farrar, Straus and Giroux, 1999.

Journalist Lemann's history of the Scholastic Aptitude Test and its role in U.S. education and society is both thorough and highly critical. The book includes detailed source notes. For an adaptation, see *Newsweek*, Sept. 6, 1999, p. 52.

Peterson, Julia J., *The Iowa Testing Program: The First Fifty Years*, University of Iowa Press, 1983.

The book provides a detailed and celebratory history of the Iowa Test of Basic Skills, the once dominant and still widely used battery of standardized tests.

Ravitch, Diane, *Left Back: A Century of Failed School Reforms*, Simon & Schuster, 2000.

Ravitch, a leading education historian and policy analyst, gives a comprehensive overview of attempts at educational "reform" during the 20th century. The book includes detailed notes and a three-page select bibliography. Ravitch served as assistant secretary of Education under President George Bush; she is now a professor at New York University.

Articles

Cloud, John, "Should SATs Matter?" *Time*, March 12, 2001, p. 62.

The article updates the debate over the SAT following the proposal by the president of the University of California to stop requiring the test for all applicants.

Danitz, Tiffany, "Education Debate Set to Begin in Congress as States Battle for Control," stateline.org, April 3, 2001 (www.stateline.org).

The article comprehensively sets the stage for the impending debate in Congress over President Bush's education reform package. It includes a link to stateline's survey that put the states' total spending on testing at $422 million last year.

Koch, Kathy, "National Education Standards," *The CQ Researcher*, May 14, 1999, pp. 401-424.

The report gives an overview on setting academic standards at the state and national levels through the 1990s.

"SAT Debate," Talk of the Nation, National Public Radio, Feb. 26, 2001 (www.npr.org).

The hour-long program featured a thorough debate on the SAT between College Board official Gretchen Rigol and FairTest Executive Director Monty Neill.

Reports and Studies

Campbell, Jay R., Catherine M. Hombo and John Mazzeo, "NAEP 1999 Trends in Academic Progress: Three Decades of Student Performance," National Assessment of Educational Progress, August 2000.

The report gives a detailed analysis of NAEP scores since 1971, which generally show declines in the 1970s, increases in the '80s and early '90s and mostly stable performance since then. The report can be found on the Web site of the National Center for Education Statistics (www.nces.gov/nationsreportcard/pubs).

"Quality Counts 2001: A Better Balance: Standards, Tests, and the Tools To Succeed," *Education Week*, Jan. 11, 2001.

The 196-page report by the respected weekly newspaper — the fifth in an annual series — provides an overview of developments regarding standards and testing and individual reports, with statistics, on each of the 50 states.

3 Mental Health Insurance

JANE TANNER

Actor Russell Crowe (right) won the 2002 British Academy of Film and Television Arts best actor award for his portrayal of Nobel Prize-winning mathematician John Nash Jr. (left) in the Oscar-winning film "A Beautiful Mind." The film's empathetic portrayal of Nash's struggle with schizophrenia has increased the public's understanding of the disease.

As a whiz in finance, the petite, attractive woman had no trouble landing a job on Wall Street after graduating from college in 1993. But there was a problem.

Despite being lauded as a dynamic, high-energy employee who worked long hours and eagerly took on extra projects, she often slipped into dark moods. She moved through seven jobs in seven years, often getting fired. Employers and co-workers could not deal with her angry flare-ups and door slamming.

"People get afraid of you," the woman says. "I'm pint-sized — 5 feet 1 inch and 105 pounds. So for people to say, 'We're scared of you,' I never could believe it." (The woman agreed to talk to a reporter but fears that if her name is used in this report it may jeopardize her job.)

Two years ago, on the verge of another job disaster, her life suddenly changed. A firm with generous mental health benefits bought out her employer, and she decided to seek expert help. During previous years of counseling, she had been told that her mood swings were due to the stress of being young and single in Manhattan. But it turned out she was suffering from bipolar disorder (also called manic depression), and today, on medication, she is stable and productive.

"When I look back on it now, I think I was just going to fail and fail and fail until we tackled the nucleus," she says.

She is not alone. An estimated 16 to 17 percent of Americans between 18 and 54 suffer from a mental dis-

From *The CQ Researcher,* March 29, 2002.

order each year. [1] The figure rises to 21 percent if alcoholism and drug abuse are included. Almost half the money paid out by private health insurers for all types of health care is spent to treat depression. [2]

There are other costs attached to mental illness. Besides the estimated $69 billion spent in 1998 in direct treatment expenses, the U.S. economy lost $79 billion due to lower or lost worker productivity, according to a 1999 surgeon general's report on mental health. [3]

About 84 percent of Americans have some sort of health insurance coverage — mostly through private insurance provided by their employers — but the adequacy of the mental health benefits in those insurance policies is "extremely variable," the report said. [4]

Historically, mental health has been the neglected stepchild in the health-benefits family — receiving much less coverage than physical ailments. For example, until 1998 many policies had $50,000 lifetime caps for mental health treatment, but $1 million for medical care. [5]

Then Congress passed a law to force companies to offer equal lifetime and

annual dollar limits for treating both mental and physical problems — a concept called mental health "parity." This year, lawmakers are debating whether to expand that parity to other aspects of insurance plans.

"Parity laws are necessary because without a mandate for equal coverage, insurers often place arbitrary restrictions on mental health coverage without placing similar restrictions on coverage for physical illness," according to political scientist Daniel Gitterman and Darcy Gruttadaro, an attorney with the National Alliance for the Mentally Ill (NAMI). [6]

A House panel on March 13 heard passionate pleas to expand existing parity requirements. "Today's hearing is really all about discrimination," said Rep. Marge Roukema R-N.J., co-chair of the House Working Group on Mental Illness and Health Issues. "For too long, we in Congress have allowed health plans to openly and legally discriminate against one group of patients, by making them pay more out of pocket for their health care, allowing them fewer visits to their treating mental health clinician, arbitrarily limiting their hospital stays and in some cases denying care altogether."

But Honeywell International Vice President Jane F. Greenman, representing a group of large, self-insured employers, said adding new expenses to already rising health costs would hurt both workers and employers. "Employers are already being forced to make very hard decisions about significantly increasing employee premium contributions . . . as well as making other reductions in coverage," she testified.

A bill in the Senate, the Mental Health Equitable Treatment Act of 2001, also would have increased parity but it was dropped from an appropria-

Majority of States Require Parity

Thirty-four states have various versions of mental health "parity" laws, which require health insurers to provide the same level of coverage for mental illness as for physical illness. The 16 states without their own parity laws abide by a less generous 1996 federal law, which Congress may expand.

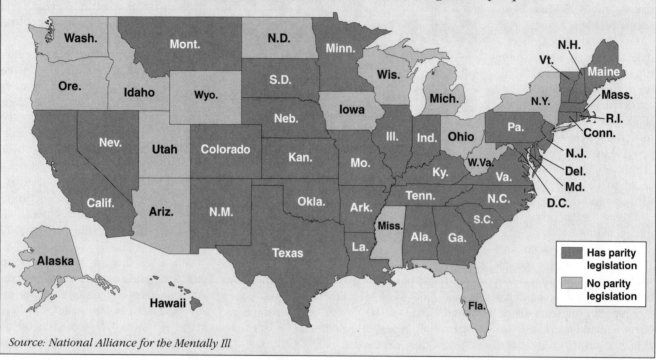

Has parity legislation

No parity legislation

Source: National Alliance for the Mentally Ill

tions bill on Dec. 18 by a House-Senate conference committee, despite unanimous approval by the full Senate last October. Republican House conference members, convinced that it would cost too much, killed the proposal in a 10–7 party-line vote.

The bill's sponsors, Sen. Pete V. Domenici, R-N.M., whose daughter has schizophrenia, and Sen. Paul Wellstone, D-Minn., whose brother also suffers from mental illness, had championed expanded parity coverage for years with little success.

But Domenici was undeterred. He said President Bush had urged him to wait until this year to tackle the issue. [7] Bush wrote to Domenici Dec. 13, promising to push for parity this year, but raising concerns about rising health-care costs. "We have lost this battle, but we haven't lost the war," Domenici said. [8]

While the Mental Health Parity Act of 1996, which went into effect in 1998, required equal annual and lifetime dollar limits for mental and physical health care, it exempted firms with 50 or fewer employees, leaving 35 million workers uncovered, says NAMI. [9] Another 40 million Americans — those without health insurance — are not covered by the law either. [10] And, since 1981, federal funding for the public mental health system — where many people go when their private benefits run dry — has been flat in the face of rising costs. In 1983, federal contributions accounted for 10.7 percent of state mental health spending, but only 2.9 percent in 1997, according to the National Association of State Mental Health Program Directors Research Institute. [11]

A 2000 General Accounting Office (GAO) study found that the federal par-

ity law did little to improve access to mental health treatment. "Although most employers' plans now have parity in dollar limits for mental health coverage, 87 percent of those that comply contain at least one other plan-design feature that is more restrictive for mental health benefits than for medical and surgical benefits," the report said. [12]

For example, in order to get around the restrictions of the 1996 bill, many health plans in 1998 increased co-payments and deductibles for mental health therapy. They also limited covered office visits to 20 and hospital stays to 30 days per year, even though lifetime and annual dollar limits were equal, as required by the 1996 law.

Even opponents of expanding parity concede that existing law has done little to erase the imbalance between coverage for emotional and physical disorders. "The problem [still] exists," wrote Sen. Judd Gregg, R-N.H. [13] "Today, access to mental health services is more limited than it is for non-mental health services."

Yet, Gregg warned that businesses and workers could be priced out of health insurance altogether if they are forced to absorb both the cost of mental health parity and a Patients' Bill of Rights, which Congress might adopt this year, amid already rising healthcare costs. Last year, health insurance premiums rose 11 percent on average, more than double the increase from a year earlier, according to Jeanne Lambrew, a health expert at George Washington University. [14]

But parity proponents cite a slew of studies and the experiences of both states and large businesses with parity in place, both of which show that parity increases costs only nominally and that expanded mental health benefits often produce lower overall health costs, because people with mental problems tend to use more medical services.

"People with anxiety may not be seeing a counselor, but they are going to the emergency room for panic attacks or to a doctor's office for gastrointestinal problems," says Tara Wooldridge, manager of the employee-assistance program at Delta Airlines.

Rep. Roukema, who just introduced an expansive parity bill that mirrors the Senate bill passed last fall, predicts that with congressional elections only months away, it is likely to pass. "It is clear to everyone that health-care issues are extraordinarily important in election years," says Roukema, whose husband is a psychiatrist. "Both in the House and Senate, they are going to want to be on the right side of the issue."

Recent events also have thrust mental health care into the limelight. For instance, the terrorist attacks of Sept. 11 have increased the demand for depression and anxiety treatment, particularly in New York City, where thousands of residents are still suffering from post-traumatic stress disorder

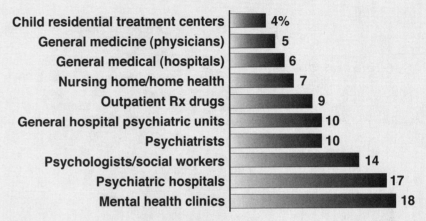

Spending on Mental Health

Nearly three-quarters of the money spent on mental health in the United States goes to psychologists, psychiatrists and in-patient care.

Spending by Category

- Child residential treatment centers — 4%
- General medicine (physicians) — 5
- General medical (hospitals) — 6
- Nursing home/home health — 7
- Outpatient Rx drugs — 9
- General hospital psychiatric units — 10
- Psychiatrists — 10
- Psychologists/social workers — 14
- Psychiatric hospitals — 17
- Mental health clinics — 18

Sources: "Mental Health: A Report of the Surgeon General," Department of Health and Human Services, 1999; T. Mark, D. McKusick, E. King, H. Harwood and J. Genuardi, Substance Abuse and Mental Health Services Administration

after witnessing the destruction of the World Trade Center. [15]

Mental health parity may also get a more favorable public reception thanks to other recent news events. The Oscar-winning movie "A Beautiful Mind," about a Nobel Prize-winning mathematician's struggle with schizophrenia, may increase public understanding of mental illness. The movie was lauded by NAMI for its sympathetic view of tormented schizophrenic John Nash. "I mean, people were actually applauding at the end of this movie," said Frank Ryan, president of NAMI in Wisconsin. "Can you believe that?" [16]

Meanwhile, the high-profile story of Andrea Yates — the Texas mother suffering from postpartum depression and psychosis recently convicted of drowning her five children — has also increased the public's awareness of mental illness.

Tipper Gore, wife of former Vice President Al Gore, has been a strong advocate for mental health issues. She spoke publicly in 1999 about her own struggles with depression and hosted a White House conference on mental illness that same year. She has been an outspoken advocate for parity laws. "For too long, diseases of the brain have had second-class status," she said from the podium at the Democratic National Convention in 1996.

Indeed, new discoveries about brain chemistry have refuted long-held beliefs that diagnoses for the most serious mental illnesses are fuzzy and their treatments dubious. "The scientific basis for understanding mental disorders is accelerating at equal or faster rates than for other medical and surgical disorders," said Darrel Regier, a former research director at the National Institute of Mental Health and now head of the American Psychiatric Association's (APA) research arm. [17]

But some of the 300-plus other diagnoses in the bible of the mental health profession, the APA's *Diagnostic and Statistical Manual of Mental Disorders* (*DSM*), are still controversial. Parity opponents worry that requiring parity for all those disorders

Only 7 Percent Spent on Mental Health

Only a small percentage of the $943 billion spent on health care in 1996 was for treatment of mental disorders.

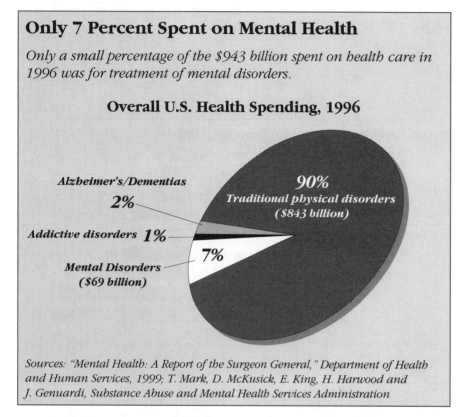

Overall U.S. Health Spending, 1996

Alzheimer's/Dementias **2%**

Addictive disorders **1%**

Mental Disorders ($69 billion) **7%**

90% *Traditional physical disorders ($843 billion)*

Sources: "Mental Health: A Report of the Surgeon General," Department of Health and Human Services, 1999; T. Mark, D. McKusick, E. King, H. Harwood and J. Genuardi, Substance Abuse and Mental Health Services Administration

— as the House and Senate bills dictated — would open a Pandora's box of indulgent therapy. Proponents contend, however, that in this era of tightly managed health plans, with strict pre-approval requirements for mental health benefits, overuse is unlikely.

As Congress considers expanding mental health parity, here are some of the key issues being debated:

Would expanded mental health parity force employers and workers to drop health insurance?

Several large business groups argue that increasing mental health coverage will push health costs over the top, forcing companies to drop health benefits or increase employees' out-of-pocket expenses.

Citing escalating health-care costs over the past three years, Kate Sullivan, health-care policy director for the U.S. Chamber of Commerce, said, "This is not the time for Congress to impose more requirements on health plans." [18]

The Senate proposal, Sullivan said, would force some companies to ratchet up co-payments and employee premium contributions. Workers' out-of-pocket costs already are rising steeply, said Helen Darling, president of the Washington Business Group on Health, which estimates the average cost of family coverage for current employees will rise to $10,000 in 2004 compared with $7,000 today. [19]

Neil Trautwein, health-care lobbyist for the 14,000-member National Association of Manufacturers, which represents 18 million employees, says some companies have reported 15–20 percent increases in health-insurance costs. "It's a very volatile, if not hostile, environment for employers who are trying to do the right thing and provide health coverage," he says.

Businesses have strong incentives to offer generous benefits, Trautwein says, because they are a key tool for attracting and keeping quality employees. "Manufacturers will hang on as

long as they possibly can in providing coverage," he says. "They'll tinker with the co-pay; encourage employees to make more cost-conscious choices." But in some cases, he notes, they have had to retreat from covering dependents.

A spokesman for Sen. Gregg cites mid-1990s studies by the Lewin Group, a health-care consulting firm, projecting that 300,000–400,000 people might drop or lose health coverage for every 1 percent increase in health premiums. [20]

But William J. Scanlon, GAO director of health financing, told the House Subcommittee on Employer-Employee Relations last July that the Lewin report and similar studies lacked sufficient data. "No study adequately estimates the coverage loss that might result from new legislative mandates," Scanlon told lawmakers. [21]

The Congressional Budget Office (CBO) estimated average premium increases of 0.9 percent under the Senate bill. [22] The National Mental Health Advisory Council estimated average premium increases of 1.4 percent in a June 2000 report to Congress. But Scanlon said the links between premium increases and loss of insurance are inconclusive.

Meanwhile, businesses insist expanding parity would increase their costs. "We are confident this type of expansion will more than double our plan costs in this area," said Richard W. Wright, manager of health-plan designs at heavy-equipment maker Caterpillar Inc., which has 150,000 employees. [23] Wright was urging U.S. representatives to stick to current law.

Honeywell's Greenman testified on March 13 that larger employers likely could absorb the increasing cost, while employers who only offer minimal coverage probably will drop it altogether. Indeed, federal laws don't compel companies to offer mental health coverage. But if they do offer it, the law says mental health benefits must equal medical benefits.

On the other hand, some large employers report that parity in mental health

Managed Care Changing Psychiatrists' Role

The bestseller *Who Moved My Cheese?* examines employee reactions to change. In mental health treatment, a companion book could be, *Who Moved My Money?*

In the last decade, the earnings of psychiatrists, psychologists and other mental health-care providers have plummeted. Partly due to managed-care cost-saving measures, the whole system of delivering mental health services in America has been radically altered, often leaving psychiatrists and psychologists out in the cold.

Social workers are now the counselors who often sit opposite troubled people in talk therapy. Instead of spending hours listening to people pour out their troubles, psychiatrists now spend most of their days in 15-minute appointments to evaluate medication regimes for patients receiving counseling elsewhere, usually from practitioners that charge less. [1]

Health plans typically pay $45 for a 15-minute medicine check, but they only reimburse $40 to $80 for an hour-long psychotherapy session, says Dr. Deborah Peel, president of the Coalition for Mental Health Care Professionals and Consumers, which opposes managed care.

Some psychiatrists eschew managed-care networks because of their bureaucracy, decision oversight and low reimbursements. Instead, they see only cash-paying clients. "Some see themselves as highly trained, bright people who don't want to work for discounts," says Stephen Etkind, Boston-based account manager for United Behavioral Health. "[Some] providers only work with the wealthy. Philosophically, they don't think insurance should be involved in psychotherapy."

Often that leaves the psychiatrists who remain in managed-care programs overloaded with the sickest patients, who need their doctors to be on call. All of these changes have made the profession less appealing. [2]

Psychiatrists have also seen their once sacrosanct role eroding as the primary prescribers of psychotropic drugs. In recent years, family practice and other physicians have been doling out more and more drugs for psycho-emotional problems like depression, anxiety and attention-deficit disorder.

Now, in an affront that psychiatric and medical lobbies fought for a decade, New Mexico has allowed psychologists — who do not have medical degrees — to prescribe psychotropic drugs. Despite an aggressive 11th-hour lobbying effort by the American Psychiatric Association (APA) and the American Medical Association (AMA), Gov. Gary Johnson signed the measure into law on March 5. [3]

"With this bill, patients will get care from the least-skilled professionals," Peel says. "No doubt, psychologists are skilled and intelligent, but their total absence of medical training is the problem." Similar bills are pending in Georgia, Hawaii, Illinois and Tennessee, even though state legislatures have voted them down more than a dozen times over the last decade. [4]

"This is a turf war with a great deal of money at stake," says William Goldman, a psychiatrist and senior vice president for behavioral health sciences at United, the third-largest mental-health benefits management company in the United States.

"The legislature and the governor in New Mexico have placed patient health and safety at risk," said APA President Richard K. Harding. "No crash course in drug prescribing can substitute for the comprehensive knowledge and skills physicians achieve through medical education and rigorous clinical experience." [5]

But psychologists argue that 450 hours of coursework, followed by two years of supervision by a psychiatrist or physician, equip them to prescribe drugs. The law also fills a void, they say, especially in rural areas where suicide rates are high and the number of psychiatrists low. "Being able to prescribe psychotropic drugs would give us an additional tool to help many patients who are not getting that help at all," said Elaine LeVine, a psychologist in Las Cruces, N.M.

Like psychiatrists, psychologists have been having their own survival struggles. Many have been priced out of the talk-therapy business by social workers and others offering less expensive services, and, until now, psychologists were not able to prescribe medication. Before the popularity of drug therapy, psychologists did as well financially as psychiatrists, Goldman says.

Psychologists have been pushing for prescribing rights since the late 1980s, when they lobbied and succeeded in helping set up a pilot program where psychologists could prescribe within the U.S. military, Goldman says. That program was subsequently closed down, under pressure from the medical community.

Goldman points out that potential problems because of drug interactions have become so complex that even medical doctors often cannot keep up. As a result, clinical pharmacists now review medication selections, he says. "All psychiatry medical directors are using them as consultants," he adds.

[1] William Goldman, "Is There a Shortage of Psychiatrists?" *Psychiatric Services*, Vol. 52, No. 12, December 2001, p. 1588.

[2] *Ibid.*

[3] Andrew Caffrey, "New Mexico May Let Psychologists Prescribe Drugs," *The Wall Street Journal*, March 6, 2002.

[4] *Ibid.*

[5] Press release, March 6, 2002.

benefits lowers overall health-care costs and increases worker productivity.

Delta Airlines increased mental health benefits for its 69,000 employees in 1994, when it switched to managed benefits for all health care. Despite increased usage of mental health treatment, costs in that area remained flat, says Delta's Wooldridge. But spending was lower on medical ailments, and people missed work less, she says.

"Yes, treatment costs money, but what's the cost of having an impaired person in the workplace?" Wooldridge asks. "What kind of productivity do they lose?"

Mental health claims are a small

The Top 5 Managed-Care Companies

The five largest companies offering managed mental-health treatment accounted for 67 percent of the more than 158 million Americans who were enrolled in mental health programs in 2001.

Organization	Enrollment (in millions)	Market Share
Magellan Behavioral Health Services	55.2	34.9%
ValueOptions	19.1	12.1
United Behavioral Health	18.5	11.7
CIGNA Behavioral Health	9.7	6.1
First Health Services of Tennessee	6.0	3.8

Source: Open Minds: Yearbook of Managed Behavioral Health Market Share in the United States, 2000–2001

fraction of Delta's health spending, she says. "There's much more cost on the physical side; that is really what is driving" costs up.

Mental health treatment accounts for 7 percent of overall health-care spending, compared to the 90 percent spent on medical care. [24]

"For companies with a lot of resources, there's a strong business case for generous mental health benefits," says Steven Wojcik, public policy director of the Washington Business Group on Health, representing 160 of the largest U.S. companies. Yet the group staunchly opposes mandates. "We prefer to keep it on a voluntary basis."

California, with its huge, varied population, instituted parity in 2000. An analysis of the first year's expenses in the bellwether state revealed spending for mental disorders increased only marginally — less than 1 percent of overall health-care dollars, says health economist Roland Sturm, of the Rand Corp., a think tank in Palo Alto. "The change in costs never gets close to 1 percent of medical costs." [25]

In states with parity laws, cost increases tied to the new laws were between 0.2 percent and 0.8 percent, ac-

cording to a recent article in *The New England Journal of Medicine.* [26]

Sen. Gregg is concerned that future federal patients' bill of rights legislation could add considerably to medical costs overall, since insurance enrollees could sue over disagreements about treatment. Gregg said this would push health costs up by 4 percent. [27]

Yet, Henry Harbin, head of Magellan Behavioral Health Services, the largest U.S. managed mental-health company, says current parity cost estimates reflect adjustments insurers already made to compensate for potential higher costs from legal appeals and looser treatment restrictions resulting from enactment of 10 state patients' rights laws and establishment of state panels to arbitrate disputed managed-care decisions. "You've already seen the market move to cope with these changes," Harbin says.

Finally, some costs for mental illness treatment are rising because of supply-and-demand issues. Fewer and fewer psychiatrists are willing to work in managed-care networks, which dominate treatment delivery, because of lower reimbursement rates, close oversight of decisions and burdensome administrative work. [28] (*See sidebar, p. 45.*)

A shortage of intermediate treatment

facilities for mentally ill adolescents also increases costs, says Lisa Boodman, an attorney with the Massachusetts Group Insurance Commission, which is considered a model in instituting parity for its coverage of state employees and retirees. "These are kids who need to leave a hospital, but outpatient treatment from home is not a viable option. They end up staying inpatient for a longer time."

Should mental health parity only apply to severe disorders?

Some lawmakers, business lobbies and health insurers are pushing for a narrow definition of mental illness in any new legislation. In order to avoid opening the floodgates to dubious complaints of less severe problems, only the most clear-cut, debilitating diseases — such as schizophrenia, bipolar disorder and major depression — should require parity, they argue

In essence, the debate in Congress comes down to whether parity should be expanded to include all 300 diagnoses in the most recent version of the APA's diagnostic manual, the *DSM IV.* Both the Senate and House legislation would cover all diagnoses in the manual except substance abuse.

John F. Kihlstrom, a psychology professor at the University of California, Berkeley, says restricting parity to a select few diagnoses is tantamount to having medical benefits cover only serious physical diseases like cancer or diabetes. "When you've got the flu, you go to your doctor and your insurance pays for the treatment because the flu is a real disease and the treatment works," he says.

Mental health experts argue that covering only major mental illnesses is pennywise and pound foolish, because when left untreated, milder forms of emotional illnesses often worsen into more serious, costly disorders. In 2001, federal employees were offered full parity. Administrators of the Federal Employees Health Benefits Program (FEHBP) — the medical-benefits program for federal workers — argue that limiting parity for major mental problems only perpetuates prejudices that have kept mental health coverage low.

"We believe that to actually end discriminatory treatment of coverage for mental illness, we must provide coverage for all diagnoses of mental illness," the FEHBP Web site tells enrollees. The plan covers all *DSM IV* categories as well as substance abuse. In fact, members of Congress are covered under this expansive parity.

Rep. Anne M. Northup, R-Ky, perhaps the most outspoken lawmaker opposing parity expansion, says people will overuse therapy for personal problems. "Nobody elects to have a heart attack," she says. "They don't elect to have a root canal. Whereas there are many people who go to mental health providers for stress or guidance with their kids even when they have no coverage. It is more elective. You have to have some limit."

Don Young, president of the Health Insurance Association of America (HIAA), said expanding mental health parity to broad *DSM* definitions would open insurers to claims for such things as malingering to avoid work or jet lag. "It would cover, for example, academic skill disorders," he said. "If you have a child with that problem, it's a meaningful problem, but should your insurance cover academic skill disorders for everybody?"

Yet, while the problems Young names are in the *DSM-IV*, listed as "Occupational Problem" and "Academic Problem," Regier says they are not official disorders but merely problems to watch. He says Young is raising a red herring for a good sound bite.

"Why would your managed-care company [approve] people [for] treatment for those diagnosis?" Regier says. "If challenged, you have to back it up that you meet the criteria. It's a lot

Comparing Group Health Plans

Benefits are generally far better for medical coverage than for mental health care under typical employer-sponsored group-health plans. Hospital stays, for example, are limited to 30 days for mental problems but unlimited for other medical problems.

Selected Features for a
Typical Employer-Sponsored Plan

Design Feature	Mental Health	Medical and Surgical
Lifetime dollar limit	$1 million combined with medical and surgical	$1 million combined with mental health
Hospital day limit	30 days	Unlimited
Outpatient office visit limit	20 days	Unlimited
Outpatient office visit coinsurance	50%	20%

Source: General Accounting Office, "Mental Health Parity Act: Despite New Federal Standards, Mental Health Benefits Remain Limited," May 2000

more than just slapping down a diagnoses of a neurotic patient and getting paid."

Ronald Bachman, an actuary and partner at PricewaterhouseCoopers who advises insurance carriers on plan designs, like vetting mechanisms, says the screenings that occur before a health-care provider is reimbursed exceed what's in the *DSM-IV*. "Are carriers paying for jet lag? No," he says.

Yet, Young maintains insurers would be required to cover all diagnoses if the law specifies all diagnoses in the *DSM IV*. "The individual comes in and says he needs to see a psychiatrist because of his sleep disorder or academic problems or work dissatisfaction, and we have to pay for it," Young says.

Congressional advocates of expanded parity say most treatment money is devoted to the most serious mental conditions, so adding intermediate and milder problems would not cost much more.

Bachman analyzed the parity bill Roukema introduced last year (HR 162), which would cover all *DSM* diagnoses, including substance abuse. He estimated serious mental illnesses would

absorb 90 percent of the mental health costs. In similar projections for parity advocates in more than 30 states, he found that serious mental illness accounted for 80-90 percent of total mental health costs.

United Health Group — the third-largest mental health managed-care administrator — analyzed a pool of 10 million of its members and found that serious mental illness accounted for only 60 percent of mental health costs for that group, says William Goldman, senior vice president of Behavioral Health Sciences, a United subsidiary. "We're sweeping in people at the early end [when it's cheaper to treat them], and that's exactly what employers want," he says.

Bachman says that in the 11 years that states have had parity laws, no one has produced a study to show that the costs are prohibitive. "The other side has had plenty of time to do it," he says. "If they have statistical proof, I'd love to see it."

Many state parity laws cover the entire *DSM-IV*, but others restrict coverage to serious illnesses. The National Mental Health Association (NMHA) argues that restricting parity to the severest mental illnesses discriminates against children and adults who suffer from the early stages of an illness that likely will worsen and eventually become more costly to treat. [29]

Yet, disputes exist within psychiatry and psychology about the validity and reliability of some diagnoses.

"What probably most frightens third-party payers is the risk of costly claims for treatment of 'problems of living' that are not severe mental illness," says Everett Dulit, 72, emeritus associate professor of psychiatry at the Albert Einstein School of Medicine in New York City. "The whole parity business makes the most sense when you are talking about biological illness when the person can't do anything about it."

Others agree. "Frankly, with the loose standards that apply to mental health, I share some of the business community's concern that mental-health parity can become a sinkhole," says the University of California's Kihlstrom. "But, I suspect that this is just a smoke screen for people who would rather not pay any benefits at all."

The reliability of the *DSM* remains under attack in some quarters. Stuart Kirk, chairman of the social welfare PhD program at the University of California at Los Angeles (UCLA) School of Public Policy and Social Research, has coauthored several books condemning the *DSM*, which he says has become heavily politicized. For instance, the gay rights movement fought a long (and successful) battle to remove homosexuality from its listing as a sexual perversion, and Vietnam veterans lobbied fiercely to get post-traumatic stress disorder recognized. [30]

But Regier notes that the rigor and validity of the *DSM IV's* diagnostic criteria are constantly being improved. "They are the most rigorous criteria that national and international scientists have been able to come up with to date," he says.

Is quality treatment available under managed benefits?

Mental health parity laws have advanced in tandem with the increasing dominance of managed behavioral health organizations (MBHOs), which provide oversight and screen patients for mental health treatment eligibility.

When states pass parity laws, they usually encourage cost controls used by firms that manage benefits with front-end approvals by "gatekeepers" and ongoing evaluation of treatments. Companies like Delta Airlines, which instituted parity in 1994, usually adopt parity in the context of managed plans. And when former President Bill Clinton in 1999 directed that all federal employees, retirees and families — including members of Congress — be offered full mental health parity by Jan. 1, 2001, he instructed administrators to rely on managed programs. [31]

Close scrutiny under managed programs has allowed companies to increase mental health coverage dramatically, says United's Goldman. Companies and state lawmakers were willing to adopt parity as long as these cost controls were in place, he says. "They wouldn't otherwise. So, that is no small thing."

Of the 250 million privately insured Americans in 2000, 158 million were covered under MBHOs, according to OPEN MINDS, a Gettysburg, Pa., firm that tracks the industry.

Most agree that state parity laws would not exist today without managed benefits. But psychiatrists and other treatment providers fear aggressive cost containment reduces the quality of care. "Managed care has helped convince many lawmakers that mental health parity is affordable," wrote Gruttadaro and Gitterman. "The question is: Does managed care undermine the purpose of parity laws?" [32]

NAMI works closely with large managed behavioral-care firms. "I personally take the view that as an advocate for parity we can't have it both ways," says Andrew Sperling, NAMI's

public policy director. "We can't argue that costs are affordable but then say we don't want managed care."

Managed benefits offer a big advantage, Sperling says: Instead of imposing tight caps on therapy visits and hospitalization, each patient's problems are given individual consideration.

In addition, separating out mental health services offers specialized treatment, Goldman says. "Lots of research shows that if you try to get depression taken care of by your primary-care doctor, it's done badly," he says.

Also, the "gatekeepers" used by MBHOs are specialists, Magellan's Harbin says. When subscribers' requests for medical and mental health coverage are vetted by the same people, someone without any psychiatric training might make treatment-access decisions about mental problems, he points out. "You would have a medical nurse with no psychiatric training calling up to do a review of a suicidal patient in a mental hospital," says Harbin, a psychiatrist. "You're not going to have a psych nurse calling up and trying to review a heart attack case; imagine how that would go over."

Goldman, also a psychiatrist with a long career in public health, says doctors don't like someone standing over their shoulders. It may annoy doctors to be accountable, he says, "But what is your alternative?"

United Health Group, he points out, has opened its records to independent researchers at UCLA's Neuropsychiatric Institute and RAND Corp., who are studying managed-care outcomes. "We have not just shared our data with them," Goldman says, "but have dumped our data into their mainframes."

Nonetheless, managed benefits have come under heavy attack. The National Coalition of Mental Health Care Professionals and Consumers, largely made up of psychiatrists, says profit motives have gutted quality treatment and rely on the least-talented providers. "You are [trying] to find the people willing to take

Chronology

1940s–1960s
Federal government defines its role in treating mental illness.

1946
President Truman signs the National Mental Health Act, creating the National Institute of Mental Health.

1952
American Psychiatric Association publishes the first *Diagnostic and Statistical Manual of Mental Disorders*. The anti-psychotic medication chlorpromazine is introduced, helping fuel the de-institutionalization movement of the 1960s-70s.

1962
Research on twins establishes schizophrenia's strong genetic component, helping to establish medical validity of mental disorders.

1963
President Kennedy signs Community Mental Health Centers Construction Act, funding local programs to reduce state mental hospital populations by half.

1965
Medicare and Medicaid are created, giving patients vouchers to use in the expanding private-care industry.

———•———

1970s–1980s
Brain science and pharmacology advance. U.S. reduces funding for community mental health.

1970
Food and Drug Administration approves lithium to treat bipolar disorder. Suicides and inpatient spending drop dramatically.

1972
Vice presidential candidate Sen. Thomas Eagleton, D-Mo., withdraws after press coverage and political pressure concerning three hospitalizations for depression.

1979
Wisconsin families with mentally ill adult children organize the National Alliance for the Mentally Ill (NAMI). By 2002, the group has 210,000 members in 50 states.

1981
President Reagan repeals prior community mental health laws, reducing federal funding for mental health. A landmark NIMH study reveals that 22–23 percent of U.S. adults have mental disorders.

1988
Prozac hits the market. With reduced side effects and risks, it is the first antidepressant general-practice doctors can prescribe.

———•———

1990s–Present
Advocates win partial victories for equal insurance coverage; cost containment in managed benefits expands and draws fire.

1991
North Carolina and Texas pass mental health parity laws for state and government workers. Six other states enact their own versions of parity within the next five years.

1996
Passage of Mental Health Parity Act, effective Jan. 1, 1998, requiring lifetime and annual dollar limits on mental health care to equal medical limits.

1997
Magellan joins a new breed of independent companies managing treatment for mental illness and addiction. By 2000 it has 55 million enrollees. Americans with Disabilities Act is extended to cover mental illness.

1999
First-ever surgeon general's report on mental illness issued.

2000
Twenty-eight additional states have passed parity legislation.

2001
The 9-million-member Federal Employees Health Benefit Program (FEHB) offers parity benefits under a directive from President Clinton.

Dec. 18, 2001
A House-Senate conference panel kills the Senate's 2001 Mental Health Equitable Treatment Act expanding parity requirements.

Feb. 26, 2002
A federal judge rules that bipolar disorder is a physical, rather than mental, condition.

March 5, 2002
New Mexico's governor signs first state law to allow certified psychologists to prescribe mental health drugs.

March 13, 2002
A House panel holds hearing on mental health parity.

March 20, 2002
Rep. Marge Roukema, R-N.J., introduces parity bill in the House, companion to the Senate measure.

The Bible of Mental Illness

Mental health practitioners rely heavily on one book to help them diagnose mental problems: the *Diagnostic and Statistical Manual of Mental Disorders* (*DSM*), published by the American Psychiatric Association (APA).

Found in just about every setting that deals with mental illness — from doctors' offices to prisons — the most recent edition, *DSM IV*, has sold nearly 1.2 million copies.

It lists the diagnostic criteria and identifying code for each of the more than 300 mental illnesses. The classifications create a common vocabulary for clinicians, who view the manual as a distillation of the most recent rigorous clinical and scientific consensus about mental illness.

But to critics, its reliability is questionable, and it is seen as a tool to add muscle to political causes or profits — or both.

"The mental health profession or any mental health group has a certain stake in having a larger turf," says Stuart Kirk, co-author of the 1997 book, *Making Us Crazy: DSM: The Psychiatric Bible and the Creation of Mental Illness*. "It makes a difference if you say there are 2 million mentally ill or 10 million mentally ill."

With just a few "simple changes in the wording" of the definition of a mental disorder, the psychiatric profession can inflate the number of people suffering from a particular mental illness, complains Kirk, who is also chairman of the social welfare PhD program in the School of Public Policy and Social Research at University of California, Los Angeles.

The first *DSM* was printed in 1952. The word "statistical" in the title is a holdover from the earliest U.S. Census accounting for the number of people with mental illness. The 1880 census included seven categories of mental illness: mania, melancholia, monomania, paresis, dementia, dipsomania and epilepsy. [1]

Not until 100 years later, when the third edition of the *DSM* was published, did the manual gain wide use. "*DSM III* was a breakthrough," says Darrell Regier, longtime research director at the National Institute of Mental Health (NIMH) and now head of the APA's research arm. That volume provided explicit diagnostic criteria and defined neurosis as "interpsychic conflicts" that cause certain symptoms, he says.

It was psychiatry's first major push for scientific descriptions of mental conditions. Until then — as is still sometimes thought today — diagnoses of mental illness were suspect. "There is no definitive lesion, laboratory test or abnormality in the brain tissue that can identify the illness," according to a 1999 surgeon general's report on mental illness. [2] "The diagnosis of mental disorders must rest with the patients' report of the intensity and duration of symptoms, signs from mental status examination and clinical observation of their behavior, including functional impairment."

The *DSM* does not use the word "disease" because it refers to "conditions with known pathology," while "disorder," used for mental conditions, is based on "clusters of symptoms and signs associated with distress and disability." [3]

Yet, many inside the field say the added veneer of science is just that. "The field of psychiatry has some guilty feelings about not being more scientific," says Everett Dulit, 72, emeritus associate professor of psychiatry at the Albert Einstein School of Medicine in New York City. "Working in a medical setting, there's tremendous pressure from the more measurement-oriented surgeons and internists. There isn't anyone who is thoughtful in the field who doesn't wince about *DSM*," says Dulit, who started his career imbedded in hard sciences as a nuclear physicist.

In the late 1970s, Dulit was on the APA committee that revised the *DSM-II* into the *DSM-III*. He remembers political battles over the definition of "adjustment disorder."

One contingent wanted the diagnosis removed, arguing it was an umbrella category that interfered with research because it often was used to label both bipolar disorder and schizo-

the lowest fee," says Barry Herman, a coalition executive board member. "Many times these insurance administrators are scraping the bottom of the barrel in terms of their provider networks."

He says the MBHOs save money by pushing patients to family practitioners or public health systems. The APA and the American Medical Association both recently approved policies urging members to discourage health plans from using MBHOs, or "carveouts" as they are known in the industry.

Goldman concedes that there are some bad apples among managed behavioral-care firms, but he says quality is uneven in all health-care areas.

The problems, he argues, stem from tight business and government purse strings, along with overheated competition among carveouts. "[Some] employers, including states, want bargain-basement care with minimum benefits," Goldman says. "There are managed-care companies who will take those contracts. Underbidding has been steadily progressing since the late 1990s."

State governments and courts have taken managed behavioral-care plans to task. The first state malpractice lawsuit against an HMO involved a Texas managed-care company accused of discharging a suicidal man too soon from a hospital despite protests from his treating psychiatrist.

The Fort Worth family of Joseph Plocica, 68, sued Merit Behavioral Care (later bought by Magellan), after he killed himself in 1998 shortly after his discharge from a Texas hospital. Within 24 hours of being sent home, Plocica drank a half-gallon of antifreeze and died in a coma nine days later. The case was settled for an undisclosed amount in September 2000. [33]

During 2001, the first year Massachusetts' new patients' bill of rights was in effect, more complaints were filed over mental health coverage than any other area of heath care. Of 137 consumer requests for reviews, 35 were phrenia, making it difficult to account properly for those ill-nesses, he says. Dulit says doctors often wanted to call what was clearly schizophrenia an "adjustment disorder," in order to avoid the stigma.

Just when the *DSM* committee seemed poised to delete adjustment disorder, another contingent made a successful 11th-hour appeal and the definition stayed in, laments Dulit. "It's still causing trouble by tossing things into one bin without differentiating," he says.

Elliot Valenstein, an emeritus University of Michigan professor of psychology and neuroscience, says drug makers' have an interest in an expansive view of mental illness. "Pharmaceutical companies have a financial stake in the popularity [of mental disorders], and promote them heavily among doctors and patients," Valenstein said. [4]

Political pressure also plays a role in defining mental illness, Kirk says. For example, in the early 1970s, gay-rights advocates exerted intense pressure on the APA to delete the listing of homosexuality as a sexual deviation. In 1974, the word "homosexuality" was erased from the *DSM* and replaced by "sexual orientation." But, in 1980 it was changed to ego-dsytonic homosexuality disorder. Finally, in 1987 ego-dsytonic homosexuality was removed. [5] Yet the psychiatric community still debates whether sexual orientation can be altered through therapy. [6]

On the other hand, Vietnam veterans fought for years to have post-traumatic stress disorder recognized and included in *DSM-III*. In *DSM-I*, "gross stress reaction," was the diagnosis for what was commonly known as battle fatigue. But it had been deleted in the *DSM-II*, published in 1968. [7]

Kirk complains that some definitions of mental disorders are really varied human reactions to normal stress. "The problem [occurs when] the rubber meets the road," he says. "Where a person comes in and spills out messy human problems."

Often, it is not at all clear whether those problems constitute a mental disorder or are just normal problems that people have, Kirk says. "It's almost as if it's not legitimate to have other kinds of human problems," he says.

Regier acknowledges that diagnoses are still evolving. "We are at a disadvantage [compared] with endocrinologists, who understand the molecular basis of diabetes," he says. "We're not that far off from cardiologists, who don't understand the cause of essential hypertension (high blood pressure)."

"Everybody would like to improve the rigor and validity of diagnostic criteria," he says. "*DSM IV* is one way of trying to do that. Until we have a different classification of genetic causes, clear environmental [causes] or biological markers, we are approximating what we believe."

However, a recent explosion in scientific discoveries about how chemistry and genetics influence mental health have begun providing clear-cut evidence of the biological bases of mental illnesses. This research, coupled with new, effective drug treatments, is becoming a powerful weapon against the public stigma and misconceptions about mental illnesses. [8]

[1] Herb Kutchins and Stuart A. Kirk, *Making Us Crazy: DSM: The Psychiatric Bible and the Creation of Mental Illness* (1997), pp. 38-39.

[2] U.S. Department of Health and Human Services, "Mental Health: A Report of the Surgeon General," 1999, p. 44.

[3] *Ibid.*

[4] Elliot Valenstein, "Rethinking the Brain's Biochemistry," *The Chronicle of Higher Education*, Dec. 4, 1998, p. A10.

[5] Kutchins and Kirk, *op. cit.*, chapter 3.

[6] Robert L. Spitzer, editorial, "Psychiatry and Homosexuality," *The Wall Street Journal*, June 23, 2001, A26. (Spitzer led the APA revision from *DSM-II* to *DSM-III*.)

[7] Kutchins and Kirk, *op. cit.*, Chapter 4.

[8] HHS, *op. cit.*, p. 454.

mental health appeals. Officials at two health plans noted that these appeals "represent a tiny fraction of the hundreds of thousands of consumers who received treatment for mental illness." [34]

Last June, Blue Cross and Blue Shield of Minnesota consented to expand access to mental health services and allow a three-person panel to review patient appeals. The agreement was a response to a lawsuit filed against the firm by Minnesota Attorney General Michael Hatch, who alleged that children were being denied essential treatment. [35]

Goldman admits substandard care exists within the industry. "There's still too much inconsistency, just like there is in the unmanaged world," he says. "I'd like someone to show me an alternative where there isn't substandard care in any area of medicine." ∎

BACKGROUND

Rise of Federal Programs

In the early part of the 19th century in the United States, those suffering from severe mental illnesses — then known as "lunatics" or "distract-ed" persons — were sent to poorhouses along with debtors and others. Their behaviors were not recognized as health problems, and no special care was provided. By the 1820s, concerns about disruptive or violent behavior prompted states to begin building asylums for the "dangerously insane." [36]

But, while the states built the asylums, local communities were responsible for providing day-to-day care. Not surprisingly, local governments did not want to incur the costs, so they continued to send people to the almshouses.

Asylum conditions were deemed inhuman and deplorable. Public pressure mounted, and between 1894 and World War I individual states passed legislation forcing state governments to pay for care for those in asylums. As a result, local communities became eager to send people to the asylums. The states have had the paramount role in mental health policy ever since. [37]

In the early 20th century, concepts about mental illness advanced. The asylums were renamed mental hospitals, and reformers who created what is now the National Mental Health Association, began calling for a more scientific approach to mental illness. [38]

After World War II, the trend was away from long-term institutional care in large, state-run mental hospitals — which were seen as "neglectful, ineffective, even harmful" — and treatment shifted to community mental health centers. [39]

But because the states could not afford to build the necessary number of local treatment centers, the federal government stepped in. On Oct. 31, 1963, President John F. Kennedy signed the Community Mental Health Centers Construction Act, creating a funding stream for community-based centers, with a goal of cutting state mental hospital populations by half.

At the signing ceremony, Kennedy was as optimistic as he was eloquent: "It was said, in an earlier age, that the mind of a man is a far country which can neither be approached nor explored. But, today, under present conditions of scientific achievement, it will be possible for a nation as rich in human and material resources as ours to make the remote reaches of the mind accessible. The mentally ill and the mentally retarded need no longer be alien to our affections or beyond the help of our communities." [40]

The law ushered in an era of de-institutionalization. "Many mental hospital patients were shifted to nursing homes, jails and streets as a result of the reduction in public mental hospital capacity during the 1960s and 1970s,"

Harvard University economist Richard Frank wrote. [41] In 1969, 55 percent of health-care spending for treating mental illness was poured into state mental hospitals; by 1994, it had dropped to 25 percent. [42]

During the same period, several other factors contributed to the mass de-institutionalization of the mentally ill, says NIMH science writer Paul Sirovatka. Court rulings around the country — based on civil rights concerns — limited involuntary commitments to asylums. Congress provided an infusion of federal dollars for community mental health treatment programs, but lawmakers excluded treatment in state hospitals, so state governments saved money by shifting patients to outpatient community-based programs. And new medications enabled the mentally ill to function better outside hospital walls, he says.

In the 1960s, two new federal programs sparked private-sector participation in mental illness treatment. In 1965, Congress created the Medicare and Medicaid programs, which provide health care for the elderly and the poor, respectively. Federal dollars, including limited resources for mental health services, were provided in the form of vouchers redeemable by hospitals or doctors. [43]

Private-sector providers began competing for Medicare dollars. Private, nonprofit hospitals, for instance, had incentives to clear out traditional medical wards and install furniture for low-tech psychiatric units.

Efforts to tilt Medicaid patients to private settings were less successful. Low payouts limited the number of providers motivated to serve them, and Medicaid recipients had less mobility to shop around. [44]

Before the two programs became law, arguments for equal coverage of mental illness during congressional hearings were similar to today's parity debates. "Among the points . . . were the difficulty in defining mental

illness, the lack of evidence on effective treatments, the high cost of covering mental health care, and the uncertainty in making actuarial estimates of costs," wrote Harvard's Frank. [45]

Push for State Parity

In the wave of deinstitutionalization, adults with serious mental disorders went from state hospitals back to their families. The families had no training and little outside support. Parents of discharged patients from state hospitals also bore the weight of the disease stigma. Psychological theories largely accepted at the time pinned blame for diseases like schizophrenia on the behaviors of mothers and fathers — a view, of course, now discredited. [46]

In 1979 a group of families in Madison, Wis., banded together to form the National Alliance for the Mentally Ill. Today, NAMI has 210,000 members in 50 states who rally in the interest of people with the most severe mental illnesses. NAMI representatives long have pushed for parity in insurance coverage.

North Carolina and Texas passed the first state parity laws in 1991, but they were just for government employees. Maryland, New Hampshire and Rhode Island enacted parity laws in 1994, and Maine and Minnesota followed the next year.

By 1996, as momentum for state parity laws was building, Domenici and Wellstone pushed for passage of the federal Mental Health Parity Act, which originally proposed a broad expansion of coverage. House Republicans drastically reduced the scope. [47]

The final version, which went into effect on Jan. 1, 1998, prohibited annual and lifetime dollar caps on mental health benefits that were lower than medical-care caps. But the law applied only if companies chose to offer mental health benefits.

Furthermore, the law allowed companies to opt out of the requirements if they could show that the changes had increased their health costs by 1 percent or more. But by March 2000, only nine companies had applied for the exemption. [48]

Instead, many employers raised out-of-pocket deductibles and co-payments and capped the number of therapy visits (average 20) and hospital days (30) enrollees could use in any given year. Meanwhile, the medical-surgical side enjoyed unlimited office visits and hospital days. [49] Only annual and lifetime dollar limits were imposed by the 1996 law.

While mental health advocates were disappointed in the law's limited scope, they were happy that it advanced the issue. "It was a rhetorical victory, but an important rhetorical victory to say that effective mental health treatments have to be paid on the same basis as other treatments," says Howard Goldman, a professor of psychiatry at the University of Maryland School of Medicine.

Between 1996 and 2000, an additional 25 states enacted some form of parity. But the laws vary greatly: Some only cover public workers, and many only apply to severe mental illnesses. Despite the narrow legislation, however, insurers in some states cover a broad sweep of diagnoses, Bachman says.

States also define severe mental illness differently. Most agree on a core group of illnesses, such as schizophrenia, bipolar disorder, major depression, schizoaffective disorder and obsessive-compulsive disorder. Some exclude eating disorders, such as anorexia nervosa and bulimia nervosa. The Minnesota attorney general's lawsuit against Blue Cross and Blue Shield alleged that the insurer had systematically refused to pay for several children's mental health problems, including anorexia. [50]

In many cases, states refused to pass parity legislation without limitations, but later went on to broaden

coverage after they found that the costs did not skyrocket.

Yet, since self-insured companies do not fall under state laws, advocates kept pushing for broader federal legislation. Federal law exempts the benefit plans of self-insured companies from state lawsuits over treatment challenges. That's why many large companies choose to self-insure, or, in other words, create a pool of money to cover treatment costs and risks. Meanwhile, companies that provide health coverage indirectly through health insurers would fall under state laws. Even so, some state laws exempt small businesses of 50 or fewer employees.

Raising the Profile

In 1999, the first-ever Surgeon General's Report on mental health stated unequivocally that mental and physical illnesses are inseparable and should be reimbursed equally. It condemned disparities in coverage and the antiquated stigma that persists despite advanced scientific understanding. [51]

Then-Surgeon General David Satcher wrote in the preface: "The report makes evident that the neuroscience of mental health — a term that encompasses studies extending from molecular events to psychological, behavioral and societal phenomena — has emerged as one of the most exciting arenas of scientific activity and human inquiry. [Yet] even more than other areas of health and medicine, the mental health field is plagued by disparities in the availability of and access to its services."

Shortly after the report came out, President Clinton directed that all federal employees, retirees and their families — including members of Congress — be offered full mental health parity by Jan. 1, 2001.

Even without government pressure, in the early 1990s, many large U.S. companies began offering generous

mental health benefits in tandem with managed plans, which gave them some assurance that costs would be monitored. "They had begun to believe studies indicating that workers with severe depression or other mental illnesses, or with alcohol or drug addiction, were costing their companies heavily in absenteeism, poor productivity, disability benefits, even at-work violence," wrote Alan L. Otten, in a 1998 report on parity for the *Milbank Quarterly*. [52] "Earlier and more extensive treatment of these problems might actually save the employers money in the long run."

Administrators of the federal employees health insurance program wrote to its 200-plus insurance carriers emphasizing that full parity would be delivered best under a "fully coordinated managed behavioral-health environment." [53]

Before that, management of mental illness benefits had been a market response to escalating mental health treatment costs, due partly to opportunism, if not outright abuse. "In the 1980s, mental health-care costs started to spiral totally out of control," says United's Goldman. Mental health costs had floated at a steady 7 percent of overall health premiums for years. Then, they rose to around 15 percent, he says. "There were some egregious things, a lot of scandals," he says.

Private chains offering mental health and substance-abuse treatment — mostly for adolescents — sprung up like mushrooms, he says. General medical hospitals jumped in by converting empty wards into treatment units.

"All you've really got to do is change the furniture and paint," says Goldman, who at the time was Massachusetts' commissioner of mental health. Treatment centers advertised heavily, he says. "I'm not exaggerating, the advertising was: 'We'll cure your children of adolescence, just drop them off here.' "

Companies clamped down with stricter limits and higher out-of-pocket costs and hired MBHOs to oversee and control mental health treatment. The rise of MBHOs has been swift: In 1993, about 70 million Americans were covered under MBHOs; by 2000, the number had more than doubled, to 158.2 million. [54] Today 97 MBHOs have at least a 1 percent market share. The top three — Magellan, ValueOptions and United — control 59 percent of the market. [55]

MBHOs have been the target of complaints and lawsuits, not unlike general health-management organizations. Yet, top experts recognize that this system is not going away, and they are seeking improvements. "Managed-care companies are a fact of life," says the APA's Regier. "You have abuses on both sides. They have brought down the cost; now we have to study to what detriment."

New Medications

Increased understanding of the brain's biochemistry and the development of new effective medications for brain disorders have helped change the way mental disease is treated. In 1989, the release of the antipsychotic medication Clozapine was a breakthrough, partly because it lacked risky and disruptive side effects. Similar new drugs have followed.

The 1988 development of Prozac was seen as a major leap forward in the treatment of depression. Related drugs, such as Zoloft and Paxil, followed. Today, drugs for mental illness are big business. Prozac manufacturer Eli Lilly & Co., brought in $3 billion last year in worldwide sales of the antipsychotic drug Zyprexa. [56] The company is waging a battle against the Department of Veterans Affairs' (VA) new, cost-saving guidelines that encourage use of similar, less expensive drugs made by competitors. [57]

"This is a multibillion [dollar] issue

for a company trying to protect market share," said Robert Lynch, a VA regional director. "[But] we are a multi-billion-dollar health-care institution trying to stretch tax dollars."

Some providers and advocates complain that today's treatment relies too much on drugs, while short-changing other approaches.

"We're much more obsessed, of course, with getting places quickly, and that's what drugs are supposed to do," said Alex Beam, author of *Gracefully Insane*, the history of the private Massachusetts mental hospital, McLean, where singer James Taylor, poets Robert Lowell and Anne Sexton and Nobel Prize-winner Nash, among others, were treated. [58]

A former McLean staffer disparages the shrinking amount of time patients spend with therapists. "You get no attention," he said recently, after calling in to a National Public Radio show. "They bring you in, they make a very quick evaluation, they try to pick from maybe 26 drugs. These drugs do have side effects and need to build up in the blood while the person is watched. It doesn't happen. They're sent back out and . . . the person is so frightened the very first thing that they do is throw out their pills. ∎

CURRENT SITUATION

New Push

On March 20, Rep. Roukema and co-sponsor Rep. Patrick Kennedy, D-R.I., introduced mental health parity legislation — a companion of the Domenici-Wellstone bill.

"We cannot in good conscience allow discrimination against mental illness to continue," Roukema said as

she introduced the bill. She compromised by dropping a previous provision that included substance abuse. "I recognize that [my previous version of] the legislation is not likely to move forward in the House. This bill responds directly to the concerns of business and insurance groups."

Noting that the bill codifies the coverage already enjoyed by federal employees and Congress, she said, "Surely if it is good enough for Congress and [its] staff, it ought to be good enough for millions of Americans who desperately need to be free from artificial and discriminatory limits on their mental health care!"

Last December, President Bush gave assurances that he would support a parity law this year. Earlier this month, a Bush spokesperson, Mercy Viana, said: "The president will work with Congress to move this issue forward and pass a bipartisan bill that he can sign."

As in previous years, lawmakers are expected to battle over cost exemptions and which illnesses to cover. They are also closely watching what happens in the 9-million-person federal employee health benefits plan, using it as a case study of the impact of parity insurance. A $4 million federal study is underway, but results will not be available until the late fall of 2003. Researchers plan to examine changes in usage of mental health treatment, how accessible it is and the level of satisfaction among federal employees and their families, he says.

Court Breaches Wall

Meanwhile, a federal court decision recently reaffirmed the biological nature of severe mental illness. In late February, U.S. District Judge Henry H. Kennedy, in Washington, D.C., ruled that the Federal National Mortgage Association (Fannie Mae) and its long-term disability insurance provider,

At Issue:

Can mental health care be adequately delivered in a managed-care environment?

HENRY T. HARBIN, M.D.
CHAIRMAN OF THE BOARD, MAGELLAN HEALTH SERVICES; FORMER CHAIR, AMERICAN MANAGED BEHAVIORAL HEALTHCARE ASSOCIATION

WRITTEN FOR THE CQ RESEARCHER, MARCH 2002

*p*erhaps the better question to ask is — can mental health care be delivered adequately in the absence of managed care? While the question seems provocative, I would argue that it is reasonable to ask it, since managed care in the mental health arena has improved access to care and put into place many needed reforms and efficiencies.

Our society and our health-care system historically have discriminated against those suffering from mental illness. For example, employers who offered comprehensive general medical care to their employees often provided only meager benefits for the treatment of mental illness. Yet despite such limitations, mental health care costs still rose dramatically in the 1970s and '80s. With the advent of managed mental health care, it became possible to moderate costs without reducing or eliminating needed benefits.

The good news is that managed mental health care brought more to the table than simply cost controls (which benefit consumers as well). Outpatient treatment typically has expanded, encouraging people to seek care early in the development of a problem, before the need for intrusive and more costly care. In addition, managed care has helped the system to move away from a clinically detrimental overreliance on inpatient care. And, it has encouraged the development of alternative treatment settings that make it possible to treat patients safely and effectively outside of the hospital.

The experiences of the 1980s and '90s made it clear that the provider community, most of whom do not practice in organized systems of care, did not develop intensive quality-assurance and cost-efficiency measures on their own. Managed care filled that void. Like it or not, this has benefited all of the system's stakeholders. While behavioral health practitioners chafe at the oversight, the fact is that practice patterns have changed in a positive way by motivating providers to focus on their ultimate goal — helping patients get better in a cost-effective manner.

Although it is not perfect, managed care has made possible many improvements in the mental health system; parity would not be possible without managed care — costs simply would be prohibitive, and most of the care would be delivered in less than optimal settings. Until peer review and practitioner accountability become an accepted part of the process and clear guidelines for treatment and outcomes exist, managed care will continue to be a critical quality-monitoring and cost-management mechanism in the mental health arena.

DEBORAH C. PEEL, M.D.
PRESIDENT, NATIONAL COALITION OF MENTAL HEALTH PROFESSIONALS AND CONSUMERS

WRITTEN FOR THE CQ RESEARCHER, MARCH 2002

*w*e're a nation in denial: All American families have experiences with mental health or addiction problems, but denial interferes with our ability to even recognize these devastating illnesses, let alone seek treatment.

Managed behavioral health care organizations (MBHOs) do not administer benefits the way other medical benefits are administered. MBHOs restrict and deny far more treatment, substitute inferior care and personnel and use more plan dollars for overhead. Market domination by MBHOs has forced the competition to operate in the same harmful ways.

Patient privacy is violated as a condition of obtaining care. MBHOs share sensitive information with employers, law enforcement, marketers, etc., so many people won't seek help. In *Jaffee v. Redmond* (1996), the U.S. Supreme Court recognized that effective psychotherapy cannot exist without privacy of psychotherapy communications (therapist-patient "privilege"). Vice President Cheney argues that government cannot operate unless communications with energy officials are protected by "executive privilege." Surely, the mental health of our citizens is as important as Cheney's ability to consult with Enron.

Imagine the following scenario if cancer were handled by cancer MBHOs: Cancer patients would call an 800 number for help. Non-physicians would decide what care is provided. Patients would be referred to community services, self-help and peer groups, or to state programs for treatment or disability. Patients would be diagnosed and treated by the least-trained medical professionals in the field of oncology.

Few patients would ever be seen by medical-specialist oncologists, radiation oncologists or cancer surgeons. Outpatient treatment would be "capped" at a few visits per year. Older and cheaper treatments would be recommended before newer or more effective options.

Specialty cancer units or radiation/oncology treatment centers would not exist in most communities. Instead, patients would be admitted to generic medical-surgical units, where staff have no oncology training. A full course of chemotherapy or radiation therapy would never be authorized, even for incapacitating, aggressive or chronic cancers. Patients would live in constant fear that their next chemo would be denied.

As incredible as this scenario seems, patients with mental illness face these obstacles each time they seek treatment.

Managed care reinforces the stigma against mental illness, and preys upon people too ashamed and too fragile to fight back. There is a better system. When will we finally admit it?

Rates of Mental Disorders in the U.S.

More than 30 million Americans suffer from a mental disorder in any given year, according to new statistics. A total of 37.5 million Americans have a mental or substance abuse disorder.

Prevalence Estimates for Mental Disorders

Disorder	Ages 18-54	All Ages	Population (millions)
Any anxiety disorder	13.3%	11.8%	23.9
Any phobia	8.0	7.8	15.8
Social phobia	3.7	3.2	6.5
Agoraphobia	2.2	2.1	4.0
Panic disorder	1.7	1.4	2.8
Obsessive-compulsive disorder	2.4	2.1	4.3
Post-traumatic stress disorder	3.6	--	5.2
Any mood disorder	5.7	5.1	10.3
Major depressive episode	5.2	4.5	9.1
Bipolar disorders	0.9	0.7	1.4
Schizophrenia	1.2	1.0	2.0
Antisocial personality disorder	1.2	1.5	3.0
Anorexia nervosa	0.1	0.1	0.2
Any mental disorder	16.5	14.9	30.2
Any substance use disorder	7.6	6.0	12.1
Any mental or substance use disorder	20.9	18.5	37.5

Note: Subtotals add to more than the overall total because sufferers can be counted in more than one category.

Sources: William E. Narrow, et al, American Psychiatric Institute for Research and Education; Department of Psychiatry, Washington University School of Medicine, February 2002

barraged with fake claims. [61]

But mental health advocates say that stigma, not just costs, is behind the opposition to parity. "Although less severe than in the past, the stigma associated with mental illness undoubtedly persists," says D.C. attorney Bret Koplow, who is also a clinical psychologist. "Animus on the part of some employers may lead them to restrict mental health coverage as an indirect means of dissuading the mentally ill from seeking or continuing employment with a particular firm."

Afraid to reveal illnesses, employees or job candidates won't press for better mental illness benefits, he says. Most people simply keep quiet, giving employers the impression that emotional disorders are rare, when they are not, he says.

Wooldridge at Delta Airlines concurs. "We hear all the time about a family member who is diagnosed with cancer," she says. "We don't hear people talking about a family member diagnosed with schizophrenia or major depression. They're not comfortable talking about that. As long as they're not comfortable, we're limiting people's access to care." ∎

OUTLOOK

Unum Life Insurance Co. of America, erroneously classified former Fannie Mae attorney Jane Fitts' bipolar disorder as a mental, rather than physical illness. Fitts, 52, quit her job seven years ago when mood swings, depression and hyperactivity made it impossible for her to work. [59]

Her disability insurance only offered a percentage of her salary for two years, even though benefits are paid for physical disabilities up to age 65.

"The U.S. District Court for the District of Columbia has opened a breach in the artificial wall that has long separated coverage of physical and mental illness in insurance policies," said a NAMI report on the court decision. [60]

However, attorneys representing employers said this ruling, which is being appealed, would invite dubious, costly claims. Jeffrey Adelson, a Santa Ana, Calif., attorney whose firm represents employers in workers' compensation cases, pointed out that years ago states limited workers' compensation claims based on psychological injuries after companies were

Band-Aid Approach?

Mental health advocates say complete mental health parity is still far off. New laws enacted in the past decade have moved incrementally toward equalizing insurance coverage for physical and psychological ails.

State laws mandated various levels of parity. The 1996 federal parity law only required parity for lifetime and annual dollar limits, but left insurers and companies with other ways to reduce spending for mental problems.

The latest parity bill passed in the Senate and introduced this month in the House would restrict only some of the strategies by requiring equal co-payments, deductibles, number of hospitals days and office visits for either the flu or depression.

"You are making things better, but you are not solving the problem," says Harvard's Frank. "There are other problems to solve. That's why we refer to it as necessary but not sufficient. Insurers and companies will find other tactics to avoid the high costs of treating the seriously mentally ill."

Among the tactics, he says, will be to make treatment sites inconvenient or requiring enrollees to first move through a gauntlet of steps. "They'll make you jump through 5,000 hoops to get it," he says.

Frank says parity can be achieved only if incentives to cut treatment costs are removed. Currently, most insurers or mental health administrators receive fixed monthly payments per enrollee. Insurers start with that pot of money and they can elevate profit margins by keeping treatment spending low by denying or cutting down on care.

The Massachusetts Group Insurance Commission, which administers health insurance for state workers, retirees and their families, created a model of mental health coverage in 1994 that eliminates incentives to cut treatment.

Commission attorney Boodman, who helped design the plan, says it was created on the heels of bad publicity for egregious cases of denying treatment for state workers. Massachusetts started a new self-insured plan that pays for treatment claims and maintains a pool to cover the risk of higher than expected claims. A mental health benefit administrator is hired for a flat fee to approve and monitor treatment.

The state consulted with actuaries to determine a dollar figure that indicated its enrollees were receiving a high level of care. If the benefits administrator spent less than that figure, it was penalized by losing 2 percent of the flat annual fee.

Since its inception, this insurance plan has not seen cost overruns or heard complaints of undertreatment. In fact, the financial experience has been so good that co-payments for therapy sessions were lowered this year from $20 to $10, says United's Stephen Etkind, who oversees the plan. "It costs more if we limit care for the most seriously ill, and they end up in the hospital," he says.

Massachusetts also offers six conventional health maintenance organizations (HMOs) as an option to state workers. If the HMOs are under-treating enrollees, their premium payments are cut, Boodman says.

Frank says that until systems like these are made standard, parity laws like those proposed by Sen. Domenici and Rep. Roukema only offer a partial solution.

"If you are going to solve the problem, at the end of the day these laws don't do it," Frank says. ■

Notes

[1] William Narrow, Donald Rae and Darrel Regier, "Revised Prevalence Estimates of Mental Disorders in the United States," *Archives of General Psychiatry*, February 2002, Vol. 59, p. 119.

[2] Richard G. Frank, *et al.*, "The Value of Mental Health Care At the System Level: The Case of Treating Depression," *Health Affairs*, September/October 1999, p. 85.

[3] "Mental Health: A Report of the Surgeon General," U.S. Department of Health and Human Services, 1999, pp. 411, 413.

[4] *Ibid.*, p. 419.

[5] *Ibid.*

[6] Darcy E. Gruttadaro and Daniel P. Gitterman, "Variation in Mental Health Parity Laws," working paper for the Center for Mental Health Services Research, University of California, Berkeley, 2000, p. 2. (Gruttadaro was an independent attorney when the paper was written.)

[7] "Conferees Drop Mental Health Parity From Fiscal 2002 HHS Appropriations Bill," *Health Plan & Provider Report*, Bureau of National Affairs (BNA), Jan. 2, 2002.

[8] News release, Dec. 18, 2001.

[9] Alan L. Otten, "Mental Health Parity: What Can It Accomplish in a Market Dominated by Managed Care?" *Milbank Quarterly*, June 1998, published by the Millbank Foundation.

[10] Milt Freudenheim, "Alarmed at Rising Number of Uninsured Americans, Coalition Forms to Reverse Trend," *The New York Times*, Feb. 9, 2002, p. A10.

[11] Hirad Lutterman and B. Poindexter, "Funding Sources and Expenditures of State Mental Health Agencies, Fiscal Year 1997," National Association of State Mental Health Program Directors Research Institute, July 1999.

[12] "Mental Health Parity Act: Despite New Federal Standards, Mental Health Benefits Remain Limited," General Accounting Office, May, 2000, p. 16

[13] Judd Gregg, "Mental Health Equitable Treatment Act of 2001: Report Together with Additional Views," Committee on Health, Education, Labor and Pensions, Report 107-61, Sept. 6, 2001, p. 18.

[14] Freudenheim, *op. cit.*

[15] For background, see Sarah Glazer, "Treating Anxiety," *The CQ Researcher*, Feb. 8, 2002, pp. 97-120.

[16] Rob Zaleski, "Communities: Up Close: Those Aiding Mentally Ill Praise 'Mind,' " *The Capital Times* (Madison, Wis.), Feb. 18, 2002, p. B1.

[17] His comments were made in a hearing last July before the Senate committee.

[18] Quoted by Barbara Martinez, "Senate Passes Bill To Match Mental, Medical Coverage," *The Wall Street Journal*, Nov. 11, 2001, p. B1.

[19] Quoted in Freudenheim, *op. cit.*

[20] Testimony of William J. Scanlon, director, Health Financing and Public Health Issues, Health Education and Human Services Division of the General Accounting Office. Printed version: GAO/T-HEHS-99-147, "Private Health Insurance: Impact of Premium Increases on Number of Covered Individuals Is Uncertain," June 11, 1999, p. 2.

[21] *Ibid.*

[22] Jennifer Bowman, Alexis Ahlstrom, Leo Lex, Stuart Hagen and James Baumgardner, "Congressional Budget Office Cost Estimate: S. 543 Mental Health Equitable Treatment Act of 2001," Aug. 22, 2001.

[23] Letter from Richard Wright, Caterpillar manager of plan design, to Rep. Roger Wicker, R-Miss., Nov. 13, 2001.

[24] Surgeon General's report, *op. cit.*, p. 412.

[25] The study results will be published in the June issue of *Psychiatric Services* magazine.

[26] Sources quoted in Richard G. Frank, Howard H. Goldman and Thomas G. McGuire, "Sounding Board: Will Parity In Coverage Result In Better Mental Health Care?" *The New England Journal of Medicine*, Vol. 345, No. 23, Dec. 6, 2001, p. 1702.

[27] Gregg, *op. cit.*

[28] William Goldman, "Is There a Shortage of Psychiatrists?" *Psychiatric Services*, Vol. 52, No. 12, December 2001.

[29] Daniel Gitterman, Roland Sturm, Rosalie Liccardo Pacula and Richard M. Scheffler, "Does the Sunset of Mental Health Parity Really Matter?" *Administration and Policy in Mental Health*, Vol. 28, No. 5, May 2001.

[30] Herb Kutchins and Stuart Kirk, *Making Us Crazy? DSM: The Psychiatric Bible and the Creation of Mental Disorders* (1979), Chapters 3, 4.

[31] *FEBH Program Carrier Letter*, No. 1999-027, Office of Personnel Management.

[32] Gruttadaro and Gitterman, *op. cit.*

[33] Hang Nguyen, "Landmark HMO Lawsuit Ends in Settlement," *The Dallas Morning News*, July 7, 2000, p. D2.

[34] Liz Kowalczyk, "Mental Coverage Gets Most Complaints: 3 State Officials To Prod Insurers," *The Boston Globe*, Feb. 14, 2002, p. A1.

[35] Maura Lerner and Josephine Marcotty, "Advocates Cheer Blue Cross Settlement on Mental Health Care," *The Minneapolis Star Tribune*, June 20, 2001.

[36] Richard G. Frank and Thomas G. McGuire, "Economics and Mental Health," *Handbook of Health Economics* (2000), Vol. 1, Chapter 16, pp. 941-942.

[37] *Ibid.*

[38] Surgeon General, *op. cit.*, p. 78.

[39] *Ibid.*, p. 79.

[40] John F. Kennedy, "Remarks Upon Signing Bill for the Construction of Mental Retardation Facilities and Community Mental Health Centers," *Public Papers of the Presidents of the United States: John F. Kennedy, January 1 to November 22, 1963*, United States Government Printing Office, p. 826.

[41] Frank and McGuire, *op. cit.*, p. 900.

[42] *Ibid.*, p. 903.

[43] Richard G. Frank, "The Creation of Medicare and Medicaid: the Emergence of Insurance and Markets for Mental Health Services," *Psychiatric Services*, Vol. 51, No. 4, April 2000, p. 467.

[44] *Ibid.*

[45] *Ibid.*

[46] Surgeon General, *op. cit.*, p. 96.

[47] Otten, *op. cit.*

[48] "Mental Health Parity Act: Despite New Federal Standards, Mental Health Benefits Remain Limited," U.S. General Accounting Office, May 2000, p. 16.

[49] *Ibid.*

[50] Josephine Marcotty, "Hatch, Blue Cross Settle Mental-Health Lawsuit," *Minneapolis Star Tribune*, June 19, 2001.

[51] Surgeon General, *op. cit.*, p. 3.

[52] Otten, *op. cit.*

[53] FEHB, *op. cit.*

[54] Monica Oss, "Open Minds: Yearbook of Managed Behavioral Health Market Share in the United States, 2000-2001," *Behavioral Health Industry News*, Oct. 4, 2000, p. 19. (Updated figures will be published by Open Minds in April.)

[55] *Ibid.*

[56] David Rogers, "VA Bid to Trim Costs May Rile Firms — Eli Lily Objects to Policy Promoting Less-Costly Treatments," *The Wall Street Journal*, Feb. 13, 2002.

[57] *Ibid.*

[58] Neal Conan, National Public Radio, "Analysis: Evolution and Future of American Mental Hospitals," transcript, "Talk of the Nation," Jan. 17, 2002.

[59] Michael Orey, "Bipolar Disorder Is a Physical Ill, U.S. Judge Rules," *The Wall Street Journal*, March 12, 2002, p. B1.

[60] "Federal Court Strikes Down Boundary Between Physical and Mental Illness: Precedent has Implications for Both Health and Long-Term Disability Insurance," NAMI news release, Feb. 28, 2002.

[61] Orey, *op. cit.*

FOR MORE INFORMATION

National Institute of Mental Health, Public Inquiries, 6001 Executive Boulevard, Rm. 8184, MSC 9663, Bethesda, MD 20892-9663; (301) 443-4513; nimhinfo@nih.gov; www.nimh.nih.gov/home.cfm.

Center for Mental Health Services Research, University of California Berkeley and San Francisco, 2020 Milvia St., Suite 405 #5610, Berkeley, Calif., 94720-5610; (510) 643-3555; www.haas.berkeley.edu. This center, one of seven funded by the NIMH, studies the structure and financing of care for severely mentally ill persons.

Insure.com, 76 LaSalle Road, West Hartford, Conn., 06107; www.insure.com. A World Wide Web site with updated insurance information.

National Alliance for the Mentally Ill (NAMI), Colonial Place Three, 2107 Wilson Blvd., Suite 300, Arlington, VA 22201-3042; (703) 524-7600; http://www.nami.org/poc.htm. A grass roots, self-help, support and advocacy organization of consumers, families and friends of people with severe mental illnesses.

Washington Business Group on Health, 50 F St., NW, Suite 600, Washington, D.C. 20001; (202) 628-9320; www.wbgh.org/index.html. Founded in 1974, WBGH represents large employers on health-care issues; it produced a report on its members' experiences in introducing mental health parity into the workplace.

Bibliography

Selected Sources

Books

Frank, Richard G., and Thomas G. McGuire, "Economics and Mental Health," Chapter 16, *Handbook of Health Economics*, Vol. I, Elsevier Science B.V., 2000.

Two economists outline the history of how mental health treatment has been financed from asylums in the 1880s to modern private insurance.

Kutchins, Herb, and Stuart Kirk, *Making Us Crazy: DSM: The Psychiatric Bible and the Creation of Mental Disorders*, The Free Press, 1997.

Two social work professors argue that political and financial interests often influence the mental health profession's key diagnostic tool.

Articles

"Conferees Drop Mental Health Parity From Fiscal 2002 HHS Appropriations Bill," *Health Plan & Provider Report*, Bureau of National Affairs, Jan. 2, 2002.

This report describes events last December when the Mental Health Equitable Treatment Act of 2001 was killed in a Senate-House committee.

Frank, Richard G., Howard H. Goldman and Thomas G. McGuire, "Sounding Board: Will Parity In Coverage Result In Better Mental Health Care?" *The New England Journal of Medicine*, Vol. 345, No. 23, Dec. 6, 2001, p. 1702.

Economists Frank and McGuire and Goldman, a psychiatry professor and leading expert, argue that even if the latest bill to expand parity passes, it will not ensure expanded treatment for mental illness because incentives to discourage use of treatment will remain intact.

Frank, Richard G., "The Creation of Medicare and Medicaid: The Emergence of Insurance and Markets for Mental Health Services," *Psychiatric Services*, Vol. 51, pp. 465-468, April 2000.

The Harvard economist outlines how the two large federal programs expanded the private-market segment of mental health treatment.

Narrow, William, Donald Rae and Darrel Regier, "Revised Prevalence Estimates of Mental Disorders in the United States," *Archives of General Psychiatry*, Vol. 59, p. 119, February 2002.

The most up-to-date estimates indicate 16 or 17 Americans of every 100 between 18 and 54 are likely to suffer from a mental disorder every year.

Rogers, David, "VA Bid to Trim Costs May Rile Firms — Eli Lily Objects to Policy Promoting Less-Costly Treatments," *The Wall Street Journal*, Feb. 13, 2002.

The author outlines the battle by a leading drug maker to hold onto a large share of the market for treating U.S. veterans. It outlines the enormous scale and profits in psychotropic medications.

Reports and Studies

"Mental Health Equitable Treatment Act of 2001: Report Together with Additional Views" Committee on Health, Education, Labor and Pensions, Report 107-61, Sept. 6, 2001, p. 18.

This Senate report outlines state and federal parity efforts to date, offering detailed discussion of the legislation, cost estimates and contrary views.

"Mental Health Parity Act: Despite New Federal Standards, Mental Health Benefits Remain Limited," U.S. General Accounting Office, May 2000.

The GAO reports that the Mental Health Parity Act of 1996 did little to increase access to mental health treatment, citing adjustments insurers and companies made to plan designs to continue to discourage use of treatment.

Oss, Monica, "Open Minds: Yearbook of Managed Behavioral Health Market Share in the United States, 2000-2001," *Behavioral Health Industry News*, Oct. 4, 2000.

This report outlines the status of the managed behavioral-health-firm industry, ranks the industry leaders and reports on the number of Americans whose benefits fall into this industry and other trends.

Otten, Alan L., "Mental Health Parity What Can It Accomplish in a Market Dominated by Managed Care?" *Milbank Quarterly*, June 1998.

Otten, a former *Wall Street Journal* reporter, provides a comprehensive overview of mental health parity laws and their effects through 1998, and describes generous benefits offered by private businesses without government mandates.

U.S. Department of Health and Human Services, "Mental Health: A Report of the Surgeon General," 1999.

Former Surgeon General David Satcher argues that the days of discriminating against people suffering from mental disorders either financially or through stigma has no grounds in the modern science of mental illness. The 458-page report provides a detailed review of the history, science, financing and politics of mental illness.

4 Rating Doctors

SARAH GLAZER

The Newark hospital had one of New Jersey's highest death rates for cardiac surgery. But that's where John Tryneski's ailing 72-year-old mother was taken last March, and she refused to be moved.

So Tryneski logged onto the state health department's Web site, where he made a potentially life-saving discovery: While his mother's surgeon did not have an impressive success rate for open-heart surgery, another doctor at the hospital did.

Tryneski persuaded his mother to shift doctors, and she came through the operation feeling "better than she's felt in years," he says.

New Jersey is one of only three states — the others are Pennsylvania and New York — that report doctors' success rates and experience for specific types of operations. New Jersey not only publishes the patient death rate for surgeons who perform coronary-artery bypass surgery* but also reports on how many operations each surgeon performs, since busy doctors tend to get better results. [1]

Actually, Tryneski's mother had needed a heart-valve replacement, and the state didn't report on those kinds of operations. But when Tryneski asked the highly rated doctor how many valve replacements he performed, the surgeon turned out to be quite experienced.

Switching to a more experienced

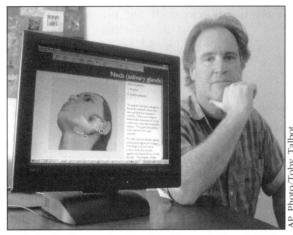

Medical software developed by Howard Pierce's PKC Corp. compares a patient's condition to constantly updated medical literature and then offers a diagnosis and a recommended treatment.

surgeon was crucial, Tryneski believes, because his mother's condition was much more serious than anyone had anticipated. "She was a heart attack waiting to happen, and she didn't know that," Tryneski says. "The doctor did an excellent job."

For most consumers, picking a doctor is more art than science. In fact, most people rely on the word of friends and family, surveys show, rather than objective ratings. Even when patients trust their doctors, they still have no sound way of judging their performance relative to others in the field.

But consumer advocates say distinguishing good doctors from bad shouldn't be guesswork, especially since many states already collect the vital data from hospitals needed for good decision-making. Consumer groups in New York have been in the forefront in pushing states to publicize more information on the risks of choosing one physician over another for medical procedures.

The Center for Medical Consumers in New York City recently publicized state data showing how often each New York physician performs common surgical procedures. The center

posted the physicians' names on its Web site for 29 common operations, including mastectomy and knee replacement.

"If you were going to have this procedure, would you rather go to a doctor who has done two in the last year or done 42?" asks Arthur Levin, the center's director. Until his group posted the figures, the state had compiled the data in a form inaccessible to the average New York consumer, according to Levin. For most consumers in the rest of the country, information of that kind is almost never made public. "I don't know if it will change consumer behavior," Levin says. "I just have a very passionate belief that if the state has the information, it should be made public."

Doctors and hospitals, however, traditionally have been hostile to public ratings, at least initially. Among doctors, the most common objection is that public scorecards discourage surgeons from operating on sicker patients for fear of upping their mortality rates. [2] Some physicians question the accuracy of such ratings and fear they will unfairly hurt their reputations.

"Often, people who have been well-trained and have an unfortunate report are good doctors," says Yank D. Coble, a Florida doctor and trustee of the American Medical Association (AMA). Though Coble says the way ratings are collected is improving, he contends that by their very nature they are flawed because they don't include equally important factors like the doctor's skills in relating to a patient.

Hospitals have responded to public state ratings by improving the quality of their staffs and programs, several studies indicate. [3] When Tryneski questioned his mother's hospital about its poor showing in

---

* Coronary-bypass surgery, or open-heart surgery, is a common treatment for heart disease, the nation's leading killer. The procedure involves taking an artery or vein from another part of the patient's body and using it to carry blood around the clogged portion of a vessel supplying the heart. Among the 16,548 patients who had bypass surgery in New Jersey in 1996 and 1997, 557 people died.

From *The CQ Researcher,*
May 5, 2000.

state rankings, the medical staff told him the negative publicity had stimulated major improvement efforts, including hiring new staff.

Especially dramatic improvements have been reported in New York, where deaths from bypass operations plunged by 41 percent from 1989 to 1992 after the state instituted public reporting. [4] That improvement has been attributed largely to hospital initiatives, such as restricting operating privileges of poorly rated doctors and recruiting more qualified personnel for cardiac teams.

In another potentially influential move, large employers in Pennsylvania and California are beginning to give economic breaks to patients and health plans that use doctors and hospitals with high ratings.

Despite objections from some in the medical community, the trend toward public ratings seems unstoppable. "I think the genie is out of the bottle," says Arnold M. Epstein, a professor at the Harvard University School of Public Health. "We're going to see more public reporting."

In a recent commentary in the *Journal of the American Medical Association* (*JAMA*), Epstein noted that the publicity over public reporting seems to have caught the attention of doctors and galvanized hospitals to improve the quality of their services. [5]

American Hospital Association spokesman Richard Wade agrees that it's "inevitable" that performance ratings will become increasingly public. "Many hospitals are uncomfortable with it," he says. "But it's a world we're going to have to become comfortable with."

A driving force behind the inevitability is the Internet, which has become a major repository and exchange for health information. Consumer groups and independent companies are starting to post information on doctors and hospitals that was never accessible before. The data

is still extremely limited. And experts question its reliability. But consumer advocates predict that this is only the beginning of a new trend encouraging patients to demand information that they would be too timid to ask their doctors for directly.

Judging a doctor's or hospital's quality raises the thorny question of what constitutes good quality medical care. For years, critics have assailed physicians for being slow to adapt their procedures to current scientific findings. While medical mistakes have received widespread media attention recently, consumers should be equally concerned about doctors' overuse of inappropriate treatment, according to Mark Chassin, chairman of the Department of Health Policy at Mount Sinai School of Medicine in New York. [6]

Over the last decade, government agencies and medical-specialty societies have issued hundreds of "best-practice" guidelines to try to encourage doctors to adopt scientifically proven practices. But most of these tomes have gathered dust on the shelves.

New hope for influencing doctors to change now rests partly with computer software programs that give doctors "real time" information as they make decisions about a patient. Will doctors pay attention to the information this time, or resist it as a simplistic kind of guidebook that interferes with their autonomy? The advent of doctors' performance ratings could increase their willingness to change their practices to conform to scientific findings.

As the medical community comes under increasing pressure to improve its performance, these are some of the issues being debated by consumers, employers and medical practitioners:

Do doctors treat patients based on scientific findings?

When a new test for detecting prostate cancer for men was devel-

oped in the late 1980s, prostate-removal operations surged — but only in certain parts of the country. In the Pacific Northwest, where doctors were enthusiastically recommending screening, a rising number of cancer cases were detected and the operation became increasingly common. In Connecticut, physicians screened for prostate cancer much less frequently, and rates of surgery were much lower. [7]

Yet there was no difference in death rates from prostate cancer.

Prostate cancer can remain clinically silent — undiscovered and symptom-free for a man's entire life. Thus, the scientific evidence indicates, prostate removal does not increase the length of life and may actually shorten it because of the risks posed by surgery. In addition, men undergoing surgery develop incontinence and impotence at high rates.

Why would doctors in some regions recommend a procedure for which there was so little scientific evidence of benefit and so much significant suffering for many men?

Dartmouth Medical School researchers, who have been studying regional variations in treatment since 1992, have raised such questions. Their findings suggest that doctors often make recommendations based not so much on scientific evidence as on other factors, such as the local professional culture, a failure to consult with patients about their preferences and professional uncertainty about the evidence.

Physicians treat patients every day with surgical procedures that have never been rigorously evaluated according to scientific standards, the Dartmouth researchers observe. By contrast, drugs must undergo extensive clinical trials before the Food and Drug Administration will grant approval to doctors to dispense them.

"Indeed, if prostate cancer surgery were a drug, rather than a procedure,

Most Americans 'Satisfied' With Their Doctor

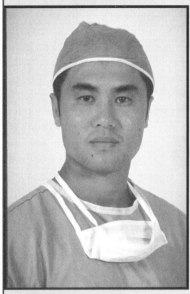

Nearly three-quarters of the Americans polled last year about health-care issues said they are "very satisfied" with their physician. Among the 20 percent who were "dissatisfied" or "somewhat satisfied" with their doctor, one in five said they had not changed doctors because they lacked information on selecting a better physician.

Q: Why are you not more satisfied with your doctor?

■ Doctor is too busy/Hard to get an appointment.	16%
■ Limited choice of doctors/My doctor is not on my health plan.	7
■ Inefficient/Doesn t help me/Not thorough.	6
■ Doctor seemed not to care/I don t get any answers.	4
■ Too long/Hard to get referrals.	1

Q: Given that you are not entirely satisfied with your doctor, which of the following best describes why you do not switch doctors?

■ I do not have enough information to know which other doctor might be better.	20%
■ No doctor is perfect, and mine is as good as any.	19
■ I do not have enough time to find another doctor who s better.	16
■ The health plan I have does not offer another doctor I like better.	11
■ There s no one I can consult to find a better doctor.	6

Q: When you have switched doctors in the past, which of the following information was most important in finding a new doctor?

■ Recommendations from friends or family.	34%
■ Getting a recommendation from another doctor.	22
■ Location of the doctor.	15
■ Doctor s hospital affiliation.	6
■ Where the doctor received education and training.	3
■ Reviews of doctors in magazines or newspapers	1
■ Seeing the doctor s name in an advertisement	1

Source: Democratic Leadership Council survey of 500 registered Democrats, Republicans and Independents

its use would be forbidden by law until proof of efficacy had been established," the authors of the *Dartmouth Atlas of Health Care* assert. [8]

Two years ago, an expert panel expressed similar alarm about doctors' tendency to use treatments without scientific basis as well as the common failure to apply treatments known to work.

"Serious and widespread quality problems exist throughout American medicine," a panel of experts convened by the Institute of Medicine (IOM) concluded in 1998 after citing an alarming trend in physicians' overuse of inappropriate treatment, underuse of appropriate treatment and medical errors. "Very large numbers of Americans are harmed as a direct result." [9]

According to panel member Chassin, "Overuse is a tremendous quality problem that harms people every day," and underuse is an equally serious problem. But neither problem has succeeded in attracting the public attention recently lavished on medical errors. "Every proven, effective treatment is underused," he says. "The list is as long as your arm. I think the public should be up in arms about the level of quality problems we have."

Underused treatments cited by the IOM panel included the failure to:

• detect and treat hypertension or depression;

• immunize children; and

• provide effective known treatments for diabetes, heart attack and asthma.

The failure alone to treat heart attacks effectively may lead to as many as 18,000 preventable deaths each year in the United States, the panel concluded. [10]

As for overused treatments, the panel cited studies finding 16 percent of hysterectomies inappropriate and 32 percent of carotid endarterectomies — a treatment for preventing stroke by removing plaque from the artery — inappropriate. The most common surgical procedure in childhood — the insertion of tubes in the ears — is inappropriate for about one-quarter of the children advised to undergo it, the panel reported. [11]

The IOM panel also cited research indicating that one-fifth of all antibiotic prescriptions were issued inappropriately during visits to the doctor to treat colds and other viral infections— for which antibiotics are ineffective. [12] The inappropriate prescription of antibiotics to some 24 million Americans "is the single most preventable cause of bacterial resistance that kills people in our intensive care units every day," Chassin says. "It's the single most important factor predicting who will become a carrier of resistant organisms and a threat to the rest of us."

Some inappropriate surgery occurs because doctors impose their biases on patients without consulting them on their preferences. For example, when two health maintenance organizations (HMOs) told patients the trade-offs of prostate surgery and giving them a choice on whether to proceed, procedures dropped by more than 40 percent. [13]

Dartmouth researchers found widespread regional variations in the rate of radical mastectomy for breast cancer as opposed to breast-conserving surgery (lumpectomy) accompanied by radiation. Extensive clinical trials have shown that improvement for survival is about the same with both options. Yet the rural Midwest tended to have much higher rates of

HealthGrades.com Inc. is one of a burgeoning number of Web sites that track medical care. It collects public and private medical data to develop report cards that rate more than 5,000 hospitals, 17,000 nursing homes, 400 health plans and physicians in 59 specialties.

mastectomy than lumpectomy. Megan McAndrew Cooper, editor of the *Dartmouth Atlas of Health Care*, recalls a newspaper interview with a small-town South Dakota doctor who told a reporter that most of his patients were farm wives and didn't care about their bodies that much.

"If the one guy in town puts his hand on your shoulder and says, 'If you were my mother, I'd recommend a total mastectomy,' a lot of women don't have the option of saying, 'I'm going somewhere else-or I'm going to get a procedure out of you that you don't do very often,' " Cooper observes.

The influence of a doctor's peers locally may also account for regional variations like that found for prostate cancer. Cooper notes, "Physicians tend to settle and practice fairly close to where they're trained, so you get a cluster effect."

In response to these criticisms and findings, physicians frequently complain that they are caught in a bind when there are gaps in the medical science. Sometimes conflicting evidence produces professional uncertainty about the rewards of using new treatments. Furthermore, doctors may be stuck in a science-knowledge limbo during the many the years it takes for clinical trials to be completed.

As a result, the AMA's Coble says, "We don't want to remove opportunities or access [to a medical treatment] until we have the right data." Sometimes physicians are aware of a medication's effectiveness before results have been published, he argues. For example, he notes that beta-blockers, a medication originally approved for blood pressure, turned out to be an important preventive measure for heart attacks.

Doctors also note that sometimes the act of giving some treatment, any treatment, to a patient is more important than the treatment itself because of the power of the placebo effect. The placebo effect probably explains why Coble felt better when his grandmother put a mustard plaster on his chest for a cold — even though no scientific evidence supports its curative powers, he notes.

"Physicians have to do some things that give hope and reassurance," Coble says, "and that does enhance healing."

Of course, it can also turn out that highly touted treatments undergoing testing don't work. For example, so many women with breast cancer were convinced that bone-marrow transplants were a life-saving procedure that few women were willing to volunteer in clinical trials for a control group receiving traditional chemotherapy. As a result, it took many years before clinical trials found bone marrow treatments ineffective. In the meantime, thousands of women had suffered through the treatment.

Physicians' growing tendency to prescribe stimulants and anti-depressants to preschool children diagnosed with behavioral problems has come under sharp criticism because there is practically no research evidence that these medications are helpful or appropriate for that age group. More troubling, almost nothing is known about whether the drugs could do lasting harm to the developing brains of small children. [14]

The way doctors treat heart attacks is widely cited as a failure to follow scientific evidence. For example, heart attack survivors should get a beta-blocker, a type of medicine that slows the heart rate, beginning right in the hospital, according to numerous studies and guidelines issued by the American College of Cardiology and the American Heart Association. [15] Yet doctors fail to prescribe beta-blockers to more than half the eligible patients, though it has been estimated that they can reduce the risk of death and second

heart attacks by at least 20 percent. [16]

On the other hand, some researchers contend, sometimes doctors may be right to be skeptical of using a widely recommended treatment for a patient with special problems.

"For beta-blockers, many times the patient has a contraindication or is not able to tolerate the drug," says David Bates, chief of the division of general medicine at Brigham and Women's Hospital in Boston, who is studying why doctors don't always adhere to scientifically based guidelines.

Have "best-practice" guidelines made medical care more effective?

In the late 1980s, many researchers who criticized medicine as insufficiently scientific advocated guidelines to help doctors determine which medical procedures were appropriate. Since then, federal agencies, expert panels and medical specialties have issued hundreds of so-called best-practice guidelines on scientifically approved treatments for given conditions. But many agree guidelines didn't succeed because, for the most part, doctors ignored them.

"Guidelines don't work. I've received hundreds of guidelines, and I put them in a file. For most doctors, it's their circular file," says Timothy G. Ferris, an internist and pediatrician at Massachusetts General Hospital in Boston.

A review of the literature published last year in *JAMA* concurred. "Despite wide promulgation, clinical practice guidelines have had limited effect on changing physician behavior," [17] the authors stated. Physicians' own reasons for not following guidelines vary depending on the recommendation. In surveys, they range from lack of awareness of the guideline to lack of confidence in the advice to inertia in changing a previous practice.

For example, as many as 90 percent of physicians said they did not

believe they could successfully counsel patients against alcohol, which many guidelines recommend. Similarly, although most physicians are aware that the federal government recommends that physicians provide counseling to stop smoking, and although studies show counseling can reduce smoking, many physicians do not follow the guideline because they do not believe it will succeed. In addition, the ever-expanding research makes it increasingly difficult for physicians to be aware of every guideline, the authors noted.

Yet the literature suggests that lack of knowledge of the guidelines is not the major problem. Only a minority of physicians are completely unaware of the most publicized recommendations, the review found. So why don't doctors follow them?

One puzzling example is the failure of most doctors to recommend aspirin for patients who have had heart attacks. It has been well-known since the 1988 publication of a major international study that heart-disease patients who take aspirin daily are at about one-third the risk of another heart attack. Yet only 26 percent of heart-disease patients were prescribed aspirin by their doctor in office visits, a recent study found. [18]

"I don't think it's a matter of physicians needing to be better educated about the role of aspirin," says the study's author, Randall S. Stafford, of Harvard Medical School. It's true that some doctors have an exaggerated idea of the drug's dangerous side-effects based on old information, Stafford says. But drug companies are unwilling to promote a new use for an old, low-cost drug like aspirin, and that's the information source many doctors rely upon for adopting new practices, according to Stafford

"It's clear that dispensing free samples to physicians is a very large area of promotional drug information," says Stafford of the 15-minute visits by drug salesmen toting sample cases to doctors' offices. To get the same information from a search of the medical literature, for example, would "take doctors a lot more work," Stafford notes.

A more important factor in ignoring guidelines, Stafford and others suggest, is pressure on doctors to deal with the instant emergency problems that patients bring to their attention. Most doctors' offices lack computerized information systems to remind a doctor that the patient who has come in with an asthma attack may also be a heart-attack patient who should be on aspirin.

"In the real-life hubbub, little things get lost," Ferris says. "When you go from room to room with patients, you don't [have time to] jump to your guidelines."

As clinical director of a disease-management program for Partners Community Health Care, a cooperative effort at several hospitals in Boston, Ferris is part of the wave of quality improvement efforts that grew out of the guideline movement — person-to-person campaigns with physicians aimed at bringing practice into line with scientific evidence. One of the most successful campaigns — involving a consortium of doctors and hospitals in Maine, New Hampshire and Vermont — used site visits by doctors to call medical staffs' attention to problems with coronary-bypass surgery and to superior methods that could reduce deaths. After the site visits, rates of death among patients who had the operation declined 24 percent among the five hospitals involved. [19]

Yet doctors say they often feel overwhelmed by all the organizations that are trying to alert physicians to the latest quality improvements. For a typical doctor, that can include as many as a half-dozen health insurers with whom the doctor is enrolled and administrators at the hospitals where they practice. "I present my program to doctors and they say, 'There are so many programs I can't keep them straight,'" Ferris reports. "We [at Partners] have our program, the local insurance companies have their own programs. The doctors don't know which to use, so they don't use either."

Doctors are also rightly suspicious of the origin and objectivity of some managed-care campaigns, Ferris says, because an increasing number are underwritten by pharmaceutical companies interested in marketing a profit-making drug. [20]

HMOs were among the first to use clinical guidelines to approve or disapprove insurance reimbursement for medical procedures. Some cases of HMO nurses denying emergency medical care over the phone have become notorious. Such cases helped spur the growing patients'-rights movement, which has often attacked managed-care guidelines as self-serving, cost-cutting measures, not efforts to improve quality. [21]

The AMA has attacked what it dubs "black box" guidelines — undisclosed criteria used by managed-care companies to deny payment for medical treatment without identifying the source of expertise (see p. 72). "AMA has made a policy statement that any guidelines should be based on evidence and list people whose reputations are attributed to those guidelines. You need to know on what grounds they're made," says AMA trustee Coble.

Robert W. Dubois, a former RAND researcher who in 1988 helped found one of the first companies to provide guidelines to HMOs and health insurers, defends the integrity of the guidelines but agrees they were often used more for cost-cutting than quality improvement. Dubois is chief executive officer of Protocare Sciences, a consulting company in Santa Monica, Calif., which has provided guidelines to some 65 HMOs and health insurance clients.

Dubois was one of a group of prominent RAND researchers who reported in 1987 that a high proportion of medical treatments in the United States were being conducted inappropriately. He hasn't lost the fervor of the early days.

"Guidelines can help us make better decisions," Dubois says. "Tonsillectomy varies sixfold to eightfold depending on the town you live in. It's unlikely to be due to scientific evidence." But he agrees that HMOs sometimes apply the guidelines in an overly simplistic fashion. "A good idea done wrong makes the idea look wrong."

Some doctors say the desire to cut costs still dominates many quality-improvement campaigns. "All too often, there's a focus on areas where there are cost savings," from the insurers' or hospital administrator's point of view, Ferris contends, "not where the public would benefit the most" from a health perspective. "I don't see a lot of quality improvement in adolescent mental health, where there's a huge need in improved services — because it will cost more."

Other physicians say they are so burdened with checklists of recommended prevention efforts that they aren't spending enough time listening to patients the old-fashioned way or extending sympathy for a patient's discomfort. "A lot of doctors do feel besieged by our charts here at the VA: Are we screening for alcohol, cigarette smoking, obesity? So the primary-care physician feels more like a traffic cop; it makes the visit more mechanical," says H. Gilbert Welch, an internist and senior research associate at the Department of Veterans Affairs in White River Junction, Vt.

Unlike some doctors, Welch argues that guidelines have worked, but they're limited in what they can do because they are by nature simplistic measures of things that can be counted. "They pervade our practice in everything we do; there are much more explicit guidelines. And more and more physicians are being measured on meeting them," says Welch, editor of the journal *Effective Clinical Practice.*

In a recent editorial in the journal, Ferris questioned whether the impressive quality improvements reported from a recent campaign aimed at chronic respiratory conditions meant doctors were robbing time from other important medical areas, were spending less time with patients with other conditions and were putting less stress on human interaction in general. [22]

Ferris also questions whether involvement in studies like this "decrease the physicians' sense of autonomy and their willingness to involve patients in diagnostic and treatment decisions." If doctors are carrying out recommendations resentfully, they can communicate their reluctance to their patients and undermine any new effort, Ferris observes.

Some hospitals and private companies are employing software to make it easier for doctors to consult the scientific literature for certain conditions. Some offer to tailor the information to individual patients' profiles by computer (*see p. 76.*) Many believe that the sheer quantity of information is so overwhelming today and physicians are so pressed for time, that computers may be the only way for a doctor to apply the latest research for a patient's condition efficiently.

"The reason the guidelines failed is because doctors can't process all that information during the short patient visits typical of a busy managed-care practice," says Lawrence L. Weed, professor of medicine emeritus at the University of Vermont, who markets his own diagnostic software program as president of the PKC Corp. in Burlington, Vt. To cope with the numerous diagnostic possibilities,

Weed says, a doctor typically limits the number of possible causes he considers for a patient's medical problem. "That's where mistakes happen."

Would public report cards rating doctors and hospitals improve care?

The common perception among Americans that their doctor is "better than average" reminds Harvard physician Epstein of public radio's fictional town of Lake Wobegone, where, it boasts, "all the children are above average."

"Without publicly reported data, a similar myth is relived every day in health care," Epstein asserted in a recent editorial. [23]

But things could be different, some consumer advocates have argued. If consumers had the same ratings in choosing a doctor or hospital that they bring to shopping for a washing machine, market demand would force up the quality of medical services, they say. Bolstering their optimism have been recent improvements in survival rates from open heart surgery in the three states — New York, New Jersey and Pennsylvania — that publicize doctors' and hospitals' death rates from the operation. [24]

The most dramatic improvements occurred in New York, where death rates plunged 41 percent after the state began publicizing hospitals' death rates from cardiac bypass surgery in 1990. Although death rates from the operation have been dropping nationwide, New York experienced the most rapid rate of decline, according to Chassin, who was New York state health commissioner from 1992 to 1994. However, skeptics have argued that comparable decreases in mortality occurred in Massachusetts, which has no reporting program.

Contrary to some consumer expectations, however, public reports have not produced any noticeable shift in patients to highly rated hos-

pitals from those with poor performance. Instead, the strongest influence of report cards has been on hospitals at the bottom of the rankings. Some of those hospitals improved practices, such as the way they prepared patients for surgery, or weeded out poor-performing staff in response to the negative publicity. [25]

In his 1999 book *Demanding Medical Excellence,* Michael L. Millenson, a health-care consultant, describes how Winthrop-University Hospital in Mineola, N.Y., was stung by its ranking — 26th out of the 30 New York hospitals performing cardiac bypass surgery. The hospital rose to 15th after recruiting an experienced team of surgeons, upgrading equipment and improving teamwork between doctors and nurses. [26]

In the years following New York's initial scorecard in 1990, which received wide news coverage, six hospitals publicly acknowledged that the performance report had spurred them to start quality improvements. [27]

Some observers believe the crucial factor was publicity. "I doubt the level of attention we've seen [among hospitals] would have been devoted had the data not been made public," Chassin says. In his role as health commissioner, Chassin held press conferences highlighting the hospitals that had made improvements and says he regularly phoned hospital presidents asking what changes they were planning to make to investigate their poor performance.

Some hospitals in New York responded to the negative publicity by restricting operating privileges of their least competent doctors. The result was an exodus of doctors with the least experience and the highest mortality rates for the operation, studies found. [28]

A similar effort in Cleveland, the Cleveland Health Quality Choice project, reported improvements in patients' recovery after death rates were published for six common medical procedures and two operations.[29] That may be because hospitals are extremely sensitive to their public image and respond to report cards as a "competitive opportunity," the *JAMA* authors suggested.

AHA spokesman Wade isn't willing to attribute all such improvements to public report cards, but agrees publicity can help. "Internally, it gives hospitals some leverage for dealing with physician performance and other quality issues," he says.

Patrick Romano, associate professor of medicine and pediatrics at University of California School of Medicine at Davis, has studied the impact of public reports in New York and in California, which reports survival rates for heart attack patients for hospitals but not for individual doctors. Romano's studies are among several that find little impact on switching consumers' choice of hospital. That's largely because the choice of hospital is usually determined by health plans or a physician's hospital affiliation, Romano suggests.

While consumers may deliberate carefully before choosing a health plan or a doctor, they "don't choose a hospital deliberately," he says. "They wind up in a hospital almost against their will." On the other hand, Romano says, "We've found numerous anecdotes of hospitals reassigning staff or changing programs in response to outcome reports."

Unfortunately, a recent study suggests, health plans are unlikely to patronize the New York hospitals with the lowest death rates from cardiac surgery. New Yorkers who belong to managed-health care plans were more likely to receive coronary surgery at the hospitals with higher death rates for the operation than patients in traditional fee-for-service plans, the study found. One possible reason suggested by the authors is that managed-care organizations may choose hospitals that give them the best deal on prices and ignore the public information on quality.[30]

State report cards have not exactly been welcomed by physicians. In New York, the reports were originally intended to publicize death rates only by hospital. In 1991, the state began releasing doctor-by-doctor data in response to a Freedom of Information request from a reporter at the Long Island newspaper *Newsday*. The state's Cardiac Advisory Committee of physicians at first reacted angrily, recommending an end to the entire state data-collection effort.[31] "It created an enormous amount of animosity and hostility that was totally unnecessary," says Chassin, adding "There's still a significant minority of surgeons who hate the system."

Speaking for the AMA, Coble grades heart surgery report cards as "imperfect" but "improving." However, he questions whether patients can rely solely on death counts and the numbers of operations performed to find the best doctor. "One has to be concerned with compassion and continuity," he stresses, among other less easily quantified qualities in a doctor.

But it's exactly the statistical information that's lacking in today's health marketplace, advocates of public reports respond. "You don't need a report card to tell if a doctor has a good bedside manner," Romano says. "But when you go in for a consultation, you don't have a clue whether the doctor has a good surgical technique or not." ∎

BACKGROUND

Questionable Variations

Dartmouth Medical School professor John E. Wennberg, who founded the *Dartmouth Atlas* series, attracted national attention in 1984 when he raised questions about the scientific basis of American medical practice. His article in the journal *Health Affairs* drew on research undertaken in Vermont, Maine and Iowa. A child had an 8 percent chance of getting his tonsils removed in one town and a 70 percent chance in another. There was a 20 percent chance that women would undergo a hysterectomy by age 70 in one region and a 70 percent chance elsewhere. These variations raised questions about the scientific basis upon which doctors make decisions about treatment.[32]

Members of Congress welcomed the information. In 1984, 10 percent of the federal budget was going for health care, double the 1961 level. Sen. William Proxmire, D-Wis., who held hearings prompted by Wennberg's article, declared, "We simply don't know if more [money] is better."[33] Wennberg's findings suggested that Congress could reduce Medicare spending and improve health-care quality at the same time.

The latest *Atlas of Health Care* continues to raise questions about the variations in surgical practice around the country and the basis on which doctors choose to do surgery. A surgical decision should be based on the gold standard for scientific evidence, the randomized clinical trial, authors of the *Atlas* contend, not local whim.

The results of the first randomized clinical trial-testing the effect of streptomycin on tuberculosis — was published in a 1948 issue of the *British Medical Journal*.[34] A British researcher, Austin Bradford Hill, gave streptomycin to 50 people while a control group received a placebo. Hill concealed who was getting which therapy from the trial's clinical investigators. After six months, Hill's trial proved the effectiveness of the drug. Fourteen of the 52 patients receiving

Chronology

1900s *The medical establishment takes up the call to make medical education scientific but ignores a similar proposal for medical practice.*

1910
A landmark report by educator Abraham Flexner and backed by the Carnegie Foundation calls for standardizing medical education around scientific principles.

1912
Harvard-trained surgeon E. A. Codman proposes that patients receive reports on hospitals' and doctors' success rates.

⎯⎯ • ⎯⎯

1960s *Thalidomide scandal prompts legislation requiring stringent clinical studies for medications, but surgery is not included.*

1962
Congress passes the Kefauver-Harris amendments to the Food, Drug and Cosmetic Act requiring drug companies to prove that a drug is effective as well as safe.

⎯⎯ • ⎯⎯

1970s–1980s
Unnecessary surgeries become a hot topic. Spiraling medical costs and Medicare spending spur interest in scientifically backed medical care.

1970
Sociologist Eliot Friedson's landmark study finds physicians emphasize intuition over science.

1984
An influential article by Dartmouth College physician John Wennberg shows wide geographic variations in surgical procedures like tonsillectomies, raising questions about whether the government is wasting money on unneeded treatments.

⎯⎯ • ⎯⎯

1990s *States publish doctors' and hospitals' death rates from operations. Expert panel's warnings on quality of medical care receive little public attention. Consumer backlash against managed care leads some HMOs to offer "report cards."*

1990
New York becomes the first state to publish death rates of individual hospitals performing open-heart surgery.

1991
The National Committee for Quality Assurance begins accrediting health plans. Xerox and other large employers tell health plans they must get accreditation or get kicked out of network.

1993
Family of breast cancer patient Nelene Fox wins $89 million judgment against her HMO, Health Net, for refusing Fox a bone-marrow transplant.

1994
President Clinton's proposal to require that all health plans disclose how good a job they do of treating patients dies with health-reform legislation.

1997
Under congressional pressure, the federal agency charged with issuing "best-practice" medical guidelines stops issuing guidelines.

1998
Institute of Medicine panel reports that quality of medical care is inadequate.

1999s
Proposal during patients'-rights legislative debate to require health plans to publicly report on their quality dies under opposition from health insurers.

November 1999
United Health Care announces it will no longer deny doctor-recommended treatments but will give its patients comparative information on the quality of doctors in its plan.

⎯⎯ • ⎯⎯

2000 *Congress and Clinton administration officials study ways to implement Institute of Medicine proposals to reduce medical errors. But quality problems receive little attention.*

February 2000
Aetna/US Healthcare announces it will no longer pay for bone-marrow transplants because studies find no improvement in breast-cancer survival.

Feb. 22, 2000
President Clinton calls for mandatory reporting of medical errors.

Who Pays Attention to Report Cards?

Although consumer advocates praise medical report cards, the medical community has expressed concern that mortality counts may unfairly tarnish the reputation of a hospital or a surgeon that takes on sicker-than-average patients.

For example, would the ratings hurt a hospital located near a nursing home whose elderly patients have particularly poor prospects for surgery?

Patrick Romano, associate professor of medicine and pediatrics at the University of California School of Medicine at Davis, says that remains a concern for numerous procedures — although cardiac specialists have come up with agreed-upon methods for adjusting cardiac death statistics to account for sicker patients.

Even so, doctors have worried that specialists will turn away sicker patients for fear of compiling a high mortality rate on public report cards. In Pennsylvania, almost two-thirds of cardiologists reported increasing difficulty in finding surgeons to operate on high-risk patients after the state published death rates for cardiac bypass surgery. Almost two-thirds of cardiac surgeons reported they were less willing to operate on such patients.[1]

In New York, the release of mortality ratings spurred stories that surgeons had turned away sicker patients and that some patients were seeking surgery outside the state. However a subsequent study suggested those reports were based more on fear than on reality. The proportion of New York patients receiving out-of-state bypass operations actually declined from 1987 to 1992, the study found.[2] And the overall severity of illness in heart-attack patients got worse over that period, suggesting that sicker patients were not being driven out of state.

The publication of heart surgery mortality data can be a double-edged sword, according to a New Jersey heart specialist who helped develop the state's public reports for cardiac bypass operations.

"The psychological influence on the surgeons in my facility is that it's somewhere in the back of their mind every time they look at patients," says Charles Dennis, chairman of the Department of Cardiology at Deborah Heart and Lung Center in Browns Mills, N.J. "It pushes them to improve quality. The negative side is they're weighing, 'Should I take on this case?' If your name is going to be on the front page of *The New York Times*, you'll think twice."

As an adviser to the state of New Jersey on its public report cards, Dennis says the state has addressed doctors' concerns that they will be penalized for treating patients with a grim prognosis. The state gives every surgeon and hospital the opportunity to submit the case of any patient who died of a heart attack and for whom there was a small chance they could have been saved by cardiac bypass surgery. If the state

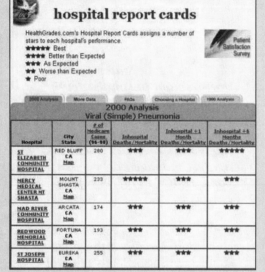

Advocates say medical report cards like these can push hospitals and physicians to improve their performance.

only bed rest had died, compared with just four of 50 patients on the drug.

In recent years, randomized clinical trials using the techniques pioneered by Hill have become the standard procedure for testing drugs in the United States. Their use expanded after landmark legislation was passed in 1962 in response to the scandal over the drug thalidomide, which was prescribed as a sleeping aid to pregnant woman but produced thousands of deformed babies. In 1962, Congress passed the Kefauver-Harris amendments to the Food, Drug and Cosmetic Act, requiring drug companies to prove that a medication was effective as well as safe.

But the new law did not apply to surgical procedures, which to this day remain largely unregulated. As a result, medical treatments outside of new drugs have tended to rely more on professional consensus and local culture.

Medical sociologist Eliot Friedson observed in his landmark study of physician culture in 1970 that physicians' training emphasized personal intuition over the skeptical testing of assumptions that is characteristic of other scientific fields. Physicians, he wrote, retained "a moral commitment to intervention" for their patients even when scientific knowledge was missing.

Today, some doctors say their medical education still treats medicine more like an idiosyncratic art than a science. Alan R. Zwerner, who agrees with the doctor's assessment, the state can eliminate such cases from a doctor's public death count. As a result, Dennis says, in New Jersey "we've not heard that complaint" that the statistics give insufficient credit to doctors who take on the riskier cases.

For the family doctor or cardiologist who has to refer a patient to a surgeon, New Jersey's public report could provide a newly objective basis for picking the right surgeon, Dennis argues. Typically, doctors' referrals are based on personal relationships or how the doctor was treated last time he called the surgeon, Dennis notes. The referring doctors rarely know how the patient survival rate for a particular surgeon compares with that of other specialists.

Unfortunately, it does not appear that doctors have made widespread use of state reports providing such information when it comes to making referrals to a surgeon. John Tryneski's experience in trying to find a good heart surgeon in New Jersey for his mother was typical, studies suggest. When Tryneski showed his mother's cardiologist the surgeon-by-surgeon mortality rates he had printed out from the New Jersey health department's Web site, the cardiologist asked for a copy. Tryneski says he realized then that the cardiologist apparently had not consulted the ratings before recommending a surgeon. Only a minority of cardiologists in New York said the report cards had influenced their referrals. And in Pennsylvania, only a minority of cardiologists had discussed the public ratings with patients.[3]

Consumers' use of report cards has been disappointing, too. In many cases, consumers are simply not aware that such report cards exist. One survey questioned 474 patients who had undergone bypass surgery in Pennsylvania, which publishes hospital- and surgeon-specific data on mortality from the operation. Of 474 patients, only 56 were aware of the performance report before their operation and less than one-quarter of those stated it had any impact on their choice of surgeon. However, when the report was described, more than half the patients said the information would have influenced their choice of surgeon if they had learned that their surgeon had a higher than expected mortality rate.[4]

Yet a patient may have little opportunity to make a choice among physicians if a coronary bypass operation is called for. A patient arriving at a hospital in the middle of a heart attack is already in the midst of an emergency. A patient who complains of pain or shortness of breath to his primary doctor usually is referred to a cardiologist who, in turn, refers the patient to a specific surgeon and a specific hospital.

"You're already into a system where it's very hard to take a step back and say, 'Excuse me, I'm going to take out my guide and decide who's going to do the bypass.' " notes Arthur Levin, who directs the Center for Medical Consumers, a consumer group in New York.

Because ratings can have such a crucial effect on a hospital's reputation, one concern of hospitals is that the "data has proper protections so it doesn't become a big lake for fishing expeditions for lawyers" pursuing malpractice cases, says Richard Wade, spokesman for the American Hospital Association.

Yet hospitals are not mounting a big campaign against publicizing ratings. One reason is that they see state-generated rating as a more reliable source of information than the many private Web site rating systems that have proliferated recently. (See sidebar, p. 73.)

[1] Martin N. Marshall, et al., "The Public Release of Performance Data: What do We Expect to Gain? A Review of the Evidence," *Journal of the American Medical Association (JAMA)*, April 12, 2000, pp. 1866-1874.

[2] *Ibid.*

[3] *Ibid.*

[4] Eric C. Schneider and Arnold M. Epstein, "Use of Public Performance Reports: A Survey of Patients Undergoing Cardiac Surgery," *JAMA*, May 27, 1998, pp. 1638-1642.

practiced as an ob-gyn for over a decade after graduating from medical school in 1974, traces this viewpoint to the way doctors are trained during internship and residency.

"What happens is they lock you up in a series of hospitals with hundreds if not thousands of physicians, all of whom do everything differently from one another. I was asked to decide what I though was best. No one asks what's most effective," recalls Zwerner, now senior vice president for strategic planning at personalmd.com, which computerizes medical records, in Pleasanton, Calif. "Much of what we do isn't evidence based. So you study like an artist — not like a scientist."

Many accepted treatments have never been studied or proven to work in clinical trials. A widespread example is "off-label" treatment — in which doctors prescribe drugs for conditions or segments of the population that have not been approved by the FDA. Antidepressants, which are widely prescribed for children, have only been studied on any significant scale in adults. In children, two widely used treatments — tonsillectomies and the insertion of tubes in the ears to prevent recurrent ear infections — lacked clinical trial data to justify them at the peak of their popularity.

But many doctors say it would be unrealistic to expect all drug uses and treatments to have undergone clinical trials, considering the expense, time and ethical hurdles involved in recruiting people to participate for long periods, especially if they involve children.

"If you wanted to practice medicine only on randomized control trials, you'd have a fairly limited practice," says Douglas B. Kamerow, director of the Center for Practice and Technology Assessment at the federal Agency for Healthcare Research and Quality (AHRQ).

Rise of Guidelines

In the late 1980s, many critics of the medical profession saw medical-practice guidelines as the solution to unscientific practices. But guidelines lost momentum as a stand-alone solution when doctors failed to use them. Advocates came to realize that doctors are more apt to change their behavior when another doctor in a position of authority presents the scientific evidence for changing a medical treatment.

"There are a lot of guidelines out there, but everyone agrees that just printing a guideline will do nothing," Kamerow says. He helped to develop 19 clinical practical guidelines for the federal agency that preceded AHRQ. But his agency soon found there were political ramifications.

Congressional pressure forced the agency out of the business of issuing guidelines after back surgeons lobbied against the agency's low-back pain guidelines, which recommended mild medication and brief bed rest as preferable to surgery. Since 1997, the agency has shifted to publishing reports summarizing the scientific evidence for specific conditions and has established an Internet clearinghouse where doctors can check out hundreds of existing guidelines.

As managed care became increasingly popular, HMOs turned to guidelines to make decisions they hoped would keep costs down. Increasingly, HMOs and insurers have been accused of misusing guidelines to reduce costs. In some cases, managed care's effort to curb use of inappropriate medical procedures could not withstand the public perception that the companies were just trying to save money by depriving people of medical care.

The most notorious example involved bone marrow transplants, an experimental and expensive treatment for breast cancer that many cancer patients saw as their best hope for survival. In 1993, the family of Nelene Fox, a woman who died of breast cancer, won an $89 million judgment against her HMO because it had refused to pay for a bone marrow transplant.

The HMO, Health Net, had balked at paying on the grounds that the treatment was unproven. The suit and the ensuing negative publicity about HMOs convinced several major insurers to pay for the treatment despite doubts about its efficacy. In February, however, Aetna/US Healthcare reversed its payment policy of the past decade and announced it would no long pay for bone marrow transplants because it is now clear the treatment does not work. Four completed studies found no improvement in survival rates for patients who receive the procedure. [35]

Over the last five years, managed-care companies have pulled back on case-by-case reviews of the kind that raised a turmoil in the Fox case, according to Dubois of Protocare Sciences. He says his company has seen a sharp fall-off in its business of advising HMOs on the use of guidelines. Managed-care organizations are relying more heavily on financial incentives to encourage doctors to make more cost-effective decisions

and selecting doctors whose practice is already more in keeping with their own cost-conscious guidelines, according to Dubois.

"What has happened in the last couple of years is a backlash against managed care and managed care's involvement" in the doctor-patient relationship, Dubois says. ∎

CURRENT SITUATION

Guidelines Controversy

Managed care's use of guidelines remains controversial, if somewhat mysterious. A recent lawsuit is emblematic of physicians' complaints that health insurers skimp on medical care under the guise of science when their primary interest is cutting costs.

Two Texas physicians are suing the consulting company that creates the guidelines for many HMO's utilization reviews — Seattle-based Milliman and Robertson — saying they want to expose the company's role in setting HMO standards used to deny coverage. The company's one-day limit on hospital stays for uncomplicated maternal deliveries created such public outrage several years ago that Congress and 41 states passed laws overriding "drive-through deliveries. [36]

The two pediatric specialists later contended in a lawsuit that Milliman and Robertson falsely listed them as co-authors in a pediatric textbook that recommends short hospital stays for several children's diseases. One said he first learned his name was

Surfing the Net to Find the Best

Most Americans get recommendations for doctors from their friends and relatives. But suppose you have just moved to a new city and don't know anyone well enough to ask for a suggestion. Now imagine that a click of your computer mouse could help you find the best family doctor and the best ob-gyn in town, as well as a top-rated local hospital to treat a relative's breast cancer.

Several private Web sites, in fact, purport to rate doctors and medical facilities. But medical experts are wary since the sites don't always reveal their methods for judging quality or make adjustments for hospitals that start out with sicker patients. In addition, there's a conflict-of-interest question for a profit-making company. Some sites offer to sell advertising to those hospitals that get highly rated. Private sites may not want to risk losing advertisers by lowering a hospital's ratings.

State health department Web sites rating doctors and hospitals are considered the most reliable, but most only touch on a few procedures.

STATE SITES

New York State Department of Health
(www.health.state.ny.us/nysdoh/research/heart)

Lists the mortality rates for coronary bypass surgery operations and angioplasty for every hospital in the state that performs the operation. In each case, it indicates whether a death rate is above or below the statewide average. It also lists death rates by physician for coronary bypass.

Pennsylvania Health Care Cost Containment Council
(www.phc4.org)

This site rates Pennsylvania hospitals for 15 common medical diagnoses or procedures including heart attack, stroke, lung cancer, adult diabetes and hip operations. For each hospital, a consumer can find out whether the mortality rate and length of stay were "greater than expected," average or "less than expected."

New Jersey Department of Health and Senior Services
(www.state.nj.us/health)

This site lists mortality rates compared to the statewide average for coronary bypass surgery by hospital and doctor.

California Office of Statewide Health Planning and Development
(www.oshpd.state.ca.us/hpp/chop/index.htm)

This site lists hospital mortality rates for heart-attack patients in the month following the operation. California plans to release mortality data by hospital for coronary bypass operations starting this spring. It also plans to release mortality rates for intensive-care units, hip fracture and pneumonia as well as maternal health following deliveries.

NONPROFITS

National Committee for Quality Assurance
(www.ncqa.org)

NCQA accredits managed care health plans and collects quality information from them. At this site, a consumer can create a report card comparing the health plans available in his or her geographic area. Note that not all health plans are included.

HealthCareChoices
(http://healthcarechoices.org)

This is a nonprofit health-information site run by former breast cancer patient Susan Rosenfeld. This site shows how many breast cancer operations were performed at individual hospitals in seven states based on the state's own data: California, Florida, Illinois, Maryland, New Jersey, New York and Pennsylvania. The volume of operations a hospital performs correlates closely with patient survival, according to some studies. However, experts note that volume should not be the sole criteria in picking a hospital or doctor since some doctors who perform a lot of surgery may have poor success rates and vice versa. This site also has links to several state databases on physician disciplinary actions.

Center for Medical Consumers
(www.medicalconsumers.org)

This nonprofit consumer organization in New York City lists the volume of operations performed by New York doctors and hospitals for 29 procedures. It also posts summaries of recent medical journal articles of interest to consumers.

OTHER SITES

www.healthgrades.com
The Web site offers ratings for individual hospitals by type of procedure. It also offers report cards on physicians, health plans and nursing homes. However the method for rating is controversial and, some experts believe, unreliable.

www.doctorquality.com
The Web site offers expert opinions on clinical questions from a panel of physicians.

http://healthscope.org
The Web site offers consumer-satisfaction ratings for California HMOs.

being used on the book 10 months after publication. The other doctor said he had never reviewed the recommended limits on hospital stays. For example, the company cuts hospital stays for serious childhood diseases like meningitis to just three days when it should be more than a week, the physicians charged.

The company's guidelines for other conditions have also been cited in class-action lawsuits against Humana Inc. in Florida and Prudential Health Plans in New York. According to the AMA's *American Medical News*, "the guidelines are widely used by [health] plans and are thought to be a top money-maker for" Milliman and Robertson.

To the extent that managed care has exerted a positive influence on medical quality, it may have reduced overuse of medical treatment, some consumers concede. But they add that HMOs had shown little interest in addressing the failure to use appropriate treatment. Indeed, the American medical system has yet to invent a payment incentive that rewards excellence from both directions, Mt. Sinai's Chassin observes.

"Overuse [of medical treatment] is fueled by fee-for-service payments," he notes, because doctors get paid more if they order more tests and treatments. On the other hand, Chassin says, underuse of appropriate medical treatments is fueled by the managed-care approach of capping the amount a doctor can spend on each patient.

Rating Health Plans

With the majority of Americans now receiving their health care through managed care, a handful of states have started to issue HMO report cards aimed at consumers. [37]

But studies find that consumers rarely use them.

"They can't read them, they can't understand them, they're not mailed to them, they don't pay attention to them," says Christina Bethell, director of research at the Foundation for Accountability (FACCT) in Portland, Ore., which represents consumers and employers. The organization aims to provide information about medical quality to the consumer.

State report cards rarely come out and tell a consumer which health plan is best, notes Mark Hocchauser, a psychologist in Golden Valley, Minn., who has evaluated more than a half-dozen report cards for readability. Hocchauser finds most of them too complicated for the average consumer. Typically, he says, the report cards are filled with technical terminology and confusing bar graphs. Frequently, they require the consumer to phone the health plans to get the additional information crucial to choosing among plans. "Try to work through them — it's like doing your taxes," he says.

For many of those reasons, Hocchauser gave Utah's first HMO report card, issued in 1996, a grade of "C." Denise Love, who helped develop the report card for the Utah State Department of Health, says the grade was fair. "The political reality was the HMO industry had to approve every word," says Love, now executive director of the National Association of Health Data Organizations in Salt Lake City, which represents state and private data collection agencies. "They were threatened by words like 'good' or 'better.' "

Most HMO report cards are based on information collected by the National Committee for Quality Assurance (NCQA), a nonprofit founded by the industry, which also accredits HMOs. In keeping with managed care's tradition of emphasizing preventive health care, the organization

asks health plans what percentage of their patients have received preventive screenings like mammograms, for example.

But Bethell says these are rarely the questions that most interest consumers. In focus groups, consumers say they're more interested in knowing how good a doctor in the plan will be. They also want to know that they're getting the medically correct treatment when they're sick.

"People only have anecdotal information, like 'Is the doctor certified' or 'Is the hospital accredited,' not 'Did the right thing happen to get the right result at the right time?' " according to Bethell.

It is not clear how much pressure NCQA ratings exert on health plans to improve their quality or on employers to pick high-quality health plans. Not all of the nation's health plans have sought NCQA accreditation. Only half of the nation's plans have NCQA accreditation. More than 20 plans failed to receive accreditation, and other health plans have reported poor scores. "Yet almost all of these health plans are still in business caring for patients," Harvard's Epstein noted in a recent editorial. [38]

Rewarding Quality

A few large employers say they want their employees to use hospitals that get the best results when patients are seriously ill. These employers say they're willing to use their purchasing power to push them in that direction.

In Pennsylvania, a coalition of large employers including Bethlehem Steel Corp. has started providing financial incentives to steer employees to area hospitals that have received high quality ratings from the state for

At Issue:

Should health-care providers be required to report to the public on the quality of their care?

DAVID LANSKY

President, Foundation for Accountability

FROM *BLUEPRINT*, THE MAGAZINE OF THE DEMOCRATIC LEADERSHIP COUNCIL, SPRING 2000

*m*any health-care insurers and providers oppose public accountability. They insist that any reporting must be voluntary and are unwilling to collect and report their own outcomes.

The three major auto manufacturers jointly asked the major national preferred provider organization (PPO) insurance plans to publish member-satisfaction data — and were refused. In a recent survey, only 2 percent of employers said they use available quality information to influence their health-care decisions.

The federal government stopped publishing hospital death rates after the hospital industry protested. The national reporting system on health maintenance organizations (HMOs) is voluntary. Indemnity insurers, including traditional Medicare and PPOs, the fastest-growing type of insurance, oppose any public information requirements. Neither Medicare nor the Federal Employee Health Benefits Program has been able to require more than the most superficial information to be disclosed — and the government has had to pay all the data-collection costs for that.

Only a standardized national reporting system will overcome this political opposition. If the federal government mandated disclosure of a minimum set of performance indicators, the information industry would eagerly compete to help consumers acquire, interpret and make decisions from those data.

These barriers won't be overcome through exhortation or incremental reform or health-plan report cards. American consumers must assert a right to know what kind of care they are getting and to choose the caregivers who meet their personal needs.

Public agencies, employers, consumers and health-care organizations must collaborate to produce information that matters to people. Government agencies should only contract with health-care organizations that disclose how public funds are spent and what health benefits are achieved by their patients and members.

Many health plans sign up the same group of doctors and hospitals, so choosing one health plan over another does not solve the quality problem. Consumers must have accurate and reliable information on cost and quality. . . .

[This will] drive us toward a health-care system that allows all Americans to understand the importance of quality care for their lives and then demand and seek it out. . . .

BLUECROSS BLUESHIELD ASSOCIATION

STATEMENT, JULY 12, 1999

*t*he Democratic Patients' Bill of Rights includes a section requiring that all types of health plans collect, report on and be accountable for improving patient clinical outcomes, i.e., enrollees' health status.

This language would narrow choice by forcing PPOs to manage care in the same way as HMOs.

PPOs appeal to people who prefer a wide selection of network physicians and free access to their physician, i.e., no gatekeeper, as opposed to people who prefer the tighter management features of HMOs.

If PPOs had to collect medical records data and be accountable for changing physicians' practices, i.e., improving patient outcomes, they would have to:

- Restrict access to out-of-network providers;
- Use primary-care "gatekeepers" to coordinate care;
- Shrink networks;
- Adopt new payment incentives to influence provider behavior; and
- Re-contract with physicians and other providers so as to enter into a much more information-intensive and management-based relationship.

Quality measurement and improvement is a young, rapidly evolving science. So, too, is the science of conveying complex information in a meaningful way to consumers.

Surveys show that in making health-plan decisions, consumers are most concerned about such matters as maintaining access to their personal physicians, ease of access to specialists and paying a small and consistent amount for services. They generally do not give much weight to standardized quality measures.

It is clearly premature to mandate that health plans collect standardized data. Indeed, research shows that if consumers are given particularly complex clinical measures that are difficult to understand, they will ignore them.

Rather than mandate the collection of extensive data of dubious value to consumers, a better approach would be to invest in research and systems to advance our knowledge of what consumers truly want to know about quality and how to measure it.

open-heart surgery. Employers in the Lehigh Valley Business Conference on Health Care, in Bethlehem, Pa., will pay 100 percent of the heart operation's cost if an employee goes to one of the recommended hospitals. Otherwise, the patient will have to pay a deductible and a copayment.

"Our employees aren't going to go to a facility just because it's there. We're saying we want to steer our employees to the best in the community," says Catherine "Kitty" Gallagher, conference president. She speaks highly of the Pennsylvania "Outcomes" reports, which have published hospital performance ratings for more than 50 procedures since 1986. "That data has done more to improve hospitals in Pennsylvania than anything else," Gallagher asserts.

Later this year, California plans to follow New York's lead in issuing mortality rates from coronary bypass surgery for California's hospitals. (The state will not list results for physicians and, since the system is voluntary, only 85 percent of hospitals have agreed to provide information.)

The Pacific Business Group on Health, a group of 34 large employers, is developing incentives for health plans that agree to channel patients to hospitals getting the lowest death rates. "The reward proposed for those plans successful at channeling members to participating hospitals with good results is a 1 percent bonus on the premium we pay them," says Arnold Milstein, medical director of the group. "I'm optimistic we will get the same excellent improvement in California that they got in New York."

The Clinton administration also has indicated interest in using performance ratings. The administration's Medicare Modernization Act, now before Congress, proposes to begin steering Medicare patients toward better-performing hospitals by offering to pay more of patients' expenses. ∎

OUTLOOK

High-Tech Solutions

High technology holds out hope for transforming medicine into a truly scientific field. "We have a scientific system that was designed in the 19th century," observes Andrew Balas, a University of Missouri health policy professor, recalling a time when a doctor could easily keep up with his field by subscribing to one or two medical journals.

Today, the quantity of research literature is so overwhelming, Balas says, that computers are the logical solution to applying scientific evidence to medical practice. In the 30 years between 1966 and 1995, more than 76,000 journal articles were published from controlled clinical trials, with the last five years contributing more than all previous 25 years. [39]

Despite the glut of information, the health-care sector spends only 2 percent of its operating budget on information systems compared with banking and insurance, which spend about one-tenth — "unacceptably low," according to Balas.

At Brigham and Women's Hospital in Boston, considered a leader in computerized information, doctors are required to enter all their prescriptions, X-ray and lab test orders into a computer. Clinical guidelines embedded in the software warn the doctor if there is a problem with the order at the time of entry.

For example, the hospital's software program informs a doctor who enters a prescription for the powerful antibiotic vancomycin that the Centers for Disease Control and Prevention recommends limited use of the drug because its overuse can contribute to resistant bacteria. The computerized guideline

has reduced the hospital's use of vancomycin by a third, according to David Bates, chief of the hospital's division of general medicine.

With the proliferation of handheld, wireless computers costing only $300 to $400, Bates envisions computer software of this type becoming far more widespread, even at low-budget community hospitals, within the next couple of years. More sophisticated programs link up prescription orders to an individual patient's medical history to provide warnings on dangerous drug interactions or allergies.

Looking into the future, Bates predicts that computer programs will link genetic screening to an individual patient's likelihood of having a bad reaction to a medication, based on his or her genetic makeup.

Helping Consumers

So far, consumers get very little information about whether their doctor is giving them the most effective treatment with the greatest skill possible.

The politically powerful health-care industry has crushed attempts that require all health plans to publicly disclose their results in treating patients. A Clinton administration proposal mandating that health plans publicly report on their performance in a nationally comparable fashion died with the president's health-reform legislation. A similar proposal aimed at managed care died during debate of patients'-rights legislation after coming under attack from health insurers. (See "At Issue," p. 75.) Better prospects for public information appear to lie with Clinton's Feb. 22 proposal that states require hospitals to report serious medical mistakes.

Frustrated with the lack of government action, some advocates see hope in the recent move by a few managed-care companies to give their patients the kind of quality information needed to choose among doctors and hospitals. Last November, Minnesota-based United Health Group, America's second-largest managed-care company, announced that it was abandoning its much-criticized practice of utilization review to deny doctor-recommended treatments. Instead, United said, it would measure the quality of doctors' performance and report their ratings to its enrollees.

Three years ago, a coalition of the Minnesota Twin Cities' biggest employers, The Buyers Health Action Group, stopped buying group policy health plans from large insurers and began contracting directly with doctors and hospitals. The group now passes its evaluations of health-care providers on to its consumers. [40]

David Kendall, senior fellow for health policy at the Progressive Policy Institute, a think tank affiliated with the Democratic Leadership Council, considers these initiatives the "most exciting development" in the effort to get health-quality information to consumers. "These are the HMOs that see themselves as brokers of information on behalf of consumers as opposed to centralized managers," Kendall says.

The role of information will become crucial in an increasingly open market for health care, some consumer advocates predict. As HMOs sign up ever-larger groups of doctors, with many of the physicians overlapping among plans, consumers will not be able to rely on a plan to select a few good doctors. Proposals by some large employers to pay their workers a lump sum for all benefits also will give consumers more responsibility for purchasing the form of health care most closely suited to their needs.

"Everyone agrees that to make that work you have to give people infor-

mation," says David Lansky, president of FACCT. "If you throw them to the wolves and say, 'The doctor won't tell you how good a job he's doing when you're sick,' I don't know how you're going to find a referral to a good cancer doctor."

Regina E. Herzlinger, a professor at the Harvard Business School, has argued that the health-care market closely resembles the stock market because consumers in both markets "need reliable information to make intelligent decisions."

Unlike the stock market, however, the health-care market has no government regulatory body to insure that prices are a fair reflection of all publicly available information. Herzlinger has proposed the creation of a health-care commission similar to the Securities and Exchange Commission, which would require health insurers to register and report comparable information on their services from both a cost and quality standpoint. [41]

Many activists within the medical community find public interest in these issues discouragingly low. "No one is beating on the door of my hospital or of medical groups demanding that performance be improved to the level of safety the airlines have," Mt. Sinai's Chassin says.

Still, many consumers are typing on their computer keyboards, judging from the proliferation of Web sites ranking doctors and hospitals. At healthcarechoices.org, it's possible to find out which hospitals do the most breast cancer surgery in a half-dozen states. And a breast cancer patient can find out which individual doctors have the most breast surgery experience in New York.

"The Internet democratizes a lot of information. It's an opportunity and a threat. The threat is you can have some really scientifically inaccurate rankings up there," says Love of the National Association of Health Data Organizations.

Susan Rosenfeld, president of healthcarechoices.org, a nonprofit health-care consumer organization, predicts that the more information becomes available on the net, the more demanding consumers will become. She envisions patients who have visited her site asking their employers, for example, why the health plan they're offered does not include a doctor who has done a high volume of breast surgeries.

"There are bad doctors and good doctors," Rosenfeld says, and "some hospitals are definitely better than others. Why should anyone in this country be forced to go to a bad doctor?" ■

Notes

[1] Julie Fields, "Surviving Bypass Surgery; Doctors' and Hospitals' Death Rates Compared," *The Record* (New Jersey), March 6, 1999, p. A1.

[2] Martin N. Marshall et al., "The Public Release of Performance Data: What do We Expect to Gain? A Review of the Evidence," *Journal of the American Medical Association* (*JAMA*), April 12, 2000, pp. 1866-1874.

[3] *Ibid*.

[4] *Ibid*. The actual mortality decreased by 21 percent during the study period. The 41 percent figure takes into account the fact that the severity of illness among patients undergoing the operation increased during this time.

[5] Arnold M. Epstein, "Public Release of Performance Data: A Progress Report from the Front," *JAMA*, April 12, 2000, pp. 1884-1886.

[6] See Sarah Glazer, "Medical Mistakes," *The CQ Researcher*, Feb. 25, 2000, pp. 138-159.

[7] For background, see Adriel Bettelheim, "Cancer Treatments," *The CQ Researcher*, Sept. 11, 1998, pp. 794-816.

[8] John E. Wennberg and Megan McAndrew Cooper, eds., *The Quality of Medical Care in the United States: A Report on the Medicare Program*; *The Dartmouth Atlas of Health Care 1999*, Dartmouth Medical School Center for Evaluative Clinical Sciences, 1999, p. 224.

[9] Mark R. Chassin et al., "The Urgent Need

to Improve Health Care Quality: Institute of Medicine National Roundtable on Health Care Quality," *JAMA*, Sept. 16, 1998, pp. 1000-1001.

[10] *Ibid.*, p. 1002

[11] *Ibid.*

[12] For background, see Adriel Bettelheim, "Drug-Resistant Bacteria," *The CQ Researcher*, June 4, 1999, pp. 473-496.

[13] Wennberg and Cooper, *op. cit.*, p. 226.

[14] Erica Goode, "Sharp Rise Found in Psychiatric Drugs for the Very Young," *The New York Times*, Feb. 23, 2000, p. A1. For background, see Kathy Koch, "Childhood Depression," *The CQ Researcher*, July 16, 1999, pp. 593-616, and Kathy Koch, "Rethinking Ritalin," *The CQ Researcher*, Oct. 22, 1999, pp. 905-928.

[15] Danny McCormick, "Use of Aspirin, Beta Blockers and Lipid-Lowering Medications Before Recurrent Acute Myocardial Infarction," *Archives of Internal Medicine*, March 22, 1999.

[16] Harlan M. Krumholz, "Early Beta-Blocker Therapy for Acute Myocardial Infarction in Elderly Patients," *Annals of Internal Medicine*, Nov. 2, 1999, pp. 648-654.

[17] Michael D. Cabana et al., "Why Don't Physicians Follow Clinical Practice Guidelines?" *JAMA*, Oct. 20, 1999. pp. 1458-1465.

[18] Randall S. Stafford, "Aspirin Use is Low Among United States Outpatients with Coronary Artery Disease," *Circulation*, March 14, 2000.

[19] Wennberg and Cooper, *op. cit.*, pp. 164-165.

[20] For background, see Adriel Bettelheim, "Managing Managed Care," *The CQ Researcher*, April, 16, 1999, pp. 305-328 and Sarah Glazer, "Managed Care," *The CQ Researcher*, April 12, 1996, pp. 313-336.

[21] For background, see Kenneth Jost, "Patients' Rights," *The CQ Researcher*, Feb. 6, 1998, pp. 97-120.

[22] Timothy G. Ferris, "Improving Quality Improvement Research," *Effective Clinical Practice*, January/February 2000, pp. 40-44, p. 41.

[23] Epstein, *op. cit.*, pp. 1884-1886.

[24] See New Jersey Department of Health and Senior Services News Release, "Cardiac

---

FOR MORE INFORMATION

Agency for Healthcare Research and Quality, 2101 Jefferson St., Suite 501, Rockville, Md. 20852; (301) 594-1364; www.ahrq.gov. This arm of the Department of Health and Human Services issues reports reviewing the scientific evidence for specific areas of clinical practice and also operates a clearinghouse for clinical guidelines.

Foundation for Accountability, 520 SW Sixth Ave., Suite 700, Portland, Ore. 97204; (503) 223-2228; www.facct.org. FACCT is dedicated to helping consumers make better health-care decisions, partly by improving health-care report cards rating health plans.

National Committee for Quality Assurance, 2000 L St., N.W., Suite 500, Washington, D.C. 20036; (202) 955-3500; www.ncqa.org. Founded by the HMO industry, this nonprofit organization accredits HMOs and collects information on the quality of their services, which it posts for consumers on its Web site in report-card format.

Center for Medical Consumers, 130 Macdougal St., New York, N.Y. 10012; (212) 674-7105; www.medicalconsumers.org. This consumer group, which lobbies for better quality in medicine at the national and local levels, recently posted how many operations each New York hospital and doctor had performed for 29 common medical procedures.

Surgery Data Shows Statewide Mortality Rate Dropping," March 5, 1999. This release reported a 13.5 percent decline in the statewide mortality rate from 1994 to 1997. Also see, Pennsylvania Health Care Cost Containment Council News Release, "New Hospital Performance Report Released," Dec. 17, 1999. This release reported a 4 percent decrease in the mortality rate in 1998 for 15 conditions.

[25] See Jennifer Steinhauer, "More Managed Care Clients Seen in Higher-Risk Hospitals," *The New York Times*, April 19, 2000, p. B4.

[26] Michael L. Millenson, *Demanding Medical Excellence* (1999), pp. 181-189.

[27] *Ibid.*, p. 201.

[28] Marshall et al., *op. cit.*

[29] *Ibid.*

[30] Lars C. Erickson et al., "The Relationship Between Managed Care Insurance and Use of Lower-Mortality Hospitals for CABG Surgery," *JAMA*, April 19, 2000.

[31] Millenson, *op. cit.*, p. 193.

[32] John E. Wennberg, "Dealing with Medical

Practice Variations: A Proposal for Action," *Health Affairs*, summer 1984, pp. 6-32.

[33] Quoted in Millenson, *op. cit.*, p. 48.

[34] Cited in Millenson, *op. cit.*, p. 101

[35] Gina Kolata and Kurt Eichenwald, "Insurer Drops a Therapy for Breast Cancer," *The New York Times*, Feb. 16, 2000, p. 24.

[36] Leigh Page, "Lawsuit puts spotlight on hospital discharge criteria," *American Medical News*, March 27, 2000.

[37] Connecticut, Florida, Maryland, Minnesota, New Jersey, Utah and Texas have all issued HMO report cards according to "Readability Analyses of Seven HMO Report Cards," presented by Mark Hocchauser, May 5-7, 1999, Employer's Managed Health Care Association.

[38] Arnold M. Epstein, "Rolling Down the Runway," *JAMA*, June 3, 1998, pp. 1691-1696.

[39] Chassin et al., *op. cit.*, p. 1003.

[40] Kerry Tremain, "Revolution in Minnesota," *Blueprint*, spring 2000, p. 33.

[41] Regina E. Herzlinger, "Leveling the Playing Field," *Blueprint*, spring 2000, pp. 22-23.

Bibliography

Selected Sources Used

Books

Millenson, Michael, _Demanding Medical Excellence: Doctors and Accountability in the Information Age_, University of Chicago Press, 1997.
Health care consultant Millenson's excellent and readable history of efforts to improve the quality of American medicine also brings the reader up to date on the ongoing debate over accountability.

Ruffin, Marshall de Graffenried Jr., _Digital Doctors_, American College of Physician Executives, 1999.
Ruffin, a physician in Charlottesville, Va., describes how information technology is transforming medicine in ways that could lead to improved quality of care.

Articles

Cabana, Michael D., et al., "Why Don't Physicians Follow Clinical Practice Guidelines? A Framework for Improvement," _JAMA_, Oct. 20, 1999, pp. 1458-1465.
Noting that clinical-practice guidelines have produced little change in physicians' behavior, the authors review 76 surveys of physicians' attitudes and find a wide range of reasons for ignoring guidelines — from inertia to lack of confidence in the results.

Chassin, Mark R., et al., "The Urgent Need to Improve Health Care Quality: Institute of Medicine National Roundtable on Health Care Quality," _JAMA_, Sept. 16, 1998, pp. 1000-1005.
This widely cited statement by an expert medical panel assembled at the Institute of Medicine concluded that "very large numbers of Americans are harmed as a direct result" of quality problems in medical care.

Epstein, Arnold M., "Public Release of Performance Data: A Progress Report from the Front," _JAMA_, April 12, 2000, pp. 1884-1886.
In this editorial, Arnold Epstein, chair of the Department of Health Policy at the Harvard School of Public Health, observes that consumer report cards heighten the sensitivity of doctors to quality issues, but that opposition by doctors could hinder the public reporting effort.

Herzlinger, Regina E., "Leveling the Playing Field," _Blueprint_, spring 2000, pp. 22-23.
Herzlilnger, a professor at the Harvard Business School, proposes creating a Securities Exchange Commission-type structure to regulate information in the health-care marketplace, which she describes as akin to the stock market in its dependence on public information. The magazine is published by the Democratic Leadership Council.

Lansky, David, "Can Consumers Judge?" _Blueprint_, spring 2000, pp. 17-19.
Lansky, president of the nonprofit Foundation for Accountability (FACCT), argues that the United States has no way of rewarding good health care because there is so little public information and because the health industry controls the evaluations of health plans.

Marshall, Martin N., et al., "The Public Release of Performance Data: What Do We Expect to Gain? A Review of the Evidence," _JAMA_, April 12, 2000, pp. 1866-1874.
In this review of studies of medical-consumer report cards, the authors conclude that the biggest impact is not on consumers but on hospitals seeking to salvage their reputations from poor ratings.

Millenson, Michael L., "Where's Mine?" _Blueprint_, spring 2000, pp. 14-15.
Tracing the history of reform efforts inside the medical profession over the past 90 years, the author argues that reform continues to be stymied by "physicians and hospitals who have a deeply vested interest in the status quo."

Pear, Robert, "White House Seeks to Curb Pills Used to Calm the Young," _The New York Times_, March 20, 2000, p. A1.
The recent sharp rise in the number of preschoolers taking psychiatric drugs prompted the White House to schedule a conference asking why the drugs are so widely prescribed.

Perez-Pena, Richard, "Data Offer a Head Count in Health Care: Numbers Provide Hints of Surgeons' Experience," _The New York Times_, Feb. 14, 2000, p. B1.
When a New York consumer group recently posted statistics on its Web site showing how often doctors and physicians perform each of more than 20 different medical procedures, experts cautioned that volume is not a completely accurate proxy for quality.

Reports

Wennberg, John E., and Megan McAndrew Cooper, eds., _The Dartmouth Atlas of Health Care 1999_, Dartmouth Medical School, Center for Evaluative Clinical Sciences, AHA Press, 1999.
"In American health care, geography is destiny," write the authors of the _Dartmouth Atlas_, who document wide geographic variations in the treatment patients get for the same condition. The findings in this third and latest version of the _Atlas_, as in the previous two, are based on the Medicare population, but most experts believe the study has broader implications for the American population.

5 Affordable Housing

JANE TANNER

C arrie Slick has always dreamed of owning her own home. But her $24,500 salary as director of social work at a nursing home barely covers her rent, food, gasoline and car and student loans. Without help, she fears she will never be able to afford the down payment on a house, at least not in her hometown — booming Charlotte, N.C., where affordable housing is scarce.

That's why she joined more than a dozen other would-be homeowners at a recent Saturday seminar on buying a home, sponsored by the nonprofit Charlotte Mecklenburg Housing Partnership. Largely funded by local banks, the group helps moderate-income people analyze their household budgets and learn about title searches and mortgage interest rates.

Above all, the partnership helps with down payments. In Slick's case, it will help her come up with the $2,000 she needs once she saves $1,000. "Financially, this is probably the only way I can do it," Slick says.

Throughout the nation, working Americans like Slick are struggling with high housing costs:

- In New York City, working families unable to keep up with high rents are among the hundreds of residents crowding into homeless shelters, many sleeping on the floor. A public school teacher was among those heading off to work after a sleepless night at a Bronx family shelter. "I'm just letting you know how discouraged I am," she said. "At 8:21 a.m., I have to be fresh for 61 New York City public-school children." [1]

Rental apartments for low- and very-low-income residents offer a view of the mountains in San Jose, Calif.

R. Thomas_Jones

- In Rochester, Minn., a shortage of low-cost housing is partly blamed for the scarcity of home health-care workers. At $7 to $9 dollars an hour, they don't earn enough to qualify for the affordable housing being built by local nonprofits. [2] The city's famed Mayo Clinic is so desperate for workers that it has committed $5 million to help build 875 moderately priced homes and townhouses.
- In California's Silicon Valley — the nation's priciest housing market — the Santa Clara Transit Authority is desperately trying to help its bus drivers and light-rail operators find homes. The median home price in the area is $505,000, and two-bedroom apartments rent for an average $2,000 a month.

Although the nation has just enjoyed the longest economic expansion in history, housing advocates say U.S. housing woes are so severe that they are affecting middle-class Americans as well as the chronically poor.

"It goes beyond the lowest income groups to the people who could afford more [upscale] housing but must move farther and farther from their

jobs to get what they want," says housing economist Robert Sheehan. Among those hardest hit are public school teachers, police officers and municipal workers.

Some 5.4 million families — nearly 13 million people — have critical housing needs, according to the U.S. Department of Housing and Urban Development (HUD). [3] Most have incomes below 50 percent of the median income for their area; don't receive government aid; pay more than half their rent for housing; or live in bad conditions. More than a quarter of those with severe housing woes are elderly, nearly a third are unemployed and another 21 percent are only marginally employed. [4]

Some housing advocates are focusing their attention on the 3 million Americans among those with critical needs who earn up to 120 percent of the national median income by either working full time or by patching together part-time jobs. They spend more than half their wages for shelter, and many can only afford to live far from their jobs in cities. The number of working families in this category has increased sharply since 1991, according to HUD.

"The affordable-housing issue has moved from the cities to the suburbs," says Michael A. Stegman, director of the Center for Community Capitalism at the University of North Carolina and co-author of "Housing America's Working Families," a study released last June by the Center for Housing Policy.

Yet, at the same time, most Americans are more comfortably housed than at any time in U.S. history. The booming economy, low unemployment, low interest rates and improvements in the housing finance system have increased homeownership rates to record levels. The prosperity, while

From *The CQ Researcher,* February 9, 2001.

Affordable Housing at Low Point

A family earning the median U.S. income could only afford 58.1 percent of the houses sold in the third quarter last year — the lowest percentage since fourth quarter 1992. The drop in the Housing Opportunity Index (HOI) since it peaked in third quarter 1999 reflected the fact that home prices rose faster than incomes.*

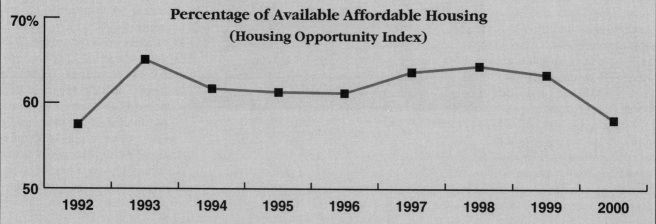

Percentage of Available Affordable Housing
(Housing Opportunity Index)

* The Housing Opportunity Index (HOI) measures the percentage of homes sold that a family earning the median income can afford to buy.

Source: National Association of Home Builders; updated data is available at www.nahb.com/facts/economics/housingopindex.html

good for housing overall, has exacerbated difficulties for those in the bottom quarter of the wage scale because their pay has failed to keep pace with housing inflation.

It's easy to point to extremes, such as hot real estate markets where home values and rents have gone through the roof. These cases aren't alarming to housing economists and others who follow the industry; they see them as simply part of a repeating cycle.

"Seattle has been through boom and bust before," says Barry Zigas, senior vice president of housing and community development at the Federal National Mortgage Corporation, better known as Fannie Mae. "I can remember a time when you couldn't give away housing in Seattle, but now it's experiencing an unbelievable crunch."

Public sympathy probably would wear thin quickly if it were just a matter of high-wage workers struggling to find homes and apartments

in hot markets. But in those very same communities cadres of lower-wage workers, who are integral to public services or general quality of life, are being shut out. [5]

Housing advocates are concerned that underlying problems in the nationwide housing market — such as increasing gentrification — are causing the shrinking supply of moderately priced and low-cost housing, especially apartments.

The situation is gravest for the poorest Americans, because the inventory of public housing is fast disappearing as HUD performs radical surgery on its properties. Since beginning to restructure its vast portfolio of properties in 1993, HUD has torn down about 33,000 public housing units, but it has built only 7,362 new ones to replace them, says HUD spokeswoman Donna White.

Under HUD's long-term plan, a total of 61,000 public housing units will be

demolished across the country. But only about 42,000 units definitely will be replaced. The remaining units will be replaced by private developers, who will be encouraged, but not required, to provide subsidized units for low-income residents. Meanwhile, private landlords are opting out of HUD contracts, while in hundreds of local communities slow-growth initiatives are making it uneconomical to build low-cost housing.

To make matters worse, as the supply of low-cost housing has dwindled wages for those at the bottom quarter of the income scale have lagged behind housing inflation, making it impossible for them to compete.

Renters are ignored by federal subsidy programs. While the federal government eagerly subsidizes homeownership through mortgage interest tax deductions, renters can't take advantage of the hefty annual subsidy, which amounted to $55 billion in fiscal

2000. And while HUD focuses attention on the poorest of the poor, there has been little support for middle-to-lower-income renters.

Although affordable-housing issues haven't registered prominently on the national political scene, local and state officials are increasingly aware of how critical the lack of moderately priced housing is to the overall well being of their communities. Businesses feel the housing pinch acutely when they try to recruit workers. They must deal with the high cost of turnover, poor worker morale and low productivity because employees face long commutes or live in unstable housing conditions.

Besides the Mayo Clinic, a long list of well-known companies like Intel and Harley Davidson are now helping to provide housing for their employees. The U.S. Conference of Mayors has made housing a top priority, and late last year it successfully pressed Congress to increase funding for rent subsidies. In Massachusetts, rapid job growth has not been matched by the construction of vitally needed apartments and low-cost housing. To spur production, Republican Gov. Paul Cellucci ordered last January that cities and towns boosting their affordable housing units should have first dibs on discretionary state grant money.

As governments and nonprofit organizations confront a housing market in which many are comfortable but millions face a housing crisis, here are some of the questions being asked:

Is there a housing crisis?

Some of the urgency over housing is tied to a few extreme cases in hot markets where prices have been bid up. Traditionally, in such overheated instances the market addresses the shortages, says John Weicher, a senior fellow at the conservative Hudson Institute.

"People see an opportunity, and you get construction," says Weicher, a former assistant secretary for policy development and research at HUD under President George Bush. "Gradually, the market catches up to the demand."

Opponents of government housing subsidies, like Howard Husock, director of the case study program at Harvard University's John F. Kennedy School of Government, contend that most people can find satisfactory housing. "If you have two incomes at not much more than minimum wage," he says, "there's a good chance that you could afford a decent house."

"Can you find a place to live?" he asks. "I think the answer is largely, yes. Is it in the best school district? No, but that's a school problem. Is it close to work? No, but that's a transportation problem."

Indeed, much of the discomfort associated with high housing costs is tied to the fact that in order to find affordable housing people must commute long distances. Some companies have begun sending out daily shuttle buses to pull in workers from outlying areas. "We see that as a decent adaptation," Husock says. "It doesn't sound ideal, but it doesn't mean that it will continue forever."

Most housing advocates, however, say there is clearly an affordability crisis among those at the lower end of the pay scale, and they blame low wages. Many would like to see a tripling of the $5.15 minimum wage and more aggressive use of earned income tax credits, which provide lower-wage workers with significant tax refunds. Housing advocates also would like to see more public money available for housing allowances and rent vouchers.

But to some economists, such initiatives indicate more of a wage problem than a housing shortage. "We would prefer people had more income, but that's not a housing problem," says Ron Seldman, assistant vice

president of the Federal Reserve Bank of Minneapolis. And if it's just that people can't afford what they'd like to have, "That's not a housing shortage," he adds.

Conventional wisdom holds that people should spend no more than 30 percent of their gross wages for housing, a benchmark used by HUD and most prime lenders. But real estate economists Richard Green and Stephen Malpezzi of the University of Wisconsin question just how a housing shortage should be defined. In a primer on U.S. housing markets, they contend that there is no affordability crisis "if households have the opportunity to spend a small fraction of their incomes on housing, but instead choose to spend a larger fraction." [6]

However, their calculations showed that even if people on the lower income rungs rented the lower-priced housing that is available, in many states they would have to spend more than 30 percent of their wages. "If low-income households are forced to spend a substantial amount of their incomes on housing," they wrote, "then we clearly have a housing-affordability problem." [7]

For renters, Green and Malpezzi found that those making the median income were not experiencing a severe housing-affordability problem, but the picture was grim for those in the lowest quartile of income distribution.

Many would argue that those at the very bottom rungs and the chronically homeless have not just a housing problem but also a litany of other chronic problems, such as addictions and mental illness.

Lately, the housing finance system has begun to open up considerably to families previously considered bad risks. Lenders are accepting more candidates from so-called "risky pools" that would have been shut out in the past. Plus, secondary markets, such as the quasi-governmental Fannie Mae and

Shuttles Go Where the Jobs Are

Last summer, Jackie Turner looked for a new job after a temporary stint with the Census Bureau. But the best-paying jobs were in the suburbs, 30 miles from her Baltimore neighborhood. Without a car and no public bus service, she figured those slots weren't options.

"I thought, there are a lot of nice-paying jobs, but how am I going to get there?" she says.

Then she learned about a free shuttle service to outlying Howard County and got a job with Home Depot in Columbia, Md. Now, Turner walks about seven blocks from the home she's renting in southeast Baltimore to pick up a shuttle to ride about 30 minutes to her $10-an-hour position.

She had briefly considered buying a home near work, but realized it would cost too much. "I want to buy my first home," she says, "but I don't want it to be $150,000."

In fact, the median price for homes in Howard County is $175,000. Besides, Turner says, she likes her neighborhood and doesn't want to live in the suburbs.

In 1999, a nonprofit, BWI Partnership, set up the Career Caravan shuttle between Baltimore's inner city and Howard County to address the mismatch between available jobs and workers like Turner.

"The inner-city workers couldn't find jobs in the city, and Howard County had all these jobs but couldn't find workers," says Janice Butler, transportation coordinator for BWI Partnership. About 120 workers use the free service to travel to 25 Howard County businesses from light manufacturing to call centers. One of the participating companies, Bagel Bin stores, had previously been providing its own private transportation because it had such difficulty finding employees.

The Career Caravan is free to both riders and businesses. It is funded largely by a $640,000 Federal Transit Administration (FTA) grant, but it also receives money through state reverse-commute money and private donations that should keep it going for another four years. In fact, the service is expanding to cover the entire city and expects to pick up several hundred more riders, Butler says.

Baltimore is not unique. "We've made these grants throughout the country — in virtually all the major urbanized areas," says Doug Birnie, the FTA's job-access coordinator. Some of the funds are used to promote car-pooling or other solutions.

Baltimore's Department of Social Services uses the job shuttle to help women who are looking for jobs get off welfare. When the department canvassed the region for potential jobs, it didn't consider neighboring Howard and Harford counties, where jobs are plentiful, because of the lack of low-cost transportation, says Cindy Theede, assistant contract manager. "We really gave up after a while. There either wasn't transportation when they needed it, or it was too costly."

Now, with the availability of Career Caravan and a similar service, Bridges to Work, women on welfare will be given the option of taking long-distance jobs. But Theede says the welfare clients may not want those jobs, because they are too far from their children's schools and daycare.

Meanwhile, taking its cue from the nonprofit shuttles, Baltimore may start to offer regular public transportation to suburban counties. As for Turner, the caravan has been a godsend, though she sometimes has to wait two hours after her shift for the shuttle to arrive. As soon as she can, she plans to buy a car.

Freddie Mac, are supporting expanded financing opportunities. * Nevertheless, people are still being shut out or are paying predatory fees.

Land-use regulations, which tend to benefit upper-income people, are also exacerbating the housing-affordability problem at the lower end of the wage scale. Green and Malpezzi don't argue that all such regulations are bad, just that they clearly push rents higher. Regulatory reforms are one way to ad-

---

* The Federal National Mortgage Corporation, or Fannie Mae, and the Federal Home Loan Mortgage Corporation, or Freddie Mac, are stockholder-owned corporations chartered by Congress to provide liquidity in the housing market. They buy loans from banks and other lenders to free up funds for additional loans, and either sell loan packages as securities or keep them in their portfolios.

dress the affordability crisis, the two economists say. But localities should consider rules case by case to determine where their costs outweigh their benefits, they add.

Is prosperity bad for housing?

The long economic expansion in the United States pushed the homeownership rate to a record 67.7 percent in the third quarter of last year. The fact that more than two-thirds of Americans are homeowners is all the more impressive considering that homeownership as an apple-pie American aspiration only became a realistic possibility about seven decades ago. In addition, because Americans' homes constitute their

single biggest source of net worth, pervasive home-value inflation has boosted the net worth of many.

Home sales and the value of residential construction set records during the late 1990s and hit record highs in 1999. Although the number of housing permits and starts cooled off a bit at the end of 2000, they still beat out a 19-year stretch from 1979 to 1997. [8]

"The United States is the best housed it has ever been in its history," says Nicolas Retsinas, director of the Joint Center for Housing Studies at Harvard University.

All the news, however, wasn't good. Thanks to basic economics, the good times wreaked havoc on the low-cost housing market. Prosperity brought increased demand, which pushed prices higher. The median sales price of existing single-family homes jumped 13.5 percent from 1997 to October 2000, from $121,800 to $138,200, according to the National Association of Realtors (NAR).

"Clearly, we have a serious affordability issue for some people, which has been exacerbated by this prosperity," says Retsinas, who served as federal housing commissioner and assistant secretary for housing during the Clinton administration. Last October, when home sales were at near-record levels, NAR's Housing Affordability Index dropped to its lowest level since the second quarter of 1992. [9]

Gentrification has added to the affordability problem. According to a popular adage, housing becomes more affordable as it ages. But as wealthier buyers have snapped up modestly priced homes in older neighborhoods and renovated them, raising their value, they have taken moderately priced housing out of the trickle-down supply.

"You can go around the country and find gentrification of downtowns, and now it has gone into the suburbs," says housing economist Sheehan. "People are getting forced out." All of the gentrification has forced lower-income homebuyers farther and farther out into the distant suburbs, where commuting costs are higher.

In addition, now, bigger is better. Starter homes — small, low-cost houses designed for first-time buyers — are out of vogue, as new homes get bigger and bigger. In 1950, about 62 percent of all new homes were less than 1,200 square feet; last year only 7 percent were. [10] The same "mansionization" is happening to newly renovated homes.

Starter homes in strong markets sell for much higher prices. Near Tyson's Corner, Va., in the Washington suburbs, homes in a post-World War II temporary housing development, built during a shortage, are in hot demand. A For Sale sign at a house in the area last year read:

"$250,000 as is, $750,000 with new house," Sheehan recalls.

Overall, the inventory of homes available for sale has shrunk. Near the end of last year, it was at the lowest level in a decade. The inventory was estimated to last only four months, compared with inventories throughout most of the 1990s that lasted six to nine months. [11] And the inventory of low-cost housing has been reduced as well. Between 1993 and 1995, for instance, the number of unsubsidized units affordable to very low-income households dropped 8.6 percent — a decrease of 900,000 units. [12]

Economic prosperity also has spurred the passage of slow-growth regulations around the country. They typically favor people at the higher income levels, because they tend to take land out of development, driving up land prices and restricting dense developments and apartments.

Meanwhile, good economic times have not closed the homeownership gap between minorities and whites. Seniors and renters have been particularly hard hit. The Joint Center's "State of the Nation's Housing: 2000" report found that the median net worth of older American minority renters was a dismal $600.

"In the midst of this remarkable prosperity, the homeownership gap between whites and minorities has hardly narrowed," the study said.

Housing advocates blame the fact that wages at the bottom quarter of the scale haven't kept pace with housing inflation. Even where employees are paid well above the current minimum wage, it's not enough.

Each year, the National Low Income Housing Coalition calculates the wage required to pay for a typical two-bedroom apartment if no more than 30 percent of a tenant's income is spent on rent. In New Jersey, which has some of the nation's highest-priced rental properties, a tenant in 2000 had to earn $16.88 an hour. In Georgia, which

ranked in the middle, the required wage was $11.13, and in West Virginia, the lowest, a worker would have to make $8.12 an hour.

Some housing advocates would like to see the minimum wage increased, but others say that could just throw fuel on the fire. Sheehan, who is president of Catholics for Housing, a Northern Virginia nonprofit, says raising wages to a level at which all families could compete in the housing market would be wildly inflationary and only further elevate prices. Others warn that employment would go down as companies reduced hiring. [13]

"The more money you pour into the economy, the more prices rise," Sheehan says. "If you are going to give that worker a raise and there's no more productivity, you are going to have inflation. That would push housing costs out of reach if it were done on a large scale."

Many cities celebrated economic booms in the last decade, but often more jobs than housing were created, especially for people in the kind of lower-wage jobs that help fuel growth. The outcome has been obvious. In Boston, for instance, in 1998 there was potential demand for 30,791 one- or two-bedroom homes in the $100,000 to $125,000 price range, but only 1,255 were vacant or available for sale. [14]

At the end of 2000, signs of an economic slowdown were popping up with greater regularity. If the marketplace softens considerably, the affordable-housing crunch likely will ease. But experts like Retsinas don't think a slower economy will bring widespread relief. Prices are much stickier coming down than going up, he says, and a recession would hit people at the lower economic rungs hardest.

Is enough being done to solve the affordable-housing problem?

There is certainly no shortage of programs aimed at solving America's housing problem. Indeed, new programs

Where Can You Afford a House?

In Springfield, Ill., workers earning the median local income ($59,100) could buy 90 percent of the homes that sold there in the third quarter last year. In pricey San Francisco, workers earning the median local income ($74,900) could only afford 5.7 percent of the houses.

The 10 Most Affordable Cities

Metro Area	Homes Affordable in 2000* for Median-Income Families	2000 Median Family Income ($000s)	2000* Median Sales Price ($000s)	2000 National Affordability Rank
Springfield, Ill.	89.6%	59.1	95	1
Davenport, Iowa; Moline-Rock Island, Ill.	87.6	51.8	75	2
Elkhart-Goshen, Ind.	86.0	54.0	112	3
Rockford, Ill.	85.8	55.3	92	4
Mansfield, Ohio	85.5	46.1	83	5
Wilmington-Newark, Del.	85.0	69.0	137	6
Dayton-Springfield, Ohio	82.4	55.9	101	7
Vineland-Millville-Bridgeton, N.J.	81.9	47.2	85	8
Des Moines, Iowa	81.6	60.0	110	9
Kansas City, Mo./Kan.	81.2	57.7	106	10

The 10 Most Expensive Cities

Metro Area	Homes Affordable in 2000* for Median-Income Families	2000 Median Family Income ($000s)	2000* Median Sales Price ($000s)	2000 National Affordability Rank
San Francisco, Calif.	5.7	74.9	505	177
Santa Cruz-Watsonville, Calif.	8.7	61.7	371	176
San Jose, Calif.	13.0	87.0	448	174
Salinas, Calif.	13.0	50.3	275	174
Santa Rosa, Calif.	13.8	58.1	287	173
San Luis Obispo-Atascadero-Paso Robles, Calif.	17.8	48.0	235	172
Oakland, Calif.	23.5	67.6	310	171
Eugene-Springfield, Ore.	23.6	41.7	136	170
San Diego, Calif.	24.6	53.7	235	169
Vallejo-Fairfield-Napa, Calif.	24.9	53.3	220	168

* Data from third quarter 2000

Note: The housing survey covered 177 cities.

Source: National Association of Home Builders; http://www.nahb.com/facts/hoi/2000_3Q/complete_ranking.htm

Where Can You Afford an Apartment?

When it comes to apartment living, New Jersey is the priciest state and West Virginia the most affordable. Workers would have to earn $16.88 an hour to rent a two-bed apartment in New Jersey without spending more than 30 percent of their wages. In West Virginia, they would only need $8.12 an hour.

10 Most Expensive States

State	Hourly Wage Needed to Rent Two-Bedroom Apt.
New Jersey	$16.88
District of Columbia	$16.60
Hawaii	$16.52
Massachusetts	$16.43
New York	$16.04
Connecticut	$15.67
California	$15.22
Alaska	$15.18
New Hampshire	$14.15
Maryland	$13.42

10 Most Affordable States

State	Hourly Wage Needed to Rent Two-Bedroom Apt.
West Virginia	$8.12
Mississippi	$8.17
Arkansas	$8.27
Alabama	$8.61
Oklahoma	$8.62
Kentucky	$8.65
North Dakota	$8.98
Louisiana	$9.03
Missouri	$9.03
Iowa	$9.10

Source: National Low Income Housing Coalition: http://www.nlihc.org/oor2000/table9.htm

and financing products are announced with great regularity and fanfare.

But while the number of strategies has proliferated, most have lacked firepower. "We don't need more tools, we've got all the tools we need," says Conrad Egan, executive director of the Millennial Housing Commission, which is expected this year to recommend expanding affordable-housing opportunities and improving public and subsidized housing. "We need more support, we need more oomph," says Egan, former policy director of the National Housing Conference. By "oomph" he means political clout, leverage for funding and legislation.

Yet, affordable housing has not been a high-profile issue. "How many times did you hear the presidential candidates talk about prescription drugs?" asks J.

Michael Pitchford, senior vice president of community development at Bank of America. "A thousand times. How many times did they talk about affordable housing? Zero."

With historically high homeownership rates and a general level of comfort among the American public, few lawmakers are motivated to examine problems facing those at the lower end of the housing market, Egan says. In addition, many perceive housing development and preservation as being too complicated. People aren't going to throw support behind something they don't understand, he adds. Also, in many cases the connection between low-cost housing and general community well being hasn't been made, he adds.

Thus, despite the seemingly endless

number of affordable-housing programs, "At the end of the day, there's not enough money," Egan says.

But clearly, low interest rates have the most powerful influence on making homeownership more affordable, and Federal Reserve Board Chairman Alan Greenspan seems committed to keeping rates low.

In addition, Fannie Mae and Freddie Mac have a strong hand to play in solving the affordability crunch. While both quasi-governmental agencies have ratcheted up their goals for influencing affordable-housing lending, the agencies have come under fire recently. A study commissioned by HUD suggests that the giant mortgage purchasers aren't doing enough to promote homeownership in low-income neighborhoods. [15]

Yet, both agencies boast scores of new innovative approaches. They also continue to offer new programs that reduce costs and dig deeper into pools of potential homeowners who may not have stellar credit but are nonetheless good risks.

A key to solving the problem, says Stegman of the Center for Community Capitalism, is to move away from tying housing issues to poverty and to recognize their impact on economic growth in cities and regions in general.

"As more and more communities realize that affordable housing is where jobs critical to their local economies go to sleep at night," he says, "we will begin to see the kinds of more broadly based coalitions of public and private stakeholders that will be required to deal with the problem."

In the meantime, there are increasing signs that affordable housing is drawing more attention and dollars. After a drought of significant legislation, Congress passed several bills at the end of 2000 described by housing advocates as a net gain for their cause.

For instance, year after year Congress had rejected attempts to increase the amount that states could allocate for federal Low Income Housing Tax Credits (LIHTCs), a key federal incentive program for boosting the supply of affordable housing. The program gives federal tax credits to banks and other investors in exchange for providing capital for new construction and the rehabilitation of low- and moderate-income apartment projects. The program had been losing steam, primarily because the amount states could allot in tax credits had been stalled at $1.25 per resident since 1987, when the program went into effect.

In a December tax measure, Congress and the White House agreed to increase the tax credit to $1.75 per person and link future increases to inflation. In addition, the cap on private bonds to fund new production was increased from $50 per resident to $75. [16]

Housing advocates also had pushed for significant legislation, such as the creation of a National Housing Trust Fund. Although no landmark laws were passed, Congress did expand homeownership and modify housing laws for seniors, the disabled and Native Americans. Lawmakers also gave manufactured homes more credibility with lenders by creating uniform, new installation regulations and enforcement provisions via the Home Ownership and Economic Opportunity Act of 2000.

Will affordable housing capture the attention of the 107th Congress and President George W. Bush? Most housing advocates hesitate to predict the future, but many suggest little new ground will be gained. Bush has pushed the idea of homeownership and likely will place his emphasis there.

On the other hand, housing insiders say apartments and multifamily projects are needed desperately, but apartments aren't as politically popular as individual homeownership.

"From a NIMBY ("Not In My BackYard") standpoint, it is easier to find support for homeownership than rentals," Egan says. "Some people think renters aren't like us, especially those getting assistance." ∎

BACKGROUND

U.S. Gets Involved

Until the 1930s, the federal government generally stayed out of the housing business. When the public sector did step in, it was local governments — most often counties — that sheltered the poor at orphanages, poor farms and veterans' homes. But it wasn't equal-opportunity housing; the shelters were mostly for whites.

The country's first housing boom occurred during the prosperous 1920s. Initially, home loans were made for large amounts, on a short-term basis and required frequent refinancing. That meant that only Americans in the upper-income echelons could participate.

But when the banking system and stock market collapsed in 1929, even those homeowners were in jeopardy of losing their properties, and many did. It was in this climate that President Franklin D. Roosevelt began getting the federal government into housing.

Roosevelt's creation of new institutions—such as the Federal Home Loan Bank System and the Federal Housing Administration (FHA)—developed an infrastructure for long-term lending and a sense of security for lenders. Thus, the thrust in America toward individual homeownership was set in motion.

Meanwhile, desperate to stimulate the moribund Depression-era economy, Roosevelt used construction of public housing as a vehicle for employment. The Housing Act of 1937 made possible the creation of local public housing authorities to construct and manage housing for the poor, using federal money funneled to states and localities. The first public housing project ever built, Santa Rita Courts in Austin, Texas, still has residents.

Private builders and conservatives opposed public housing. "Recognizing that the special interests and the courts would block a national program to build and operate housing for the poor, the Roosevelt administration sought to define a housing policy around decidedly conservative approaches," according to the Texas Low Income Housing Information Service. "It would seek to link any low-income housing built directly to the elimination of slums in the cities and to the creation of jobs and local business opportunities." [17]

Nonetheless, in 1939, the National Association of Real Estate Boards weighed in, noting in one of its

Chronology

1920s–1950s
Federal housing policy begins promoting housing construction and homeownership.

1929
Collapse of the banking system triggers a national housing crisis. Only a small minority of higher-income Americans own homes, and they are on the verge of losing them. Mortgages are short-term and must be repeatedly refinanced.

1932
President Franklin D. Roosevelt creates the Federal Home Loan Bank System to create savings and loan associations to offer long-term mortgages in communities throughout the country.

1933
The Public Works Administration clears out slum housing and constructs apartment communities for the poor, in the process creating thousands of jobs.

1934
The Federal Housing Administration (FHA) is created to insure private residential mortgage loans. With lenders protected, mortgage lending expands. The creation of the FHA and Federal Home Loan Bank System mark a shift from an emphasis on rental housing to homeownership.

1937
The Housing Act of 1937 creates local public housing authorities to construct and manage housing for the poor with federal money funneled to states and localities.

1938
The Federal National Mortgage Corporation (Fannie Mae) is created to bolster the housing market by buying up FHA loans.

1949
Promising to create a "decent home and suitable living environment for every American family," the Housing Act prompts new waves of public housing production during the 1950s and early '60s.

1960s–1980s
Public housing is elevated in the political pecking order, even as the government turns to private markets to provide low-income housing.

1965
A number of housing agencies are consolidated into the Department of Housing and Urban Development (HUD).

1970
Congress charters the Federal Home Loan Mortgage Corp. (Freddie Mac) as a stockholder-owned corporation to create and maintain a national secondary market for conventional residential mortgages.

1971
Rent subsidies are introduced as an alternative to the construction of public housing.

1977
Under President Jimmy Carter, the Community Reinvestment Act (CRA) pushes banks to provide credit in low-income neighborhoods.

1986
As part of the Tax Reform Act, Congress creates Low-Income Housing Tax Credits, which encourage private investors to invest in affordable housing.

1990s–2000s
A new political agenda reduces the housing role of the federal government.

1993
HUD begins radical revamping of public housing properties, dubbed Hope VI. Aging and decrepit units are demolished and replaced with fewer units geared to mixed-income levels.

1994
A conservative Congress vows to dismantle HUD, but does not succeed. Congress holds static the number of HUD housing vouchers for the poor from 1994-1998.

1990s
No significant legislation on affordable housing is passed. Allocations for Low Income Housing Tax Credits, the key federal program to spur production of low-cost housing, remain at 1986 levels.

2000
Congress boosts federal tax credits to promote new construction of affordable housing and passes legislation in the 11th hour to expand homeownership. At the end of the year, President-elect George W. Bush taps Florida lawyer Melquíades Martinez as new HUD secretary.

newsletters: "United States Housing Authority projects now underway are undiluted socialism." [18]

Congress Acts

At the end of the Depression, Congress created a secondary market for government-insured loans by establishing Fannie Mae to stabilize and enhance lending.

The nation experienced an acute housing shortage after World War II. That not only triggered a boom in the private housing market but also prompted President Harry S Truman to push Congress to rev up construction of public housing once again. Despite opposition from Sen. Joseph McCarthy, Congress passed the Housing Act of 1949.

According to the landmark law's preamble:

"The Congress declares that the general welfare and security of the Nation and the health and living standards of its people require housing production and related community development sufficient to remedy the serious housing shortage, the elimination of substandard and other inadequate housing through the clearance of slums and blighted areas, and the realization as soon as feasible of the goal of a decent home and a suitable living environment for every American family, thus contributing to the development and redevelopment of communities and to the advancement of the growth, wealth, and security of the Nation."

The wave of public housing construction continued into the 1960s. By 1965, several housing agencies had been consolidated into the Department of Housing and Urban Development (HUD), which was elevated to a Cabinet-level agency.

Meanwhile, during President Lyndon B. Johnson's administration, with guidance from the 1968 Kaiser Commission on Urban Housing, housing policy shifted toward private-market solutions, such as offering subsidies to developers and guaranteed rent payments to private-property managers.

In 1969, HUD lowered income-eligibility requirements for public housing. This and similar policies eventually increased economic segregation and isolation in public housing. Today, HUD's early strategy of building large high-rise housing projects for the poor has been deemed a failure by observers and those involved in housing policy. Several crime-ridden projects have been razed, and HUD now is working hard to reverse its previous pattern by creating low-density, mixed-income housing that won't end up segregating subsidized tenants into substandard ghettoes.

Nixon's Legacy

During Richard M. Nixon's presidency, significant policy changes gave public housing residents more mobility and decreased reliance on publicly owned projects, which were riddled with cost overruns and corruption. Under Section 8 of the Nixon-proposed Housing and Community Development Act of 1974, poor families could receive subsidies to help them rent privately owned apartments. These vouchers have been popular with both political parties because they avoid the cumbersome bureaucracy of public construction and ownership of properties.

In 1977, during President Jimmy Carter's administration, the Community Reinvestment Act (CRA) pushed lenders to reach out to the poor by threatening to reject bank mergers and restrict bank growth if the institutions failed to serve the low-income and high-risk areas of their communities. CRA did not carry a lot of punch initially, and debate continues over how strictly it is enforced.

However, CRA's influence grew when bank mergers heated up in recent years. For instance, Charlotte-based NationsBank made its biggest CRA and community-development push just before it announced a merger with Bank of America.

President Ronald Reagan's administration continued to favor relying on the private sector to satisfy the nation's housing needs. In 1986, for example, Congress sought to motivate private investment in affordable housing in exchange for federal tax credits. Although the state-administered LIHTC program has been popular, funding didn't keep up with inflation for the program's first 13 years.

After the 1994 takeover of Congress by a Republican majority, conservatives began attacking large government-assistance programs, such as welfare and public housing. Some even advocated dismantling HUD altogether.

Amid those debates, funding for rent vouchers was frozen for four years, from 1994 to 1998. Since then, Congress has agreed to some voucher increases, but HUD is still under pressure to reform its operations.

HUD's New Approach

Large-scale, high-rise housing projects had come under fire for high-crime rates and the long tenure of many tenants, which sometimes went back three generations. Now, the agency has revised its blueprints to create public housing models more likely to improve the tenants' prospects for moving up to homeownership, by creating housing that supports a range of incomes in small-scale settings. Rather than isolating the poor together, the newer housing brings together people who are trying to im-

Factory-Built Homes on the Rise

It's not uncommon these days to see half a house barreling down the highway, open-faced like a dollhouse, as factory-built home sections are shuttled from plants to homeowners' lots. And the phenomenon is about to become even more common.

As the cost of homes continues to rise, some housing experts predict an increasing number of people will turn to factory-built homes as cheaper alternatives.

The potential was largely overlooked until recently. But it can no longer be ignored, since 20.7 percent of all housing starts in 1999 were manufactured homes, according to the National Conference of States Building Codes and Standards. Although the National Association of Home Builders calculates that only 17.2 percent of new homes that year were manufactured, either way you look at it, manufactured homes have captured a significant share of the new-home market.

To many consumers, manufactured homes conjure images of boxy metal trailers. But that's the old era. Technology has elevated the quality of manufactured homes dramatically, and new designs blend seamlessly into conventional neighborhoods. Some are two-story homes and in rare cases boast 6,000 square feet of interior space.

As middle- and low-income homebuyers find themselves increasingly priced out of the housing market, housing advocates are turning to assembly-line homes to address the affordability crunch. Nonprofits in Seattle and other cities are using manufactured homes for many projects, including urban infill — putting homes on small, often vacant, inner-city lots.

"People should think of using manufactured housing as part of the strategy," says Michael Savage, a Washington, D.C.-based community-development consultant. He helped implement a joint program of the National Coalition for Homeless Veterans and the Miss America Corp. to promote using manufactured homes to get disabled veterans off the streets.

Cost savings are considerable. The average manufactured home is 1,450 square feet and $43,300 without a lot. Conventional homes now average 2,190 square feet and cost $136,425 for the structure alone.[1] That means a manufactured home costs about $30 a square foot to build, compared with $62.30 for a conventional home.

In portions of Sun Belt states, such as Florida, Texas, California, Georgia and Alabama, factory-built homes are fairly well accepted.[2] But communities in many other states reject them outright. Often, neighbors fear their property values will decline, especially if the manufactured homes are the modest, boxy doublewides.

Most of the newer manufactured homes are stand-alone units on foundations — nothing like the tiny rectangular mobile homes in trailer parks. Yet many communities classify all manufactured homes as trailers, abiding by decades-old zoning laws that in essence specify "no trailers." As a result, when would-be buyers of manufactured homes seek zoning variances, neighbors rally to keep them out.

Although biases against pre-manufactured homes are powerful, acceptance is growing, albeit slowly. At the end of 2000, Congress hastened the process by passing legislation standardizing installation and other regulations for manufactured homes. And 16 states prohibit discrimination against factory-built homes.[3]

Economic trends may force the issue. The shortage of construction workers and diminishing skill levels eventually will push more production into factories. And thanks to economies of scale in purchasing, assembly-line efficiencies and automation, manufactured homes are a bargain.

Demographic shifts in the next 10 years will also favor manufactured housing.[4] Of the 12 million new households expected to form in the next decade, most will be headed by people under 25 and over 55 — the age groups that buy manufactured homes in the greatest numbers.

Mark Patton, chief executive officer of the Rural Housing Institute, predicts that by the end of the decade the only two jobs left for carpenters will be remodeling or building fancy homes. "Everything else is going to be built in a factory," says Patton, whose Wilton, Iowa-based nonprofit builds modular homes for low-income people.

Today's factory-built homes are designed to blend in with traditional housing.

[1] U.S. Department of Commerce, Bureau of the Census, www.census.gov.

[2] "Estimated Stock and Sale of Existing Manufactured Homes in 1999," Manufactured Housing Institute, 2000.

[3] Ibid.

[4] Eric S. Belsky, "2000-2010: The Decade for Manufactured Housing," Joint Center for Housing Studies, Harvard University, May 2000, p. 19.

prove their circumstances with residents who are already successful.

Under a program dubbed HOPE VI, which started as a pilot in 1993, HUD is well on its way to demolishing 61,000 public housing units and replacing them with 42,000 mixed income, low-density units. The remaining units will be replaced with private housing, but developers will not be required to include units for low-income residents.

The Homeownership and Economic Opportunity Act, passed in late 2000, should help ease affordability problems by allowing rent subsidies to be applied toward buying homes. The act especially targets elderly, disabled and Native Americans. Rep. Rick A. Lazio, R-N.Y., then chairman of the House Banking and Financial Services Housing and Community Opportunity Subcommittee, had pushed this and other housing legislation for many years.

"For regions of the country where real estate and rental costs are unusually high, such as my home state, our initiatives can mean the difference between renting and owning a home, helping thousands of New Yorkers and other Americans become homeowners," Lazio said when the bill passed in the House. [19]

By the late 1990s, the booming economy had generated record-breaking homeownership rates. But the strong marketplace, coupled with stagnant wages at the lower end of the pay scale, also contributed to the current crunch in affordable housing.

At the end of 2000, signs of a slowing economy had yet to hit the housing market, which continued to produce record housing starts. A cooling economy was expected to ease the affordable housing crunch, but not alleviate it to any great extent, partly because the supply of low-cost housing has been shrinking. ∎

HUD Secretary Melquiades Rafael Martinez.

CURRENT SITUATION

Martinez to Head HUD

The new administration is bringing many changes at the federal level. At the end of 2000, President-elect Bush selected Melquiades Rafael Martinez as secretary of HUD. During his confirmation hearings, Martinez told a Senate committee on Jan. 17 that he would work to ensure that more minority families could buy their own homes.

"Despite record-high levels of homeownership, African-American and Hispanic-American homeownership rates remain below 50 percent," Martinez said. "That is not acceptable." [20]

Martinez, a wealthy personal-injury lawyer who fled to Florida from Cuba as a teenager, added, "I know the value of homeownership because I have witnessed its great power throughout my entire life."

Martinez, former chairman of the Orlando Housing Authority and the Florida Growth Management Study Commission under Gov. Jeb Bush, assured the committee that he was not part of the wing of the Republican Party that had tried to abolish HUD. "I intend to be a very active secretary," he said, suggesting that the department should take a leading role in managing the explosive urban growth precipitated by the recent economic prosperity.

The nation faces a looming housing problem in both rural areas and in cities, he said, pointing out that the number of affordable houses for sale had declined while the number of poor people seeking housing had grown.

"Unless we make sure that everyone is participating in this great economic expansion and until we ensure that barriers to home ownership are torn down for everyone . . . until then, our job is not done," he said.

Advocacy groups that once had been wary of Martinez, claiming he lacked significant experience in housing, now say they look forward to working with him. "We were encouraged that he understands the country is facing a serious problem that there is not enough affordable housing for low-income families," said Sheila Crowley, president of the National Low Income Housing Coalition.

Habitat for Humanity's Dilemma

Lori Vaclavik, head of the Habitat for Humanity affiliate in Denver, considers herself a friend of Mother Nature. Indeed, a book by noted Colorado nature photographer John Fielder adorns her coffeetable.

But last fall, in a surprising turn of events, Vaclavik found herself opposed to a proposed state constitutional amendment to slow growth and protect green space.

Vaclavik opposed the initiative because she feared it would have made it impossible for Habitat to continue its mission of building low-cost, interest-free-mortgage housing for Denver's working poor. "It's not that we are against growth management and in favor of sprawl," Vaclavik said. "It's the right problem, but the wrong solution."

Private builders and developers are vociferous opponents of the growing number of slow-growth and "smart growth" plans, contending they drive up the cost of housing by pulling land off the market and restricting housing density. Now, nonprofit affordable-housing builders like Habitat International, which otherwise have stayed outside local political machinations, are joining the fray on the side of developers.

When the Colorado measure failed to pass muster with voters last November, the defeat was attributed by some observers and pollsters

Habitat for Humanity built several homes for low-income residents in Atlanta's Edgewood neighborhood.

to public opposition by the local Habitat affiliate. Vaclavik, who appeared in anti-amendment commercials with Republican Gov. Bill Owens, says the ecumenical Christian housing ministry also would have been priced out of the land-purchase market by the measure. The average price Habitat pays for a 6,250-square-foot lot in Denver has risen from $5,000 three years ago to $20,000, she says.

Across the country, in a classic case of "strange bedfellows," other affordable-housing advocates also find themselves fighting alongside developers fending off slow-growth efforts. For example, the Sea Island Habitat for Humanity chapter, which builds housing on Johns and Wadmalaw islands outside Charleston, S.C., has been lobbying against Charleston County's comprehensive plan, which at one point required four-to-eight-acre lots for each new home. Habitat generally builds three homes to an acre in that area.

"With this regulation, it would have become another Hilton Head, where all the poor people have long commutes to jobs," says Chuck Swenson, Habitat's local executive director.

"We're interested in preserving the rural nature, but the plan has to include low-income housing."

Habitat for Humanity was created in 1976 by Millard Fuller, a Georgia businessman and lawyer, who believed that poor people hungering for their own home would gladly work hundreds of hours to build it. The organization gets corporations, churches and individuals to donate building materials, and prospective owners and volunteers do the actual construction work. Since its creation, Habitat chapters have completed about 100,000 homes around the world.

The organization has also become a considerable force in U.S. housing. The typical Habitat house covers 1,000 square feet and costs about $46,600. In 1999, with 3,893 successful closings, Habitat was the 15th largest U.S. homebuilder in volume.[1] Fuller and other housing experts estimate it may eventually move into the top spot.[2]

Throughout the nation, most of the hundreds of proposed and already-enacted growth management plans are well-intentioned attempts to protect the environment and preserve quality of life. But the constraints they impose on affordable housing are often overlooked by those not involved in housing advocacy.

"Land-use and growth-management controls probably have the largest aggregate effects on housing," says Stephen Malpezzi, a professor of real estate economics at the University of Wisconsin at Madison. "Regulations raise prices."

Malpezzi says it's difficult to accurately measure the true costs and benefits of growth-management components and regulations. "Yet, any time we put a regulation in place, we're deciding that the benefits are worth the costs," he says.

When Vaclavik stepped into the growth management debate, her telephone voice mail quickly filled with angry calls. Some of her volunteers quit; some donors told her they'd never write another check to the cause. But Vaclavik says that by raising the red flag, she brought low-cost housing into the debate. "Now the environmental groups are going to consider affordable housing and the consequences," Vaclavik says. "I think they figured that out."

---

[1] *Builder* magazine, "Builder 100" ranking, May 2000.

[2] Howard Husock, "It's Time to Take Habitat for Humanity Seriously," *City Journal*, Manhattan Institute, summer 1995, p. 36.

"Suddenly You Belong Somewhere"

President George W. Bush made the following remarks about his support for homeownership in a speech in Cleveland in April during the campaign:

[In] the spirit of the Homestead Act, we will help many Americans to buy their first home. Just as Lincoln gave immigrants fresh from Europe a piece of land, we will help Americans to own a part of the American Dream.

Everyone who owns a home can remember that first day when the loan was approved, the check cleared and they stepped foot into their very own house.

It's different from renting. Suddenly you belong somewhere. Just like that, you're not just visitors to the community anymore but part of it — with a stake in the neighborhood and a concern for its future.

Looking at today's construction boom, it's easy to forget that many Americans are still waiting for this experience. The homeownership rate among whites in America is 73 percent. Among African-Americans and Hispanics, it is 47 percent.

President George W. Bush

AP Photo/Harry Cabluck

This is a good aim, as far as it goes — but we should extend it further. Instead of receiving monthly voucher payments to help with the rent, I propose a path to ownership.

Under my plan, low-income families can use up to a year's worth of rental payments to make a down payment on their own house. And for five years after that, as they pay their mortgage and build equity, they can still receive housing support, just as they would if they were still renting.

It makes a lot more sense to help people buy homes than to subsidize rental payments forever. They are not only gaining property but independence and the sense of belonging that ownership brings.

For the millions of low-income families not enrolled in Section 8, we will create a new program — called the "American Dream Down Payment Fund." When a low-income family is qualified to buy a house but comes up short on the down payment, we will help them. If they and the bank can come up with 25 percent of the down payment, the government will pay the rest, up to $1,500.

Right now the government offers help to low-income families, but mainly in the rental market. Through what's known as the Section 8 program, the federal government makes up the difference between fair-market rents and what a given family is able to pay.

This simple reform could help over 650,000 families in five years purchase homes.

I believe in private property. I believe in private property so strongly, and so firmly, I want everyone to have some.

"He also understands the need for more affordable rental units." [21]

Sen. Paul S. Sarbanes, D-Md., announced at the hearing that HUD had been removed from the government's "high-risk" category because of management changes made by departing Secretary Andrew M. Cuomo. "You're inheriting a better HUD," he told Martinez.

In October, Congress approved a $32.4 billion budget for HUD, including a record $1 billion in new grants to help the estimated 200,000 homeless people nationwide. Martinez indicated he would like to shift some HUD programs to state and local governments, partly to eliminate red tape that bedeviled him as a local official applying for HUD grants.

Echoing Bush's campaign theme of "compassionate conservatism," Martinez said he hoped to create partnerships with faith-based and non-profit organizations to help solve the nation's housing problems. He also said he would promote Bush's plan to provide tax credits to financial institutions that help low-income families finance houses.

Regardless of what happens at the federal level, state and local governments are already taking matters into their own hands. Realizing that only so much aid is going to trickle down from the federal government, many communities have created housing trusts to fi-

At Issue:

Should the government help poor people pay the rent?

ROBERT J. REID
EXECUTIVE DIRECTOR
NATIONAL HOUSING CONFERENCE

WRITTEN FOR THE CQ RESEARCHER, JANUARY 2001

*f*ederal rental assistance for lower-income households helps the impoverished, disabled and elderly. It also enables families to attain the stability, security and proximity to jobs they need in order to climb the ladder of success. Affordable housing contributes to health, education, economic growth and strong neighborhoods. It also attracts the involvement of private and government capital.

It is a normal, although painful, feature of real estate that lower-income households are priced out of the regular markets. Those households can find affordable housing only in soft real estate markets or in substandard properties. Government intervention is thus necessary to help develop and preserve good quality properties with long-term affordability.

Federal support comes in three forms: subsidies that contribute to equity or reduce debt service; default protection; and rental subsidies paid to public and private landlords, which make up the difference between the actual rent and the amount residents can pay with 30 percent of their income. Over 5 million households currently receive supports.

The supports almost always provide good quality housing. The cost to taxpayers is in line with the public benefits provided, and the end result is public-private partnerships, as well as partnerships between federal, state and local participants. However, the formulas for distributing supports are complex, and as a result they reach only about a third of America's households with critical housing needs.

Future rental assistance should include the following lessons gleaned from 70 years of experience: mixed-income developments compatible with their neighborhoods are more successful; subsidies should include both those tied to specific properties and those that move with the residents; high-quality landlords, who emphasize long-term viability, are crucial; and appropriate supportive services should be linked to the rental assistance.

To supplement federal assistance, local and state governments should be encouraged to reduce fees and taxes for affordable housing and expand development opportunities through inclusionary zoning. Local and state expenditures on affordable housing should be increased and leveraged with private contributions, using trust funds when appropriate.

Finally, we can only hope the growing recognition that at least 14 million American families still face critical housing needs — and that more than 3 million of those are working families — will build the broad public support necessary to continue these efforts.

HOWARD HUSOCK
CONTRIBUTING EDITOR
MANHATTAN INSTITUTE

WRITTEN FOR THE CQ RESEARCHER, JANUARY 2001

*t*he $13 billion federal housing voucher program may look good at first blush, compared with public housing projects. But replacing an old failure with a new one should not be confused with success. Vouchers now serve 1.7 million households — more than are served by public housing. But they pose significant problems of their own.

For instance, in south suburban Chicago, middle-class minority homeowners are up in arms over the fact that inner-city households are being relocated, via vouchers, into their neighborhoods. "Their lifestyle doesn't blend with our suburban lifestyle," complains African-American hospital administrator Kevin Moore. His concern embodies many of the unforeseen consequences of vouchers.

By subsidizing poor households to relocate in lower-middle-class neighborhoods, we devalue the effort those newly emergent middle-class families have made to buy into such neighborhoods. We assume, wrongly, that moving families into "better" neighborhoods will encourage them to adopt better habits, rather than acknowledging that good lifestyle choices should come first in order for the poor to reach the middle class. In the Chicago case, two-parent minority families, who fought to leave the problems of too-often-troubled families behind, complain that the government now is paying those same families to move next door.

What's more, because 75 percent of vouchers must go to households earning 30 percent of the median income — a group dominated by unmarried mothers — 84 percent of vouchers go to female-headed households. Yet, contrary to welfare reform's time-limited approach to public assistance, there is no time limit on such support. Thus, we are providing unlimited assistance to single-parent families.

But what about the claims that housing costs everywhere are outstripping the ability of working families to pay? We should not confuse price spikes in a few hot markets with a generalized affordability crisis. Homeownership is at an all-time high. Even HUD figures acknowledge that two-income families do not face a housing crisis.

Thus the housing crisis is closely related to our illegitimacy crisis. It is bad social policy to provide the resultant single-parent households with unlimited housing vouchers in neighborhoods others have struggled to reach. If we feel we must provide support for such households, better to do so through existing public housing — coupled with job training and a time limit on their stay. Let's not undermine welfare reform through the back door in the name of a non-existent housing crisis.

nance low-cost housing projects and make loans and down-payment grants to individual homebuyers. At least 150 such housing trusts already have been launched throughout the country.

"They are becoming a prevalent strategy," says Egan of the Millennial Housing Commission

In Charlotte, where a population boom has put a squeeze on housing, the local housing authority plans to begin building its own apartments. Other local and state governments are making idle public lands available for affordable-housing developments. Massachusetts, for instance, recently put more than 1,000 acres of surplus state property on the market for private developers to build affordable housing. New York City is putting thousands of buildings acquired by the city through tax delinquencies back into private hands. Many of the buildings are targeted for moderate-income housing.

Mayor Rudolph Giuliani also promised on Jan. 8 to spend $600 million to build or renovate low-cost housing during the next four years. Housing advocates in New York were disappointed that none of the money is to be used for rental vouchers.

"We remain concerned about the ground that has been lost," said Mary Brosnahan, executive director of the Coalition for the Homeless. Previous administrations had spent $600 million to $700 million each year, she said, but Giuliani had let spending drop to $100 million to $200 million a year. [22]

In California, appropriations for affordable housing were increased by 800 percent last year, to $570 million. To deal with a boom in the population of low-wage earners in Colorado, the state created its own housing-credit program to allow investors in affordable housing to offset state tax liabilities.

And Baltimore, like many other cities, is encouraging workers — especially public servants — to move back into the city to be closer to their jobs. Two years ago, the city began offering cash incentives to help cover closing costs or down payments for police officers, teachers and others who buy homes in the city.

Public-Private Efforts

Preserving existing affordable housing is another priority for state and local governments. About a million rental units tied to federal rent subsidies will expire by 2004, and many housing experts fear that landlords, who now can make more money in the private market, may opt out of the federal program. Even though HUD is increasing the value of the vouchers given to the landlords to keep those properties in the program, it is unclear how many will stay.

Colorado did some creative financing in order to issue $96 million in housing bonds, many of which will be used to refinance and preserve more than 4,300 units of affordable rental housing in 22 counties. Recent federal laws increasing the cap on so-called private-activity bonds should help Colorado and other states raise more money for housing.

In Washington, D.C., the public housing agency also applied unconventional means to raise money. At the end of last year, it used the prospect of future funding from HUD as leverage for a $29 million loan to complete renovations started five years ago. Issued in conjunction with Bank of America and Fannie Mae, it is the first loan transaction ever made based on forthcoming federal funding.

Congress encouraged such public-private partnerships in 1998, when it passed legislation prodding HUD and local housing authorities to create more partnerships with the private sector and to structure loans so they would give more confidence to lenders.

"Housing authorities and communities around the country will benefit from loans of this nature, allowing them to accomplish in one year what would have otherwise taken several years," said William Cooper, president of Bank of America of Greater Washington. [23]

On another front, the National Equity Fund (NEF) — the country's largest nonprofit syndicator of low-income housing tax credits — is getting directly involved in preserving older buildings. NEF acts as a middleman between developers and bankers. Developers who need cash give their tax credits for building low-income housing to NEF, which sells them to banks and gives the money to the developers.

In Missouri, 12 properties that have been part of the federal rent-subsidy program were turned over to the NEF in exchange for tax credits offered by Missouri. "With tens of thousands of affordable homes at risk nationwide, innovative solutions like the Missouri model are becoming critical to preservation" of older buildings, said NEF President Joseph Hagan. [24]

Corporate Initiatives

Faith-based nonprofits are also getting more active in housing preservation. Sheehan of Catholics for Housing says such groups look for private multifamily housing units whose HUD contracts are poised to run out and make purchase offers to the landlords. "We're looking for opportunities to acquire property and preserve it," he says. "It's too difficult to buy land and build in cities."

In addition, employers are taking on more responsibilities for their employees' housing needs. In Northern California, the Silicon Valley Manufacturers Group, made up of 190 companies from tiny startups to Hewlett Packard and Intel along with government agencies and nonprofits, has made housing one of its key initiatives.

"With rents up so high, we are concerned that churches are seeing their members driven away and nonprofits and small businesses being forced out of the area," says Laura Stuchinsky, the group's director of transportation and land use.

The group's housing committee actively lobbies city and county commissions for approval of high-density housing projects near public transportation and other services. It also helped boost the Santa Clara Housing Trust's housing kitty to $20 million to help develop housing projects and provide loans to first-time homebuyers.

Companies like Bank of America, the nation's largest consumer bank, have begun to offer employees grants toward down payments or closing costs. If they stay on the job five years, the bank's grants of up to $5,000 are forgiven.

Predatory Lending

Meanwhile, the lending industry is reaching deeper into the pool of potential borrowers to find low-income families who will make good prospects for homeownership. Low- and zero down-payment mortgages are becoming more common. And so-called sub-prime lenders, who offer financing to people with poor credit histories but at higher than prime interest rates, have been playing a bigger role in the housing market. Sub-prime lending for home purchases in cities grew from 1 percent in 1993 to 5 percent in 1998. [25]

Although traditionally underserved populations are beginning to get financing, many housing experts are concerned about the higher rates and fees they are paying. Indeed, many note that some of the borrowers could have been accepted by prime lenders in the first place but were turned down, possibly because of racial or other forms of discrimination.

According to a 1996 study by Freddie Mac, between 10 percent and 35 percent of sub-prime borrowers could have qualified for a lower-cost loan. Lawmakers have pushed to restrict Freddie Mac and Fannie Mae from purchasing loans from predatory lenders. In recent years, the two secondary-market institutions have been helping more underserved populations get access to better credit.

At the end of the 1990s, the nation's immigrant population was the fastest-growing subset of new U.S. households; but in this decade, immigrants are expected to represent the largest share of population growth. [26] As a result, Freddie Mac has begun to tailor lending products to the new population. For example, instead of having to wait until they get green cards, immigrants now can qualify for homeownership as long as they are legal residents.

In addition, since many immigrants don't have bank accounts, they will be permitted to count cash on hand as part of their assets. And friends and family members living together — a common practice among immigrants — can contribute toward 30 percent of the down payment.

"When we looked at the immigrant issue, we realized that the whole environment had changed and we needed to change," says Craig Nickerson, vice president of community development lending at Freddie Mac. ∎

OUTLOOK

President Bush's Focus

Retsinas at the Harvard Joint Studies program says he's relatively bullish about the prospects for the housing market in general over the next decade. His optimism is based in part on the likelihood that new immigrants are likely to fuel a strong housing market when they eventually reach home-buying age.

But on the affordable-housing front, Retsinas and others are not as sanguine. If there is an economic downturn, he notes, low-income people are the first to be affected. Moreover, federal support is likely to continue its retreat, he says, while the supply of existing low-cost housing will undoubtedly continue to shrink. In that event, state and local leaders will have to pull more weight and continue to direct resources to moderately priced housing.

If President Bush follows through on his campaign statements, he will focus on increasing homeownership rather than programs to boost rental housing. Among other things, he proposed allowing low-income families to use up to a year's worth of federal rental subsidies for down payments on a house. In addition, they would still receive subsidies during the first five years that they are paying mortgages.

"It makes a lot more sense to help people buy homes than to subsidize rental payments forever," Bush said in Cleveland on April 11. "It's different from renting. Suddenly you belong somewhere."

Another key component of Bush's housing agenda is boosting savings accounts for those in the lowest 20 percent of the income bracket. Under Bush's proposed individual development accounts program, banks would be encouraged to match up to $300 in savings put away by a low-income savings-account holder, in exchange for federal tax credits. Critics have pointed out that the plan would require education and counseling since many low-income Americans don't have banking experience.

The idea is to broaden welfare reform into asset building, says Stegman of the University of North Carolina's Center for Community Capitalism. "But all of this requires more sophistication among lower- and moderate-income working families," he says. "When you step back and look at the fact that one in 10 families have no bank account at all, financial education is hugely important to this."

For families that don't receive federal housing aid, Bush proposed that the federal government kick in up to $1,500 toward a down payment if would-be homeowners and their lenders could come up with at least 25 percent of the total down payment. Bush suggests the plan could help 650,000 families buy homes in the next five years.

Bush's proposals, and others, of course, depend on financial support from Congress. And with the nearly even split between Republicans and Democrats, it remains to be seen how much bipartisan cooperation will prevail.

Few who closely follow affordable-housing issues predict monumental shifts in the near future. Top housing experts expect only pilot programs to emerge in the next administration.

"It doesn't look like housing affordability is a priority for this administration," says Patrick Markee, senior policy analyst for New York City's Coalition for the Homeless, although he says it's a perfect time to make major investments. "It's an opportunity to use the benefits of the strong economy. It will be a shame if we don't see it as a priority." ■

FOR MORE INFORMATION

Joint Center for Housing Studies, Harvard University, 1033 Massachusetts Ave., Cambridge, Mass., 02138; (617) 495-7908; www.gsd.harvard.edu/jcenter. This collaborative center aligned with Harvard's Design School and the Kennedy School of Government analyzes housing policies, practices and demographic trends.

National Low Income Housing Coalition, 1012 14th St., N.W., Suite 610, Washington, D.C. 20005; (202) 662-1530; www.nlihc.org. Established in 1974, this nonprofit advocates for decent, affordable housing by disseminating information, formulating policy and providing public education programs.

National Housing Conference, 815 15th St., N.W., Suite 538, Washington, D.C., 20005; (202) 393-5772; www.nhc.org. Founded in 1931, the nonprofit advocacy group is made up of developers, lenders, nonprofits and public-sector housing agencies. It advocates housing policy changes.

National Association of Home Builders, 1201 15th St. N.W., Washington, D.C., 20005; (800) 368-5242; www.nahb.com. The NAHB represents some 800 state and local builders associations and 203,000 individual firms.

National Association of Realtors, 700 11th St. NW, Washington, D.C., 20001; (202) 383-1000; http://nar.realtor.com. Founded in 1908, the association represents 750,000 residential and commercial Realtors and others engaged in the real estate industry. Its economists provide up-to-date reports and data useful in monitoring housing trends and home values.

Notes

[1] Quoted in Nina Bernstein, "Changing Course, Giuliani Proposes Rent subsidies for Homeless Families," *The New York Times*, Oct., 12, 2000.

[2] Luke Shockman, "Addressing the Workers Shortage," *Post-Bulletin*, Rochester, Minn., Jan. 19, 2000.

[3] "Rental Housing Assistance: The Worsening Crisis: A Report to Congress on Worst Case Housing Needs," U.S. Department of Housing and Urban Development, 1999.

[4] American Housing Survey, 1997.

[5] Michael A. Stegman, Roberto Quercia, and George McCarthy, "Housing America's Working Families," *New Century Housing*, Volume 1, Issue 1, The Center for Housing Policy, June 2000.

[6] Richard Green, and Stephen Malpezzi, draft, "A Primer on U.S. Housing Markets and Housing Policy," Center for Urban Land Economics Research, University of Wisconsin-Madison, Feb. 23, 2000.

[7] *Ibid.*

[8] U.S. Housing Market Conditions, U.S. Department of Housing and Urban Development, Office of Policy Development and Research. Third-Quarter 2000.

[9] National Association of Realtors. Up-to-date figures on median home prices and Housing Affordability Index can be found at http://nar.realtor.com/.

[10] Joint Center for Housing Studies, Harvard University, "The State of the Nation's Housing: 2000," June 2000.

[11] NAR, *op. cit.*

[12] *Ibid.*

[13] Michael Verespej, "Can Living Wage Work?" *Industry Week*, Sept. 18, 2000.

[14] American Housing Survey, 1998, along with calculations by Michael Stegman, *et al.*, in Stegman, *op. cit.*

[15] Patrick Barta, "Fannie Mae, Freddie Mac Are Chided On Low-Income Homeownership Effort," *The Wall Street Journal*, Nov. 30, 2000.

[16] Jean Cummings and Denise DiPasquale, "The Low-Income Housing Tax Credit: An Analysis of the First Ten Years," *Housing Policy Debate*, Volume 10, Issue 2, Fannie Mae Foundation, 1999.

[17] From their Web site, at www.texashousing.org.

[18] *Ibid.*

[19] From prepared statements by Lazio, Oct. 24, 2000.

[20] Quoted in Elizabeth Becker, "HUD Candidate Would Seek More Homes for Minorities," *The New York Times*, Jan. 18, 2001.

[21] *Ibid.*

[22] Quoted in Bruce Lambert, "Housing: Lowering Costs Seen as Crucial to Building Plan," *The New York Times*, Jan. 9, 2001.

[23] Quoted in Kovaleski, Serge F., "D.C. Housing Agency Lands Repair Loans: $29 Million Deal Uses Private Money," *The Washington Post*, Dec. 21, 2000.

[24] Quoted in "NEF Affiliate Acquires Sec. 8 Projects Donated in Return for State Tax Credit," *Affordable Housing Finance*, p. 54, Sept. 2000.

[25] Joint Center for Housing Studies, *op. cit.*

[26] *Ibid.*, p. 4.

Bibliography

Selected Sources Used

Articles

Bernstein, Nina, "Rent Subsidies Proposed for Homeless Families: Giuliani Changes View on Housing Aid," *The New York Times*, Oct. 12, 2000.

New York City Mayor Rudolph Giuliani proposes rent subsidies to ease crowding at emergency shelters, which increasingly house working parents and their children.

Oppel, Richard Jr., "Efforts to Restrict Sprawl Find New Resistance From Advocates for Affordable Housing," *The New York Times*, Dec. 26, 2000, p. A18.

Oppel documents opposition by Habitat for Humanity and other affordable-housing groups to anti-growth measures, which the nonprofits say would limit their outreach.

Shockman, Luke, "Addressing the Worker Shortage," *Post-Bulletin* (Rochester, Minn.), Jan. 19, 2000.

A shortage of health-care workers is tied to the lack of affordable housing.

Verespej, Michael, "Can Living Wage Work?" *Industry Week*, Sept. 18, 2000, p. 11.

There's little empirical data to indicate whether living-wage bills requiring employers to pay higher-than-minimum wages have improved the economic status of entry-level workers or led to fewer workers being hired, or both.

Reports and Studies

Burchell, Robert C., *et al.*, "Inclusionary Zoning: A Viable Solution to the Affordable Housing Crisis?" New Century Housing, The Center for Housing Policy, Vol. 1, Issue 2, October 2000.

The report advocates using inclusionary zoning ordinances to increase the affordable homes available in communities. Such ordinances typically set minimum percentages of affordable units required in new developments and give developers incentives to include low-cost housing, such as waiving zoning requirements.

Cummings, Jean, and Denise DiPasquale, "The Low-Income Housing Tax Credit: An Analysis of the First Ten Years," Housing Policy Debate, Volume 10, Issue 2, Fannie Mae Foundation, 1999.

The study generally concludes that low-income housing tax credit projects — the major federal program to produce affordable rental housing — fail to reach the very poor.

Green, Richard K., and Stephen Malpezzi, "A Primer on U.S. Housing Markets and Housing Policy" (draft), Center for Urban Land Economics Research, School of Business, University of Wisconsin-Madison, Feb. 23, 2000.

Housing economists conclude that Americans at the bottom quarter of the income ladder face the most difficulties in finding affordable housing.

"Out of Reach," National Low Income Housing Coalition, 2000.

The annual study determines that minimum-wage earners would be unable to rent a two-bedroom house in any city without spending over 30 percent of their income.

Pill, Madeleine, "Employer-Assisted Housing: Competitiveness Through Partnership," Joint Center for Housing Studies and Neighborhood Reinvestment Corporation, September 2000.

This study argues that housing is a crucial component of economic competitiveness and that employers should play a role in creating housing opportunities.

"Rental Housing Assistance: The Worsening Crisis: A Report to Congress on Worst Case Housing Needs," U.S. Department of Housing and Urban Development, 1999.

The housing-affordability crisis facing very-low-income renters continues to worsen as a record high 5.4 million renter households pay a disproportionately large share of their wages for housing or live in substandard conditions

Stegman, Michael A., *et al.*, "Housing America's Working Families," *New Century Housing*, The Center for Housing Policy, Vol. 1, Issue 1, June 2000.

This study argues that the critical housing needs of working families are growing and impacting suburban communities. It calls for increased emphasis on the housing needs of moderate- and middle-income families, instead of a narrow focus on the very poor.

"The State of the Nation's Housing: 2000," Joint Center for Housing Studies, Harvard University, June 2000.

In its annual report, the center explores the homeownership gap between whites and minorities and the affordability crisis for low-wage earners and renters.

6 Welfare Reform

SARAH GLAZER

After more than five years on welfare, Connie Rounds — the divorced mother of two teenagers — went to work as an aide at a residential facility for the elderly in Oregon. It was 1998, and she was paid $6.30 an hour. [1]

When Rounds' boss required her to work overtime, her income went over the monthly eligibility limit for Medicaid and state health insurance, a major disaster for Rounds, who is in her 40s and suffers from chronic health problems.

Losing health insurance saddled Rounds with more than $3,000 in medical bills, which she must pay from a monthly income that has no room for luxuries. After her old car gave out, Rounds purchased a better used car, which put her over the eligibility limit for food stamps. * For several months, Rounds had to choose between buying the daily pain killers that enabled her to work or paying for basic expenses such as car insurance, the electric bill for her trailer and food.

Although her income has gone up $1.60 an hour since she started working, Rounds and her family are no better off financially than when she first left welfare because her increased wages make her ineligible for health insurance and food stamps. [2]

When Rounds first left welfare, she only worked half-time. One of her teenage daughters was doing poorly in school, smoking and staying out late. About a year ago, Rounds

---

* Last October Congress raised the cap on how much cars owned by food stamp recipients could be worth without disqualifying them from the program.

From *The CQ Researcher,*
August 3, 2001.

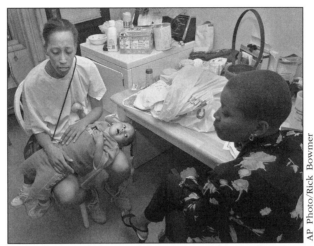

Marquita Chisholm, 27, left, was cut off from welfare last fall and began working for McDonald's in Cleveland. But when she had her third child, she quit her job. McDonald's wanted to hire her back, but she could not find child care. On her lap is daughter Rainah. They are being visited by social worker Diana Merriweather.

began working 32 hours a week to boost her income, but she worried about losing time she could spend with her daughter. The extra hours also kept Rounds continually exhausted and strapped for time to complete a recertification course she needed to qualify for a higher-paying job as a licensed practical nurse.

Looking back, Rounds feels lucky that welfare enabled her to stay home with her children when they were young. That's something her co-workers are not able to do under the tougher work requirements that came with the sweeping welfare reforms passed in 1996. Citing a co-worker whose milk dried up because she had to work when her nursing baby was 3 months old, Rounds says, "Working full-time is too hard when you are a single parent." [3]

When Congress passed the welfare reform bill, conservatives had high hopes for breaking what they saw as a culture of dependence on welfare while liberals predicted destitute children in the streets. Now, five years later, the liberals' dire predictions of vastly increased poverty

have not come to pass. But experts disagree whether the dramatic behavioral changes touted by reform advocates are the result of a newfound work ethic triggered by the law or were the result of the booming economy.

Moreover, the complex process of leaving welfare has raised new issues. As Rounds' story illustrates, the average $6.75 per hour wage earned by former welfare mothers is so low that many are no better off than when they were on welfare. [4] And if a welfare mother loses welfare-associated benefits, like health insurance and food stamps, she can end up even worse off. In addition, long working hours — coupled with obstacles to obtaining child-care subsidies promised when the law was passed — often result in children and teens being left unsupervised.

Studies have found that teens with parents in early welfare-to-work programs did worse in school and had more behavior problems than adolescents in other welfare households, perhaps because working parents have less time to monitor their teens' behavior and may saddle them with more responsibilities at home. [5] By contrast, studies of elementary children have found either positive or neutral effects on children's behavior and school performance, which some researchers attribute to the boost in pride a working mother passes on to her young children. [6]

The landmark 1996 law — officially the Personal Responsibility and Work Opportunity Reconciliation Act (PRWORA) — ended the open-ended entitlement to cash benefits, guaranteed to single mothers under the old welfare system. Now no one can receive a monthly welfare check for

Welfare Rolls Have Been Declining

The nation's welfare rolls have dropped by more than half from their peak of 14.2 million recipients in 1994 — two years before the 1996 welfare reform bill passed. Conservatives tend to credit the law's toughened time limits and work requirements, which many states had already enacted on a trial basis. Liberals generally credit a strong economy that provided a wealth of low-wage jobs. Economists credit both factors.

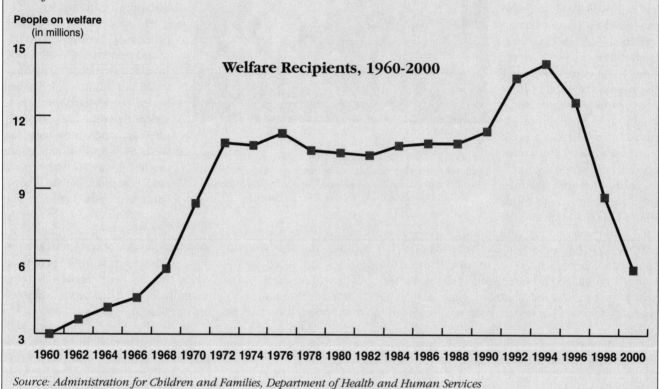

People on welfare (in millions)

Welfare Recipients, 1960-2000

Source: Administration for Children and Families, Department of Health and Human Services

more than five years in a lifetime, except in hardship cases as defined by the states. However, states were allowed to impose even earlier deadlines, and some did so. The law also required welfare recipients to work, or be involved in activities leading to work, within two years after receiving welfare.

Federal welfare funding to the states, which had been based on the welfare population in each state, was converted to a single block grant of $16.5 billion annually over six years to be distributed to all the states. Because the block grant expires in October 2002, Congress is expected to revisit many of these issues when

lawmakers reauthorize the program in 2002.

Nationally, welfare reform has had dramatic effects: Welfare rolls have declined by more than half since their peak in 1994; more poor, single mothers are working than ever before; single-parent families are seeing their earnings rise and child poverty is at its lowest level ever.

But plenty of problems remain, in addition to low wages and lost health benefits for some:

- About half the welfare recipients who left welfare in 1996 and 1997 had lower household incomes in the year they left — more than $50 a month lower

— than their last months on the rolls, according to a study based on a national sample of more than 30,000 households. [7]

- Some welfare recipients have lower net earnings than they had on welfare because they do not keep their job for the entire year, or they lose food stamps and Medicaid, sometimes erroneously, when they leave the welfare rolls.

- Up to a third of those who left welfare for low-wage jobs were back on welfare within a year, largely because of the lack of steady work and the difficulty of keeping a job while maintaining a patchwork of child-care arrangements. [8]

- About 40 percent of former recipients who have left the welfare rolls are not working, leaving welfare officials scratching their heads as to how they are surviving.

Nevertheless, champions of welfare reform say the law's success should be judged by the dramatic number of recipients who have gone to work, not by how many are still in poverty.

"Welfare reform is about altering the culture of poverty, not reducing poverty," argued journalist Mickey Kaus, a long-time critic of welfare, at a recent Brookings Institution forum. [9] Rather than achieve "equal income" for the poor, he writes, the aim is to provide "equal respect . . . the respect our society reserves for workers, even if they gain not a cent of income." [10]

"We're showing that — at least in a good economy — we can promote work," boasts Ron Haskins, a senior fellow at Brookings who helped write the 1996 law as former chief welfare adviser to Republicans on the House Ways and Means Committee. "We've had a huge impact," he says, noting that never-married mothers are now more likely to be working than receiving welfare — a reversal from pre-reform years.

Some reform advocates say that even if former welfare recipients are worse off in the short-term, the long-term dismantling of a system that

encouraged an urban underclass of idle, unmarried mothers is worth it, citing the leveling off in the 1990s of births to unmarried mothers.

Skeptics doubt it was the welfare law that caused out-of-wedlock births to level off, noting that the percent

Johnnie Cartledge, Cessna Aircraft Co. plant manager in Wichita, Kan., teaches blueprint reading to former welfare recipients and recovering substance abusers who are training to be aircraft mechanics. The Cessna program is part of the Welfare to Work Partnership, a nonprofit association of businesses that helps retrain former welfare recipients.

of single-mother births leveled off in 1994 — more than two years before the law was enacted. But reformers point out that during the early '90s — when the unwed-births began declining — many states already were experimenting with time limits and work requirements for welfare recipients.

Even so, the huge increases in homelessness, foster care and hunger that liberals predicted would follow welfare reform have not materialized, admits Christopher Jencks, a sociologist at Harvard University's John F. Kennedy School of Government, who opposed the reforms when they passed. "It's hard to argue there's an increase in material hard-

ship through this period," he concedes. "That's telling me that the gloom-and-doom set — of whom I number myself — overdid it a bit."

Nevertheless, say welfare reform critics, the largest economic expansion in decades has been far more influential in getting welfare recipients into the work force than any cultural conversion to the work ethic. Contrary to the popular stereotype, critics argue that many welfare moms had prior work experience, only used welfare between jobs and would have left the welfare rolls even without welfare reform.

"I don't think these welfare mothers were as out-to-lunch as conservatives think," Jencks says. He says the welfare rolls shrank so rapidly because state welfare offices discouraged new applicants from coming onto the rolls by requiring them to seek employment first.

Many experts worry about what will happen if there is a recession. Typically, a 1 percent rise in unemployment translates into a 5 percent rise in the welfare rolls for single mothers and a 10 to 15 percent rise for married couples, notes economist Rebecca Blank, dean of the Gerald R. Ford School of Public Policy at the University of Michigan. And, if families that lose their jobs come knocking at the welfare office doors, they may be turned away if they have reached their five-year time limit. Furthermore, many won't qualify for unemployment insurance because they only had part-time jobs or won't have worked long enough.

Out-of-Wedlock Births Stopped Rising

The steady rise in out-of-wedlock births flattened out in 1994, but experts are unsure what role the 1996 welfare reform bill or earlier state reforms played. Some experts suggest that increased use of the contraceptive Depo Provera and concern about AIDS and other sexually transmitted diseases played the key role.

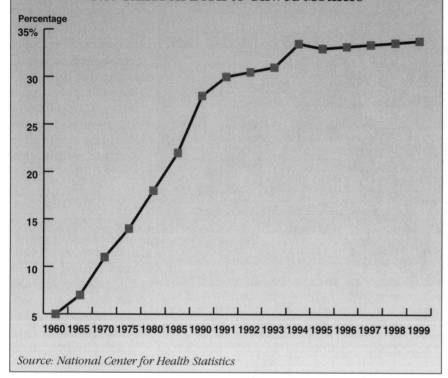

U.S. Children Born to Unwed Mothers

Source: National Center for Health Statistics

An economic downturn could be devastating to poor children, who compose about two-thirds of the welfare caseload, notes Ann Segal, former deputy assistant secretary for policy initiatives in the Health and Human Services Department under President Bill Clinton. "What happens when the time limits come and Mom can't find a job?" asks Segal, who now studies children's issues for the David and Lucile Packard Foundation in Los Altos, Calif. "I can't believe the country would write off that number of children. It's a scary thought to me."

Conservatives say state and federal governments haven't "written off" anybody. Instead, they have more than doubled the amount spent on the poor over the $30 billion per year they spent on the old welfare program at its peak. Total aid to the working poor increased to about $65 billion by 1999, primarily through state and federal earned-income tax credits (EITC) — tax refunds only available to low-income working families. A mother with two children leaving welfare and earning $10,000 a year can supplement her income by $4,000 in cash from the tax credit and by more than $2,000 in food stamps, bringing her total income to $16,000 — lifting her above the official poverty line. But in most states

that income is still marginal. A child-care crisis, broken-down car or ailing family member could cause a newly working parent to lose that first job. "They're one disaster away from destitution," Blank says.

When re-funding for welfare reform comes up for debate in 2002, Congress is expected to clash over how much federal money states should continue to receive for welfare. Democrats are expected to push for more exemptions from the time limits, while Republicans are likely to seek measures encouraging marriage and discouraging out-of-wedlock births — two goals of the 1996 law that the Bush administration strongly supports.

As lawmakers and policy experts debate the law, here are some of the issues they will tackle:

Did welfare reform move recipients off the welfare rolls and into employment?

After years of steady increases, the nation's welfare rolls have dropped by more than half from their peak of 5.1 million families in 1994. But the downward trend began more than two years before the 1996 federal welfare reform bill passed and several years before most states implemented those reforms. Does the welfare reform bill deserve the credit?

Conservatives tend to credit the law's toughened time limits and work requirements for transforming welfare recipients' attitudes toward work. Liberals generally give more weight to the strong economy, which provided a flood of low-wage jobs and the lowest unemployment rate in 25 years. Economists credit a mixture of both factors.

The employment rate among never-married mothers, who typically have little education or work experience and spent the most time on welfare, shot up to 65 percent in 1999, compared with 49 percent in

1996. [11] New York University politics Professor Lawrence M. Mead III, who has long criticized welfare's failure to emphasize work, cites those statistics as evidence of the success of the welfare reform program, called Temporary Assistance for Needy Families (TANF). "It's the first large increase in work levels since the 1960s," he says. "A key part of that story is eliminating the welfare entitlement and requiring adults to function. There's no denying the success of TANF."

Ironically, most people left the rolls long before time limits actually begin to kick in this fall, which Mead attributes to the word getting out on the street that the deadlines were approaching.

"You make it no longer acceptable to be dependent, and a lot of people get the message," Mead says. "Now the caseworkers are saying, 'The clock is ticking. You should bank your hours because you're really going to need them.'" By "banking hours," recipients conserve their lifetime limit of five years of welfare eligibility for a future emergency, such as a health problem or getting laid off or fired.

But sociologist Jencks says conservatives are wrong to think the law somehow transformed welfare mothers from idlers into workers for the first time. "Even without welfare reform, nearly half the single mothers on the rolls in 1994 would have left by 1999 simply because their children grew older, they found work or they got married," he says. However, he concedes that without welfare re-

form most of the mothers who left welfare would have been replaced by other mothers who had just had their first baby, split up with their husband or lost their job. [12]

Welfare reform made its biggest difference in state welfare offices, which tended to open fewer new cases. In some states, caseworkers handed newspaper "Help Wanted"

Doris Saunders, mother of five, tells a Welfare to Work Partnership conference in Washington, D.C., last May about her journey from being a welfare recipient to manager of special projects at the Sears store in New Castle, Del.

sections to applicants, telling them to return after making 30 calls, Jencks says. A lot of mothers never came back, he thinks, and word of mouth probably discouraged other mothers from applying.

Moreover, work is not foreign to most welfare mothers, he contends. According to survey data, 60 percent of all welfare recipients had worked in the previous two years. "Making Ends Meet," a study of 214 welfare-reliant women in four cities, found that mothers had an average of five years of job experience. But the mothers who were on welfare had concluded that returning to the kinds of jobs they had in the past would

not make them better off or that the job might vanish and leave them without income to support their small children. Many had plans to return to work when their children were older. [13]

Critics of welfare reform say the economy has been so strong in recent years that it's hard to know what the law's effect would have been in its absence. After 1996, the nation experienced its lowest unemployment rate in 25 years: The annual rate fell from 6.9 percent in 1993 to 4 percent in 2000. And during this longest-running expansion in U.S. history, real hourly wages for the lowest-paid workers (adjusted for inflation) began to rise after falling for two consecutive decades. [14]

Mark Greenberg, a senior attorney at the liberal Center for Law and Social Policy who opposed welfare reform, worries about what will happen in a recession. "The way the welfare system has worked during a strong economy gives us very little information about what the picture will be in a deteriorating economy," he says.

Experts from both camps agree that a large chunk of the declining caseloads is attributable to recently passed laws that make work pay, such as expanding the EITC. The credit, available only to low-wage workers with children, can have as much value as a $2 per-hour raise. Some call the EITC the government's largest anti-poverty program.

Other policies that helped the working poor include health insurance for low-income children not

How Much Is Welfare Worth?

The monthly welfare benefit for a single parent with two children ranges from a low of $120 per month in Mississippi to a high of $923 in Alaska, according to Pamela Loprest, a welfare expert and senior research associate at the Urban Institute. Pennsylvania, which lies in the middle of the TANF (temporary assistance for needy families) benefits range, pays $403 per month. The monthly food stamp grant for a single mother with two children and no work income would add approximately $330. Only about a quarter of TANF recipients receive a government housing subsidy. Ron Haskins of the Brookings Institution estimates the annual value of Medicaid insurance at about $4,000. But liberal experts are reluctant to place a dollar value on Medicaid since it does not add dollars to a family's income that can be spent on something else like food. Also, its value is highly dependent on the health of an individual family.

receiving welfare, increased spending on child-care subsidies and increased earned-income "disregards," which permit welfare recipients to keep more of their earnings while remaining on welfare. [15]

In a recent summary of economic studies, Douglas J. Besharov, a resident scholar at the conservative American Enterprise Institute (AEI), concluded that aid to the working poor explained 30 percent to 45 percent of the caseload decline. He thinks welfare reform accounted for another 30 percent to 45 percent of the drop, and credits the healthy economy with 15 percent to 25 percent of it. [16]

Conservatives like Haskins say that if the booming economy were mainly or even solely responsible for the dropping welfare rolls, past economic booms should have produced similar reductions, but they didn't. Instead, caseloads rose even in the best labor markets. During economic expansion in the 1980s, when the American economy added 20 million jobs, welfare rolls still grew by nearly half a million families, notes Haskins, of Brookings. [17] Similarly, caseloads continued to rise by 700,000 families between December 1991 and March 1994, the first couple of years of the most recent recovery, even as the economy added 6 million jobs.

Welfare rolls did not begin their sustained decline until 1994, when more than half the states implemented work-requirement programs that predated the 1996 reforms. In the 1990s, Haskins argues, it was the new welfare-assistance deadlines and tougher work requirements that pushed families into the job market.

A report just released by the conservative Manhattan Institute in New York City concludes that TANF accounts for more than half the decline in welfare participation and more than 60 percent of the rise in employment among single mothers. By contrast, the report by two Baruch College economists also finds that the booming economy of the 1990s explains less than 20 percent of either trend. [18]

Many economists argue that it was both the booming economy and the harder line coming from welfare offices. In 1999, the Council of Economic Advisers (CEA) estimated that welfare reform accounted for one-third of the caseload reduction from 1996 to 1998, and the robust economy for about 10 percent.

By contrast, from 1993 to 1996, when unemployment was dropping even more sharply, most of the decline was due to the strong labor market, the CEA concluded. Tough,

new state work requirements during that period accounted for only about 10 percent of the drop, the CEA said. Increases in state and federal minimum wages also accounted for about 10 percent of the caseload decline, the CEA said. [19]

"The bottom line is we could not have had the dramatic decline in caseloads if we hadn't had the biggest social policy change in decades," says the University of Michigan's Blank, a former CEA member under President Clinton, who counts herself as one of the early liberal skeptics of welfare reform. She says the reforms were more successful than she expected because "states have been more serious than I expected in . . . changing their bureaucracies."

Are welfare recipients and their children better off after they leave the rolls?

Much of the upcoming reauthorization debate will no doubt center on whether those leaving welfare are better off than they were while receiving benefits. No one disputes that as the caseload declined, so did overall child poverty. By 1999, child poverty had fallen to its lowest rate since the government started measuring it in 1979 — to 19.6 percent of all children (14 million children), compared with the peak of 26.3 percent in 1993. [20] Black child poverty declined more in 1997 and 1999 than in any previous year, reaching its lowest level ever in 1999. [21]

But, these numbers don't tell the story of those at the bottom of the income scale. Welfare-reform critic Wendell E. Primus, director of income security at the Center on Budget and Policy Priorities, stresses that the decline in poverty has not been as steep as the drop in the welfare caseload. And deep poverty — defined as having an income below 50 percent of the poverty level — has been growing. [22]

Female-headed families appear to be leaving welfare because they can earn more money now than before, Primus points out. Earnings have risen for the bottom 40 percent of these families, and annual earnings for the bottom 20 percent increased nearly 82 percent from 1993 to 1999. Earnings for the next lowest 20 percent rose almost 100 percent. [23]

Despite the higher incomes, those leaving welfare more recently appear to be having a harder time making ends meet in some respects. According to a recent study by the Urban Institute, a liberal Washington-based think tank, about a third of those who left welfare in both 1997 and 1999 say they have had to skip or scrimp on meals in the past year. The study also found that the most recent welfare-leavers tend to have more health problems than those who left earlier.

Furthermore, rising housing costs appear to be causing trouble for the most recent welfare graduates. A significantly higher percentage of those who left welfare in 1999 have housing worries. Forty-six percent were unable to pay mortgage, rent or utility bills in the past year, compared with 39 percent of those who left welfare in 1997. The study suggested that this could reflect rising housing costs driven up by tight housing markets. [24]

In addition, many of those who left welfare earliest may have been less capable of working than more

recent leavers. Many left welfare not to work, but because their benefits were terminated when they failed to meet welfare reform's work requirements or because health problems prevented them from working. [25]

Furthermore, critics of reform say that once work expenses like child care and transportation are factored in, many families are only marginally better off when they leave welfare, and some are actually worse off. For instance, the poorest two-fifths of

Former welfare recipients tell their stories at a 1999 Faces of Welfare Reform panel in Chicago, Ill., during a seminar sponsored by the Welfare to Work Partnership. From the left are New York City Citigroup office manager Gail Hagan; Chicago Sears sales associate Kelly Shaheed; Cessna Aircraft assembly mechanic Chris Wilcox and CEO of Children of the Rainbow Day Care Center Gale Walker. Local NBC-TV anchorman Art Norman, right, hosted the discussion.

families headed by single mothers increased their average earnings by about $2,783 per family between 1995 and 1999, but their disposable incomes increased only $643 after inflation and work expenses were factored in, according to Primus.

Moreover, those at the very bottom of the income ladder — 700,000 families — appear to be worse off, he says. The average disposable income of the poorest one-fifth of single

mothers fell 3 percent in real terms from 1995 to 1999, he notes.

Primus also notes that while some working families leaving welfare are making higher incomes on paper, their net earnings are less. For instance, some do not continue to receive Medicaid and food stamps for which they are eligible, or their rising incomes make them ineligible for such supports. Or they fail to work a full year, either because their jobs are unstable or their lives are too chaotic.

The Urban Institute found after researching welfare families in 12 states that many families leaving welfare are eligible for food stamps but aren't receiving them. Families leaving welfare often lose both their Medicaid and food stamps, either because they don't know they are still eligible or because claiming them requires repeated in-person visits to a welfare office during work hours. [26]

A recent University of Wisconsin study found that less than a third of the mothers who left welfare for work in that state had higher incomes a year later, and more than 60 percent remained in poverty because the loss of food stamps and other benefits outweighed their increased earnings. [27] "The glass is half-full," says Maria Cancian, lead author of the study and a professor of public affairs and social work at the University of Wisconsin-Madison. "You've seen big increases in employment and earnings. But these women are not [earning] incomes to bring children out of poverty."

Even with higher wages, many of

Wisconsin's "Workfare" Experiment...

Policy-makers have long flocked to Wisconsin to figure out how the state managed to cut its welfare rolls more than any other urban state in the nation. [1] Wisconsin has reduced its monthly caseload by more than 93 percent since 1987, when it began its first experiments with a work-based system. [2]

"Welfare is gone in Wisconsin," says Demetra Smith Nightingale, director of the Welfare and Training Research program at the Urban Institute in Washington, D.C., who has surveyed research on the state's welfare experiment. About 85 percent of Wisconsin's welfare cases are now concentrated in Milwaukee, a heavily black and Hispanic city that is one of the most depressed in the nation. [3]

Wisconsin abolished the welfare entitlement check altogether in 1997 and replaced it with a new program called Wisconsin Works, or W-2. It requires virtually everyone to work and pays a cash subsidy only to those in government jobs or treatment programs. Almost everyone has to work — including the disabled, drug abusers and mothers with young children. [4]

Then-Gov. Tommy G. Thompson, who oversaw the creation of the program before being tapped by President Bush as secretary of Health and Human Services, calls his state's program "the standard for welfare reform in America." Conservatives have hailed the state's tough work policies and the influence of conservative theorist Charles Murray, who has argued that traditional welfare created a culture of non-work among the poor. [5]

But what often gets overlooked in the political compromise brokered between a Republican governor and Democratic legislators is financial help for low-income workers on a scale so generous that it has been compared with a European welfare state. [6]

Wisconsin subsidizes child care and health care for all working families with incomes up to 165 percent of poverty — not just former welfare recipients — adds a state tax credit on top of the federal earned-income tax credit and has massively increased health insurance for children.

"They're more progressive on the services side while tougher on the work side" than any other state, Nightingale says.

"W-2 redefined who the government helped," says Milwaukee Director of Administration David Riemer, one of the Democratic architects of the program. "The old AFDC [Aid to Families with Dependent Children] system was very narrow: It took the poorest of single parents and ignored all above the poverty line and ignored people with no kids. W-2 created a de facto entitlement to child care and health care for the entire working poor."

In his 1988 book *The Prisoners of Welfare: Liberating America's Poor from Unemployment and Low Wages*, Riemer argued for replacing government aid with government jobs as a progressive goal. Today, he contends that Wisconsin's program approaches the liberal ideal of providing a guaranteed minimum income for the working poor.

"The key to political success in Wisconsin was a concordat where the Democrats abandoned the idea of entitlement to welfare and the Republicans abandoned the idea of downsizing government," says Lawrence M. Mead, a professor of politics at New York University, who is writing a book on the Wisconsin experience. "They junked the old system and created a new one that is simultaneously very severe and very generous. It says, 'You've got to work, but if you work, we'll help you in all these ways.'"

However, only a small proportion of the working poor take advantage of all the generous supports, according to Lois Quinn, senior research scientist at the University of Wisconsin-Milwaukee Employment and Training Institute, which has been studying W-2. Child-care subsidies, for example, reach less than one-quarter of the eligible children in Milwaukee, according to the institute. "There's been a dramatic increase in child care, but it's not serving the

Many were opposed to Wisconsin's groundbreaking welfare reform program. The state began experimenting with a work-based system in 1987, but it abolished the welfare entitlement check altogether in 1997 and replaced it with a new program called Wisconsin Works, or W-2. A Milwaukee group called Welfare Warriors shows its concern about the 1997 policy change.

AP Photo/Morry Gash

. . . Miracle or Mirage?

majority of working poor families. And it's not going to, because it would break the bank," says Quinn, who doubts the legislature would support the funding if all eligible families claimed it.

Although the legislature initially passed what looked like massive increases in spending for the poor, the welfare caseload plunged so dramatically that the program quickly became self-financing, Mead says. [7]

"Gov. Thompson went out in a burst of glory because he had these programs that looked like they served the entire working poor," Quinn says, "but the price tag, had it been utilized, would have been very expensive."

One reason more eligible parents don't take advantage of the child-care subsidies is that many of them — especially former welfare mothers — rely on informal babysitting arrangements with neighbors and relatives, which often don't qualify for subsidies.

Wisconsin's child-care subsidies go only to licensed or certified day care. Few qualified centers stay open on nights and weekends, when many former welfare mothers work in fast food, retail and nursing homes. They "need you on the weekend and maybe Tuesday night because Becky can't come in. Informal care is about the only thing that works for that," Quinn says. Only 24 licensed child-care providers with 458 slots were open after 7 p.m. in Milwaukee's central city, according to an institute study conducted from 1996 to 1999. [8]

Moreover, former welfare recipients have a hard time keeping steady work. The Urban Institute reported that while at least 75 percent of former recipients work some of each year after they leave the rolls, less than half are continuously employed. [9] And a study by the University of Wisconsin-Madison found that more than 60 percent of those who left welfare in 1995 and 1997 remained in poverty. [10]

In addition, as Wisconsin gets down to a welfare population that may be hard to employ, people are hitting the 24-month point without getting jobs. "What does it mean for the safety net?" Nightingale asks.

Riemer contends that as a result of W-2, Milwaukee's low-income population is better off. Some data bear out his contention. In nine Milwaukee neighborhoods with the highest concentrations of former welfare families, incomes have risen since the advent of W-2, and the number of single parents filing income taxes continues to increase, according to Quinn.

But, Quinn notes, "The largest [income] increases came before welfare reform in Milwaukee County, likely due to the economy" in Wisconsin, which has been blessed with a low unemployment rate following W-2. Currently, Quinn reports, the number of working poor families is declining in Milwaukee. But the number of near-poor (earning incomes at 100 to 125 percent of poverty) is growing. "The big challenge," she says, "will be moving beyond that."

As Wisconsin governor, Tommy G. Thompson, now secretary of Health and Human Services, pushed through landmark welfare reforms.

Health and Human Services Dept.

[1] Lawrence M. Mead, "The Politics of Welfare Reform in Wisconsin," *Polity*, summer 2000.

[2] Tommy G. Thompson, "Welfare Reform's Next Step," *Brookings Review*, summer 2001, pp. 2-3.

[3] Amy L. Sherman, "The Lessons of W-2," *Public Interest*, summer 2000, p. 36.

[4] *Ibid.*

[5] Mead, *op. cit.*

[6] *Ibid.*

[7] Mead, *op. cit.*

[8] John Pawasarat and Lois M. Quinn, "Impact of Welfare Reform on Child Care Subsidies in Milwaukee County, 1996-1999," October 1999, University of Wisconsin-Milwaukee Employment and Training Institute; www.uwm.edu/Dept/ETI.

[9] Demetra Smith Nightingale and Kelly S. Mikelson, *An Overview of Research Related to Wisconsin Works (W-2)*, Urban Institute, March 2000; http://urban.org/welfare/wisc_works.html.

[10] Maria Cancian *et al.*, *Before and After TANF: The Economic Well-Being of Women Leaving Welfare*, May 2000, Institute for Research on Poverty, University of Wisconsin-Madison.

these women rarely reach above $10 an hour, Cancian says. Many have sporadic employment because either the job does not last a full year or personal crises force them to quit before the year is out. Other studies show that about 20 percent of mothers leaving welfare go through long periods without work, and many more are sporadically unemployed. [28]

Still another study found that about half of the women who left welfare remained below the poverty level 18–21 months later, primarily because only a minority got good-quality jobs with benefits, reliable hours and decent wages, says Sandra Morgen, director of the University of Oregon's Center for the Study of Women in Society, which conducted the study for Oregon state. [29] "What we've done in most states is force people into a problematic labor force," she says.

In addition, small raises frequently cause these mothers to become ineligible for food stamps and Medicaid. And because state-required copayments for child care are based on income, a small wage increase can jack up the copayment so high that mothers are forced to "pull the kid out of decent child care and stick him with grandma or the boyfriend," she adds.

The study also raised serious concerns about the poor quality of child care that former welfare mothers can afford and the precarious, patched-

President Franklin D. Roosevelt delivers one of his popular "Fireside Chats" in 1937. Two years earlier, Congress passed the Aid to Dependent Children program to help widows with children.

together arrangements many moms rely upon. If one thing goes wrong in that complicated structure, Morgen says, it can lead to job loss. "We have families who wake up at 5:30 a.m. to take a sleeping kid to Aunt Lola, who gets the kid to school; someone else picks the kid up and later takes the kid somewhere else," she says. "The kid may have three different child-care arrangements, and if any one of them gets screwed up, it can send the whole system out of whack." In addition, for many women, child care becomes unaffordable in the summer when children need all-day care.

"An awful lot of families want to work and think they're better off. But a significant percentage — who don't want to be working and think their kids need them — think they're worse off," Morgen says.

But welfare-reform advocates say

that even if newly working mothers are poor, it is better than being on the dole because it boosts their self-esteem, creates a better role-model for their children and gives them a first step toward a better job.

Welfare critic Mead argues that, "over several years, if people keep working, they usually do escape poverty. But it's a long and painful climb."

The University of Michigan's Blank suggests that even if a former welfare mother loses her first job, she may persist in looking for a second job because she will have figured out how to cope with child care and transportation.

Robert Rector, a senior research fellow at the conservative Heritage Foundation, disputes the idea that a family's income determines a child's well being. "The worst thing about welfare is that it destroyed the marital and work ethic and damaged children's life prospects," Rector says. "A child in a working single-mother household will do better than where the mother is collecting a welfare check."

But the research on children of working mothers remains equivocal. About half the studies find significant improvements in children's behavior or academic achievement, while the other half find no effects. [30]

Another puzzle is the so-called "missing 40 percent." When Congress takes a close look at welfare funding next year, it will no doubt look at the large percentage of women who do

Chronology

1930s *During President Franklin D. Roosevelt's administration, widows are classed with the disabled as unable to work.*

1935
Congress passes Aid to Dependent Children to help widows with children.

1936
Less than 1 percent of families with children are on welfare.

———— • ————

1960s *Welfare rolls surge, welfare-rights movement reduces welfare's stigma, divorce and illegitimate birth rates rise.*

1962
Welfare program is renamed Aid to Families with Dependent Children (AFDC).

1964
President Lyndon B. Johnson declares "war on poverty," establishing anti-poverty programs.

———— • ————

1970s *As the U.S. economy slows, Congress begins tightening eligibility for welfare and requiring more AFDC parents to take jobs or enroll in job training.*

1971
Congress requires all AFDC parents to register for work or job training unless they have children under age 6.

1974
The earned-income tax credit is enacted to provide tax refunds for the working poor.

———— • ————

1980s *The federal government starts granting waivers to states to experiment with welfare-to-work programs.*

July 31, 1981
Congress cuts cash benefits for the working poor and allows states to require welfare recipients to work.

Oct. 31, 1988
President Ronald Reagan signs the Family Support Act requiring states to implement education, job training and placement programs for welfare recipients.

———— • ————

1990s *Most states are allowed to experiment with work requirements and penalties. Congress passes major welfare-reform bill. Poverty and unemployment drop to historic lows.*

1992
Democratic presidential candidate Bill Clinton promises to "end welfare as we know it."

1993
Newly elected President Clinton raises the amount paid to poor working families under the earned-income tax credit.

1994
Welfare rolls reach peak of 5.1 million families. Republican majority takes over Congress and begins debating ways to reform welfare.

1996
President Clinton signs the landmark welfare-reform law on Aug. 26 removing the open-ended entitlement to welfare and converting the program to a block grant to states. Congress raises the minimum wage from $4.25 to $4.75 an hour.

Sept. 1, 1997
The minimum wage is increased again to $5.15 an hour. Falling welfare caseloads enable states to begin amassing a $5 billion surplus in unspent federal welfare funds.

1998
Child poverty drops to its lowest level since 1989.

1999
Employment of never-married single mothers rises to all-time high of 65 percent.

———— • ————

2000s *Amid historic lows in welfare cases and unemployment, Congress prepares to debate welfare-reform reauthorization.*

September 2000
Welfare caseload drops to 2.2 million families, a 50 percent decrease from its 1994 peak. Jobless rate drops to historic low of 4 percent.

October 2001
Five-year time limit on welfare benefits begins to kick in.

Oct. 1 2002
Congress must reauthorize welfare-reform legislation.

not go to work after leaving welfare, according to a recent analysis by AEI scholar Besharov. Studies suggest that some have other forms of government aid or are getting help from family members, friends or boyfriends.

But Harvard's Jencks thinks the non-working welfare-leavers may be the one-third or more of welfare recipients who are unemployable because of poor job skills, mental health issues or drug problems. Democrats are expected to question whether this unemployable population will need more assistance to stay out of dire poverty after their five-year limits expire. If they are unable to exploit a social network, Jencks suggests, this population will be worse off after the time limits hit.

Welfare reform has been so successful at pushing adults into work in some states that their welfare rolls now consist mostly of children who are in the custody of someone other than their biological parents. Dea Shanute, 2, went to live with her disabled grandmother, Betty Burke, when her mother could no longer care for her. Burke receives $116 a month from the state to care for the child.

BACKGROUND

Widows' Relief

The original aim of cash welfare in the 1930s was to enable widows to stay home and raise their children. In 1935, Congress passed the Aid to Dependent Children bill. The goal, as stated in a report to President Franklin D. Roosevelt, was to "release from the wage-earning role the person whose natural function is to give her

children the physical and affectionate guardianship necessary . . . but more affirmatively to rear [her children] into citizens capable of contributing to society." [31]

But in the 1970s, when the single-mother population rose dramatically and became dominated by divorced, separated and never-married women, Americans became increasingly hostile to aid for single mothers. In the 1930s, single mothers were grouped with the aged and disabled as citizens who should not be asked to work, and most married mothers did not work at the time. By the 1990s,

work had become the norm for U.S. mothers.

Polls consistently show that two-thirds or more of Americans support policies to help "the poor" who cannot help themselves, especially children and the disabled. But the same number also say they do not support "welfare." [32] And polls show that Americans have traditionally opposed government aid for the able-bodied. [33] As the public increasingly perceived single mothers as fully capable of working, opposition seemed to mount in tandem with growing welfare rolls.

For nearly 60 years, it seemed that welfare rolls could only grow, regardless of the economy's health. Except for a few brief declines, the rolls grew from 147,000 families in 1936 to about 5 million in 1994 — from less than 1 percent of the families with children to about 15 percent.

After President Lyndon B. Johnson declared war on poverty in 1964, the rolls surged 230 percent from 1963 to 1973. The rise largely reflected two factors, according to the AEI's Besharov: administrative changes that made it easier for income-eligible families to get benefits, and the welfare-rights movement, which removed some of the stigma of being on welfare. [34] But this period also saw a rise in divorce and concern about the decline of traditional families.

After remaining roughly steady for the next 15 years, the welfare rolls shot up 34 percent between 1989 and 1994. Fears that welfare was discouraging work and encouraging illegitimate births resurfaced with new urgency during this period. Much of the caseload rise was due to the major economic downturn of the late 1980s and early '90s, according to Besharov. But there were other important influences: a spike in out-of-wedlock births, government efforts to get single mothers to sign up for Medicaid — and therefore also for welfare benefits — and an increase in child-only welfare cases, perhaps resulting from the crack epidemic that rendered addicted parents incapable of caring for their children. [35]

Since the 1970s, welfare policy has been "a tug-of-war between those trying to protect children and families from penury and those who believe that welfare dependency is even worse for families than poverty is," writes Gordon Berlin, senior vice president at the Manpower Demonstration Research Corporation, and author of numerous welfare studies. [36] But until the 1990s, he notes, neither side gained much of an edge in changing welfare.

Until the early 1970s, most changes in the program — renamed Aid to Families with Dependent Children (AFDC) in 1962 — tended to expand eligibility and liberalize benefits. Grants grew slightly during the 1970s and '80s, but not enough to keep up with inflation.

Beginning around 1972, as the economy slowed and poverty increased, public resentment grew against the tax burden needed to support large federal anti-poverty programs. Efforts to reform welfare over the next 20 years revolved around reducing benefits, tightening eligibility and requiring more AFDC parents to take jobs or enroll in job training.

But none of the changes dramatically affected welfare caseloads. In a last-ditch effort Congress passed the Family Support Act of 1988, requiring states to place most mothers with

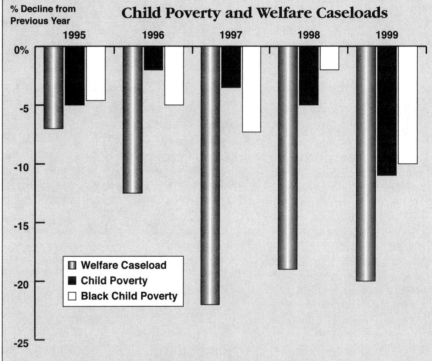

Child Poverty and Welfare Caseloads Declined

Child poverty and welfare caseloads both declined after passage of the 1996 welfare-reform law. By 1999, child poverty was at its lowest rate since the government started measuring it in 1979 — 19.6 percent of all children (14 million children), compared with the peak of 26.3 percent in 1993. Black child poverty reached its lowest level ever in 1999. However, welfare-reform critics say that the decline in poverty has not been as steep as the drop in caseloads.

Child Poverty and Welfare Caseloads

% Decline from Previous Year

Legend:
- Welfare Caseload
- Child Poverty
- Black Child Poverty

Sources: Congressional Research Service; Census Bureau; Wendell E. Primus, Center on Budget and Policy Priorities, "TANF Reauthorization," National Governors Association Briefing, June 6, 2001, Washington, D.C.

children over age 3 in education, work or training.

The public's dissatisfaction with welfare stemmed partly from the growing size and costs of AFDC and partly from resentment that it was supporting a large proportion of unwed mothers, most of whom were assumed to be African-Americans. In fact, more whites than blacks received AFDC. [37] In addition, by the 1990s it had become more common for mothers to work than to stay home — a reversal from the societal position of mothers in 1935.

Welfare Reform

On the presidential campaign trail in 1992, Democratic candidate Clinton promised to "end welfare as we know it." After the election, his administration granted waivers from federal welfare regulations to many states, allowing them to experiment with toughening work requirements and imposing time limits on benefits. Both approaches became cornerstones of the Repub-

"I'm Grateful I'm Not on Welfare Today"...

When New York City's welfare office told Gregory Cannon he would have to clean city buildings to work off his $34 weekly welfare check, he bought crack cocaine with the bus fare they gave him. Today Cannon is drug free and working, thanks to Binding Together Inc. (BTI), a job-training program for former welfare recipients.

"I had plenty of jobs where I told off the boss and walked away," he says. "At Binding Together, I learned to get along with people. BTI gave me what [New York City's Work Experience Program] didn't — pride and dignity."

Binding Together mainly serves the hard-to-employ. About 75 percent of its trainees have prison records, and many were drug users. But in the past two years, clients have had multiple problems — including lower literacy levels, untreated mental health problems and less experience living a sober life, according to Program Director Angelia Holloway.

Because New York state limits how long an individual can receive welfare assistance — including time spent in drug treatment — many people now arrive at the program with much shorter periods of sobriety under their belt — as little as three months compared with 18 months previously. Thus, they still have to learn basic skills like getting along with co-workers and arriving at work on time. The program is also finding higher rates of depression and learning disabilities. The average reading level has dropped — from eighth grade to about a fifth-grade level. And the program is getting an increasing number of women navigating their first job for whom child care is a major logistical issue.

Nationally, some welfare experts expect to see more such problems as the country's welfare caseload shrinks to a hard core of people who have little work experience and multiple health and substance-abuse problems.

As a result, BTI does a lot more counseling and hand-holding to get people ready for work, Holloway says. Constance Hayes, 40, who came to BTI directly from a drug-treatment program, says she was "still in a shell" when she first arrived. "Since I've been here," she says, "I'm able to open up and socialize better with people. BTI taught me I can live in a productive way and can get money." She is counting on BTI to find her a copying job for

Two hundred former welfare recipients and other hard-to-employ people a year learn to operate sophisticated copiers at a training program run by Binding Together Inc. in New York City.

Binding Together Inc.

lican-backed 1996 welfare-reform law.

The changes ultimately adopted were based more on a Republican plan than on an administration bill. Both bills imposed time limits on benefits, but the Clinton proposal included an entitlement to a public job afterward, and that was not in the final bill. The Republican bill changed the program from one in which all recipients were entitled to a benefit under AFDC — and states received open-ended funds as their caseload grew — to a capped block grant, which gave states an incentive to cut caseloads because they would get to keep any unspent money.

It was largely this change — and the fear that states would not have either the money or the incentive to support welfare recipients adequately — that led to several high-profile resignations of welfare policy-makers from Clinton's Department of Health and Human Services (HHS), including Primus.

TANF was seen as a cut in federal funding because states would get funding based on their 1995 caseloads, recalls Greenberg, of the Center for Law and Social Policy.

"Our question was: How will states manage with fixed funding and rising caseloads? But caseloads had begun falling in 1994, so TANF resulted in a significant increase in funding to the states," he says. "If you compare TANF to AFDC in 1997, the states had an additional $4.7 billion."

The result was more positive than Greenberg had expected, he says, because the states used the extra money to support families leaving the welfare rolls with additional child-care subsidies, child health insurance and other assistance, ameliorating the dire situation foreseen under low wages.

...Job-Training Graduate Says

about $8 an hour.

Several recent BTI graduates say they were motivated to find job training because they could barely make ends meet on welfare, and they knew their time limits on welfare assistance were approaching.

Desiree Dennis, 39, the mother of five, had been on public assistance for more than seven years when New York City assigned her a "workfare" job cleaning highways. She found the work "disgusting and degrading," and decided to find a job-training program. She recently started working as a copier operator at a print shop next door to Binding Together.

Yet at the $8 hourly wages typically paid to copy operators, some mothers aren't much better off than on welfare. Joann Gonzalez, 25, who was on public assistance for almost eight years, decided to get job training because she couldn't support her two children on the $390 per month she received from workfare for collecting trash in city offices. "I just decided to get up and start working because public assistance wasn't giving me enough money to live off," she says.

Gonzalez had not looked for work when her children were younger, she says, because she had no job experience and lacked a high school diploma. After training at BTI, she got work in January as a copy operator.

She makes $220 a week, working from 2-10 p.m. That sum is quickly gobbled up by the $150 she pays to her babysitter and her $75 contribution to her subsidized rent. "I can't live off $220," she says. "Besides the rent and the light bill, you've got expenses for the kids: clothes, school pictures, notebooks." But her husband recently moved back in with her, which makes the job viable. He picks the kids up at 9 p.m. from the babysitter when he gets home from his job.

Graduates generally agree there should be time limits on welfare.

Vanessa Ratliff, 40, a mother of three, described herself as a "dedicated and sincere" cocaine user since high school. Today she works at BTI. "I'm grateful I'm not on welfare today," she says. "I was on it for a good 20 years, and it was OK with me. It shouldn't be that way, where I should be comfortable on it for 20 years."

Binding Together Inc.

Vanessa Ratliff, a mother of three, now works at BTI after abusing drugs and receiving welfare for 20 years.

A recent study in Cleveland, Los Angeles, Miami-Dade and Philadelphia concluded that "the worst fears'" of welfare reform's critics — that states would slash benefits and services — "have not materialized." On the contrary, the study found, states are actually keeping some people longer on the rolls because they are permitting working people both to earn money and receive cash assistance. Under the old rules, a mother would be cut from the rolls once her caseworker discovered she had a job that earned significant income. [38]

The Working Poor

The massive increases in aid to the working poor initiated by Clinton and passed by the Republican Congress also helped prevent the grim forecast of the bill's opponents. Such subsidies now exceed the amount spent on the old AFDC program.

The most important support is the EITC, available only to working parents. Between 1993 and 1999, the income supplement for a single mother of two more than doubled

from $1,700 to about $3,900 per year. [39]

Clinton also pushed through a two-stage increase in the minimum wage — from $4.25 to $4.75 an hour in 1996 to the current $5.15 an hour in 1997. In addition, real hourly wages for the lowest-paid workers began to rise after falling for two consecutive decades. [40] The prospects for welfare-leavers also brightened during this period as the annual unemployment rate fell from 6.9 percent in 1993 to 4 percent in 2000, its lowest rate ever.

Child care and Medicaid subsidies also expanded to record highs. Between 1996 and 1999, millions more children have become eligible for health insurance through the Medicaid program, and child-care subsidies have been expanded, essentially becoming an entitlement for families leaving welfare. Total annual federal and state child-care expenditures rose from $8 billion to more than $12 billion from 1993 to 1999, Besharov calculates, providing subsidies for more than 1 million additional children. [41]

However, advocates for the poor say child-care subsidies often buy poor quality care, and that only a fraction of the eligible low-income families take advantage of them. ■

CURRENT SITUATION

Reauthorizing TANF

B ecause the states' TANF block grant of $16.5 billion annually for six years expires in October 2002, the welfare-reform law must be reauthorized before then. Some hearings have been held, but serious legislative action is not expected until mid-2002.

The size of the block grant is the biggest issue to be resolved. Because the grant was established before caseloads plummeted, several states have had large unspent surpluses. In 1999, federal lawmakers were shocked to learn not only that there was an unprecedented $7.4 billion in federal welfare funds sitting unspent, left over from fiscal 1997 and 1998, but also that some states had used their surpluses for

non-welfare uses like reducing middle-class taxes. [42]

Since then, much of the surplus has melted away, with only about 4 percent remaining unobligated, says Gretchen Odegard, legislative director for human services at the National Governors' Association (NGA). Moreover, many states are holding their surpluses in reserve in case of an economic downturn. Others are using them to provide child care and transportation for the newly working poor.

"Those structures are in place," Odegard says. "They're the reason the funding needs to continue. The governors will fight reductions in funding."

While Republican lawmakers are likely to argue that the unspent surpluses indicate that federal welfare assistance should be cut, Democrats will argue that states should keep the money as a contingency fund for leaner times or for child care and health insurance for the working poor.

Time limits are another major issue to be debated. Democrats and liberals are expected to propose more generous exemptions from TANF's five-year time limit for former recipients working part-time or completing their education and job training, as well as those considered the hardest-to-employ. Some studies suggest that many who are still on welfare are currently unemployable due to multiple problems, including drug or alcohol addiction, depression, disabled children and lack of work experience. [43]

States already are permitted to exempt up to 20 percent of their caseloads. So far, few states have defined who will be eligible for exemptions. According to ongoing research, a significant number of people who do not qualify for disability benefits, such as people undergoing treatment for cancer, cannot meet existing work requirements. [44]

Republicans are expected to argue that the 20 percent exemption should be sufficient to take care of problem cases.

Work Requirements

T ANF required welfare recipients to work — or take up to 12 months of vocational education — within two years of receiving benefits. States were required to have half of their recipients involved in such activities by 2002.

Because caseloads have fallen so dramatically — more than 50 percent in some states — states have been able to meet those targets without having to create the kinds of extensive work programs envisioned by the bill. Republicans, led by HHS Secretary Tommy G. Thompson, argue that states should not be released from the requirement to establish good work or work-plus-training programs.

Democrats will argue that the bill should have a broader definition of what qualifies as work, including a broader definition of what kind of education is allowed. Republicans are likely to argue that only work works, pointing to past failures of government-funded job-training programs.

Democrats also would like to see the law include an explicit new goal: reducing poverty. The law should not just aim to get a welfare recipient the first job available, but a well-paying job, they will contend.

Most states have allowed welfare recipients to keep most of their earnings from a job — up to a certain salary — without losing supplemental cash support. [45] Democrats will argue that recipients who are in the transition between welfare and work should not have to risk hitting their five-year time limit on assistance and becoming ineligible for benefits if they need them in the future.

There is also a growing momentum in both parties in Congress to let welfare mothers keep a larger

Are Welfare Time Limits Unfair?

Two of the most controversial provisions of the 1996 welfare reform law were its five-year time limit on benefits and financial penalties for families not complying with the work requirements.

So far it is hard to gauge the effects of the time limits, since most families have left the rolls before their time limits kick in. Many families, however, will be affected starting this October and in subsequent years.

Although time limits are unlikely to be challenged, Democrats are expected to push for provisions to soften the limits' effects.

A recent University of Michigan study found high rates of depression and physical health problems among Michigan welfare recipients. Moreover, the women who reported the problems tended to work fewer months out of the year. High school dropouts and those with little work experience tended to have trouble keeping a job. [1]

Democrats will point to such studies to argue that a high proportion of welfare recipients may not be able to start working before the time limits hit and that exceptions should be made for hardship cases.

But Republicans can be expected to resist. Ron Haskins former chief welfare adviser to Republicans on the House Ways and Means Committee when they were crafting the welfare reform bill and currently a senior fellow at the Brookings Institution, notes that current law permits states to exempt 20 percent of their caseload from the time limit. "There's no evidence that any state will press up against the time limit," he says. Moreover, he points out that a surprisingly high proportion of women with mental health and other problems manage to work at least part of the year, suggesting they may not have insuperable barriers to work.

The changes Democrats are expected to propose include:

- Stopping the clock on the five-year time limit for welfare recipients who are working but still receiving TANF (temporary assistance to needy families) benefits. Under some state policies, recipients continue to receive reduced welfare benefits while working to encourage their transition to working. Democrats will argue that such recipients should not be penalized by lifetime welfare limits while they are making the transition toward self-sufficiency and that states should have the option of subsidizing low wages.
- Changing the basis for the 20 percent hardship exemption. Under the law, states are currently permitted to exempt 20 percent of their welfare caseload from the time limits. Few states have actually defined who will count under the 20 percent. Democrats will argue that the 20 percent should be based on the higher caseloads states had at the time

of welfare reform's passage, not today's drastically reduced caseloads. Such a recalculation would permit a higher number of recipients to be exempted from the time limits.

- Loosening restrictions on training and education. Under current law, welfare recipients are permitted to enroll in vocational education for a maximum of one year under the federal work requirement. Democrats will argue that welfare recipients should be allowed to extend their education for longer than that and for a wider array of educational programs, such as college and English classes, before facing sanctions for not participating in work.

Advocates working with the poor at the community level say they're opposed to the entire concept of time limits. "Poverty doesn't have time limits, so helping people shouldn't have time limits," says Don Friedman, senior policy analyst with the Community Food Resource Center, a social service agency in New York City. "It's inhumane and outrageous to arbitrarily decide someone isn't entitled to assistance."

Friedman claims that, in practice, the time-limit exemptions aren't helping the people they should. For example, New York City requires even people with serious disabilities to come into its offices to be re-evaluated to see if they are exempt from the time limits. "I predict 10 percent of the caseload will be sanctioned for non-participation because they can't understand the rules or they can't make it in," he says.

For Nancy Nay, who suffers from sickle cell anemia and cancer, it is not clear that she can be defined as one of the 20 percent of hardship cases, because the number of slots keeps shrinking as the caseload declines, *The New York Times* recently reported. [2]

Federal law also allows states to exempt welfare mothers who are coping with domestic violence. But in New York, which opted for such a provision, more than half the women were never screened for domestic violence, and of those who said they were victims fewer than half were referred for help, according to Marcellene Hearn, an attorney at the NOW Legal Defense and Education Fund.

"Many states have adopted laws that are pretty good" for welfare recipients who are victims of domestic violence, Hearn says, but "caseworkers are just not following through."

---

[1] Mary Corcoran *et al.*, University of Michigan Program on Poverty and Social Welfare Policy, "Predictors of Work Among TANF Recipients: Do Health, Mental Health and Domestic Violence Problems Limit Employment?" Unpublished paper for Brookings Institution press briefing, May 21, 2001.

[2] Nina Bernstein, "As Welfare Deadline Looms, Answers Don't Seem So Easy," *The New York Times*, June 25, 2001, p. A1.

TANF Provisions for Reauthorization

Here are the major funding provisions of the current TANF (temporary aid to needy families) program, which Congress must reauthorize by Oct. 1, 2002.

Provision	Description	Funding	In Baseline?
Basic TANF block grant to states	To help needy children, reduce non-marital births and other purposes	$16.5 billion annually, FY1996–FY2002	Yes
Illegitimacy bonus for up to 5 states	To reward greatest reductions in out-of-wedlock birth rates	$100 million annually, FY1999–FY2002	Yes
Performance bonuses	To reward high performance by states	$1 billion for FY1999–FY2003	Yes
Population and poverty adjustor for 17 states	Grants for states with high population growth and low welfare spending	Up to a total of $800 million for FY1998–FY2001	No
Contingency fund	Matching grants for needy states	$2 billion for FY1997–FY2001.	No
Native Americans	Grants for tribes	$7.6 million annually, FY1997–FY2002	Yes
Territories	Grants for TANF, foster care and other programs	About $116 million, FY1997–FY2002	Yes
Loan fund	Interest-bearing loans for state welfare programs	Total amount of loans may not exceed $1.7 billion	N/A
Medicaid for families leaving welfare	Federal payments for up to 12 months of Medicaid	About $0.5 billion per year	Yes
Additional Medicaid costs	Funds to compensate for computing Medicaid eligibility	$500 million total	No
Research by Census Bureau	To study impact of TANF on poor families	$10 million annually, FY1996–FY2002	No
Research by Dept. of HHS	Funds to study costs/benefits of TANF	$15 million annually, FY1997–FY2002	No

Source: Brookings Institution

Note: If a TANF provision is in the baseline, then Congress will not need to find a funding mechanism (either a tax increase or a program cut) to reauthorize the provision. If funding is not in the baseline, Congress must find a funding mechanism.

TANF at a Glance

The 1996 welfare-reform law replaced the old AFDC (Aid for Families with Dependent Children) program with the radically different TANF program (temporary aid to needy families). TANF's five key provisions are:

1) The individual entitlement to benefits provided by AFDC was repealed. The right to cash welfare was replaced by a system of mutual responsibilities in which cash benefits are conditioned on attempts to prepare for self-support.

2) The funding mechanism of open-ended federal payments for every person added to the welfare rolls by states was replaced by a block grant with a fixed amount of funding for each state for 6 years. States were given far more discretion than under AFDC law, to spend funds for purposes other than cash assistance, such as transportation, wages subsidies, pregnancy prevention and family formation.

3) States were required to place an escalating percentage of their caseload in work programs.

4) Financial sanctions were placed both on states and individuals who fail to meet the work standards. In the case of individuals, states must reduce the cash TANF benefit and sometimes the food stamp benefit of adults who fail to meet the work requirements designed by states. Similarly, the federal government will reduce the block grant of states that fail to meet the percentage work requirement. This requirement stipulates that states must have 50 percent of their caseload involved in work programs for a minimum of 30 hours per week by 2002.

5) States are generally not allowed to use federal dollars to pay the benefits of families who have been on welfare for more than 5 years.

---

share of child-support payments paid by absent fathers. Under current law, the state and federal governments retain all of a father's child-support payments while mothers are on welfare and about half the payments on overdue child support after mothers leave welfare. The provision has discouraged some unwed mothers from cooperating with state and federal agencies trying to find so-called "deadbeat dads," because often the father is paying some support to the mother unofficially.

Both conservative and liberal advocacy groups argue that families should get more of these collections in order to benefit the children involved.

Non-custodial fathers of children on welfare often do not pay child-support regularly because they are unemployed or employed in low-wage jobs. Helping such fathers get good-paying jobs is high on the agenda of several progressive groups, who point out that most federal employment efforts have so far been aimed only at mothers.

Unwed Mothers

Promoting marriage and reducing out-of-wedlock pregnancies ranked among the 1996 law's key goals. The virtual disappearance of married families from many poor, urban neighborhoods worries the administration, according to HHS Secretary Thompson, who pushed through one of the earliest welfare-to-work experiments as governor of Wisconsin. (*See sidebar, p.118.*) "The nation has clearly had major success in rolling back the culture of not working," he wrote in a recent article, "but the incidence of single-parent families, especially those formed by births outside of marriage, is still too high." [46]

Any proposals delving into the private arena of marriage, however, will be viewed as government intrusion and likely will face strong opposition from the National Organization for Women (NOW) and other progressive groups. It's not clear what proposals might be offered, other than exhorting the states to try harder to reduce unmarried births and possibly setting aside a fixed pot of money to encourage state experiments.

Although many states have used federal funds — provided under the 1996 law — to prevent teen pregnancy, congressional Republicans are disappointed at how little states have done to promote marriage. Lawmakers are expected to discuss whether states should be offered federal money to encourage more marriage. Rector of the Heritage Foundation proposes paying a $1,000 annual bonus over five years to reward at-risk women who wait to have a child until they are 20 and married — as long as they remain married and off welfare for five years.

Most states have been leery of plunging into this controversial territory, although West Virginia adds a $100 marriage incentive to the monthly cash welfare benefit of any family that includes a legally married man and women living together. [47]

Timothy Case of the NOW Legal Defense and Education Fund condemns both West Virginia's approach and Rector's proposal as "rank discrimination against families where

Child-Care Aid Goes Unused

Most former welfare recipients who are working do not receive the child-care subsidies they are eligible to receive. In many parts of the country, subsidies go to less than one-third of the former recipients, according to a study by the liberal Center for Law and Social Policy (CLASP). [1]

Study co-author Mark Greenberg, a senior CLASP attorney, says 40 percent are simply unaware that they could get child-care assistance. When families leave welfare, the state welfare office may not know that they have gone to work and may not get an opportunity to inform parents face-to-face that the aid is available. Meanwhile, parents receiving or just leaving welfare are actually more likely to receive child-care subsidies than other poor parents, probably because they have greater contact with government offices.

Many parents don't apply for the subsidy because states often don't pay for the kind of informal, unlicensed care that many welfare recipients must rely upon to cover their night and weekend work shifts, when few child-care centers are open. By contrast, families that are receiving the subsidies are more likely to use organized, center-based care than those using a neighbor or relative. Still other families may be overwhelmed by the administrative and paperwork hassles of applying for the aid.

The child-care subsidy, which varies from state to state, may not be enough to provide a mother with the child care of her choice. The federal government requires each state to pay a day-care subsidy high enough to meet the fees at 75 percent of that state's child-care providers, based on the most recent market survey. But only 23 percent of the states meet this requirement, Greenberg says.

According to the Department of Health and Human Services, only 12 percent of the 15 million eligible low-income children benefit from the major source of federal child-care funds — the $13.9 billion, six-year Child Care and Development Block Grant. Another study, of low-income workers in Santa Clara, Calif., showed that a third of the parents were unable to work because they could not afford child care, while another third reduced their work hours. [2]

The child-care block grant is underutilized because it does not provide enough federal funding to cover all the eligible families, so there are few state outreach or information programs aimed at getting more families signed up for benefits, Greenberg says. "Why have a big outreach campaign if you can't respond to the need?" he asks.

About 20 percent of federal welfare funds, called Temporary Aid to Needy Families (TANF), now goes to paying for child care, Greenberg says. Much of that comes from surpluses of federal welfare money realized by the states after their caseloads declined dramatically following reform efforts. But the number of children benefiting from the child-care subsidy hasn't increased as fast as the number of mothers leaving welfare to go to work.

If Republicans succeed in cutting TANF during the welfare-reform reauthorization next year, it could have a "huge impact on the child-care system," Greenberg says.

---

[1] Rachel Schumacher and Mark Greenberg, "Child Care After Leaving Welfare: Early Evidence from State Studies," October 1999; www.clasp.org.

[2] Linda Giannarelli and James Barsimantov, "Child Care Expenses of America's Families," December 2000, Urban Institute; www.urban.org. Spending was $3.45 billion in 2000. See U.S. Department of Health and Human Services, "Fact Sheet: Administration for Children and Families Child Care Development Fund," Jan. 23, 2001, www.acf.dhhs.gov, and HHS press release, "New Statistics Show Only Small Percentage of Eligible Families Receive Child Care Help," Dec. 6, 2000.

parents are unmarried. The government should not try to coerce people into marrying. Marrying or not marrying is a private decision."

Rector argues that welfare currently creates a "profound [financial] anti-marriage incentive," even though mothers are no longer required to be unmarried in order to qualify for benefits. As long as a man earning $7-$8 an hour doesn't marry the woman he loves who is on welfare, she keeps her benefits. Once they marry, his income gets counted, pushing the wife over the income eligibility line and forcing

her to lose almost all benefits, Rector observes.

Eloise Anderson, former director of social services for California's welfare system, argues that the married family environment prepares a child for citizenship and adulthood "better than any other social arrangement." She is among those who have proposed that unmarried couples be urged to consider marriage in the hospital as soon as their child is born. [48]

Wade F. Horn, who as President Bush's new assistant secretary of HHS for children and families will admin-

ister TANF, actively supports government programs advocating marriage. He points out that most children born in single-parent families will experience poverty before they turn 11 and that fatherless children are more likely to fail at school, engage in early sexual activity and develop drug and alcohol problems. [49]

In hospital interviews conducted in a national survey, 80 percent of unwed couples reported being "romantically involved" at the "magic moment" of their child's birth. [50] Usually it is the father's poverty or unemployment that prevents them from marrying, says study co-author Sara S. McClanahan, a professor of sociology and public affairs at Princeton University's Woodrow Wilson School of Public and International Affairs. "I don't think signing them up for marriage will solve the problem. They're just going to split up," unless the husband's unemployment and the couple's lack of parenting and relationship skills are addressed, she says.

Other welfare experts worry that such policies could have dire consequences if the father is physically abusive. It's also not clear that marriage produces better futures for children or if the kinds of couples who decide to get married already have the kinds of relationship and parenting skills that are better for children.

AEI's Besharov suggests that increased use of the long-acting contraceptive Depo Provera and concern about AIDS probably has had a larger influence on curbing out-of-wedlock births than any changes in welfare policy. It's too early to say, many agree, whether welfare reform can affect sexual behavior. ■

OUTLOOK

Decline Tapering Off?

M any welfare experts are concerned that as welfare rolls fall the population of recipients will be composed increasingly of those who are harder to employ. But statistics paint a mixed picture.

For example, it now appears that less than 10 percent of the welfare population has a drug abuse problem, far lower than the 25 percent assumed during the welfare-reform

debate, notes Peter Reuter, a visiting scholar at the Urban Institute. And, he adds, it's not clear that addiction should keep welfare recipients from working. "Most people who have substance abuse problems who are not on welfare are employed," Reuter says. "They find jobs and on the whole keep them."

Moreover, Urban Institute studies have found that 1999 welfare recipients were no more disadvantaged than those on the rolls two years earlier. [51] One reason may be that those least able to work have been among the first forced off the rolls by work requirements, while those with jobs sometimes are permitted to stay on the rolls under new state rules.

However, some employers and job-training companies say they're now seeing a less educated, more troubled population, with higher levels of depression among former welfare recipients undergoing job training or entering the work force.

"Businesses we work with say they are having a more difficult time finding work-ready applicants [among former welfare recipients] than two or three years ago," says Dorian Friedman, vice president for policy at the Welfare to Work Partnership in Washington, D.C. The partnership is comprised of employers committed to hiring ex-welfare recipients.

At CVS drugstores, which have hired some 12,000 former welfare recipients, newer applicants have lower literacy levels and are more likely to have prison records, notes Wendy Ardagna, who specialized in working with former welfare recipients at CVS and is now on loan to the Welfare to Work Partnership.

Nevertheless, companies will continue to be interested in hiring former welfare recipients because they foresee a shortage of entry-level workers at least through 2020, according to Ardagna. Former long-time welfare recipients may have trouble getting

promotions and more pay, she says, because of their low level of education — frequently no more than an eighth-grade reading level.

Political Consensus?

B oth liberals and conservatives say they detect an increased willingness among legislators and voters to improve the lot of the working poor, who enjoy much greater support in national polls than non-working welfare recipients. [52]

"If you redefine single moms as working, the public's willingness to support them increases," says Harvard's Jencks, who argues for raising the minimum wage and increasing child-care subsidies.

By transforming so much of the welfare population into the working poor, conservatives may have handed liberals the kind of consensus they need to get more government help for workers.

As evidence, welfare critic Mead of New York University notes that some provisions in the tax-cut bill recently signed by President Bush were aimed at helping the working poor. The bill increased by $88 billion over 10 years the tax refunds that low-income families with children will receive. [53]

A similar consensus is gathering in the states, where governors will fight to keep the programs they established to subsidize health insurance and child care.

Many experts think the consensus will spill over to the reauthorization of the food stamp program, which also comes up for review next year. Advocates for the hungry would like to see it made easier for the working poor to receive food stamps, and for restrictions on working families to be relaxed. [54]

In a supreme political irony, Mead foresees enlarged support for improving job quality through an increased minimum wage and other pro-labor measures traditionally associated with the political left — as a result of welfare reform's conversion of welfare mothers to workers.

"Now we're going back to the 'me too' politics of the 1950s and '60s, where Republicans were competing with Democrats to do good things for ordinary people," Mead predicts. "We're going to see child care and all kinds of things coming from Washington to help out all those struggling workers.

"But," he points out, "if they had not become workers it would never have happened." ∎

Notes

[1] Connie Rounds is a fictitious name used in the following report to protect the confidentiality of the person interviewed by the study authors. Center for the Study of Women in Society Welfare Research Team, University of Oregon, "Oregon Families Who Left Temporary Assistance to Needy Families (TANF) or Food Stamps: A Study of Economic and Family Well-Being from 1998 to 2000, January 2001," Vol. II, pp. 65-68.

[2] Ibid.

[3] Ibid., p. 67. For background on the 1996 law, see Christopher Conte, "Welfare, Work and the States," The CQ Researcher, Dec. 6, 1996, pp. 1057-1080.

[4] Ron Haskins et al., Welfare Reform: An Overview of Effects to Date, January 2001, Policy Brief No. 1, Brookings Institution.

[5] Tamar Lewin, "Surprising Result in Welfare-to-Work Studies," The New York Times, July 31, 2001, p. A16.

[6] Pamela Morris et al., "Welfare Reform's Effects on Children," Poverty Research News, Joint Center for Poverty Research, July-August 2001, pp. 5-9; www.jcpr.org.

[7] Richard Bavier, "An Early Look at Welfare Reform in the Survey of Income and Program Participation," Monthly Labor Review, forthcoming.

[8] House Ways and Means Committee, 2000 Greenbook.

[9] Kaus spoke at a Brookings Institution forum on May 17, 2001, in Washington, D.C.: "Beyond Welfare Reform — Next Steps for Combating Poverty in the U.S." Transcript at www.brook.edu/com/transcripts/20010517/htm

[10] Mickey Kaus, "Further Steps toward the Work-Ethic State," Brookings Review, summer 2001, pp. 43-47.

[11] Ron Haskins, "Giving is Not Enough," Brookings Review, summer 2001, pp. 13-15.

[12] Christopher Jencks and Joseph Swingle, "Without a Net," The Prospect Online, Jan. 3, 2000; www.prospect.org.

[13] Kathryn Edin and Laura Lein, Making Ends Meet: How Single Mothers Survive Welfare and Low-Wage Work (1997), pp. 63-64. National Survey data cited in Edin is from the Panel Study of Income Dynamics.

[14] Wendell Primus, "What Next for Welfare Reform? A Vision for Assisting Families," Brookings Review, summer 2001, pp. 17-19.

[15] Ibid.

[16] Douglas J. Besharov and Peter Germanis, "Welfare Reform-Four Years Later," The Public Interest, summer 2000, pp. 17-35.

[17] Haskins, op. cit.

[18] June E. O'Neill and M. Anne Hill, Gaining Ground? Measuring the Impact of Welfare Reform on Welfare and Work, July 2001, The Manhattan Institute; www.manhattan-institute.org

[19] The White House, "The Effects of Welfare Policy and the Economic Expansion on Welfare Caseloads: An Update," Council of Economic Advisers, August 3, 1999; http://clinton4.nara.gov/WH/EOP/CEA/html/welfare/.

[20] Wendell E. Primus, Center on Budget and Policy Priorities, "TANF Reauthorization," NGA Briefing, June 6, 2001, Washington, D.C. According to Primus, counting the additional income received by low-income families from tax and government benefits, the percentage of children in poverty is even lower — 12.9 percent in 1999, compared to 20 percent in 1993.

[21] Ibid.

[22] Ibid.

[23] Haskings et al., op. cit., p. 5.

[24] Pamela Loprest, How are Families that Left Welfare Doing? A Comparison of Early and Recent Welfare Leavers, April 2001, pp. 5-6.

[25] Ibid., p. 6.

[26] Ron Haskins, Isabel Sawhill and Kent Weaver, "Welfare Reform Reauthorization: An Overview of Problems and Issues," Welfare Reform and Beyond Policy Brief No. 2, January 2001, Brookings Institution.

[27] Maria Cancian et al., "Before and After TANF: The Economic Well-Being of Women Leaving Welfare," Institute for Research on Poverty, Special Report No. 17, May 2000.

[28] Haskins et al., op. cit., Policy Brief No. 2, p. 4.

[29] Center for the Study of Women in Society, op cit.

[30] Haskins et al., op. cit., Policy Brief No. 1, pp. 6-7.

[31] "Report of the Committee on Economic Security," January 1935, cited in John E. Hansan and Robert Morris, eds., Welfare Reform, 1996-2000 (1999), p. 6.

[32] Gordon Berlin, "Tug-of-War," Brookings Review, summer 2001, p. 35.

[33] Ibid., pp. 9-10.

[34] Besharov, op. cit., p. 18.

[35] Ibid., pp. 18-19.

[36] Berlin, op. cit.

[37] In 1992, 38.9 percent of families receiving AFDC were white, 37 percent were black and 17.8 percent were Hispanic. See Hansan and Morris, op. cit., p. 9.

[38] Manpower Demonstration Research Corporation, "Big Cities and Welfare Reform: Early Implementation and Ethnographic Findings from the Project on Devolution and Urban Change," April 1999; www.mdrc.org.

[39] Besharov, op. cit., p. 24.

[40] The hourly wage rate for the 20th percentile rose from $6.58 in 1993 to $7.13 in 2000 for female workers. See Primus, op. cit.

[41] Besharov, op. cit.

[42] For background, see Kathy Koch, "Child Poverty," The CQ Researcher, April 7, 2000, p. 295.

[43] Haskins, op. cit., p, 4.

[44] Berlin, op. cit., p. 38.

[45] Ibid.

[46] Tommy G. Thompson, "Welfare Reform's Next Step," Brookings Review, summer 2001, pp. 2-3.

[47] See testimony of Theodora Ooms, senior policy analyst, Center for Law and Social Policy, before the House Committee on Ways and Means Subcommittee on Human Resources, May 22, 2001; www.clasp.org/marriagepolicy/toomstestimony.htm.

Should the government encourage welfare recipients to marry?

WADE F. HORN
*Assistant Secretary for Children and Families,
Department of Health and Human Services*

FROM THE *BROOKINGS REVIEW*, SUMMER 2001

*m*arriage is in trouble, especially in low-income communities. It is no accident that communities with lower marriage rates have higher rates of social pathology. Unfortunately, [federal and state governments] have been reluctant even to mention the word, let alone do something to encourage it. Public policy . . . needs to show that [society] values marriage by rewarding those who choose it. . . .

Congress should make clear that the intent of the 1996 [welfare reform] law was to promote marriage, not cohabitation or visits by non-resident parents. . . .

Second, states should be required to indicate how they will use Temporary Aid to Needy Families (TANF) funds to encourage marriage. Anyone who has ever spent any time in a state welfare office can attest to the . . . not-so-subtle message that marriage is neither expected nor valued.

Third, Congress should reduce the financial disincentives for marriage [by requiring states] to eliminate the anti-marriage rules . . . in the old [welfare] program. The law that established the TANF block grant to states allowed, but did not require, states to eliminate the old rules. Congress should also reduce or eliminate financial penalties for marriage in other programs, like the earned-income tax credit.

Fourth, Congress should implement marriage incentives, [such as] suspending collection of child-support arrearages if the biological parents get married . . . and requiring states to provide a cash bonus to single welfare mothers who marry the child's father.

Fifth, Congress should fund programs that enhance the marital and parenting skills of high-risk families. Many men and women lack [such skills] because they grew up in broken homes without positive role models [or] . . . had inadequate or abusive parents themselves. Congress should provide resources to religious and civic groups offering meaningful premarital education to low-income couples applying for or on public assistance.

Finally, [Congress should] earmark some TANF funds for a broad-based public awareness campaign to publicize the importance of marriage and the skills necessary to form and sustain healthy marriages.

When it comes to promoting healthy, mutually satisfying marriages, doing nothing hasn't worked. Perhaps doing something might.

**JACQUELINE K. PAYNE, POLICY ATTORNEY, AND
MARTHA DAVIS, LEGAL DIRECTOR**
NOW Legal Defense and Education Fund

**TESTIMONY SUBMITTED TO HOUSE WAYS AND MEANS HUMAN
RESOURCES SUBCOMMITTEE HEARING, JUNE 28, 2001**

*m*arriage is not the solution for everyone, nor is it the solution to poverty. Our country consists of diverse family structures: those in which parents are married, single, remarried, gay and lesbian, foster and adoptive. These families . . . deserve to be valued and respected as they are.

Marriage is a constitutionally protected choice. The Supreme Court has long recognized an individual's right to privacy regarding decisions to marry and reproduce as "one of the basic civil rights of man, fundamental to our very existence and survival." (*Skinner v. Oklahoma*) Significantly, this constitutional right equally protects the choice not to marry. This right of privacy protects an individual from substantial governmental intrusion into this private decision. Marriage promotion mandates in [proposed] bills essentially coerce economically vulnerable individuals to trade in their fundamental right to privacy regarding marital decisions in exchange for receiving job and life-skills training. . . .

Supportive services should be made available to all families, regardless of their marital status or family composition, including services to help improve employment opportunities, budget finances, promote non-violent behavior, improve relationships and provide financial support to children. Where parents choose to engage in an intimate relationship, resources should be available to help ensure that it is a safe, loving and healthy one.

Promotion of marriage requirements endangers lives. Violence against women both makes women poor and keeps them poor. Over 50 percent of homeless women and children cite domestic violence as the reason they are homeless. Many depend on welfare to provide an escape from the abuse. [Studies] demonstrate that a significant proportion of the welfare caseload — consistently between 15 percent and 25 percent — consists of current victims of serious domestic violence.

For these women and their children, the cost of freedom and safety has been poverty. Marriage is not the solution to their economic insecurity. For them marriage could mean death; it will almost undoubtedly mean economic dependence on the abuser or economic instability due to the abuse.

Where the very lives of these women and children are at stake, we cannot afford to encourage the involvement of [abusive] fathers without taking every reasonable precaution, and without recognizing that in some cases father involvement is not appropriate.

[48] Anderson quote is from the May 17 Brookings forum; www.brook.edu/com/transcripts/20010517.htm.

[49] Wade F. Horn and Isabel V. Sawhill, *Making Room for Daddy: Fathers, Marriage, and Welfare Reform*, Brookings Institution, written for the New World of Welfare Conference, February 2001, p. 2.

[50] This analysis comes from a new study "Fragile Families and Child Well-Being," which will follow 3,600 children born to unmarried parents and 1,100 children born to married parents in 20 cities. Information about the study is at http://opr.princeton.edu/circw/ff.

[51] See Sheila R. Zedlewski and Donald W. Alderson, "Before and After Reform: How Have Families on Welfare Changed?" The Urban Institute, April 2001.

[52] "A National Survey of American Attitudes Towards Low-Wage Workers and Welfare Reform," April 27-30, 2000, by Lake Snell Perry and Associates; http://www.jff.org/pdfs%20and%20downloads/FinalSurveyData.pdf.

[53] See Robert Greenstein, *The Changes the New Tax Law Makes in Refundable Tax Credits for Low-Income Working Families*, Center on Budget and Policy Priorities, June 18, 2001; http://www.cbpp.org/6-14-01tax.htm.

[54] See Kathy Koch, "Hunger in America," *The CQ Researcher*, Dec. 22, 2000, pp. 1048-1051.

FOR MORE INFORMATION

Brookings Institution, 1775 Massachusetts Ave., N.W., Washington, D.C. 20036; (202) 797-6105; www.brookings.edu/wrb. This think tank's Welfare and Beyond project sponsors forums and issues reports on controversial issues relating to welfare reform and the upcoming reauthorization bill.

Center on Budget and Policy Priorities, 820 First St., N.E., Suite 510, Washington, D.C. 20002; (202) 408-1080; www.cbpp.org. This nonpartisan research group analyzes government policies affecting low-income Americans and has been in the forefront in arguing that the poorest families are worse off after welfare reform.

Center for Community Change/National Campaign for Jobs and Income Support, 1000 Wisconsin Ave., N.W., Washington, D.C. 20007; www.communitychange.org. The center and the National Campaign represent grass-roots welfare-rights advocates across the country and have released reports critical of state welfare-reform efforts.

Center on Law and Social Policy, 1015 15th St., N.W., Washington, D.C. 20005; (202) 906-8000; www.clasp.org. CLASP is a research and advocacy organization for the poor that provides analyses of many welfare-related issues from a perspective that is critical of welfare reform.

Heritage Foundation, 214 Massachusetts Ave., N.E., Washington, D.C. 20002; (202) 546-4400; www.heritage.org. This conservative think tank has been a vocal critic of welfare and a supporter of policies to encourage marriage in welfare-prone communities.

House Human Resources Subcommittee, House Ways and Means Committee, U.S. House of Representatives; waysandmeans.house.gov/humres.htm This subcommittee has primary jurisdiction over welfare in the House. Its Web site includes links to hearing documents and witness testimony.

Joint Center for Poverty Research, Northwestern University/University of Chicago, 2046 Sheridan Rd., Evanston, Ill. 60208; (773) 271-0611; www.jcpr.org. The center summarizes its own and others' research on welfare reform in its newsletter.

Manpower Demonstration Research Corp. (MDRC), 16 E. 34th St., New York, N.Y. 10016; (212) 532-3200; www.mdrc.org. This nonprofit, nonpartisan research organization has a reputation for objective, influential studies of welfare and welfare reform.

Senate Finance Committee, U.S. Senate; www.senate.gov/~finance/. The committee with primary jurisdiction over welfare reform in the Senate is expected to hold hearings on welfare reform as the reauthorization deadline approaches.

Urban Institute, 2100 M St., N.W., Washington, D.C. 20037; (202) 833-7200; www.urban.org. This nonpartisan think tank has issued numerous influential reports regarding welfare reform.

U.S. Department of Health and Human Services, Administration for Children and Families (ACF), 901 D St., S.W., Washington, D.C. 20447; (202) 401-9215; www.acf.dhhs.gov. ACF is the federal agency with primary jurisdiction over temporary aid to needy families. Its welfare reform Web site includes links to HHS policy documents and data.

Bibliography

Selected Sources Used

Books

Edin, Kathryn, and Laura Lein, *Making Ends Meet*, Russell Sage Foundation, 1997.

Hundreds of interviews convince the authors that poor single mothers are usually worse off once they leave welfare for low-wage jobs.

Articles

Besharov, Douglas J., and Peter Germanis, "Welfare Reform — Four Years Later," *The Public Interest*, summer 2000, pp. 17-35.

Besharov, a scholar at the American Enterprise Institute, and Germanis, assistant director of the University of Maryland's Welfare Reform Academy, largely credit falling welfare rolls to the good economy and government supports to the working poor.

Boo, Katherine, "After Welfare," *The New Yorker*, April 9, 2001, pp. 93-107.

The profile of this single mother who made it off welfare by working two full-time jobs has raised questions about whether children and teens are better off when their mothers are in the work force.

Haskins, Ron, "Giving is not Enough," *Brookings Review*, summer 2001, pp. 12-15.

Haskins, a principal aide to House Republicans in the crafting of the welfare reform bill, argues that the 1996 law produced the reductions in the caseload and record high employment levels among single mothers.

Primus, Wendell, "What Next for Welfare Reform?" *Brookings Review*, summer 2001, pp. 16-19.

Primus, who resigned in protest from the Clinton administration over the 1996 welfare reform law and is now at the liberal Center for Budget and Policy Priorities, argues that the reauthorization bill should shift its focus from reducing caseloads to reducing poverty.

Sawhill, Isabel, "From Welfare to Work," *Brookings Review*, summer 2001, pp. 4-8.

In this special issue devoted to welfare reform, the senior Brookings Institution fellow summarizes the broad range of views on welfare reform.

Sherman, Amy L., "The Lessons of W-2," *The Public Interest*, summer 2000, pp. 36-48.

This positive report assesses Wisconsin's work-based welfare experience, which reduced welfare caseloads by more than 80 percent.

Reports and Studies

Boushey, Heather, and Bethney Gundersen, "When Work Just Isn't Enough: Measuring Hardships Faced by Families after Moving from Welfare to Work," Economic Policy Institute, June 2001. http://epinet.org

Families who have left welfare experience levels of hardship similar to other poor families.

Center for the Study of Women in Society, Welfare Research Team, University of Oregon, "Oregon Families Who Left Temporary Assistance to Needy Families (TANF) or Food Stamps: A Study of Economic and Family Well-Being from 1998 to 2000," January 2001.

About half the women had incomes below the poverty level a year and a half after leaving welfare. Volume 2 contains individual profiles of women interviewed.

Haskins, Ron, Isabel Sawhill and Kent Weaver, "Welfare Reform: An Overview of Effects to Date," Policy Brief No. 1, The Brookings Institution, January 2001.

A former architect of the welfare-reform bill and a liberal economist summarize the effects of the 1996 welfare reform law.

Haskins, Ron, Isabel Sawhill and Kent Weaver, "Welfare Reform Reauthorization: An Overview of Problems and Issues," Policy Brief No. 2, The Brookings Institution, January 2001.

A good summary of issues likely to be debated in Congress during the welfare-reform bill's reauthorization.

Horn, Wade F., and Isabel V. Sawhill, "Making Room for Daddy: Fathers, Marriage, and Welfare Reform," The Brookings Institution, February 2001.

Horn, President Bush's new assistant secretary for children and families, and Brookings scholar Sawhill argue that public policy must help "bring fathers back into the family picture."

Loprest, Pamela, "How are Families that Left Welfare Doing? A Comparison of Early and Recent Welfare Leavers," The Urban Institute, April 2001.

This report finds little evidence that recent welfare leavers are less capable of working than those who left several years earlier.

Rector, Robert, "Issues 2000, Welfare: Broadening the Reform," Heritage Foundation.

A scholar at the conservative foundation argues that the welfare system "bribed individuals" into having children out of wedlock.

7   Affirmative Action

KENNETH JOST

Jennifer Gratz wanted to go to the University of Michigan's flagship Ann Arbor campus as soon as she began thinking about college. "It's the best school in Michigan to go to," she explains.

The white suburban teenager's dream turned to disappointment in April 1995, however, when the university told her that even though she was "well qualified," she had been rejected for one of the nearly 4,000 slots in the incoming freshman class.

Gratz was convinced something was wrong. "I knew that the University of Michigan was giving preference to minorities," she says today. "If you give extra points for being of a particular race, then you're not giving applicants an equal opportunity."

Gratz, now 24, has a degree from Michigan's less prestigious Dearborn campus and a job in San Diego. She is also the lead plaintiff in a lawsuit that is shaping up as a decisive battle in the long-simmering conflict over racial preferences in college admissions.

On the opposite side of Gratz's federal court lawsuit is Lee Bollinger, Michigan's highly respected president and a staunch advocate of race-conscious admissions policies.

"Racial and ethnic diversity is one part of the core liberal educational goal," Bollinger says. "People have different educational experiences when they grow up as an African-American, Hispanic or white."

Gratz won a partial victory in December 2000 when a federal judge agreed that the university's admissions system in 1995 was illegal. But the

From *The CQ Researcher,*
September 21, 2001.

First-year engineering students at the University of Michigan-Ann Arbor gather during welcome week last year. A federal judge ruled in December 2000 that the school's race-based admissions system in 1995 was illegal but that a revised system adopted later was constitutional. The case is widely expected to reach the Supreme Court.

ruling came too late to help her, and Judge Patrick Duggan went on to rule that the revised system the university adopted in 1998 passed constitutional muster.

Some three months later, however, another federal judge ruled in a separate case that the admissions system currently used at the university's law school is illegal. Judge Bernard Friedman said the law school's admissions policies were "practically indistinguishable from a quota system."

The two cases — *Gratz v. Bollinger* and *Grutter v. Bollinger* — were argued together in December 2001 before the federal appeals court in Cincinnati.[1] And opposing lawyers and many legal observers expect the two cases to reach the Supreme Court in a potentially decisive showdown. "One of these cases could well end up in the Supreme Court," says Elizabeth Barry, the university's associate vice president and deputy general counsel, who is coordinating the defense of the two suits.

"We hope the Supreme Court resolves this issue relatively soon," says

Michael Rosman, attorney for the Center for Individual Rights in Washington, which represents plaintiffs in both cases. "It is fair to say that there is some uncertainty in the law in this area."

The legal uncertainty stems from the long time span — 23 years — since the Supreme Court's only previous full-scale ruling on race-based admissions policies: the famous *Bakke* decision. In that fractured ruling, *University of California Regents v. Bakke,* the high court in 1978 ruled that fixed racial quotas were illegal but allowed the use of race as one factor in college admissions.[2]

Race-based admissions policies are widespread in U.S. higher education today — "well accepted and entrenched," according to Sheldon Steinbach, general counsel of the pro-affirmative action American Council on Education.

Roger Clegg, general counsel of the Center for Equal Opportunity, which opposes racial preferences, agrees with Steinbach but from a different perspective. "Evidence is overwhelming that racial and ethnic discrimination occurs frequently in public college and university admissions," Clegg says.[3]

Higher-education organizations and traditional civil rights groups say racial admissions policies are essential to ensure racial and ethnic diversity at the nation's elite universities — including the most selective state schools, such as Michigan's Ann Arbor campus. "The overwhelming majority of students who apply to highly selective institutions are still white," says Theodore Shaw, associate director-counsel of the NAACP Legal Defense Fund, which represents minority students who intervened in the two cases. "If we are not con-

Despite Progress, Minorities Still Trail Whites

A larger percentage of young adult African-Americans and Hispanics have completed college today than 20 years ago. But college completion rates for African-Americans and Hispanics continue to be significantly lower than the rate for whites. Today, the national college completion rate — 30 percent — is more than triple the rate in 1950.

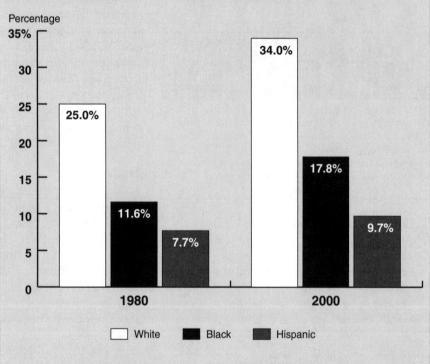

Percentages of College Graduates, Ages 25–29

Percentage

- 1980: White 25.0%, Black 11.6%, Hispanic 7.7%
- 2000: White 34.0%, Black 17.8%, Hispanic 9.7%

White / Black / Hispanic

Source: U.S. Department of Education, "Digest of Education Statistics," 2001 edition.

scious of selecting minority students, they're not going to be there."

Opponents, however, say racial preferences are wrong in terms of law and social policy. "It's immoral. It's illegal. It stigmatizes the beneficiary. It encourages hypocrisy. It lowers standards. It encourages the use of stereotypes," Clegg says. "There are all kinds of social costs, and we don't think the benefits outweigh those costs."

The race-based admissions policies now in use around the country evolved gradually since the passage of federal civil rights legislation in the mid-

1960s. By 1970, the phrase "affirmative action" had become common usage to describe efforts to increase the number of African-Americans (and, later, Hispanics) in U.S. workplaces and on college campuses.[4] Since then, the proportions of African-Americans and Hispanics on college campuses have increased, though they are still underrepresented in terms of their respective proportions in the U.S. population. (*See chart, p. 129.*)

Michigan's efforts range from uncontroversial minority-outreach programs to an admissions system that ex-

plicitly takes an applicant's race or ethnicity into account in deciding whether to accept or reject the applicant. The system formerly used by the undergraduate College of Literature, Science and the Arts had separate grids for white and minority applicants. The current system uses a numerical rating that includes a 20-point bonus (out of a total possible score of 150) for "underrepresented minorities" — African-Americans, Hispanics and Native Americans (but not Asian-Americans). The law school's system — devised in 1992 — is aimed at producing a minority enrollment of about 10 percent to 12 percent of the entering class.

Critics of racial preferences say they are not opposed to affirmative action. "Certainly there are some positive aspects to affirmative action," Rosman says, citing increased recruitment of minorities and reassessment by colleges of criteria for evaluating applicants. But, he adds, "To the extent that it suggests that they have carte blanche to discriminate between people on the basis of race, it's not a good thing."

Higher-education officials respond that they should have discretion to explicitly consider race — along with a host of other factors — to ensure a fully representative student body and provide the best learning environment for an increasingly multicultural nation and world. "Having a diverse student body contributes to the educational process and is necessary in the 21st-century global economy," Steinbach says.

As opposing lawyers prepare for the appellate arguments next month in the University of Michigan cases, here are some of the major questions being debated:

Should colleges use race-based admissions policies to remedy discrimination against minorities?

The University of Michigan relies heavily on high school students' scores on standardized tests in evaluating applications — tests that have been widely criticized as biased against African-Americans and other minorities. It gives preferences to children of Michigan alumni — who are disproportionately white — as well as to applicants from "underrepresented" parts of the state, such as Michigan's predominantly white Upper Peninsula.

Even apart from the university's past record of racial segregation, those factors could be cited as evidence that Michigan's current admissions policies are racially discriminatory because they have a "disparate impact" on minorities. And the Supreme Court, in *Bakke*, said that racial classifications were constitutional if they were used as a remedy for proven discrimination.

But Michigan is not defending its racial admissions policies on that basis. "Every public university has its share of decisions that we're now embarrassed by," President Bollinger concedes. But the university is defending its use of race — along with an array of other factors — only as a method of producing racial diversity, not as a way to remedy current or past discrimination.

Some civil rights advocates, however, insist that colleges and universities are still guilty of racially biased policies that warrant — even require — explicit racial preferences as corrective measures.

"Universities should use race-conscious admissions as a way of countering both past and ongoing ways in which the admission process continues to engage in practices that perpetuate racism or are unconsciously racist," says Charles Lawrence, a professor at Georgetown University Law Center in Washington.

Opponents of racial preferences, however, say colleges should be very wary about justifying such policies on the basis of past or current discrimination against minorities. "The Supreme Court has been pretty clear that you can't use the justification of past societal discrimination as a ground for a race-based admissions policy at an institution that did not itself discriminate,"

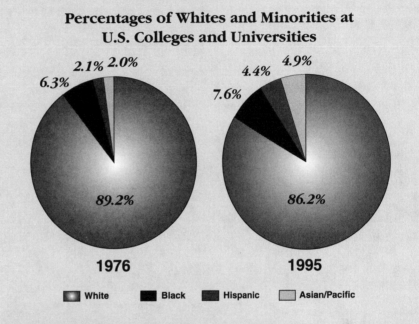

Minority Enrollments Increased

African-Americans and Hispanics make up a larger percentage of the U.S. college population today than they did in 1976, but they are still underrepresented in comparison to their proportion of the total U.S. population. Hispanics comprise 12.5 percent of the population, African-Americans 12.3 percent.

Percentages of Whites and Minorities at U.S. Colleges and Universities

2.1% 2.0%
6.3%
89.2%
1976

4.4% 4.9%
7.6%
86.2%
1995

White Black Hispanic Asian/Pacific

Note: Percentages do not add to 100 due to rounding.

Source: U.S. Dept. of Education, "Digest of Education Statistics," 2001 edition .

says Stephen Balch, president of the National Association of Scholars, a Princeton, N.J.-based group of academics opposed to racial preferences.

Balch defends alumni preferences, the most frequently mentioned example of an admissions policy that disadvantages minority applicants. "It's not at all unreasonable for colleges and universities to cultivate their alumni base," Balch says. In any event, he adds, "As student bodies change, the effect of that policy will change."

For his part, Rosman of the Center for Individual Rights says racial preferences are not justified even if colleges are wrong to grant alumni preferences or to rely so heavily on standardized test scores. "If you have criteria that discriminate and are not

educationally justified, then the appropriate response is to get rid of those criteria, not to use 'two wrongs make a right,'" Rosman says.

Minority students intervened in both the undergraduate and law school suits to present evidence of discrimination by the university and to use that evidence to justify the racial admissions policies. In the undergraduate case, evidence showed that the university refused to desegregate fraternities and sororities until the 1960s, allowed white students to refuse to room with black students and did not hire its first black professor until 1967. The evidence also showed that black students reported continuing discrimination and racial hostility through the 1980s and into the '90s.

In a Feb. 26 ruling, Judge Duggan acknowledged the evidence but rejected it as a justification for the admissions policies. The racial segregation occurred too long ago to be a reason for current policies, Duggan said. He also rejected the minority students' argument that the racial impact of alumni pref-

Should colleges use race-based admissions policies to promote diversity in their student populations?

Michigan's high schools graduated some 100,000 students in 1999. Out of that number, only 327 African-American students had a B-plus average

minority applicants, Barry says the number of African-American and Hispanic students "would drop dramatically" from the current level of about 13 percent of undergraduates to "somewhere around 5 percent."

Opponents of racial preferences dismiss the warnings. "It's certainly not inevitable that the number of students from racial and ethnic minorities will decline" under a color-blind system, Rosman says. In any event, he says that diversity is "not a sufficiently powerful goal to discriminate and treat people differently on the basis of race."

The dispute between supporters and opponents of racial admissions policies turns in part on two somewhat rarefied issues. Supporters claim to have social-science evidence to show that racial and ethnic diversity produces quantifiable educational benefits for all students — evidence that opponents deride as dubious at best. (*See story, p. 138.*) The opposing camps also differ on the question of whether the *Bakke* decision allows colleges to use diversity as the kind of "compelling government interest" needed to satisfy the so-called strict-scrutiny standard of constitutional review. (*See story, p. 132*)

Apart from those specialized disputes, opponents of racial preferences argue simply that they constitute a form of stereotyping and discrimination. "We don't believe that there is a black outlook or an Asian outlook or a white experience or a Hispanic experience," Clegg says. "Students are individuals, and they should be treated as individuals, not as fungible members of racial and ethnic groups."

Some critics — including a few African-Americans — also say racial preferences "stigmatize" the intended beneficiaries by creating the impression that they could not be successful without being given some advantage over whites. "There is no way that a young black at an Ivy League university is going to get credit for

---

Gratz v. Bollinger: Race and College Admissions

Jennifer Gratz, a white woman, sued the University of Michigan contending she was improperly denied admission because of race. The lawsuit is shaping up as a key battle in the long-simmering conflict over racial preferences in college admissions.

"I see benefits from different opinions, different thoughts on any number of subjects. But I don't think that's necessarily race coming through. I don't think like every other white person. . . . Your race doesn't mean that you're going to think this way or that way."

Jennifer Gratz, B.S., University of Michigan, Dearborn

"You get a better education and a better society in an environment where you are mixing with lots of different people — people from different parts of the country, people from different parts of the socioeconomic system, people from abroad, and people from different races and ethnicities."

Lee Bollinger, President, University of Michigan

---

erences, standardized test scores and other admissions criteria justified preferences for minority applicants.

Judge Friedman rejected similar arguments in the final portion of his March 26 ruling in the law school case. "This is a social and political matter, which calls for social and political solutions," Friedman wrote. "The solution is not for the law school, or any other state institution, to prefer some applicants over others because of race."

and an SAT score above 1,000 — the kind of record needed to make them strong contenders for admission to the University of Michigan's Ann Arbor campus based on those factors alone.

University officials cite that stark statistic to underline the difficulty they face in admitting a racially diverse student body — and to justify their policy of giving minority applicants special consideration in the admissions process. Without the current bonus for [doing well]," says Shelby Steele, a prominent black critic of racial preferences and a research fellow at the Hoover Institution at Stanford University. "There's no way that he's going to feel his achievements are his own."

Supporters of racial admission policies, however, say that race plays an independent and important role in American society that colleges are entitled to take into account. "It is reasonable for educational institutions to believe that race is not a proxy for something else," Bollinger says. "It is a defining experience in American life — and therefore an important one for this goal" of educational diversity.

White supporters of affirmative action generally deny or minimize any supposed stigmatization from race-conscious policies. Some blacks acknowledge some stigmatizing effects, but blame white racism rather than affirmative action. "The stigmatizing beliefs about people of color," Professor Lawrence writes, "have their origin not in affirmative action programs but in the cultural belief system of white supremacy." [5]

The two judges in the Michigan cases reached different conclusions on the diversity issue. In his ruling in the undergraduate case, Duggan agreed with the university's argument that a "racially and ethnically diverse student body produces significant education benefits, such that diversity, in the context of higher education, constitutes a compelling governmental interest under strict scrutiny."

Ruling in the law school case, Judge Friedman acknowledged that racial diversity may provide "educational and societal benefits," though he also called for drawing "a distinction . . . between viewpoint diversity and racial diversity." Based on his interpretation of *Bakke*, however, Friedman said these "important and laudable" benefits did not amount to a compelling interest sufficient to justify the law school's use of race in admissions decisions.

Should colleges adopt other policies to try to increase minority enrollment?

Texas and Florida have a different approach to ensuring a racial mix in their state university systems. Texas' "10 percent plan" — adopted in 1997 under then-Gov. George W. Bush — promises a spot in the state university to anyone who graduates in the top 10 percent of any high schools in the state. Florida's plan — adopted in 1999 under Gov. Jeb Bush, the president's brother — makes the same commitment to anyone in the top 20 percent.

The plans are drawing much attention and some favorable comment as an ostensibly race-neutral alternative to racial preferences. But major participants on both sides of the debate over racial admissions policies view the idea with skepticism.

"It's silly to suggest that all high schools are equal in terms of the quality of their student body," Clegg says. "And therefore it makes no sense to have an across-the-board rule that the top 10 percent of every high school is going to be admitted."

Both Clegg and Rosman also say that a 10 percent-type plan is dubious if it is adopted to circumvent a ban on explicit racial preferences. "Any neutral policy that is just a pretext for discrimination would have to survive strict scrutiny," Rosman says.

Supporters of race-based admissions are also unenthusiastic. "The only reason they work is because we have segregated high schools, segregated communities," Shaw says. "From a philosophical standpoint, I'd rather deal with race in a more honest and upfront way and make a more principled approach to these issues."

In the Michigan lawsuits, the university cited testimony from a prominent supporter of racial admissions policies in opposition to 10 percent-type plans. "Treating all applicants alike if they finished above a given high school class rank provides a spurious

form of equality that is likely to damage the academic profile of the overall class of students admitted to selective institutions," said former Princeton University President William G. Bowen, now president of the Andrew W. Mellon Foundation in New York City.

Rosman looks more favorably on another alternative: giving preferences to applicants who come from disadvantaged socioeconomic backgrounds. "It's not a bad idea to take into account a person's ability to overcome obstacles," he says. "That's useful in assessing a person's qualifications."

In his testimony, however, Bowen also criticized that approach. Youngsters from poor black and Hispanic families are "much less likely" to excel in school than those from poor white families, Bowen said. On that basis, he predicted that a "class-based" rather than race-based admissions policy "would substantially reduce the minority enrollments at selective institutions."

For its part, the university stresses that its current system gives up to 20 points to an applicant based on socioeconomic disadvantage — the same number given to minority applicants. "We consider a number of factors in order to enroll a diverse student body," Barry says, "because race is not the only element that's important to diversity in education."

In their rulings, Duggan and Friedman both favorably noted a number of alternatives to race-based admissions policies. Friedman suggested the law school could have increased recruiting efforts or decreased the emphasis on undergraduate grades and scores on the Law School Aptitude Test. He also said the school could have used a lottery for all qualified applicants or admitted some fixed number or percentage of top graduates from various colleges and universities. Friedman said the law school's "apparent failure to investigate alternative means for increasing minority enroll-

What Does *Bakke* Mean? Two Judges Disagree

The Supreme Court's 1978 decision to prohibit fixed racial quotas in colleges and universities but to allow the use of race as one factor in admissions was hailed by some people at the time as a Solomon-like compromise.

But today the meaning of the high court's famous *Bakke* decision is sharply disputed. And the disagreement lies at the heart of conflicting rulings by two federal judges in Michigan on the legality of racial preferences used at the University of Michigan's flagship Ann Arbor campus.

In upholding the flexible race-based admissions system used by the undergraduate College of Literature, Science and the Arts in December, Judge Patrick Duggan said *Bakke* means that colleges can evaluate white and minority applicants differently in order to enroll a racially and ethnically diverse student body.

But Judge Bernard Friedman rejected that widely held interpretation in a March 27 decision striking down the law school's use of race in admissions. Friedman — like Duggan an appointee of President Ronald Reagan — said that racial and ethnic diversity did not qualify as a "compelling governmental interest" needed under the so-called strict scrutiny constitutional standard to justify a race-based government policy.

The differing interpretations stem from the Supreme Court's unusual 4-1-4 vote in the case, *University of California Regents v. Bakke*. Four of the justices found the quota system used by the UC-Davis Medical School — reserving 16 out of 100 seats for minorities — to be a violation of the federal civil rights law prohibiting racial discrimination in federally funded institutions. Four others — led by the liberal Justice William J. Brennan Jr. — voted to reject Alan Bakke's challenge to the system.

In the pivotal opinion, Justice Lewis F. Powell Jr. found the UC-Davis admissions system to be a violation of the constitutional requirement of equal protection but said race could be used as a "plus" factor in admissions decisions. The "attainment of a diverse student body," Powell wrote, "clearly is a constitutionally permissible goal for an institution of higher education."

Under Supreme Court case law, it takes a majority of the justices — five — to produce a "holding" that can serve as a precedent for future cases. In a fractured ruling, the court's holding is said to be the "narrowest" rationale endorsed by five justices. But Brennan's group did not explicitly address the question of diversity. Instead, they said that race-based admissions decisions were justified to remedy past discrimination — a proposition that Powell also endorsed.

Critics of racial preferences in recent years have argued that the Brennan group's silence on diversity means that they did not join Powell's reasoning. On that basis, these critics say, Powell's opinion cannot be viewed as a controlling precedent. They won an important victory when the federal appeals court in New Orleans adopted that reasoning in the so-called *Hopwood* case in 1996 striking down the University of Texas Law School's racial preferences.

In his ruling in the Michigan law school case, Friedman also agreed with this revisionist view of *Bakke*. "The diversity rationale articulated by Justice Powell is neither narrower nor broader than the remedial rationale articulated by the Brennan group," Friedman wrote. "They are completely different rationales, neither one of which is subsumed within the other."

But in the undergraduate case, Duggan followed the previous interpretation of *Bakke*. Brennan's "silence regarding the diversity interest in *Bakke* was not an implicit rejection of such an interest, but rather, an implicit approval of such an interest," Duggan wrote.

The two judges also differed on how to interpret later Supreme Court decisions. Duggan cited Brennan's 1990 majority opinion in a case upholding racial preferences in broadcasting — *Metro Broadcasting, Inc. v. Federal Communications Commission* — as supporting the use of diversity to justify racial policies. But Friedman said other recent rulings showed that the Supreme Court had become much more skeptical of racial policies than it had been in 1978. Among the decisions he cited was the 1995 ruling, *Adarand Constructors v. Peña* that overruled the *Metro Broadcasting* holding.

Reporters follow Allan Bakke on his first day at the University of California-Davis Medical School on Sept. 25, 1978. The Supreme Court ordered him admitted after ruling that the school violated his rights by maintaining a fixed quota for minority applicants.

AP Photo/Walt Zeboski

ment" was one factor in rejecting the school's admissions policies.

For his part, Duggan noted the possibility of using race-neutral policies to increase minority enrollment when he rejected the minority students' critique of such policies as alumni preferences. "If the current selection criteria have a discriminatory impact on minority applicants," Duggan wrote, "it seems to this court that the narrowly tailored remedy would be to remove or redistribute such criteria to accommodate for socially and economically disadvantaged applicants of all races and ethnicities, not to add another suspect criteria [sic] to the list." ■

BACKGROUND

Unequal Opportunity

African-Americans and other racial and ethnic minority groups have been underrepresented on college campuses throughout U.S. history. The civil rights revolution has effectively dismantled most legal barriers to higher education for minorities. But the social and economic inequalities that persist between white Americans and racial and ethnic minority groups continue to make the goal of equal opportunity less than reality for many African-Americans and Hispanics.

The legal battles that ended mandatory racial segregation in the United States began with higher education nearly two decades before the Supreme Court's historic ruling in *Brown v. Board of Education*.[6] In the first of the rulings that ended the doctrine of "separate but equal," the court in 1938 ruled that Missouri violated a black law school applicant's equal protection rights by offering to pay his tuition to an out-of-state school rather than admit him

to the state's all-white law school.

The court followed with a pair of rulings in 1950 that similarly found states guilty of violating black students' rights to equal higher education. Texas was ordered to admit a black student to the state's all-white law school rather than force him to attend an inferior all-black school. And Oklahoma was found to have discriminated against a black student by admitting him to a previously all-white state university but denying him the opportunity to use all its facilities.

At the time of these decisions, whites had substantially greater educational opportunities than African-Americans. As of 1950, a majority of white Americans ages 25–29 — 56 percent — had completed high school, compared with only 24 percent of African-Americans. Eight percent of whites in that age group had completed college compared with fewer than 3 percent of blacks. Most of the African-American college graduates had attended all-black institutions: either private colleges established for blacks or racially segregated state universities.

The Supreme Court's 1954 decision in *Brown* to begin dismantling racial segregation in elementary and secondary education started to reduce the inequality in educational opportunities for whites and blacks, but changes were slow. It was not until 1970 that a majority of African-Americans ages 25–29 had attained high school degrees.

Changes at the nation's elite colleges and universities were even slower. In their book *The Shape of the River*, two former Ivy League presidents — Bowen and Derek Bok — say that as of 1960 "no selective college or university was making determined efforts to seek out and admit substantial numbers of African-American students." As of 1965, they report, African-Americans comprised only 4.8 percent of students on the nation's college campuses and fewer than 1 percent of students at select New England colleges.[7]

As part of the Civil Rights Act of 1964, Congress included provisions in Title IV to authorize the Justice Department to initiate racial-desegregation lawsuits against public schools and colleges and to require the U.S. Office of Education (now the Department of Education) to give technical assistance to school systems undergoing desegregation. A year later, President Lyndon B. Johnson delivered his famous commencement speech at historically black Howard University that laid the foundation for a more proactive approach to equalizing opportunities for African-Americans. "You do not take a person," Johnson said, "who, for years, has been hobbled by chains and liberate him, bring him up to the starting line of a race and then say, 'You are free to compete with all the others,' and still justly believe that you have been completely fair."[8]

Affirmative Action

Colleges began in the mid-1960s to make deliberate efforts to increase the number of minority students. Many universities instituted "affirmative action" programs that included targeted recruitment of minority applicants as well as explicit use of race as a factor in admissions policies. White students challenged the use of racial preferences, but the Supreme Court — in the *Bakke* decision in 1978 — gave colleges and universities a flashing green light to consider race as one factor in admissions policies aimed at ensuring a racially diverse student body.

The federal government encouraged universities to look to enrollment figures as the criterion for judging the success of their affirmative action policies. By requiring universities to report minority enrollment figures, the Nixon administration appeared to suggest that race-conscious admissions were "not only permissible but mandatory," according to Bowen and Bok. But universities were also motivated, they say, to remedy past racial discrimination, to educate minority leaders and to create diversity on campuses.

As early as 1966, Bowen and Bok report, Harvard Law School moved to increase the number of minority students by "admitting black applicants with test scores far below those of white classmates." As other law schools adopted the strategy, enrollment of African-Americans increased — from 1 percent of all law students in 1965 to 4.5 percent in 1975. Similar efforts produced a significant increase in black stu-

President Lyndon B. Johnson signs the Civil Rights Act on July 2, 1964. Race-based admissions policies now in use around the country evolved gradually from the landmark law.

dents in Ivy League colleges. The proportion of African-American students at Ivy League schools increased from 2.3 percent in 1967 to 6.7 percent in 1976, Bowen and Bok report.[9]

Critics, predominantly but not exclusively political conservatives, charged that the racial preferences amounted to "reverse discrimination" against white students and applicants. Some white students challenged the policies in court. The Supreme Court sought to resolve the issue in 1978 in a case brought by a California man, Alan Bakke, who had been denied admission to the University of California Medical School at Davis under a system that explicitly reserved 16 of 100 seats for minority applicants. The 4–1–4 decision fell short of a definitive resolution, though.

Justice Lewis F. Powell Jr. cast the decisive vote in the case. He joined

four justices to reject Davis' fixed-quota approach and four others to allow use of race as one factor in admissions decisions. In summarizing his opinion from the bench, Powell explained that it meant Bakke would be admitted to the medical school but that Davis was free to adopt a more "flexible program designed to achieve diversity" just like those "proved to be successful at many of our great universities."[10]

Civil rights advocates initially reacted with "consternation," according to Steinbach of the American Council on Education. Quickly, though, college officials and higher-education groups took up the invitation to devise programs that used race — in Powell's terms — as a "plus factor" without setting aside any seats specifically for minority applicants. The ruling, Steinbach says, "enabled institutions in a creative man-

ner to legally provide for a diverse student body."

The Supreme Court has avoided re-examining *Bakke* since 1978, but has narrowed the scope of affirmative action in other areas. The court in 1986 ruled that government employers could not lay off senior white workers to make room for new minority hires, though it upheld affirmative action in hiring and promotions in two other decisions that year and another ruling in a sex-discrimination case a year later. As for government contracting, the court ruled in 1989 that state and local governments could not use racial preferences except to remedy past discrimination and extended that limitation to federal programs in 1995.[11]

All of the court's decisions were closely divided, but the conservative majority made clear their discomfort with race-specific policies. Indeed, as legal-affairs writer Lincoln Caplan notes, none of the five current conservatives — Chief Justice William H. Rehnquist and Associate Justices Sandra Day O'Connor, Antonin Scalia, Anthony M. Kennedy and Clarence Thomas — has ever voted to approve a race-based affirmative action program.[12]

Negative Reaction

A political and legal backlash against affirmative action emerged with full force in the 1990s — highlighted by moves in California to scrap race-conscious policies in the state's uni-

Chronology

Before 1960
Limited opportunities for minorities in private and public colleges and universities.

1938
Supreme Court says Missouri violated Constitution by operating all-white law school but no school for blacks.

1950
Supreme Court says Texas violated Constitution by operating "inferior" law school for blacks.

1954
Supreme Court rules racial segregation in public elementary and secondary schools unconstitutional; ruling is extended to dismantle racially segregated colleges.

1960s–1970s
Civil rights era: higher education desegregated; affirmative action widely adopted, approved by Supreme Court if racial quotas not used.

1964
Civil Rights Act bars discrimination by federally funded colleges.

1978
Supreme Court rules in *Bakke* that colleges and universities can consider race as one factor in admissions policies.

1980s
Supreme Court leaves Bakke *unchanged.*

1986
Supreme Court limits use of affirmative action by employers if plan leads to layoffs of senior workers, but upholds racial preferences for union admission and promotions.

1987
Supreme Court rules, 6–3, that voluntary affirmative action plans by government employers do not violate civil rights law or Constitution.

1989
Supreme Court says state and local governments can adopt preferences for minority contractors only to remedy past discrimination.

1990s
Opposition to race-based admissions policies grows.

1995
Supreme Court, in *Adarand* case, limits federal minority-preference programs for contractors; President Clinton defends affirmative action; University of California ends use of race and sex in admissions.

1996
University of Texas law school's use of racial preferences in admissions ruled unconstitutional in *Hopwood* case; California voters approve Proposition 209 banning state-sponsored affirmative action in employment, contracting and admissions.

1997
Texas Gov. George W. Bush signs law guaranteeing admission to University of Texas to top 10 percent of graduates in state high schools.

1998
Washington state voters approve initiative barring racial preferences in state colleges and universities.

1999
Gov. Jeb Bush of Florida issues executive order banning racial preferences but granting admission to state colleges to top 20 percent of graduates in all state high schools.

2000s
Legal challenges to affirmative action continue.

Dec. 4, 2000
University of Washington Law School's former admissions system — discontinued after Proposition 200 — is upheld by federal court.

Dec. 13, 2000
University of Michigan undergraduate admissions policies upheld by federal judge, though former system ruled illegal.

March 26, 2001
Supreme Court agrees to hear new appeal in *Adarand* case.

March 27, 2001
University of Michigan Law School admissions policies ruled unconstitutional by federal judge.

June 2001
Supreme Court declines to review conflicting rulings in *University of Washington, University of Texas* cases.

Aug. 27, 2001
Federal appeals court in Atlanta rules University of Georgia admissions system giving bonuses to all non-white applicants is unconstitutional.

October 2001
Supreme Court to hear *Adarand* case Oct. 31.

December 2001
Federal appeals court in Cincinnati hears appeals in *University of Michigan* cases on Dec. 6.

Should Minority Contractors Get Preferences?

Six years ago, the Supreme Court cast doubt on the constitutionality of federal preferences for minority-owned road contractors. Now a white Colorado contractor, Randy Pech, is asking the court to rule that a revised program approved by Congress during the Clinton administration also doesn't pass constitutional muster.

The justices will hear arguments on Oct. 31 in a renewed challenge by Pech, whose company, Adarand Constructors, Inc., waged an earlier battle against a Department of Transportation (DOT) program giving contractors a 10 percent bonus for awarding subcontracts to minority-owned firms.

In a 5–4 decision in *Adarand Constructors, Inc. v. Peña*, the court in 1995 held that minority set-asides, or preferences, are constitutional only if they serve a compelling government interest and are narrowly tailored to meet that goal.[1] Applying that standard, lower courts later ruled the subcontractor-compensation clause unconstitutional.

The federal government then revised the overall program somewhat. Among other things, the revision allows white-owned businesses to apply for status as a disadvantaged company. The government dropped the subcontractor-compensation clause, but retained a provision setting aside 10 percent of federal highway contractors for "disadvantaged business enterprises." The Denver-based 10th U.S. Circuit Court of Appeals ruled last year that the revised program satisfied the "strict scrutiny" standard of constitutional review.

The new case, *Adarand Constructors, Inc. v. Mineta*, finds the Bush administration in the unanticipated position of defending an affirmative action program. President Bush was critical of racial preferences during his presidential campaign. But his newly appointed solicitor general, Theodore Olson, filed a brief in late August defending the DOT program as constitutional. Court observers note that it would have been unusual for the government to change positions after the justices agreed to review the case.[2]

In its brief, *Adarand* asks the court to rule that racial preferences are "intolerable, always." As an alternative, the company urges the justices to rule that the government did not have adequate evidence of racial discrimination against minority contractors to justify the program and that the mandatory presumption of disadvantage in favor of minority-owned firms was not narrowly tailored to remedy past discrimination.

In its brief, however, the government contends that Congress had "extensive evidence of public and private discrimination in highway contracting" and created the preferences system "only after race-neutral efforts . . . had proved inadequate."

---

[1] The legal citation is 515 U.S. 200 (1995). For background, see Kenneth Jost, *The Supreme Court Yearbook*, 1994–1995, pp. 27–32.

[2] The Mountain States Legal Foundation, the public interest law firm representing Adarand, has a summary of the case on its Web site: www.mountainstateslegal.org. The government's brief can be found at www.usdoj.gov/osg.

---

versity system and a federal appeals court decision barring racial preferences in admissions in Texas and two neighboring states. But President Bill Clinton rebuffed calls to scrap federal affirmative action programs. And colleges continued to follow race-conscious admissions policies in the absence of a new Supreme Court pronouncement on the issue.

In the first of the moves against race-conscious admissions, the 5th U.S. Circuit Court of Appeals in New Orleans in March 1996 struck down the University of Texas Law School's system that used separate procedures for white and minority applicants with the goal of admitting a class with 5 percent African-American and 10 percent Mexican-American students.[13] The ruling in the *Hopwood* case unanimously rejected the university's attempt to justify the racial preferences on grounds of past discrimination. Two

judges also rejected the university's diversity defense and directly contradicted the prevailing interpretation of *Bakke* that diversity amounted to a "compelling governmental interest" justifying race-based policies.[14]

The ruling specifically applied only to the three states in the 5th Circuit — Louisiana, Mississippi and Texas — but observers saw the decision as significant. "This is incredibly big," said John C. Jeffries Jr., a University of Virginia law professor and Justice Powell's biographer. "This could affect every public institution in America because all of them take racial diversity in admissions."[15]

Four months later, the University of California Board of Regents — policymaking body for the prestigious, 162,000-student state university system — narrowly voted to abolish racial and sexual preferences in admissions by fall 1997. The 14–10 vote approved a res-

olution submitted by a black businessman, Ward Connerly, and supported by the state's Republican governor, Pete Wilson. Connerly was also the driving force behind a voter initiative — Proposition 209 — to abolish racial preferences in state government employment and contracting as well as college and university admissions. Voters approved the measure, 54 percent to 46 percent, in November 1996.

In the face of opposition from UC President Richard Atkinson, the move to scrap racial preferences was delayed to admissions for the 1998–1999 academic year. In May 1998, the university released figures showing a modest overall decline in acceptances by non-Asian minorities to 15.2 percent for the coming year from 17.6 percent for the 1997–1998 school year. But the figures also showed a steep drop in the number of black and Hispanic students in the entering classes at the two most prestigious campuses — Berkeley and UCLA. At Berkeley, African-American and Hispanic acceptances fell to 10.5 percent from 21.9 percent for the previous year; at UCLA, the drop was to 14.1 percent from 21.8 percent.

The Supreme Court did nothing to counteract the legal shift away from racial preferences in education. It declined in 1995 to review a decision by the federal appeals court in Richmond, Va., that struck down a University of Maryland scholarship program reserved for African-American students. A year later, the justices refused to hear Texas' appeal of the *Hopwood* decision; and a year after that they also turned aside a challenge by labor and civil rights groups to Proposition 209. Instead, the high court concentrated on a series of rulings beginning in June 1993 that limited the use of race in congressional and legislative redistricting.[16] And in June 1995 the court issued a decision, *Adarand Constructors, Inc. v. Peña*, that limited the federal government's discretion to give minority-owned firms preferences in government contracting.[17]

With affirmative action under sharp attack, Bowen and Bok came out in 1998 with their book-length study of graduates of selective colleges that they said refuted many of the criticisms of race-based admissions. Using a database of some 80,000 students who entered 28 elite colleges and universities in 1951, 1976 and 1989, the two former Ivy League presidents confirmed the increase in minority enrollment at the schools and the impact of racial preferences: More than half the black students admitted in 1976 and 1989 would not have been admitted under race-neutral policies, they said. But they said dropout rates among black students were low, satisfaction with their college experiences high and post-graduation accomplishments comparable with — or better than — white graduates.[18]

The Bowen-Bok book buttressed college and university officials in resisting calls to scrap racial preferences.

While voters in Washington state moved to eliminate race-based admissions with an anti-affirmative action initiative in 1998, no other state university system followed the UC lead in voluntarily abolishing the use of race in weighing applications.

In Texas, then-Gov. George W. Bush sought to bolster minority enrollment in the UT system after *Hopwood* by proposing the 10 percent plan — guaranteeing admission to any graduating senior in the top 10 percent of his class. (Florida Gov. Jeb Bush followed suit with his 20 percent plan two years later.) Many schools — both public and private — re-examined their admissions policies after *Hopwood*. But, according to Steinbach, most of them "found that what they had was satisfactory."

Legal Battles

C ritics of race-based admissions kept up their pressure on the issue by waging expensive, protracted legal battles in four states: Georgia, Michigan, Texas and Washington. The cases produced conflicting decisions. The conflict was starkest in the two University of Michigan cases, where two judges both appointed in the 1980s by President Ronald Reagan reached different results in evaluating the use of race at the undergraduate college and at the law school.

The controversy in Michigan began in a sense with the discontent of a longtime Ann Arbor faculty member, Carl Cohen.[19] A professor of philosophy and a "proud" member of the American Civil Liberties Union (ACLU), Cohen had been troubled by racial preferences since the 1970s. In 1995 he read a journal article that described admissions rates for black college applicants as higher nationally than those for white applicants. The article prompted Cohen to begin poking around to learn about Michigan's system.[20]

As Cohen tells the story, administrators stonewalled him until he used the state's freedom of information law to obtain the pertinent documents. He found that the admissions offices used a grid system that charted applicants based on high school grade point average on a horizontal axis and standardized test scores on a vertical axis — and that there were separate grids or different "action codes" (reject or admit) for white applicants and for minority applicants. "The racially discriminatory policies of the university are blatant," Cohen says today. "They are written in black and white by the university. It's just incredible."

Cohen wrote up his findings in a report that he presented later in the year at a meeting of the state chapter of the American Association of University Professors. The report also found its way to a Republican state legislator, Rep. Deborah Whyman, who conducted a hearing on the issue and later held a news conference to solicit unsuccessful applicants to challenge the university's admission system. They forwarded about 100 of the replies to the Center for Individual Rights, a conservative public-interest law firm already active in challenging racial preferences.

Gratz and a second unsuccessful white applicant — Patrick Hamacher — were chosen to be the named plaintiffs in a class-action suit filed in federal court in Detroit in October 1997. The center filed a second suit against the law school's admission system in December 1997. The lead plaintiff was Barbara Grutter, who applied to the law school in December 1996 while in her 40s after raising a family and working as a health-care consultant. Grutter, who is white, thought she deserved admission based on her 3.8 undergraduate grade-point average 18 years earlier and a respectable score on the law school admission test (161, or 86th percentile nationally). Since the rejection, she has not enrolled elsewhere.

Evidence of Diversity Benefits Disputed

The University of Michigan is defending its race-based admissions policies not only with law but also evidence of the educational benefits of having a racially mixed student body. But opponents of racial preferences dismiss the evidence as distorted and biased.

The largest of the studies introduced as evidence in the two federal court lawsuits over the university's undergraduate and law school admissions policies runs 850 pages. Written by Patricia Gurin, chairman of the Psychology Department, it contains detailed statistics derived from a national student database and surveys of Michigan students. Gurin contends that students "learn more and think in deeper, more complex ways in a diverse educational environment."[1]

In addition, Gurin says students "are more motivated and better able to participate in an increasingly heterogeneous and complex democracy." And students who had "diversity experiences" during college — such as taking courses in Afro-American studies — also had "the most cross-racial interactions" five years after leaving college.

The National Association of Scholars, which opposes racial preferences, released two lengthy critiques of Gurin's study after the trials of the two suits. The studies were included in a friend-of-the-court brief filed in the appeals of the rulings.[2]

In the major critique, Thomas E. Wood and Malcolm J. Sherman contend that the national student database actually shows "no relationship" between the proportion of minorities on campus and educational benefits. They also say that "diversity activities" had only a "trivial impact" on educational outcomes.

The university also included "expert reports" from William G. Bowen and Derek Bok, the two former Ivy League university presidents who co-authored the pro-affirmative action book *The Shape of the River.* Bowen and Bok repeat their conclusions from the 1998 book that black students admitted to the "highly selective" colleges and universities studied did "exceedingly well" after college in terms of graduate degrees, income and civic life.[3] About half of the blacks admitted to the schools would not have been admitted under race-neutral policies, Bowen and Bok say.

University of Michigan student Agnes Aleobua speaks out against a court ruling last March that the law school's race-based admission policy is illegal.

AP Photo/Paul Sancya

In their reports for the Michigan suits, Bowen and Bok briefly acknowledge that black students at the schools had lower grades and lower graduation rates than whites. In an early critique of the book, two well-known critics of racial preferences — Abigail and Stephan Thernstrom — call Bowen and Bok to task for glossing over the evidence of poor performance by black students. They note that the dropout rate for black students — about 20 percent — was three times higher than for whites and that black students' grades overall were at the 23rd percentile — that is, in the bottom quarter.[4]

The studies are the tip of a large iceberg of academic literature that has sought to examine the effects of diversity in colleges and universities. In the most recent of the studies to be published, a team of authors from Pennsylvania State University concludes that the evidence is "almost uniformly consistent" that students in a racially or ethnically diverse community or engaged in "diversity-related" activities "reap a wide array of positive educational benefits."[5] In their own study of students at seven engineering schools, the scholars found what they called "a small, if statistically significant, link between the level of racial/ethnic diversity in a classroom and students' reports of increases in their problem-solving and group skills."

[1] Gurin's report can be found on the university's Web site: www.umich.edu.

[2] Thomas E. Wood and Malcolm J. Sherman, "Is Campus Racial Diversity Correlated With Educational Benefits?", National Association of Scholars, April 4, 2001 (www.nas.org). Wood is executive director of the California Association of Scholars; Sherman is an associate professor of mathematics and statistics at the State University of New York in Albany.

[3] William G. Bowen and Derek Bok, *The Shape of the River: Long-Term Consequences of Considering Race in College and University Admissions,* 1998. Bowen is a former president of Princeton University, Bok a former president of Harvard University.

[4] Stephan Thernstrom and Abigail Thernstrom, "Reflections on The Shape of the River," *UCLA Law Review,* Vol. 45, No. 5 (June 1999), pp. 1583–1631. Stephan Thernstrom is a history professor at Harvard; his wife is a senior fellow at the Manhattan Institute and a member of the Massachusetts Board of Education.

[5] Patrick T. Terenzini *et al.,* "Racial and Ethnic Diversity in the Classroom: Does It Promote Student Learning?", *Journal of Higher Education* (September/October 2001), pp. 509–531. Terenzini is a professor and senior scientist with the Center for the Study of Higher Education at Pennsylvania State University.

The cases proved to be long and expensive. By last fall, the university said it had spent $4.3 million defending the two suits, not counting personnel costs; the center had spent $400,000, including salaries, and also received the equivalent of $1 million in pro bono legal services from a Minneapolis firm helping to litigate the suits. Among the key pieces of evidence was a long report by an Ann Arbor faculty member — psychology Professor Patricia Gurin — concluding that diversity in enrollment has "far-reaching and significant benefits for all students, non-minorities and minorities alike." The center countered with a lengthy study issued under the auspices of the National Association of Scholars that analyzed the same data and found "no connection . . . between campus racial diversity and the supposed educational benefits."

In the meantime, the university revised its undergraduate admissions system, beginning with the entering class of 1999. The race-based grids and codes were replaced by a numerical system that assigned points to each applicant based on any of a number of characteristics. An applicant from an "underrepresented minority group" — African-Americans, Hispanics and Native Americans — is given 20 points. (One hundred points is typically required for admission, according to Cohen.) The same number is given to an applicant from a disadvantaged socioeconomic status, to a white student from a predominantly minority high school or to a scholarship athlete, according to university counsel Barry. The most important single factor, she adds, is an applicant's high school grades.

Judge Duggan's Dec. 13 ruling in the undergraduate case sustained the plaintiffs' complaint against the system used when Gratz and Hamacher had been rejected. Duggan said that the "facially different grids and action codes based solely upon an applicant's race" amounted to an "impermissible use of race." But Duggan said the revised sys-

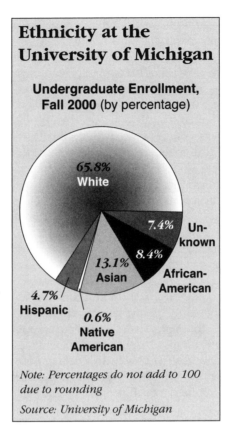

Ethnicity at the University of Michigan

Undergraduate Enrollment, Fall 2000 (by percentage)

- 65.8% White
- 7.4% Unknown
- 8.4% African-American
- 13.1% Asian
- 4.7% Hispanic
- 0.6% Native American

Note: Percentages do not add to 100 due to rounding

Source: University of Michigan

tem was on the right side of what he called "the thin line that divides the permissible and the impermissible."

Three months later, however, Judge Friedman on March 27 struck down the law school's admission system. Evidence showed that the school had used a "special admissions" program since 1992 aimed at a minority enrollment of 10 percent to 12 percent.

Friedman relied on a statistical analysis that showed an African-American applicant's relative odds of acceptance were up to 400 times as great as a white applicant's. Friedman rejected the use of diversity to justify the racial preferences, but in any event said the law school's system was not "narrowly tailored" because there was no time limit and there had been no consideration of alternative means of increasing minority enrollment.

The two Michigan cases took on added significance in June when the Supreme Court declined for a second time to hear Texas' appeal in the *Hop-*

wood case or to hear the plaintiffs' appeal of a ruling by the 9th U.S. Circuit Court of Appeals upholding a discontinued system of racial preferences at the University of Washington Law School. As the lawyers in the Michigan cases prepared for their scheduled appellate arguments, the 11th U.S. Circuit Court of Appeals issued a ruling on Aug. 27 striking down the University of Georgia's admissions system. With less extensive evidence in the Georgia case, however, legal observers viewed the two Michigan cases as the most likely to be accepted by the Supreme Court for its first full look at race-based admissions since *Bakke*.[21] ■

CURRENT SITUATION

Legal Confusion

A half-decade of legal and political challenges to race-based admissions policies has forced changes at some of the country's biggest state universities and produced widespread uncertainty throughout higher education.

"Colleges and universities are mystified with the confusing landscape as to what is and what is not permissible when it comes to admission practices," says Barmak Nassirian, associate executive director of the American Association of Collegiate Registrars and Admissions Officers. With the law unclear, Nassirian says, "institutions are essentially left to fend for themselves when it comes to compliance."

State universities in Texas and Florida are implementing new policies that eliminate explicit preferences for minority applicants but substitute guaranteed admission to high-ranking graduates of all high schools in the state — the top

10 percent of graduates in Texas, top 20 percent in Florida. The University of California in June approved a similar plan — guaranteeing admission to the top 12.5 percent of any high school class — that is to go into effect in fall 2003.

Both California and Texas reported significant declines in minority enrollment immediately after Proposition 209 and the *Hopwood* decision forced the state universities to eliminate racial preferences. Officials in Texas and Florida say the new policies are proving effective in minimizing the impact on minority enrollment.

Black and Hispanic enrollment dropped at the University of Texas and Texas A&M University immediately after *Hopwood*, but is now said to be back to levels immediately before the ruling. "It's maintained our course," state Rep. Irma Rangel, a Democrat and one of the authors of the 10 percent law, told the *Fort Worth Star-Telegram* earlier this year.[22]

University of Florida officials braced for reduced minority enrollment under the top 20 percent plan that first went into effect for the freshman class entering this fall. In June, university officials were projecting a drop in the number of African-American students — from 12 percent the previous year to 9 percent for the incoming class — but a modest increase in Hispanic students. "We expected we would have reductions here, but we've done everything we know how to keep it from happening," Charles E. Frazier, the university's vice provost, told The Associated Press.[23]

Public universities have the biggest problem in devising acceptable admissions policies, Nassirian says, because of the large number of applications they receive. Elite private universities have the resources to make a "very comprehensive assessment of an applicant's full portfolio," Nassirian explains. With more applications and fewer resources, he concludes, big state universities have to use less individualized ways "to make

a first cut as to whose application moves up and gets reviewed."

The University of Georgia — which receives about 14,000 applications a year — defended its racial system by noting the difficulty of individual review, but the appeals court rejected the defense. "If UGA wants to ensure diversity through its admissions decisions, and wants race to be part of that calculus," Judge Stanley Marcus wrote, "then it must be prepared to shoulder the burden of fully and fairly analyzing applicants as individuals and not merely as members of groups." [24] For its part, the University of Michigan says every application is individually reviewed by one of 21 admissions counselors assigned to specific geographic areas.

Nassirian contends racial preferences are an issue only for a minority of colleges with selective admissions policies. For those schools, though, he says he hopes the Supreme Court will take up the issue soon.

"It is regrettable that the law of the land has to get so overly complicated that you need a whole team of attorneys to guess what is allowable and what is not," Nassirian says. "That is not generally a sign of health — when people cannot get definitive answers as to what the law is."

Legal Appeals

Opposing lawyers for the two major sides in the University of Michigan cases projected confidence as they prepared for arguments in the most closely watched case on racial preferences in college admissions since *Bakke*.

The federal appeals court in Cincinnati scheduled a total of 90 minutes to hear from lawyers representing the university, the plaintiffs and the minority intervenors in the undergraduate and law school cases — 15 minutes for each lawyer in each case. The three judges

who heard the case were picked at random shortly before the arguments: The court's 11 judges include five appointed by Republican presidents and six named by Democrats.

Representing the unsuccessful applicants, Rosman of the Center for Individual Rights says he is "cautiously optimistic" about the outcome. "We think we have a strong case, but you can never predict what a court will do," Rosman says. The university's attorney — John Payton, a lawyer with a prominent Washington law firm — says, "I feel very good about where we are."

Payton says *Bakke* is the key to the case, and he discounts the significance of the court rulings that have questioned its status as a precedent for using diversity to justify race-conscious admissions policies. "I don't think you can find a trend in that small group of cases," he says, "and I don't think there is a trend."

For his part, Rosman warns that justifying racial admissions policies on the basis of diversity could invite similar policies elsewhere in government. "If you think that racial diversity leads to intellectual foment that leads to new and better ideas, it's not clear why you wouldn't want to have different perspectives from different races in a lot of different areas of government," he says.

Payton thinks the evidence introduced by the university to defend its policies may influence the judges. "The social-science evidence confirms the consensus among educators that there is a very significant educational impact [from having] a diverse student body," he says. Rosman is dubious. "I don't think they're going to be too overwhelmingly fascinated by the social-science evidence," he says.

Both sides have drawn support from outside groups in the form of friend-of-the-court briefs, but the university rallied a more impressive list of allies. More than a dozen briefs supporting the university's position were filed by, among others, the American Bar As-

At Issue:

Should colleges eliminate the use of race in admissions?

THOMAS E. WOOD
EXECUTIVE DIRECTOR, CALIFORNIA ASSOCIATION OF SCHOLARS, CO-AUTHOR OF CALIFORNIA PROP. 209

WRITTEN FOR THE CQ RESEARCHER, SEPTEMBER 2001

Colleges should eliminate the use of race in admissions. One cannot prefer on the basis of race without discriminating against others on the basis of race. Treating people differently on the basis of their race violates the Constitution's guarantee of equal protection under the laws.

There is only one national database for higher education that is in a position to adequately address this question whether, or to what extent, campus racial diversity is a necessary component of educational excellence. So far, the American Council on Education/Higher Education Research Institute database has failed to find any connection between campus racial diversity and any of the 82 cognitive and non-cognitive outcome variables incorporated in the study.

Proponents claim that the abandonment of racial classifications will result in the resegregation of higher education. Since preferences have been used to increase the number of minorities in the past, their abandonment will lead in the near term to lower numbers for minorities (though only in the most elite institutions of higher education).

But the claim that abandoning the use of race in college admissions will lead to resegregation implies that all or virtually all minorities who are presently enrolled in the most elite institutions are there only because they have been given preferences, which is both untrue and demeaning. The claim also ignores the fact that the country was making significant progress toward diversity *before* the advent of racial preferences in university admissions in the mid-to-late 1970s.

This analysis is confirmed by the experience of Texas, California and Washington, which already have bans on racial classifications in university admissions. The experience in these states has been that while there is an initial decline when racial classifications are abandoned (though only in the most elite institutions), the underlying trend toward greater diversity resumes after the initial correction.

For some, of course, any regression from the numbers that are obtainable through the use of preferences is unacceptable. At its heart, this is the view that racial diversity is a value that trumps all others. But that is a view that has clearly been rejected by the courts, and for good reason. Diversity is an important public policy goal, but there is a right way and a wrong way to pursue it. Racial classifications are the wrong way.

ANGELO ANCHETA
DIRECTOR, LEGAL AND ADVOCACY PROGRAMS, CIVIL RIGHTS PROJECT, HARVARD LAW SCHOOL

WRITTEN FOR THE CQ RESEARCHER, SEPTEMBER 2001

Affirmative action policies advance the tenet that colleges, like the workplace and our public institutions, should reflect the full character of American society. Race-conscious admissions policies not only promote the integration ideal first realized in *Brown v. Board of Education* but also help create educational environments that improve basic learning and better equip students for an increasingly diverse society.

The U.S. Supreme Court upheld race-conscious admissions over 20 years ago in *Regents of the University of California v. Bakke*. Yet, affirmative action opponents, armed with the rhetoric of quotas and tokenism for the unqualified, persist in trying to undermine *Bakke*. Educators know that quotas are illegal under *Bakke* and that granting admission to the unqualified serves no one's interest. Colleges have been highly circumspect, employing carefully crafted policies that consider all applicants competitively and that use race as only one of many factors in admissions decisions.

Nevertheless, recent litigation challenging affirmative action in Texas, Washington, Georgia and Michigan portends that the Supreme Court will soon revisit *Bakke*. But the case that promoting educational diversity is, in the language of the law, "a compelling governmental interest" and that race-conscious admissions policies can best serve that interest has only strengthened in recent years.

The latest findings show that student-body diversity significantly improves the quality of higher education. Studies at the University of Michigan have found that diverse learning environments can enhance students' critical-thinking skills, augment their understanding and tolerance of different opinions and groups, increase their motivation and participation in civic activities and better prepare them for living in a diverse society. Several studies support these findings and further show that interaction across races has positive effects on retention rates, satisfaction with college, self-confidence and leadership ability.

Without race-conscious admissions, the student-body diversity necessary to advance these educational outcomes would be lost. The declining enrollment of minority students at public universities that have abandoned affirmative action strongly suggests that the "color-blind" path is not the path to equal opportunity; nor is it the path to the highest-quality education.

Affirmative action policies reflect the reality that race has always shaped our educational institutions. Justice Blackmun's admonition in *Bakke* thus remains as vital as ever: "In order to get beyond racism, we must first take account of race. There is no other way."

sociation, General Motors, a group of 33 other *Fortune* 500 companies, and a long roster of higher education and civil rights groups. The eight briefs in support of the plaintiffs came from such conservative groups as the National Association of Scholars, the Center for Equal Opportunity and the Independent Women's Forum.

The minority intervenors will also repeat their arguments that the race-conscious admissions policies are justified as a remedy for the university's overt discrimination in the past and the disparate impact of other admissions policies on minorities. They face an uphill fight since both judges rejected their arguments. But Miranda Massie, the Detroit lawyer representing minority students in the law school case, says pro-affirmative action groups will mount a march and rally in Cincinnati on the day of the appeals court hearing.

Whatever the three-judge panel decides, the losing parties are certain to appeal to the Supreme Court. "Eventually, the Supreme Court will decide in all probability," Univeristy of Michigan President Bollinger says. Rosman agrees: "To the extent that the Supreme Court can resolve the uncertainty, it would be appropriate." ■

OUTLOOK

Ideals and Reality

M ichigan graduate Jennifer Gratz and President Bollinger agree that someday colleges should stop using race as a factor in admissions decisions. "They can make up whatever policy they want as long as they as don't discriminate," Gratz says.

Bollinger, too, says he views color-blind admissions as an ultimate goal. "If it eventually came about that we got

racial and ethnic diversity without taking race or ethnicity into account, we would no longer do so," Bollinger says.

Critics think the time for abolishing racial preferences has come. "We don't think institutionalized discrimination against African-Americans any longer exists," says Clegg of the Center for Equal Opportunity. "So institutionalized discrimination in their favor shouldn't exist."

Supporters say the critics overestimate the racial progress made since the peak of the civil rights era in the mid-1960s. "Thirty-five years — when you stack it up against 300 years — is peanuts," says Shaw of the NAACP Legal Defense Fund. "To think that we have solved all of these problems in 35 years is shortsighted and just wrong."

Public opinion and political sentiment on the issue appear to be somewhat malleable. Polls generally register support for "affirmative action" and opposition to "racial preferences." At Michigan, Cohen says he has few faculty allies in opposing race-conscious admissions. As for students, "it seems to me plain that a majority supports the university's position," he says.

Democrats in Congress have generally defended affirmative action even when the issue was hot in the mid-1990s. Republican leaders initially staked out positions against preferences after taking control of Congress following the 1994 elections, but then put the issue on a back burner.

The Supreme Court has also charted an uncertain course on the issue. The justices are divided along ideological lines on the issue, with the five conservatives generally opposed to racial policies and aligned against the four more liberal justices: John Paul Stevens, David H. Souter, Ruth Bader Ginsburg and Stephen G. Breyer.

Two of the conservatives — Scalia and Thomas — have staked out the strongest position against considering race in government policies. But O'Connor has a pivotal vote on the subject and has consistently stopped short of flatly

prohibiting the government from taking race into account in employment, contracting or redistricting.

Bollinger — a legal scholar as well as university administrator — says *Bakke* remains "a firm constitutional precedent" for the university's policy. He says he is optimistic about the outcome of the two lawsuits — and about the future course of race relations in academia and beyond.

"I really do believe people of good sense will see the importance of maintaining the course that *Brown v. Board of Education* put us on — to work very hard on issues of race and ethnicity in this society," Bollinger says. "We have much to learn, much to overcome, and our great educational institutions are one of the most meaningful ways of addressing the experience of race."

For her part, Gratz says she had a "diverse group" of friends in high school and college, but acknowledges they were predominantly other whites. Still, she believes race relations in the United States today are "pretty good."

"I think that the more emphasis that we put on race, the more people are going to look at race," she concludes. "And I would like to see that in the future we really do have equal opportunity for all, regardless of race."

Does she think that will happen? "Yes," Gratz says, "it can happen." ■

Notes

[1] For extensive information on both cases, including the texts of the two rulings and other legal documents, see the University of Michigan's Web site (www.umich.edu) or the Web site of the public-interest law firm representing the plaintiffs, the Center for Individual Rights (www.cir-usa.org).

[2] The legal citation is 438 U.S. 265; Supreme Court decisions can be found on a number of Web sites, including the court's official site: www.supremecourtus.gov. For background, see Kenneth Jost, "Rethinking Affirmative Action," *The CQ Researcher*, April 28, 1995, pp. 369-392.

[3] See Robert Lerner and Althea K. Nagai, "Pervasive Preferences: Racial and Ethnic Discrimination in Undergraduate Admissions Across the Nation," Center for Equal Opportunity, Feb. 22, 2001 (www.ceo-usa.org).

[4] For background, see David Masci, "Hispanic Americans' New Clout," *The CQ Researcher*, Sept. 18, 1998, pp. 809-832; David Masci, "The Black Middle Class," *The CQ Researcher*, Jan. 23, 1998, pp. 49-72; and Kenneth Jost, "Diversity in the Workplace," *The CQ Researcher*, Oct. 10, 1997, pp. 889-912.

[5] Charles R. Lawrence III and Mari J. Matsuda, *We Won't Go Back: Making the Case for Affirmative Action* (1997), p. 127. Matsuda, Lawrence's wife, is also a professor at Georgetown law school.

[6] For background, see Joan Biskupic and Elder Witt, *Guide to the U.S. Supreme Court* (3d ed.), 1997, pp. 362-363. The cases discussed are *Missouri ex rel. Gaines v. Canada*, 305 U.S. 337 (1938); *Sweatt v. Painter*, 339 U.S. 629 (1950); and *McLaurin v. Oklahoma State Regents for Higher Education*, 339 U.S. 637 (1950).

[7] William G. Bowen and Derek Bok, *The Shape of the River: Long-Term Consequences of Considering Race in College and University Admissions* (1998), pp. 4-5. Bowen, a former president of Princeton University, is now president of the Andrew W. Mellon Foundation in New York City; Bok is a former president of Harvard University and now University Professor at the John. F. Kennedy School of Government at Harvard.

[8] Reprinted in Gabriel J. Chin (ed.), *Affirmative Action and the Constitution: Affirmative Action Before Constitutional Law, 1964-1977*, Vol. 1 (1998), pp. 21-26.

[9] Bowen and Bok, *op. cit.*, pp. 6-7.

[10] Description of the announcement of the decision taken from Bernard Schwartz, *Behind Bakke: Affirmative Action and the Supreme Court* (1988), pp. 142-150.

[11] The cases are *Wygant v. Jackson Bd. of Education*, 476 U.S. 267 (1986); *Johnson v. Transportation Agency of Santa Clara County* 480 U.S. 646 (1987); *City of Richmond v. J.A. Croson Co.* 488 U.S. 469 (1989); and *Adarand Constructors, Inc. v. Peña* 575 U.S. 200 (1995).

[12] Lincoln Caplan, *Up Against the Law: Affirmative Action and the Supreme Court* (1997), p. 16.

[13] The case is *Hopwood v. Texas*. Some background on this and other cases in this section drawn from Girardeau A. Spann, *The Law of Affirmative Action: Twenty-Five Years of Supreme Court Decisions on Race and Remedies* (2000).

[14] The legal citation is *Hopwood v. Texas*, 78 F.2d 932 (5th Cir. 1996). In a subsequent decision, the appeals court on Dec. 21, 2000, reaffirmed its legal holding, but upheld the lower court judge's finding that none of the four plaintiffs would have been admitted to the law school under a race-blind system. See *Hopwood v. Texas*, 236 F.2d 256 (5th Cir. 2000).

[15] Quoted in Facts on File, March 28, 1996.

[16] For background, see Jennifer Gavin, "Redistricting," *The CQ Researcher*, Feb. 16, 2001, pp. 113-128; Nadine Cahodas, "Electing Minorities," *The CQ Researcher*, Aug. 12, 1994, pp. 697-720.

[17] The legal citation is 515 U.S. 200.

[18] For a critique, see Stephan and Abigail Thernstrom, "Reflections on the Shape of the River," *UCLA Law Review*, Vol. 46, No. 5 (June 1999), pp. 1583-1631.

[19] For a good overview, see Nicholas Lemann, "The Empathy Defense," *The New Yorker*, Dec. 18, 2000, pp. 46-51. See also Carl Cohen, "Race Preference and the Universities — A Final Reckoning," *Commentary*, September 2001, pp. 31-39.

[20] "Vital Signs: The Statistics that Describe the Present and Suggest the Future of African Americans in Higher Education," *The Journal of Blacks in Higher Education*, No. 9 (autumn 1995), pp. 43-49.

[21] The Washington case is *Smith v. University of Washington Law School*, 9th Circuit, Dec. 4, 2000; the Georgia case is *Johnson v. Board of Regents of the University of Georgia*, 11th Circuit, Aug. 27.

[22] See Crystal Yednak, "Laws Meant to Boost Diversity Paying Off," *Fort Worth Star-Telegram*, Jan. 13, 2001, p. 1.

[23] Ron Word, "State Universities Have Differing Results Recruiting Minorities," The Associated Press, June 19, 2001.

[24] See Edward Walsh, "Affirmative Action's Confusing Curriculum," *The Washington Post*, Sept. 4, 2001, p. A2.

FOR MORE INFORMATION

American Council on Education, 1 Dupont Circle, N.W., Suite 800, Washington, D.C. 20036; (202) 939-9300; www.acenet.edu. The council was the lead organization in a friend-of-the-court brief filed by 30 higher-education groups in support of the University of Michigan's race-conscious admissions policies.

Center for Equal Opportunity, 14 Pidgeon Hill Dr., Suite 500, Sterling, VA 20165 (703) 421-5443; www.ceousa.org. The center filed a friend-of-the-court brief in support of the plaintiffs challenging University of Michigan admissions policies.

Center for Individual Rights, 1233 20th St., N.W., Suite 300, Washington, D.C. 20036; (202) 833-8400; www.cir-usa.org. The public-interest law firm represents plaintiffs in the University of Michigan cases and others challenging race-conscious admission policies.

NAACP Legal Defense Fund, 99 Hudson St., Suite 1600, New York, N.Y. 10013; (212) 965-2200; www.naacpldf.org (under construction, September 2001). The Legal Defense Fund represents the minority student intervenors in the two suits contesting admission policies at the University of Michigan.

National Association of Scholars, 221 Witherspoon St., Second Floor, Princeton, N.J. 08542-3215; (609) 683-7878; www.nas.org. The organization studies and advocates on academic issues including race-based admissions policies.

Bibliography

Selected Sources Used

Books

Bowen, William G., and Derek Bok, *The Shape of the River: Long-Term Consequences of Considering Race in College and University Admissions*, Princeton University Press, 1998.

The book analyzes data on 80,000 students admitted to 28 selective private or public colleges and universities in 1951, 1976 and 1989 to examine the impact of race-based admissions on enrollment and to compare the educational and post-graduation experiences of white and minority students. Includes statistical tables as well as a nine-page list of references. Bowen, a former president of Princeton University, heads the Andrew W. Mellon Foundation; Bok is a former president of Harvard University and now a professor at Harvard's John F. Kennedy School of Government.

Caplan, Lincoln, *Up Against the Law: Affirmative Action and the Supreme Court*, Twentieth Century Fund Press, 1997.

The 60-page monograph provides an overview of the Supreme Court's affirmative action rulings with analysis written from a pro race-conscious policies perspective. Caplan, a longtime legal-affairs writer, is a senior writer in residence at Yale Law School.

Chin, Gabriel J. (ed.), *Affirmative Action and the Constitution: Affirmative Action Before Constitutional Law, 1964–1977* (Vol. 1); *The Supreme Court "Solves" the Affirmative Action Issue, 1978–1988* (Vol. 2); *Judicial Reaction to Affirmative Action, 1988–1997* (Vol. 3), Garland Publishing, 1998.

The three-volume compendium includes a variety of materials on affirmative action from President Lyndon B. Johnson's famous speech at Howard University in 1965 to President Bill Clinton's defense of affirmative action in 1995 as well as the full text of the federal appeals court decision in the 1995 *Hopwood* decision barring racial preferences at the University of Texas Law School. Chin, who wrote an introduction for each volume, is a professor at the University of Cincinnati College of Law.

Edley, Christopher Jr., *Not All Black and White: Affirmative Action, Race, and American Values*, Hill & Wang, 1996.

Edley, a Harvard Law School professor, recounts his role in overseeing the Clinton administration's review of affirmative action in 1995 as part of a broad look at the issue that ends with measured support for affirmative action "until the justification for it no longer exists."

Schwartz, Bernard, *Behind Bakke: Affirmative Action and the Supreme Court*, New York University Press.

Schwartz, a leading Supreme Court scholar until his death

in 1997, was granted unusual access to the private papers of the justices for this detailed, behind-the-scenes account of the *Bakke* case from its origins through the justices' deliberations and final decision.

Spann, Girardeau A., *The Law of Affirmative Action: Twenty-Five Years of Supreme Court Decisions on Races and Remedies*, New York University Press, 2000.

The book includes summaries — concise and precise — of major Supreme Court decisions from *Bakke* in 1978 to *Adarand* in 1995 Spann is a professor at Georgetown University Law Center.

Steele, Shelby, *A Dream Deferred: The Second Betrayal of Black Freedom in America*, HarperCollins, 1998.

Steele, a prominent black critic of affirmative action and a research fellow at the Hoover Institution at Stanford University, argues in four essays that affirmative action represents an "extravagant" liberalism that "often betrayed America's best principles" in order to atone for white guilt over racial injustice.

Articles

Lawrence, Charles R. III, "Two Views of the River: A Critique of the Liberal Defense of Affirmative Action," *Columbia Law Review*, Vol. 101, No. 4 (May 2001), pp. 928–975.

Lawrence argues that liberals' "diversity" defense of affirmative action overlooks "more radical substantive" arguments based on "the need to remedy past discrimination, address present discriminatory practices, and reexamine traditional notions of merit and the role of universities in the reproduction of elites." Lawrence is a professor at Georgetown University Law Center.

PBS NewsHour, "Admitting for Diversity," Aug. 21, 2001 (www.pbs.org/newshour).

The report by correspondent Elizabeth Brackett features interviews with, among others, Barbara Grutter, the plaintiff in the lawsuit challenging the University of Michigan Law School's race-based admissions policies, and the law school's dean, Jeffrey Lehman.

Thernstrom, Stephan, and Abigail Thernstrom, "Reflections on The Shape of the River," *UCLA Law Review*, Vol. 46, No. 5 (June 1999), pp. 1583–1631.

The Thernstroms contend that racial preferences constitute a "pernicious palliative" that deflect attention from real educational problems and conflict with the country's unrealized egalitarian dream. Stephan Thernstrom is a professor of history at Harvard University; his wife Abigail is a senior fel

8 Nuclear Waste

BRIAN HANSEN

F ew signs of civilization can be seen from the windswept crest of Yucca Mountain, a flat-topped volcanic ridge about 100 desert miles northwest of Las Vegas.

The closest humans live 15 miles to the south, at a desolate crossroads known as Lathrop Wells — population eight.

But deep inside the 6,000-foot-tall mountain, the scene is straight out of science fiction. Five miles of ghostly, fluorescent-lit tunnels wind through the mountain, pock-marked with boreholes crammed with instruments. And all around, hard-hatted scientists conduct sophisticated experiments.

Yucca Mountain is the controversial centerpiece of the government's plan for disposing of thousands of tons of deadly nuclear waste. The scientists are studying whether the site will safely hold the 42,000 metric tons of nuclear waste being stored at nuclear power plants across the country, plus another 4,300 tons of radioactive military waste. [1]

Under federal law, the Department of Energy (DOE) should have begun storing nuclear waste at Yucca by Jan. 31, 1998. But the DOE testing of the site is years behind schedule, thanks in part to lawsuits filed by environmental groups and Nevada politicians opposed to the project. Indeed, Yucca Mountain — the only site being considered as a federal nuclear waste repository — won't be ready until at least 2010. And that's only if Congress and the Nuclear Regulatory Commission (NRC) approve DOE's final storage plan.

Nuclear energy proponents have long been frustrated over the delays at Yucca Mountain. At a hearing last September,

From *The CQ Researcher,*
June 8, 2001.

Deep inside Nevada's Yucca Mountain, a technician conducts a test on a container for radioactive wastes.

Department of Energy

Sen. Frank H. Murkowski, R-Alaska, then chairman of the Senate Energy Committee, argued that the site must be brought online as soon as possible to ensure the continued viability of the nuclear power industry, which supplies about one-fifth of the nation's power. Murkowski also noted that nuclear utilities could sue the federal government for up to $80 billion in damages for failing to take charge of the nation's spent nuclear fuel by the Jan. 31 deadline.

"This country is choking on its own nuclear waste," Murkowski thundered. "If we don't solve the problem of our spent nuclear fuel soon, the American taxpayer will bear the cost of the financial liability . . . and the environmental damages from losing 20 percent of clean, emissions-free electricity generation."

But critics maintain that Yucca Mountain poses grave risks to human health and the environment. Some 50,000 truck-loads of nuclear waste would have to be transported across the country to the site over 25 years, and critics say the inevitable highway accidents would release radiation. Moreover, they warn, once the waste is entombed in the mountain, plutonium and other radioactive materials would ultimately leach into the aquifer below, contaminating drinking water

used throughout the desert Southwest.

"If this flawed scheme goes through, generations of people who will live in the region over the coming decades and centuries will have to face the very real possibility that one day a nuclear genie will be uncorked," says Joan Claybrook, president of the consumer watchdog group Public Citizen.

If approved, Yucca Mountain would serve as a permanent disposal facility for two types of nuclear waste: spent nuclear fuel used by the nation's 103 operating commercial nuclear reactors and high-level radioactive waste generated by the military during the manufacture of nuclear weapons.

Spent nuclear fuel — which would make up 90 percent of the wastes at Yucca Mountain — consists of finger-tip-size enriched uranium pellets used during nuclear fission. One pellet can generate as much electricity as 149 gallons of oil, 1,780 pounds of coal or 17,000 cubic feet of natural gas. [2] In nuclear power plants, the pellets are sealed in long metal tubes known as fuel rods, which are bundled together in groups called fuel assemblies.

Every 12 to 24 months, nuclear plants replace their oldest fuel assemblies with new ones. Because they are still intensely radioactive, depleted fuel assemblies must be isolated from humans for thousands of years.

The military nuclear waste slated for Yucca Mountain is in liquid form — about 55 million gallons. Most is stored in 177 underground tanks at the DOE's Hanford Nuclear Reservation near Richland, Wash. Large volumes are also stored in Idaho, South Carolina and New York state. [3]

Before permanent storage, the liquid waste must first be turned into glass or other solid forms — a dan-

Temporary Storage Sites for Nuclear Waste

Some 42,000 metric tons of radioactive commercial waste and 4,300 tons of military waste are being stored on a temporary basis in pools and reinforced canisters around the U.S. The government is studying a plan to bury the waste under Yucca Mountain in Nevada.

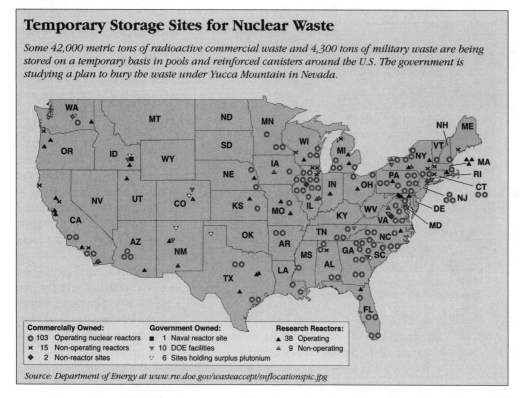

Commercially Owned:
- ⊙ 103 Operating nuclear reactors
- ✕ 15 Non-operating reactors
- ◆ 2 Non-reactor sites

Government Owned:
- ■ 1 Naval reactor site
- ▽ 10 DOE facilities
- ▽ 6 Sites holding surplus plutonium

Research Reactors:
- ▲ 38 Operating
- ▲ 9 Non-operating

Source: Department of Energy at www.rw.doe.gov/wasteaccept/snflocationspic.jpg

gerous and technologically challenging process. Then, because of the deadly radiation exuded by high-level waste for thousands of years, it must be shielded with concrete and lead.

The DOE has spent nearly $7 billion since 1982 trying to solve the nuclear-waste dilemma, much of the money on the Yucca Mountain site. "We have found nothing in our scientific studies that would prove the [Yucca] site unsuitable," says Alan Benson, a DOE spokesman in Nevada.

But critics say the site would be vulnerable to earthquakes, flooding and volcanic eruptions over the thousands of years it would be in use and that it was selected for political — not scientific — reasons.

"Yucca Mountain is an unsuitable site for an unsuitable project," says Lisa Gue, a policy analyst with Public Citizen. "The nuclear power industry is anxious to get Yucca Mountain open so the nation's ever-increasing nuclear waste problem will be out of sight, out of mind."

Without a permanent repository,

nuclear power plants have stored their used fuel in steel-lined concrete vaults filled with water, which acts as a radiation shield and coolant. But many of these pools are now full, so some plants have begun to store their spent fuel in above-ground casks. Though designed to withstand everything from earthquakes and tornadoes to sabotage, the casks are not designed for long-term storage.

"We can store spent nuclear fuel on-site in a very safe, efficient and cost-effective way, but that doesn't mean DOE should ignore its obligation to move the material to a permanent repository," says Steven P. Kraft, director of used-fuel management at the Nuclear Energy Institute.

Most nuclear plants are seeking 40-year renewals of their operating licenses. But even if Yucca Mountain is approved, the site is not large enough to accommodate the additional radioactive waste that would be generated. If all existing plants are relicensed, 84,000 metric tons of waste would re-

quire storage by 2035. Yucca Mountain's capacity is 70,000 tons.

And the nation's stockpile of nuclear waste would increase even faster if President Bush's newly announced energy policy is implemented. Bush has called for additional nuclear plants to be built to combat what he calls a national "energy crisis."

As policy-makers debate the nation's nuclear waste dilemma, here are some of the issues they will consider:

Is Yucca Mountain a safe repository?

The Yucca Mountain project grew out of the Nuclear Waste Policy Act of 1982, which required the DOE to design an underground "geologic repository" for disposing of nuclear waste.

The most immediate danger under the DOE's preliminary plan, critics say, would be transportation accidents. Nuclear wastes would be transported to Yucca Mountain via truck or train — or a combination of both — in thousands of shipments over highways and rail lines in 43 states.

The DOE acknowledges that transportation-related accidents would almost certainly occur during the vast operation, but it says special shipping casks would all but eliminate the danger of radiation being released.

"Will there be accidents? That's certainly a possibility," Benson says. "But we haven't been able to come up with a credible, real-world scenario where there would be any kind of catastrophic release."

But some critics have dubbed the transportation scheme "Mobile Chernobyl," after the catastrophic 1986 nuclear plant explosion in the former Soviet Union. These critics fear a transportation accident could trigger a similar airborne contamination release in the United States, especially if a damaged shipping cask were engulfed in a high-temperature diesel fire.

"Transporting high-level nuclear waste increases the risk of radioactive release and disperses this risk along transportation routes where emergency responders may lack the capacity to respond effectively to a radiation emergency," says Diane D'Arrigo, director of the radioactive waste project at the Nuclear Information and Resource Service, an environmental group.

At the mountain, wastes would be placed in containers designed to last at least 10,000 years. Remotely operated rail cars would transport the containers down a ramp and into 100 miles of tunnels 1,000 feet below the surface. There, because of the high levels of radiation and the resulting heat, robots would position them for disposal.

The DOE would monitor the repository for at least 50 years after disposal of the last wastes and then would seal the tunnels and post guards at the site for as long as necessary. Because government, society and language could change radically in the thousands of years it would take the wastes to decay to safe levels, monuments would be placed around the site to warn future generations of the danger.

Yucca Mountain backers say its safety will be assured by the combination of natural geologic features and radiation barriers being added. That view received a significant boost in 1998, when a six-volume DOE study summarized 15 years of scientific data on the site.

The study found that the mountain's arid climate and stable geology would reduce the chance that water would leach radioactive waste out of the repository. [4] Even if water did seep in and corrode the specially designed waste containers, the radioactive material would have to pass through 1,000 feet of rock before it could contaminate the underlying aquifer, the report notes.

Using mathematical models, the report concluded that people living near Yucca Mountain would receive little or no increase in radiation exposure for 10,000 years after the repository was closed, with maximum exposure occurring after 300,000 years. By that time, the metal waste containers probably would have deteriorated, but the radioactive materials would have become far less toxic. Then, people approximately 12 miles from the mountain might receive additional radiation equivalent only to present-day "background" radiation levels, the report said.

But critics are quick to cite other studies suggesting that the site would pose far greater risks. [5] They note it sits in an active earthquake zone sliced by 33 known geologic faults, where scientists have recorded more than 600 seismic events of magnitude 2.5 or greater.

Finally, the critics also note that recent studies indicate water would penetrate the repository and transport radioactive particles off-site much more rapidly than previously believed.

"The site itself is pretty poor from a scientific perspective, and we believe it should be disqualified for that reason," says Robert Loux, director of the Nevada Agency for Nuclear Projects, the state's DOE watchdog group.

The state maintains that Yucca Mountain does not meet the qualifications of a geologic repository as mandated by federal law because it would rely on human-engineered barriers — high-tech nickel and titanium waste containers — for more than 95 percent of its performance. [6] Loux bases that figure on the computer-driven mathematical models the DOE is using to analyze performance at the site. [7]

"We don't see the waste containers lasting until the wastes are no longer dangerous," Loux says. "That's why the law and the National Academy of Sciences and others insist that geology has to be the primary barrier."

"I don't know where [Nevada's] figures come from," says the DOE's

Benson. "We're still in the process of determining whether we have a suitable site right now, and that's what we're focused on."

Should the U.S. invest in transmutation to solve its nuclear waste disposal problem?

Some experts believe that a still experimental waste-reprocessing technique known as "transmutation" someday may reduce the required isolation time for spent nuclear fuel from thousands of years to just a few centuries. [8]

Proponents acknowledge that the technology would not eliminate the need for an underground repository. But subjecting nuclear waste to transmutation before storing it, they argue, would eliminate the chance that future generations would be threatened by an ill-conceived repository.

That's a big plus for Sen. Pete Domenici, R-N.M. Last year, Domenici secured $34 million in federal funds to launch a transmutation research program at the DOE's national laboratory near Los Alamos, N.M. In March, he introduced legislation to provide $120 million in additional federal funds to the fledgling program next year. [9]

"There's no question that transmutation is technically feasible," says Peter Lyons, Domenici's science adviser. "It could dramatically change the arguments about what could happen with a repository, in terms of possible scenarios for future impact on humans."

But critics say transmutation is not only scientifically dubious but also far too expensive. They also note that the process would contribute to nuclear proliferation because it extracts plutonium — a key component in nuclear weapons — from the nuclear waste. Disposing of unprocessed radioactive waste underground, however, "protects" the plutonium in the fuel. [10]

"Transmutation is just another name for reprocessing, and reprocessing is a bad idea that was abandoned by the United States years ago because of its high costs and adverse proliferation consequences," says Rep. Edward J. Markey, D-Mass., a longtime anti-nuclear voice in Congress. "At a time when we are concerned about Iraq, North Korea, Iran and other countries acquiring nuclear explosives, we should not be reviving a plutonium economy that makes weapons-grade material more readily available" to rogue nations or terrorists.

President Bush downplayed those concerns in May when he unveiled his proposed energy policy. Bush maintains that transmutation and other reprocessing technologies can be carried out in a "proliferation-resistant" manner that "continues to discourage the accumulation of separated plutonium."

Transmutation proponents maintain that the remaining uranium waste material could be buried in shallow landfills, claiming it would be no more radioactive than the uranium ore mined to manufacture nuclear fuel. But many critics say that would be risky.

"Putting uranium in shallow dumps is a very, very bad idea," says Arjun Makhijani, president of the Institute for Energy and Environmental Research, an environmental advocacy group. "It's very long-lived and would [still] be contaminated with some plutonium, neptunium and technetium."

Cost is still another stumbling block for transmutation, according to critics. A 1999 DOE study estimates it would take $280 billion — and 117 years — to transmute all the spent nuclear fuel generated by the nation's nuclear power plants during their current 40-year license periods. [11] However, most of those costs could be recouped by selling the surplus electricity generated in the process, the DOE concluded.

But critics dismiss the transmutation initiative as "nuclear alchemy" and say, moreover, that it smacks of "pork barrel politics" being practiced by Domenici to benefit the national laboratory in his state.

"There are so many ill-advised research programs that can't be stamped out because of the political clout [of

their supporters]," said Edwin Lyman, scientific director of the Nuclear Control Institute, a non-proliferation group. "This is a perfect example." [12] ∎

BACKGROUND

The Arms Race

America's nuclear waste dilemma grew out of the World War II-era quest to build an atomic bomb, which sparked a 45-year-long nuclear arms race between the United States and the former Soviet Union.

The commercial nuclear power industry, in turn, grew out of the arms race. The first commercial nuclear reactor to generate electricity, a joint venture between a private company and the federal government, was an experimental unit known as the EBR-1. On Dec. 20, 1951, it produced enough power to illuminate four light bulbs. Seven years later, the first full-scale nuclear power plant went online in Shippingport, Pa., producing enough power for 38,500 households. [13]

In the late 1950s and early '60s, little fuss was made over the radioactive wastes that began piling up at the nation's nuclear power plants. Most plant owners and government policymakers viewed nuclear waste as a short-lived problem that would be solved — someday — by technology.

In 1957, for example, the National Academy of Sciences concluded that nuclear wastes could be safely deposited in various geologic media, such as underground salt beds. The academy noted, however, that significant research would be required to locate, design and build such a repository. As a result, the Atomic Energy Commission (AEC) — a predecessor of the DOE — launched a nationwide search for a suitable site.

That effort culminated in 1970, when the AEC recommended storing defense waste in salt deposits near Lyons, Kan. But two years later, that proposal was abandoned for political and technical reasons. [14]

The AEC then recommended the use of a "retrievable surface storage" facility at the government's Hanford facility. But that proposal also was abandoned because of concerns that it would defer future efforts to build a geologic repository, a favored solution. [15]

Meanwhile, the fledgling nuclear power industry was building more and more power plants, each of which could store only a few decades' worth of spent fuel in on-site storage pools. However, the lack of a long-term waste-management solution didn't seem to bother U.S. utility companies, which ordered 41 nuclear power plants in 1973 alone, the year of the so-called Arab oil embargo. [16]

But the industry's halcyon days wouldn't last. In the late 1970s, power-plant operators began to realize that some reactors might have to be shut down in the mid-1990s unless additional waste-storage options were found.

At the same time, the public began to question the shortsighted nuclear waste disposal plans. Several states prohibited further nuclear power plant construction until the federal government demonstrated that nuclear waste could be disposed of safely and permanently. [17]

The partial meltdown of the Three Mile Island nuclear power plant near Harrisburg, Pa., brought new plant construction to a screeching halt. Although no one was injured in the 1979 accident, no U.S. nuclear power plants have been built since.

With spent nuclear fuel piling up at power plants around the country, the government considered a variety of disposal alternatives, including burying radioactive waste below the ocean floor or in the Antarctic ice sheet or rocketing it into space.

Chronology

Congress Acts

Research into other disposal schemes was abandoned for good in 1982, when Congress passed the Nuclear Waste Policy Act. [18] The measure made geologic disposal the nation's official disposal strategy and established a timetable for locating sites for two potential repositories and completing construction of one. The measure also established a tax-payer-supported fund to pay for building the repository and required the DOE to assume control of the nation's spent nuclear fuel by the Jan. 31, 1998, deadline.

Because the government has missed the deadline, federal courts have ruled that utilities can tap into that fund to recoup their on-site storage costs. Estimates of how much that could cost range up to the $80 billion mentioned by Murkowski.

Three locations — Yucca Mountain, Hanford and Deaf Smith County, Texas — were ultimately selected as potential locations for the first repository. Nevada, Washington state and Texas opposed nuclear waste facilities inside their borders, although a few local groups welcomed them for economic reasons. States that found themselves on the DOE's short list to host the second repository also balked. Indeed, they formed a political alliance with the "first-round" states and together managed to get all repository-related funds eliminated from the 1988 federal budget. [19]

In 1987, to contain the meltdown of its carefully designed nuclear waste disposal scheme, Congress significantly amended the Nuclear Waste Policy Act. The amendment ended all research at the Washington and Texas sites, leaving Yucca Mountain as the nation's lone potential disposal site. [20]

Nevada objected vigorously to the designation, which it viewed as a political rather than a scientific move. A legal battle quickly ensued, as Nevada refused

1950s Nuclear power industry begins to flourish, using weapons technologies.

May 26, 1958
First nuclear power plant opens at Shippingport, Pa.

———•———

1970s Nuclear power industry declines after 1979 accident.

April 7, 1977
President Jimmy Carter bans reprocessing of spent nuclear fuel to prevent stockpiling of plutonium used in weapons.

March 28, 1979
A reactor accident at Three Mile Island nuclear plant in Pennsylvania prompts a moratorium on new nuclear plants and forces greater federal oversight over the industry.

———•———

1980s A catastrophic accident in the Soviet Union further undermines U.S. confidence in nuclear power.

Jan. 7, 1983
Nuclear Waste Policy Act requires Department of Energy (DOE) to take control of spent nuclear fuel by Jan. 31, 1998.

April 26, 1986
Chernobyl nuclear power station in Ukraine explodes, killing 31 people. Thousands more con-

tract thyroid cancer and other radiation illnesses.

1987
Congress directs DOE to study Yucca Mountain as the nation's only nuclear-waste repository.

———•———

1990s Government falls behind in constructing a nuclear waste disposal site.

Dec. 27, 1996
Utah tribe agrees to store nuclear waste on its reservation.

Jan. 31, 1998
DOE misses the deadline for removing nuclear wastes from commercial reactor sites.

Dec. 18, 1998
DOE concludes that Yucca Mountain is a promising site.

———•———

2000s Nevada intensifies efforts to block Yucca Mountain site.

2000
Nevada denies DOE water permit, prompting a U.S. suit.

Jan. 22, 2001
Gov. Kenny Guinn says Nevada will spend $5 million to oppose Yucca Mountain.

May 2001
DOE says it needs more funds to apply for an operating license for Yucca Mountain.

to issue the DOE the permits necessary to begin studying the site. [21] But federal courts ruled that Nevada could not block the proposed repository until it is formally approved by Congress.

Just last year, Nevada denied the DOE's request for a supply of well water large enough to build the repository. The federal government immediately sued the state, claiming the decision violated both the Constitution and the nuclear-waste law. Last September, after a U.S. District Court ruled in favor of Nevada, DOE officials said they would simply truck the water in from outside.

That didn't sit well with Republican Gov. Kenny Guinn, who threatened to impose a $1 million-per-gallon fine on every gallon the DOE imported. [22] But the DOE refused to back down and appealed the case to the 9th U.S. Circuit Court of Appeals.

Not to be outdone, Guinn in January dedicated $5 million in state funds to "fight the Department of Energy and those in Congress who are determined to make Nevada the nation's nuclear waste dump." [23]

But in February, President Bush countered that move when he unveiled his budget for the coming fiscal year. The budget earmarks $445 million for Yucca Mountain site studies — a $55 million increase. [24] ∎

CURRENT SITUATION

Opposition in Nevada

With a final decision on Yucca Mountain drawing closer, Nevada lawmakers are ramping up efforts to block the controversial project.

Last December, Sen. Harry Reid, D-Nev., asked the DOE's inspector general, Gregory H. Friedman, to investigate whether the agency violated any criminal laws in considering the site. Reid's request followed reports in the *Las Vegas Sun* suggesting that the DOE and the nuclear power industry have secretly worked together to win congressional approval for Yucca. [25] Federal law prohibits the DOE from taking sides during the site-selection process.

On April 23, the DOE narrowly dodged that bullet when Friedman concluded that while the DOE and its contractors made several "questionable statements" that could be construed as "inappropriately advocating" the Yucca Mountain site, he "could not substantiate the concern that bias compromised the integrity of the site-evaluation process." [26]

But Reid said he was troubled that Friedman was unable to obtain all of the electronic mail messages he needed for his investigation. Friedman said a DOE contractor told him the messages had disappeared following a "computer malfunction." [27]

On April 25, Reid and the rest of the Nevada congressional delegation asked the General Accounting Office to investigate the missing e-mail. The agency says it will look into the matter as part of an ongoing investigation into a whistleblower's allegations that the Yucca Mountain project is fraught with waste and fraud.

Utah Indians' Deal

As the fight over Yucca Mountain continues, several power companies are trying to stash spent nuclear fuel at an impoverished Indian reservation in the Utah desert. The proposal is a collaborative venture between Private Fuel Storage (PFS) — a consortium of eight large U.S. utility companies — and the Skull Valley Band of the Goshute Indian Tribe, a federally recognized sovereign nation of 112 people.

The Goshutes have accepted an undisclosed amount of money to temporarily stockpile the spent fuel on their reservation 60 miles southwest of Salt Lake City for at least 25 years. Up to 40,000 metric tons would be shipped to the isolated reservation, where it would be kept in 4,000 concrete and steel storage casks on an above-ground concrete pad. The NRC is currently reviewing the proposal, which could get under way in as little as two years. [28]

The Goshute/PFS proposal grew out of a 1987 amendment to the nuclear waste law, which Congress enacted when it became clear that a permanent geologic repository would not be built by Jan. 31, 1998. The amendment authorized construction and use of a temporary storage facility on Indian lands until the DOE completed the underground facility.

The Goshutes received $300,000 to conduct studies and visit nuclear power plants around the world.

"Initially, it bothered us that they seemed to be targeting Indian reservations," said Leon Bear, chairman of the Skull Valley Band. "Then we went through the studies and decided it was feasible to store it, that it was safe." [29]

Bear won't disclose the financial terms of the deal, but he said it will greatly benefit the impoverished tribe. "It will allow our tribal government to provide social programs for our tribal members, [such as] housing needs, health needs," he says. "For a long time, the tribe has been pretty much distressed over revenues they don't have."

But Margene Bullcreek opposes the proposed deal, which she says Bear made without most members' knowledge. She is leading a small group of "traditionalists" who don't want their ancestral homeland turned into a nuclear waste dump.

"The real issue is not the money," Bullcreek says. "The real issue is who

Measuring the Radiation From Nuclear Waste

Exposure to radiation can alter the chemical balance of cells, resulting in cancer and genetic damage, but often the effects may not be evident for years. *

Scientists know a lot about the effects of extremely high doses of powerful ionizing radiation, because they have studied the effects on victims of the 1945 atomic bombings of Hiroshima and Nagasaki, Japan, as well as the 1986 nuclear plant explosion in Chernobyl, Ukraine. Such high doses can cause acute radiation sickness, extensive cell damage, death and inheritable genetic mutations.

But scientists disagree over the potential health effects — and even the definition — of lower doses of ionizing radiation.

Radiation exposure is measured in units called millirem. The Nagasaki and Hiroshima victims were exposed to 300,000 to 500,000 millirem of radiation, and the Chernobyl workers received up to 1.6 million millirem.

The average American is exposed to 360 millirem annually, most of it coming from "background" radiation emitted from natural sources, like cosmic rays that bombard the Earth from outer space and radon gas filtering up through the soil from underground uranium deposits. The Environmental Protection Agency estimates that background radiation causes 1 to 3 percent of the cancer cases in the United States each year.

Because exposure to natural sources is largely uncontrollable, the government tries to minimize exposure from manmade sources, like X-rays, color TVs, smoke detectors and computer monitors. Of the 360-millirem doses the average American is exposed to each year, only 60 millirem comes from manufactured sources.

Nuclear waste emits three main kinds of radiation that can change the chemical balance inside human cells in different ways, depending on the radiation's penetrating power.

---

* There are two types of radiation energy: Non-ionizing radiation is emitted by radios, color TVs and wireless phones; ionizing radiation is emitted by microwaves, ultraviolet light, and X-rays and gamma rays.

- Alpha radiation is the least-penetrating form. It can travel only a few inches through the air and can be stopped by a sheet of paper. Although alpha particles cannot penetrate human skin, they may be extremely harmful if inhaled, ingested or enter the body, for instance, through a cut in the skin.
- Beta particles can travel several feet through the air but can be stopped by a layer of clothing or a thin sheet of aluminum foil. They cause their most serious health effects when swallowed or inhaled.
- Gamma radiation can easily pass through the human body and severely damage internal organs. It must be shielded with concrete, lead, steel or water.

In the United States, less than 1 percent of the average person's annual radiation exposure comes from nuclear power plants. According to the Nuclear Regulatory Commission, someone living next door to a nuclear power plant would receive one additional millirem of radiation per year. A person working inside such a facility would receive 300 additional millirem per year — far below the 5,000-millirem federal limit for occupational radiation exposure.

If nuclear waste is stored at Yucca Mountain, exposure to ionizing radiation would be increased both from the repository itself and from transporting waste to the facility. But the Department of Energy says the increased exposure will not exceed federal standards.

Furthermore, says the DOE, the maximum increased exposure from operating the repository will occur 300,000 years after the facility is closed, after the canisters of waste likely have deteriorated. At that time, people in the area could receive an additional 260 millirem per year, says the DOE, still well below levels received by some people living in other parts of the United States.

Transporting waste to the repository would increase radiation exposure by an even smaller amount, says the DOE. Someone standing 100 feet from a vehicle transporting the heavily shielded nuclear waste would receive a radiation dose of 0.0004 millirem, the DOE estimates.

---

we are as Native Americans and what we believe in. If we accept these wastes, we're going to lose our tradition."

Utah politicians are also fighting the proposal, fearing that the ostensibly "temporary" nuclear waste dump would become a permanent blight on their state. Republican Gov. Michael O. Leavitt has vowed to utilize "all lawful and appropriate means" to keep nuclear wastes out of his state. [30] On March 13, he signed

two laws designed to derail the proposal, bringing to six the total of anti-dumping laws now on the books.

But the Goshutes and the power companies are fighting back. On April 19, they sued to overturn the six laws.

Bear says the Goshutes were forced to join the lawsuit because of the state's "direct attack on [the tribe's] constitutional rights."

"The state laws attempt to take away our inherent sovereignty and

our rights recognized by the federal government," Bear says. "We have been forced by the state into this action to preserve our sovereignty."

Meanwhile, the Goshute/PFS proposal is moving through the licensing process. A series of public hearings will be held in Salt Lake City in November. The NRC's licensing decision is expected in April 2002, pending completion of environmental and other studies by the Goshutes and PFS.

More Waste?

With President Bush calling for more nuclear power plants, the nation's stockpile of nuclear waste will probably grow before a permanent disposal scheme is finalized. [31] Two proposals pending on Capitol Hill would significantly bolster the nuclear power industry.

One measure, an omnibus energy bill proposed by Sen. Murkowski, would give the nuclear power industry at least $500 million in tax breaks over the next 10 years and would require the NRC to streamline its licensing process for new and existing nuclear power plants. [32]

The other bill, sponsored by Sen. Domenici, declares that electricity generated by nuclear power is "environmentally preferable" to energy produced by burning fossil fuels. [33] In remarks in March on the Senate floor, Domenici said that nuclear energy is "essentially emissions free" and makes an "immense contribution to the environmental health of our nation." And in an effort to forestall some of the "scientifically inaccurate stigmas" that Domenici said have vilified nuclear energy, the bill would make it illegal for the federal government to "discriminate" against nuclear energy when making purchasing decisions. [34]

Critics have sharply denounced Domenici's bill. "It is thoroughly irresponsible to promote the use of nuclear power when there is still no technically feasible means of assuring that long-lived radioactive wastes can be isolated from the environment," says Wenonah Hauter, director of Public Citizen's Critical Mass Energy and Environment Program.

Domenici's measure also proposes construction of the kinds of advanced nuclear power plants being developed in other parts of the world, such as the Pebble Bed Modular Reactor (PBMR) currently undergoing testing in South Africa. If the feasibility tests are favorable, the U.S.-based Exelon Corp. plans to seek a license to begin building PBMR plants here by 2004. [35]

Exelon maintains that PBMR technology poses fewer long-term waste disposal risks than reactors currently in use. Critics, however, say it remains intrinsically dangerous. ∎

OUTLOOK

The Jeffords Factor

The final decision on Yucca Mountain is likely to be made by Congress by next year. First, Energy Secretary Spencer Abraham must formally make a recommendation about the site to President Bush — which he is expected to do later this year.

Abraham unabashedly supported the Yucca Mountain dump during his stint as a Republican senator from Michigan. But under the Nuclear Waste Policy Act, his formal recommendation must be based on the results of the DOE site studies and must be accompanied by a final environmental impact statement.

If Abraham recommends the site and Bush concurs, the president would then ask Congress to approve it. The state of Nevada would then have 60 days to object, which it has already indicated it will do. At that point, the site would be temporarily "disapproved," but Congress could override Nevada's disapproval by adopting a joint resolution with a simple majority of both houses.

It is difficult to predict how many members of Congress would side with the Nevada delegation. That question became even more intriguing on May 24, when Vermont Sen. James M. Jeffords announced that he was leaving the Republican Party to become an independent. Jeffords' defection tipped control of the previously evenly divided Senate to the Democrats, and is expected to put him in charge of the Senate Environment and Public Works Committee, which has jurisdiction over Yucca Mountain.

According to several news reports, Jeffords' switch was facilitated by the ranking Democrat on that panel, Sen. Reid, who offered to step aside as new chairman for Jeffords. As chairman, Reid would have been gatekeeper for Yucca Mountain-related legislation. Environmental lobbyists say it's highly unlikely that Reid would have given the committee to someone who wasn't prepared to block the project.

"No one is saying so publicly, but Sen. Reid obviously has come to an understanding with Sen. Jeffords," says Hauter of Public Citizen. "As chairman, Jeffords could really slow things down."

"I think the Yucca Mountain issue is dead as long as we're in the majority," Sen. Tom Daschle, D-S.D., the new majority leader, told the *Las Vegas Review-Journal*.

Erik M. Smulson, Jeffords' press secretary, refused to comment on the senator's plans for Yucca Mountain. But he noted that Jeffords said on May 24 that he would continue to vote the same way and be the same senator he was.

Last year, Jeffords supported a bill to expedite shipment of nuclear waste to Yucca. The measure passed both houses of Congress but was vetoed by President Clinton on April 25, 2000.

If Jeffords does change his position on Yucca Mountain, as many expect, he also would be breaking ranks with the governor of his home state and five other New England chief executives. On March 28, Gov. Howard Dean, D-Vt., and the governors of four other neighboring states asked Abraham to facilitate an "expeditious resolution" of their long-term nuclear waste-storage problem.

Still, Hauter predicts the political tide will turn against Yucca Mountain once the Energy Department designates the extensive road and rail routes to be used to transport nuclear waste to Nevada. Congress will come under tremendous pressure to reject the site once mem-

At Issue:

Should nuclear wastes be buried under Yucca Mountain in Nevada?

JOE F. COLVIN
PRESIDENT AND CEO, NUCLEAR ENERGY INSTITUTE

FROM TESTIMONY BEFORE THE HOUSE COMMERCE SUBCOMMITTEE ON ENERGY AND POWER, JULY 7, 2000.

Yucca Mountain is one of the most studied pieces of property in the world. A deep geologic repository, located at an isolated, arid location, remains the cornerstone of the nation's used-fuel management policy. There is no scientific basis for concluding that Yucca Mountain cannot fulfill the role of being a safe, environmentally responsible facility for commercial used nuclear fuel, and for the high-level radioactive waste from defense and other national programs stored in 40 states.

Based on repeated promises from the federal government, electric utilities that built nuclear power plants expected used fuel to be stored for a short period of time at their plants, then shipped for disposal at a federal government facility. Fuel storage facilities at nuclear power plants were never intended to provide long-term storage capacity. Because of Department of Energy delays in developing a federal repository, electricity consumers have been forced to pay twice for used nuclear fuel storage. Several hundred million dollars has been spent to develop additional on-site storage facilities at nuclear power plants since the late 1980s, and more are in the planning process.

Meanwhile, electricity consumers continue to pay an additional $700 million every year into the Nuclear Waste Fund for DOE to manage used nuclear fuel. To date, they have committed more than $16 billion for the program.

In some cases, building a temporary storage facility has subjected companies to unacceptably high political and financial costs. As difficult as they are today, these issues will only get more complex with further delay.

America's 103 nuclear power plants provide 20 percent of our electricity in a manner that produces no harmful air pollution. It is up to us, who enjoy the benefits of that electricity, to manage the byproducts of those facilities safely and responsibly. We simply cannot defer this problem to future generations. The time for promises has long passed — now is the time for action.

Unparalleled scientific study at Yucca Mountain should be sufficient for DOE to make a site recommendation to the president in 2001. The industry fully expects them to do so without further delay. Congressional leadership is essential to hold DOE accountable for completing its critically important tasks and breaking the cycle of perpetual delay that has been the unfortunate history of this program.

NEVADA COMMISSION ON NUCLEAR PROJECTS

FROM A REPORT PRESENTED TO THE GOVERNOR AND STATE LEGISLATURE, DECEMBER 2000.

Today, Nevada and the nation must contend with what has become a single-minded, coercive federal effort to turn Yucca Mountain into a radioactive-waste disposal site at any cost, while the program's uncertainties continue to mount.

Over the years, science has given way to raw politics as the U.S. Department of Energy and supporters of DOE's repository project in Congress have sought to obfuscate and compensate for an ever-multiplying set of flaws and problems with the site and with the notion of transporting unprecedented amounts of deadly spent nuclear fuel and high-level nuclear waste across the country.

Yucca Mountain is located in a geologically active area in southern Nevada. The site is known to contain numerous geologic and hydrologic characteristics that would, on initial examination, be features that would ordinarily be avoided in looking for viable sites for long-term geologic disposal. However, because the site was selected by Congress in a political process instead of a scientific one, these geologic/hydrologic features were either ignored or masked by the Department of Energy in congressional deliberations.

The many technical deficiencies of the Yucca Mountain site and DOE's flawed approach to geologic disposal notwithstanding, the most potentially explosive aspect of the federal program is the reality that tens of thousands of shipments of deadly radioactive waste will travel the nation's highways and railroads — through 43 states and thousands of communities, day after day for upwards of 40 years. A severe transportation accident or successful terrorist attack in an urban area could release radioactive materials to the environment, causing hundreds of latent cancer fatalities and costing hundreds of millions, or even billions, of dollars for cleanup and compensation.

The most serious and possibly catastrophic economic risk for Nevada stemming directly from the Yucca Mountain project is the potential for stigma impacts on the tourist industry. Such impacts could produce significant losses to an economy dominated by visitor-based revenues

The commission believes that the Yucca Mountain program poses significant and unacceptable risks not only for the state of Nevada but also for the nation as a whole. It is a strong and compelling case that clearly calls for a change in national nuclear waste policy and direction. Neither Nevada nor the nation can afford the risks or the costs of the current program.

bers' constituents realize the transportation scheme will expose "50 million Americans to dangerous levels of radiation in their communities," Hauter says.

However, the DOE says the shipping containers will be strong enough to prevent any radiation from being released in an accident, even a conflagration of diesel fuel.

Meanwhile, more clouds are forming over Yucca Mountain. In May, the Energy Department announced that it could not apply to the NRC for a license for the repository in 2002 without more money from Congress. The department needs $1 billion a year for the next seven years to get the project through the NRC's rigorous licensing procedure, it says. [36] Currently, the department's Yucca Mountain funding stands $98 million short of that mark, which could jeopardize its projected 2010 opening, said Victor W. Trebules, manager of the DOE's Office of Project Control. [37]

But Nevada lawmakers vow to block the project.

"We're going to fight back," said Gov. Guinn. "We are going to put up the best fight you've ever seen." [38] ■

Notes

[1] More information about spent nuclear fuel can be found on the Department of Energy's Web site at http://www.rw.doe.gov/homejava/homejava.htm.

[2] For more information, see the Nuclear Energy Institute's Web site at http://www.nei.org.

[3] For background, see Mary H. Cooper, "Nuclear Arms Cleanup," *The CQ Researcher*, June 24, 1994, pp. 553-576.

[4] The Viability Assessment for the Yucca Mountain project can be viewed on the Department of Energy's Web site at http://www.ymp.gov/timeline/va/index.htm.

[5] Nevada's Agency for Nuclear Projects has posted several scientific reports critical of the Yucca Mountain project at http://www.state.nv.us/nucwaste.

[6] For more information, see the "Report and Recommendations of the Nevada Commission on Nuclear Projects," December 2000.

[7] For more information on this mathematical modeling approach, which the Department of Energy calls the Total System Performance Assessment, see http://www.ymp.gov/documents/sl921m3_b/index.htm.

[8] For a comprehensive look at transmutation technologies, see National Research Council, *Nuclear Wastes: Technologies for Separations and Transmutations*, 1996.

[9] Domenici's bill, the Nuclear Energy Electricity Supply Assurance Act of 2001, was introduced on March 7, 2001.

[10] For background on proliferation, see Mary H. Cooper, "Missile Defense," *The CQ Researcher*, Sept. 8, 2000, pp. 689-712; David Masci, "U.S.-Russia Relations," *The CQ Researcher*, May 22, 1998, pp. 457-480. and Mary H. Cooper, "Nuclear Arms Cleanup," *The CQ Researcher*, June 24, 1994, pp. 553-576.

[11] Department of Energy, Office of Civilian Radioactive Waste Management, *A Roadmap for Developing Accelerator Transmutation of Waste (ATW) Technology*, October 1999.

[12] Quoted in Chuck McCutcheon, "Byproducts and Bad Chemistry," *CQ Weekly*, April 7, 2001, p. 764.

[13] For more information, see the Nuclear Energy Institute's Web site at http://www.nei.org.

[14] For background, see Department of Energy, "History of the Civilian Radioactive Waste Management Program," at http://www.rw.doe.gov/program/pprev3hist.pdf.

[15] *Ibid.*

[16] According to statistics compiled by Nuclear Energy Institute.

[17] See, for example, League of Women Voters, *The Nuclear Waste Primer: A Handbook for Citizens*, 1993, p. 5.

[18] The act can be viewed on the Department of Energy's Web site at http://www.rw.doe.gov/progdocs/nwpa/nwpa.htm.

[19] League of Women Voters, *op. cit.*, pp. 48-49.

[20] Department of Energy, "History of the Civilian Radioactive Management Program."

[21] For background, see the state of Nevada's "Report and Recommendations of the Nevada Commission on Nuclear Projects," December 2000.

[22] See Brendan Riley, "Gov Threatens $1 Million-a-Gallon Fine if Water Imported for Nuke Dump," The Associated Press, Sept. 26, 2000.

[23] Guinn made his remarks during his "State of the State" address on Jan. 22, 2001.

[24] See The Associated Press, "More Funds Proposed to Study Nuclear Waste Dump Site in Nevada," April 11, 2001.

[25] See Jeff German, "DOE Wants Yucca," *Las Vegas Sun*, Dec. 1, 2000.

[26] The Inspector General's report can be viewed online at http://www.ig.doe.gov/pdf/yucca.pdf.

[27] Press release, April 25, 2001.

[28] More information about the PFS/Goshute proposal is available online at http://www.privatefuelstorage.com/project/project.html.

[29] Quoted in Jerry D. Spangler and Donna Kemp Spangler in "Toxic Utah: Goshutes Divided Over N-Storage," the *Deseret News*, Feb. 14, 2001.

[30] For background, see Tom Arrandale, "Hot Stuff on Ice," *Governing*, April 2000, p. 32.

[31] For background, see Mary H. Cooper, "Energy Policy," *The CQ Researcher*, May 25, 2001, pp. 441-464.

[32] The National Energy Security Act of 2001 was introduced on Feb. 26, 2001.

[33] The Nuclear Energy Electricity Supply Assurance Act of 2001 was introduced on March 7, 2001.

[34] Senate floor remarks on March 6, 2001.

[35] According to the testimony of Ward Sproat, Exelon Corp. vice president of international programs, before the House Energy and Air Quality Subcommittee, March 27, 2001.

[36] For background, see Mary Manning, "DOE Seeks Delay in Yucca License: Budget Shortfall May Hinder 2010 Opening of Site," *Las Vegas Sun*, May 7, 2001.

[37] *Ibid.*

[38] *Ibid.*

Bibliography

Selected Sources Used

Books

League of Women Voters Education Fund, *The Nuclear Waste Primer: A Handbook for Citizens,* **Lyons & Burford, 1993.**
Explains the sources, types and hazards of nuclear waste transportation and disposal.

National Research Council, *Nuclear Wastes: Technologies for Separations and Transmutations,* **National Academy Press, 1996.**
Examines technologies for transmuting long-lived nuclear wastes into more stable materials.

Articles

Arrandale, Tom, "Hot Stuff on Ice," *Governing,* **April 2001, pp. 32-34.**
Reports on a proposal to store spent nuclear fuel on a Utah Indian reservation.

German, Jeff, "DOE Wants Yucca," *The Las Vegas Sun,* **Dec. 1, 2000.**
German reports that confidential documents suggest the Department of Energy secretly collaborated with the nuclear industry to win approval for Yucca Mountain.

Kerr, Richard A., "Science and Policy Clash at Yucca Mountain," *Science,* **April 28, 2000, p. 602.**
Examines allegations that science has taken a back seat to politics in the study of Yucca Mountain.

McCutcheon, Chuck, "Byproducts and Bad Chemistry," *CQ Weekly,* **April 7, 2001, pp. 764–765.**
A prominent U.S. senator says the nation's nuclear waste problem can be mitigated through transmutation, but critics say the process is technologically dubious.

McCutcheon, Chuck, "High-Level Acrimony in Nuclear Storage Standoff," *CQ Weekly,* **Sept. 25, 1999, pp. 2204–2208.**
McCutcheon takes readers inside Yucca Mountain.

Reports and Studies

Department of Energy, "A Roadmap for Developing Accelerator Transmutation of Waste (ATW) Technology: A Report to Congress," October 1999.
Synthesizes information from worldwide experts on developing transmutation technologies.

Department of Energy, "Yucca Mountain Science and Engineering Report: Technical Information Supporting Site Recommendation Consideration," May 2001.
Examines the hundreds of scientific studies conducted over the past 20 years at Yucca Mountain.

Nevada Commission on Nuclear Projects, "Report and Recommendations of the Nevada Commission on Nuclear Projects," December 2000.
Concludes that the Yucca Mountain repository should be disqualified for scientific reasons.

FOR MORE INFORMATION

Department of Energy, Office of Civilian Radioactive Waste Management, Yucca Mountain Site Characterization Office, P.O. Box 30377, North Las Vegas, Nev. 89036; (800) 225-6972; www.ymp.gov. The office was established to determine if Yucca Mountain is suitable for a national nuclear-waste repository.

Nevada Agency for Nuclear Projects, 1802 North Carson St., Suite 252, Carson City, Nev. 89701; (775) 687-3744; www.state.nv.us/nucwaste. A state agency highly critical of the Yucca Mountain project.

Nuclear Control Institute, 1000 Connecticut Ave., N.W., Suite 410, Washington, D.C. 20036; (202) 822-8444; www.nci.org. An independent advocacy group that works to curtail the reprocessing of spent nuclear fuel and the proliferation of nuclear weapons.

Nuclear Energy Institute, 1776 I St., N.W., Washington, D.C. 20006; (202) 739-8000; www.nei.org. The nuclear power industry's advocacy organization promotes beneficial uses of nuclear energy and technologies.

Nuclear Regulatory Commission, 1 White Flint North, 11555 Rockville Pike, Rockville, Md. 20852-2738; (301) 415-7000; www.nrc.gov. Regulates nuclear reactors and the transport, storage and disposal of nuclear materials.

9 Energy Security

MARY H. COOPER

Ever since the 1973 Arab oil embargo, concern about cutoffs of oil imports by foreign suppliers has been a major focus of U.S. energy policy. Now there's a new threat: sabotage of pipelines, nuclear power plants and other energy facilities.

"The Sept. 11 terrorist attacks greatly widened what are considered credible threats to the energy system," says Arjun Makhijani, president of the Institute for Energy and Environmental Research (IEER). "Before Sept. 11, this was a discussion about energy policy. After Sept. 11, it should be primarily a discussion about security."

In a recent report, the Takoma Park, Md., institute warned that:

- Growing dependence on Middle Eastern oil imports increases the United States' military commitment in an unstable region of the world;

- The country's 103 working nuclear power plants are potential targets for attacks that could release lethal levels of radiation;

- Sabotage anywhere in the centralized electricity grid could cause extensive blackouts; and,

- Much of the nation's extensive network of oil and gas pipelines is in remote areas, where terrorists could wreak havoc on both the fuel supply and the surrounding environment. [1]

President Bush cited the attacks on New York City and the Pentagon as one more reason Congress should pass the energy plan he proposed last May.

From *The CQ Researcher*, February 1, 2002.

Caribou graze under the 800-mile-long Trans-Alaska Pipeline. Conservationists say the pipeline disturbs animals in the region. But others argue the pipeline has been a benign presence and that, similarly, President Bush's plan to allow drilling in the Arctic National Wildlife Refuge won't be harmful.

AP Photo/Al Grillo

Bush's plan calls for more domestic energy production, notably by opening the Arctic National Wildlife Refuge (ANWR) and other federal lands to oil and gas production, expanding nuclear power and increasing coal production.

"The less dependent we are on foreign sources of crude oil, the more secure we are at home," Bush said on Oct. 11. "We've spent a lot of time talking about homeland security, and an integral piece of homeland security is energy independence."

Not surprisingly, many congressional Democrats reject Bush's plan, especially drilling in the Arctic, for its potentially harmful environmental impact. Environmentalists have long advocated more federal support for developing cleaner alternatives to fossil fuels — oil, coal and natural gas — not only to reduce America's energy dependence but also to reduce emissions of both air pollutants and the gases that are thought to contribute to global warming, mainly CO_2. [2]

Senate Majority Leader Tom Daschle, D-S.D., has promised that early this year — perhaps in February — he will be ready to ask the Senate to consider a Democratic alternative to Bush's plan. The measure, introduced by Daschle on Dec. 5, is based on a bill formulated before the September attacks by Senate Energy and Natural Resources Committee Chairman Jeff Bingaman, D-N.M. It focuses more on conservation and development of alternative-energy sources. Rejecting the Bush plan as "drill, dig and burn," Daschle described the Democrats' alternative as a "balanced energy plan that will strengthen our economy, protect our environment and provide energy security." [3]

Some proponents of energy conservation found both proposals wanting. "Some provisions in the [Democrats'] bill would encourage some conservation," says Mark Hopkins, vice president of the Alliance to Save Energy, a business, consumer and government coalition. "But I actually don't find that much difference between the two approaches."

The terrorist attacks have prompted environmentalists to add a new argument to their energy conservation agenda. Brent Blackwelder, president of Friends of the Earth, wants policymakers to make national security the watchword for all energy policy. In a Nov. 20 letter to Tom Ridge, director of the new Office of Homeland Security, Blackwelder asked that "every energy provision in proposed legislation be subject to a basic security screen that asks: 'Does the proposed measure or action make our energy system more or less vulnerable to terrorism, war, natural disasters and accidents?' "

Experts say there are many things the government could do to enhance energy security. First, Makhijani says, it should phase out nuclear power — the

Fossil Fuels Generate Most U.S. Energy

Oil and other fossil fuels provide about 85 percent of all the energy used in the United States. Conservationists and other critics of U.S. energy policy want greater use of renewable domestic sources, especially geothermal, solar and wind. Renewables, including hydropower, currently provide 7 percent of the nation's total energy needs.

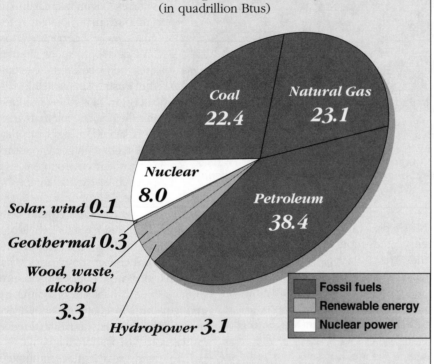

U.S. Energy Consumption in 2000 by Source
(in quadrillion Btus)

Coal **22.4**

Natural Gas **23.1**

Nuclear **8.0**

Petroleum **38.4**

Solar, wind **0.1**

Geothermal **0.3**

Wood, waste, alcohol **3.3**

Hydropower **3.1**

Fossil fuels
Renewable energy
Nuclear power

Source: "Monthly Energy Review," Energy Information Administration, December 2001.

only way, in his view, to eliminate potentially catastrophic terrorist attacks on plants, on pools of spent nuclear fuel stored onsite or on trucks and trains carrying radioactive waste across the country for more secure disposal. [4]

"The consequences of a complete loss of containment by accident or attack," the IEER report said, "could very well be on the same scale as the 1986 Chernobyl accident" in Ukraine, which released lethal amounts of radioactive iodine-131 into the atmosphere and caused 30 deaths as well as a rise in cancer incidence and environmental damage in Belarus, Ukraine, Russia and

beyond. [5]

The nuclear power industry rejects Makhijani's assessment of the threat, and Bush himself has called for expanding nuclear power as a reliable source of electricity.

The government could also decentralize the nation's electric power grid into regional and local grids — so-called distributed power systems — centered around smaller generating plants that could generate electricity from alternative, less-polluting energy sources such as solar, geothermal or biomass power.

But the most urgently needed policy change, most critics agree, is to

curb Americans' appetite for oil. Because nearly half of the oil consumed by Americans is gasoline, Americans would have to change entrenched driving habits. Hybrid cars that run on gas and electricity and easily get twice the mileage of today's fleet are just coming on the market. Hydrogen fuel cells may soon make the gasoline-powered internal-combustion engine obsolete altogether. (*See box, p. 162.*)

But conservationists say there's no need to wait for new technology to reduce Americans' demand for oil. If the federal government were to provide more support for conservation measures, they say, it would enhance energy security and reduce pollution at the same time. Fuel-economy standards, for example, have not changed since the 1980s, despite technological developments that would enable automakers to improve efficiency. The Sierra Club calls increasing gas mileage "the biggest single step to curbing global warming and saving oil." [6]

But Detroit argues that consumers prefer gas-guzzling trucks, vans and sport-utility vehicles — SUVs — which now account for about half of auto sales.

Other experts call for an increase in gasoline taxes, which are much lower in the United States than in other industrial countries. "I don't know of any experts who pay attention to energy and environmental policy who don't think that the best way of all to deal with the problem is to increase the price of energy," says Paul R. Portney, president of Resources for the Future. "That would stimulate conservation on the part of consumers and stimulate industry to look for new sources domestically and internationally on the production side."

Other policy tools that could save energy today include tax breaks for investment in renewable energy, direct funding of research and development of alternative fuels and selective procurement of items that incorporate leading-edge technology, such as hybrid vehicles for government fleets.

Amid the outpouring of post-9/11 patriotism — symbolized by the nationwide display of American flags — some experts say now is the time for a radical shift in energy policy. Americans appear eager to do their part to protect national security, they point out, but today's leaders are not tapping into that patriotism by asking this generation to make sacrifices like their parents and grandparents did during World War II.

"Everybody is looking for something they can do to help, but that message is not being sent to the people," Hopkins says. "Most politicians are a little scared of recommending change, for fear that potential voters may be upset with the idea that somehow we can't have it all."

Many lawmakers wonder whether American consumers are really ready to take drastic steps to curb their energy appetites. Many of those flags, after all, are flying from the antennas of SUVs that only get 13 miles to the gallon.

As lawmakers consider energy policy in the new post-Sept. 11 world, these are some of the issues they are considering:

Can nuclear power plants be made safe from terrorist attack?

President Bush's plan encourages further development of nuclear energy. When the plan was drawn up last spring, an electricity shortage in California was causing widespread blackouts and price hikes, cited by the administration as evidence of a new U.S. energy "crisis."

Although the shortage quickly passed, the administration did not alter its call for more electricity generators, including nuclear power plants. If enacted, Bush's plan would provide the biggest boost to the beleaguered nuclear power industry since an accident at Pennsylvania's Three Mile Island plant in 1979 sparked fears of serious radiation leaks. Though the accident was contained with no apparent harm,

Manufacturing Uses the Most Energy

Manufacturing and other industrial uses accounted for 36 percent of U.S. energy consumption in 2000 — as much as the residential and commercial sectors combined. Transportation consumed slightly more than a quarter of the energy used.

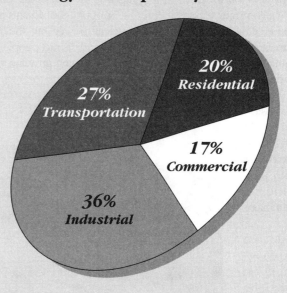

Energy Consumption by Sector

Source: "Monthly Energy Review," Energy Information Administration, December 2001

public concern was so high that no new nuclear plants were licensed after that date.

However, seven years later, the nuclear accident at Chernobyl reinforced public opposition to nuclear power. In the years that followed, several plants closed down, mainly because they were not economically viable. Today, the 103 nuclear reactors in 31 states produce about 20 percent of the electric power used in the United States.

The events of Sept. 11 raised new fears that nuclear plants could be tempting targets for terrorist attack. "It's imperative that the potential of catastrophic nuclear accidents and attacks be actually factored into energy-policy thinking," says Makhijani, of the Institute for Energy and Environmental Research. He argues that nuclear power plants are so vulnerable to attack that they

should be phased out altogether as their operating licenses expire.

Industry officials insist that such fears are unwarranted, though they concede that no actual tests have been performed to determine whether a nuclear power plant could sustain an attack by a large, fully fueled airliner.

According to Mitch Singer, a spokesman for the Nuclear Energy Institute, nuclear plants are hardened to withstand almost any foreseeable attack. The reactor core, he says, is housed inside a steel container, which in turn is surrounded by a containment building covered by a 45-inch-thick dome of reinforced concrete and lined with steel and additional concrete shielding.

"The odds of an airliner the size of a Boeing 757 or 767 hitting the containment dome at just the precise angle it would need to possibly breach the dome itself are almost infinitesimal," Singer says. "If the plane did impact at that exact angle, there probably would not be any significant damage to the reactor core itself. There's no question that the area outside would sustain a lot of damage, but the fire from the fuel igniting would basically fall off the concrete dome and burn out."

Makhijani calls Singer's assessment "dangerous speculation coming from the pocketbook and not from the head. Just think of the physical shock of a major deposition of kinetic energy and the explosion and fire that would follow. I don't even think an airliner would have to penetrate the core to create the risk of a major accident."

Without a detailed analysis based on experimentation on scale models, he says, "Industry assertions that a full-speed, full-fuel attack by a 747 on a nuclear reactor would not result in catastrophic damage are not responsible."

The industry says that new "pebble-bed modular reactors," currently under development, will be safer because they are smaller and use less fuel. But as currently designed, to be constructed without secondary containment buildings, they would be even more vulnerable to sabotage than conventional plants, many critics say. [7]

Critics of nuclear power also cite the dangers posed by spent nuclear fuel, usually stored in waste pools on site. Controversy over where to permanently dispose of this highly radioactive material has raged since the 1950s. On Jan. 10, Energy Secretary Spencer Abraham recommended that President Bush formally designate Yucca Mountain in Nevada as the nation's centralized repository for nuclear waste. The facility is currently under construction. [8] But even if the repository opens on schedule, in 2010, critics say transporting nuclear waste across the country would present the risk of accident or attack against the trucks or trains carrying it.

Supporters of Bush's plan to expand nuclear power say the risks are overstated and distract people from the country's disturbing growing reliance on foreign energy sources. Luke Popovich, a spokesman for the business-oriented Alliance for Energy and Economic Growth, says that the need to lessen U.S. dependence on foreign oil and develop more domestic resources is "the single most important lesson that can be learned from Sept. 11."

What the nation should not be doing, Popovich says, is using the terrorist attacks as "a license to condemn or boost any particular fuel source."

Some critics of Bush's nuclear-expansion proposal say terrorism is only part of the reason to oppose it. "The reason we're not expanding our nuclear capacity is simply that it's ridicu-

The House has approved oil drilling in the Arctic National Wildlife Refuge's coastal plain, but the Bush administration plan faces a battle in the Senate. Proponents and critics disagree over whether drilling will despoil the region known as America's Serengeti.

AP Photo/Arctic National Wildlife Refuge

lously expensive to build a nuclear power plant today," says Jerry Taylor, director of natural resources studies at the Cato Institute. When capital costs are taken into consideration, he says, "It is twice as expensive to generate power from a nuclear power plant as it is to generate it from a gas-fired or a coal-fired power plant. For that reason alone, we're not building nuclear power plants, and we'll never build nuclear power plants."

But Taylor stops short of supporting Makhijani's call to phase out existing nuclear plants out of security concerns. "If we're worried that terrorists may figure out a way to shut down the electricity grid, and we unilaterally start shutting down nuclear power plants, we may well do that for them," he says. "You may well cut off your nose to spite your face."

Would drilling for oil in the Arctic National Wildlife Refuge enhance energy security?

Because oil accounts for about 40 percent of U.S. energy consumption — and about 60 percent of that oil is imported — the Bush energy plan focuses on coaxing more crude out of American soil. [9]

But after more than a century of aggressive oil production, there are few promising places left to drill in the United States. Deposits in Texas and Oklahoma are petering out. Even Alaska's North Slope, which helped the United States weather earlier oil crises, is nearing the end of its productive life. Thousands of wells scattered mostly around the West still could yield oil, but at current world petroleum prices extraction would cost more than the oil would bring on the market.

Over the past decade, domestic oil production has fallen from more than 7 million barrels a day to just under 6 million, while consumption has grown to almost 20 million barrels a day. Since the mid-1990s, imports have risen to about 11 million barrels a day. [10]

Environmental-protection laws enacted decades ago have restricted oil and gas drilling on most public lands. But as domestic reserves on private lands have dwindled, the industry has sought to have those rules relaxed.

Preliminary research indicates that the biggest untapped reserves on U.S. soil are under ANWR's 1.5-million-acre coastal plain, where no energy production is currently allowed. Citing the urgent need for alternatives to oil imports, the Bush administration plan would allow oil companies to drill for oil on about 2,000 acres of the reserve.

"The mid-range estimates for reserves in ANWR are the equivalent of 10 years of oil from the Persian Gulf," wrote Energy Secretary Abraham. "That's 10 years to let diplomacy work in the event of a serious disruption in supply. Not a bad investment, I would say." [11]

Environmentalists say drilling in ANWR would disrupt wildlife migration patterns as well as pose the risk of an environmental catastrophe from potential oil spills.

Environmentalists also cite General Accounting Office (GAO) estimates that drilling for oil in ANWR would satisfy U.S. demand for no more than six months. Moreover, even if measurable reserves are found in ANWR, critics point out, it would be a decade before it would begin to flow to consumers in the Lower 48.

"What we get from the Arctic Natural Wildlife Refuge amounts to about what this country uses in six months," Daschle said. "So we [would] wait 10 years to get a six-month supply. I just

don't think that's a very good deal." [12]

The Democratic alternative to Bush's plan would continue barring ANWR oil drilling and emphasize federal support for conservation and accelerated development of renewable energy sources like geothermal, solar and wind power. Under the Democrats' plan, a tenth of all domestic electricity would have to be produced from renewable sources by 2020. By 2012, refiners would have to triple the amount of corn-derived ethanol that they produce. Ethanol is a renewable gasoline additive that increases the gasoline supply and curbs air pollution. However, ethanol critics say it takes more energy to produce than it replaces.

Other experts say both the Bush and Democrats' plans have it all wrong because they ignore the economic realities of the global oil market, in which no consuming nation can isolate itself.

"The conversation about oil imports is really no more intellectually serious than a conversation about food independence," Taylor says. "Even if all the oil we consume came from Texas and not a drop of it came from abroad, it wouldn't matter because if OPEC production were to go down, [world crude prices would skyrocket and] that would increase the price of domestic crude just as high as it would increase the price of [imported] crude."

For that reason, he says, both sides are looking at drilling in ANWR for the wrong reasons. "Even if we drill in ANWR it's not going to reduce our vulnerability to OPEC," he says. "The case for drilling in ANWR has absolutely nothing to do with national security. The case for drilling in ANWR is whether the oil beneath some of that tundra is more valuable than the wilderness above it."

Taylor proposes letting oil companies and environmental organizations bid for rights to the ANWR tracts. "If people really care about conserving ANWR they can send their checks to a Save the ANWR Fund, and maybe those checks

will be larger than what the oil industry is willing to pay for drilling rights. If it's true, as the environmentalists say, that there is very little oil there, the industry won't bid so much. It's not in their interest to overbid."

Supporters of drilling in ANWR say environmentalists ignore the industry's success in minimizing the environmental impact of their activities, especially since the disastrous *Exxon Valdez* oil spill in 1989.

"Companies are taking steps to police themselves because ever since the *Exxon Valdez* accident, shareholders don't want to be associated with a company that is routinely irresponsible," Popovich says. "The don't-explore-don't-develop crowd seems to be either believing its own propaganda or exaggerating the threat of accidents to wildlife habitat."

Should conservation play a more prominent role in energy policy?

While the Bush and Democratic energy plans both stress increasing domestic energy supplies, many experts say a better approach to solving the country's energy problems — including its vulnerability to attack — would be to emphasize conservation.

"Energy efficiency is not only the fastest, cheapest, least-polluting energy resource, but it also has a potentially major impact on energy security by reducing the energy demand on our system," says Hopkins of the Alliance to Save Energy. "It allows us to minimize the energy infrastructure's vulnerability to attack."

Conservation plans have been on the books since the mid-1970s, when a series of disruptions in Middle East oil exports caused energy prices to spike. The decade's energy crises sparked tax breaks to improve home insulation, the federal Energy Guide efficiency rating system for appliances and several other incentives to reduce energy consumption.

One of the most controversial mea-

Battle of the Energy Plans

The Bush administration and Senate Democrats have presented radically different plans to protect U.S. energy resources. The Bush plan was submitted in May and incorporated into the 2001 Securing America's Future Energy (SAFE) Act, which was passed by the House on Aug. 1. The Democrats' 2002 Energy Policy Act was introduced on Dec. 5 by Senate Majority Leader Tom Daschle, D-S.D., who plans action on the legislation in February. Here are highlights of the two competing proposals:

The Bush Plan

- Opens 2,400 acres of Alaska's Arctic National Wildlife Refuge (ANWR) to drilling for oil and gas.
- Encourages deep-water drilling in the Gulf of Mexico.
- Loosens restrictions on oil and gas production on federal lands.
- Provides $33.5 billion in tax cuts and other incentives over 10 years to encourage oil and gas exploration, nuclear power generation and research into cleaner-burning coal technology, nuclear-fuel reprocessing and renewable-energy sources.
- Provides tax breaks to purchasers of hybrid cars and other energy-efficient products.
- Sets slightly higher fuel-economy standards for sport-utility vehicles (SUVs) between 2004 and 2010.
- Calls for a 20 percent increase in air-conditioner and heat-pump efficiency instead of the 30 percent sought by the Democrats.
- Increases home-energy assistance to low-income families.

The Senate Democrats' Plan

- Continues to bar drilling in ANWR.
- Provides federal loan guarantees to build a $20 billion natural gas pipeline from Alaska to the Lower 48 states.
- Streamlines permitting of oil and gas drilling on federal lands, consistent with environmental regulations.
- Boosts research-and-development funding for renewable energy from $400 million to $733 million by 2006.
- Bans the clean-air gasoline additive MBTE, found to pollute groundwater and requires refiners to triple use of renewable ethanol, a clean-air additive made from corn, by 2012.
- Contains no provisions to improve vehicle fuel economy, expected to be addressed in separate legislation.
- Provides tax incentives, as yet unspecified, expected to be far less than the Bush plan's $33.5 billion and focused more heavily on conservation and efficiency programs than on energy production..
- More than doubles energy assistance available to low-income families.

Deep-water drilling in the Gulf of Mexico is encouraged by President Bush's energy plan, which was passed by the House in August.

AP Photo/Corpus Christi *Caller-Times*/George

More funding for research and development of wind power and other renewable energy sources is called for in the Senate Democrats' plan.

AP Photo/Don Ryan

sures, the Corporate Average Fuel Economy (CAFE) standards, required automakers to improve their products' fuel efficiency. By building smaller models, they succeeded.

But when oil prices later dropped thanks to new discoveries of deposits, consumers began buying bigger, less fuel-efficient cars and SUVs.

As oil imports continued to climb in recent years, many experts argued that the CAFE standards — which have remained unchanged for 15 years — should be tightened. However, Detroit's hottest sellers in a time of relatively low oil prices are gas-guzzling SUVs, and the industry is resisting the regulatory change for fear of losing customers. (*See "At Issue," p. 171*)

In 1996, under pressure from the automakers, Congress actually prohibited the National Highway Traffic Safety Administration (NHTSA) from even studying the possibility of raising the CAFE standards. Last year, however, lawmakers lifted the ban and required the agency to issue a new standard for the 2004 model year of SUVs, vans and other light trucks by April 1. But on Jan. 18, NHTSA announced it would maintain the current light-truck standard of 20.7 miles per gallon through 2004, saying it would be hard for the industry to make the needed improvements by the deadline.

"The automakers have scared people into believing that the only way to increase fuel efficiency is to downsize into little cars that smack into trucks and get people killed," Hopkins says. "But that's completely false. There's an array of new technologies that can be applied to cars to make them much more fuel-efficient while maintaining auto safety."

Indeed, many experts say technology exists to permit the tightening of CAFE standards to 40 miles per gallon for both cars and light trucks by 2010. But the IEER's Makhijani says the technology is available to raise it much higher — even to 100 miles per gallon by 2020. In fact, General Motors already has made a prototype fuel-cell car that gets the equivalent of that mileage. [13] Adopting such a high standard, he says, would not only reduce air pollution but increase energy security as well.

"It would even reduce the incentive

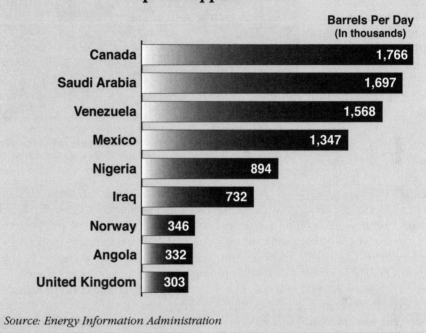

Leading U.S. Petroleum Suppliers

Canada is America's leading supplier of crude oil. Of the top five suppliers to the U.S., only Saudi Arabia is from the Middle East. Overall, the United States imported 8.9 million barrels daily from non-Arab suppliers in 2000, compared with 2.7 million barrels from Arab producers, or about 31 percent.

Top Oil Suppliers to U.S.

Barrels Per Day (In thousands)

Country	Barrels Per Day
Canada	1,766
Saudi Arabia	1,697
Venezuela	1,568
Mexico	1,347
Nigeria	894
Iraq	732
Norway	346
Angola	332
United Kingdom	303

Source: Energy Information Administration

for terrorists to blow up pipelines in Saudi Arabia," he says, "because it would show a tremendous determination by the United States not to be held hostage to Persian Gulf oil supplies and to invest enough in its domestic energy policy that it could do without."

Free-market advocates say conservation programs distort the self-correcting power of market forces. "When prices get high, people conserve," Taylor says. "They don't have to have Ralph Nader tell them to do so; they'll do it out of their own self-interest." Furthermore, he says, when prices for certain fuels are high, companies will invest in new energy supplies because it will be profitable to do so. "Those two things working together bring prices back down."

In any case, Taylor says, fuel-effi-

ciency standards are not the most effective tools to achieve energy conservation. "CAFE standards actually decrease the marginal cost of using energy," he says. "If I sell my SUV that gets 20 miles to the gallon and buy a Dodge Neon that gets 42 mpg, you've made it cheaper for me to drive, and so I'll drive more. If your idea is to reduce consumption, the only way you're going to get people to use less energy is to make it more expensive for them to use it. And the best way to do that is to increase the tax on energy."

Portney, of Resources of the Future, agrees that raising energy taxes would conserve energy more effectively than CAFE standards. "By itself, CAFE would do very little, and it would take a long time to do it," says

Portney, who chaired a National Academy of Sciences transportation panel that recently issued a report on CAFE standards. [14] That's because the tougher fuel-economy standards would only apply to new cars, which make up only 16 million of the approximately 200 million vehicles on the road. "It will take 15 or 20 years before we would have a whole fleet that gets substantially better fuel economy than today," Portney says.

Democrats are divided on the standards, with lawmakers from auto-manufacturing states siding with the industry. The Democratic alternative to Bush's energy blueprint would add up to $15 billion in tax credits and incentives to encourage energy production and conservation.

"While it is vital that we increase domestic production of traditional and alternative sources of energy," said Sen. Byron L. Dorgan, D-N.D., "it is also important, on the consumption side of the equation, that we stop wasting energy." [15] ∎

BACKGROUND

Oil Shocks

For most of America's history, abundant deposits of fossil fuels have powered the country's industrial economy and transportation system. Vast deposits of coal, long the chief energy source for factories, trains and heat-

Long lines at U.S. service stations were common in 1973, after the Organization of Petroleum Exporting Countries embargoed oil exports to the U.S. because of its support for Israel in the Yom Kippur war.

ing plants for large buildings, seemed virtually inexhaustible. After the Texas oil boom at the turn of the century, oil replaced coal in many applications, notably as the fuel of choice for the new internal combustion engine.

Oil remained abundant through the skyrocketing post-World War II demand for cars. Although domestic oil production peaked in the late 1950s and the country began to import oil, energy-security concerns were virtually absent from the policy debate.

All that changed in the 1970s, with the nation's first energy shocks and a resulting policy designed to reduce U.S. dependence on outside sources of energy. The shocks began on Oct. 20, 1973, when Arab members of the Organization of Petroleum Exporting Countries (OPEC) placed an embargo on oil exports to the United States in retaliation for its support of Israel in the Yom Kippur War earlier that month. [16]

Crude prices skyrocketed as once-abundant supplies were disrupted, triggering a surge in heating-oil prices and panic buying of gasoline. The widespread public anxiety led President Richard M. Nixon to form the Energy Research and Development Ad-

ministration (ERDA), the precursor of today's Energy Department, which was charged with making the United States energy-independent.

The chaos at gas pumps and the fear of even greater economic turmoil if supplies were disrupted prompted Congress in 1975 to create the Strategic Petroleum Reserve, a federally owned stockpile of crude stored in underground salt caverns in Louisiana and Texas. Capable of holding 700 million barrels, the reserve provided a critical buffer to oil cutoffs and constituted one of the first efforts to enhance energy security.

The first energy crisis also spurred development of new domestic oil deposits, notably in Alaska's Prudhoe Bay, where production began in the late 1970s. To curb demand, Congress in 1975 created the innovative CAFE standards requiring automakers to improve fuel consumption in new cars. By 1987, the standards required a company-wide average threshold on all new cars of 27.5 miles per gallon and 20.7 mpg for light trucks.

While automakers could continue to sell the gas-guzzlers that were so popular at the time, the rules essentially required them to produce more fuel-efficient vehicles as well in order to meet the company average. Japanese automakers specializing in small, energy-efficient cars, like Toyota and Honda, quickly stepped in to meet Americans' sudden demand for their vehicles.

OPEC's "oil weapon" had dealt a harsh blow to the United States, by then the world's biggest oil consumer. Although the embargo was short-lived, its imposition had awakened U.S. policy-makers to the threat of energy dependence.

Chronology

1970s Energy crises spur new policies to enhance U.S. energy security.

Oct. 20, 1973
Arab oil producers impose an embargo on exports to the United States, hiking oil prices and plunging the country into its first energy crisis.

1975
Congress sets up the Strategic Petroleum Reserve, a federally owned stockpile of crude oil aimed at cushioning the impact of future disruptions of oil imports. Congress also sets Corporate Average Fuel Economy (CAFE) standards requiring automakers to improve fuel efficiency in new cars.

1977
Newly elected President Carter unveils his National Energy Plan calling its goal — reduced dependence on foreign oil — the "moral equivalent of war." He asks Congress to establish a Cabinet-level Department of Energy and encourages conservation and energy-efficiency standards for appliances. The Trans-Alaska pipeline opens enabling oil produced in Alaska's Prudhoe Bay to reach U.S. markets.

1978-79
Iranian Revolution leads to cutoff of some Mideast oil, triggering the nation's second major energy crisis in a decade.

1979
An accident at Pennsylvania's Three Mile Island nuclear power plant sparks fears of a catastrophic radiation leak, bringing further nuclear plant construction to a halt.

1980s New oil becomes available from non-OPEC sources discovered in the 1970s, triggering lower world crude prices and loosening OPEC's control of prices. Amid low oil prices, the Reagan administration reverses many energy-conservation measures.

January 1981
Following the Iranian Revolution of 1978-79, oil prices peak at $34 a barrel, setting off a round of inflation and economic stagnation that lasts for much of the decade.

1986
Oil prices reach their lowest level since 1973.

1989
The oil tanker *Exxon Valdez* runs aground off Alaska, causing a disastrous oil spill.

1990s Robust economic growth spurs growing reliance on oil imports.

Aug. 2, 1990
Iraq occupies Kuwait, interrupting the flow of 1.6 million barrels of oil a day from the Persian Gulf. In retaliation, the U.N. approves an embargo barring oil exports from Iraq, a major oil producer. In the ensuing panic, oil prices rise from $13 a barrel to $40.

Jan. 16, 1991
After Iraq ignores a Jan. 15 U.N. deadline for withdrawal from Kuwait, a coalition of 31 nations and the United States launches Operation Desert Storm. Iraq is defeated after 44 days.

1992
The 1992 Energy Policy Act calls for restructuring the electric power industry, more conservation, development of renewable energy sources and alternative fuels and construction of new nuclear power plants.

1996
Congress bars the National Highway Traffic Safety Administration (NHTSA) from considering raising vehicle fuel-efficiency standards, unchanged since 1987.

2000s The Sept. 11 terrorist attacks raise new concerns about the security of U.S. energy supplies.

May 2001
President Bush declares a new energy crisis after California suffers electricity shortages. His administration unveils an energy blueprint that would open the Arctic National Wildlife Refuge (ANWR) in Alaska to oil drilling.

Dec. 5, 2001
Senate Majority Leader Tom Daschle, D-S.D., introduces a Democratic energy plan barring drilling in ANWR.

Jan. 10, 2002
Energy Secretary Spencer Abraham recommends that President Bush formally designate Nevada's Yucca Mountain as the central repository for spent nuclear fuel from the country's nuclear power plants.

Jan. 18, 2002
NHTSA declines to set stricter standards for SUVs and other light trucks beginning with the 2004 model year.

Hybrids Offer Fuel-Efficient Choices

As lawmakers prepare to debate national energy policy, new-car buyers can now make a statement of their own about energy security.

With a quarter of U.S. oil consumption coming from the troubled Middle East, many energy experts say the best way Americans can reduce the energy system's vulnerability is by using less gasoline. One way is by forsaking gas-guzzling sport-utility vehicles (SUVs) and vans — and there are now more energy-efficient models than ever before to choose from. The ultimate energy-saving, non-polluting vehicle — powered by hydrogen fuel cells — is not yet on the market.

Vehicles using cleaner-burning and more abundant natural gas have been around for some time. But because there aren't enough refueling stations around the country for their wider use, they have been almost entirely limited to fleets of delivery or service vans for government and commercial entities with their own fueling facilities.

With natural gas vehicles not yet widely available, the first commercially viable alternative to the internal-combustion engine is the so-called hybrid car, which pairs the traditional, gasoline engine with an electric engine. Unlike fully electric cars, which have to be plugged in for recharging and carry heavy, cumbersome batteries, the small batteries in hybrid cars are charged by a device that converts the energy generated during braking into electricity. By substituting electric power for gasoline for part of the driving time, hybrid cars can get up to 65 mpg — better than anything else on the road today.

Japanese automakers have beat Detroit to the punch with hybrids — just as they did during the 1970s when American consumers abandoned their big cars for smaller, fuel-efficient models. Last year, Honda came out with the Insight, a small two-seater that gets 65 mpg. Toyota was close behind with its slightly roomier, four-passenger Prius, which gets 48 mpg.

A massive switch to hybrids would greatly enhance U.S. energy security. According to one estimate, if everyone used hybrids today, the United States would save 1.6 billion barrels of oil each year — much more than the country imports from the Middle East. [1]

Although SUVs continue to dominate American new-car sales, demand for both Japanese hybrids is high. Both Toyota and Honda plan to add more models to their U.S. lineups, including a hybrid version of the popular Honda Civic, due out this year.

For its part, Detroit plans to bring hybrids to the market by 2004. But consumers' tastes continue to discourage U.S. automakers from shifting away from big vehicles. Indeed, SUVs, pickups and minivans outsold passenger cars for the first time in 2001.

Detroit automakers argue that better mileage means smaller, lighter cars that aren't as safe in collisions. But energy experts insist that SUV-lovers can have it both ways. "People don't want to have bad mileage, but unfortunately the auto industry has cried wolf, telling people with several kids that they won't be able to have the kind of big car they want [and still get good mileage]," says Mark Hopkins, vice president of the Alliance to Save Energy. "That's completely false. The same technology that's in the Prius could be applied to SUVs."

Jimmy Carter's Plan

No one seemed to have learned the energy-dependence lesson better than President Jimmy Carter. In 1977, shortly after taking office, he unveiled his National Energy Plan to help America become more energy self-sufficient. He called the goal "the moral equivalent of war." Carter asked Congress to combine various energy-related agencies, including ERDA, into the Department of Energy, with a Cabinet-level secretary of Energy.

In addition, Carter urged citizens to conserve energy, appearing on national television clad in a cardigan sweater. Carter urged Americans to turn down their thermostats in winter and up in summer, take public transportation, drive fuel-efficient cars, insulate their houses and take other steps to reduce energy consumption.

A spurt of patriotic conservation resulted, with many Americans improving their home insulation and buying more fuel-efficient cars. But they largely ignored, and sometimes ridiculed, the president's more inconvenient or uncomfortable proposals, such as taking public transportation and lowering the thermostat. Memories of the public's adverse reaction to Carter's conservation initiatives still haunt some lawmakers, who say the Carter experience proves Americans would never accept radical conservation proposals.

However, environmentalists point out that many industries and homes became much more energy efficient as a result of a variety of efficiency regulations imposed during the Carter administration. In fact, home owners and businesses alike found that energy efficiency saved them money. Congress also passed tax incentives to spur research and development of alternative energy sources for electricity generation, including such renewable sources as solar, wind and geothermal energy.

Carter's warnings about the folly of overdependence on foreign oil came true in the winter of 1978-79, when the Iranian Revolution swept the militant Muslim fundamentalist leader Ayatollah Ruhollah Khomeini to power, again disrupting the flow of oil from the Middle East. Although this second oil shock did not come as the result of an intentionally imposed embargo,

Critics say the Bush administration's energy policies discourage the development of more fuel-efficient cars. Last month, Energy Secretary Spencer Abraham announced that the administration was abandoning the Partnership for a New Generation of Vehicles, a federal program established by former President Bill Clinton that funded research that helped produce the hybrid car.

In its place, Abraham announced a new Freedom Car program, aimed at developing hydrogen as a primary fuel for cars and trucks. Fuel cells, which use hydrogen and oxygen to generate electricity and emit only water vapor, have been in development for decades. The Bush plan is aimed at giving a vital boost to fuel-cell development, in partnership with Detroit.

While applauding efforts to boost development of non-polluting cars that use an energy-secure fuel, critics fault the administration for abandoning the Clinton program, and with it, a chance to achieve immediate gains in fuel efficiency.

"It will be at least another 10 years before fuel-cell vehicles will become a serious response to the need to conserve energy," said Therese Langor, transportation director for the American Council for an Energy-Efficient Economy. "My concern is that we don't

AP Photo/Damian Dovarganes

Hybrid cars use gasoline and electric engines to achieve better mileage. Toyota says its four-seater Prius gets 48 mpg. Honda's two-seater Insight promises 65 mpg.

let the long-term objectives interfere with the desperately needed short-term goals." [2]

Abraham defended his action, saying the partnership had cost taxpayers $1.5 billion but was far from reaching its goal of creating an 80-mpg family sedan by 2004. The new administration program will produce hydrogen fuel cells suitable for all vehicles, and thus will "move us beyond fossil fuels and free us from dependence on imported oil," he wrote. "Such a vehicle can be a reality and would indeed be my dream car." [3]

Meanwhile, Japanese automakers continue to fill the "green" vehicles niche that Detroit has for now, at least, left open. Every major Japanese carmaker presented at least one less-polluting, higher-efficiency vehicle at last November's Tokyo Auto Show. And, both Honda and Toyota plan to put fuel-cell cars on the market by 2003.

It remains to be seen whether American consumers will bite.

---

[1] See "The Year in Ideas," *The New York Times Magazine*, Dec. 9, 2001, pp. 78-79.
[2] Quoted by John Gartner, "Is Bush's Fuel Cell Plan Hot Air?" *Wired News*, Jan. 22, 2002.
[3] Letter to the editor, *The New York Times*, Jan. 20, 2002.

its impact was equally damaging to the U.S. economy. Price hikes again triggered long lines at service stations, many of which imposed 10-gallon quotas per vehicle. A gasoline-allocation system introduced earlier by President Nixon — designed to facilitate deliveries and control prices — exacerbated the situation.

Carter was roundly defeated by Ronald Reagan in 1980, largely as a result of a year-long unresolved "hostage crisis" that ensued after Khomeini loyalists kidnapped 52 Americans from the U.S. Embassy in Tehran, highlighting again for Americans the instability of the Middle East.

By January 1981, oil prices had reached $34 a barrel, setting off a round of inflation and economic stagnation that would last for much of the decade.

President Reagan reversed Carter's focus on alternative fuels, demonstrating his preference for fossil fuels by opening up federal lands to oil exploration and sending U.S. warships to protect Persian Gulf shipping lanes. He allowed government subsidies for alternative fuels to expire in 1985, and federal funding for alternative fuels research dropped from $1 billion in 1981 to $116 million in 1989. [17]

Domestic Risks

The search for alternative energy sources led to renewed interest in nuclear power. The nuclear industry received generous government subsidies in the hope that it could pro-

vide a safe and reliable source of electricity. But after the 1979 accident at Three Mile Island, the government halted new reactor construction. The far more serious accident at Chernobyl only added to fears of devastating nuclear mishaps.

Despite the far-reaching policy responses to the oil disruptions of the 1970s and '80s, some energy experts warned that policy-makers had ignored important vulnerabilities in the U.S. energy system. According to a 1980 report by the Federal Emergency Management Agency (FEMA), the centralized nature of the electricity grid and fuel pipelines left these essential energy conduits open to potentially debilitating attacks.

Indeed, the 800-mile Trans-Alaska Pipeline, which in 1977 began carrying oil from the North Slope oil fields to the port of Valdez, had already been attacked in 1978 by an unknown vandal, resulting in a 700,000-gallon spill. To reduce this type of risk, the report called for the rapid development of solar and other non-fossil-fuel energy sources to generate electricity and the construction of smaller, regional grids to transmit it to consumers. "Dispersed, decentralized and renewable energy sources can reduce national vulnerability and the likelihood of war by substituting for vulnerable centralized resources," the FEMA report concluded. [18] The report failed to prompt any action by the federal government.

Another report that failed to result in significant policy changes came out in 1981. Commissioned by the Defense Department, it concluded that the domestic energy infrastructure — such as pipelines, nuclear power plants and transmission lines — was even more vulnerable to disruption, accidental or intentional, than supplies of foreign oil. [19]

Energy Use

During the 1980s the United States and other major industrial powers continued to try to reduce their vulnerability to Middle East political instability by seeking alternative sources of oil. Rich deposits of non-OPEC oil, which had been discovered in Mexico, Nigeria and the North Sea in the 1970s, were contributing sizable exports by the early 1980s. In addition to its Alaska oil fields, the United States turned to neighboring Mexico and Venezuela for an increasing share of its ever-growing imports of crude. Although Venezuela is an OPEC member, its proximity to the United States reduces the risk of unintentional supply interruptions resulting from turmoil in the Middle East.

Largely as a result of this diversification, OPEC lost much of its ability to control the output and price of oil on world markets. The increase in crude supplies caused prices to fall during most of the 1980s, reaching their lowest level in 1986 since the first oil shock in 1973.

Energy conservationists say national leaders should tap into the patriotism that blossomed after the terrorist attacks last Sept. 11 and ask Americans to trade in their gas-guzzling SUVs and light trucks for more fuel-efficient vehicles.

AP Photo/April L. Brown

Gasoline became cheaper, prompting many U.S. motorists to abandon the conservation effort and to purchase bigger, less-efficient cars, especially the new and wildly popular additions to the light-truck category — SUVs — and passenger vans. These large vehicles, held to less stringent fuel economy standards than cars, are high consumers of fuel.

Growing gasoline consumption and dwindling domestic petroleum reserves led to greater U.S. dependence on foreign oil. The security threat posed by increasing oil imports returned to the fore on Aug. 2, 1990, when Iraq invaded its Persian Gulf neighbor Kuwait, cutting off the flow of 1.6 million barrels of oil a day from the region. In retaliation for the invasion, a U.S.-led coalition eventually went to war in January 1991 and expelled Iraq from Kuwait, and the United Nations approved an embargo on oil exports from Iraq, a major producer. Oil prices rose from $13 a barrel to $40.

Action in Congress and the States

Though the oil-price spike surrounding the Persian Gulf War was short-lived, concern over U.S. vulnerability to oil shocks prompted Congress to pass sweeping energy legislation, the first major attempt to reduce the country's dependence on foreign oil since the 1970s.

Based on an energy blueprint issued by President George Bush, the 1992 Energy Policy Act called for restructuring the electric power industry, encouraging conservation, developing renewable energy sources and alternative fuels and facilitating construction of new nuclear power plants. But aside from a new research program to reduce the hazards of nuclear waste from civilian reactors, the law contained few new provisions to enhance security around energy facilities. [20]

In fact, the law's biggest impact was on electricity markets, since it opened the door for deregulation of electric utilities, the last heavily regulated energy sector. Beginning with New Hampshire in 1996, several states began to free up their electric utilities to competition.

The same year, California became

the first state to deregulate the retail side of the utility industry. The poorly executed transition in 2000 and early 2001 gave Californians a taste of what a catastrophic disruption in electricity supplies would look like. Power providers, many of them out of state, were free to withhold electricity from the California market and profit from the resulting higher prices. State utilities suddenly were unable to buy all the power they needed, even at higher prices, triggering four blackouts and more rate hikes to dampen demand.

Gasoline prices also spiked in 2001, reaching their highest levels — around $1.70 per gallon — since the gulf war. A shortfall in natural gas supplies, increasingly the fuel of choice for home heating and new power plants, also pushed up energy prices last year. The price hikes and uncertainties surrounding utility deregulation prompted President Bush to declare that the country faced the worst energy crisis since the late 1970s. In May he unveiled his energy plan, based largely on increasing domestic production of oil, gas and nuclear power. ∎

CURRENT SITUATION

Competing Energy Plans

The main difference between the Bush energy plan, passed by the House last August, and the Democratic alternative introduced in December, boils down to a distinction between supply and demand. (*See sidebar, p. 162.*) The House bill stresses the supply side of the energy equation by boosting domestic production of traditional fossil fuels — oil, gas and coal. In addition to opening federal

lands to more oil and gas drilling, it would help fund development of technology to make coal, American's most abundant fossil fuel, burn more cleanly. The measure also would encourage more nuclear power to generate electricity.

The Democrats' plan emphasizes reducing Americans' demand for imported oil and other fossil fuels. The bill's tax incentives and programs are weighted toward conservation and development of alternative energy sources. It would require that by 2020, 10 percent of the nation's electricity be generated by non-hydroelectric renewable sources, which today make up less up than 5 percent.

Curbing pollution is another major goal of the Democrats' proposal. Fossil fuels not only pollute the air, but also are considered by most scientists to be the primary contributor to global warming. Recognizing that the country will not soon wean itself entirely from its reliance on oil, the bill would encourage drilling on all federal lands already open to oil and gas production, but pointedly would not allow drilling in ANWR.

Despite the rhetoric, many experts say the two approaches are more alike than they are at odds. "There is probably a greater commonality in these two plans than the conventional wisdom would admit," says Popovich, of the Alliance for Energy and Economic Growth. "ANWR is the single largest difference, and CAFE standards are another, but there are areas where both approaches increase energy efficiency [and] conservation efforts and modernize the infrastructure."

The sudden collapse in December of Enron Corp., the Texas energy giant, has complicated the Bush administration's job of selling its energy plan. Enron's bankruptcy, the largest in U.S. history, left thousands of employees and small investors holding worthless Enron stock in their retirement plans.

Congressional and Justice Depart-

ment investigations into alleged wrongdoing by Enron executives, who had funneled large campaign contributions to influential lawmakers of both parties, promised to muddy the energy-policy debate with questions about the company's influence in policy proposals. Former Enron CEO Kenneth L. Lay, for example, reportedly had a large and perhaps inappropriate role in crafting the Bush energy blueprint last spring under Vice President Dick Cheney's direction. In addition, questions were being raised about Enron's contacts with the Bush administration shortly before the company collapsed. [21]

Citing executive privilege, the White House has refused to release records of the energy task force proceedings, which included six meetings with Enron and other energy companies.

The controversy intensified on Jan. 25, when U.S. Comptroller General David M. Walker, head of the General Accounting Office, Congress' investigative arm, said he would sue the White House, if necessary, to gain access to the records. Two days later, Cheney said he would not hand them over.

The vice president based his forceful rejection of the GAO's demand for information on his desire to restore presidential power to its previous level. "I have repeatedly seen an erosion of the powers and the ability of the president of the United States to do his job," he told the ABC News program "This Week." "We are weaker today as an institution because of the unwise compromises that have been made over the last 30 to 35 years," he added.

Meanwhile, President Bush went on the offensive last month to shore up union support for his energy plan. Opening ANWR to oil exploration and production, he said, would create new union jobs at a time of economic hardship. "This energy bill that we're working on is a jobs bill," he told union leaders in a visit to the Teamsters Union headquarters in Washington. "It will be good for our foreign policy, good for our national security and, more importantly, it will be good for jobs." [22] The Teamsters, contending the new drilling could employ hundreds of thousands of new workers, have endorsed the proposal.

On Jan. 22, Sen. John F. Kerry, D-Mass., tried to gain the upper hand in the energy debate by announcing he would soon introduce a new Democratic bill that would increase CAFE standards by an unspecified amount and increase tax breaks aimed at developing new energy sources. "If we enact the entire Bush energy plan, we will find ourselves 20 years from now more dependent on foreign oil than we are today," he said. By 2020, under Kerry's plan, alternative and renewable fuels would account for 20 percent of energy use in the United States — twice as much as under the earlier Democratic proposal. [23]

"Many politicians may feel that we need to increase the fuel efficiency of vehicles," says Hopkins of the Alliance to Save Energy. "That's almost a given of a smart policy."

The prospects for passage of either Bush's energy plan or the Democrats' alternative are far from certain.

After receiving endorsement for his plan by the Teamsters Union — traditionally allied with the Democrats — Bush predicted optimistically that he had the 60 votes in the Senate needed to ensure congressional approval. [24]

But Senate Democrats are unlikely to approve any measure that allows drilling in ANWR, and Sen. Ted Stevens, R-Alaska, has said he would filibuster any bill that does not allow it. Daschle plans to bring his party's alternative plan to the floor the week of Feb. 11. But both Sens. Joseph Lieberman, D-Conn., and Kerry, who calls it a "status quo" plan, have vowed to filibuster the measure as it stands. [25]

Adding to the uncertainty is the political fallout from the Enron collapse, which Rep. John Dingell, D-Mich., and

After more than a century of domestic oil exploration and production, there are few promising places to drill in the United States. Even Alaska's North Slope is nearing the end of its productive life.

AP Photo/Tim Sharp

other Democratic lawmakers have cited as reason to reconsider electric utility deregulation, which they already were considering doing as a result of the California deregulation fiasco. [26]

Increasing Security

One of the few non-controversial actions President Bush has taken since Sept. 11 to shore up energy security was his Nov. 13 directive to keep the Strategic Petroleum Reserve filled to its 700-million-barrel capacity, up from the current level of 549 million barrels. At current consumption levels of almost 20 million barrels a day, about 60 percent of which is imported, the move would enable the United States to weather a cutoff of foreign oil supplies for a couple of weeks beyond the 54 days the reserve currently covers.

"Our current oil inventories, and those of our allies who hold strategic stocks, are sufficient to meet any potential near-term disruption in supplies," Bush said in announcing his decision. "Filling the SPR up to capacity will strengthen the long-term energy security of the United States."

But critics continue to insist that neither the Republican nor the Democratic energy plans sufficiently address the new kinds of energy-security threats made clear on Sept. 11. "The ideas in the public debate are too timid and don't correspond to the magnitude of the problem," says Makhijani, who estimates that it would take about $20 billion a year over 10 years to achieve his goals of phasing out nuclear energy, speeding the switch from oil to renewable sources, decentralizing the electricity grid and taking other steps to reduce the energy system's vulnerability. His plan would cost "a fraction" of the Bush tax cut and "a tiny fraction of current military expenditures," he says. Instead of tax breaks to advance these goals, as

At Issue:

Should auto fuel-economy standards be tightened to reduce dependence on foreign oil?

DAVID FRIEDMAN
SENIOR ANALYST, CLEAN VEHICLES PROGRAM,
UNION OF CONCERNED SCIENTISTS

FROM TESTIMONY BEFORE THE SENATE COMMERCE, SCIENCE AND TRANSPORTATION COMMITTEE, DEC. 6, 2001

u.S. drivers consumed 121 billion gallons of gasoline in 2000. . . [which is] 40 percent of the oil products that the nation consumes. . . . Vehicle travel is expected to increase nearly 50 percent over the next 20 years. . . .

SUVs and other light trucks are allowed to use one-third more fuel than cars under current CAFE . . . requirements. This "light truck loophole" caused consumers to use about 20 billion more gallons of gasoline in 2000 and cost consumers about $30 billion more than if the fuel economy standards of light trucks [were] the same as that of cars. . . .

Raising fuel economy standards is the fastest, least expensive and most effective thing Congress can do to reduce our future dependence on oil. The oil savings associated with reaching an average fuel economy of 40 mpg by 2012 for all new cars and light trucks would be 1.9 million barrels per day in that year alone — four times the expected peak output from the Arctic National Wildlife Refuge at today's oil prices and over three times the oil we imported from Iraq last year (and more than we imported from Saudi Arabia).

The cumulative oil savings would be about 3 billion barrels of oil or 125 billion gallons of gasoline. That means that in 10 years we would save almost as much oil as is recoverable at today's oil prices from the whole Arctic refuge in its 50-60 year lifetime. That is also 25 times the oil savings called for in the House energy bill. . . . At the same time we [would be] significantly cutting our oil dependence, consumers [would be] saving $12.6 billion in 2012 and close to $100 billion per year by 2015, while the auto industry will see a growth of over 40,000 jobs in the U.S. . . .

[I]t is clear that the technology exists to cost-effectively increase fuel economy with resulting benefits to oil use, consumers and the environment. These significant improvements in fuel economy can be achieved with existing technology, enabling us to achieve progress in fuel economy in the near term as we watch the market for hybrid electric and fuel-cell vehicles grow.

[B]oth near- and longer-term increases in fuel economy . . . can be accompanied by the same safety, comfort and performance consumers expect today, and could even improve the overall safety of America's highways if the light-truck loophole is closed.

THOMAS J. DAVIS
VICE PRESIDENT, NORTH AMERICAN PRODUCT DEVELOPMENT, GENERAL MOTORS CORP.

FROM TESTIMONY BEFORE THE SENATE COMMERCE, SCIENCE AND TRANSPORTATION COMMITTEE, DEC. 6, 2001

*a*s the Congress has examined energy policy this year, a number of statements have been made about the continuing need for the U.S. to conserve energy, to increase and diversify energy supplies and to enhance energy security. We share these concerns. . . .

We see the ultimate vision for a sustainable energy future in vehicles powered by hydrogen fuel cells. Hydrogen fuel made from renewable sources of energy can be used to power fuel-cell vehicles that are more than twice as energy efficient as today's vehicles and emit only pure water. . . .

For those who argue for more high-fuel-economy vehicles, many such vehicles are available today. In fact, over 50 models . . . offer fuel economy above 35 mpg, but they attract less than 1 percent of sales. Hence, they have an insignificant impact on Corporate Average Fuel Economy, or CAFE. . . .

What does our long-term vision for hydrogen-based, clean, efficient, personal mobility have to do with CAFE policy? Well, CAFE is actually an obstacle to the realization of this vision. With relatively low gasoline prices, CAFE works against the market, the consumer and long-term technology development. . . .

We are investing significant engineering resources to create a completely revolutionary technical capability. A near-term shift in CAFE pulls engineering resources back to incremental advancements in internal-combustion-engine systems and to reductions in vehicle power, weight and size. . . .

There are better ways than CAFE to conserve petroleum in the transportation sector. With over 200 million passenger vehicles already on American roads today, reducing their fuel consumption would be the best policy to pursue. For example, we see opportunities in incentives to scrap older, less-efficient vehicles and to reduce fuel-consuming congestion on U.S. roads.

In addition, fuel savings can be encouraged through incentives to deploy hybrid buses for urban mass transit — since the fuel savings of hybrid powertrains are greatest in stop-and-go urban driving and in high-consumption vehicles like buses — and the purchase of hybrid vehicles for government fleets. . . .

These types of policies would . . . reduce fuel consumption by the large number of vehicles already on the road. Advances in the energy efficiency of future vehicle[s] can also contribute, though at a slower pace, because new vehicles [only] replace approximately 5 percent of the on-road fleet each year.

the proposed energy plans would provide, Makhijani would use federal money to buy renewable energy, fuel cells, more efficient cars and other leading-edge technology to hasten its commercialization.

Meanwhile, energy companies have increased security around hundreds of power plants and refineries and thousands of miles of pipelines and transmission lines since the attacks. In late November the Federal Bureau of Investigation (FBI) warned gas companies that Osama bin Laden had made arrangements for attacks on North American natural gas pipelines if he was captured or killed. [27]

However, guarding these lines, which stretch over 260,000 miles, is a daunting task. In an unrelated incident on Oct. 4, an intoxicated man took a potshot at a remote section of the Trans-Alaska Pipeline, causing a 286,000-gallon oil spill and shutting down the oil flow until workers could find and stop the leak. [28]

Some Critics Dismiss Concerns

Of all the components of the energy system, nuclear power plants and their spent-fuel pools may hold the greatest potential for cataclysmic damage from terrorist attack, critics say. Since Sept. 11, security measures have been tightened around nuclear plants, including contingents of National Guardsmen patrolling the perimeters, but the efforts have not always been enough to allay fears of neighboring residents. A group of New York residents recently petitioned the Nuclear Regulatory Commission to shut down the two reactors at Indian Point on the Hudson River until security measures are tightened. Meanwhile, the NRC last month announced plans to dispense free doses of potassium iodide — thought to protect against radiation poisoning — to neighbors of the nation's nuclear power plants, in case of an accident or sabotage. [29]

But some conservative economists

say the concern about sabotage against most of the energy system is overblown. "There are only so many human bullets that bin Laden can fire at us; in fact, we haven't seen any since Sept. 11 in the United States," says Taylor of the Cato Institute, who says fears of attack on the power grid or most utility plants are unwarranted. "One has to assume that there is a finite number of agents he can send on suicide missions, which means the opportunity costs of any of these actions are quite steep from his perspective. So if you've got maybe 15 agents who are capable of being human bombs, would you really fire them at some gas-fired power plant in Kentucky? I can think of 100 targets that would be more psychologically and economically important than most of the power plants or most of the electricity grid."

In Taylor's view, beefing up security around energy infrastructure at government expense actually would make the energy system more vulnerable to terrorist attacks. "Most of the risks of terrorism in the energy markets would be internalized quite nicely if you didn't have the federal government constantly picking up the tab for security and suggesting they it may well bail out industries that find themselves on the receiving end of terrorism," he says, adding that the marketplace is a better guardian of energy security. "If energy investors were to find that the costs of providing security for their plants were their cost to bear, and not the federal government's, I think you'd find investors naturally putting their money in places which are less likely to be at risk."

But in view of the massive airport security lapses that occurred on Sept. 11 under the auspices of private security agencies, many have questioned the ability and willingness of the private sector to provide adequate security for various terrorist targets.

Even state and local law enforcement agencies may not be up to the task of safeguarding the nation's ener-

gy system. Joseph Tinkham II, Maine's commissioner of emergency management, recently appealed for federal help after a security audit uncovered numerous lapses around nuclear power plants and other key facilities.

"While we in the states take great pains to protect our citizens from the natural perils which may befall us," Tinkham said, "protection from attack by a foreign enemy upon our people in their homes and in their places of business has, for almost two centuries, been within the purview of the federal government." [30] ∎

OUTLOOK

Changing Alliances

N ow in its fourth month, the war on terrorism may affect U.S. relations with some of its major foreign oil suppliers in unpredictable ways. About a quarter of U.S. oil imports come from the Persian Gulf, the epicenter of fundamentalist Islam. Saudi Arabia, where bin Laden and most of the suicide hijackers implicated in the Sept. 11 attacks were born, is also the third-largest source of oil imports to the United States. Bin Laden, living in exile, has repeatedly called for the overthrow of the Saudi royal family for allowing some 5,000 American troops in the country, an affront, he says, to the Muslim holy cities of Mecca and Medina.

According to a recent *Washington Post* story, due to pressure from conservative Muslims, the Saudi government may soon ask the United States to withdraw its forces from the Prince Sultan Air Base, which has served as a key command-and-control post for the U.S. military since the Gulf War. [31] Although Saudi officials deny the report and Secretary of State Colin L. Powell says he has received no such request, some lawmakers suggest that a withdrawal might help quell instability in that vital oil-producing country.

"We need a base in that region, but it seems to me we should find a place that is more hospitable," said Senate Armed Services Committee Chairman Carl M. Levin, D-Mich. "I don't think they want us to stay there." [32]

The United States maintains other bases in Kuwait, Bahrain and Oman along the Persian Gulf oil transit routes, as well as in Turkey.

As the region's biggest oil producer, Saudi Arabia continues to dominate OPEC and its production decisions. But some experts downplay the country's ability to wreak havoc on the U.S. energy system again. "OPEC needs our money more than we need its oil," the Cato Institute's Taylor says. "One of the reasons why there is instability in Saudi Arabia is that the oil dole is much lower today than it was 20 years ago. If Saudi Arabia were to cut production by half, they'd find themselves in a revolution before we'd find ourselves in a depression."

The war on terrorism has enhanced U.S. standing in other potentially key oil supplying countries, notably Russia — the world's second-largest oil exporter — and the former Soviet republics of Kyrgyzstan, Uzbekistan and Tajikistan, which ring the Caspian Sea and are considered to cover the world's last sizable reservoir of untapped oil. The recent thawing of U.S. relations with Russia has raised hopes that the former Cold War enemy could become a reliable energy supplier for the West. [33]

Plus, the United States has been involved in ongoing negotiations for construction of a major oil pipeline out of the Caspian region, which the United States hopes will be routed to the Mediterranean through NATO ally Turkey. Russia and the three Caspian republics have supported the United States' intervention in Afghanistan.

At the same time, the anti-terrorism campaign is complicating relations with Iran, which has significant oil supplies. While Iran has not been a source of U.S. imports for more than a decade, the rise over the past several years of political moderates less hostile to the United States had fueled hopes for improving relations with this major Persian Gulf producer.

However, reports that bin Laden's Al Qaeda militants may recently have fled from Afghanistan into neighboring Iran has prompted concern in Washington that Tehran may try to influence the delicate nation-building effort under way in Afghanistan under U.S. leadership. In a thinly veiled threat against interference, Bush said that if Iranian officials "in any way, shape or form try to destabilize the [Afghan] government," the United States would "deal with them . . . in diplomatic ways — initially." [34]

However the fight against terrorism shifts allegiances in the major oil-exporting regions, no one expects the United States to wean itself entirely from foreign oil, or indeed from Middle Eastern oil.

"I don't think it is necessary or even desirable to get rid of oil imports altogether," says Makhijani of the Institute for Energy and Environmental Research. "So many regions of the world would become bankrupt that it would cause a lot of harm, because the West has been the one to cultivate oil-exporting countries, and that cannot suddenly be changed. What is necessary, I think, is to eliminate the leverage that one region has on world supplies." ∎

Notes

[1] Arjun Makhijani, "Securing the Energy Future of the United States: Oil, Nuclear, and Electricity Vulnerabilities and a Post-September 11, 2001, Roadmap for Action," Institute for Energy and Environmental Research (IEER), November 2001.

[2] For background, see Mary H. Cooper, "Global Warming Treaty," *The CQ Researcher*, Jan. 26, 2001, pp. 41-64.

[3] "Senate Democrats Unveil Broad-Based Energy Policy Bill," Dow Jones International News, Dec. 5, 2001.

[4] For background, see Brian Hansen, "Nuclear Waste," *The CQ Researcher*, June 8, 2001, pp. 489-504.

[5] IEER, *op. cit.*, p. 30.

[6] Sierra Club Global Warming and Energy Program, www.sierraclub.org.

[7] For background, see Mary H. Cooper, "Energy Policy," *The CQ Researcher*, May 25, 2001, pp. 441-464.

[8] See Chuck McCutcheon, "Energy Secretary's Recommendation to Use Yucca Mountain as Waste Site Signals Start of Climactic Fight," *CQ Weekly*, Jan. 12, 2002, p. 132.

[9] "National Energy Policy," Report for the National Energy Policy Development Group, May 2001.

[10] U.S. Department of Energy, Energy Information Administration, "Short-Term Energy Outlook," January 2002.

[11] Spencer Abraham, "Drill ANWR Now," *The Wall Street Journal*, Nov. 8, 2001.

[12] Quoted in Dennis Gale, "Daschle: Senate Democrats' Energy Bill Would Be Good for South Dakota," The Associated Press, Dec. 6, 2001.

[13] IEER, *op. cit.*, p. 50.

[14] National Research Council, Transportation Research Board, "Effectiveness and Impact of Corporate Average Fuel Economy (CAFE) Standards," 2001.

[15] Quoted by Tom Doggett, "Senate Democrats Push U.S. Energy Conservation," Reuters English News Service, Dec. 5, 2001.

[16] For background, see David Masci, "Middle East Conflict," *The CQ Researcher*, April 6, 2001, pp. 273-296.

[17] For background, see Rodman D. Griffin, "Alternative Energy," *The CQ Researcher*, July 10, 1992, pp. 573-596.

[18] Environmental Policy Institute/Friends of the Earth, "Dispersed, Decentralized and Renewable Energy Sources: Alternatives to National Vulnerability and War," December 1980.

[19] Amory B. Lovins and L. Hunter Lovins, *Brittle Power: Energy Strategy for National Security* (1981), republished in 1982 by the Rocky Mountain Institute.

[20] For information on the act, see 1992 *CQ Almanac* (1993), pp. 231-258. See also Adriel Bettelheim, "Utility Deregulation," *The CQ Researcher*, Jan. 14, 2000, pp. 1-16.

[21] See Dana Milbank and Paul Blustein, "White

House Aided Enron in Dispute," *The Washington Post*, Jan. 19, 2002.

[22] Quoted by James Gerstenzang, "Bush Gets Union Allies in Arctic Drilling Drive," *Los Angeles Times*, Jan. 18, 2002.

[23] See Dana Milbank, "Sen. Kerry to Offer Alternative to Bush Energy Proposal," *The Washington Post*, Jan. 22, 2002.

[24] See Alex Keto, "Bush Moves to Bolster Energy Plan," *Dow Jones International News*, Jan. 18, 2002.

[25] "Bush Calls for More Mining — Kerry Rips 'Status Quo' Plan," *Chicago Tribune*, Jan. 23, 2002.

[26] See Jackie Calmes and Tom Hamburger, "Cast Prepares for Congressional Curtain to Rise on Enron Scandal," *The Wall Street Journal*, Jan. 23, 2002.

[27] See "Natural Gas Lines May Be Targets if Bin Laden Falls, FBI Warns," *Los Angeles Times*, Nov. 27, 2001.

[28] See Kim Murphy, "Alaskan Pipeline Poses Special Kind of Security Risk," *Los Angeles Times*, Oct. 14, 2001.

[29] See Randal C. Archibold, "In Shadow of Reactors, Parents Seek Peace of Mind in a Pill," *The New York Times*, Jan. 21, 2002.

[30] Tinkham testified on Dec. 11, 2001, before the Senate Governmental Affairs Committee.

[31] See David B. Ottaway and Robert G. Kaiser, "Saudis May Seek U.S. Exit," *The Washington Post*, Jan. 18, 2002.

[32] *Ibid.*

[33] For background, see David Masci, "The Future of U.S.-Russia Relations," *The CQ Researcher*, Jan. 18, 2002, pp. 25-48, particularly, "Russia Flexes Its Oil Muscles," p. 40.

[34] See Eric Schmitt, "Bush Tells Iran Not to Undercut Afghan Leaders," *The New York Times*, Jan. 11, 2002.

FOR MORE INFORMATION

American Council for an Energy-Efficient Economy, 1001 Connecticut Ave., N.W., Suite 801, Washington, D.C. 20036; (202) 429-0063; www.aceee.org. Dedicated to advancing energy efficiency as a means of promoting both economic prosperity and environmental protection.

Competitive Enterprise Institute, 1001 Connecticut Ave., N.W., Suite 1250, Washington, D.C. 20036; (202) 331-1010; www.cei.org. This conservative research group advocates free enterprise and limited government. It calls for broader deregulation of energy markets and more domestic energy production.

Energy Information Administration, U.S. Department of Energy, 1000 Independence Ave., S.W., Washington, D.C. 20585; (202) 586-8800; www.eia.doe.gov. Collects and publishes a vast compendium of information on national and international energy trends, reserves, production, demand, consumption and prices.

League of Conservation Voters, 1920 L St., N.W., Suite 800, Washington D.C. 20036; (202) 785-8683; www.lcv.org. Supports candidates who call for strong environmental-protection measures. It is highly critical of the Bush administration's new energy proposals.

National BioEnergy Industries Association, 1616 H St., N.W., 8th Floor, Washington, D.C. 20006; (202) 628-7745; www.bioenergy.org. Represents landowners, foresters, equipment manufacturers and others involved in developing technologies to generate electricity from wood and other plant waste, or biomass.

National Highway Traffic Safety Administration, 400 Seventh St., S.W., Washington, D.C. 20590; (202) 366-9550; www.nhtsa.dot.gov. This agency issues vehicle mileage and safety standards.

Natural Resources Defense Council, 1200 New York Ave., Suite 400, Washington, D.C. 20005-4709; (202) 289-6868; www.nrdc.org. Staffed by lawyers and scientists, the NRDC undertakes litigation and research to protect the environment.

Nuclear Energy Institute, 1776 I St., N.W., Suite 400, Washington, D.C. 20006; (202) 739-8000; www.nei.org. Promotes expansion of the nuclear energy industry.

Resources for the Future, 1616 P St., N.W., Washington, D.C. 20036; (202) 328-5000; www.rff.org. Conducts studies on the economic and policy aspects of energy and the development of natural resources.

Solar Energy Industries Association, 1616 H St., N.W., 8th Floor, Washington, D.C. 20006; (202) 628-7745; www.seia.org. Represents industries with interests in the production and use of solar energy and monitors legislation and regulations on renewable energy.

Union of Concerned Scientists, 2 Brattle Square, Cambridge, Mass. 02238; (617) 547-5552; www.ucsusa.org. Supports the development of non-fossil fuels to help improve air quality and reduce emissions of greenhouse gases implicated in global warming.

Bibliography

Selected Sources

Books

Deffeyes, Kenneth S., *Hubbert's Peak: The Impending World Oil Shortage*, Princeton University Press, 2001.

As global oil reserves dwindle, the author predicts that petroleum production will peak within five years and fall below demand by the end of the decade. He advises policy-makers to encourage development of alternative sources before then.

Hoffmann, Peter, *Tomorrow's Energy: Hydrogen, Fuel Cells, and the Prospects for a Cleaner Planet*, MIT Press, 2001.

The development of a "hydrogen economy," in which the most abundant element in the universe would largely replace fossil fuels, is drawing closer. This review of the research and development of hydrogen fuel cells paints a hopeful scenario for achieving economic growth without pollution or dependence on foreign energy sources.

Yergin, Daniel, *The Prize: The Epic Quest for Oil, Money & Power*, Simon & Schuster, 1991.

Published over a decade ago, this exhaustive account remains the best, single source of information about the rise of the oil industry, the United States' steady reliance on this fuel for its economic well-being and its impact on national security.

Articles

Begley, Sharon, "Driving Toward Independence: Yes, the U.S. Can Live without Saudi Oil — and Even Keep Its SUVs," *Newsweek*, Nov. 19, 2001.

This year SUV sales were up 40 percent over 2000, even after the Sept. 11 terrorist attacks suggested to some experts that the United States needs to use less gasoline to reduce its vulnerability to disruption of oil imports from the Persian Gulf. Though domestic production could help reduce oil imports, conservation may hold the greatest promise for energy security.

"How Much Would It Help?" *The Economist*, Oct. 20, 2001.

President Bush's plan to drill for oil in Alaska's Arctic National Wildlife Refuge (ANWR) would barely make a dent in U.S. oil imports. It may take a decade to ready the site for production, but industry supporters say it can increase domestic production without harming the environment.

Lovins, Amory B., and L. Hunter Lovins, "Fool's Gold in Alaska," *Foreign Affairs*, July/August 2001.

Rising oil imports are the legacy of policy-makers' failure to enact rigorous conservation measures over the past 15

years. Relatively low oil prices during this period have hidden from consumers the threat to energy security posed by the country's growing demand for oil imports.

Milbank, Dana, "Cheney Refuses Records' Release," *The Washington Post*, Jan. 28, 2002, p. A1.

The vice president says he won't give congressional investigators records from the administration's energy-policy development meetings.

Schwartz, Nelson D., "Breaking OPEC's Grip: Forget about Energy Independence," *Fortune*, Nov. 12, 2001.

The United States will never achieve energy independence, but it can reduce its reliance on oil imports from the politically volatile Middle East, thanks to technology allowing new access to deep, underwater deposits.

Reports and Studies

Energy Information Administration, U.S. Department of Energy, "Monthly Energy Review," January 2002.

The monthly reports feature historical data on domestic energy consumption, including sources of foreign oil and uses of fossil and renewable resources.

Makhijani, Arjun, *Securing the Energy Future of the United States: Oil, Nuclear, and Electricity Vulnerabilities and a Post-September 11, 2001, Roadmap for Action*, Institute for Energy and Environmental Research, November 2001.

The terrorist attacks should spur the government to take urgent action to protect the U.S. energy system, including a phaseout of nuclear power plants, decentralization of the electricity grid and rapid development of renewable energy sources.

National Energy Policy Development Group, *National Energy Policy*, The White House, May 2001.

President Bush's energy task force, led by Vice President Dick Cheney, recommends increasing domestic production of fossil fuels by opening Alaska's Arctic National Wildlife Refuge and other federal lands to oil and gas production.

National Research Council, Transportation Research Board, *Effectiveness and Impact of Corporate Average Fuel Economy (CAFE) Standards*, National Academy Press, 2001.

This review of fuel-efficiency standards in place since the 1970s counters industry arguments that improving fuel economy reduces auto safety by requiring automakers to build lighter, smaller cars. It concludes that efficiency could be improved using existing technology.

10 Civil Liberties in Wartime

DAVID MASCI AND PATRICK MARSHALL

As a Republican senator from Missouri, Attorney General John Ashcroft served on the Judiciary Committee. So when he testified on Capitol Hill on Dec. 6 before his old panel, the camaraderie was palpable as he joked and reminisced with his former colleagues.

But the smiles quickly disappeared when the hearing — on civil liberties following the Sept. 11 terrorist attacks on the World Trade Center and the Pentagon by Middle Eastern airplane hijackers — began in earnest. Democrats and Republicans alike closely questioned and even criticized Ashcroft on some of the tough, new policy changes made by the Bush administration in the name of national security — changes that critics say restrict cherished freedoms.

In particular, committee members worried that the Justice Department's continued detention of more than 600 mostly Muslim men may infringe on their rights. They also questioned Ashcroft's recent order permitting federal agents to eavesdrop on conversations between inmates and their attorneys. Until now, such communications have been considered privileged, or protected by law from disclosure. In addition, many senators worried that the president's plan to try foreigners charged with terrorist acts in secret military tribunals might lead to "victor's justice" at the expense of due process.

"The Constitution does not need protection when its guarantees are popular," said Committee Chairman Patrick Leahy, D-Vt. "But it very much

From *The CQ Researcher,*
December 14, 2001.

President Bush and Attorney General John Ashcroft, at left, defend their tough, new policies as vital to combating terrorism, but civil libertarians say they undermine cherished American freedoms.

needs our protection when events tempt us to, 'just this once,' abridge its guarantees of our freedom."

Ashcroft repeatedly dismissed panel members' concerns. "Our efforts have been crafted carefully to avoid infringing on constitutional rights, while saving American lives," he said.

In fact, the attorney general turned the tables and criticized his critics, arguing that they help the enemy when they oppose efforts to give the government more tools to fight terrorism. "To those who scare peace-loving people with phantoms of lost liberty, my message is this: Your tactics only aid terrorists — for they erode our national unity."

The impulse to restrict liberties has always been and still is especially strong during wartime, and not just among the military and law enforcement communities. Polls show that the American people generally support the steps taken by the administration since Sept. 11, just as they backed the last great raft of security measures — President Franklin D. Roosevelt's internment of

Japanese-Americans and other restrictions enacted during World War II. [1]

For instance, according to a recent *Washington Post*/ABC News survey, 73 percent of Americans favor allowing the federal government to eavesdrop on normally privileged conversations between suspected terrorists and their attorneys. The new rules — which so far affect only 16 suspects — would be used in cases where the attorney general believed the person might be passing information to his lawyer that would further a terrorist act by their co-conspirators still at large. Ashcroft claims that discussions not involving terrorist plans will still be privileged and will not be used against the suspect.

But civil libertarians and others counter that lawyers and their clients need absolute privacy in order to speak freely when planning defense strategy. "An inmate won't feel like there is privacy, since the people who are prosecuting you are also the people who are listening into the conversation and deciding what is and isn't privileged," says Irwin Schwartz, executive director of the National Association of Criminal Defense Lawyers. Moreover, Schwartz says, there is an existing process — which involves acquiring a warrant from a judge — that allows officials to breach attorney-client privilege, but it at least requires the approval of a third, independent party.

Schwartz and others also have strongly criticized the Justice Department's initial arrest of more than 1,200 immigrants — mainly from predominantly Muslim countries — in the weeks following the attacks and the continuing detention of about half of them. Most are being held on immigration

Public Attitudes Toward Censorship

Public support for military censorship is almost as high as it was during the 1991 Persian Gulf War. By a 53 percent to 39 percent margin, respondents in late November said it is more important for the government to be able to censor stories than for the media to be able to report news it sees as in the national interest.

	1985	1991	Nov. 2001
What is more important:	Percent Responding		
Government censorship of news it believes a threat to national security?	38%	58%	53%
Media's ability to report news it believes is in national interest?	50	32	39
In covering war news:			
Give military more control?	29	57	50
Media should decide how to report?	64	34	40
News coverage should be:			
Pro-American	--	--	20
Show all points of view	--	--	73

Source: The Pew Research Center For The People & The Press, Nov. 28, 2001

violations, but a small number are also being detained as possible material witnesses to terrorist acts.

Critics charge that in its efforts to prevent another attack, the department has essentially gone on a fishing expedition, rounding up Arabs and others without giving any real reasons that justify such a mass detention. "The federal government needs to explain what it's doing here, needs to publicly show that these people are planning criminal activity or have engaged in criminal activity, instead of just throwing them in jail and not saying anything," says James Zogby, president of the Arab American Institute, an advocacy group for Americans of Arab descent. * The secrecy surrounding the detentions is causing loyal Arab-Americans to feel threatened and disillusioned in their own country, he adds.

Zogby and others are also disturbed

by charges that some detainees have been held for weeks or even months with little or no evidence to link them to terrorist acts or groups. They point to Al Bader al-Hazmi, a San Antonio physician who was held for 13 days before being cleared, and Tarek Abdelhamid Albasti, an Arab-American and U.S. citizen from Evansville, Ind., who was detained for a week because he has a pilot's license. [2] His deten-

---

* On Dec. 11, a federal grand jury indictment charged that Zacarias Moussaoui, a French Moroccan, conspired with terrorist Osama bin Laden in the Sept. 11 attacks — the first U.S. charges in the case. Moussaoui had sought pilot training in Minnesota last summer, but school officials became suspicious when he only wanted to learn to steer a plane. He was arrested shortly afterward on immigration charges. Moussaoui had trained in bin Laden terrorist camps in Afghanistan, the indictment alleges.

tion came at the time authorities were investigating reports that Middle Eastern men were taking flying lessons in the United States, or seeking to rent crop-duster planes.

But Ashcroft has argued that his strategy of "aggressive detention of lawbreakers and material witnesses" has very possibly prevented new attacks. [3] "This is an entirely appropriate reaction," agrees Kent Scheidegger, legal director at the conservative Criminal Justice Legal Foundation. "Given what happened on Sept. 11 and the shadowy nature of the perpetrators, we need to look at a lot people in order to effectively stop future acts of terrorism."

The Justice Department also says that none of the detainees have been denied their rights. "All persons being detained have the right to contact their lawyers and their families," Ashcroft told the Judiciary Committee.

At the same hearing, Ashcroft was called on, repeatedly, to explain and defend the administration's plan to possibly use military courts to try high-ranking, foreign terrorism suspects. The attorney general and other defenders of the proposal say that such courts may be needed because much of the evidence presented against defendants may be highly classified and not appropriate for use in an open court. In addition, they say, using traditional courts to try terrorists may endanger the lives of all of those involved, including the jury, prosecutors and judges. (*See sidebar, p. 182.*)

But military courts, with their lower standards of due process, might not guarantee defendants a full and fair trial, says Ralph Neas, president of People for the American Way, a liberal civil liberties advocacy group. "This looks like a star chamber to me," he says. In particular, Neas worries that defendants may not be allowed to confront all of the evidence presented against them and that juries, made up of military officers, will be able to convict someone with a two-thirds vote rather than the usual unanimous verdict.

Civil libertarians also are concerned about some of the provisions of the USA Patriot Act, which cleared the Congress and was signed into law by President Bush just six weeks after the Sept. 11 attacks. The new law creates new terrorist-related offenses as well as giving the federal government new powers to conduct surveillance and detain non-citizens (see p. 192).

Opponents say the new law's provisions allowing the detention of immigrants are particularly worrisome because non-citizens can be held indefinitely so long as the attorney general believes they threaten national security. "They've gone way overboard here because the government can hold someone as long as they like. Period," says Stephen Henderson, an assistant professor of law at Chicago's Kent Law School.

But Clifford Fishman, a professor of law at Catholic University, says the new law is necessary to protect the country in a time of war. "This is not some great expansion of government authority," he says. "And besides, people who come here are still going to be much freer here than where they came from."

The performance of the news media also has been swept up in the raging post-9/11 civil liberties vs. security debate. Media-watchers of all political stripes have complained that some editors and reporters at times have acted more like patriots than journalists and thus have failed in their "free-press" mission to keep the public fully informed, especially since the war in Afghanistan began.

The debate over the proper balance between liberty and security is as old as the American Republic. In 1798 President John Adams' Federalist Party passed the Alien and Sedition Acts, which restricted free speech and the rights of immigrants. Enactment of the law produced a storm of criticism and it was largely overturned during the first term of Adams' suc-

Evaluating the War on Terrorism

In early November, the vast majority of Americans approved of the way top administration officials and major governmental institutions were handling the war on terrorism, but they gave a low rating to the performance of the news media.

Do you approve or disapprove of the way the following people and institutions are handling the war on terrorism since September 11?

Percent who approve

President Bush	89%
Secretary of State Colin Powell	87
Defense Secretary Donald Rumsfeld	80
Attorney General John Ashcroft	77
Congress	77
U.S. Postal Service	77
Vice President Dick Cheney	75
Centers for Disease Control and Prevention	71
Homeland Security Director Tom Ridge	60
The news media	43

Source: The Gallup Organization, Nov. 8-11, 2001

cessor in the White House, Thomas Jefferson. Similar questions were raised during the Civil War and during both world wars, when the federal government curtailed certain liberties in the name of protecting the nation. (See "Background," p. 186.)

As the United States prepares to enter the fourth month of its latest war, here are some of the questions lawyers, national security experts and others involved in the debate over civil liberties and security are asking:

Should the Justice Department monitor conversations between lawyers and defendants in the interest of preventing further terrorist attacks?

For defense lawyers, the ability to

communicate confidentially with clients is tantamount to a sacred right. The "attorney-client privilege," as it is known, "is one of the most significant and oldest rules governing" what is and isn't admissible in court, says Schwartz of the criminal defense lawyers association. "It's one of our most cherished and long-recognized rights."

On Oct. 30, though, the Department of Justice instituted new rules, which took effect immediately, that limit the attorney-client privilege for certain criminal defendants in federal custody. The changes permit the department to listen in on communications between inmates and their lawyers when "reasonable suspicion exists . . . that a particular inmate may use the communications with attorneys or their agents to further or facilitate acts of terrorism." [4]

The inmate and attorney would be notified of the monitoring, which would be conducted by a special "taint team" that would disclose only information that might be used to prevent future attacks. Other information, such as discussions of the inmate's guilt or innocence and defense strategy, would remain confidential and would not be made available to federal prosecutors, the department said. [5]

In explaining the new procedure, Attorney General Ashcroft said that given the threats currently facing the nation, the new rules were needed to "thwart future acts of violence or terrorism." [6] He gave assurances that the power to eavesdrop would be used sparingly, noting that only 16 out of 158,000 federal prisoners are now subject to the special monitoring. [7]

Still, many lawyers, lawmakers and civil libertarians immediately condemned the new rule as unnecessary and unconstitutional. They contend that by eliminating the attorney-client privilege for some suspected terrorists the Justice Department has denied inmates both their Sixth Amendment right to an attorney and their Fourth Amendment right to unreasonable search and seizure. *

"A client in a criminal case can't trust his lawyer and really can't work with him unless he believes that whatever he's saying is being said in confidence," Schwartz says. "So we're taking away one of the fundamental rights of criminal defendants."

"It's absolutely impossible to defend someone if you can't speak to them in private," agrees Henderson at Kent Law School. "If someone is listening

---

* Notably, recent polls have shown that Americans overwhelmingly believe that U.S. citizens charged with terrorism, like Oklahoma City bomber Timothy McVeigh, should be afforded constitutional rights, while non-citizens should not.

in, you simply can't speak your mind, which of course is crucial when planning your defense."

Opponents also worry that the so-called taint team won't be able to adequately protect inmates because it may reveal more to Justice Department officials than is proper under the disclosure guidelines. "Look, the problem with this is that the team is made up of Justice Department officials," Henderson says. "How can an inmate feel confident when the people who are listening work for the same organization as the people who are prosecuting the case?"

In addition, Henderson and others say, there is a means, under the old rules, by which prosecutors can break the attorney-client privilege while still affording constitutional protections. "If you have 'probable cause' to believe that the [attorney-client] privilege is being exploited to further criminal ends," says David Cole, a law professor at Georgetown University, "then you can go to a judge and get a warrant to listen in to the conversation."

Requiring the government to show "probable cause" is more demanding than the "reasonable suspicion" standard required under the new anti-terrorist rule, but it makes it more likely that a breach of the attorney-client privilege will be justified, Cole says.

More important, the old rules give final authority to an independent judge while the new procedure puts the entire decision in the hands of the attorney general, says Neas of People for the American Way. "This change gives the attorney general unbridled powers because he's become the only real arbiter in this process," Neas says. "We've cast off the role of the judiciary and in doing so have cast off the checks and balances given to us by the founders."

But supporters of the new powers echo the attorney general, arguing that they are needed to prevent another major terrorist attack. "One thing that we know for sure is that the enemy is planning more and worse attacks,"

Fishman says. "The other thing we know is that we didn't do enough to prevent the Sept. 11 attacks."

Indeed, supporters of the new rules say, there are many examples of inmates directing criminal activity from prison, making the possibility that terrorists would do the same quite high. "Violent criminals — especially gang members — order murders and attacks from prison all the time," Scheidegger of the Criminal Justice Legal Foundation says.

Scheidegger, Fishman and others say that the taint team and other safeguards built into the new rules are adequate to protect a client's right to consult with his attorney in confidence. "We know that there's always a possibility for abuse or mistakes because there are people involved, and people aren't perfect," Fishman says. "But I think that, in general, everything that doesn't involve plotting a new attack" will still be confidential.

Supporters also argue that the less rigorous "reasonable suspicion" standard is needed because Justice Department officials should have the authority to follow hunches when the fate of the nation is at stake.

"One could imagine a legitimate situation where important information discovered because of a 'reasonable suspicion' would not have been discovered using 'probable cause,' " Fishman says. "I'm not happy that the government has to [lower the standard], but I'll sleep better at night knowing they have more tools to prevent the next attack."

Is the detention of hundreds of terrorism suspects an overreaction to the events of Sept. 11?

Following the attacks on New York City and the Pentagon, the Justice Department rounded up more than 1,700 people possibly connected to terrorist acts or groups. And while many were released in subsequent weeks, more than 600 remained in custody in early

December. [8] In addition, the department is currently engaged in questioning an additional 5,000 recent immigrants who could also be detained. (*See sidebar, p. 187.*)

The current detainees are mostly male, foreign born and from predominantly Muslim countries like Egypt, Saudi Arabia and Pakistan. According to figures cited by the attorney general on Dec. 7, 563 people are being held for violations of their immigration status and another 60 are in federal custody for other reasons. Of these 60, roughly two dozen are being detained as "material witnesses," indicating that investigators believe they may have some information about past or future terrorist attacks.

Critics of the detentions say the government initially prevented the detainees from contacting defense attorneys, often for several days. In addition, the government has not revealed the identities of some of those being held, what they are being charged with or where they are being detained.

While polls show that most Americans support the detentions, many civil libertarians and Arab-American advocates point to the stories of those who have been released, as proof of the haphazard and heavy-handed nature of the operation. Countless Arab-Americans now out of prison have told of spending weeks or even months in jail, often based on very tenuous evidence. For instance, two Palestinian-Americans were held for more than two months because a federal agent at an airport in Houston determined that their passports looked like they could have been tampered with. Tests later showed that nothing had been altered and the men were finally released.

But Fishman defends the policy as a necessary element in the government's efforts to bring those responsible for past attacks to justice and to stop future terrorist acts. Indeed, Fishman and other detention supporters say, the fact that some innocent people may have to spend weeks or even months in jail is a price worth paying, since the detentions may prevent future terrorist activity.

"It's clearly better to err on the side of sweeping too broadly than not sweeping broadly enough," Fishman says. "The worst that will happen is that someone will be wrongfully detained for a few weeks or months, and frankly that pales in comparison with the consequences of not detaining legitimate suspects."

Attorney General Ashcroft alluded to this argument recently when he compared the current detention strategy to Attorney General Robert F. Kennedy's efforts to snuff out organized crime in the early 1960s.

"Robert Kennedy's Justice Department, it is said, would arrest mobsters for spitting on the sidewalk if it would help in the battle against organized crime," he said. "It has been and will be the policy of the Department of Justice to use the same aggressive arrest and detention tactics in the war on terror." [9]

Supporters also point out that the net is not cast as wide, or as carelessly, as it might at first seem. "It's important to remember that there are hundreds of thousands of young Arab men in this country right now," says Orin Kerr, an associate professor at the George Washington University School of Law. "Sure, the government has made mistakes — detaining people they have since let go — but this idea that they're pulling all of them off the street is incorrect. They've arrested only a very small fraction of them."

Finally, defenders of the policy argue that it is dangerous to second-guess the Justice Department — especially at this early stage in the investigation. "Frankly, it's hard to know what is and isn't appropriate because we don't know what Ashcroft and the others know," Kerr says.

Fishman agrees. "At this stage we have to trust the people in charge because they have the best information available to make these decisions. The way I see it, we really don't have a choice."

But opponents argue that lack of information about the nature of the threat the United States faces is not an excuse for trampling on the civil liberties of hundreds of possibly innocent people.

"Everyone knows we're going through a troubled and tense time and that the situation is very difficult," says Neas of People for the American Way. "But that doesn't mean that we can't bring some standards and accountability to the process."

"There needs to be more transparency here," agrees the Arab American Institute's Zogby. "The government needs to start showing probable cause for keeping those people they decide to detain."

Neas and Zogby find the secrecy surrounding the detentions especially troubling. Not only are names and locations not being revealed, they point out, but also no one is really sure that the rights of the detainees are being respected.

"It's not good enough for the Department of Justice to say, 'Trust us,' " Neas says. "Right now, all of the big decisions are essentially being made by the attorney general, and we don't know what those decisions are. It's as if there were only one branch of government."

"We've heard a lot of troubling stories," Zogby adds, "like some people are being denied access to their lawyer, or detainees have no idea why they're being held."

Opponents also contend that the detentions are reinforcing negative stereotypes that all Arab-Americans cannot be trusted and might be terrorists. "This kind of behavior on the part of the federal government is feeding the impression that if someone's young, Arab and male, they're guilty," Zogby says. "I think the Justice Department wants to look like they're doing something, so they detain a lot of people and go to the American people and say, 'We have 600 Arabs in jail, so you can feel safer.' "

Military Tribunals Play by Different Rules

"These are extraordinary times," President Bush said after authorizing the creation of secret military tribunals to try suspected terrorists. "And I would remind those who don't understand the decision I made that Franklin Roosevelt made the same decision in World War II. Those were extraordinary times, as well."

Military tribunals have a long history in the United States as well as in other countries. Most countries typically try members of the armed forces in a different court system than civilians. And, in times of war, military tribunals have judged civilians and military personnel of other nationalities. Military courts have also substituted for domestic civilian courts in the United States under conditions where the civilian court system could not function.

Neither international nor U.S. law sets procedures for military tribunals. Historically, however, U.S. military courts have provided fewer protections for the accused than civilian courts. Generally, military courts do not require a presumption of innocence, nor do they require a jury of one's peers or proof of guilt "beyond a shadow of a doubt." In recent history, U.S. military courts have required only a two-thirds vote of the officers on the tribunal to convict, and there are no provisions for appeal.

Revolutionary War

The first and most notable instance of an American military court passing judgment on a foreign national occurred during the Revolutionary War. Officers chosen by Gen. George Washington convicted British secret agent Major John Andre of collaborating with Benedict Arnold and sentenced him to be hanged. The British government did not object to the use of a military tribunal in judging Andre.

Civil War

During the Civil War, not only was the right of habeas corpus suspended by President Lincoln but also many civilians were judged by military courts. Accused civilians, thus, were denied their constitutionally protected right of a trial by jury, and there was no procedure available for them to challenge the legality of the proceedings.

In 1866, the attorney general of the United States argued that the legal protections established in the Bill of Rights were "peacetime provisions." But the Supreme Court ruled that the Lincoln administration had no authority to take away civilians' right to a trial by jury: "[U]ntil recently no one ever doubted that the right to trial by jury was fortified in the organic law against the power of attack. It is now assailed; but if ideas can be expressed in words, and language has any meaning, this right — one of the most valuable in a free country — is preserved to every one accused of crime who is not attached to the army, or navy, or militia in actual service. The Sixth Amendment affirms that 'in all criminal prosecutions the ac-

cused shall enjoy the right to a speedy and public trial by an impartial jury,' language broad enough to embrace all persons and cases." [1]

World War I

In a case recalling that of Major Andre, a German spy caught near the Mexican border in 1918 was tried in secret by the U.S. Army. Lothar Witzke, a lieutenant in the German Navy, was found guilty and sentenced to hang. In 1920, with the war over, President Woodrow Wilson commuted his sentence to life imprisonment. As it happened, in 1923 Witzke rescued a number of fellow inmates during a prison fire. He was then set free and returned to Germany.

World War II

Two particularly notable uses of military tribunals occurred during the Second World War. In 1942, eight German saboteurs were tried in a secret by a military commission. German submarines had landed them on beaches in Long Island and Florida, and they were captured after one of their party, George Dasch, turned himself in. The government may have used military trials both to ensure conviction and to apply the death penalty, a punishment not available in civilian courts. Six of the eight were convicted and electrocuted on Aug. 8, 1942. Dasch and another defendant who cooperated received prison terms and were released after the war.

Lawyers for the defendants did manage to get their case before the Supreme Court on the grounds that one of the defendants was the son of naturalized American citizens. In its decision, however, the Court held that both citizens and non-citizens lose the protection of the American legal system when they become agents of the enemy in time of war. [2]

Military tribunals also judged foreign nationals at Nuremberg, Germany, after the war. The International Military Tribunal, established by the United States, Great Britain, the Soviet Union and France, indicted and tried 24 former Nazi leaders for a variety of war crimes. Three were acquitted, eight received long prison sentences and the rest were sentenced to death.

While the International Military Tribunal reflected the tradition of Anglo-American civil law, it differed from civilian courts in several critical areas. Most notably, the tribunal did not offer trial by jury. Also, hearsay evidence — evidence provided by those not available for questioning by the defense — was admissible. And there was no way to appeal the tribunal's judgment.

A similar postwar tribunal in Tokyo tried 25 Japanese nationals for war crimes. Seven were sentenced to hang — including General Hideki Tojo, the prime minister from 1941-44; 16 were sentenced to life imprisonment.

---

[1] *Ex Parte Milligan*, 71 U.S. (4 Wall.) 2 (1866).
[2] *Ex Parte Quirin*, 317 U.S. 1 (1942).

Finally, opponents argue that in a large, open society, the detention — even of several hundred people — is not a very effective way of preventing future terrorist attacks.

"With more than 4 million aliens who have overstayed their visas currently residing in the country, and 5,000 miles of largely unprotected borders, detaining a thousand people probably isn't making too much of a dent in the threat," says Michael Ratner, a lecturer at the Columbia University School of Law and vice president of the Center for Constitutional Rights in New York City. "On top of this, we don't really know if any of these people we've detained are dangerous."

Zogby goes so far as to say the department's strategy is probably backfiring, since it is alienating an ethnic community that might be able to offer all kinds of help in tracking down the real terrorists. "We are loyal Americans, and we want to cooperate with the investigation," he says. "But when you do this, you create so much ill will that people are much less inclined to help."

But Kerr cautions that it is unrealistic to expect that no one will be unjustly detained during what has become the largest criminal investigation in U.S. history. "Look, they've been trying to prevent another attack, using sketchy information, so they're bound to make mistakes," he says. "But that's the price of doing business when you're trying to save thousands, maybe tens of thousands of lives."

Should the federal government try suspected terrorists in a military court?

In 1996, Sudan offered to arrest Osama bin Laden and hand him over to Saudi Arabia for eventual extradition to the United States. The suspected mastermind of the terrorist actions of Sept. 11, 2001, ultimately left Sudan a free man, in part because the United States could not convince Saudi Arabia to take him.

But even if the Saudis had cooperated, another obstacle prevented bin Laden's extradition to the United States. "The FBI did not believe we had enough evidence to indict bin Laden [in a civilian court] at that time, and therefore opposed bringing him to the United States," said then deputy national security adviser Samuel R. "Sandy" Berger. [10]

The failure to nab bin Laden in 1996 is often cited as a reason for supporting President Bush's plan to set up military tribunals to try foreigners suspected of terrorism. Bush has not said that he will use military courts, only that he wants the option. In addition, the administration has yet to explain how the courts will operate, since the Pentagon hasn't finished drafting operational guidelines for the tribunals, according to William J. Haynes II, the Defense Department's general counsel. [11]

Still, if military tribunals are established, they probably would require less rigorous evidentiary standards than a civilian court, allowing prosecutors to offer information against a defendant that would be barred from a traditional trial. For example, the secondhand recounting of a conversation, or "hearsay" evidence, could be used against a defendant in a military court, though such evidence is generally prohibited in federal criminal judicial proceedings

In addition, evidence culled from classified information could be offered in secret in a military trial in order to protect national security — and defendants could be prevented from challenging the information, even if it led to their conviction.

Moreover, in a military trial, defendants would be denied judgment by a jury of their peers and instead would face a panel made up of American military officers. The usual requirement of a unanimous jury verdict for conviction also would be set aside. Defendants could be convicted and sentenced on a two-thirds jury vote. Appeals would also be limited: Only the Supreme Court could review a verdict.

In the face of domestic and international criticism, President Bush has defended the use of military tribunals as "the absolute right thing to do." [12] Even as the government of Spain announced that it would not hand over terrorist suspects to the United States without assurances that they would be tried in civilian courts, the president insisted that he "must have the option of using a military tribunal in times of war." [13]

Douglas W. Kmiec, dean of the Catholic University School of Law, agrees with Bush that revealing classified information at a public trial could severely compromise national security.

"Frankly, we can't always reveal how and what we know and the identities of the people who help provide us with this information in open court," he says.

In addition, Kmiec says, trying terrorists in federal court could put the lives of judges, prosecutors, jurors and others at risk.

"I'd be concerned for my safety if I were on a jury that convicted an Al Qaeda member," he says. "These trials would even endanger the cities they were held in because they might be bombed in retribution for the conviction of a terrorist."

Beyond practical considerations, tribunal supporters say, terrorists simply are not entitled to civilian trials, and the president has complete authority to use military tribunals.

"Foreign terrorists are unlawful combatants, and they do not have a right to civilian trial," says Todd Gaziano, director of the Center for Legal and Judicial Studies at the Heritage Foundation, a conservative think tank. "The Constitution gave Congress the authority to set up a military justice system to deal with military personnel and others in the theater of war, and Congress has delegated the president the authority to use this military justice system."

Supporters also point out that the United States has a long history of using military tribunals during past conflicts to try foreign nationals and that the

Supreme Court has upheld their use.

"I would remind those who don't understand the decision I made that Franklin Roosevelt made the same decision in World War II," Bush said, referring to the use of military courts to try German nationals who had been caught on U.S. soil in 1942 trying to commit acts of sabotage. [14]

But opponents counter that using military tribunals against certain defendants runs counter to American notions of justice and is completely unnecessary. "In no way does this comport with our idea of due process," says Columbia University's Ratner. "If we go forward on this, we'll look back on it as a dark day in American history."

Ratner is troubled by the fact that much evidence that is inadmissible in a regular court could be used against a defendant in a military trial. "People say that such and such a conversation wouldn't be admissible in a regular court," he says. "There's a reason why it wouldn't be admissible: It's unreliable. All of a sudden that doesn't matter anymore?"

Ratner says it is possible to present classified evidence in open court without jeopardizing national security. "In the 1993 [World Trade Center] bombing case, we used a lot of classified information to help convict the defendants," he says. "In cases like this, you enter or present the evidence in private and then present a non-classified version of the evidence to the jury."

In fact, Georgetown's Cole says, the public trials and convictions of the bombers of the World Trade Center, the two American embassies in East Africa as well as the federal building in Oklahoma City show that it is possible to effectively try domestic and even foreign terrorists in an open, non-military court. "Have we shown that we can't try terrorism suspects in open court?" Cole asks. "No. The opposite is true, because we've already tried horrendous crimes of terrorism in open court, and on more than one

occasion."

Finally, opponents argue that trying terrorism suspects in military courts will make any convictions suspect. "When you have a trial where people are being tried in secret and they are unable to confront the evidence against them, they lack the kind of legitimacy that an open court would give," Cole says.

This lack of legitimacy will tarnish America's moral standing in the world and erode its reputation as a nation that respects human rights and the rule of law, according to Judiciary Committee Chairman Leahy. In his view, President Bush's order "sends a message to the world that it is acceptable to hold secret trials and summary executions, without the possibility of judicial review, at least when the defendant is a foreign national."

But supporters counter that if handled properly, military courts will not hurt America's reputation, nor deny defendants their most basic rights.

"This is not going to be some sort of barbaric process, like you see in countries like Peru," Kmiec says. "Our military has a history of following fair guidelines and procedures, and I think that anyone who appears before one of these tribunals will have a fair chance to defend himself."

Has the press bowed to patriotic fervor and not reported critically on U.S. efforts to fight terrorism?

Some conservatives have joined liberals in complaining that journalists have failed to fulfill their responsibility to properly inform the public. Other media analysts argue that the system is working just as it should.

Critics of the media's performance point to three major issues. First, the general compliance, and lack of an outcry, when the government asked TV networks to broadcast only limited portions of speeches by bin Laden. Second, critics cite the firings of journalists who have criticized President

Bush's behavior immediately following the incidents of Sept. 11. Third, critics complain of the limited attention paid by the press to policies and legislation, such as the USA Patriot Act, that would potentially infringe on Americans' civil liberties.

Marvin Kalb, executive director of the Joan Shorenstein Center on the Press, Politics, and Public Policy at Harvard University, believes that some press failings are explained by the fact that immediately after the terrorist attacks, the press responded with patriotic emotion, like the rest of the country.

"Right after Sept. 11, everyone was caught up in a rush of patriotism," Kalb says. "The idea of criticizing your country was something that most reporters didn't want to do. And they didn't. It was a patriotic press."

Soon, however, Kalb says that the press returned to its proper, questioning role. "Once the bombing began and the Taliban began to fall apart, the coverage changed," he says. "Before, the reporters were almost totally dependent upon whatever [Defense Secretary Donald H.] Rumsfeld told them. Now reporters are in the field covering the story, seeing it and being exposed to terrible danger."

Far from being uncritical of the government, reporters are doing their jobs vigorously, some observers say. "I don't think the press is being too submissive," says Neil Hickey, editor-at-large at the *Columbia Journalism Review*. "I've talked to eight or nine Pentagon correspondents, and they're mutinists down there over the problem they're having of penetrating the Pentagon. The curtain has come down, and the word has gone out that nobody is supposed to talk to them except Rumsfeld, [Pentagon spokesman Rear Adm. John] Stufflebeam and Gen. Meyers, the chairman of the Joint Chiefs of Staff."

Hickey complains that similar restrictions on access to information are in place overseas. "Foreign editors and newspaper executives are extremely

Chronology

1776–1864
The new nation struggles to define and protect citizens' rights, but the government clamps down on civil liberties during the Civil War.

Dec. 15, 1791
The Bill of Rights is ratified.

1798
Congress passes the first Alien and Sedition Act, which restricts immigrants' free speech and other rights.

April 27, 1861
President Abraham Lincoln suspends the right of habeas corpus, allowing the government to hold arrested persons indefinitely without explaining the reasons for detention to the courts.

September 1862
Lincoln orders citizens suspected of disloyal practices to be tried under military jurisdiction.

1870–1922
Economic problems and waves of labor unrest plague the country and state and local officials, often aided by federal resources, use their power to break the unions. World War I brings the threat of foreign influence and domestic agitation.

1886
Labor protests in Chicago lead to the Haymarket bombing and riots in which seven policemen are killed and 70 wounded, along with many civilian casualties. The affair marks the beginning of new actions curtailing the rights of domestic labor and radical groups.

1894
A strike at the Pullman railway car factory in Chicago is broken up by 16,000 federal troops.

March 1917
War Department authorizes Army officers to repress acts committed "with seditious intent."

1918
Congress passes the Sedition Act, making virtually all criticism of the government and the war effort illegal.

November 1919
In America's first "Red Scare," Attorney General A. Mitchell Palmer begins cracking down on individuals and organizations suspected of communist leanings. The so-called Palmer raids reach their climax on Jan. 2, 1920, when federal agents in more than 30 cities arrest 5,000 to 10,000 alien residents.

1941–1945
World War II offers new challenges for domestic and international law.

1941
Japan attacks Pearl Harbor on Dec. 7. Hawaii's governor places the territory under martial law for three years.

1942
In February, President Franklin D. Roosevelt interns ethnic Japanese on the West Coast.

1945
House Un-American Activities Committee (HUAC) becomes a standing committee.

1950–1975
Red scares return, and America tries to protect itself.

1950
Sen. Joseph R. McCarthy, R-Wis., launches a series of investigations into alleged communist sympathizers in the federal government.

1954
Congress censures McCarthy.

1956
FBI launches COINTELPRO, a secret program of intelligence gathering and disruption of legal organizations in the United States.

2001
Terrorism strikes on U.S. soil.

Sept. 11
Middle Eastern terrorists hijack four civilian airliners. Two crash into the World Trade Center; a third hits the Pentagon and the fourth crashes in rural Pennsylvania.

Oct. 26
President Bush signs the USA Patriot Act, aimed at deterring terrorist acts.

Oct. 30
New Department of Justice rules limit the attorney-client privilege for certain criminal defendants.

Nov. 13
President Bush authorizes military tribunals to try suspected terrorists.

Dec. 6
Attorney General John Ashcroft appears before lawmakers on Capitol Hill to defend the crackdown on terrorism.

irate that their reporters have been excluded from contact with those in the staging areas in Pakistan," he says. Hickey says most reporters also have been excluded from the aircraft carrier *Kitty Hawk*, from which many of the commando raids have been launched. The exception, he says, was "a tiny [media] pool that is with the Marines in Kandahar — and that consists of an AP guy, a Reuters guy, a still photographer, a TV cameraman and, of all things, a reporter from the *Marine Times*."

Other observers criticize the press for being too lax in covering potential threats to civil liberties at home, especially the antiterrorism legislation and the proposed military tribunals.

"Rumsfeld, Ashcroft and Powell keep saying, 'We are going to protect our basic values,' while they're really shredding them," columnist Nat Hentoff says. "Well, most people don't see the contradiction. And the press is not illuminating that contradiction."

Hentoff blames two factors for the limited coverage. First, he says, the pressure of deadlines and the 24-hour news cycle cause reporters to rush material to print without doing as much research as they should. Secondly, he says, "Many reporters and editors don't know that much about the Constitution, about past precedent."

Reed Irvine, director of Accuracy in Media, a conservative watchdog group, generally agrees with Hentoff's assessment. "There's a tendency on the part of journalists today to accept the word of the government as being the word of God," Irvine says. "They don't challenge it. One of the reasons for that, I believe, is that most of the reporters that cover these things are beat reporters. If you're assigned to cover aviation, for example, you'd better be on good terms with the FAA. You'd better not make people mad at you by revealing that they've been lying."

Hentoff also points to the firing of two journalists — Tom Guthrie of the *Texas City* (Texas) *Sun* and Dan Guthrie

of the *Grants Pass* (Ore.) *Daily Courier* — over columns critical of President Bush as signs of an overly submissive press.

"In both cases, publishers appeared to be responding to furious reader reaction to criticism of the commander in chief in time of war," Hentoff wrote in a recent column. "Fear had conquered freedom of the press." [15]

Daily Courier Editor Dennis Roler says that Guthrie's criticism of Bush for flying around the country instead of immediately returning to the White House in the wake of the Sept. 11 attacks wasn't the only reason he was fired. Still, Roler felt compelled to write an editorial apologizing for Guthrie's column, stating, "Criticism of our chief executive and those around him needs to be responsible and appropriate. Labeling him and the nation's other top leaders as cowards as the United States tries to unite after its bloodiest terrorist attack ever isn't responsible or appropriate." [16]

Most press observers, however, disagree with the proposition that controversial columns should be vetted. "The antidote to controversial speech is not less controversial speech, it's more controversial speech," Hickey says. "Let the public be exposed to a whole range of ideas and let them make up their own minds. The public doesn't need protection." ∎

BACKGROUND

Lincoln's Action

The greatest dangers to liberty lurk in insidious encroachment by men of zeal, well meaning but without understanding," wrote Supreme Court Justice Louis Brandeis in a court decision in 1928. [17]

Indeed, throughout America's his-

tory, with the notable exception of racist acts, the greatest challenges to civil liberties have come at the hands of well-meaning politicians and government officials during wartime or in response to other perceived dangers to national security.

The first such acts by federal officials that attracted significant attention were during the Civil War. Southern states began seceding from the Union shortly after, and partly due to, the election of Abraham Lincoln as president in 1860. On April 12, 1861, Confederate forces began firing on Fort Sumter, a Union garrison near Charleston, S.C.

Fully aware that the nation's capital was surrounded by states sympathetic to the Confederacy — Lincoln even had to enter Washington surreptitiously for his inauguration to avoid the violence of pro-South mobs — the president felt it necessary on April 27 to issue a proclamation suspending the right of habeas corpus. The carryover from English common law requires the government to explain to the court why it is detaining a prisoner and, if the court decides the reason is not sufficient, to free the prisoner.

In one of the more notable incidents, in the fall of 1861 the suspension of habeas corpus was used to detain more than a dozen Maryland legislators who the federal government thought favored secession. They were arrested to prevent them from voting their sentiments. [18]

Lincoln knew the step was of questionable legality. "Are all the laws, but one, to go unexecuted and the government itself go to pieces, lest that one be violated," Lincoln asked Congress in a special message on July 4, 1861, in an attempt to quiet critics.

Perhaps surprisingly, Lincoln's suspension of habeas corpus provoked little public outcry. Today, Chief Justice William Rehnquist suggests that this may be because the court opin-

Is Questioning Immigrants Fair?

The government's plan to prevent future terrorist attacks on American soil relies to a large extent on the Justice Department's ongoing efforts to interview thousands of recent immigrants from the Middle East. But critics charge the plan is unconstitutional and racist.

When the Bush administration began conducting the interviews in early November, it portrayed the operation as an effort to gather information, not a massive dragnet intended to arrest thousands of suspects. "Terrorist activity rarely goes entirely unnoticed," Attorney General John Ashcroft said on Nov. 29. "Non-citizens are often ideally situated to observe the precursors to, or early stages of, terrorist activity." [1]

Some 5,000 people who have arrived in the U.S. since Jan. 1, 2000, mostly Middle Eastern men between the ages of 18 and 33, have been asked to voluntarily submit to questioning at their homes.

"We're being as kind and fair and gentle as we can in terms of inviting people to participate," Ashcroft said. [2] Indeed, on Nov. 29, the attorney general tried to sweeten the pot by announcing that the government would help those who provide useful information to remain in the country and even become citizens. [3]

The Fifth Amendment to the Constitution protects a suspect's right against self-incrimination, including the right not to answer questions from police. In addition, the Fourth Amendment protects privacy by prohibiting "unreasonable searches and seizures."

"The government has the right to ask questions," said Norman Dorsen, former president of the American Civil Liberties Union. "But people have a right not to answer questions." [4]

In 1973, the Supreme Court fleshed out the Constitution's protections against self-incrimination, stating that consent to be searched or answer questions must be "voluntarily given and not the result of duress or coercion, express or implied."

But some civil liberties advocates worry that a number of factors could make those interviewed feel compelled to cooperate, regardless of their legal protections. For instance, they argue that since all the interviewees are recent immigrants, many could be concerned that the Immigration and Naturalization Service would detain or even deport them depending on whether and how they decide to cooperate. "My sense is that many of these people will only talk to the government because they think they'll be arrested or deported if they don't," says Michael Avery, an associate professor of law at Suffolk University in Boston. "That sounds like coercion to me."

Others might be intimidated because they feel like they are one of the targets of what has become a massive investigation in the wake of the Sept. 11 attacks, Avery says. "The government is already holding a lot of people, and these folks know it," he says. "That fact has to be in the back of their minds when they talk to federal officials."

Opponents also say that targeting Middle Eastern immigrants amounts to racial profiling on a mass scale. "You're stigmatizing a whole community when you do this," says James Zogby, executive director of the Arab American Institute.

But others defend the administration's efforts as well-directed and within the bounds of the law. "Look, we need to cast a wide net and suck in as much information as possible, and these people could be well suited to help us do that," says Kent Scheidegger, legal director for the Criminal Justice Legal Foundation, a conservative think tank in Sacramento, Calif. "Asking people to come in voluntarily and answer questions is not unconstitutional. It's what police investigators do."

Scheidegger also defends the decision to focus on people from Middle Eastern countries. "The terrorist threat is from the Middle East, so you don't want to waste your time interviewing recent immigrants from Norway," he says. "It's appropriate to look a certain group when, as in this case, there's a substantial connection between national origin and the threat."

---

[1] Quoted in Neil A. Lewis, "Immigrants Offered Incentives to Give Evidence on Terrorists," *The New York Times*, Nov. 30. 2001.

[2] Quoted in William Glaberson, "Legal Experts Question Legality of Questioning," *The New York Times*, Nov. 30, 2001.

[3] Lewis, *op. cit.*

[4] Quoted in Glaberson, *op. cit.*

ion that held Lincoln did not have the authority to do so was authored by Chief Justice Roger B. Taney, who was also the author of the infamous Dred Scott decision. Rehnquist notes that the case "inflamed the North and would cast a cloud over the High Court for at least a generation." [19]

Suspending habeas corpus was not the only violation of citizens' civil rights. First Amendment protections were also abused. Newspapers that were not sufficiently sympathetic to the Union cause were banned from the mails, which was the major means of delivery at the time.

The New York News tried to fight the policy by hiring newsboys to deliver it locally. The government ordered U.S. marshals to seize copies of the paper and one newsboy was arrested for selling it.

"Remarkably, other New York papers did not rally round the sheets that were being suppressed," writes Rehnquist. "Instead of crying out about an abridgement of First Amendment rights — as they would surely do today — their rivals simply gloated." [20]

Worse still, President Lincoln went much farther than suspending habeas corpus in September 1862 — just a month after the Emancipation Proclamation. He issued a proclamation holding that citizens found "discouraging volunteer enlistments, resisting militia drafts, or guilty of any disloyal practice affording aid and comfort to rebels," would be subject to trial and punishment under military law. Rehnquist commented that, "Such people faced, in other words, stringent penalties for actions that were often not offenses by normal civilian standards, and faced them, moreover, without the right to jury trial or other procedural protections customarily attending a criminal trial in a civil court." [21]

Attacks on Labor

In the years after the Civil War, periodic economic crises were the occasion for federal actions against what were perceived to be radical labor unions that threatened the economic stability of the country.

"Union organization depended on the constitutional freedoms of speech, press and assembly, but employers consistently abridged these rights. Their reliance on espionage, blacklisting, strikebreakers, private police and, ultimately, armed violence, nullified the Bill of Rights for those workers who had the temerity to resist their employers' unilateral exercise of power," a historian wrote. [22]

Not only did the federal government not do anything to defend the constitutionally protected rights of workers, but on a number of occasions it actually took action against workers.

"During the 1870-1900 period, all of the various techniques used to repress labor were gradually developed and institutionalized by business and governmental elites: the company town, the use of private police, private arsenals and private detectives, the deputization of private police, the manipulation of governmental police agencies, the revival of conspiracy doctrine and the labor injunction," writes Robert Justin Goldstein, professor of political science at Oakland University in Rochester, Mich. [23]

During a strike against the Pullman

railway car company in 1894, for example, federal troops were sent to Chicago to quell the strike. "Federal troops were also sent to Los Angeles; Sacramento; Ogden, Utah; Raton, New Mexico, and many other areas, especially in the West, and often on the thinnest of excuses," writes Goldstein. In all, 16,000 federal troops were sent.

"In a number of cases the actions of the troops were so reckless that local officials protested bitterly," Goldstein notes. "Thus, the Sacramento Board of City Trustees adopted a resolution condemning the 'tyranny and brutality which has characterized the conduct of the U.S. soldiers who have wounded and assaulted unoffending persons upon the streets,' and condemned troops for free and unprovoked use of their bayonets and guns and for the reckless wounding of innocent citizens." [24]

The Palmer Raids

The threat of world war brought the next wave of federal erosions of civil liberties.

"The story of civil liberties during World War I is a dreary, disturbing and, in some respects, shocking chapter out of the nation's past," writes Paul L. Murphy, professor of history and American studies at the University of Minnesota. "Americans, committed through their president, Woodrow Wilson, to 'make the world safe for democracy' — a phrase which implied that the nation and its allies bore a responsibility to free the world to adopt America's traditional 'liberal' commitment to liberty and justice — stood by on the domestic scene and saw liberty and justice prostituted in ways more extreme and extensive than at any other time in American history." [25]

As early as March 1917, the War Department authorized Army officers to repress acts committed with "sedi-

tious intent." The guidelines were so vague that abuses were widespread. "Military intelligence agents participated in a wide range of dubious activities, which involved a wholesale system of spying on civilians that would be unmatched in scope until the late 1960s. Military intelligence activities included surveillance of the International Workers of the World (IWW), the Pacific Fellowship of Reconciliation and the National Civil Liberties Bureau, forerunner of the American Civil Liberties Union." [26]

The Sedition Act, passed in May 1918, made illegal virtually all criticism of the government or of the war effort.

The Wilson administration also helped organize the American Protective League, a privately funded organization that was intended to help the government with, among other things, food rationing and investigating the loyalty of soldiers and government personnel.

"The organization quickly became a largely out-of-control, quasi-governmental, quasi-vigilante agency which established a massive spy network across the land," writes Goldstein. [27]

The assault on civil liberties didn't end with the armistice. The Bolshevik Revolution and the Red Scare that ensued in the United States resulted in a series of further measures.

Under pressure from Congress to take steps against anarchists and communists, Attorney General A. Mitchell Palmer launched a series of raids, which came to be known as "Palmer Raids," against groups with suspected communist leanings, such as the Union of Russian Workers, the Communist Party and the IWW. Alien residents associated with the groups were arrested and detained while deportation proceedings were conducted. The raids, which began in November 1919, reached their climax on Jan. 2, 1920, when federal agents raided organizations in more than 30 cities and arrested between 5,000 and 10,000 alien residents.

Japanese Internment

During World War II, barely more than two months after Japanese forces bombed Pearl Harbor on Dec. 7, 1941, President Roosevelt signed Executive Order 9066, which authorized the removal of ethnic Japanese — many of them U.S. citizens — from West Coast communities.

At the time, at least, the action seemed understandable to many. There was widespread fear of Japanese attacks on the coast and of sabotage of critical facilities. And, unlike ethnic Italian and German populations in the United States, ethnic Japanese were not seen as integrated into American society.

"Both federal and state restrictions on the rights of Japanese emigrants had prevented their assimilation into the Caucasian population and had intensified their insularity and solidarity," writes Rehnquist. "Japanese parents sent their children to Japanese-language schools outside of regular school hours, and there was some evidence that the language schools were a source of Japanese nationalistic propaganda. As many as 10,000 American-born children of Japanese parentage went to Japan for all or part of their education. And even though children born in the United States of Japanese alien parents were U.S. citizens, they were under Japanese law also viewed as citizens of Japan." [28]

While the internment of Japanese-Americans during World War II has since come to be seen as an injustice, the Supreme Court decided in several cases in 1943 and 1944 that the internment was justified, given the threats facing the country.

Internment was the most dramatic civil rights issue during World War II, but it was not the only issue. In the wake of the attack on Pearl Harbor, the governor of Hawaii placed the is-

Sen. Joseph R. McCarthy, R-Wis., made unsubstantiated accusations against suspected communists in the movie industry and the U.S. and foreign governments in the early 1950s, giving rise to the term "McCarthyism." Here he holds up a picture of former British Prime Minister Clement Attlee and suggests that his communist salute during the Spanish Civil War 20 years earlier marked him as a sympathizer.

AP Photo

lands under martial law and suspended habeas corpus. At the same time, and with Gov. Poindexter's blessings, Lt. Gen. Walter Short, commander of the Military Department of Hawaii, declared himself military governor of Hawaii.

Short issued a series of ordinances, and violations could and did land many civilians in military rather than civilian courts. The military rule of Hawaii continued for three years until President Roosevelt ordered it revoked.

Cold War McCarthyism

At the end of World War II, civil liberties advocates were hopeful that the climate was improving. "In July 1945," writes Goldstein, "the ACLU reported that its caseload had 'markedly declined' and that it foresaw its post-war activities as revolving much less around court cases that involved challenges to individual civil liberties. Instead it looked forward to building 'institutional arrangements to protect civil liberties' such as fighting monopolistic practices in communications and promoting 'the wider participation of faculties and students in educational control.' " [29]

By August 1947, however, the ACLU reported "the national climate of opinion in which freedom of public debate and minority dissent functioned with few restraints during the war years and after, has undergone a sharply unfavorable change." [30]

Historians credit two factors with the turnaround. First, there was a wave of labor strikes in 1946, which resulted in a rise of anti-labor sentiment. Secondly, and even more significantly, it became apparent that America was involved in a new kind of war, a Cold War with the Soviet Union. The United States now had global responsibilities, and it had an enemy with global reach. Espionage was a major fear.

The House Un-American Activities Committee (HUAC) was made a standing committee of the House in January 1945. Soon after, a series of spy

Limiting Free Speech Online

When terrorists crashed two airliners into the World Trade Center on Sept. 11, Stuart Biegel tried to reach friends in Manhattan. He couldn't get through using a telephone or a cell phone, but he was able to reach them via e-mail.

"So much for the Internet being a vulnerable medium," says Biegel, a professor at the University of California-Los Angeles (UCLA) who specializes in cyberspace law. "The Internet is like water flowing. If it's blocked from one direction it goes around."

And it's not just e-mail that's circulating on the Web. Americans following events in Afghanistan and the nation's war on terrorism can find a wealth of information. Neither Osama bin Laden nor the now-deposed Taliban regime have Web sites, but at www.rawa.org readers can read about the heroic efforts of the Revolutionary Association of the Women of Afghanistan (RAWA). In addition to a calendar of protests and press conferences and a history of the organization, a pop-up window on the site hawks RAWA T-shirts and coffee mugs.

Online visitors also can participate in a chat with a journalist just back from Afghanistan on CNN's Web site. (http://www.cnn.com/2001/COMMUNITY/08/24/shah/.)

The Internet is coming into its own, much like talk radio, as a public medium for citizens to voice their opinions on the issues. The lively chat rooms maintained by America Online, Yahoo and Microsoft Network feature strong opinions on all sides — but only up to a point.

"Certainly, there were a lot of very strong emotions that were expressed in the days after Sept. 11, which is exactly what our service is designed for," says Nicholas Graham, a spokesperson for AOL.

Biegel agrees that people seem more inclined to speak their minds on the Internet than in other places, including his classroom. "People tend to feel more comfortable because they perceive anonymity when they take a screen name, and also because they're doing it in the privacy of their own home," he says. "I even see this with my students in on-line discussion forums. Some who may not speak out in class are suddenly very articulate in an online discussion forum. They're not sitting there in a room with everybody around, so they feel more relaxed."

Discussions have been so lively, in fact, that online services have stepped in to moderate the language in some chat room conversations. "We draw a very, very fine line between expressing heartfelt emotions and hate speech," Graham says. "When we are made aware of hate speech online, or if we see it ourselves, we take immediate action ranging from a disciplinary warning to termination of service."

But some chat-room visitors say the censoring isn't even-handed. "We have had several cases reported to us of postings by people with Arab-sounding names being taken down because they expressed a different point of view," said Laila Al-Qatami, a spokeswoman for the Arab-American Anti-Discrimination Committee. "Likewise, we've been told of harassing messages against people of Arab descent not being taken down." [1]

Indeed, according to *The Washington Post*, "Yahoo has deleted a note calling someone a "Zionist Israeli [expletive]." But the following message has remained up for weeks despite several complaints lodged by users and copied to *The Washington Post*: "Muslims are against the Jews because Muslims are too greedy. They want to take Israel's teeny-weeny land. That's how greedy and parasitic these Muslims are. America should wipe them all out." [2]

Biegel notes that while the Internet is a public medium and people can says just about anything they want on their own Web site, the online services actually are private.

"Companies such as AOL and Yahoo are private companies and are not subject to the First Amendment in the same way that public entities are," Biegel says. "AOL can restrict speech and make rules that would not withstand First Amendment scrutiny."

Online services generally rely on staff "chaperones" to screen out overly offensive messages. They visit chat rooms to check on what's going on. "Our guides are trained very carefully to deal with discrimination, whether it's religious, ethnic or whatever," Graham says. "They're very familiar with terms that might be offensive to a given community."

Given the large number of chat groups and messages, however, chaperones or moderators find it very difficult to keep up with the huge flow of messages. Accordingly, most actions by the online services are initiated in response to a user complaint.

Since chat rooms take place in real time, however, monitoring and controlling content is very difficult, as indicated by a Dec. 10 spot check of AOL's chat room on the World Trade Center. In addition to several instances of extremely vulgar language, there was even a user proposing to drive an armored tank to Washington, D.C.

---

[1] Quoted in Ariana Eunjung Cha, "Screening Free Speech? Online Companies Draw Fire for Removing 'Offensive' Postings," *The Washington Post*, Nov. 18, 2001, p. H01.
[2] *Ibid.*

---

scares rattled the American public, including the case of Alger Hiss, a State Department employee accused, and eventually convicted, of spying for the Soviet Union. Then, in 1951, Julius and Ethel Rosenberg were convicted of spying for the Soviet Union and electrocuted at Sing Sing Prison in New York state.

On March 21, 1947, President Harry S. Truman announced the creation of a new government-loyalty program, under which all current or prospective government employees were to undergo loyalty investigations.

It was in an environment of fear, then, that Sen. Joseph R. McCarthy of Wisconsin rose to public prominence when, beginning in early 1950, he warned of rampant communist influence in government.

At Issue:

Should airports use racial profiling to screen passengers?

CLIFFORD S. FISHMAN
PROFESSOR OF LAW, THE CATHOLIC UNIVERSITY OF AMERICA

WRITTEN FOR THE CQ RESEARCHER, DEC. 6, 2001

*a*irport and airline security in this country — or more accurately, the lack of it — has been an open scandal for decades. On September 11, we paid the price.

Now it is proposed that airport security personnel should "profile" airline passengers from Moslem and Middle Eastern countries for special scrutiny.

To target an entire ethnic group, the overwhelming majority of whom are good, decent, innocent people, because of the crimes committed by a tiny handful of them, is immoral, in most instances illegal and violates fundamental American values.

Nevertheless, in the aftermath of September 11, airport security officials are temporarily justified in doing so, for three reasons:

First, because since 1993, the perpetrators of every terrorist act committed or attempted by foreigners within the U.S. — the World Trade Center car bomb, September 11 and several unsuccessful conspiracies in between — have been from the Middle East, Algeria or Pakistan.

Second, September 11 taught us that failing to prevent terrorists from boarding an airliner can cost thousands of lives and significantly disrupt our way of life.

Third, because we do not yet have in place the resources or personnel to properly scrutinize every individual who boards and every package loaded onto a plane, it would be irresponsible not to focus most of our attention on people who fit the "profile" of those most likely to attempt another September 11.

This justification is temporary, for two reasons: Permanently profiling any group violates our ideals and values. And the next group of hijackers might not fit the profile. They might be from Somalia or Indonesia (where allegedly there are Al Qaeda cells in each country). Or they could be members of Aum Shinrikyo, the Japanese sect that a few years ago released a deadly chemical in the Tokyo subway.

Or they might be "all-American guys" like Timothy McVeigh and Terry Nichols, who blew up the federal building in Oklahoma City. Until adequate security resources are put in place to properly screen everyone, we can only hope that security personnel who "profile" Middle Easterners will act professionally and courteously. Inevitably, though, thousands of innocent, decent people will be singled out unfairly, and many will be harassed and humiliated — and that is an outrage, even though it is temporarily necessary.

Let us pray that those who are singled out or mistreated will have the grace to understand, and to forgive us for the wrongs that will be done to them.

JEAN ABINADER
MANAGING DIRECTOR, ARAB AMERICAN INSTITUTE

WRITTEN FOR THE CQ RESEARCHER, DEC. 10, 2001

*i*n poll after poll taken after September 11, Arab Americans indicated their overwhelming desire to cooperate with the authorities to improve airline security. This desire to cooperate, however, does not justify the rude and abusive behavior by airline crews, ground personnel and security staff.

Many of the improvements in procedures and technology can be implemented in a non-discriminatory fashion. Recommendations ranging from baggage matching to better equipment and training for security personnel can be applied to all passengers equally, thus ensuring greater security without the need to single out passengers because of perceived ethnic origin, or other characteristics such as clothing or accents.

There is a continuing need for airlines to restate their policies against racial profiling, especially to inform and advise passengers and crew that federal and state statutes do not permit "vigilantism," particularly if the person in question has passed the common screening procedures for all passengers. Perhaps a variation of the "passenger bill of rights" regarding profiling needs to be included in the materials available to passengers in their seat pockets.

Finally, racial profiling presents more complications than solutions. Based on testimony by security officials, profiling does not make a measurable difference in the prevention of crimes, although it is helpful in investigating criminal activities once there has been a crime. This is not to suggest that law enforcement officials should be passive because of ethnic or racial considerations. Rather, it requires that great caution be exercised if racial or ethnic factors are to be included as one of a number of variants that may warrant that a security person investigate further.

Basing security procedures solely on racial or ethnic characteristics leads to discriminatory behaviors by the officials involved and reinforces stereotypes that damage the government's ability to reach out and coordinate its efforts with the affected communities.

We recommend that the government work diligently to improve its screening of all travelers and their belongings. Equally applied procedures and reminders that racial profiling is unhelpful can also be useful in reducing the potential for disruptive behavior by passengers intent on independently assuming the role of air police.

Efforts should also be made to hire more Arab-Americans and American Muslims. Qualified and trained Arab-Americans can be resources to the security services and to the airlines by validating non-discriminatory practices and helping to deal with passengers from Arab and Muslim countries who may feel overwhelmed by enhanced security procedures.

The anti-communist hysteria resulted in extensive hearings over the next two years by HUAC and its Senate counterpart, the Permanent Investigations Subcommittee. By the time McCarthy was finally censured by his colleagues in 1954, countless careers and reputations had been needlessly ruined.

COINTELPRO and the Vietnam War

It wasn't much of a step from the anti-communist hysteria and blacklistings of the early 1950s to federal actions against suspected domestic radical opponents of the Vietnam War in the 1960s and early '70s. In fact, the most dramatic federal violation of citizens' civil rights actually began in 1956 when the FBI launched COINTELPRO, a counterintelligence program designed to disrupt what remained of the Communist Party in the United States.

The initial FBI memo that formalized COINTELPRO indicated that the agency would explore a number of tactics to combat communist influences in domestic organizations, including using the Internal Revenue Service to investigate suspected citizens, planting informants and attempting to create dissention within the groups and to disrupt their activities. [31]

Between 1964 and 1968 alone, the FBI conducted more than 1,000 undercover operations against antiwar, white supremacy, civil rights and other domestic groups. ∎

CURRENT SITUATION

USA Patriot Act

Within hours of the Sept. 11 attacks, lawmakers and commentators were calling for Congress to give new powers to the federal government to fight terrorism. And in spite of warnings by civil libertarians and some members of the House and Senate to tread carefully, Congress quickly complied, sending legislation to the president six weeks after the attacks.

Attorney General Ashcroft had asked for a variety of new powers in the weeks after the tragedy. In particular, Ashcroft requested new authority to conduct searches and detain suspects.

Exactly a month after the attacks, the Senate easily passed an anti-terrorism bill that had been crafted by Republican and Democratic leaders that encompassed many of Ashcroft's proposals. The following day, the House passed its own tougher version. Less than two weeks later, on Oct. 25, the Senate cleared a compromise bill, 98–1. President Bush signed the USA-Patriot Act the next day.

Although the bill was tempered somewhat by more liberal members of Congress, especially Senate Judiciary Committee Chairman Leahy, it gave Ashcroft much of what he had asked for, including provisions that:

- Allow "roving wiretaps" that follow suspects no matter what telephone they use. Old rules required law enforcement officers to acquire a new warrant each time a suspect used a different phone. The provision "sunsets" in 2005.
- Give law enforcement the authority to conduct "secret searches" of a suspect's residence, including computer files. Authorities can delay telling the suspect of the search for "a reasonable time" if such information would adversely affect the investigation. Previously, law enforcement had to inform suspects of any search.
- Allow the attorney general to detain any non-citizen believed to be a national security risk for up to seven days. After seven days the government must charge the suspect or begin deportation proceedings. If the suspect cannot be deported, the government can continue the detention so long as the attorney general certifies that the suspect is a national security risk every six months.
- Make it illegal for someone to harbor an individual they know or should have known had engaged in or was about to engage in a terrorist act.
- Give the Treasury Department new powers and banks and depositors new responsibilities in tracking the movement of money.
- Allow investigators to share secret grand jury information or information obtained through wiretaps with government officials if it is important for counterintelligence or foreign intelligence operations.
- Allow authorities to track Internet communications (e-mail) as they do telephone calls.

While not entirely happy with the new law as written, many civil libertarians and others applauded Congress for not including all of the provisions requested by the attorney general. For instance, under Ashcroft's initial proposal, evidence obtained overseas in a manner that would be illegal in the United States would still have been admissible in an American court if no laws had been broken in the country where the evidence was gathered.

"So if you had a wiretap in Germany that would have been illegal here, but is legal there, the evidence would have been admissible here," law Professor Henderson says. "Congress said 'no way' and tossed that out."

And yet, Henderson and Georgetown's Cole argue, even though it doesn't contain some of the most

> "Under this law, we impose guilt by association on immigrants. We make them deportable not for their acts but for their wholly innocent associations."
>
> — *Professor of Law David Cole, Georgetown University*

> "It's a gross overreaction to say that this new law is going to take away vital freedoms. It gives the government a bit more power than it had."
>
> — *Professor of Law Clifford Fishman, Catholic University*

troubling provisions proposed by the Justice Department, the bill still goes too far. They particularly object to those parts of the law that allow the government to detain and deport or hold immigrants.

"I think the most radical provisions are those directed at immigrants," Cole says. "Under this law, we impose guilt by association on immigrants. We make them deportable not for their acts but for their associations, wholly innocent associations with any proscribed organization and you're deportable."

But George Washington University's Kerr argues that the Patriot Act does not, as critics contend, go too far. "Overall, I think this is a very balanced act, giving the government just what it needs in this fight," Kerr says. "I'm actually impressed at how narrowly tailored this language is. The administration could have gotten even more authority, but they asked just for what they needed."

"It's a gross overreaction to say that this new law is going to take away vital freedoms," agrees Catholic University's Fishman. "It gives the government a bit more power than it had. And remember, this is a government that has generally shown that it can be trusted with power." ∎

OUTLOOK

Back to Normal Soon?

On more than one occasion, President Bush has warned the American people that the struggle to defeat Al Qaeda and other terrorist groups will last years, even decades. But some critics of the administration predict that many of the tough steps taken to prevent terrorism domesically will be short-lived. They base their prediction on past actions, when the American people reacted to curtailments of civil liberties by eventually reasserting their rights.

"We have a long history of overreacting during times of crisis, whether it be the Alien and Sedition Acts or the internment of the Japanese during World War II," says Neas of People for the American Way. "After a while, we usually look back on those actions and realize that they were a mistake, and I think that's what will happen here.

"Congress put sunset provisions in the Patriot Act for a reason. But I wouldn't be surprised if popular pressure forced the government to sunset the law and some of these other changes before five years passed."

Schwartz of the criminal defense lawyers' association agrees that after the initial shock of the attacks wears off, Americans will want the government to relinquish the new powers it has acquired. "The American people are not going to let the government burn the Constitution in the name of fighting terrorism," he says. "Look at the Congress and the press: They're already challenging the administration on many of its policies. This, only three months after attacks."

But others, on both sides of the civil liberties debate, say that the terrorist attacks on New York and Washington have thrust the United States into a long struggle, similar to the Cold War, and that new limits on freedoms could remain in place for years.

"Everything is different now," says Columbia University's Ratner. "The fact that serious people are now talking about using torture means that the [civil liberties] bar has been lowered dramatically since Sept. 11, and I don't see it being raised any time soon."

"Unless there are very visible abuses of this new authority, I doubt there will be a groundswell of support for repeal of these new powers any time soon," agrees Catholic University's Fishman. He points out that most people supported giving the government more crime-fighting authority even before Sept. 11, because they don't see the changes as a direct threat to their personal freedom. "They say, 'I'm not a criminal so I have no problem with the government taking more power to get the bad guys.' "

In addition, Fishman says, new terrorist attacks would make Americans even more supportive of tough, new measures to fight terrorism. "Another great disaster would further solidify opinion behind these changes."

But Scheidegger of the Criminal Justice Legal Foundation predicts only modest changes in future U.S. civil liberties.

"There's always this great push for new authority when something dramatic happens," he says, "and then things always settle down and we take it back a little. While I don't think we'll go back to where we were before Sept. 11, I also don't think the long-term changes will be as far-reaching as it might appear they'll be right now." ■

Notes

[1] Cited in Richard Moran and Claudia Deane, "Most Americans Back U.S. Tactics," *The Washington Post*, Nov. 29, 2001.

[2] Amy Goldstein, "A Deliberate Strategy of Disruption," *The Washington Post*, Nov. 4, 2001, and Deborah Sontag, "Who Is This Kafka That People Keep Mentioning?," *The New York Times Magazine*, Oct. 21, 2001.

[3] Quoted in "Disappearing in America," *The New York Times*, Nov. 10, 2001.

[4] Quoted in George Lardner Jr., "U.S. Will Monitor Calls to Lawyers," *The Washington Post*, Nov. 9, 2001.

[5] *Ibid.*

[6] Quoted in David G. Savage and Robert L. Jackson, "Response to Terror Defendants: Ashcroft Eavesdropping Rule Assailed Law," *Los Angeles Times*, Nov. 10, 2001.

[7] Cited in *Ibid.*

[8] Christopher Drew and William K. Rashbaum, "Opponents' and Supporters' Portrayals of Detentions Prove Inaccurate," *The New York Times*, Nov. 3, 2001.

[9] Goldstein, *op. cit.*

[10] Quoted in Barton Gellman, "U.S. Was Foiled Multiple Times in Efforts to Capture Bin Laden or Have Him Killed," *The Washington Post*, Oct. 3, 2000.

[11] Vernon Loeb and Susan Schmidt, "U.S. Wants Custody of Enemy Leaders," *The Washington Post*, Dec. 1, 2001.

[12] Quoted in Mike Allen, "Bush Defends Order for Military Tribunals," *The Washington Post*,

Nov. 20, 2001.

[13] Quoted in "Taking Liberties," "The News Hour with Jim Lehrer," Nov. 27, 2001, www.pbs.org/newshour.

[14] Quoted in *Ibid.*

[15] Nat Hentoff, "Between Freedom and Fear: A Self-censored Press?" *Editor & Publisher*, Nov. 6, 2001.

[16] Reprinted in The Associated Press wire, Sept. 26, 2001.

[17] *Olmstead v. United States* (1928), 277 U.S. 438 at 479:

[18] Rehnquist, William H., *All the Laws But One: Civil Liberties in Wartime*, Vintage Books, 1998, p. 45.

[19] *Ibid.*, p. 45.

[20] *Ibid.*, p. 47.

[21] *Ibid.*, p. 60.

[22] Jerold S. Auerbach, "The Depression Decade," in Alan Reitman, (ed.), *The Pulse of Freedom* (1975), p. 73.

[23] Robert Justin Goldstein, *Political Repression in Modern America: From 1870 to 1976* (1978), p. 23.

[24] *Ibid.*, p. 55.

[25] Paul L. Murphy, *World War I and the Origin of Civil Liberties in the United States* (1979), p. 15.

[26] Goldstein, *op. cit.*, p. 110.

[27] *Ibid.*, p. 111.

[28] Rehnquist, *op. cit.*, p. 107.

[29] Goldstein, *op. cit.*, p. 287.

[30] American Civil Liberties Union, "Annual Report, 1946-1947," p. 4.

[31] Goldstein, *op. cit.*, p. 407.

FOR MORE INFORMATION

Accuracy in Media, 4455 Connecticut Ave., N.W., Suite 330, Washington, D.C. 20008; (202) 364-4401; www.aim.org. AIM analyzes print and electronic news media for bias.

American Civil Liberties Union, 122 Maryland Ave., N.E., Washington, D.C. 20002; (202) 544-1681; www.aclu.org. The ACLU initiates court cases and lobbies for legislation with the aim of protecting civil liberties.

Arab American Institute, 1600 K. St., N.W., Suite 601, Washington, D.C. 20006; (202) 429-9210; www.aaiusa.org. An advocacy group concerned with issues affecting Arab-Americans.

Criminal Justice Legal Foundation, P.O. Box 1199, Sacramento, Calif. 95816; (916) 446-0345; www.cjlf.org. Advocates victims' rights and a strengthening of the ability of law enforcement to fight crime.

The Heritage Foundation, 214 Massachusetts Ave., N.E., Washington, D.C. 20002; (202) 546-4400; www.heritage.org. A think tank that advocates the promotion of individual freedom and strong law enforcement.

National Association of Criminal Defense Lawyers, 1025 Connecticut Ave., N.W., Suite 901, Washington, D.C. 20036; (202) 872-8600; www.criminaljustice.org. Represents the interest of criminal-defense attorneys.

People for the American Way, 2000 M St., N.W., Suite 400, Washington, D.C. 20036; (202) 467-4999; www.pfaw.org. Promotes the protection of civil liberties.

Bibliography

Selected Sources

Books

Goldstein, Robert Justin, *Political Repression in Modern America: From 1870 to 1976*, University of Illinois Press, 1978.
Goldstein, a political science professor at Oakland University, details the history of repressive actions against U.S. citizens, especially the little-covered actions against labor unions in the late 1800s and the early 1900s. Includes extensive footnotes and a lengthy bibliography.

Linfield, Michael, *Freedom Under Fire: U.S. Civil Liberties in Time of War*, South End Press, 1990.
Linfield, a Los Angeles attorney, chronicles the dangers to civil liberties during wartime, with special focus on actions during the Revolutionary War.

Murphy, Paul L., *World War I and the Origin of Civil Liberties in the United States*, W. W. Norton, 1979.
A professor of history and American studies at the University of Minnesota readably explores the severe erosion of Americans' civil rights during World War I and the Red Scare afterwards.

Rehnquist, William H., *All the Laws But One: Civil Liberties in Wartime*, Vintage Books, 1998.
This readable work by the chief justice of the United States deals heavily with the Civil War and its aftermath and the Japanese internments during World War II, paying close attention to Supreme Court actions.

Articles

Glaberson, William, "Use of Military Court Divides Legal Experts," *The New York Times*, Nov. 14, 2001, p. A1.
Glaberson details the debate over the administration's proposed use of military tribunals.

Goldstein, Amy, "A Deliberate Strategy of Disruption," *The Washington Post*, Nov. 4, 2001, p. A1.
Goldstein looks in detail at the government's detention of potential terrorism suspects.

Lane, Charles, "Liberty and the Pursuit of Terrorists," *The Washington Post*, Nov. 25, 2001, p. B1.
A Supreme Court reporter argues that President Bush's recent steps in the war against terrorism are consistent with those taken by his predecessors in similar situations.

Lardner, George Jr., "U.S. Will Monitor Calls to Lawyers," *The Washington Post*, Nov. 9, 2001, p. A1.
Lardner explains the Justice Department decision to monitor attorney-client communication when the defendants are suspected terrorists.

Palmer, Elizabeth A., "Terrorism Bill's Sparse Paper Trail May Cause Legal Vulnerabilities," *CQ Weekly*, Oct. 27, 2001, p. 2533.
The article chronicles the legislative course of the U.S.A. Patriot Act and details its provisions.

Posner, Richard A., "Security Versus Civil Liberties," *The Atlantic*, Dec. 2001, p. 46.
A noted federal judge urges Americans not to overreact to possible curtailing of freedoms as the government gears up to combat terrorism.

Safire, William, "Seizing Dictatorial Power," *The New York Times*, Nov. 15, 2001, p. A31.
The conservative columnist argues that military tribunals are a tragic mistake. "Intimidated by terrorists . . . we are letting George W. Bush get away with the replacement of the American rule of law with military Kangaroo courts," he writes.

Thomas, Evan, *et al*, "Justice Kept In the Dark; Closed military tribunals," *Newsweek*, Dec. 10, 2001, p. 37.
In the past few weeks, Ashcroft has led such an aggressive campaign to stamp out subversion that even old-time G-men are wondering whether the attorney general is trying too hard to fill the shoes of the late J. Edgar Hoover.

Toner, Robin, "Civil Liberty vs. Security: Finding a Wartime Balance," *The New York Times*, Nov. 18, 2001, p. A1.
Toner examines recent steps to strengthen government authority in the fight against terrorism in light of historical precedent as well as popular attitudes.

Willing, Richard and Toni Locy, "U.S. Now a Less-Forgiving Host to Illegal Immigrants," *USA Today*, Nov. 30, 2001, p. A1.
More than 1,200 people have been detained in the probe into the attacks on the World Trade Center and the Pentagon, and 548 of them are illegal aliens, most of them young Muslim men, who likely never would have come to the attention of immigration officials had they not been scooped up by the FBI.

Reports and Studies

"Bringing Al-Qaeda to Justice: The Constitutionality of Trying Al-Qaeda Terrorists in the Military Justice System," Heritage Foundation, Nov. 5, 2001.
The conservative think tank argues that military tribunals make sense and are probably constitutional.

11 Cyber-Crimes

BRIAN HANSEN

Carlos Salgado Jr. walked into San Francisco International Airport carrying a tote bag containing an ordinary CD-ROM disk and Mario Puzo's popular Mafia novel *The Last Don*. He passed through security without incident and strolled down the concourse to a passenger lounge near Gate 67. But Salgado, 36, wasn't there to catch a plane.

The freelance computer technician had stolen more than 100,000 credit-card numbers by hacking into several e-commerce databases on the Internet. It was an easy heist for Salgado, who simply used a ready-made computer-intrusion program that he found on the Web. Using a pirated e-mail account to conceal his identity, Salgado arranged to sell the information to an online fence for $260,000. The exchange was set for May 21, 1997.

As a precaution, Salgado put the stolen data on a CD-ROM, but with Hollywood-like flair he encoded the information based on a passage in Puzo's novel. Salgado's story, too, would someday make good reading: He was about to pull off one of the largest cyber-crimes in the Internet's short history. All told, the bank data that Salgado had electronically liberated from the Internet had a combined credit line of more than $1 billion.

Unfortunately for Salgado, he was walking into an FBI sting operation. The bureau had started monitoring Salgado's online machinations after being tipped off by an alert technician at one of the companies Salgado had pilfered. Initially, the FBI knew Salgado only as "SMACK," his online "handle." But when

From *The CQ Researcher,*
April 12, 2002.

Onel de Guzman, a 23-year-old hacker from the Philippines, has been tied to the "Love Bug," an Internet "worm" that caused an estimated $10 billion in damage worldwide in 2000. Guzman, pictured with his sister, claims he did not know the bug would be so devastating.

he handed over the encrypted CD to an undercover agent, the feds finally had their man. Salgado pleaded guilty to breaking into a computer network and trafficking in stolen credit cards. He was sentenced to two and a half years in prison.

Few cyber-attacks are as serious as Salgado's. Nonetheless, experts say unauthorized incursions into government and private computer systems are part of a larger — and growing — cyber-crime trend.

"This is the 21st-century equivalent of the armored-car robbery," says Computer Security Institute (CSI) Editorial Director Richard Power. "Why should the bad guys bother dealing with armored cars and police with machine guns when they can knock off a [network] server and get tens of thousands of live credit cards? This is happening all the time now. The Salgado case was just the beginning."

Riptech, Inc., an Internet security firm in Alexandria, Va., verified 128,678 cyber-attacks on just 300 of the companies it serves in the last six months of 2001. [1] To be sure, only a small fraction of these attacks successfully breached the organizations' front-line security measures. Still, 41 percent of

Riptech's clients had to patch holes in their computer-security systems after "critical" attacks. And nearly one in eight suffered at least one "emergency" attack requiring some form of data-recovery procedure. (*See graph, p. 203.*)

"Our findings strongly suggest that once companies connect their systems to the Internet, they are virtually guaranteed to suffer some form of attack activity," Riptech recently reported. "The Internet security threat is real, pervasive and perhaps more severe than previously anticipated." [2]

An annual survey conducted by the FBI and CSI confirms the explosion of cyber-crime to epidemic proportions. More than 91 percent of the corporations and U.S. government agencies that responded reported a computer-security breach in 2001, and 64 percent acknowledged financial losses because of the attacks. [3]

Some cyber-crimes, like Salgado's caper, are committed primarily for money. Others are "inside" jobs perpetrated by disgruntled employees like Timothy Lloyd, a revenge-minded network administrator in New Jersey. After being demoted and reprimanded in 1996, he wrote six lines of malicious computer code that caused $10 million in financial losses for the Omega Engineering Corp.

Lloyd was convicted of sabotaging the company's computer network and last February was sentenced to 41 months in prison and ordered to pay more than $2 million in restitution. At Lloyd's trial, an Omega executive said the firm "will never recover" from the attack. [4]

Many computer attacks are essentially online vandalism. Hackers have defaced countless Web pages, greatly embarrassing major corporations and government agencies. Hackers some-

How to Avoid Internet Scams

Con artists have been quick to seize upon the Internet for new ways to separate consumers from their money. According to the Federal Trade Commission (FTC), the nation's chief consumer-protection agency, the best way to avoid getting taken is to buy with a credit card from a reputable Web site, and to use common sense. The following list of the most popular scams is based on more than 285,000 fraud complaints filed last year on a centralized database utilized by hundreds of law-enforcement agencies. To report Internet scams to the FTC, call 1-877-FTC-HELP (1-877-382-4357), or use the online complaint form at www.ftc.gov/ftc/consumer.htm.

The Scam	The Bait	The Catch	The Safety Net
Internet Auctions	Shop in a "virtual marketplace" that offers a huge selection of products at great deals.	You receive an item that is less valuable than promised, or, worse yet, you receive nothing at all.	When bidding through an Internet auction, particularly for a valuable item, check out the comments about the seller and insist on paying with a credit card or through a reliable payment service such as PayPal or BillPoint.
Internet Access Services	Free money, simply for cashing a check.	You get trapped into long-term contracts for Internet access or another Web service, with big penalties for cancellation or early termination.	If a check arrives at your home or business, read both sides carefully for the conditions you're agreeing to if you cash the check. Monitor your phone bill for unexpected or unauthorized charges.
Credit-Card Fraud	View adult images online for free, just for providing your credit-card number to prove you're over 18.	Fraudulent promoters make charges using your credit-card number, or sell your card number to other online hucksters.	Share credit-card information only with a company you trust. Dispute unauthorized charges on your credit-card bill by complaining to the bank that issued the card. Federal law limits your liability to $50 in charges if your card is misused.
Modem Hijacking	Get free access to adult material and pornography by downloading a "viewer" or "dialer" computer program.	The program you download surreptitiously disconnects your computer's modem from your local Internet Service Provider and reconnects you to a high-priced service overseas. You don't find out until you get a huge phone bill in the mail.	Don't download any program in order to access a so-called "free" service without reading all the disclosures carefully for cost information. Just as important, read your phone bill carefully, and challenge any charges you didn't authorize or don't understand.

Source: Federal Trade Commission

times act to advance social or political views. Last year, Chinese hackers defaced a host of U.S. government Web sites after a Chinese pilot died in a collision with an American spy plane over the South China Sea. American hackers retaliated by defacing 2,500 Chinese sites. Similar cyber-warfare broke out between American and Middle Eastern hackers after the Sept. 11 terrorist attacks.

To be sure, not all hackers are viewed as criminals. So-called ethical or white-hat hackers who try to break into computer systems at the behest of security-conscious companies are often lauded for advancing the state of computer technology. But "black-hat" hackers, or "crackers," seek to wreak havoc or illegally profit from their cyberspace forays.

"Gray-hat" hackers occupy a shadowy niche somewhere in between these two extremes. While they have no qualms about illegally breaking into computer systems, gray hats generally don't pilfer or damage assets but inform their victims about the security flaws they discover.

Many hackers embrace a controversial philosophy: They show the general public how they compromised particular computer systems by posting their hacking codes, or "scripts," to public areas of the Internet. The hackers say this forces careless com-

The Scam	The Bait	The Catch	The Safety Net
Web Cramming	Get a free, custom-designed Web site for a 30-day trial period, with no obligation to continue.	Charges appear on your telephone bill, or you receive a separate invoice, even if you never accepted the offer or agreed to continue the service after the trial period.	Review your telephone bills, and challenge any charges you don't recognize.
Multilevel Marketing Plans/ Pyramid Schemes	Make money through the products and services you sell as well as those sold by the people you recruit into the program.	After paying to join the program and purchase inventory, you learn that your "customers" are other distributors, not the general public. Some multilevel marketing programs are actually illegal pyramid schemes. When products or services are sold only to distributors like yourself, there's no way to make money.	Avoid plans that require you to recruit distributors, buy expensive inventory or commit to a minimum sales volume.
Travel and Vacation Scams	Get a luxurious trip with lots of "extras" at a bargain-basement price.	You get lower-quality accommodations and services than advertised, or no trip at all. Or, you get hit with hidden charges or additional requirements after you've paid.	Get references on any travel company you're planning to do business with. Then, get details of the trip in writing, including the cancellation policy, before signing on.
Bogus Business Opportunities	Be your own boss and earn big bucks.	You get scammed in any number of ways. The bottom line: If it looks too good to be true, it probably is.	Talk to other people who started businesses through the same company, get all the promises in writing, and study the proposed contract carefully before signing. Get an attorney or an accountant to look at it, too.
Online Investment Scams	Make an initial investment in a day-trading system or service, and you'll quickly realize huge returns.	Big profits always mean big risk. Consumers have lost money to programs that claim to be able to predict the market with "100 percent accuracy."	Check out the promoter with state and federal securities and commodities regulators, and talk to other people who invested through the program to find out what level of risk you're assuming.
Health-Care Products/ Services	Items sold over the Internet or through other non-traditional suppliers that are "proven" to cure serious and even fatal health problems.	You put your hopes — and your money — on a marketing company's "miracle" product instead of getting the health care you really need.	Consult a health-care professional before buying any "cure-all" product that claims to treat a wide range of ailments or offers quick cures and easy solutions to serious illnesses.

panies and slipshod software manufacturers to take computer security more seriously.

Not surprisingly, many organizations don't like having their vulnerabilities publicized in this manner. Law-enforcement agencies typically don't endorse the philosophy, either.

"Thanking hackers who violate the privacy of networks or network users [by] pointing out our vulnerabilities is a little bit like sending thank-you notes to burglars for pointing out the infirmity of our physical alarms," said Martha Stansell-Gamm, chief of the Department of Justice's Computer Crime and Intellectual Property division. [5]

Many of the hacker-crafted scripts that circulate in cyberspace are viruses or worms — programs that can corrupt computer files and spread themselves across the Internet. (*See glossary, p. 209.*) Novice hackers known as "script kiddies" unleash thousands of viruses and worms every year, often without realizing the potential impact of their actions. Onel de Guzman, the 23-year-old Filipino hacker who has been tied to the "Love Bug," claimed he had no idea the worm would be so devastating. It caused an estimated $10 billion in damage worldwide in May 2000. [6]

Con artists, meanwhile, are using the Web to perpetrate various types of fraud schemes in record numbers, according to law-enforcement officials. "The number of [fraud] complaints has increased steadily over the last two or three years," says Timothy Healy, director of the Internet Fraud Complaint Center (IFCC), operated by the FBI and the National White Collar Crime Center.

Internet auction fraud was the most frequently reported type of complaint handled by the IFCC last year, according to Healy. Fraudsters can rig Internet auctions in a number of ways, such as using shills to drive up the bidding process. Con men also use the Internet to perpetrate a wide variety of investment scams, bogus e-commerce opportunities and confidence rackets. "It's amazing what's out there," Healy says.

One of the most prevalent and insidious Internet-assisted scams is identity theft — stealing credit card and Social Security numbers and other personal information. Some identity thieves hack into e-commerce Web sites to pilfer such data. Others set up bogus Internet sites of their own to dupe unwitting consumers into revealing their credit-card numbers.

Armed with stolen identities, thieves can perpetrate a variety of crimes, from opening bogus bank accounts and writing bad checks to taking out car loans and mortgages in their victims' names.

Under federal law, consumers who use credit cards are liable only for the first $50 of fraudulent charges made on their accounts, and many credit-card companies even waive that amount. Still, identity-theft victims typically incur more than $1,000 in out-

FBI agent Doris Gardner heads the bureau's computer crimes unit in Charlotte, N.C., one of several throughout the country. The unit focuses on both e-commerce fraud and cyber-predators who target children.

AP Photo

of-pocket expenses trying to restore their mangled credit ratings, according to the Federal Trade Commission. (Debit-card purchases do not receive automatic fraud protection.) [7]

Lenders are hit even harder. Identity theft cost financial institutions some $2.4 billion in direct losses and related mopping-up expenses in 2000, according to Celent Communications, a Boston consulting firm. [8]

Controversies abound over how best to deal with Internet hucksters, hackers and virus writers. Some policymakers, wary of Internet-facilitated terrorist attacks, are calling for tough new laws to prevent computer crimes — including life sentences for some offenses (*see p. 212*). Others fear that

such initiatives will trample on civil liberties. Still others want legislation to make software companies such as Microsoft liable for damages caused by computer-security failures.

As the debate rages, here is a closer look at some of the key questions being asked:

Is it safe for consumers and merchants to do business online?

Only about 40 percent of all adult Internet users in the United States use the Web to shop or pay bills, according to the Census Bureau. [9] Many Americans eschew online shopping, banking and other types of Internet commerce because they fear having their credit card or Social Security numbers stolen, numerous studies have found. For example, 85 percent of the Internet users polled recently by Washington-based SWR Worldwide cited security as the biggest deterrent to e-commerce. A poll by GartnerG2, a Stamford, Conn., firm, put the number worried about security at 60 percent. [10]

According to Gartner, U.S. e-commerce fraud losses in 2001 exceeded $700 million, constituting about 1.14 percent of the $61.8 billion in total online sales. That ratio was 19 times higher than the fraud rate for traditional in-store transactions, which hovered at less than one-tenth of 1 percent during the same time period, Gartner said. Since the e-commerce era began in the mid-1990s, Gartner estimates that one in every six online consumers has been victimized by credit-card fraud, and one in 12 has been hit with identity theft.

"We're not going to see low fraud rates like we have in the brick-and-mortar world until we make some serious changes in the way that online business is conducted," says Avivah Litan, Gartner's vice president for research. "There are some big issues to deal with."

For merchants, the Internet is a double-edged sword. While they can broaden their customer bases and increase their revenues by going online, merchants also expose themselves to cyber-criminals.

Some law-enforcement officials concede that they can't keep pace with the number of e-commerce fraud scams already on the Internet. "There's no way that we can police the entire Web with the small staff that we have at this agency," says an official at the FTC, which investigates Internet fraud. "We go after things that are particularly egregious or pernicious, but we really have to strategically target our limited resources."

Other experts downplay the risks associated with online commerce. "I think we're doing quite well in terms of protecting buyers and sellers in the virtual marketplace," says Emily Hackett, executive director of the Internet Alliance, a Washington-based trade group. "The vast majority of online transactions are carried out without any problems at all."

Consumers can protect themselves when shopping online (as well as in traditional brick-and-mortar stores) by using a credit card. Under federal law, consumers are liable for only the first $50 of fraudulent charges made on their credit-card accounts, and many card issuers waive that amount. Users of debit cards, checks or other payment methods are not necessarily protected. Consequently, more than 95 percent of all e-commerce transactions are made with credit cards, Gartner says.

Credit-card companies are liable for fraudulent in-store transactions accompanied by signed (albeit forged) receipts. However, merchants are typically on the hook for any transactions they process without validating the purchaser's signature — which is rarely

Internet Fraud Complaints

Auction and communications fraud and non-delivery of merchandise are the most common fraud complaints reported to the Internet Fraud Complaint Center (IFCC.) Losses were especially high with identity theft and investment fraud.

Complaint Type	% of Complainants Who Reported Dollar Loss	Average (median) $ Loss per Typical Complaint
Auction fraud	78.4%	$230
Non-delivery (of purchases or payment)	73.8	225
Credit card/debit card fraud	58.3	207
Confidence fraud	63.1	339
Nigerian letter scam	01.1	3,000
Investment fraud	69.1	469
Check fraud	56.4	194
Business fraud	55.8	192
Identity theft	14.4	520
Communications fraud	78.7	145

Source: "IFCC Annual Internet 'Fraud Report,'" National White Collar Crime Center and FBI

done over the Internet. Consequently, merchants — not consumers or credit-card companies — bear most of the costs of e-commerce fraud.

Most Internet merchants utilize a fraud-prevention program. But programs vary widely in effectiveness and customer convenience. Many small merchants screen their online orders manually, flagging those with unusually high dollar volumes, suspicious billing information or other indicators of fraud. Large merchants often use sophisticated computer software programs to identify potentially fraudulent transactions. Best Buy Co., a consumer electronics retailer, can program its system to red-flag or automatically reject any online orders that originate from countries with high fraud rates.

Many Internet merchants also protect their online sales through the Secure Socket Layer protocol, or SSL. This technology encrypts consumers' credit-card numbers and other personal information so that it can be safely transmitted to merchants' databases. But while SSL allows consumers and merchants to exchange payment information through a secure "electronic pipe," the technology does not protect the database. And since all merchants don't encrypt their customers' data, they provide juicy targets for ill-intentioned hackers. Meredith Outwater, an e-commerce fraud expert at Celent Communications, says fraud-minded hackers constantly surf the Internet looking for these kinds of opportunities.

"Merchants aren't securing their servers enough," Outwater says. "There are merchants who have their [customers'] credit-card data just sitting on servers, waiting to be hacked. That happens more often than data getting intercepted in transmission."

Nonetheless, Kenneth Kerr, a senior analyst at Gartner, does not consider e-commerce to be riskier than shopping in traditional brick-and-mortar stores. "It takes a sophisticated thief to hack into a Web server," Kerr said. "It is a lot simpler to steal identity information in a physical environment like a restaurant." [11]

Many computer-security experts say that consumers should avoid doing business with small e-commerce merchants. "Stay away from the mom-and-pop e-tailers, because they typically don't have the resources to implement a comprehensive, layered approach to security," says Victor Keong, a Toronto-based business consultant at Deloitte & Touche. "Merchants that rely only on one layer of security are very vulnerable."

Alfred Hunger, vice president of engineering at SecurityFocus, in San Mateo, Calif., agrees that there is a wide range of security among Internet merchants. "The publicly held e-tailers take [security] much more seriously than the mom-and-pop shops," Hunger says. "The small shops still represent a significant risk."

Should computer network security problems be publicly disclosed?

Hackers and virus writers regularly cause problems in cyberspace by exploiting flaws, or "bugs," in software programs. The computer-security community has long debated the wisdom of informing the general public about these vulnerabilities. Some experts argue that software security bugs should be publicly disclosed as soon as they are detected. Advocates of "full disclosure" say that by publicizing software vulnerabilities immediately, computer users can protect themselves against hackers and cyber-criminals who will inevitably discover and exploit the flaws. Full disclosure also compels vendors to promptly engineer and disseminate software "patches" to fix computer-security problems engendered by their flawed products, these advocates say.

"I'm very big on disclosure because it advances the security posture of everyone," Keong says. "The earlier

that [software vendors] get the patches out there, the better."

Salt Lake City-based BugNet is one of several firms that hunts for software flaws and posts warnings about vulnerable systems on its Web site. Eric Bowden, BugNet's general manager, says that such disclosures get software companies to address computer security problems. Bowden denies that his bug hunters are out to embarrass, vilify or extort money from software giants such as Microsoft, as some critics contend.

"BugNet is very solutions-oriented," Bowden says. "We're not in it to point fingers or play the blame-game with [software] developers as much as we're trying to find solutions to serious problems."

Unlike other bug-hunting organizations, BugNet does not immediately publicize detailed information about every software vulnerability it finds. Depending on the type of the bug at hand, BugNet may or may not give a vendor time to engineer a patch before posting a vulnerability warning, Bowden says. Bugs that pose only minor problems usually get posted immediately, he concedes. However, BugNet typically delays publicizing serious security flaws if vendors agree to develop workable patches, he says.

"It's important to get [vulnerability] information out there early, but I also believe in giving vendors enough time to develop some kind of work-around for security bugs," Bowden says. "You can cause a lot of damage by calling attention to a security bug before a patch is available."

Moreover, unlike some other bug-hunting organizations, BugNet does not publish "exploit scripts" — step-by-step instructions that hackers can use to exploit security vulnerabilities. Indeed, novice hackers known as "script kiddies" often download these ready-made scripts and run them without realizing the consequences of their actions, Bowden notes.

"There are millions of script kiddies out there, and I don't want to arm them with the tools to do all kinds of destructive things," Bowden says.

Microsoft couldn't agree more. Scott Culp, manager of Microsoft's security response center, blasted the full-disclosure policy in an essay published last October.

"It's simply indefensible for the security community to continue arming cyber-criminals," Culp wrote. "We can and should discuss security vulnerabilities, but we should be smart, prudent and responsible in the way we do it." [12]

Microsoft advocates a policy of full disclosure but not full exposure. "Our policy on disclosure of security problems is intended to keep our customers safe," a spokesperson says. "If we were to publicize a problem without being able to offer a solution, that would make potential attackers aware of the hole but not give our customers a way to protect themselves."

Last fall, in a controversial move, Microsoft formed an alliance with several bug-hunting firms in an effort to curtail the publication of software-security flaws. At Microsoft's request, the firms agreed to wait at least 30 days before publicizing detailed information about any security-related bugs they discover.

"We want to create an atmosphere where people are more responsible with the disclosure of vulnerability information," said Eddie Schwartz, an analyst at Guardent Inc., a Waltham, Mass., firm that joined the alliance. "Right now, it is way too ad hoc." [13]

Other security experts are less enthusiastic about the alliance's efforts.

"I think the 30-day grace period is just another way for Microsoft and others to once again remove themselves from their responsibility for developing quality software before it hits the streets," said John Cowan Jr., of Louisville, Ky.-based Caldwell Industries Inc. [14]

Bruce Schneier, chief technology

officer at Counterpane Internet Security Inc., in Cupertino, Calif., agrees.

"Microsoft's motives in promoting bug secrecy are obvious: It's a whole lot easier to squelch security information than it is to fix problems or design products securely in the first place," Schneier said. "Disclosure doesn't create security vulnerabilities — programmers create them, and they remain until other programmers find and remove them." [15]

Should software companies be liable for Internet security breaches?

Hackers and virus writers frequently launch attacks over the Internet by exploiting security flaws in commercial software. The Boston consulting company @Stake found that 70 percent of the security gaps that plagued its customers' computer networks last year were due to software bugs. [16]

Many computer-security experts say that software manufacturers know about most of these flaws before they put their products on the market. Mark Minasi, an investigative journalist who specializes in technology issues, claims that 90 percent of the bugs that consumers report to software vendors were already known to the vendors at the time of release. [17] Yet, many studies have found that businesses and government agencies that have been attacked via these types of software security gaps have incurred billions of dollars in damages. [18]

There are no laws requiring software vendors to manufacture hack-proof or virus-resistant products. Likewise, no software company has ever been held responsible for damages stemming from a known security flaw in a product. Software vendors have long avoided this type of liability by inserting disclaimers in the so-called end-user licensing agreements (EULAs) that customers must consent to before using a product. In general, EULAs require users to assume all risks associated with the product. The EULA for Microsoft's Windows 2000 operating system is typical of this type of liability waiver. It states, in part:

"In no event shall Microsoft or its suppliers be liable for any damages whatsoever . . . arising out of the use of or inability to use the software product, even if Microsoft has been advised of the possibility of such damages." [19]

Given the crucial role that software plays in the modern world, many computer-security experts say it's high time that software companies take responsibility for producing hack-prone products.

"Software is deployed in places where it's absolutely critical for safety, like in much of our infrastructure," says Hunger of SecurityFocus. "It's totally unreasonable to give software vendors immunity from liability when every other industry — the Fords and the Boeings of the world — are held to a much, much higher standard."

Some legal experts predict that consumers will use the courts to force software vendors to accept liability for unsafe products, as occurred with the tobacco industry. "I think where you're going to see reform come is through lawsuits," said Jeffrey Hunker, dean of the H. John Heinz III School of Public Policy and Management at Carnegie Mellon University in Pittsburgh. "So much of our economic structure depends on computers that it's unsustainable to hold software companies blameless." [20]

Michael Erbschloe, vice president for research at Computer Economics, in Carlsbad, Calif., says the modern world "doesn't have any choice economically" not to require secure software. "People are getting very tired of the hack attacks and the lax security," Erbschloe adds. "The economic consequences of this run very high, and go to many levels."

Since 1995, computer viruses and

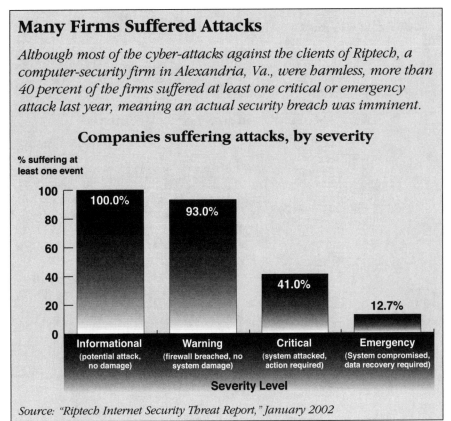

Many Firms Suffered Attacks

Although most of the cyber-attacks against the clients of Riptech, a computer-security firm in Alexandria, Va., were harmless, more than 40 percent of the firms suffered at least one critical or emergency attack last year, meaning an actual security breach was imminent.

Companies suffering attacks, by severity

% suffering at least one event

- Informational (potential attack, no damage): 100.0%
- Warning (firewall breached, no system damage): 93.0%
- Critical (system attacked, action required): 41.0%
- Emergency (System compromised, data recovery required): 12.7%

Severity Level

Source: "Riptech Internet Security Threat Report," January 2002

Many Firms Keep Mum About Attacks

A significant percentage of the firms and organizations that suffer security incidents don't report them because they fear negative publicity, according to a recent survey.

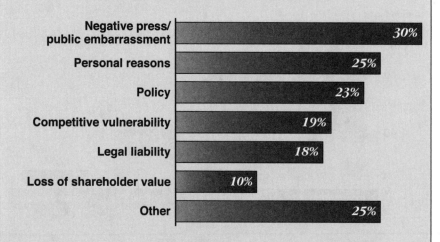

Why security incidents are not reported
(by percentage of firms reporting)

Negative press/ public embarrassment	30%
Personal reasons	25%
Policy	23%
Competitive vulnerability	19%
Legal liability	18%
Loss of shareholder value	10%
Other	25%

Note: Includes multiple responses; 4,500 security professionals were polled.

Source: InformationWeek, *"Global Information Security Survey, 2001,"* September 2001

worms have caused more than $54 billion in economic damages, Erbschloe estimates. That figure, he notes, does not include the damages inflicted by other types of cyber-crimes, such as computer-facilitated credit-card theft. [21]

A recent National Academy of Sciences report declares that the state of the nation's cyber-security is "far worse than what known best practices" could provide. The report says that "market incentives" have failed to push software companies and other private-sector interests toward creating a secure computing climate. Consequently, the report recommends that policymakers consider "legislative responses" to improving cyber-security, including making vendors liable for security breaches. [22]

But Mark Bohannon, general counsel and vice president for government affairs at the Software and Information Industry Association, says it would be impossible to hold software ven-

dors responsible for security breaches, because software programs must interact with myriad other computer network systems.

"The notion of holding software vendors liable for security breaches when their products must interoperate with other things that they don't even control just boggles my mind," Bohannon says. "The people who are making these proposals really need to carefully examine how the industry really works."

Microsoft continues to oppose efforts to make software vendors liable for security breaches. However, CEO Bill Gates says security is now the company's highest priority. In a Jan. 15 e-mail to all Microsoft employees, Gates launched the company's "trustworthy computing" initiative, which he described as "more important than any other part of our work. Our products should emphasize security right out of

the box, and we must constantly refine and improve that security as threats evolve. Eventually, our software should be so fundamentally secure that customers never even worry about it." [23]

Gates acknowledged that in the past, Microsoft's biggest priority was adding new features and "functionality" to its products. That can no longer be the case, Gates wrote. "All those great features won't matter unless customers trust our software," he declared. "So now, when we face a choice between adding features and resolving security issues, we need to choose security." [24]

To that end, Microsoft sent every one of its more than 9,000 software developers through advanced security-training courses earlier this year. But many security experts question whether Microsoft will follow through.

"Issuing a statement doesn't solve any problems," said Schneier of Counterpane Internet Security. "Microsoft is notorious for treating security as a public-relations problem. Gates said all the right words. If he does that, it will be a sea change. I'd like to believe him, but I need proof. [25]

BugNet's Bowden offered a similar assessment. "It may or may not be lip service," Bowden said. "But it's obvious that they have been bloodied up enough by critics who claimed that their products were too insecure." ∎

BACKGROUND

Early Hackers

Many of today's computer-facilitated crimes were inspired, in part, by a technology-centered counterculture that emerged in the United States in the late 1950s. Led by ambitious students at the Massachusetts Institute of Technology and other top

Chronology

1960s–1970s

The first hackers advance computer technology, sometimes with illegal activities.

1961
Hackers at MIT known as the Tech Model Railroad Club write advanced programming code for an early minicomputer.

1971
Esquire magazine publishes detailed instructions for "phone-phreaking," or making free long-distance calls.

1972
California phone-phreaker John Draper ("Captain Crunch") uses a toy whistle from a cereal box to produce the 2,600-hertz tone needed to make free long-distance calls.

1975
Hackers produce one of the first personal computers, the Altair 8800.

1977
Hackers Stephen Wozniak and Steven Jobs form Apple Computer.

1980s
Hackers help launch the personal computer revolution. Congress cracks down on computer criminals.

1981
Philadelphia hacker Pat Riddle ("Captain Zap") uses a pre-Internet computer network called ARPANET to break into computer systems at the Pentagon and White House.

1983
"War Games," a movie about a teenage hacker who nearly starts a nuclear war, is released. Real-life hacker Kevin Mitnick, 17, is arrested in Los Angeles for hacking into the Pentagon.

1984
2600: The Hacker Quarterly, is founded.

1986
The Computer Fraud and Abuse Act (CFAA), the first federal computer-crime law, makes it a felony to enter computer systems operated by the government or federally insured financial institutions.

1988
Cornell University graduate student Robert Morris creates an experimental computer program, later dubbed a "worm," that cripples thousands of computer systems. The Computer Emergency Response Team (CERT) is formed.

1989
Mitnick is arrested again and convicted of stealing software and long-distance access codes from two corporations. After a year in prison, he resumes hacking.

1990s
Cyber-crime explodes with the development of the Internet.

1993
Hackers discover myriad vulnerabilities in Microsoft's new Windows NT Web server operating system.

1994
Music student Richard Price ("Datastream Cowboy") is charged with hacking into NASA and Korean Atomic Research Institute computers.

1994
Russian hacker Vladimir Levin breaks into Citibank's computer system and steals more than $10 million from customers' accounts. Levin is eventually convicted of bank and wire fraud.

1995
Tsutomu Shimomura helps the FBI track down Mitnick, who is imprisoned for four years while he awaits trial. Hackers deface popular Web sites, including *The New York Times*, to protest Mitnick's imprisonment. He eventually pleads guilty to seven counts and is released in January 2000 but prohibited from using computers and mobile phones.

1999
The "Melissa" virus shuts down computers around the world. David L. Smith, a New Jersey programmer, gets five years in prison for releasing the malicious code.

2000–Present

Hackers and virus writers continue to cause billions in damages. The Sept. 11 attacks against the United States spark fears of cyber-terrorism.

2000
A 15-year-old hacker known as "Mafiaboy" cripples popular e-commerce sites. The attacks cost some $1.7 billion in lost sales and damages. Hackers access Microsoft's proprietary source code.

2001–2002
Hackers deface pro-Muslim Web sites in the wake of the Sept. 11 terrorist attacks. The White House orders government agencies to remove certain information from public Web sites, fearing it could aid cyber-terrorists.

A Tale of Two Hackers

Kevin Mitnick called himself the "Condor," after the 1975 thriller about a man on the run. It was a suitable alias: At the time of his arrest in 1995, he was the most wanted computer hacker in cyberspace history.

Mitnick, now 38, is out of prison and living in California. His hacking spree cost his victims tens of millions of dollars over the course of two decades. It all began in 1981, when Mitnick and two other "phone phreakers" stole passwords and operating manuals for the Pacific Bell telephone company's computer system and used the information to hack into the system and get free calls. The three were arrested after a jilted girlfriend turned them in to the police. Mitnick, then 17, was placed on probation.

In 1983, Mitnick gained national notoriety by hacking into a Pentagon computer via the ARPNET, a pre-Internet computer network operated by the Defense Department. This time, he was sentenced to six months in a juvenile detention facility. After his release, Mitnick put custom license plates on his car that read "X HACKER." But his hacking days were far from over.

In 1988, he and a friend, Lenny DiCicco, hacked into the Digital Equipment Corp., a Palo Alto, Calif., software company. The company discovered the incursion immediately, but the FBI couldn't pinpoint the source of the attacks. Anticipating the surveillance, Mitnick had hacked into the phone system and scrambled the source of his computer's modem calls.

The electronic subterfuge worked — until DiCicco, under pressure, confessed to the FBI. Mitnick was accused of stealing $1 million worth of proprietary software and causing $4 million in damages. He eventually pleaded guilty to two charges and was sentenced to a year in prison. Under the terms of his release, he was told to stay out of trouble. He didn't.

The FBI came looking for Mitnick in 1992 in conjunction with yet another computer break-in. But before they could arrest him, he vanished. Still, it didn't take long for the FBI to pick up his trail. Later that year, a caller purporting to be a law-enforcement officer asked the California Department of Motor Vehicles (DMV) office in Sacramento to fax a photograph of a confidential police informant to a non-government phone number in Los Angeles. A suspicious DMV official traced the number to a Kinko's copy shop. Police rushed to the shop, but the suspect bolted across a parking lot and disappeared around the corner, dropping the documents as he fled. Fingerprints confirmed it was Mitnick.

Mitnick's undoing began on Christmas Day in 1994, when he broke into files belonging to Tsutomu Shimomura, a scientist at the San Diego Supercomputer Center. Shimomura began monitoring Mitnick's movements through cyberspace as the outlaw hacker broke into myriad computer systems around the world. Shimomura eventually traced Mitnick to an apartment in Raleigh, N.C. The FBI moved in on Feb. 15, 1995.

After more than two years on the run, the Condor was again in custody. Mitnick faced a multitude of charges, including 23 counts of computer and wire fraud. He pleaded guilty to one count and was extradited back to California, where he was hit with an additional 25 charges. Prosecutors argued that Mitnick had cost his victims more than $290 million during his two-year hacking spree. [1]

To prepare his defense in the complicated case, Mitnick waived his right to a speedy trial. As a result, he sat in prison for four years awaiting trial. The hacker underground protested Mitnick's long pre-trial detention by defacing some of the most popular Web sites on the Internet, including Yahoo! and *The New York Times*.

On March 16, 1999, Mitnick pleaded guilty to five felony counts of computer and wire fraud and was sentenced to 46 months in prison, with time off for months served. He received an additional 22 months for crimes committed in North Carolina. To date, Mitnick's composite 68-month prison sentence is the longest yet imposed on a computer hacker.

Mitnick was released from California's Lompoc federal penitentiary on Jan. 21, 2000. Under his unusually stringent parole conditions, he is prohibited from using a computer or cell phone until Jan. 20, 2003.

universities, it was grounded in a belief that technology should be liberated from the control of governments and private industry.

The technology junkies who spearheaded this revolution were known as "hackers." Back then, the term was a laudatory moniker bestowed on people who were skilled at improving the capabilities of computer systems.

To be sure, the early hackers sometimes ran afoul of the law. However, they were motivated primarily by the promise of new technologies, not the pursuit of ill-gotten gains. The early hackers wanted to advance computer technology beyond the level of hulking, room-sized machines and punch cards. They often carried out their electronic experiments surreptitiously and without authorization. Then as now, they justified their unlawful actions on the grounds that they were working for the betterment of everyone.

Steven Levy, chief technology writer for *Newsweek*, dubbed this notion the "hacker ethic." In a seminal book on the subject, Levy described the mindset of the hacker community in the late 1950s:

"Access to computers should be unlimited and total. All information should be free. You can create art and beauty on a computer. Computers can change your life for the better." According to Levy, bona fide hackers "believe that essential lessons can be learned . . . from taking things apart, seeing how they work, and using this knowledge

Testifying before a Senate committee hearing on cyber-crime shortly after his release from prison, Mitnick sounded an ominous warning: "My motivation was a quest for knowledge, the intellectual challenge, the thrill and the escape from reality," he said in March 2000. "If somebody has the time, money and motivation, they can get into any computer." [2]

Adrian Lamo: Hero or Criminal?

Adrian Lamo has hacked into some of the largest corporations in the world, but unlike Kevin Mitnick, he's never been arrested. After he breaches a computer network, Lamo, 21, informs his "victims" and offers to help fix the flaws he finds for free. Some computer-security experts praise so-called ethical hackers like Lamo.

"Ethical hackers who don't do damage and push the state of the art in security [provide] a valuable service," said Jonathan Couch Sr., a network security engineer at Sytex Inc., a Doylestown, Pa., technology-consulting firm. "The government needs to have the discretion not to prosecute." [3]

But Marcus Ranum, chief technology officer at NFR Security, in Rockville, Md., calls Lamo a "sociopath" whose behavior is indefensible.

"It's against the law — how much more cut and dried can you get?" said Ranum. "If society was comfortable with what he's doing, they'd change the law." [4]

Lamo himself doesn't put much stock in society's norms and conventions. He lives largely out of a backpack, spending most of his time in San Francisco and the suburbs of Washington, D.C. Sometimes he stays with friends; other times he sleeps in abandoned buildings. Armed with his laptop, he does much of his hacking from Web kiosks at all-night copy shops and Internet cafes.

Adrian Lamo, left, and Kevin Mitnick

WBG Links

Lamo prefers the vagabond lifestyle because he likes to put himself in situations where "interesting things" can happen. "All the interesting things that have happened to me have been the result of synchronicity and organized chaos," he said. "I do what I do; there's no particular motive I can describe." [5]

Although Lamo has yet to be prosecuted for his unauthorized forays, one of his recent victims hasn't been so quick to thank him. Earlier this year, Lamo hacked into a cache of confidential information at *The New York Times*, but the newspaper has not sought Lamo's assistance in plugging the hole in its network. On the contrary, the company is contemplating pressing charges. "We're still investigating and exploring all of the options," *Times* spokesperson Christine Mohan says.

Lamo acknowledges that it's illegal to hack into a computer system without permission. But unauthorized hacking is not necessarily wrong, he says.

Obviously, [no organization] wants to be compromised and it's never a one-hundred-percent pleasant experience," he said. "But I'd like to see more receptivity to processing compromises that don't result in damage, without necessarily destroying the life of the person involved." [6]

[1] Cited in Richard Power, *Tangled Web: Tales of Digital Crime From the Shadows of Cyberspace*, Que/MacMillan, 2000.

[2] Quoted in John Schwartz, "Hacker Gives a Hill How-To," *The Washington Post*, March 3, 2000. Mitnick testified before the Senate Committee on Governmental Affairs.

[3] Quoted in Kevin Poulsen, "Panel Debates Hacker Amnesty," *SecurityFocus*, March 25, 2002.

[4] *Ibid.*

[5] Quoted in Kevin Poulsen, "Lamo's Adventures in WorldCom," *SecurityFocus*, Dec. 5, 2001.

[6] *Ibid.*

to create new and even more interesting things." Hackers also "resent any person, physical barrier, or law" that stands in the way of this objective, a philosophy that continues to thrive in the hacker community today. [26]

"As long as the human spirit is alive, there will always be hackers," said Eric Corley, a.k.a. Emmanuel Goldstein, an editor at *2600: The Hacker Quarterly*.* "We may have a hell of a fight on our hands if we continue to be imprisoned and victimized for exploring, but that

will do anything but stop us. I'm the first to say that people who cause damage should be punished, but I really don't think prison should be considered for something like this unless the offender is a true risk to society." [27]

---

* Corley borrowed his computer handle from the name of a character in George Orwell's futuristic novel *1984*, which warned that the government, or "Big Brother," would take over society if permitted. The character Emmanuel Goldstein fought the system.

But computer-security experts generally reject such reasoning. "Hacking is a felony — for good reason," said Charles C. Palmer, of IBM. "Some [hackers] . . . think it's harmless [if they] don't do anything besides go in and look around. But if a stranger came into your house, looked through everything, touched several items, and left — after building a small, out-of-the-way door to be sure he could easily enter again — would you consider that harmless?" [28]

Phone "Phreaks"

The early hackers did not limit their technological forays to computers. In the 1960s and '70s, many hackers tried to exploit telephone systems. Known as phone "phreaks," they made devices known as "blue boxes" that allowed them to make free long-distance calls. The boxes could duplicate the high-pitched, 2,600-hertz tone that AT&T used to control its long-distance switching system.

Blue boxes quickly became hot commodities in the United States. Two enterprising phone phreaks, Stephen Wozniak and Steven Jobs, the future founders of Apple Computer, pedaled blue boxes in college dormitories. Another phreak, John Draper, discovered that he could hack into the phone system using a toy whistle from a box of Cap'n Crunch breakfast cereal.

"Cap'n Crunch," as Draper was called, quickly became a legend in the phreaking community. He outfitted his Volkswagen van with a high-tech blue box and roamed the highways in California in search of isolated telephone booths from which he could practice his craft. He spent hours at these booths, "sending calls around the world, bouncing them off communications satellites, leapfrogging them from the West Coast to London to Moscow to Sydney and then back again." [29]

The phone-phreak community was never very large, numbering a few hundred die-hards, at most. In 1971, they formed an alliance with the Yippies, an anarchist, anti-capitalist, anti-Vietnam War group. The Yippies' chief agitator, Abbie Hoffman, believed that phreaking could play an important role in fomenting a social revolution. Together, the groups published an underground newsletter that provided detailed phone-phreaking instructions to about 1,000 subscribers around the world.

Several widely circulated magazine articles brought the phone-phreaking craze to the attention of the general public — and the police. In June 1972, *Ramparts* magazine printed schematic diagrams for ripping off the Bell Telephone Co. Police seized copies of the magazine from newsstands, which helped to drive it out of business.

The *Ramparts* article and a similar piece in *Esquire* sparked a crackdown on phone phreakers. The police were especially eager to take down "Cap'n Crunch," who was convicted on federal wire-fraud charges and sentenced to four months in prison. He made good use of his time.

"Jails are the perfect venue for transferring hacking knowledge," Draper later wrote. "Inmates have a lot of spare time on their hands, and a patient teacher can teach just about anyone anything, given enough time." [30]

Hacking With PCs

The personal computer revolution of the early 1980s ushered in a new hacking era. Hackers equipped their PCs with modems and began communicating via a rudimentary electronic bulletin-board system, the precursor to modern e-mail. Hackers used bulletin boards to gossip, trade tech tips and exchange software — and also to traffic stolen computer passwords and credit-card numbers.

Hackers also began to break into online computer systems. Pat Riddle, a hacker in Philadelphia, used the ARPANET — a pre-Internet computer network — to hack into computers at the Pentagon, the White House and other high-profile institutions. At the time, the ARPANET was still controlled by the government. Riddle, whose online handle was "Captain Zap," also used his PC to pilfer more than $500,000 in merchandise from several large computer companies.

The FBI caught up with Riddle in 1981. There was no comprehensive computer-fraud law at the time, so Riddle, then 24, was indicted for stealing property and telephone service. Incredibly, he plea-bargained his way to a $1,000 fine and probation after the high-priced legal team retained by his prominent family warned prosecutors that "no jury will ever understand" the technical evidence needed to convict him. [31]

Meanwhile, hacking groups began to pop up everywhere. The U.S-based Legion of Doom and a German group, Chaos Computer Club, were started in 1984 along with *2600: The Hacker Quarterly*.

Anti-Hacking Law

The proliferation of hacker clubs, the Captain Zap incident and several other high-profile computer-intrusion cases caused great trepidation among policymakers and law-enforcement officials. The media and the entertainment industry did much to fuel — or exaggerate, according to some critics — the hacker threat and mystique. The 1983 movie "War Games," for example, portrayed a teenage hacker who nearly triggered a nuclear war by breaking into Defense Department computers. The movie led to a spike in modem sales — as well as a congressional inquiry to see if the Hollywood scenario could really happen.

In Washington, lawmakers scrambled to address the threats posed by computer crime, although some critics said they overreacted because of the hyped media coverage. In 1986, Congress passed the Computer Fraud and Abuse Act, the first federal computer-crime law. The CFAA made it a felony, punishable by up to five years in prison, to enter computer systems operated by the federal government or federally insured financial institutions.

The law also made it a crime to

Speaking the Language of Cyber-Crime

Black Hat — a hacker who breaks into a computer system to steal or destroy information. White Hat, or "ethical," hackers are hired by corporations or government agencies to look for vulnerabilities in computer systems. Somewhere in between are Gray Hats, who unlawfully break into systems and then tell their victims how they did it. Black Hats and Gray Hats are sometimes called crackers.

Bug — an unintended design flaw in a software program that may cause a computer to malfunction or crash. A security bug, according to software giant Microsoft, is "a flaw in a product that makes it infeasible — even when using the product properly — to prevent an attacker from usurping privileges on the user's system, regulating its operation, compromising data on it, or assuming ungranted trust."

Distributed Denial of Service (DDoS) Attack — an attack that renders a Web site unavailable to Internet users by overloading it with high volumes of data.

Firewall — a hardware or software device designed to keep hackers from accessing a computer system.

Hacker — originally, a laudatory term used to describe highly skilled computer programmers. Today, it usually describes people who break into computer systems to steal or destroy data.

Password Cracker — a software program that helps hackers gain access to a computer system by automatically sending thousands or millions of words — usually taken from dictionaries — against password fields.

Phreak — someone who hacks into telephone systems, usually to make free long-distance calls.

Script — A computer code used by a hacker.

Social Engineering — a method by which hackers trick or coerce gullible computer users into revealing their passwords or other confidential information that can be used to gain access to their systems. Often done with a phone call to an unsuspecting administrative aide.

Trojan Horse — a seemingly innocuous program containing code designed to damage, destroy or alter files in an unsuspecting user's computer; normally spread by e-mail attachments.

Virus — a self-replicating computer program that spreads itself across a network, usually via an e-mail attachment. Some viruses are designed to damage files or otherwise interfere with normal computing functions, while others don't do anything but spread themselves around. Computer worms differ from viruses in that they do not spread through e-mail attachments, but rather by exploiting software flaws common to individual computers linked to a network.

---

exchange computer passwords with the intent of committing interstate fraud. The provision was designed to outlaw the "pirate" bulletin boards that hackers often used to exchange pilfered confidential information.

The first hacker prosecuted under the new measure was Robert T. Morris, a 22-year-old graduate student at Cornell University. Morris wrote an experimental, self-replicating computer program called a "worm" and on Nov. 2, 1988, injected it into the newly launched Internet. A flaw in the program allowed the worm to reproduce itself far faster than Morris had anticipated, and it shut down or seriously crippled thousands of computer systems at universities, military installations and medical research facilities, mainly in the United States.

Dealing with Morris' worm cost millions of dollars. Morris was convicted, fined $10,050 and sentenced to three years of probation and 400 hours of community service. Critics said he got off too easily, but the trial judge maintained the light sentence was appropriate because he had only been experimenting and meant no harm.

The Morris worm demonstrated that the Internet had several gaping security flaws. Over the next few years, it was inundated by worms and viruses, another type of malicious computer code. By 1992, some 1,300 computer viruses existed — a 420 percent increase from just two years earlier. While the vast majority were harmless, a few caused tremendous damage. [32]

One of the worst was unleashed on March 26, 1999. The virus spread over the Internet through an e-mail attachment that, when opened, forwarded itself to 50 other people in a victim's e-mail address book. The multiplying effect of the virus shut down thousands of e-mail systems around the world. It was dubbed "Melissa," a name that investigators found embedded in the malicious code.

Federal authorities quickly tracked Melissa to David L. Smith, a 30-year-old computer programmer in New Jersey who did contract work for AT&T and Microsoft. Smith admitted that he created and unleashed the virus, named after an exotic dancer he had met in Florida.

Smith pleaded guilty to federal and state charges in December 1999 and was sentenced to five years in prison. Experts estimated that Melissa had inflicted $400 million in actual damages.

At Smith's sentencing, Robert J. Cleary, the U.S. attorney who prosecuted the case, said the virus "demonstrated the danger that business, government and personal computer users everywhere face in our technological society."

Hackers and malicious code writers have continued to vandalize cyberspace. In February 2000, a hacker crippled Yahoo! and several other popular e-commerce Web sites by bombarding them with thousands of simultaneous data requests. The so-called distributed denial of service (DDoS) attacks prevented customers from accessing the sites for several hours. Experts estimated that the attacks cost more than $1.7 billion in lost sales and damages.

Law-enforcement officials eventually linked the attacks to a 15-year-old Canadian who called himself "Mafiaboy." On Jan. 18, 2001, the teen hacker pleaded guilty to 56 charges, including mischief and illegal use of a computer service. He was sentenced to eight months in a youth detention center and ordered to donate $250 to charity. Under Canadian law, the maximum sentence he could have received was two years detention.

"The [Mafiaboy] case demonstrates . . . that the entire Internet is vulnerable to the machinations of a 15-year-old kid," said Mark Rasch, vice-president for cyber-law at Global Integrity Corp., in Reston, Va. "It demonstrates that the Internet, for security purposes, is only as strong as its weakest link." [33] ∎

CURRENT SITUATION

Cyber-Crime and FOIA

Many companies are tight-lipped about attacks on their computer systems. For example, only 36 percent of the firms and organizations that responded to the latest CSI/FBI computer-crime survey called the police after being victimized by hackers. The secrecy is understandable, says CSI Director Patrice Rapolus.

"They didn't want to make themselves more of a target, and they don't want the publicity," Rapolus said. [34]

In addition, says Patricia McGarry, a prosecutor in the Justice Department's Computer Crime and Intellec-

tual Property division, companies often don't disclose cyber-attacks for fear of hurting their bottom lines.

"There are some companies that have been reluctant to report, especially those that have publicly traded stock, because they have a perception that it may affect their standing in the stock market and their economic growth," McGarry says. "We try to encourage them to come forward no matter what, but there are many that choose not to."

Some experts argue that companies would be more willing to report attacks if the government would better protect the information from public disclosure. At present, however, computer attack information reported to the FBI or other federal law-enforcement agencies is subject to release to the general public through Freedom of Information Act (FOIA) requests.

The Bush administration and some lawmakers on Capitol Hill want to exempt from FOIA laws any organization that shares computer-attack information with the government. Advocates of exemptions say they are necessary because the entire nation is at risk when companies fail to report cyber-attacks.

One such proposal would exempt from FOIA disclosure any information about computer attacks waged against companies that form the nation's "critical infrastructure." The measure, sponsored by Sen. Robert Bennett, R-Utah, and Jon Kyl, R-Ariz., defines critical infrastructure as the "physical and cyber-based systems and services essential to the national defense, government, or economy of the United States."

The bill notes that much of the nation's critical infrastructure — such as power plants, communications companies and the banking and finance industry — is owned and operated by the private sector. The government, Bennett said, must give these organizations an incentive — in the form of a FOIA exemption — to report cyber-attacks. "No company is going to voluntarily

provide information in a forum where competitors, critics and attackers can get hold of it," Bennett said. [35]

The Bennett/Kyl measure also would exempt participating companies from antitrust laws so they could legally work together to develop technologies for stemming future cyber-attacks. Reps. Thomas M. Davis III, R-Va., and James P. Moran, D-Va., have introduced similar legislation in the House.

Richard A. Clarke, the president's special adviser on cyber-security, says a FOIA exemption might entice companies to report more computer attacks to the FBI. "Companies might not immediately start telling the [FBI] what they need to tell them, but at least they won't have that excuse anymore," Clarke told a Senate Judiciary subcommittee in February.

Several of the nation's largest industries are lobbying in favor of the exemption — including energy, manufacturing and pharmaceutical firms.

Critics dismiss the measure as unnecessary because other laws already protect the disclosure of sensitive information. Moreover, the critics say, the proposed exemption could prevent citizens from obtaining information completely unrelated to cyber-security, such as environmental data.

"This [FOIA exemption proposal] goes way beyond cyber-attacks," said Rena Steinzor, an academic fellow at the Natural Resources Defense Council, an environmental group. "It's basically nothing more than an avenue for industry to receive amnesty for voluntarily giving the government information about blatant law violations."

Eric Sobel, general counsel at the Electronic Privacy Information Center, agrees. "It seems like the industry is trying to use this issue as a basis for closing down a whole range of public disclosure," he said. "The people on [Capitol Hill] don't understand the unintended consequences." [36]

At Issue:

Are e-tailers doing enough to make online shopping safe?

EMILY HACKETT
EXECUTIVE DIRECTOR, INTERNET ALLIANCE

WRITTEN FOR THE CQ RESEARCHER, APRIL 2002

*t*he Internet is a safer place for shopping than the neighborhood mall or downtown department store. And online retailers are working to improve consumer confidence so the Internet can become the marketplace of the 21st century.

In online transactions, there are no carelessly discarded or duplicate credit-card receipts for thieves to pull from the trash can; no sales clerks or waiters to steal your name and credit-card numbers and no pickpockets lurking in crowded department store elevators. The online marketplace is secure because merchants have invested in technology, like VeriSign's verification and encryption systems and eBay's charge-back protection guarantee.

Internet transactions increasingly are paid with credit cards, the most secure method of online payment. Consumers are right to be concerned about protecting credit-card information. But while fraud has occurred online, identity theft primarily remains an offline crime. An identity stolen offline is often used online to defraud a consumer and a marketer. It is this fraudulent online activity with data stolen offline that retailers are working hard to combat.

Merchants are doubly motivated: They need to calm consumer fears, and they themselves are the ultimate victims of credit-card fraud. The major credit-card companies, by law, never expose the consumer to more than a $50 loss. In fact, VISA and MasterCard guarantee zero liability for consumers.

Technology is just the first step. Education is critical. An informed consumer, armed with the latest technology, is a powerful weapon against online fraud. Here is how smart consumers shop online:

- Shop with vendors whose reputation is sound.
- Shop only with vendors who use a secure server.
- Use a credit card.
- Use the secure payment mechanisms offered online.
- Report problems to the FTC at http://www.consumer.gov/idtheft/.

Industry has supported the passage of identity-theft legislation in an effort to give states the tools they need to capture online criminals. Internet companies have supported tough spam laws that make it illegal to fraudulently sell in the rapidly growing online marketplace. Industry has established a tough set of guidelines for ethical behavior on the Internet.

Technology is the key to solving the problems of Internet security and safety, but common sense and thoughtful legislation also have their roles to play.

EDMUND MIERZWINSKI
CONSUMER PROGRAM DIRECTOR,
U.S. PUBLIC INTEREST RESEARCH GROUP

WRITTEN FOR THE CQ RESEARCHER, APRIL 2002

*p*olls do show some increases in online shopping, but I'm sure that e-tailers are disappointed in its modest growth. Why? Consumers don't trust the Internet. And, they shouldn't.

First, consumers don't always get what they paid for. A recent "secret shopper" survey conducted by Consumers International found that too many sites failed to deliver — goods ordered failed to arrive, sites charged for goods that never turned up and where goods were returned, the retailer never sent a refund. Credit-card company data support these findings — chargebacks are much higher when consumers shop cyber-sites than when they shop stores or catalogs. Many chargebacks are refund requests when merchandise is shoddy or doesn't arrive.

Second, consumers are wary of card fraud. While the notion that hackers might nab your numbers as they hurtle through space is largely false, the problem of hackers or thieving employees breaking into poorly designed Web-merchant computers is real.

Worse, if I only have a debit card, I don't have the same legal $50-fraud limit as I do when I use a credit card, nor do I have the same legal rights to dispute goods that are shoddy or don't arrive. When I go on the radio or television to talk about debit cards, my advice is: "Never use these risky cards on the Internet." Why shouldn't consumers have the same billing-dispute protection and $50-fraud limit when they use a debit card?

Third, consumers have a real fear that e-tailers will share or sell their secrets to the highest bidder. I can shop in a store, and pay cash, if I want to be anonymous. Why not on the Net? Instead, everyone's business model is designed around capturing customer information. Consumers have a right to shop without giving up their privacy.

I'm encouraged by some Internet ideas — trusted third-party escrow systems show some potential, for example — but more needs to be done to make the Internet a safe place to shop. Advocates want the Internet to offer innovative small companies low-cost-of-entry opportunities to compete with the big boys. We want consumers to have more choices. To get there, we need help from e-tailers.

Join our call for strengthened consumer rights when we use any payment card — credit, debit or even stored value. Second, strengthen alternative-dispute resolution and Internet trusted-seal programs by basing them on laws. Third, change business models to respect our privacy.

Terrorism by Computer?

Since the Sept. 11 terrorist attacks on New York City and the Pentagon, computer-security experts and government officials have feared another type of attack: cyber-terrorism. White House cyber-security adviser Richard A. Clarke said terrorists could use the Internet to snarl the air-traffic control system, open floodgates on dams, cripple power grids or sabotage nuclear power plants.

"When I look at the vulnerabilities of the Internet, I lose sleep," Clarke said. "Why is any of that stuff connected to the Internet in the first place?" [1]

The Bush administration has ordered a number of federal departments to remove certain information from their Web pages, on the theory that terrorists could use the data to plan additional attacks. The White House also has asked for the cooperation of several private organizations — a move that has drawn fire from civil liberties groups.

Testifying before a Senate panel earlier this year, Clarke acknowledged that the United States had yet to catch a foreign government or terrorist group using Internet warfare. Still, Clarke said, several nations are gearing up to wage Internet warfare, including Iraq, Iran, North Korea and China. He warned that any nation or terrorist group that launches a cyber-attack against the United States should expect serious repercussions.

"We reserve the right to respond in any way appropriate: through covert action, through military action, [or] any one of the tools available to the president," Clarke told lawmakers. [2]

Clarke would not say what level of cyber-attack might provoke a military response. "That's the kind of ambiguity that we like to keep intentionally to create some deterrence," he said.

The Bush administration has budgeted about $4.2 billion for cyberspace security in 2003, a 64 percent increase over the present spending level. The private sector must also dramatically increase its computer-security budget in order to keep the U.S. economy on solid ground, Clarke said.

"The Internet . . . was not designed to have the entire economy of the United States built onto it," Clarke said. "We need to be hardened against attack." [2]

---

[1] Quoted in Thomas Peele, "Web Called Vulnerable to Terror," *The Contra Costa Times*, Feb. 20, 2002.
[2] Clarke testified before the Senate Judiciary Committee on Feb. 13, 2002.
[3] Quoted in Alan Goldstein, "U.S. Attorney General, Others Discuss Fragile Nature of Computer Networks," *The Dallas Morning News*, Feb. 13, 2002.

Tougher Sentences

Washington lawmakers also are debating a bill that would curb cyber-crime by punishing hackers and virus writers with longer prison terms — including life sentences for some crimes. Under current laws, sentences for computer crimes are capped at a maximum of 10 years in prison and are determined primarily by calculating the actual economic damages caused by each incident — which is difficult to prove in most cases.

The proposed Cyber Security Enhancement Act would require judges to consider several factors when sentencing computer criminals, including the judicial system's need to provide an "effective deterrent" to the "growing incidence" of cyber-crime. Under the measure, sponsored by Rep. Lamar Smith, R-Texas, judges could impose life sentences on any hacker or virus writer who "knowingly causes or attempts to cause death or serious bodily injury."

The Justice Department favors an even broader measure. Earlier this year, Deputy Assistant Attorney General John G. Malcolm told a House panel that hackers should be imprisoned for life for acting in a "reckless" manner — not just in a knowingly dangerous fashion. Malcolm said an example of such "reckless" behavior would be hacking into a telephone company and knocking out a community's 911 emergency system.

"It is easy to envision . . . that somebody might die or suffer serious injury as a result of this conduct," Malcolm told lawmakers. "Although the hacker might not have known that his conduct would cause death or serious bodily injury, such reckless conduct would seem to merit punishment greater than the 10 years permitted by the current statute." [37]

Microsoft, which is frequently accused of putting product functionality ahead of security concerns, also favors tougher sentences for cyber-criminals. Susan Kelley Koeppen, a Microsoft lawyer, told the House panel that society must stop coddling hackers and virus writers.

"Cyber-crime will never be effectively curbed if society continues to treat it merely as pranksterism," Koeppen said. "While our society does not tolerate people breaking into brick-and-mortar homes and businesses, we inexplicably seem to have more tolerance for computer break-ins. Computer attacks need to be treated as the truly criminal activities that they are." [38]

Jennifer Stisa Granick, a San Francisco attorney who has represented several well-known hackers, says harsher sentences won't curb cyber-crime. Like all criminals, people who commit computer crimes don't think they're going to get caught, Granick says. Tougher sentencing laws would only induce "false guilty pleas" by innocent defendants who don't want to risk trial, she says.

Granick is especially concerned that tougher sentencing laws would be unjustly applied to all types of computer crimes — no matter how minor.

"I think the punishment should fit the crime, and not all computer crimes are equal," Granick says. "Some are the equivalent of vandalism, and some could be the real-world equivalent of terrorism. We shouldn't paint all computer-intrusion incidents with the same brush."

Power, of CSI, agrees that tougher laws won't cut down on computer attacks. Indeed, Power says that throwing the book at hackers whose only crime is curiosity would diminish — not bolster — Internet security.

"It's crazy to indict somebody for pointing out the vulnerabilities of a supposedly secure [computer] system," Power says. "We're in an era where everybody's experimenting, including the people who write the laws. And some of these laws are not going to work very well." ∎

OUTLOOK

Losing Battle?

P olice never will keep up with hackers and virus writers, in the view of some computer security experts.

"I don't think that law enforcement will ever have the upper hand," says BugNet's Bowden. "Hackers are researching new ways of doing things that law enforcement can't even imagine how to protect against at this point."

But the police do have one thing going for them, according to Bowden: Once hackers do launch attacks, their methods can be scrutinized so that organizations can protect themselves the next time around.

"There's a pretty small window that [any one particular] hack can be used," Bowden says.

Power concedes Bowden's point. But he notes that the argument is only true if computer-users make use of the latest security technology — which he says many are not doing.

"Companies are not doing enough to defend themselves," Power says. "They're not staffing for information security, they're not dedicating enough resources for information security and they're not organized in the right way to make information security effective."

A recent *InformationWeek* survey of some 4,500 private and public-sector organizations around the world bears out Power's argument. It concludes that "few businesses have taken the necessary steps to guard themselves adequately against break-ins and espionage." Moreover, at most companies, spending on computer security falls far short of business objectives, the report found. [39] It recommends increased spending on security.

Many security experts say law-enforcement agencies, too, must boost spending if they want to keep pace with hackers and virus writers. Hunger, of SecurityFocus, says law enforcement has been, and will continue to be, hindered by "brain drain."

"When people in law enforcement become technically apt enough to be on par with the game, they're able to get jobs in the civilian world that pay significantly more," Hunger says. "That's a hurdle they need to overcome if they want to get up to speed and stay up to speed."

The Justice Department's McGarry concedes that cyber-crime is "only going to grow to be a larger problem" in the future. But she rejects the notion that the federal law-enforcement community is losing the battle, noting that Justice maintains specialized cyber-crime units in New York, Los Angeles and Washington — cities with high incidences of computer-facilitated crimes.

"I don't think we are behind the eight ball in any fashion," she says. "We're devoting a great amount of resources in terms of manpower and technical expertise, so I don't think we're lagging in any respect." ∎

Notes

[1] "Internet Security Threat Report," *Riptech, Inc.*, February 2002. For related coverage, see Brian Hansen, "Cyber-Predators," *The CQ Researcher*, March 1, 2002, pp. 169-192, and Ellen Perlman, "Digital Nightmare," *Governing*, April 2002, pp. 20-24.

[2] *Ibid.*

[3] "Computer Crime and Security Survey 2001," Computer Security Institute (CSI) and Federal Bureau of Investigation (FBI), January 2002.

[4] Quoted in Sharon Gaudin, "Computer Sabotage Case Back in Court," *Network World Fusion*, April 4, 2001.

[5] Quoted in Linden MacIntyre, "Hackers," PBS "Frontline," Feb. 13, 2001.

[6] For background, see Richard Power, *Tangled Web: Tales of Digital Crime from the Shadows of Cyberspace* (2000), pp. 150-151.

[7] Top 10 Consumer Fraud Complaints of 2001, Federal Trade Commission, Jan. 23, 2002.

[8] "Identity Theft and its Effect on the Financial Services Industry," Celent Communications, September 2001.

[9] U.S. Census Bureau, *Current Population Survey*, September 2001.

[10] GartnerG2, "Privacy and Security: The Hidden Growth Strategy," August 2000.

[11] Quoted in Mark W. Vigoroso, "Online Mugging a Threat, but no Showstopper," *E-Commerce Times*, Feb. 1, 2002.

[12] Scott Culp, "It's Time to End Information Anarchy," Microsoft Security Response Center white paper, October 2001.

[13] Jaikumar Vijayan, "Vendors Lead Effort to Delay Reporting of Security Vulnerabilities," *Computerworld*, Nov. 19, 2001.

[14] *Ibid.*

[15] Bruce Schneier, "Is Disclosing Vulnerabilities a Security Risk in Itself?" *Internetweek*, Nov. 19, 2001.

[16] From "The Injustice of Insecure Software," @Stake white paper, February 2002.

[17] Mark Minasi, *The Software Conspiracy: Why Companies Put Out Faulty Software, How They Can Hurt You and What You Can Do About It* (1999).

[18] See, for example, CSI and FBI, *op. cit.*, and "Security Review 2002," Computer Economics Inc., 2002.

[19] From "End-User License Agreement for Mi-

crosoft Software," as posted on Microsoft's Web site.

[20] Quoted in Dennis Fisher, "Software Liability Gaining Attention," *Eweek*, Jan. 14, 2002.

[21] Computer Economics, *op. cit.*

[22] From "Cybersecurity Today and Tomorrow: Pay Now or Pay Later," The Computer Science and Telecommunications Board of the National Research Council (a branch of the National Academy of Sciences), January 2002.

[23] Bill Gates, "Trustworthy Computing" memo, Jan. 15, 2002, as posted on Microsoft's Web site.

[24] *Ibid.*

[25] Quoted in Kristi Helm and Elise Ackerman, "Gates Makes Security Top Focus," *The San Jose Mercury News*, Jan. 17, 2002.

[26] Steven Levy, *Hackers: Heroes of the Computer Revolution* (1984).

[27] CNN special report on hackers, May 1999.

[28] *Ibid.*

[29] Paul Mungo and Bryan Clough, *Approaching Zero: The Extraordinary Underworld of Hackers, Phreakers, Virus Writers and Keyboard Criminals* (1992).

[30] Quoted in Winn Schwartau, *Cybershock: Surviving Hackers, Phreakers, Identity Thieves, Internet Terrorists and Weapons of Mass Destruction* (2000).

[31] Quoted in Mungo and Clough, *op. cit.*, p. 67.

[32] For background, see *Security of the Internet*, Froehlich/Kent Encyclopedia of Telecommunications, Vol. 15, Marcel Dekker, New York, 1997, pp. 231-255. Also available online at www.cert.org/encyc_article/tocencyc.html.

[33] Quoted in "Canadian Internet Hacker 'Mafiaboy' Pleads Guilty," Reuters, Jan. 19, 2001.

[34] Quoted in Randy Barett, "Trust Me!" *Eweek*, Aug. 20, 2001.

[35] Quoted in Matt Richtel, "In an Era of Tighter Security, How Much Cyberfreedom Are We Willing to Surrender?" *The New York Times*, Dec. 3, 2001.

[36] *Ibid.*

[37] Malcolm testified before the House Judiciary Subcommittee on Crime on Feb. 12, 2002.

[38] *Ibid.*

[39] "Global Information Security Survey," *Information Week*/PricewaterhouseCoopers, 2001.

FOR MORE INFORMATION

BugNet, 385 South 520 West, Lindon, UT 84042; (801) 226-8200; www.bugnet.com. A division of Key Labs Inc. that finds flaws in commercial software and posts vulnerability warnings on its Web site.

Business Software Alliance, 1150 18th St., N.W., Suite 700, Washington, DC 20036; (202) 872-5500; www.bsa.org. A membership group representing personal computer software publishing companies. Operates toll-free anti-piracy hotline (800) 667-4722.

Computer Emergency Response Team (CERT), Software Engineering Institute, Carnegie Mellon University, Pittsburgh, PA 15213; (412) 268-7090; www.cert.org. Collects and distributes detailed technical information about computer security breaches and posts information for computer neophytes on its Web site.

Computer Security Institute, 600 Harrison St., San Francisco, CA 94107; (415) 947-6320; www.gocsi.com. An organization for computer-security professionals that works with the FBI to produce an annual report cataloging the cost of computer-facilitated crimes.

Cult of the Dead Cow, 1369 Madison Ave., N.Y., NY 10128; www.cultdeadcow.com. A quasi-underground computer-security organization that publishes hacking techniques on its Web site. Created "Black Orifice," a computer program that allows users to remotely take control of computers with certain Microsoft operating systems.

Federal Trade Commission, 600 Pennsylvania Ave., N.W., Washington, DC 20580; (202) 326-2222; www.ftc.gov. The federal agency responsible for preventing fraudulent, deceptive and unfair business practices in the marketplace, including Internet fraud and identity theft.

FBI National Infrastructure Protection Center (NIPC), 935 Pennsylvania Ave., N.W., Washington, DC 20535; (202) 323-3205; www.nipc.gov. Investigates intrusions into government, educational and corporate computer networks and provides information on major computer-crime investigations on its Web site.

Information Technology Association of America, 1401 Wilson Blvd., Arlington, VA 22209; (703) 522-5055; www.itaa.org. A trade organization for IT professionals that works to advance Internet and e-commerce security.

2600: The Hacker Quarterly, P.O. Box 752, Middle Island, NY 11953; (631) 751-2600; www.2600.com. A magazine written by hackers, for hackers, that publishes techniques for hacking computer and telephone systems. Online version provides archived speeches and presentations from the annual Hackers on Planet Earth (HOPE) conference.

Bibliography

Selected Sources

Books

Levy, Steven, *Hackers: Heroes of the Computer Revolution*, Anchor Press/Doubleday, 1984.

Many experts consider this the most complete account of the personal-computer revolution in the late 1950s. Packed with anecdotes and scientific details about the hacker clubs at top schools. Levy is chief technology writer for *Newsweek.*

Mungo, Paul, and Bryan Clough, *Approaching Zero: The Extraordinary Underworld of Hackers, Phreakers, Virus Writers, and Keyboard Criminals*, Random House, 1992.

This anecdotal, non-technical overview of computer-facilitated crimes provides good detail about the evolution of computer hacking in Europe. Mungo is a British journalist, Clough an accountant who specializes in international computer-security issues.

Power, Richard, *Tangled Web: Tales of Digital Crime from the Shadows of Cyberspace*, Que/Macmillan, 2000.

This comprehensive study of cyber-crimes includes more than 50 tables, charts and diagrams, a glossary and the full text of major U.S. computer-crime laws. Power is editorial director of the Computer Security Institute in San Francisco.

Shimomura, Tsutomu, with John Markoff, *Takedown: The Pursuit and Capture of Kevin Mitnick, America's Most Wanted Computer Outlaw*, Hyperion, 1996.

Shimomura, a senior fellow at the San Diego Supercomputing Center, began tracking Mitnick in 1994 after he stole files from his work station. Shimomura outsmarted Mitnick, leading the FBI to his doorstep. Markoff covers computer crime and technology for *The New York Times.*

Stephenson, Peter, *Investigating Computer-Related Crime*, CRC Press, 2000.

A fairly technical account of how police catch cyber-criminals. An excellent resource for students interested in careers in law. The author is a network consultant and lecturer.

Articles

Bettelheim, Adriel, "Emerging Players: Sen. Robert F. Bennett, R-Utah," *CQ Weekly*, Jan. 5, 2002.

A profile of one of Washington's leading cyber-security advocates.

Bettelheim, Adriel, and Rebecca Adams, "Threats and Priorities," *CQ Weekly*, Oct. 20, 2001.

Examines how Congress is dealing with the fact that much of the national infrastructure is vulnerable to computer-facilitated attacks.

Cohen, Adam, "The Identity Thieves are Out There — and Someone Could be Spying on You," *Time*, July 2, 2001.

A journalist who specializes in science and technology issues provides a non-technical overview of how personal and financial information can be compromised on the Internet.

Docherty, Neil (producer and director), and Linden MacIntyre (correspondent), "Hackers," PBS "Frontline," Program No. 1910, Feb. 13, 2001.

This public television program offers a good overview of hackers and cyber-crime. Printer-friendly transcripts of the program are at www.pbs.org/wgbh/pages/frontline/shows/hackers.

Mandelblit, Bruce D., "Clicks & Crime: The Inside Story of Internet Fraud," *Security*, Sept. 1, 2001.

A computer-security professional warns readers about the most common Internet fraud scams.

Vigoroso, Mark W., "Online Mugging a Threat, but No Showstopper," *E-Commerce Times*, Feb. 1, 2002.

A technology writer reports that e-commerce continues to grow despite the public's security concerns.

Vijayan, Jaikumar, "Vendor Led Effort to Delay Reporting of Security Vulnerabilities," *Computerworld*, Nov. 19, 2001.

A technology writer reports on Microsoft's effort to prevent the disclosure of flaws in its software.

Studies and Reports

Computer Emergency Response Team (CERT) Coordination Center, *2001 Annual Report*, Feb. 19, 2002.

A technical overview of the Internet-security vulnerabilities reported in 2001 to CERT, a federally funded organization based at Carnegie Mellon University.

Computer Security Institute/San Francisco FBI Computer Intrusion Squad, *2001 Computer Crime and Security Survey*, January 2002.

The annual CSI/FBI survey is based on data reported by 538 U.S. corporations, government agencies, financial and medical institutions and universities. Annotated with charts, graphs and tables; an executive summary is at www.gocsi.com/prelea/000321.html.

Riptech, Inc., "Internet Security Threat Report," January 2002.

A broad analysis of Internet-based attacks on hundreds of organizations during the last six months of 2001. Annotated with numerous charts, graphs and tables; discusses technical aspects of virus attacks and computer-intrusion events. Executive summary is at www.riptech.com/newsevents/release020127.html.

12 Reparations Movement

DAVID MASCI

Rep. John Conyers Jr. is not a man who gives up easily. Six times since 1989, the feisty 19-term Michigan Democrat has introduced a measure in the House of Representatives to create a commission to study paying reparations to African-American descendants of slaves. Each time, the bill has died.

But Conyers is optimistic. He claims that beating the same legislative drum so long has helped bring the reparations issue to the attention of the American people.

"Twelve years ago, most people didn't even know what reparations were, and now it's a front-burner issue," he says. "It's like those first [unsuccessful] bills making Martin Luther King's birthday a holiday: You have to build up a critical mass of support, or you don't get anyplace."

Indeed, several local governments have passed resolutions favoring reparations, and the issue has caught the attention of a growing cadre of prominent black advocates and scholars, who have begun holding conferences and symposia on the subject. "It's time to address this issue we've so long denied — the lingering effects of slavery," said Johnnie Cochran, former counsel for O.J. Simpson and a member of a "dream team" of attorneys preparing to sue the federal government and others for slavery reparations. [1]

In addition, several African nations are trying to put the issue on the agenda of the upcoming United Nations World Conference Against

From *The CQ Researcher,*
June 22, 2001.

A memorial at the Nazi concentration camp at Buchenwald honors the hundreds of thousands of Jews who were murdered there. Billions of dollars have been paid to Holocaust survivors.

AP Photo/Eckehard Schulz

Racism, in Durban, South Africa. They hope the United States and former colonial powers like Britain and France will increase aid to African countries to compensate for centuries of slave trading.

Until 50 years ago, debates over reparations for victims of persecution were largely theoretical. But in the wake of World War II, reparations increasingly have been seen as a viable means of addressing past injustices — not just to Jews slaughtered in the Holocaust but to Japanese-Americans, Native Americans and even Australian Aborigines. In fact, the debate over slavery reparations comes on the heels of a string of victories for groups seeking restitution.

In 1988, for instance, Congress passed a law authorizing the U.S. government to apologize for interning Japanese-Americans during the war and award $20,000 to each surviving victim. More recently, European countries and companies from Bayer AG to Volkswagen have paid billions of dollars to victims of Nazi Germany's effort to exterminate Europe's Jews and other "undesirables."

Now it is time for slavery reparations, proponents say. Randall Robinson, author of the bestseller

The Debt: What America Owes to Blacks, argues that acknowledging the nation's debt to African-Americans for slavery and a subsequent century of discrimination will help heal the country's existing racial divide. "We cannot have racial reconciliation until we make the victims of this injustice whole," says Robinson, president of TransAfrica, a Washington, D.C.-based black advocacy group.

Besides raising a moral question, reparations for slavery is also an economic issue, Robinson says. Many of the problems facing black America are directly linked to slavery and the 100 years of forced segregation that followed emancipation in 1865, he says. "It's foolish to argue that the past has nothing to do with the present," Robinson says. "There's a reason why so many African-Americans are poor: It's because a terrible wrong occurred in our history that produced a lasting inequality." Reparations will help right that wrong, advocates say, by helping black Americans reach social and economic parity.

But other black Americans warn that paying reparations for slavery will drive a new wedge between blacks and whites, leading to greater racial polarization. "Doing something like this would create a tremendous amount of resentment among whites," says Walter Williams, chairman of the Economics Department at George Mason University in Fairfax, Va.

Williams says whites and other Americans would understandably be opposed to paying restitution for a crime that ended more than 135 years ago and to a community now making great social and economic strides. "Blacks have come so far; this is

Seeking Justice for Australia's Aborigines

Australian Olympic gold medal winner Cathy Freeman knew all about the "stolen generation" of Aborigines. Her grandmother was one of the thousands of youngsters taken from their parents by white authorities.

Winning the 400-meter dash at last year's Summer Games gave Freeman a chance to speak out on the centuries of mistreatment of Australia's indigenous people.

Aborigines have lived in Australia for at least 40,000 years, most likely migrating from Southeast Asia. Their downfall as a people began in 1788, when British ships brought 1,000 settlers, including more than 500 convicts from overcrowded jails. Clashes began almost immediately, but the Aborigines' primitive weapons were no match for British guns and mounted soldiers.

Because the convicts provided free labor, the white settlers treated the Aborigines as little more than useless pests. Those who were not killed were driven away to fenced reser-vations in the most inhospitable parts of the "outback" territory. Crimes against Aborigines often went unpunished.

Aborigines, who make up 2 percent of Australia's largely white population of 19 million, were not allowed to vote until 1962; they were not counted in the census until 1967. Moreover, Aborigines' life expectancy is 20 years less than the national average and they occupy the lowest rung of the nation's economic ladder.

But in 1992, they won a significant victory when courts recognized that the Aborigines had "owned' Australia before whites arrived. Today, they own more than 15 percent of the continent, mostly in the remote northern territory.

Nevertheless, some Aboriginal leaders are seeking

Olympic gold medalist Cathy Freeman has used her celebrity to call attention to her fellow Aborigines.

Reuters Photo/Jerry Lampen

reparations for perhaps the worst injustice perpetrated against their group — the state-sponsored abduction of Aboriginal children from their parents.

From the early 1900s until the 1970s, as many as 100,000 Aboriginal children were taken from their parents to be raised among whites in orphanages or foster families. State and federal laws that permitted the practice were based on the belief that full-blooded Aborigines would eventually die out and that assimilating the children into white society was the best way to save them.

In 1997, the Australian Human Rights and Equal Opportunity Commission reported that many of the children had been physically and sexually abused and suffered long-term psychological damage from the loss of family and cultural ties.

But Australian Sen. John Herron called the 1997 report "one-sided" and said the stories about removing Aboriginal children from their families was greatly exaggerated." [1]

His comments stung Aden Ridge-way, the only Aborigine senator in Parliament, who angrily compared Herron's statements to "denying the Holocaust." [2]

"They were denying they had done anything wrong, denying that a whole generation was stolen," Freeman said. "The fact is, parts of people's lives were taken away." [3]

Herron recognizes the removal of Aboriginal children as a blemish on Australia's history, but he claims many were taken with their parents' consent and for their own welfare. He believes amends are the responsibility of states and churches and has suggested that reparations claims be filed individually via the courts.

nothing but counterproductive," he says.

Opponents also argue that, rather than correcting economic disparity, reparations would take money and attention away from more pressing social and economic issues facing black Americans, such as a substan-dard education system and high in-

carceration rates for young African-American men. "This would be such a huge waste of resources, at a time when so much needs to be done in education and other areas," Williams says.

To counter such arguments, sla-very reparations advocates have be-gun modeling their efforts on suc-

cessful techniques used by Holo-caust victims. Recent battles for Holocaust-related reparations have netted survivors and their families more than $10 billion in compensa-tion for slave labor, recovered bank accounts and unclaimed life insur-ance policies.

But some argue that compensat-

But reparations proponents say it is difficult to prove abuse in the absence of documents and witnesses. They cite the first stolen-generations case, brought last year, which was dismissed for lack of evidence.

Many advocates for the Aborigines favor creation of a national compensation board to adjudicate all "stolen generation" claims.

But Prime Minister John Howard dismisses the idea. He refuses to issue an apology, stating today's Australians should not be held responsible for the mistakes of past generations. He also points to a $63 million government program designed to reunite families of the stolen generation.

However, former Prime Minister Malcolm Fraser says an apology is essential. "We can't undo the past, but we can, in an apology, recognize the fact that many actions in the past did a grave injustice to the Aboriginal population of Australia. We have a commitment to recognize that and other past injustices in walking together into a new future." [4]

Last year, the government spent $1.5 billion on health, education, housing and job-training programs for Aborigines.

But monetary payments and programs are not enough, say some reparations supporters. Geoff Clark, chairman of the Aboriginal and Torres Strait Islander Commission, which oversees indigenous affairs, wants the government not only to apologize but also to sign a treaty with the indigenous population that would provide limited autonomy for Aboriginal communities. His group cites similar treaties in the United States and Canada.

Howard says a treaty would be too divisive. "One part of Australia making a treaty with another part is to accept that we are in effect two nations," he said in a radio interview last year." [5]

Ridgeway supports the treaty. "I think the prime minister's kidding himself if he thinks that a treaty's going to be divisive. The goal is about a formal document that better defines black and white relations and the unfinished business of re-conciliation." [6]

A national election later this year is widely expected to usher in a new prime minister. Howard's rival has supported the idea of a government apology to the Aborigines.

— *Scott Kuzner*

Australians protesting outside the federal court in Darwin in August 2000 call for government compensation for indigenous Australians of the "stolen generations."

AP Photo/David Guttenfelder

[1] "Separated, But Not a Generation," *Illawarra Mercury*, Aug. 19, 2000, p. 9.

[2] Mitchell Zuckoff, "Golden Opportunity, Australian Aboriginal Activists Hope to Exploit the Olympics to Publicize Their De-mands for an Apology, Cash Reparations and Limited Sov-ereignty," *The Boston Globe*, Sept. 18, 2000, p. 1E.

[3] Michael Gordon, "Beginning Of The Legend," *Sydney Morning Herald*, Sept. 25, 2000, p. 10.

[4] Malcolm Fraser, "Apology Must Be First Step," *Sydney Morning Herald*, April 8, 1999, p. 15.

[5] Tony Wright and Kerry Taylor, "PM Rules Out 'Divisive' Treaty," *The Age*, May 30, 2000, p. 2.

[6] *Ibid.*

ing victims of injustice cheapens their suffering. Indeed, a group of mostly Jewish-American scholars and journalists has criticized some of the efforts to obtain relief for Holocaust survivors. They say the lawyers and Jewish groups involved have turned the legitimate quest for restitution into a shameless money grab that

degrades the memory of the millions who perished.

"Fighting for money makes it much harder to see a tragedy in the right light," says Melissa Nobles, a professor of political science at the Massachusetts Institute of Technology (MIT) in Boston.

"They have hijacked the Holo-

caust and appointed themselves saviors of the victims — all in the name of money," says Norman Finkelstein, a history professor at Hunter College in New York City and author of *The Holocaust Industry: Reflections on the Exploitation of Jewish Suffering.*

Finkelstein points out that those

representing the victims have used hardball tactics to "blackmail" Germany, Switzerland and other countries into paying huge sums to satisfy what are often dubious claims. Besides cheapening the historical legacy of the Holocaust, he argues, such actions could potentially trigger an anti-Semitic backlash in Europe.

Supporters say they are only working aggressively to obtain some small measure of justice for the victims. "We are trying to compensate slave laborers and return the assets of survivors," says Elan Steinberg, executive director of the World Jewish Congress, one of the groups leading the Holocaust reparations efforts. "In doing this, we must uncover the truth, which is often hard for these countries to confront."

He says Holocaust victims should not be denied their assets or rightful compensation just because confronting European countries with their past might lead to an anti-Jewish backlash. "Survivors have a right to pursue legitimate claims," he insists. "This is about justice."

"It is good that we try to make some effort to acknowledge someone's suffering, even if it is inadequate," says Tim Cole, a professor of 20th century European history at the University of Bristol in England. At the very least, reparations are important symbolic gestures to the victims from the victimizers, he adds.

As the debate over reparations continues, here are some of the questions experts are asking:

Should the United States pay reparations to African-American descendants of slaves?

For much of its 250-year history on these shores, slavery was America's most divisive and contro-versial issue. The Founding Fathers fought over the status of African slaves when drafting both the Declaration of Independence and the Constitution. And of course, in 1861 slavery helped trigger the nation's most costly conflict, a four-year Civil War that tore the country apart.

Today, few Americans of any race would disagree that slavery was the most shameful and tragic episode in American history. Many would also agree that African-Americans as a

---

> "Whites need to realize that we'll have no chance of cohering as a nation in the future unless we deal with this issue now."
>
> — *Randall Robinson, President, TransAfrica*

---

whole, including the descendants of slaves, are still suffering from its effects.

Proponents say compensation is justified on a variety of levels, beginning with the fact that African-Americans remain severely handicapped by the legacy of slavery, lagging behind the nation as a whole in virtually every measure. As a result, supporters say, they need and deserve extra help to overcome the economic and social disadvantages they face.

"Our entire economic sector has been and remains truncated because of slavery," says Ronald Walters, a political science professor at the University of Maryland. "We need

something to help reverse this terrible harm done to blacks in this country."

"You have an enormous, static and fixed inequality in America due to a 350-year human-rights crime," Robinson says. "We have an obligation to compensate the people still suffering for the wrong that occurred."

Robinson, Walters and others argue that reparations are justified by the fact that the United States grew prosperous largely through the toil of unpaid African-Americans. "Exports of cotton, rice and tobacco swelled the coffers of the U.S. Treasury, yet the people who produced it were never paid," Robinson says.

However, an overwhelming majority of Americans do not believe the nation owes black Americans reparations. A March poll found that 81 percent of registered voters oppose reparations, while only 11 percent support them. [2]

Some Americans feel that the nation has already paid reparations for slavery by passing civil rights and affirmative action laws and by funding myriad social programs designed to help African-Americans and other disadvantaged peoples. "Since the War on Poverty in the 1960s, the nation has spent $6 trillion on fighting poverty," Williams says.

Others dismiss the whole idea of reparations for slavery out of hand, citing the potentially astronomical cost. Compensating for slavery's injustices could cost as much as $10 trillion, according to some estimates, dwarfing the estimated $10 billion paid to Holocaust victims so far.

Nevertheless, supporters say, reparations would ease African-Americans' feeling that the nation cares little about their plight. "The socio-economic inequality that exists today because of slavery means that the American promise of egalitarianism remains unfulfilled for blacks," Walters says. "It would make the idea of America and American democracy meaningful to blacks."

Paying reparations would benefit the entire nation by creating a more conducive environment for racial reconciliation, supporters say. "We'll never have any harmony or stability between the races until there is commitment to make the victim whole," Robinson says. "Whites need to realize that we'll have no chance of cohering as a nation in the future unless we deal with this issue now."

Conyers agrees that paying reparations would encourage racial healing — for both blacks and whites. "This could create a bridge that unlocks understanding and compassion between people," he says.

But opponents say compensating slavery victims will have exactly the opposite effect — creating new grounds for racial polarization. "I can't think of a better fortification for racism than reparations to blacks," says George Mason University's Williams. "To force whites today, who were not in any way responsible for slavery, to make payments to black people — many of whom may be better off [than the whites] — will create nothing but great resentment."

"It would create a huge backlash against black people, which is something they don't really need," says Glen Loury, director of the Institute of Race and Social Division at Boston University. "It would also be seen as just another example of black people's inability 'to get over it and move on.' "

Indeed, opponents say, reparations might even have the reverse effect: They could significantly weaken the nation's commitment to lifting poor black Americans out of poverty. "This would be a Pyrrhic victory for African-Americans," says Loury, who is black. "It would undermine the claim for further help down the road, because the rest of America will say: 'Shut up: You've been paid.' "

In addition, Loury says, pushing for restitution detracts from the real

---

"I can't think of a better fortification for racism than reparations to blacks."

— Walter Williams, Chairman, Economics Department, George Mason University

---

issues facing the black community. "This whole thing takes the public's attention away from important issues, like failing schools and the fact that so many African-Americans are in jail."

Have efforts to collect reparations for Holocaust victims gone too far?

In the last five years, efforts to compensate and recover stolen property for Holocaust victims and their heirs have increased dramatically. What started in the mid-1990s as an action to recover money in long-dormant Swiss bank accounts has snowballed into a host of lawsuits and settlements against European insurance companies, German and American manufacturers and art galleries around the world. [3]

By and large, these actions have been hailed as a great victory for victims of oppression. Yet a small but growing circle of critics questions the efforts. They charge the lawyers working on behalf of Holocaust victims — as well as the World Jewish Congress, the International Commission on Holocaust Era Insurance Claims (known as the Claims Conference) and other groups — with exploiting a historical tragedy for monetary gain.

"This whole thing has gone way too far," says Gabriel Shoenfeld, senior editor of *Commentary*, a conservative opinion magazine that examines issues from a Jewish perspective. "This is a case of a just cause that has been traduced by overzealous organizations and some rather unscrupulous lawyers." Hunter College's Finkelstein goes further, branding those who work on behalf of survivors as "the Holocaust industry" and their actions "nothing short of a shakedown racket."

Shoenfeld and Finkelstein are troubled by the fact that Jewish groups and attorneys working on the cases have taken it upon themselves to represent Holocaust survivors. "Groups like the World Jewish Congress don't really represent anyone," Finkelstein says. "They weren't elected by anyone to do this, and most Jews don't even know who they are."

He argues that such groups are using the survivors' high moral status as a cudgel to beat countries and corporations into submission. "They've wrapped themselves in the mantle of the needy Holocaust victims against the greedy, fat Swiss bankers and Nazi industrialists," Finkelstein says. "They are out of control and reckless."

Shoenfeld says the claims often are either overblown, dubious or

For Native Americans, a Different Struggle

Unlike African-Americans, Native Americans are not seeking a huge settlement to right the wrongs of the past. Instead, they're working on the present.

"We don't want reparations," says John Echohawk, executive director of the Native American Rights Fund, an Indian advocacy group in Boulder, Colo. "What we do want is the government to honor its duty to us — and we want our land and our water back." They also want up to $40 billion they say the government owes them.

Tribes have been making land claims against the government for more than a century. Today, dozens of claims are being dealt with (see p. 226).

But the biggest fight for restitution has come over allegations of government mishandling of a huge trust fund for Native Americans. Indian advocates say the federal government will end up owing between $10 billion and $40 billion to Native Americans when the matter is cleared up.

Since 1887, the federal government's Bureau of Indian Affairs (BIA) has managed many of the natural resources on Indian lands, such as oil and mineral deposits and grazing and water rights. Proceeds from the sale or use of these resources are, in theory at least, put into a trust fund administered by the government on behalf of members of the tribes who own the assets — some 500,000 Native Americans throughout the country.

Penny Manybeads stands beside her hogan at the Navajo Indian reservation in Tuba City. Ariz., in 1993. Native Americans want the government to pay for the mismanagement of their natural resources trust fund.

In the 1970s, Elouise Cobell, a member of the Blackfoot tribe, began to question the government's management of these accounts. Other Indians had long suspected mismanagement, but no one had challenged the BIA officials who controlled the fund.

Over the next two decades, Cobell, who has an accounting background, concluded that billions of dollars had been lost, and that many Indians were being cheated out of money that was rightfully theirs. Her efforts to get BIA officials to pay attention to the problem came to naught. "They tried to belittle me and intimated that I was a dumb Indian," she says.

In 1996, after years of what Cobell calls stonewalling by federal officials, she and four other Native Americans filed a class action suit in federal court against the Department of the Interior, which controls BIA. "The suit was a last resort, because no one would listen to us," Echohawk says. "No one did anything."

The plaintiffs charged that many records had been destroyed; that officials had improperly invested much of the money coming into the trust; and that no effort was made to keep individual Indians informed about the individual accounts the government kept for them. [1] These claims were later buttressed by a government official, who acknowledged that trust managers could not locate some 50,000 account holders because of poor recordkeeping.

Even before the suit was filed, the federal government had made some attempts to address the problem. In 1994, Congress passed the Native American Trust Fund Accounting and Management Reform Act, authorizing the appointment of a special trustee to manage and reform the fund. But the first such trustee, former Riggs Bank President Paul Homan, resigned in protest in 1999, complaining that the Interior Department was not adequately committed to reform.

Meanwhile, Cobell's suit against the government succeeded. In December 2000, a federal court ruled against the Interior Department and took control of the trust fund. "The government kept arguing that they were doing the best they could, but that just wasn't true," Echohawk says. "Fortunately, the court didn't believe them."

The government lost a subsequent appeal. Most recently, the new Bush administration decided not to continue to appeal the ruling, ending resistance to a court-administered solution.

The parties now must decide how much the government owes the trust fund. "We hope we can avoid a protracted legal battle over damages and settle out of court," Echohawk says, adding that Bush's decision not to continue appealing the ruling is a good sign the administration is committed to solving the problem.

Still, Echohawk is wary. "I'm cautious because until now, the government has fought us every inch of the way," he says. "Federal stonewalling and neglect are part of the story of the American Indian."

---

[1] Colman McCarthy, "Broken Promises Break Trust," *The Baltimore Sun*, March 7, 1999.

simply not valid. "It's clear that they're trying to humiliate these countries into giving in," he says.

Shoenfeld cites a recent case against Dutch insurers, who had already settled with the Netherlands' Jewish community for unpaid wartime insurance policies. "These guys then came in and tried to unfairly blacken Holland's reputation by painting their behavior during the war in an unfavorable light, without acknowledging all of the good things Dutch people did for Jews during that time," he says. "It was all an effort to blackmail them, to extract more money from them."

Even the much-publicized victory against the Swiss banks was marred by unscrupulous tactics, Finkelstein contends. After forcing the banks to set up a commission headed by former U.S. Federal Reserve Chairman Paul A. Volcker to investigate claims, they demanded a settlement before the commission finished its work, he says.

The Swiss caved in and paid $1.25 billion, Finkelstein says, because the groups were creating public hysteria and had American politicians threatening an economic boycott. "They honed this strategy against the Swiss and then turned to the French, Germans and others and used it successfully against them."

Such heavy-handed tactics create unnecessary ill will against European Jews, critics say. "By bludgeoning the Europeans into submission, the Holocaust industry is fomenting anti-Semitism," Finkelstein says.

Shoenfeld says the tactics have already spurred an anti-Semitic backlash in Germany and Switzerland. "Don't Jews have enough problems in the world without bringing upon themselves the wrath of major European powers?" he asks.

But groups pursuing Holocaust reparations say their opponents are misguided. "How can anyone ask [if] we are going too far in attempting to get restitution for people who were driven from their homes, forced into hiding, persecuted and forced to work?" asks Hillary Kessler-Godin, director of communications for the Claims Conference in New York City.

Supporters also argue that their tactics are not "heavy-handed" or designed to blackmail European countries. "We're not out to humiliate anyone," says the World Jewish Congress' Steinberg. "But sometimes the truth is hard and difficult for everyone to accept."

For instance, it would not serve the truth or the victims to sugarcoat Holland's dismal record of protecting Jews during the Holocaust, Steinberg says. "Holland had the worst record of any Western European country," he argues. "Eighty percent of its Jews were wiped out."

He also points out that his group rushed to settle the Swiss case before the Volcker commission finished its work in order to begin repaying survivors before they died. "Many survivors are very old and dying at such a rapid rate — some 10,000 to 15,000 a year. We had to move on this," he says. The commission will continue its work, so that all 55,000 Holocaust-era accounts can be investigated and paid out, he adds.

Proponents also counter the criticism that their actions foment anti-Semitism. "Anti-Semitism is not caused by Jewish actions, but by people who don't like Jews," Kessler-Godin says. "To temper our actions on behalf of people who have suffered the worst form of anti-Semitism possible in the name of not causing anti-Semitism defies logic."

"Holocaust survivors should not have to abrogate their rights simply for political expediency," Steinberg adds, pointing out that most people, regardless of their religious background, understand and support his group's efforts. "At the end of the day, most non-Jews — except those who represent the banks or insurance companies — see this as an act of justice."

Does putting a price tag on suffering diminish that suffering?

On Dec. 7, 1998, the leader of one of the pre-eminent Jewish organizations in the United States shocked many American Jews by publicly questioning efforts to obtain reparations for Holocaust survivors. In a *Wall Street Journal* editorial, Abraham Foxman, national director of the Anti-Defamation League, argued that when "claims become the main focus of activity regarding the Holocaust, rather than the unique horror of 6 million Jews, including 1.5 million children, being murdered simply because they were Jewish, then something has gone wrong." [4]

Foxman worried that the drive to obtain restitution would shift modern attitudes about the Holocaust from one of reverence for the victims and their suffering to an accounting of their material losses.

"I fear that all the talk about Holocaust-era assets is skewing the Holocaust, making the century's last word on the Holocaust that the Jews died, not because they were Jews, but because they had bank accounts, gold, art and property," he wrote. "To me that is a desecration of the victims, a perversion of why the Nazis had a Final Solution, and too high a price to pay for a justice we can never achieve." [5]

Foxman's editorial provoked an immediate response from many prominent Jews. Nobel Peace Prize winner Elie Wiesel argued that compensating Holocaust survivors does not sully their memory but is the right thing to do.

"It is wrong to think of this as about money," said Wiesel, a Holocaust survivor himself. "It is about justice, conscience and morality." [6]

But critics point out that reparations, almost by their nature, are tainted, because they mix the sacredness of a people's suffering and pain with the world's greatest source of corruption: money. "Although there might be a way to handle this whole thing with dignity, it inexorably becomes a sordid business," Finkelstein says. "I believe money always corrupts things."

"There is a real danger here that most people will say: Hey wait a minute. This is all really about money," says MIT's Nobles. "Money can profoundly obscure the nature of a tragedy."

Some critics also contend that monetary reparations can do victims more harm than good. "People who have been victimized need to become free internally in order to move beyond the tragedy that has occurred," says Ruth Wisse, a professor of Yiddish and comparative literature at Harvard University. "In this sense, reparations can be harmful because they make victims less dependent on themselves."

Instead of monetary payments, she says, nations should take steps to resolve the political problems that led to the suffering in the first place. "Reparations should be made on political terms, not economic terms," she says. For example, she said a country like Turkey, which many historians say exterminated more than a million Armenians at the beginning of the 20th century, might want to help protect Armenia from outside threats.

But advocates for reparations argue that the money is more a powerful symbol than a primary motive. "We're really talking about justice," says the University of Bristol's Cole. "It's a symbolic act, a gesture."

Although, Cole says, "no amount of money can ever compensate for the suffering of history's victims," restitution can aid them in some small way. "There are things we can do to ease people's suffering or bring them some sense that justice is being done."

"Of course you can't put a price tag on suffering," says the University of Maryland's Walters. "But what you can do is ask: What will bring the victims a measure of dignity? Isn't that the most important thing?"

Proponents also contend that, in the real world where victims of past oppression may still be suffering, monetary compensation can make a huge difference in their lives. For instance, says Kessler-Godin, many Eastern European Holocaust survivors live in poverty and need assistance. "It's OK for Abraham Foxman, living his comfortable American life, to say that it cheapens the memory of victims, but there are people who are living hand to mouth who don't have that luxury."

Finally, supporters say, forgoing reparations allows the victimizers to retain their financial wealth. "When you argue that a victim shouldn't pursue restitution, you are essentially rewarding the oppressors," Steinberg says. ∎

BACKGROUND

Ancient Notion

The payment of reparations for genocide or other injustices is a relatively new phenomenon, which began with Germany's 1951 pledge to aid Israel and to compensate individual victims of the Holocaust. "Be-

fore World War II, nations saw what they did to other people during wartime as a natural byproduct of war," MIT's Nobles says. "The vanquished simply had to accept what had happened to them."

But while the use of reparations may be a relatively new remedy, the ideas behind them have a long, if circuitous, intellectual pedigree stretching back for millennia. For instance, the ancient Greeks and Romans explored the notion that the weak and oppressed deserve sympathy and possibly assistance. The 4th century B.C. Athenian philosopher Plato addressed this issue in his most famous dialogue, *The Republic*. A generation later Aristotle, another Athenian philosopher, wrote that the best kind of government was one that helped those who had been deprived of happiness. [7]

Judeo-Christian doctrine also grappled with what individuals and society owe to the downtrodden and oppressed. For instance, in the *New Testament*, Jesus Christ singled out the persecuted as being particularly deserving of compassion and assistance. [8]

The first modern articulation of these principles came in the 18th century during the Enlightenment. Ironically, it was the intellectual father of free market economics — Scottish philosopher Adam Smith — who wrote most forcefully and eloquently about guilt and the resulting sympathy it causes.

In his 1759 treatise, *The Theory of Moral Sentiments*, he wrote: "How selfish soever man may be supposed, there are evidently some principles in his nature, which interest him in the fortunes of others, and render their happiness necessary to him, though he derives nothing from it, except the pleasure of seeing it. Of this kind is pity or compassion, the emotion we

Chronology

1945–1980

After World War II, West Germany moves to pay restitution to Jewish survivors of the Holocaust.

1948
Congress passes the Japanese-American Evacuations Claims Act to compensate Japanese-Americans who lost property as a result of being interned during World War II.

1951
West German Chancellor Konrad Adenauer proposes paying assistance to Israel and reparations to Jewish survivors of the Nazi Holocaust.

1953
Israel and West Germany agree on payment of reparations and aid. Over the next nearly 50 years, Germans will pay more than $60 billion in Holocaust-related restitution.

1956
Swiss government asks banks and insurers to reveal their Holocaust-related assets. The companies say such "dormant accounts" hold less than 1 million Swiss francs.

1962
A second request for an accounting of Holocaust-related assets leads to the discovery of about 10 million Swiss francs in dormant accounts.

1965
West Germany ends state-to-state payments to Israel. Holocaust survivors continue to receive payments from German government through the present.

1980s–Present

Oppressed groups begin seeking reparations.

1980
Congress creates the Commission on Wartime Relocations and Internment of Civilians to study possible reparations for Japanese-Americans interned during World War II.

1987
National Coalition of Blacks for Reparations in America (N'COBRA) is founded.

1988
Congress passes the Civil Liberties Act, which apologizes for the wartime internment of Japanese-Americans and authorizes the payment of $20,000 to surviving internees. Eventually, 80,000 Japanese-Americans receive an apology and a check.

1989
Rep. John Conyers Jr., D-Mich., introduces legislation to create a commission to study the African-American reparation issue. He will reintroduce the bill five more times in the coming years.

1990
The first Japanese-American internees begin receiving reparations checks.

1995
European and American media exposés document the role of Swiss banks in financing the Nazi war effort and in failing to make restitution to Holocaust survivors.

October 1996
Class action suit is filed in New York federal court against Swiss banks, seeking funds from "dormant accounts" of Holocaust victims.

1998
Though not an apology, President Clinton says in a speech at a Ugandan village school that it was wrong for European Americans to have received "the fruits of the slave trade."

August 1998
Swiss government agrees to pay $1.25 billion to settle claims against Swiss banks.

December 1998
In a *Wall Street Journal* op-ed piece, Anti-Defamation League national director and Holocaust survivor Abraham Foxman questions the tactics employed by those seeking reparations for Holocaust survivors.

December 1999
The German government and corporations that used slave labor during the war establish a $4.3 billion fund to compensate surviving slave laborers.

2000
TransAfrica founder Randall Robinson publishes *The Debt: What America Owes to Blacks*, a bestselling book arguing for reparations for slavery.

2001
Conservative commentator David Horowitz creates a controversy on many American campuses when he tries to publish an ad in college newspapers entitled "Ten Reasons Why Reparations for Slavery is a Bad Idea — and Racist, Too."

2002
Prominent African-American attorneys promise to sue the federal government and private companies for slavery reparations.

THE WHITE HOUSE
WASHINGTON

A monetary sum and words alone cannot restore lost years or erase painful memories; neither can they fully convey our Nation's resolve to rectify injustice and to uphold the rights of individuals. We can never fully right the wrongs of the past. But we can take a clear stand for justice and recognize that serious injustices were done to Japanese Americans during World War II.

In enacting a law calling for restitution and offering a sincere apology, your fellow Americans have, in a very real sense, renewed their traditional commitment to the ideals of freedom, equality, and justice. You and your family have our best wishes for the future.

Sincerely,

GEORGE BUSH
PRESIDENT OF THE UNITED STATES

OCTOBER 1990

In October 1990, Japanese-Americans interned during World War II received this letter of apology from President George Bush, in addition to a check for $20,000.

feel for the misery of others, when we either see it, or are made to conceive it in a very lively manner." [9]

Smith argued further that this sympathy is a cornerstone of justice. It is necessary for creating and maintaining general social order, he believed.

Native Americans

In the 18th and 19th centuries, compassion for the plight of others — whether out of Christian duty or to promote the greater good — fueled movements to abolish slavery and the slave trade in Europe and the United States. Later, these impulses led the United States, albeit very slowly, to consider compensating Native Americans for the government's taking of their land and the resulting destruction of much of their population and culture.

The expansion of the American frontier during the 19th century resulted in American Indians being forcibly moved to reservations, where many remain today. Millions of acres, primarily in the Great Plains, were taken from tribes with little or minimal compensation.

But the U.S. government did not consider compensating Native Americans for the loss of this property until 1946, when Congress established a Claims Commission to handle Indian land claims. The body soon became bogged down in the flood of claims, many of which were substantial. When the commission was eliminated in 1978, it had adjudicated only a fraction of the disputes between tribes and the government and had paid Native Americans only token compensation for the lost land. [10]

Meanwhile, the courts became much more sympathetic to Indian claims. In 1980, for instance, the Supreme Court awarded the Sioux $122 million for the theft of lands in South Dakota's Black Hills. It remains the largest award for a Native American land claim in U.S. history. (*See story, p. 222.*)

Today, Native Americans are still pressing land claims, particularly in the Eastern United States. "Many of these claims revolve around treaties made between states and Indian nations early in the country's history," says John Echohawk, executive director of the Native American Rights Fund, an Indian advocacy group in Boulder, Colo. Since the U.S. Constitution leaves the power to negotiate Indian treaties with the federal government, many of these agreements with the states are now being challenged, he adds.

One of the biggest such disputes involves three bands of Oneida Indians, who are trying to recover 300,000 acres of land in central New York state. The case hinges on a treaty negotiated in 1838.

Restitution to "Comfort Women"

On the other side of the globe, victims of a more recent tragedy — Japan's sexual enslavement of thousands of Asian women during World War II — are also seeking restitution. An estimated 200,000 "comfort women" were forced to serve the Japanese military at its far-flung outposts. They claim they were kidnapped or tricked into working as sexual slaves for the Japanese soldiers, who beat and raped them.

In 1995, then Japanese Prime Minister Tomiici Murayama officially apologized for the practice, but the government has yet to pay any reparations to the surviving women.

Other groups that have been victimized, like Armenians, also want restitution. And still others — like Latinos, Chinese-Americans and women in the United States — who suffered varying degrees of discrimination over the years, have not organized significant reparations movements, in part because their suffering is perceived as being different from the official policies that led to genocide or slavery.

Japanese-Americans

On Feb. 19, 1942, less than three months after the Japanese bombing of Pearl Harbor, President Franklin Delano Roosevelt signed Executive Order 9066, authorizing the removal of Japanese immigrants and their children from the western half of the Pacific coastal states and part of Arizona.

South Korean "comfort women" who were forced to provide sex for Japanese soldiers in World War II demand compensation during a protest at the Japanese Embassy in Seoul last March.

Reuters Photo/Yun Suk-bong

Within days, the government began removing 120,000 Japanese-Americans — two-thirds of them U.S. citizens — from their homes and businesses. Many were forced to sell their property at far below market value in the rush to leave. All were eventually taken to hastily built camps in Western states like California, Idaho and Utah, where most remained until the war was almost over. Some young Japanese-American men were allowed to leave the camps to serve in the armed forces — and many did so with valor — and a handful of mostly young internees were also permitted to relocate to Midwestern or Eastern states.

The camps were Spartan, but in no way resembled Nazi concentration camps or Stalinist Russia's gulags. Still, the internees were denied their freedom and, in many cases, their property.

During this time, internee Fred Korematsu and several other Japanese-Americans challenged the constitutionality of the internment. Korematsu's case ultimately found its way to the Supreme Court, which ruled that during national emergencies like war Congress and the president had the authority to imprison persons of certain racial groups.

After the war, Congress passed the Japanese-American Evacuations Claims Act of 1948 to compensate those who had lost property because of their internment. Over the next 17 years, the government paid $38 million to former internees. [11]

But efforts to make the government apologize for its wartime actions and pay reparations to internees over and above the property claims remained on a back burner until the 1970s. During that decade, Japanese-American activists — led by the community's main civic organization, the Japanese-American Citizens League (JACL) — began building support for redress.

Initially, only about a third of Japanese-Americans favored reparations. Many felt the painful war years should be forgotten. Others worried that vocal demands, coupled with growing fears among the U.S. public over the rising economic power of Japan, would provoke another backlash against Japanese-Americans. [12]

But by the end of the decade, a majority of Japanese-Americans supported the effort, and the JACL began effectively lobbying Congress for redress. In 1980, Congress created the Commission on Wartime Relocations and Internment of Civilians to study the issue.

During public hearings over the next two years, the commission heard emotional testimony as former internees shared their personal sagas. Publicity generated by the hearings helped awaken the American public to the injustice done to the internees.

One former internee, Kima Konatsu, told about her family's experience while incarcerated near Gila River, Ariz. "During that four years we were separated [from my husband] and allowed to see him only once," Konatsu told the commission. Eventually he became ill and was hospitalized, she said. "He was left alone, naked, by a nurse after having given him a sponge bath. It was a cold winter and he caught pneumonia. After two days and two nights, he passed away. Later on, the head nurse told us that this nurse had lost her two children in the war and that she hated Japanese." [13]

In 1983, the commission concluded that there had been no real national security reason to justify relocating or incarcerating the Japanese-Americans, and that the action had caused the community undue hardship. A second report four months later recommended that the government apologize for the internment and appropriate $1.5 billion to pay each surviving internee $20,000

Japanese-Americans were housed in hastily erected internment camps, like this one near Phoenix, Arizona, after the Japanese attack on Pearl Harbor. The U.S. later paid $20,000 to each person confined.

in reparations. [14]

That same year, a new National Council for Japanese-American Redress (NCJAR) emerged, which opposed what it saw as the JACL's accommodationist approach to reparations. NCJAR filed a class action suit against the government on behalf of the internees, demanding $27 billion in damages. But the suit was dismissed in 1987 on procedural grounds. [15]

Nevertheless, the lawsuit created restitution momentum in Congress, where support had been building since issuance of the commission's 1983 reports. Because many former internees were elderly, proponents argued that something should be done quickly, before most of the intended beneficiaries died. [16]

In 1988, Congress passed the Civil Liberties Act, which authorized $1.25 billion over the next 10 years to pay each internee $20,000. The law also contained an apology to Japanese-Americans who had been incarcerated [17] (see p. 226).

On Oct. 9, 1990, the government issued its first formal apologies and checks to Japanese-Americans in a moving ceremony in Washington, D.C. A tearful Sen. Daniel K. Inouye,

D-Hawaii — a Japanese-American who lost an arm fighting for the United States during World War II — told the internees and assembled guests that day: "We honor ourselves and honor America. We demonstrated to the world that we are a strong people — strong enough to admit our wrongs." [18]

Since then, some 80,000 former internees have received compensation. [19]

The Holocaust

In many ways, the modern debate over reparations began on Sept. 27, 1951. On that day West German Chancellor Konrad Adenauer appeared before the country's legislature, or Bundestag, and urged his fellow Germans to make some restitution for the "unspeakable crimes" Germany had committed against the Jewish people before and during World War II. His proposal — to provide assistance to the newly founded state of Israel as well as restitution to individual Holocaust survivors — was supported by both his own Christian Democratic party and the opposition Social Democrats.

Ironically, West Germany's offer of reparations was much more controversial in Israel, where a sizable minority, led by then opposition politician Menachem Begin, opposed taking "blood money" from Holocaust perpetrators. Begin and others argued that by receiving compensation from the Germans, Israel would literally be selling the moral high ground. [20]

Italian-Americans Were Also Mistreated

Japanese-Americans were not the only ethnic group to suffer from discrimination during World War II. Many Italian-Americans also were victimized in the name of national security.

The United States was at war with Italy from the end of 1941 until it surrendered to the Allies in 1943. During that time, some 600,000 Italian immigrants were classified as "enemy aliens," even though many had sons fighting for the United States against Italy, Germany and Japan.

Tens of thousands were subjected to search and arrest, and 250 were interned in camps. In California, an evening curfew was imposed on more than 50,000 Italian-Americans. Some 10,000 were forced to move away from areas near military installations. Authorities even impounded the boats of Italian-American fishermen.

While generally recognized as a gross violation of civil liberties, the federal government's mistreatment of Italians was much less far-reaching than the internment suffered by 120,000 Japanese. Indeed, more German-Americans were interned — about 11,000 in Texas, North Dakota and elsewhere. Perhaps that's why Italian-American groups have not demanded reparations. Instead, they have asked the government to "acknowledge" what happened.

In 2000, Congress agreed, passing legislation authorizing the Justice Department to conduct an investigation into the episode. The department's work is expected to be finished by the end of the year.

But Israeli Prime Minister David Ben Gurion argued forcefully that Israel had a duty to see that Germany did not profit from its heinous crimes. "He understood that we are obligated to ensure that murderers are not inheritors," says the World Jewish Congress' Steinberg.

Ben Gurion prevailed, in part because Israel desperately needed funds to resettle European Jews who had survived the Holocaust. The German government began paying restitution to Holocaust survivors around the world in 1953 and has since paid out about $60 billion for both individual claims and aid to Israel. The state-to-state payments ended in 1965, but the German government still sends monthly pension checks to about 100,000 Holocaust survivors.

After West Germany's agreement with Israel, little was done to obtain further restitution for Holocaust victims. Many who had survived the camps were more concerned with getting on with their new lives and wanted to forget about the past. In addition, the Soviet Union and its Eastern bloc allies — where most Holocaust victims had come from — made no effort to aid the quest for restitution. Even the United States was content to let the issue lie, partly in order to focus on integrating West Germany and other Western allies into a Cold War alliance. [21]

Still, the issue did not disappear entirely. In Switzerland — a banking and finance mecca and a neutral country during the war — the government was taking small, inadequate steps to discover the extent of Holocaust-related wealth. Many Jews killed by the Germans had opened accounts in Swiss banks and taken out insurance policies from Swiss companies before the war as a hedge against the uncertainty created by the Nazi persecution.

In 1956, the Swiss government surveyed its banks and insurance companies to determine the value of accounts held by those who had died or become refugees as a result of the Holocaust. The companies replied that there were less than a million Swiss francs in those accounts.

In 1962, the government once again requested an accounting of Holocaust-related assets. This time, the companies came up with about 10 million francs, some of which was paid to account holders or their heirs. In the 1960s, '70s and '80s, other efforts by individuals seeking to recover Swiss-held assets were largely unsuccessful because the banks and insurers required claimants to have extensive proof of account ownership, proof that often had been lost or destroyed during the war.

But in the 1990s the situation changed dramatically. First, the collapse of communist regimes throughout Eastern Europe opened up previously closed archives containing Holocaust-related records. In addition, many Holocaust survivors lost their reticence about pursuing claims, in part because films like "Schindler's List" brought greater attention to their plight and made it easier to go public.

In the mid-1990s, journalists and scholars began uncovering evidence that Switzerland had been a financial haven for Nazi officials, who had deposited gold looted from Holocaust victims in Swiss banks. The investigation stimulated new interest in dormant bank accounts and insurance policies.

In 1996 a class action suit on behalf of victims and their heirs was filed in New York against Swiss banks and insurance companies. Swiss efforts to get the suit dismissed failed. Meanwhile, pressure from the U.S. Congress and local officials threatening economic sanctions against the companies forced the banks and insurers to acknowledge the existence of a large number of dormant accounts. By 1999, the Swiss had negotiated a settlement to set aside $1.25 billion to pay out dormant accounts and fund other Holocaust-related philanthropies.

The Swiss case prompted other Holocaust claims. For instance, in 1998 U.S. and European insurance regulators, Jewish groups and others formed a commission — headed by former Secretary of State Lawrence Eagleburger — to investigate claims against European insurance companies outside Switzerland.

The commission was an attempt to bypass lawsuits and to get the insurers — which include some of Europe's largest, like Italy's Generali and Germany's Allianz — to pay elderly claimants before they died. So far, the companies have paid out very little in compensation, because of bureaucratic wrangling at the commission and unwillingness on the part of survivors to accept what have in many cases been only small offers of restitution from the companies. [22]

Meanwhile, former prisoners who had been forced to work without pay for German manufacturers during the war began seeking restitution for their labor. The Nazis had drafted an estimated 12 million people — including 6 million mostly Jewish concentration camp inmates — to provide unpaid labor for some of the biggest names in German industry, including giant automaker Volkswagen. Many were worked to death. [23]

Initially Germany and then-Chancellor Helmut Kohl resisted efforts to pay reparations to slave laborers, citing the 1953 settlement with Israel. But in 1998 the country elected a new leader, Gerhard Schröeder, who authorized negotiations to settle the issue.

Last July, the German government and companies that had used slave labor established a $4.3 billion fund to compensate an estimated 1.5 million survivors. The deal, negotiated with German and American lawyers for the slave laborers and ratified in the Bundestag on May 30, indemnifies German industry from further lawsuits on behalf of slave laborers. ■

Rep. John Conyers Jr., D-Mich., wants Congress to create a commission on reparations for descendants of slaves. "Twelve years ago, most people didn't even know what reparations were, and now it's become a front-burner issue," he says.

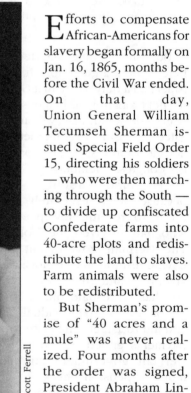

CQ/Scott Ferrell

CURRENT SITUATION

Reparations for Slavery

Efforts to compensate African-Americans for slavery began formally on Jan. 16, 1865, months before the Civil War ended. On that day, Union General William Tecumseh Sherman issued Special Field Order 15, directing his soldiers — who were then marching through the South — to divide up confiscated Confederate farms into 40-acre plots and redistribute the land to slaves. Farm animals were also to be redistributed.

But Sherman's promise of "40 acres and a mule" was never realized. Four months after the order was signed, President Abraham Lincoln was assassinated. His successor, Southerner Andrew Johnson, largely opposed reconstruction and quickly rescinded Sherman's order. More than 40,000 slaves were removed from farms they had recently occupied.

In the years since Special Field Order 15, the idea of compensating African-Americans arose only occa-

At Issue:

Should the U.S. government apologize to African-Americans for slavery?

REP. TONY P. HALL
D-OHIO

WRITTEN FOR THE CQ RESEARCHER, JUNE 2001

*a*merica's history has changed the course of humanity. As an enemy of tyrants, an advocate of liberty and a defender of freedoms, America has proven herself again and again. Our achievements stir other peoples' pride, and our history bestows upon us the courage to conquer new challenges.

But our achievements and our history are blemished by the shameful decades when U.S. laws permitted the enslavement of African-Americans. This long chapter ensured that many of the hands that built our young nation were not those of full participants in an emerging American dream, but of men, women and children forced to obey the tyranny of "masters."

In recent years, we have apologized for racist medical experiments that inflicted pain and eventually death on many young, innocent men in Tuskegee, Ala. We have paid reparations for forcibly interning thousands of Japanese-Americans during World War II. And we helped to broker an apology and reparations for victims of the Holocaust.

Of course, the fact we have acknowledged these wrongs doesn't make up for the pain of the past. But if what we've done in these cases wasn't sufficient to fulfill that impossible goal, it was necessary to restore the goodwill needed to change our future. In giving these and other Americans the dignity of an honest admission that our nation was wrong, these apologies have given us all a measure of healing.

Nearly 14 decades after slavery was abolished, its legacy still reverberates through Americans' daily lives. Neither former slaves nor slave owners are alive today, and few Americans trace their own roots to slavery. But all Americans bear slavery's bitter burdens — the lingering racial tensions, the stubborn poverty and dysfunction that is disproportionately high among African-Americans, the persistence that justice has not yet been done.

"I am sorry" are the first words uttered by anyone sincere about righting a wrong. And yet in the case of our nation's greatest moral failing, we have yet to say these words. We have pursued countless policies toward the goal of racial healing. We have been enriched by the determination of African-Americans to overcome the problems rooted in their ancestors' enslavement. But neither their success, nor the blood spilled in our Civil War, excuses our country's continuing silence.

Some critics say an apology may open old wounds. Some say that paying reparations is essential to atonement. But no one can say those three words don't ring true.

ROBERT W. TRACINSKI
FELLOW, AYN RAND INSTITUTE, MARINA DEL REY, CALIF.

JUNE 2001

*a*n apology for slavery on behalf of the nation presumes that whites today, who mostly oppose racism and never owned slaves, still bear a collective responsibility — simply by belonging to the same race as the slaveholders of the Old South. Such an apology promotes the very idea at the root of slavery: racial collectivism.

Slave owners were certainly guilty of a grave injustice. But by what standard can other whites be held responsible for their ideas and actions? By what standards can today's Americans be obliged to apologize on the slaveholders' behalf? The only justification for such an approach is the idea that each member of the race can be blamed for the actions of every other member, that we are all just interchangeable cells of the racial collective.

Critics of the proposed apology oppose it, not because it embraces this racist premise but because it does not go far enough. They want to apply the notion of racial collectivism in a more "substantial" form, by increasing welfare and affirmative-action programs designed to compensate for the wrongs of slavery. Such compensation consists of punishing random whites, by taxing them and denying them jobs and promotions in order to reward random blacks.

The ultimate result of this approach is not racial harmony or a color-blind society but racial warfare. It is precisely this kind of mentality that has devastated the Balkans, with each ethnic tribe continually exacting revenge on the other in retaliation for centuries-old grievances.

The idea of a national apology for slavery merely reinforces this same kind of racial enmity in America. By treating all whites as the stand-ins or representatives for slaveholders, it encourages the view of blacks and whites as a collective of victims pitted against an opposing and hostile collective of oppressors, with no possibility for integration or peaceful coexistence.

The only alternative to this kind of racial Balkanization is to embrace the opposite principle: individualism. People should be judged based on their choices, ideas and actions as individuals, not as "representatives" of a racial group. They should be rewarded based on their own merits — and they must not be forced to pay, or to apologize, for crimes committed by others, merely because those others have the same skin color.

Americans both black and white should reject the notion of a collective guilt for slavery. They should uphold the ideal of a color-blind society, based on individualism, as the real answer to racism.

sionally in the public arena and attracted little attention. But lately the idea has gained considerable steam, propelled by several high-profile events, such as academic conferences on the subject and the threat of reparations lawsuits by prominent black attorneys.

In addition, Chicago, Detroit and Washington, D.C., have passed resolutions supporting federal reparations legislation. And slavery reparations has become a hot topic on college campuses, as more and more scholars study the idea. "This is the fourth paper I've delivered on reparations this year alone," University of San Diego Law Professor Roy Brooks said at a May conference on the issue. "That suggests there's much to say about the subject and that reparations is a hot issue internationally." [24]

The lawsuits being prepared by several prominent black attorneys and advocates are expected to be filed early next year. They are the brainchild of a legal team that includes TransAfrica's Robinson, O.J. Simpson attorney Cochran, Harvard University Law School Professor Charles Ogletree and Alexander Pires, who recently won a $1 billion settlement from the Department of Agriculture on behalf of black farmers who were denied government loans.

"The history of slavery in America has never been fully addressed in a public forum," Ogletree said. "Litigation will show what slavery meant, how it was profitable and how the issue of white privilege is still with us. Litigation is a place to start, because it focuses attention on the issue." [25]

The team wants the federal government to officially apologize for slavery and for the century of state-supported discrimination — such as the South's segregationist "Jim Crow" laws — that followed emancipation. Moreover, the lawyers are likely to ask for some kind of monetary remedy, although no agreement has been reached either on how much is owed or how reparations would be dispersed.

Estimates vary wildly over how much black Americans are owed for slavery. Larry Neal, an economics professor at the University of Illinois at Urbana-Champaign, has calculated that the United States owes African-Americans $1.4 trillion in back wages for work completed before emancipation. Georgetown University Business School Professor Richard America, however, estimates the debt is closer to $10 trillion. [26]

Robinson doesn't want direct cash payments to African-Americans, especially people like himself, who are in the middle- or upper-income brackets. He favors establishment of a trust fund to assist underprivileged blacks. "The question we need to be asking is: How do we repair the damage?" Robinson asks. "We need a massive diffusion of capital to provide poor African-American youth with education — from kindergarten through college — and some sort of fund to promote economic development."

Most legal experts do not expect Cochran, Ogletree and the others to succeed, noting that the claim is almost 150 years old and thus the statute of limitations expired long ago.

"Even in a friendly court, there are going to be statute of limitations problems," Tulane University Law School Professor Robert Wesley says. [27] Moreover, experts point out, under the doctrine of sovereign immunity governments are protected from most legal actions.

Still, some legal scholars say the suit is not wholly a pipe dream, noting that civil rights attorneys in the 1950s and '60s also faced long odds in their battle to end race discrimination. "This will be a daunting task, but it is certainly not impossible," says Robert Belton, a

South Carolina Gov. Jim Hodges helps to break ground for an African-American monument last year in Columbia. In spite of efforts by several states to come to terms with the history and contributions of black Americans, many advocates for slavey reparations say that only restitution will close the racial divide.

AP Photo/Lou Krasky

Vanderbilt University law professor.

Even if the suit does not ultimately lead to redress or an apology, it may succeed on another level, says David Bositis, senior political analyst at the Joint Center for Political and Economic Studies, a think tank focusing on African-American issues. "Even if they just got some federal district judge to hear the case, it would become a much larger news item and so would stimulate discussion and debate," he says. "They would consider that a victory."

The black legal team is also planning to sue private companies that benefited from slavery, including banks, insurance companies, shipping firms and other businesses that may have profited from the slave trade.

Research by New York City lawyer and activist Deadria Farmer-Paellmann revealed that several insurance companies — including Aetna and New York Life — insured slave owners against the loss of their "property."

"If you can show a company made immoral gains by profiting from slavery, you can file an action for unjust enrichment," she said. [28] Her work coincides with a new California law requiring all insurance companies in the state to research past business records and disclose any connections to slavery.

In addition, a growing chorus of civil rights leaders, including the Rev. Jesse L. Jackson, has called on insurers to pay some form of restitution. "We call on the insurance companies to search their national files and disclose any and all policies issued to insure slave owners during the period of slavery," Jackson said. [29]

Some black leaders have suggested that culpable corporations establish scholarship funds for underprivileged black students.

But, while Aetna has publicly apologized for insuring owners against the loss of slaves, it has refused to provide compensation, arguing that slavery was legal when the policies were issued. New York Life is withholding comment until it finishes reviewing its historical records. ∎

OUTLOOK

Starting a Dialogue

Those working to obtain reparations for slavery often compare the fight with the long, uphill struggle faced by civil rights activists in the 1950s and '60s. "The relative powerlessness of our community is not a new thing for African-Americans," the University of Maryland's Walters says. "We've been here before and have won, and I think we're going to win this time, too."

"The uneasiness that some express about reparations is the same uneasiness that we had about integration and about a woman's right to choose," Harvard's Ogletree said. "We've gained some important mainstream viability, but these things take time." [30]

For now, reparations proponents say that they hope to get the government to consider the issue, just as it did for Japanese-American internees and Holocaust survivors. "Right now this is about process," Walters says. "With Japanese-Americans, nothing really happened until after the government took some time to study the issue."

But opponents and others are confident the effort will fail. "This is going to die out because it makes no sense," George Mason's Williams says. "Conyers' bill is languishing in Congress and will continue to languish in Congress, because white politicians cannot sell this to white America."

MIT's Nobles agrees. "The best they can hope for from Congress is some sort of formal apology," she says. A claim based on an injustice that occurred so long ago is simply too nebulous to warrant serious consideration by lawmakers or judges, she says. "This isn't like the case of Japanese-Americans, where you had direct survivors of the act in question. [The former internees'] suffering was identifiable and for a specific period of time — four years — making it much less complicated."

Efforts against private firms — like insurance companies — have a better chance of producing some monetary reward, she predicts. "Eventually, some company will feel the heat, cave in and set up some sort of trust fund or something," she says, adding that Cochran, Ogletree and the other attorneys are unlikely to quit without something to show for their efforts. "To prove that all of this [effort] was worthwhile, they're going to work for a real win."

Others agree the movement will probably achieve at least some of its goals. "The less sophisticated supporters may think that they're going to win reparations, but the more sophisticated ones know that, in the near term, the chance of this happening is very unlikely," says Bositis, of the Joint Center for Political and Economic Studies.

"For these more realistic people, the principal thing they are trying to do is to start a dialogue on the issue, to get people talking about it," he concludes. ∎

Notes

[1] Quoted in Jane Clayson, "Some Civil Rights Leaders Say Descendants of Slaves Should

Be Compensated," CBS News: "The Early Show," Jan. 11, 2001.

[2] Larry Bivins, "Debate on Reparations for Slavery Gaining Higher Profile," *Gannett News Service*, April 21, 2001.

[3] For background, see Kenneth Jost, "Holocaust Reparations," *The CQ Researcher*, March 26, 1999, pp. 257-280.

[4] Quoted in Abraham H. Foxman, "The Dangers of Holocaust Restitution," *The Wall Street Journal*, Dec. 7, 1998.

[5] Quoted in *Ibid*.

[6] Mortimer Adler, *Aristotle for Everybody* (1978), p. 126.

[7] Quoted in Arthur Spiegelman, "Leaders of Fight for Holocaust Reparations Under Attack," *The Houston Chronicle*, Dec. 27, 1998

[8] Matthew 5:10.

[9] Adam Smith, *The Theory of Moral Sentiments* (1759), pp. 47-48.

[10] Elazar Barkan, *The Guilt of Nations: Restitution and Negotiating Historical Injustices* (2000), p. 183.

[11] Mitchell T. Maki, *et al.*, *Achieving the Impossible Dream: How Japanese-Americans Obtained Redress* (1999), p. 54.

[12] Barkan, *op. cit.*, p. 34.

[13] Maki, *op. cit.*, p. 107.

[14] *Ibid*.

[15] *Ibid.*, pp. 121-128.

[16] Christine C. Lawrence, ed., *1988 CQ Almanac* (1988), p. 80.

[17] *Ibid*.

[18] Maki, *op. cit.*, p. 213.

[19] *Ibid.*, p. 214.

[20] Barkan, *op. cit.*

[21] Jost, *op. cit.*

[22] Henry Weinstein, "Spending by Holocaust Claims Panel Criticized," *Los Angeles Times*, May 17, 2001.

[23] "Key Dates in Nazi Slave Labor Talks," *The Jerusalem Post*, May 21, 2001.

[24] Quoted in Erin Texeira, "Black Reparations Idea Builds at UCLA Meeting," *Los Angeles Times*, May 12, 2001.

[25] Quoted in Tamar Lewin, "Calls for Slavery Restitution Getting Louder," *The New York Times*, June 4, 2001.

[26] Kevin Merida, "Did Freedom Alone Pay a Nation's Debt?" *The Washington Post*, Nov. 28, 1999.

[27] Quoted in Tovia Smith, "Legal Scholars Considering Class Action Lawsuit to Seek Restitution for Descendants of African Slaves," Weekend Edition Saturday, National Public Radio, April 1, 2001.

[28] Quoted in Lewin, *op. cit.*

[29] Quoted in Tim Novak, "Jackson: Companies Owe Blacks," *The Chicago Sun Times*, July 29, 2000.

[30] Quoted in Lewin, *op. cit.*

FOR MORE INFORMATION

Anti-Defamation League, 823 United Nations Plaza, New York, N.Y. 20017; (212) 490-2525; www.adl.org. Fights anti-Semitism and represents Jewish interests worldwide.

Conference on Jewish Material Claims Against Germany, 15 East 26th St., Room 906, New York, N.Y. 10010; (212) 696-4944; www.claimscon. org. Pursues reparations claims on behalf of Jewish victims of the Nazi Holocaust.

Japanese American Citizens League (JACL), 1765 Sutter St., San Francisco, Calif. 94115; (415) 921-5225. www.jacl.org. The nation's oldest Asian-American civil rights group fights discrimination against Japanese-Americans.

Joint Center for Political and Economic Studies, 1090 Vermont Ave., N.W., Suite 1100, Washington, D.C. 20005; (202) 789-3500; www.jointctr. org. Researches and analyzes issues of importance to African-Americans.

National Coalition of Blacks for Reparations in America, P.O. Box 62622, Washington, D.C. 20029; (202) 635-6272; www.ncobra.com. Lobbies for reparations for African-Americans.

Native American Rights Fund, 1712 N St., N.W., Washington, D.C. 20036; (202) 785-4166; www.narf.org. Provides Native Americans with legal assistance for land claims.

TransAfrica, 1744 R. St., N.W., Washington D.C. 20009; (202) 797-2301; www.transafricaforum.org. Lobbies on behalf of Africans and people of African descent around the world.

U.S. Holocaust Memorial Museum, 100 Raoul Wallenberg Place, S.W., Washington, D.C. 20024; (202) 488-0400; www.ushmm.org. Preserves documentation and encourages research about the Holocaust.

World Jewish Congress, 501 Madison Ave., 17th Floor, New York, N.Y., 10022; (212) 755-5770; www.wjc.org.il. An international federation of Jewish communities and organizations that has been at the forefront of negotiations over Holocaust reparations.

Bibliography

Selected Sources Used

Books

Elazar Barkan, *The Guilt of Nations: Restitution and Negotiating Historical Injustices*, W.W. Norton (2000).

A professor of history at Claremont Graduate University has written an excellent and thorough history of restitution efforts in the 20th century, from attempts by Holocaust survivors to recover stolen property to the campaign to compensate "comfort women" forced to provide sex to Japanese soldiers. Barkan also examines the intellectual origins of the reparations movement.

Finkelstein, Norman G., *The Holocaust Industry: Reflections on the Exploitation of Jewish Suffering*, Verso, 2000.

Finkelstein, a professor of political theory at Hunter College, charges lawyers and Jewish groups with exploiting the Holocaust for financial and political gain, using unethical and immoral tactics. He contends that much of the money "extorted" from European companies and countries is not going to survivors, and that the entire process is degrading the historical legacy of the Holocaust.

Maki, Mitchell T., Harry H. L. Kitano and S. Megan Berthold, *Achieving the Impossible Dream: How Japanese Americans Obtained Redress*, University of Illinois Press (1999).

The authors trace the history of efforts to get the U.S. government to pay reparations to Japanese-Americans interned during World War II.

Robinson, Randall, *The Debt: What America Owes to Blacks*, Plume, 2000.

The president of TransAfrica argues for reparations for African-Americans, writing: "If . . . African Americans will not be compensated for the massive wrongs and social injuries inflicted upon them by their government, during and after slavery, then there is no chance that America can solve its racial problems — if solving these problems means, as I believe it must, closing the yawning economic gap between blacks and whites in this country."

Articles

Bivis, Larry, "Debate on Reparations for Slavery Gaining Higher Profile," Gannett News Service, April 21, 2001.

The article examines African-Americans' growing call for reparations.

Dyckman, Martin, "Our Country has Paid the Bill for Slavery," *St. Petersburg Times*, June 25, 2000.

Dyckman makes a strong case against reparations to black Americans, arguing that the Union soldiers who died in the Civil War to free the slaves paid the country's debt to African-Americans.

Jost, Kenneth, "Holocaust Reparations," *The CQ Researcher*, March 26, 1999.

Jost gives an excellent overview of the debate over reparations for the survivors of the Nazi Holocaust. His description of the fight over dormant bank accounts and insurance policies in Switzerland is particularly illuminating.

McTague, Jim, "Broken Trusts: Native Americans Seek Billions They Say Uncle Sam Owes Them," *Barron's*, April 9, 2001.

McTague examines the Native American lawsuit against the federal government for decades of mishandling of the trust fund derived from the lease and sale of natural resources on Indian lands. The tribe recently won a judgment against the federal government, and the suit may result in native tribes receiving up to $10 billion.

Merida, Kevin, "Did Freedom Alone Pay a Nation's Debt?" *The Washington Post*, Nov. 28, 1999.

Merida examines the movement to obtain reparations for the African-American descendants of slaves, providing a good historical overview of efforts to compensate newly freed slaves after the Civil War.

Schoenfeld, Gabriel, "Holocaust Reparations — A Growing Scandal," *Commentary Magazine*, Sept. 2000.

The magazine's senior editor takes Jewish groups to task for their hardball tactics against Germany and other European countries in their Holocaust reparations efforts. He worries they will foment bad feeling in Europe against Jews and Israel.

Trounson, Rebecca, "Campus Agitator," *Los Angeles Times*, April 10, 2001.

The article chronicles the controversy surrounding recent attempts by conservative commentator David Horowitz to place ads in college newspapers that argue against reparations for African-Americans.

Zipperstein, Steven J., "Profit and Loss," *The Washington Post*, Sept. 24, 2000.

A professor of Jewish studies at Stanford University accuses author Norman G. Finkelstein of making wild and unsubstantiated charges in *The Holocaust Industry* (see above). "Imagine an old-style rant, with its finely honed ear for conspiracy, with all the nuance of one's raging, aging, politicized uncle," he writes.

13 Future Job Market

JANE TANNER

When Mark Caddell was laid off from an Austin, Texas, high-technology company last October, he became one of the estimated 468,000 people who lost their jobs in the month after the terrorist attacks on the World Trade Center and the Pentagon. [1]

But the Sept. 11 attacks only added momentum to the massive layoffs that had begun much earlier. In fact, economists say, the decade-long U.S. economic expansion — the longest in American history — ended last March when the country quietly slipped into recession.

Caddell and many of his friends became victims of the fleeting rise and fall of dot-com mania. Overblown expectations of Internet commerce had brought rapid wealth — at least on paper — to many of Caddell's buddies. "It's a big leap for them to shift from being millionaires to thinking, 'Man, I don't know if I'll be able to pay the mortgage,' " he says.

In many ways, the 38-year-old video producer and multimedia expert is symbolic of the modern worker. Since graduating from Baylor University in 1985, he has held seven jobs and done two stints as a production assistant on feature films. For five years, he ran his own production firm. But until October he always had managed to stay one step ahead of the ax. Now he advises workplace newcomers: "Stay awake."

Indeed, it's difficult to predict the prospects for young people about to enter the work force. Experts disagree about when the downturn will end, and no one can predict the long-term added costs of doing business as a result of the terrorist attacks, especially if future

From *The CQ Researcher,* January 11, 2002.

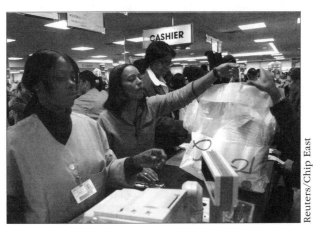

The continuing shift to a service and retail economy means more jobs with low pay and few benefits, such as cashiering. Almost 500,000 new cashier jobs will be created in the next 10 years.

attacks add to anxiety. "The future is uncertain whether this will be a problem of about the same dimensions [as it is now] and businesses will learn to cope, or whether it just gets more costly and uncertain doing business globally," says Marvin H. Kosters, director of economic policy studies at the American Enterprise Institute (AEI).

Yet, many aspects of the labor market facing today's college and high school students seem clear. Notions of stock-option jackpots and office perks like ping-pong tables and espresso machines have vanished, as students watch parents and neighbors lose their jobs.

But some trends are evident. For one thing, education matters. The unemployment rate for high school dropouts jumped from 7.1 percent to 7.7 percent from October 2000 to October 2001. For high school graduates without college educations, it jumped from 4.3 percent to 4.7 percent. Meanwhile, for workers who had some college courses but did not graduate, unemployment went from 3.8 percent to 4.1 percent during the same period last year. College graduates were idled the least: Their unemployment rate only increased slightly, from 2.5 percent to 2.7 percent. [2]

Over the next two decades, however, economists predict a worrisome

shortage of workers, as the labor pool's growth rate slows along with the growth rate of the general population. The labor force — now 119 million workers — is only expected to grow by 16 percent in the next 20 years, compared with an astonishing 50 percent increase during the last two decades, according to Harvard University Professor David T. Ellwood. [3]

Much of that growth was due to the large numbers of Baby Boomers, women and minorities who entered the work force in record numbers in the past. But experts do not predict any such surges in the future, and many of the boomers will start retiring — hence, the projected slowdown in the growth rate.

More specifically, the growth in the number of people in the prime of their working careers — those ages 25–54 — is expected to slow to a mere 3 percent growth rate, compared with a galloping 54 percent from 1980-2000. [4]

The education levels of future workers also trouble economists. Ideally, every new generation of workers would continue advancing up the educational ladder. That was certainly true of the Baby Boomers, who were vastly more educated than their parents and grandparents and who dramatically raised the overall education level of U.S. workers over the past 20 years.

However, even though colleges are bulging at the seams now, the next wave of workers will only match the educational level of the boomers. But in the future the best jobs will require more education than past jobs. Part of the problem stems from the number of Latino immigrants, who on the whole are less educated than other groups but make up an increasing percentage of the work force.

Already, there are critical shortages

The 15 Fastest-Growing Occupations

High-skilled, high-paying computer careers are growing at a fast clip, but so are low-skill, low-pay jobs that require modest education. Also, demand for workers is growing fast in medical-support fields.

Occupation	Employment (thousands of jobs)		Change %	Rank by 2000 median annual earnings*	Education or training needed
	2000	2010			
Computer software engineers, applications	380	760	100%	1	Bachelor's degree
Computer support specialists	506	996	97	2	Associate's degree
Computer, systems software engineers	317	601	90	1	Bachelor's degree
Network, computer systems administrators	229	416	82	1	Bachelor's degree
Network systems, data analysts	119	211	77	1	Bachelor's degree
Desktop publishers	38	63	66	2	Postsecondary/vocational
Database administrators	106	176	66	1	Bachelor's degree
Personal, home-care aides	414	672	62	4	On-the-job training
Computer systems analysts	431	689	60	1	Bachelor's degree
Medical assistants	329	516	57	3	On-the-job training
Social and human-service assistants	271	418	54	3	On-the-job training
Physician assistants	58	89	53	1	Bachelor's degree
Medical, health-information technicians	136	202	49	3	Associate's degree
Computer, information-systems managers	313	463	48	1	Bachelor's degree or higher plus work experience
Home health aides	615	907	47	4	On-the-job training

*Rankings of annual earnings:

1 = very high ($39,700 and over) 3 = low ($18,500 to $25,760)
2 = high ($25,760 to $39,660) 4 = very low (up to $18,490)

Source: "Occupational Employment Projections to 2010," U.S. Bureau of Labor Statistics, November 2001.

in several key occupations, including teachers, nurses and pharmacists. And the imminent retirement of the aging Baby Boomers is expected to exacerbate the shortages.

But despite labor shortages in some fields, the nation's continuing shift to a service and retail economy makes it more likely that young people will find themselves in jobs where the pay is low, benefits are few, tenure is uncertain and mobility to better positions is limited. In other words, we may be living in the "Information Age," but the reality for many future workers will be jobs that are repetitive and re-quire little creativity and imagination.

"Included among information jobs are a lot of clerical jobs," says Rob Kling, professor of information sciences at the University of Indiana.

The salary gap between low- and high-skilled workers has been widening — and is expected to diverge further. The fastest-growing job categories reflect that split. Certain hot technology jobs will demand high-level skills and will offer high pay. Thus, despite Silicon Valley's current high level of unemployment, long-term prospects for computer engineers and systems analysts are excellent. The Bu-reau of Labor Statistics (BLS), for instance, estimates that the U.S. economy will need about 760,000 computer software application engineers by 2010, double the 380,000 slots needed in 2000. [5] (*See chart, p. 239*)

At the same time, demand will be greatest for workers in low-wage, low-skill jobs, such as cashiers. The BLS estimates that by 2010, some 3.8 million cashiers will be needed, 474,000 more than were needed in 2000.

Yet, the middle ground is not barren. Many high-demand jobs will require modest education or training and still pay fairly well. Registered nurses,

Where the Most Jobs Will Be

The 15 jobs with the most new openings in the coming decade do not require a lot of higher education — nor do they pay well. Exceptions are nurses, teachers, managers and computer engineers.

Occupation	Employment (thousands of jobs)		Change %	Rank by 2000 median annual earnings*	Education or training needed
	2000	2010			
Food preparation, service	2,206	2,879	30%	4	On-the-job training
Customer-service representatives	1,946	2,577	32	3	On-the-job training
Registered nurses	2,194	2,755	26	1	Associate's degree
Retail salespersons	4,109	4,619	12	4	On-the-job training
Computer-support specialists	506	996	97	2	Associate's degree
Cashiers, except gaming	3,325	3,799	14	4	On-the-job training
Office clerks, general	2,705	3,135	16	3	On-the-job training
Security guards	1,106	1,497	35	4	On-the-job training
Software, applications engineers	380	760	100	1	Bachelor's degree
Waiters and waitresses	1,983	2,347	18	4	On-the-job training
General, operations managers	2,398	2,761	15	1	Bachelor's degree, plus work experience
Truck drivers	1,749	2,095	20	2	On-the-job training
Nursing aides, orderlies, attendants	1,373	1,697	24	3	On-the-job training
Janitors, cleaners (except maids), housekeepers	2,348	2,665	13	4	On-the-job training
Postsecondary teachers	1,344	1,659	23	1	Doctoral degree

*Rankings of annual earnings:

1 = very high ($39,700 and over)   3 = low ($18,500 to $25,760)
2 = high ($25,760 to $39,660)   4 = very low (up to $18,490)

Source: "Occupational Employment Projections to 2010," U.S. Bureau of Labor Statistics, November 2001.

computer support specialists and dental hygienists require only associate's degrees; desktop publishing and tractor-trailer truck drivers only call for on-the-job training and likely a vocational certificate. [6]

The terrorist attacks may lead more young people to look into careers they hadn't previously considered. As the federal Centers for Disease Control and Prevention (CDC) and state public health departments play increasingly bigger roles in national defense, some new graduates may be attracted to epidemiology and public health. [7] And recruiters on college campuses report

that interest has surged in both law enforcement and social advocacy since Sept. 11.

"There might be more young people who want to sign up for military service, or the FBI or CIA, " says Joyce Smith, executive director of the National Association for College Admissions Counseling. "These are areas that kids didn't necessarily aspire to, but now these careers are being pushed into the public light."

High school career counselors, on the other hand, report that more students are saying that they don't want jobs that would put them in harm's

way. "They are wary about careers where you might have to do a lot of traveling," says Renee Kersey, a counselor in Charlotte, N.C. And many parents are leaning toward nearby universities so their children won't have to fly home for holidays. "Parents are saying, 'Let's keep our son or daughter within a day's drive,' " said Gregory Branch, assistant vice president for enrollment at South Carolina State University. [8] Parents who have lost their own jobs or seen their stock portfolios shrink with the falling stock market are especially likely to pick state schools for their children.

Moreover, high school students today

are much more likely to share college classrooms with adults retooling their skills or changing careers to improve their own job prospects. Ongoing changes in technology call for updated education and training. In fact, adults are expected to make up 50 percent of total college enrollments by 2010, according to the National Association for College Admissions Counseling. At the same time, future students will be more likely to engage in distance learning or teach themselves new skills needed to stay relevant. [9]

When today's high school students finally enter the work force, they'll find a globalized market that draws skilled employees from an international labor pool. Through "electronic migration," workers in the Philippines or India or Ireland will answer helpdesk questions from computer users in Iowa City and Bangor, Maine.

Thanks to the ease of long-distance and overseas realtime communications, workers increasingly will collaborate with team members thousands of miles and many borders away. "Arrangements can be made and revised electronically, so you can't tell if you're dealing with someone across the street or in India or China," Kosters says.

The days of toiling at one company until it's time for the gold watch will largely have been over for nearly two decades by the time today's high school students punch the clock. New workers should be flexible and prepared for more job switches and even career changes than the "Generation Xers" — the generation born between the early 1960s and 1981 — who en-

tered the job market before them.

In the near future, companies will make long-term projections based on shorter periods, and payrolls will expand and contract with the whims of consumer demands. Whether workplace laws and policies will change to accommodate frequent job changes remains to be seen. For example, there's pressure from independent contractors and policy advocates to make pensions portable from one employer to the next.

Work venues are likely to become even more flexible. "By the year 2005, people will have 'anytime, anywhere' access to voice or video communications, the Internet and other networked computer systems," says the Society for Human Resource Management. [10] After

An estimated 561,000 new nurses will be needed in the next 10 years, as the Baby Boomers age. Jobs in high-demand fields like nursing, computer support and dental hygiene require modest education or training and still pay fairly well.

AP Photo/Tim Boyd

the terrorist attacks decimated several companies, many firms began re-evaluating the advisability of congregating their workers and data in one place. Employers also came to appreciate the use of home offices as backup offices.

The number of U.S. employees who work from home, from the road or other external settings rose 16.5 percent, to 28.8 million, this past year, according to the International Telework Association. In addition, many young

people poised to enter the job market virtually have their own high-tech centers. But they should be aware, the association study warns, that off-site workers don't get promoted as readily as traditional personnel.

On the other hand, young people poised to move into the job market won't be as interested in conventional, uninterrupted 40-year careers. Unlike their parents, they will retire earlier, and step off the career track to take a few sabbaticals during their working lives, according to the Employee Benefit Research Institute (EBRI). [11]

As teenagers and college graduates prepare to clock-in, employers, educators, economists, sociologists and young people themselves are asking the following questions:

Are young people out of touch with job-market realities?

Career counselors say some students' career expectations do not match job market realities. In a career-interest survey last spring of more than 13,000 Charlotte, N.C., high school students, the most popular jobs were attorney and doctor. "Law and medicine are always one and two," says Carlton Crump, who heads a Charlotte subsidiary of The Boy Scouts of America, which has conducted similar surveys for decades.

"If you look at the top 20 career choices and compare them with the number of people in our community in those jobs, it doesn't match up," Crump says. "It's unrealistic."

Television influences career ideas, counselors say. "They see all these programs with young lawyers in miniskirts," says career counselor Kersey. "TV glamorizes these careers."

For instance, many students have been asking about forensic sciences since the rise in popularity of the TV program "CSI" (Crime Scene Investigation).

Executives at Iowa City-based ACT Inc., which administers the ACT college admissions tests, worry about the disconnect between teenagers' early career choices and labor-market practicalities. "When you look at a five-year pattern, you see a consistent decline in areas where we have critical human resource needs," says Don Carstensen, vice president of educational services.

An ACT career-preference survey last year of more than 1 million graduating seniors showed declining interest in computer technology, teaching, engineering and health sciences — all fields with high demand. Meanwhile, there was an increased interest in visual and performing arts far out of proportion with available jobs.

Some argue that it is unrealistic to expect young people to make practical career decisions. After all, most people in the middle of their work lives didn't pick their current occupations when they were 17 or 18 but took indirect routes to their careers.

Yet, the stakes are higher now for students who don't make good choices. "In the past, there was a little bit less concern if students were not informed about how their interests align with workplace opportunities, because, frankly, there was a lower threshold of skill required to pursue a number of job possibilities," Carstensen says.

Moreover, high school counselors who are expected to help students pick sensible careers are overstretched. The average counselor-student ratio is 1-to-561. [12] And, when career counselors steer students toward the kinds of good-paying, paraprofessional or technical jobs that are in high demand, parents often object.

"Parents don't accept trades as an option," says Verne Farrell, career counselor at Main Township East High School in Chicago.

"It is an interesting paradox because many of the high-skilled, high-salary opportunities do not necessarily carry with them a baccalaureate credential," Carstensen says.

Others blame unrealistic job selections on the overemphasis on standardized test scores, which only indicate how much content high school students have retained. But schools fail to teach students how to apply the information, says Geoff Jones, headmaster of the Potomac School in Maryland and former principal at Thomas Jefferson High School for Science and Technology in Alexandria, Va. "There's a mismatch in terms of what we really expect of our work force," he says.

The same experts argue, however, that students shouldn't be pushed prematurely into career slots. "One of the great strengths of our society is that we provide individual latitude in pursuit of whatever our life work is going to be," Carstensen says. Yet, he, too, would like students to consider job-market realities more seriously.

"It's difficult for kids to make these decisions when they've had such limited [work] experience," says Mark Kuranz, a counselor in Racine, Wis., and past president of the American School Counselors Association. "There are certain things you can't understand and integrate until you are developmentally ready and have had life experiences."

Yet, some high school students are in touch with job realities. Besides the legions working at malls and restaurants, some have made more serious forays into the working world. Adam Roston, a senior at Deerfield High School outside of Chicago, has run a video production company since 10th grade. He pulls in as much as $1,200 each weekend he films a bar mitzvah or birthday party, and has learned to cut expenses and underbid competitors. "I'm learning business skills, people skills and how to organize," Roston says. He plans to study business and knows he will need cut-

ting-edge skills to remain in demand.

Around the country, some schools work hard to teach the skills students will need. As Thomas Jefferson's founding principal 15 years ago, Jones worked closely with the business community to develop courses designed to make students think in terms of dynamic systems, instead of stagnant pieces of information.

One semester, for example, ninth-graders at Thomas Jefferson answered a local community's request for proposals (RFP) and submitted a bid to monitor pollution in neighborhood streams most likely caused by lawn runoff, Jones says. They worked with the local government, residents and park officials. The RFP was similar to those produced by firms bidding for the project in the real marketplace.

In addition, today's vocational education courses allow students in mainstream schools to hold internships at companies and agencies in their communities. Old-style vocational courses — like welding or woodworking — have been replaced by classes that teach professional skills, such as accounting and finance.

Last summer, for instance, Charlotte high school senior Angela Campbell worked in the city's finance department as part of her plan to become a certified public accountant. She takes traditional college-prep academics, as well as vocational/technical track finance courses. (*See "At Issue," p. 251.*)

Local contributions to school spending affect the quality of the career counseling that students receive, according to Karen Isenburg, head of career and technical education at Charlotte-Mecklenburg public schools. As a result, well-heeled communities tend to offer more professional career experiences, she says.

In any case, most students eventually align themselves with the job market. Robert L. Kent, career services director at West Virginia University, sees many former students returning in

Is Public Service "In" Again?

Ambitious, young job seekers usually don't consider government work, what with the low pay, cumbersome application process and lack of public esteem.

But Sept. 11 may have changed all that. The terrorist attacks in New York City and Washington have engendered new respect for both federal and local public employees, especially those on the front lines of the war against terrorism. Following the attacks, postal workers, firemen and law enforcement officers emerged as the nation's new heroes.

As a result, some labor experts say Washington once again may see the "best and the brightest" heading for government work, just as they did during the New Deal, World War II, the Great Society programs of the 1960s and the Vietnam War.

Kristine Kippins, a senior at the University of Pennsylvania's Wharton School of Business, may be among them. She was on track for a high-paying job on Wall Street. But after the death of a high school friend in the World Trade Center collapse, Kristine decided to join the Peace Corps.

"Wall Street just doesn't seem very important anymore," she said. "Anybody in the Peace Corps is kind of an ambassador for the U.S. Hopefully, if just a couple of people could see that we're not all that bad, it could make a difference." [1] She plans eventually to run for Congress.

Although some media have interpreted such anecdotes about newly patriotic students switching to government jobs as proof of a trend, opinion polls and other indicators present a more confusing picture.

At PoliTemps, a political staffing service, applications from job seekers have jumped 40 percent since the summer, of which 15 percent occurred after Sept. 11. Founder Chris Jones thinks the post-Sept. 11 increase was due largely to a renewed sense of public service. [2]

A survey by career consultancy HotU Inc. found that 32 percent of college students nationwide are more interested in public service careers now than they were a year ago, compared with 7 percent who were less interested. [3] It was not clear how much of the newfound interest in public-sector jobs was due to patriotism and how much to a lackluster economy. As economic conditions worsened after Sept. 11, private-sector jobs have been harder to come by.

But another poll — commissioned in October by the Partnership for Public Service and the Council for Excellence in Government — shows that despite the surge of patriotism, interest in working for the federal government remains low. The poll found that before the attacks, one in six college students "expressed significant" interest in public work. Afterward, 80 percent said their interest in federal jobs had either stayed the same or decreased. Notably, among professionals, only one in six expressed strong interest, and the attraction to government work dropped as household income rose. [4]

"We apparently appreciate government workers, but we still don't want to become them," said Max Stier, president of the partnership. [5]

Indeed, federal officials were worried about the unattractiveness of federal employment even before Sept. 11. Within three years, more than half of all federal employees — average age 45 — will be eligible to retire, taking with them years of experience and potentially causing a devastating loss of skill and institutional memory.

The Agency for International Development (AID) may be hit hardest, with 50 percent eligible for retirement, according to a Government Accounting Office report. [6] "Three-quarters of the agencies are estimated to have eligibility rates of 30 percent or more," the report said.

Perhaps most disturbing is the fact that a third of the federal emergency workers who responded to the Sept. 11 attacks

their late 20s for new degrees.

"I see more of it every year," he says. "They come back and say it has been painful [out in the job market]. 'I didn't get it then,' they say. 'Now I get it.' "

Will many of today's young people end up in "bad" jobs?

Some labor market experts say finding a "good" job — offering decent wages and benefits, security and upward mobility — is harder now that technology has gutted the ranks of mid-level employees.

As satirist P. J. O'Rourke noted: "The Internet is 'flattening organiza-

tions.' All those expensive middle-management types are being fired because nowadays the CEO of Taco Bell can be in direct communication with his employees simply by logging on and e-mailing the zitty kid behind the counter in Dayton: 'Time to nuke some more Chalupas.' " [13]

Besides technology, experts blame globalization and the simultaneous shrinkage of union membership and bargaining power for the declining supply of quality jobs. Both trends have allowed many companies to slash benefits, often by "outsourcing" tasks to low-paid, non-union workers overseas or to domestic contract and temporary workers, who

usually do not qualify for benefits. [14]

"Almost 40 percent of men and 50 percent of women do not receive health insurance from their main jobs, and nearly half the men and over half the women receive no pension benefits," according to a recent study in the *American Sociological Review.* [15]

High-salary, high-tech positions are not expected to add as many new jobs as low-skill, low-compensation jobs. The food-preparation, fast-food and customer-service industries combined will create the most new jobs — 1.3 million — in the next decade. [16] (*See chart, p. 239.*) Likewise, office clerks, janitors, teachers' aides, waitresses and will reach retirement age within five years.

As a result, an anxious Uncle Sam is using patriotism to appeal to Americans to join the ranks of essential emergency response personnel. "We need people who will rise to the occasion and respond to the need for public service NOW," the top government hirer, Office of Personnel Management Director Kay Coles James, said in an open letter to students, sent to campus newspapers across the country. The letter was prompted by thousands of student inquiries about potential government jobs.

James' letter listed the areas of greatest need as FBI investigators, CIA agents, Centers for Disease Control epidemic monitors; Food and Drug Administration staffers responsible for keeping the blood supply clean; Federal Reserve Board analysts who watch for attacks on the banking system and Environmental Protection Agency monitors, who check for the presence of toxic chemicals or biohazards.

Congress is mulling reforms to make federal work more attractive. Legislation to forgive student loans for talented people who go to work for the government may come up this

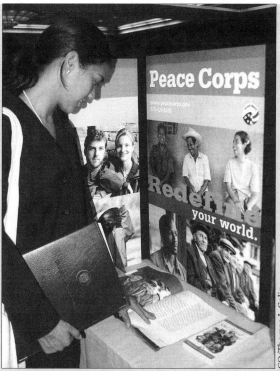

CQ/Thomas J. Colin

In a dramatic reversal, students at Georgetown University's career fair last October showed far more interest in the Peace Corps, military service and intelligence gathering than in Wall Street careers.

year. And Sens. George Voinovich, R-Ohio, and Fred Thompson, R-Tenn., have introduced the Federal Human Capital Act, calling for appointment of a chief human capital officer for each federal agency to assess labor needs, improve recruitment and enhance workplace culture.

"We can see this work force shortage coming," partnership director Stier said. "If we don't get more folks trained, we will have no one to blame but ourselves." [7]

[1] Neil Irwin and Amy Joyce, "In Pursuit of Idealism: With the Nation at War and Job Prospects Bleak, Students Consider Public Service," *The Washington Post*, Oct. 22, 2001, p. E1.

[2] *Ibid.*

[3] *Ibid.*

[4] Peter D. Hart and Robert M. Teeter, nationwide poll, "The Unanswered call to Public Service: Americans' Attitudes Before and After September 11," The Partnership for Public Service and the Council for Excellence in Government, Oct. 23, 2001.

[5] Stephen Barr, "Federal Diary: Many Feel Good About Government; Few Want to Work for It," *The Washington Post*, Oct. 24, 2001, p. B2.

[6] General Accounting Office, "Federal Employee Retirements: Expected Increase Over the Next Five Years Illustrates Need for Planning," GAO-01-509, April 2001, p.5.

[7] "US Govt. Search For Staff Becomes Urgent After Attacks," *Dow Jones International News*, Nov. 5, 2001.

groundskeepers will be in high demand.

Thus, now and at least for the next six years, job hunters will increasingly find jobs with poor pay and benefits, according to BLS estimates. [17] Jobs that require only on-the-job training and fall into the bottom half of the pay range (most in the lowest quartile) accounted for seven of 10 jobs in 2000. [18] Not only that, but by 2010, 18 of the 30 occupations expected to add the most workers fall into this category.

"Setting aside the very tragic events of Sept. 11, this is probably the best of times in some respects for individuals who have competitive skill sets

and the worst of times for those who do not," says ACT's Carstensen. "We're seeing a greater divide between the haves and the have nots."

According to the 1998 book *New Rules for a New Economy: Employment and Opportunity in Postindustrial America*, "America's New Economy has shown that it can generate jobs. It has not shown that it can generate enough good jobs." [19]

Manufacturing once offered the most good-paying, secure jobs with solid benefits. However, thanks in large part to globalization, U.S. factory jobs now account for only about 15 percent of employment. [20]

"The service sector now dominates the American economy, and the service sector is very bifurcated," says University of Oregon sociology Professor Ken Hudson. "It has created very good jobs and very bad jobs. Things that we would consider undesirable about jobs come together in the bad jobs — low wages, no benefits and no job security. At the other end are jobs like mine, with autonomy, security and interesting work."

Economist Stephen Herzenberg, a co-author of *New Rules for a New Economy*, suggests that wages are the most important factor in turning a bad job into a good one. "The minimum hourly wage would now be over $7 if it had kept pace with inflation since 1968 — and $12 if it had kept pace with productivity," he says. The current $5.15 per hour minimum wage has not been raised since 1997, and repeated attempts to raise it have failed. [21]

Education and training will remain the key to getting good jobs, according to Herzenberg and his co-authors. "Higher education reduces bad job characteristics for both sexes," they wrote. [22]

Herzenberg also sees bright spots in the labor outlook. About 40 percent of the work force heads to a good job each day, he says. Many other desirable jobs pay fairly well and don't require extensive education and training. For instance, a growing number of jobs — like paralegals and respiratory therapists — only require an associate's degree whiles others mainly call for on-the-job training, such as desktop publishing and computer repair, according to the BLS. In addition, nurses and teachers — who garner solid salaries and benefits — are always in demand.

AEI's Kosters argues that some lower-end jobs can be rewarding. "It is wrong to think exclusively in terms of good jobs and bad jobs," he says. He points out, for instance, that many of the new jobs catering to retiring Baby Boomers will require a variety of skill levels. "Some things are fairly simple, basic skills — cleaning, making beds, nursing home caretaking — but some others are more sophisticated," such as physical therapists and nursing home managers.

In addition, Kosters adds, some of the new jobs will require "a certain kind of initiative and leadership" that wasn't a requirement for a factory worker.

Herzenberg notes that it's a gross overgeneralization to say that all "service jobs" are a grind. "The teenager serving hamburgers and French fries at a local fast-food restaurant may be the stereotype of the service worker," he says, "but Michael Jordan and Michael Jackson are service workers, too, as are investment bankers and computer professionals."

And not all low-rung jobs are dead-ends, say labor experts. Some progressive employers create career tracks and training to help poorly skilled entrants move up.

For instance, home health aides — usually considered a low-paying, thankless job — are in high and growing demand. Cooperative Home Care Associates pays above the norm, offers free health insurance and pays for public transportation. It also offers training for aides who want to become licensed practical nurses. As a result, it attracts a better pool of candidates, and its turnover is below 20 percent, much lower than the industry average. [23]

Will future employees and companies be loyal to each other?

In 1982, Cyndi Pearce went straight from college to an engineering job with the ITT Corp. in Raleigh, N.C. Like her father, who spent his career as an engineer with Bell South Corp., she anticipated a long tenure.

But four years later, ITT laid off 2,000 employees. Although Pearce didn't get axed, she may have suffered an even worse fate. One day, the 26-year-old systems administrator was told to shut down the computer system at 4 p.m. Don't let anyone touch it, she was advised without explanation. Computer engineers threatened and shouted at her, but she stood her ground. Soon all employees were told to leave the building and were handed white or brown envelopes as they exited; white meant the worker still had a job.

"Those were some of the darkest days of my career," says Pearce, who got a white envelope but soon left voluntarily to work at GE Semiconductor. Six months later, then-CEO Jack "Neutron Jack" Welch decided to get out of the semiconductor business. "Half of the people around me — pooff — disappeared," she recalls.

Like legions of other workers, Pearce was caught in the restructuring and downsizing that swept corporate America from the late 1980s to the mid-'90s. And those corporate belts were being tightened largely at the expense of employee job security. [24]

"After that first layoff, there was no doubt in my mind that my loyalty needed to be to me first," says Pearce, at age 42 now working for her sixth company. "I realized that they really don't care if I am truly successful, and that I'm going to have to take care of that myself."

Companies now expand and contract their work forces based on market demand. Meanwhile, employees' commitments are tied to "the availability of other job options." [25] So, tight labor markets make for more job-hopping. Rare today is the job that promises job security in exchange for employee loyalty.

Economists say employees long for the good old days of lifetime employment. But, in reality, the old days — at least prior to World War II — weren't so good, in terms of job security. It wasn't until World War II that long tenures and in-house promotion ladders become a model.

Contrary to workplace complaints, there's evidence that loyalty survives. Two surveys — one nearly a quarter-century ago and the other more recent — show that loyalty and commitment to employers actually have increased over the past 20 years. [26] A 1977 University of Michigan poll showed that 64 percent of the respondents would, without hesitation, take the same job again. And a 1997 Harris Poll found that 69 percent would choose their current jobs again. [27]

But Karlyn Bowman, an AEI fellow, says people have adjusted their sense of loyalty to a series of shorter-term commitments to match the realities of

Chronology

1930s *Worker-protection laws are passed at federal and state levels.*

1931
Davis-Bacon Act requires prevailing wage rates for laborers on public construction projects.

1932
Norris-LaGuardia Act limits federal injunctions prohibiting unions from strikes or other coercive tactics.

1935
Social Security Act encourages all the states to enact unemployment insurance laws. Congress enacts National Labor Relations Act to govern employer/employee bargaining and union relationships.

1938
Fair Labor Standards Act recognizes division between managers and workers; sets minimum wage, time pay, the 40-hour work week and equal pay and child-labor standards. (An amendment in 1949 prohibits child labor for the first time.)

1940s *Postwar employment boom provides more employment.*

1946
Kelly Services agency for temporary workers is founded.

1947
Labor Management Relations (Taft-Hartley) Act strengthens unions.

1948
Manpower Inc., eventually the world's largest temporary-staffing service, is founded.

1960s–1970s *Technology improves white-collar work life. Worker protections increase.*

1960
"The Pill" allows women to put off motherhood to focus on work.

1964
Title VII of the Civil Rights Act creates the Equal Employment Opportunity Commission to enforce employment anti-discrimination laws.

1968
Age Discrimination in Employment Act protects workers ages 40 to 65.

1970
Occupational Safety and Health Act requires safe working conditions.

1977
Tandy Corp. begins to popularize personal computers. Apple Computer Co. produces a superior model.

1980s–1990s *Corporate America slashes payrolls in newly competitive, global economy; Internet booms.*

1989
Worker Adjustment and Retraining Notification Act requires 60-day notice before plant closings and layoffs.

1990-1991
Recession brings jobless rate to 7.8 percent.

1993
Internet use by business, media and individuals begins to grow exponentially. Xerox Corp. slashes about 10 percent of its payroll.

1994
IBM institutes its first layoffs. Bureau of Labor Statistics begins first comprehensive survey of the nation's contingent work force.

1997
Commerce Department and Information Technology Association of America declare a severe shortage of high-tech workers. Teamsters' Union strikes United Parcel Service over part-time workers and pension issues. Within two weeks, UPS gives in to most Teamster demands. First full-service, online-only bank opens.

2000s *The nation's 10-year expansion collapses into recession after the Web-based boom goes bust.*

March 2000
Average unemployment rate drops to a 30-year low of 3.9 percent; many communities experience even tighter unemployment. On March 11, the Nasdaq bear market begins, and legions of dot-com "millionaires" watch stocks drop.

March 2001
Recession begins, ending the longest expansion in U.S. history.

Sept. 11, 2001
Terrorists bomb World Trade Center and Pentagon, further weakening economy and labor market.

December 2001
Unemployment jumps to 5.8 percent, the highest since April 1995. Since the employment peak in March, job losses in the private sector total 1.4 million.

the labor market. "They expect their experiences to be different, they expect to change jobs a lot more often," Bowman says. "That doesn't mean that while they are at the firm they won't be as loyal, but they may also be looking ahead to the next opportunity."

Employees remain loyal in part because good relations are needed in order to enhance skills and polish résumés. Yet, many employees have transferred their allegiance from companies to fellow workers. "Some of the only loyalty left in the workplace is co-worker loyalty," says Texas marketing expert Caddell. "The more volatile the market and industry, the closer you become with the people around you."

Co-workers and former co-workers often become job-opportunity networkers. Since they worked together at Computer Sciences in 1999, Caddell and former co-worker Kate Goralski have played team tag, making job connections for each other. When Caddell left to join Express Digital, he soon hired Goralski to work on his team. When Express Digital relocated its Austin staff to Colorado, Goralski started looking elsewhere. She interviewed at Vignette, but didn't take the job. Yet, she mentioned Caddell in that interview and he ended up there.

Also, with frequent job changes, people never know who will play a role in their future careers. "I had a fellow working for me, and two years later when the contract changed over, I was working for him," says Raleigh engineer Pearce.

At least some young people don't relish the idea of being a swashbuckling free agent. "I would love nothing more than to get involved in a corporation and move up the ladder and pay my dues," says Chicago high school senior Roston. But after he saw a family friend fired from a longtime bank job, he's not sure it's possible. "It's scary," he says. ∎

BACKGROUND

The Bad Old Days

During the past hundred-plus years, U.S. commerce and industry were primarily based on loose, contingent arrangements between workers and companies. The notion of stable, career-ladder employment was a post-World War II phenomenon, which industry began dismantling in the mid-1980s.

"What many still see as the traditional lifetime employment relationship may well have been a transient phenomenon," wrote Peter Capelli, director of the Center for Human Resources at the University of Pennsylvania's Wharton School and author of *The New Deal at Work* (1999). [28]

In the first half of the 20th century, many companies did pretty much what they are doing today: outsourcing skilled work and using temporary workers when demand surges. [29]

In the early 1900s, for example, the Durant-Dort Carriage Co. — run by William Durant, who would later found General Motors — didn't make a single carriage. A local builder made them, and Durant put his company name on them before selling them. Business grew, and Durant decided to build the carriages in-house. Even then, he only assembled them, after obtaining the parts from local suppliers.

Similarly, early clothing and shoe companies hired hordes of independent contractors to make the goods. The companies had little overhead and could contract and expand production according to demand, avoiding having to pay workers in lean times. [30] In essence, workers were deemed interchangeable parts.

New approaches to labor changed that. In 1913, Henry Ford realized he could reduce his staggering 370 percent

turnover rate if, among other changes, he raised pay and recognized seniority and performance. Turnover dropped to 20 percent, and the idea of longevity with a company began to take hold.

During the 1930s, the Great Depression again turned the tide in favor of workers. Three key pieces of federal legislation began to give employees more power and protection:

- The National Labor Relations Act of 1935 (or Wagner Act), which allowed workers to organize to bargain with companies.
- The Social Security Act of 1935, which created the Social Security system, unemployment insurance and a structure for pension plans.
- The Fair Labor Standards Act of 1938, which established a minimum wage, overtime pay and child-labor restrictions.

The IBM Model

After World War II, a more committed, extended relationship between employer and employee flourished. International Business Machines (IBM) became the epitome of that model. "Big Blue" hired thousands of young employees who stayed for their entire careers and worked their way up.

The company offered low-skill entry points, on-the-job training and prescribed career ladders. Responsibilities were clearly described, and legions of middle managers made sure workers were complying with the rules. Managers felt secure that they could grow old working for the company, and that only an egregious error would derail their careers, or get them booted.

In fact, friendliness and getting along were rewarded more heavily, according to Capelli of the Wharton School. He cites a Purdue University study showing that bonuses were more closely tied to amiability and cooperativeness than to intellectual prowess. [31]

Robots vs. White-Collar Workers

White-collar workers, move over. Robots long have been part of the American labor force, but they generally performed difficult, messy jobs like welding automobiles and handling toxic wastes. But recently, robots have been entering the professional arena. Robotic systems now dispense medications in hospitals and big institutions, and some chain pharmacies are experimenting with them.

"Robotic technology is revolutionizing the pharmacy profession by enabling pharmacists to expedite service to inpatients," said Robert J. Weber, chairman of the pharmacy department at the University of Pittsburgh School of Pharmacy. [1]

Robot pharmacists have a huge advantage over their human counterparts: They almost never make mistakes. "The number of drug errors [made by robots] is virtually zero," says William McCormick, professor of pharmacy administration at the University of Houston. ROBOT-Rx, a drug-dispensing system used in several Dallas hospitals, purportedly filled 45 million doses without an error in its first few years. [2] The system is made by the pharmaceutical firm McKesson Inc.

Yet, most consumers won't see robots at their corner drug store anytime soon. Robotic pharmacy systems can cost nearly $1 million, so it makes sense to use them to serve large populations — like the Texas prison system, which hands out 10,000 prescriptions a day.

McCormick points out that robots merely take over the tedious dispensing function, freeing up pharmacists to spend more time on the cognitive part of their jobs — counseling patients and consulting with doctors.

Robotics is part of an automation trend that began to take off in the late 1800s with the mass assembly of Winchester rifles. "The adjectives that characterize the tasks and occupations affected by automation are the 4Ds of robotics: dull, dumb, dangerous and dirty," says Vijay Kumar, a professor of mechanical engineering at the University of Pennsylvania.

Nowadays, however, instead of only performing boring, repetitive tasks, labor-saving robotics, sophisticated software and the Internet are increasingly replacing the middlemen in business-to-business transactions, as well as other professionals.

Stocks and bonds, for instance, are often traded electronically now. The Internet has made obsolete many salesmen who once bought and sold industrial and commercial raw materials. Web-based systems are replacing human-resources personnel and meeting planners. Digitally driven online instruction is taking the place of trainers, teachers and college professors. Pilotless helicopters produce aerial photos for commercial use.

Robotics has even gone to Hollywood. Director Andrew Niccol is using a computer-generated actress to play opposite Al Pacino in the upcoming movie "Simone." And a software program makes high-quality copies of classic paintings. [3]

Yet, experts say most jobs for humans are safe, because robots and software still lack intelligence. "Any task that requires a minimum IQ level will remain out of reach of automation in the foreseeable future," Kumar says.

For example, robotic arms used by surgeons to perform certain types of delicate surgery allow tinier incisions and quicker recovery. But the surgeon is still needed to maneuver the tiny surgical arms with joysticks and make on-the-spot judgment calls.

Moreover, the human craving for contact with other people, rather than machines, apparently has stalled the march of job-stealing software in certain fields. Online mortgages, for example, have not taken off as fast as expected, presumably because consumers feel more comfortable dealing with other people. A recent study predicted that by 2004 a quarter of all mortgages would be handled online. Currently, however, only 5 percent of mortgages are handled digitally. But homeowners seem comfortable refinancing online. [4]

Humans also beat out automation when it comes to producing graphic art. The distinctive dot portraits of newsmakers featured daily in *The Wall Street Journal* — known as stipple drawings — have been done by hand for more than two decades. The task takes a graphic artist a full day. When the *Journal* tried software that creates stipple drawings much faster, editors quickly dismissed the idea because the software could not match the image created with a human hand tapping away for hours.

R. Martin Spencer, president of Atlanta-based GeckoSystems Inc., which is creating an automated system to monitor the pulse rates of elderly people living alone, says the creative arts are perhaps the safest haven from automation, especially political cartoons.

"There is always a twist," Spencer says. "I don't expect a machine to have a sense of humor for some time, or to be ironic or cynical or sarcastic, much less express that visually."

---

[1] Quoted from a University of Pittsburgh Medical Center press release, May 3, 2001.

[2] Maurice Marram, "Dallas hospitals pioneer use of robotics in O.R., pharmacy," *Dallas Business Journal*, May 29, 1998.

[3] Kevin Maney, "Artificial intelligence isn't just a movie: machines, software that 'think' no longer folly of science fiction," *USA Today*, June 20, 2001.

[4] Bob Tedeschi, "E-Commerce Report: In a shaky economic climate, mortgage refinancings have helped one segment of business: online lenders," *The New York Times*, Oct. 22, 2001, p. C8.

The cozy system also was seen as cultish. In his 1956 classic on the era, *The Organization Man*, reformist sociologist William H. Whyte examined the subjugation of the individual to the company.

Blue-collar laborers also were protected — by both heavy-handed union representation and a seniority system originally designed as an incentive for longevity. In industries where cyclical layoffs were common, the last one hired would be the first one idled, so many workers with substantial seniority could expect to work without interruption. But the protective shield soon would be penetrated.

Downsizing Dinosaurs

A combination of forces led to the IBM model's fall from grace during the economic restructuring that hit the United States in the mid-to-late 1980s. Labor-intensive companies like IBM began to be seen as industrial dinosaurs. The era's new technology enabled top-level managers to communicate directly with employees at the lowest levels of the corporation, and permitted automated monitoring of work output and quality. Almost overnight, middle managers became obsolete.

At the same time, America's postwar industrial dominance had eroded. Competition from overseas threatened nearly every industry. In addition, domestic discount retailers threatened giant department store chains, not to mention small mom-and-pop operations. Companies could no longer afford inefficiency and waste.

In an increasingly service-oriented marketplace, the power and size of labor unions have diminished. Concentrated mainly in manufacturing industries, unions find it difficult to organize cashiers, telemarketers and other workers whose ranks are swelling. To add to the upheavals, deregulation triggered the breakup of monopolies like AT&T.

The textile industry's manufacturing and clothing-assembly operations were especially hard hit by globalization. Many factories moved abroad, either to low-wage countries overseas or to *maquiladoras*, duty-free plants just across the border in Mexico, often owned by U.S. concerns.

In fall 1993, Congress approved the North American Free Trade Agreement (NAFTA), which strengthened trade relationships between the United States, Mexico and Canada. In the agreement's first seven years, 83,258 textile jobs "went south," according to the Economic Policy Institute. [32]

Manufacturers like Ford Motor Co. moved many of their jobs overseas to lower-wage countries, even as Toyota, Honda, Mercedes and other foreign firms moved manufacturing into the United States, which put production closer to millions of potential customers and provided significant tax breaks and other economic incentives offered by local and state governments.

Displaced auto and textile workers were told that their futures were in service industries and technology jobs. But by the end of the 1990s, amid the longest economic boom and lowest unemployment rates in recent history, technology jobs were being increasingly outsourced to low-wage countries like India, Ireland and the Philippines.

In addition, when technology companies complained of a dire shortage of high-tech workers, Congress created a special, six-year H-1B visa for foreign technology workers. Hundreds of thousands of so-called H-1B workers from Russia, the Philippines, India, Ireland and other nations entered the country, even as some older and higher-paid U.S. technology workers claimed they were being laid off. [33]

Meanwhile, those at the lower levels of the job market found their buying power declining in real terms, as the minimum wage moved up only about $1 (in 1999 dollars) between 1955 and 1999. [34]

"Wage inequality has grown as firms have contracted out work once performed by their own employees," economist Herzenberg wrote. [35] "Janitorial, food-service and security jobs that once paid big-company wages and benefits are more often isolated in low-cost suppliers that rely on low-paid contingent workers." [36]

In 1999, fears that catastrophic computer crashes could occur during the calendar rollover from 1999 to 2000 created an upward blip in technology employment, as companies spent millions of dollars to protect their systems from crashing in the Y-2K debacle that never materialized. To save memory, many computers had been programmed with two-digit year identification and would not register the correct year without remedies. [37]

Companies became slaves to their latest quarterly earnings. Average Americans plunged into the stock-trading game. The latest uptick or downtick of a publicly traded firm became common conversation, as new investors from all strata watched the market reach dizzying, record-breaking heights.

Businesses and entrepreneurs became infatuated with the idea of making big profits from Web sites that connected everyday necessities and interests with the Internet. Companies offering everything from online grocery shopping to Internet health advice paid employees, in part, with stock shares and options that made many millionaires, at least on paper. [38]

Then the market crashed. Among the more spectacular dot-com failures was Webvan Group, which expected many Americans to order groceries online and pay a premium for same-day delivery. Launched on June 2, 1999, the grocery service boasted vast, automated warehouses around the country costing $30 million to $40 million each.

Two years later, Webvan had an accumulated deficit of $829 million. Last fall, it held the largest dot-com liquidation sale in 2001. Webvan Group stock traded at nearly $35 a share in 1999. On Dec. 5, 2001, shares traded at $.0015, or one-tenth of a cent. [39] ∎

CURRENT SITUATION

Waiting Out a Recession

"Facing Decreased Demand for Coins, Mint Starts Layoffs." The recent newspaper headline clearly signaled that the current economy and job market is seriously ailing. The accompanying article went on to explain that the U.S. Mint will produce only 15 billion new pennies, nickels, dimes and quarters this year, down from the original target of 25 billion coins. [40]

The overall drop in demand for pocket change is due to less consumer spending, which can be traced to job layoffs, a Mint official said. And the layoffs have probably prompted many Americans to tap those jars full of coins on dresser tops.

About 1.4 million jobs were jettisoned from March 2001, when the current recession began, through the end of the year. The 468,000 private-sector jobs that disappeared in October, following the Sept. 11 terrorist attacks, represented the biggest monthly decline in more than a quarter-century. Last year, the average unemployment rate was 4.8 percent, up from 4.0 percent in 2000, according to the BLS.

As recent college graduates know, this is not a good time to look for a job. A group of 2001 MBA graduates from Babson College formed a weekly support group to share job leads and commiserate.

"I would hope this group would end by Christmas, but that might be generous given what we've seen in the market," said LaVerne Cerfolio, 33, co-founder of Babson Unemployment Support Team (BUST). [41]

Even employment recruiters are losing their jobs. Some are considering new careers, including teaching high-school science, a job chronically in high demand. [42]

Experts disagree over when the current recession — the nation's 11th in 60 years — will end. Post-World War II recessions usually lasted just over 10 months. The National Bureau of Economic Research officially put the start of the trough at last March. [43] And while bureau economists disagree over how strong the eventual rebound will be, they expect an upswing the

first half of this year. [44]

But federal lawmakers weren't able to agree on an economic stimulus package, and no final action was taken before they adjourned in December. They are expected to revisit economic-stimulus legislation this year.

Bright Spots

Not every industry is shaving workers. Security firms have expanded since the terrorist attacks. Military contractors, who produce everything from combat boots to weapon sensors, are hiring. And low-interest rates have fostered frenetic activity in the mortgage industry.

Indeed, parts of the mortgage industry are looking for workers. "Anytime we hear about a group laying off, we try to make contact with that company's human resources department to look for workers," said Leora Goren, managing director for human resources at Countrywide Home Loans. [45]

Payrolls are also rising in other industries. Health care and pharmaceutical companies are hiring and will

need more workers as the population ages. Nursing homes, assisted-living facilities and other services for the elderly will need workers.

Highly specialized fields are booming, such as bioinformatics — a hybrid of biology, mathematics and computer science. [46] Bioinformatics specialists use computers to analyze newly discovered data about human genes, thus speeding the research and development of new drugs. The fledgling industry may need as many as 20,000 scientists by 2005. [47] It's unlikely they'll be available, but universities are rushing to fill the need.

Bioinformatics also is providing a boom for computer makers and boosting their employment in specific areas. IBM, for instance, is spending $100 million to build a supercomputer that will model the processes of gene proteins. [48]

Lifelong Training

Bioinformatics scientists and other top-level workers will have to constantly upgrade their skills, as will

Survival Advice for Future Workers

For most young people, the government's job-outlook figures are just "a lot of numbers on a page," says high school guidance counselor Renee Kersey of Charlotte, N.C. Most high school seniors and college students choosing a career never even look at the projections for which jobs will be most in demand, provided free of charge on the Bureau of Labor Statistics (BLS) Web site, she says.

The students are much more interested in the numbers that will appear on their paychecks. Salary is their top consideration, guidance counselors say, and the second biggest consideration is doing what they enjoy.

But these days, when the best jobs require solid education, and entry-level jobs with career-advancement potential are relatively rare, career counselors advise young people to weigh the long-term needs of the job market.

Once students have identified their interests, commonsense should be part of the career-selection process, advises Don Carstensen, vice president of educational services at ACT Inc., a college entrance exam service. "Focusing a little bit more on the practical realities — the true employment opportunities — [needs to] play a role here," he says.

Educators and current employees have other advice for young people about to begin what eventually could become 45 years of work. Above all, they say, workers must continually upgrade their skills because the best jobs require higher levels of education. Gaining new skills "is never going to be over," says Mark Kuranz, past president of the American School Counselors Association.

Workers will need to be especially flexible, according to Geoff Jones, headmaster of the Potomac School, near Washington, D.C. "Workplaces are changing more rapidly than ever before," he says, "so individuals need to be more adaptable."

Most counselors agree that students must be ready for a rapid series of job changes. In the 1970s, the average U.S. worker held 9.2 jobs between the ages of 18 and 34, according to a BLS 20-year longitudinal survey. More than half of those jobs were held before age 24. [1]

Future workers will especially need good interpersonal and negotiating skills, because of the greater likelihood that they will change jobs frequently and will either work under contract or make contract hires.

The ability to work in teams is also critical. "Most of our work is done collaboratively," Jones says. "We don't individually and heroically carry the day. Our successes are built on teams."

Teamwork and the ability to get along with a variety of people isn't only required for high-level jobs. Career counselors say it is equally important for the legions working in the service industry, most of whom will deal face-to-face with the public every day.

Consultant Leslie Cline helps major corporations seeking to improve teamwork. "I provide them with tools for handling interpersonal conflicts, getting everyone's best ideas and putting aside personal interests for what is best for the group," she says.

New workers also will need to have a deep understanding of diversity, she adds. "Not just age, race and sex," she says. "If you and I look at things differently, that's diversity."

---

[1] "Number of Jobs Held, Labor Market Activity and Earnings Growth Over Two Decades: Results from a Longitudinal Survey," National Longitudinal Survey of Youth 1979, U.S. Bureau of Labor Statistics, April 2001.

less skilled workers.

For the last couple of generations, education opportunities have been clear-cut: Students could choose from college degrees, associate's degrees, skill-training programs or on-the-job training. Now, however, rapid technological changes and intense global competition are forcing workers to constantly update their skills and education. Workers either keep pace or find themselves relegated to low-skill, low-pay jobs.

"There's a skills/wage divide," Carstensen of ACT says. "People are really secure only to the extent that they are a value-added contributor to their employer."

With the marketplace's voracious appetite for new skills, new approaches to training will become commonplace. "There's going to be so much change in what constitutes an education," says Smith of the National Association for College Admissions Counseling. "Education doesn't just mean the pursuit of formal degrees, it means individual courses, certificates, professional education programs lasting anywhere from a few days to a few months."

Unfortunately, the need for regular re-education comes at a time when companies are less inclined to spend money on training. According to the New York City-based Century Foundation, U.S. companies have a $120 billion "training gap. [49] That is, they are spending an estimated $40 billion on worker training (just over 1 percent of payroll) but would need to spend $160 billion to make enhancing employees' skills a higher priority. [50]

The foundation also reported that only 10 percent of American workers receive any formal training from employers. Most are "white-collar executives, technicians and other already well-educated workers; lower-echelon employees typically receive little if any training."

Generally, companies spend more on training when unemployment is low, and less when it is high. But in some cases, even with tight employment, they don't want to invest in training for fear the newly skilled employee will skip over to a competitor who will benefit from the investment.

At Issue:

Should all high school students be required to take some vocational or technical courses?

N. L. McCASLIN
SITE DIRECTOR, NATIONAL CENTERS FOR CAREER AND TECHNICAL EDUCATION THE OHIO STATE UNIVERSITY

WRITTEN FOR THE CQ RESEARCHER, JANUARY 2002

*a*ll parents want their children to become financially independent and able to function as responsible members of society. Technological advances, greater international competition and changes in the way businesses and industries are managed and operated are affecting the type of skills needed by workers in the United States. If schools fail to prepare students for both employment and further education, students will find themselves unable to earn a living and thus dependent upon society for support.

Career and technical-education students develop the academic and technical skills needed in areas ranging from entry-level through professional-level positions. Recent research has found that academic performance in core subjects was similar both for students who concentrated on academic courses and those who took academic and career/technical education courses.

Career and technical-education students also learn about occupations and skills needed to locate and secure employment. Schools have begun to implement four major forms of career-development activities: (1) work-based career interventions; (2) advising interventions; (3) introductory career interventions and (4) curriculum-based career interventions. Career and technical education enables students to see their courses in a context that interests them and gives them a focus and purpose for continuing their education.

Students in career and technical education are provided the opportunity to prepare themselves to directly enter the labor market and/or to continue their education at postsecondary institutions. Today's career and technical-education programs prepare students for broad career pathways rather than narrowly focused occupations with limited opportunities.

The Census Bureau reports that approximately 15 percent of the students in grades 10, 11 and 12 dropped out of high school during 1999. However, it did not take into account students dropping out prior to the 10th grade in that year. The nation's dropout rates are most severe in big-city high schools, where more than 50 percent of freshmen drop out. Recent research found that career and technical education helped reduce the likelihood of dropping out of high school.

Only about 20 percent of high school graduates actually graduate from college. That leaves the remaining 80 percent to develop the academic and technical skills needed for employment however they can.

MARC TUCKER
PRESIDENT, NATIONAL CENTER ON EDUCATION AND THE ECONOMY

WRITTEN FOR THE CQ RESEARCHER, JANUARY 2002

*m*ost students nowadays eventually get a diploma or degree that is intended to qualify them for a job of some kind. In that sense, all education is vocational. Conversely, it is also true that a swiftly rising proportion of jobs requires strong academic skills. So, in that sense, all education is academic.

But first things first. In an age in which many automobile dealers will hire only graduates of two-year college programs, a student who is not ready to do college-level work is often condemned to a lifetime of economic struggle. It follows that the first obligation of every high school is to make sure that all students graduate ready to do college-level work without remediation.

As a practical matter, this means that they have to be able to read, write and do mathematics at the college level by the time they graduate from high school.

In many of the countries with which the United States competes, this is a standard that students must meet by the end of their 10th year in school. There is no reason why we should not set the same standard here.

A student who has met that standard by the end of their sophomore year in high school — or any time after that — should be able to proceed directly to a community or technical college to obtain a high-quality technical or vocational education, if that is what the student wants.

Why shouldn't that student stay in high school for further vocational or technical education and training? Because there are few high schools in this country that can afford the very expensive equipment that is used in modern industrial workplaces, nor can they afford to hire the kinds of people who have the skills needed to teach fully current skills to the students. Those people and that equipment are in our community and technical colleges, and that is where the students should go for that kind of education.

There is no question that we must do a much better job of vocational and technical education. The key to getting there is to let each institution do what it is best suited to do. The core business of the high school should be getting the academics right.

The local community or technical college should provide the technical and vocational skills. Following this scheme would cost no more than we are currently spending but would produce a vastly better result.

"It was difficult to find a company willing to train me," says Raleigh engineer Pearce. "They use the same excuse: 'If we train you, you are just going to leave.' They had a better chance of retaining me if they made me happy."

However, some companies have enhanced their training programs to lure and retain employees. Merrill Lynch, for instance, made its information-technology training more cost effective by putting it into standardized modules and offering it to employees. "The company has turned training into a source of competitive advantage for recruiting and retaining employees," said Wharton's Capelli. [51]

Pearce has done what many new workers will have to do: teach themselves. "The Web has been wonderful, you have all that information online," she says. Texas video producer Caddell concurs: "I taught myself Web-page design just to get by."

Career counselor Kersey has taken up the training torch. "I stress to students to get into every training opportunity they can, cross-train, train for somebody else's job, be in the mindset that you will be learning forever."

The Century Foundation advocates federal tax credits to increase companies' investments in training and expanded eligibility for student financial-assistance programs under Title IV of the Higher Education Act.

Unprepared Graduates

If today's high school students are any indication, new workers moving into the job market will need plenty of re-education and training. At a time when the market is demanding higher-level skills, student performance in key subjects, such as math and science, is dismal.

Only 18 percent of high school seniors nationwide in 2000 were "proficient" in science, down from 21 per-

cent in 1996, according to the National Assessment of Educational Progress (NAEP) — better known as the nation's "report card." However, seniors had made slight progress in math over the decade. In a similar national test on math skills, 17 percent of high school seniors in 2000 were proficient, up from 12 percent in 1990.

The NAEP science test, first administered in 1996, is given periodically to 15,000 seniors at public and private schools. Students are ranked as performing at: below basic, basic, proficient or advanced.

Education Secretary Ron Paige said it was troubling for the future job market that an overwhelming majority of the seniors were not "proficient" in math or science.

"After all, 12th-grade scores are the scores that really matter," he said. "If our graduates know less about science than their predecessors four years ago, then our hopes for a strong 21st-century work force are dimming just when we need them most." [52]

There is also a mismatch between employees' reading levels and job demands, according to a report last June by the New England Council, a business advocacy organization for six Northeastern states. The report blames the gap in part on a shortage of qualified teachers. In Massachusetts, for instance, about 28 percent of the new teachers hired for middle school and high school in 2000 did not have certification in the fields they were teaching, according to the council.

The survey found that among middle and high school teachers in 2000, 16.2 percent of those teaching technology were not certified to teach that subject. Neither were 13.8 percent of those teaching reading, 6.8 percent of science teachers and 6.6 percent of math teachers.

Unlike high-tech employers, who prefer to let jobs go unfilled rather than hire unskilled workers and train them, school districts must have someone to

run their classes, even if it's someone who lacks proper qualifications.

Educators point out that at the height of the booming technology-driven economy of the late 1990s, many math and science teachers were lured into more lucrative technology jobs at some of the same firms that complained loudest about poor math and science skills. Meanwhile, many of those same enterprises were pitting cities and counties against one another in bidding wars for the greatest tax relief to relocate. The tax breaks were often on property taxes — the source of most city and county education funds. [53]

High school students who graduate ill-equipped for work must receive remediation — either at community colleges or from their employers. Beginning about 10 years ago, declining abilities among high school graduates triggered an increase in remedial courses in colleges, says Edwin A. Trathen, assistant to the president for enrollment management at the State University of New York, North Country. Since then, community colleges have been providing increasing numbers of college remedial classes.

Trathen says his community college must teach basic punctuation and grammar and put many students through a crash course on how to use a library. "We have to teach them how to find a text in the library, how to physically locate it," he says.

"The worst way to prepare for this Third Industrial Revolution is to turn out people who have to take remedial English when they go to college," says William Niskanen, chairman of the Cato Institute.

To help solve the problem in advance, SUNY North Country sends testers into 7th-, 10th- and 11th-grade classes to assess math and English skills. Many students had respectable 80 to 85 grade averages but would have been placed into remedial courses, Trathen says. "We're giving students a wake-up call," he says.

As Niskanen puts it: "The sharpest comment I've heard to describe what's going on here is that it has only taken a century to go from teaching Latin and Greek in high school to teaching remedial English in college." ■

OUTLOOK

Labor Shortage

More than 1 million workers from throughout the labor market lost their jobs in 2001. Many have had trouble getting back onto payrolls during the current recession. Yet, perhaps ironically some experts who look further down the road are concerned about an overall shortage of well-educated young-to-middle-age workers.

Harvard's Ellwood laid out a troubling view of the labor market in the next two decades. [54] He noted that in the last 20 years the labor market grew 35 percent, as 38 million additional employees entered the work force. College-educated workers doubled during the same period to 30 percent of the labor pool, up from 22 percent. [55]

But the future labor market will be a "sputtering" one, Ellwood said. Not only will the prime-age workforce grow by only 3 percent, but the percentage of college-educated workers is expected to rise by 5 percent at best.

As a result, Baby Boomers may be encouraged by companies to delay their retirements and college-educated stay-at-home moms may be lured back into the workforce. But both strategies would be costly, according to Ellwood. [56] Employers will respond by offering incentives to older workers and more training to younger workers, or by exporting more skilled work abroad and importing more temporary workers.

Some experts are optimistic about the post-Generation X group of workers. "If most Americans aren't very hopeful about today's rising generation, it's because so many of them figure that history generally moves in straight lines," futurists Neil Howe and William Strauss wrote in their 2000 book *Millennials Rising: The Next Great Generation.* [57]

Most people assume that the young people in primary and secondary school now will share characteristics of the Baby Boomers and Gen Xers, they assert. "These trends point to more selfishness in personal manner, more splintering in public purpose, more profanity in culture and daily discourse, more risk-taking with sex and drugs, more apathy about politics, and more crime, violence and social decay."

But Howe and Strauss expect children currently on school playgrounds to become drastically different adults than their predecessors. First, they explain, today's children are experiencing an age when children are a key focus of society. While previous generations used contraceptives and abortions, many of these children were the products of fertility struggles, the authors said. Today's kids are more coddled and watched. Many need Day-Timers to keep track of schedules busy with organized sports and lessons.

Teenagers today think it's cool to be smart, the authors said, and today's grade-schoolers score significantly higher on aptitude tests. [58] These future workers, which Howe and Strauss call the "Millennials," are comfortable with technology and are expected to be more inclined toward public service and teamwork.

This view of the upcoming work force is optimistic. Yet, others are fretting about the future labor market. What do young people think? Some, like Jason Milstein, a high school senior in Chicago, don't seem too worried.

"It seems like there are always going to be ups and downs. My goal is to find a job that I'm happy with. If I find something I truly enjoy, it won't even seem like work. That's my hope and goal." ■

Notes

[1] Bureau of Labor Statistics press release, Dec. 7, 2001.

[2] Bureau of Labor Statistics, "Table A-3. Employment status of the civilian population 25 years and over by educational attainment," November 2001.

[3] David T. Ellwood, "The Sputtering Labor Force of the 21st Century: Can Social Policy Help?" National Bureau of Economic Research, Working Paper 8321, June 2001.

[4] *Ibid.*

[5] Daniel E. Hecker, "Occupational employment projections to 2010," *Monthly Labor Review*, Bureau of Labor Statistics, November 2001, pp. 79, 80.

[6] *Ibid.*

[7] Sheryl Gay Stolberg and Judith Miller, "Bioterror Role an Uneasy Fit for Disease Centers," *The New York Times*, Nov. 11, 2001, p. A1.

[8] Quoted in The Associated Press, "More Students File Early Applications to S.C. Universities," *The Charlotte Observer*, Nov. 13, 2001.

[9] For background, see Brian Hansen, "Distance Learning," *The CQ Researcher*, Dec. 7, 2001, pp. 993-1016.

[10] "Human Resources Management Environmental Scan 2000," Society for Human Resource Management, March 2000.

[11] "Trends in Early Retirement," *Facts from EBRI*, July 2001.

[12] "U.S. Student-to-Counselor Ratios," American Counseling Associations, January 2000.

[13] P.J. O'Rourke, *The CEO of the Sofa* (2001), p. 30.

[14] For background, see the following *CQ Researcher* reports by Mary H. Cooper: "Jobs in the 90s," Feb. 28, 1992, pp.169-192; "Employee Benefits," Feb. 4, 2000, pp. 65-88 and "World Trade," June 9, 2000, pp. 497-520. Also see the following *CQ Researchers*: Kenneth Jost, "Labor Movement's Future," June 28, 1996, pp. 553-576; Charles S. Clark, "Contingent Work Force," Oct. 24, 1997, pp. 937-960 and Brian Hansen, "Globalization Backlash," Sept. 28, 2001, pp. 761-784.

[15] Arne L. Kalleberg, Barbara F. Reskin and Ken Hudson, "Bad Jobs in America: Standard and Nonstandard Employment Relations and Job Quality in the United States," *American Sociological Review*, April 2000, Vol. 65, p. 264.

16 Hecker, *op. cit.*, p. 80.

17 Kalleberg, *op. cit.*, p. 264.

18 Hecker, *op. cit.*, pp. 57, 79, 80

19 Stephen A. Herzenberg, John A. Alic and Howard Wial, *New Rules for a New Economy* (1998).

20 *Ibid.*, p. 3.

21 For background, see Kathy Koch, "Child Poverty," *The CQ Researcher*, April 7, 2000, pp. 281-304.

22 Kalleberg, *op. cit.*, p. 270.

23 Herzenberg, *op. cit.*, p. 99.

24 Peter Capelli, *The New Deal at Work: Managing the Market-Driven Workforce* (1999), p. 12.

25 *Ibid.*, p. 39.

26 Karlyn Bowman, "Attitudes About Work and Leisure in America," American Enterprise Institute for Public Policy Research, Aug. 27, 2001.

27 University of Michigan survey for the Department of Labor; Louis Harris & Associates survey for the Families and Work Institute.

28 Capelli, *op. cit.*, p. 62.

29 *Ibid.*, p. 49.

30 *Ibid.*, p. 52.

31 *Ibid.*, p. 65.

32 Robert E. Scott, "NAFTA's Impact on the States: The Industries and States that Suffered the Most in the Agreement's First Seven Years," Supplement to the Economic Policy Institute Briefing Paper, "NAFTA at Seven: Its Impact on Workers in All Three Nations," April 2001.

33 For background, see Kathy Koch, "The High-Tech Labor Shortage," *The CQ Researcher*, April 24, 1998, pp. 361-384.

34 Jared Bernstein and John Schmitt, "The Impact of the Minimum Wage: Policy lifts wages, maintains floor for low-wage labor market," Economic Policy Institute, Briefing Paper, June 27, 2000, p. 3.

35 Herzenberg, *op. cit.*, p. 14.

36 For background, see Mary H. Cooper, "Income Inequality," *The CQ Researcher*, April 17, 1998, pp. 337-360.

37 For background, see Kathy Koch, "Y2K Dilemma," *The CQ Researcher*, Feb. 19, 1999, pp. 137-160.

38 The rapid rise and humiliating fall of Internet companies is clearly outlined in an award-winning documentary, *Startup.com*, by Chris Hedgedus and Jehane Noujam, released on Sept. 18, 2001.

39 Securities and Exchange Commission; Nick Winfield, "Grocer Webvan Reveals Initiatives for Recovery, Including Job Cuts," *The Wall Street Journal*, April 26, 2001; Knight-Ridder Tribune Business News, Oct. 3, 2001; Oct. 31, 2001; www.bigcharts.com, Dec. 6, 2001.

40 The Associated Press, "Facing Decreased Demand for Coins, Mint Starts Layoffs," *The New York Times*, Nov. 24, 2001.

41 Quoted in Kris Maher, "Career Journal: The Jungle," *The Wall Street Journal*, Nov. 13, 2001.

42 *Ibid.*

43 Richard W. Stevenson, "Economists Make It Official: U.S. Is in Recession," *The New York Times*, Nov. 27, 2001, p. C1.

44 *Ibid.*

45 Quoted by Barbara Whitaker, "In the Great Job Desert, Some Hidden Oases," *The New York Times*, Nov. 4, 2001.

46 Brad Stone, "Wanted: Hot Industry Seeks Supergeeks," *Newsweek*, April 30, 2001. p. 54.

47 *Ibid.*, p. 55.

48 *Ibid.*, p. 56.

49 Carl E. Van Horn, "No One Left Behind: The Report of the Twentieth Century Fund Task Force on Retraining the American Workforce," The Century Foundation, 1996.

50 *Ibid.*, 1996.

51 Capelli, *op. cit.*, p. 204.

52 Quoted in Abby Goodnough, "National Science Scores for 12th Graders Slip," *The New York Times*, Nov. 21, 2001, p. A12.

53 For background, see Kathy Koch, "Reforming School Funding," *The CQ Researcher*, Dec. 10, 1999, pp. 1052-1053.

54 Ellwood, *op. cit.*

55 *Ibid.*, p. 3.

56 *Ibid.*, p. 68

57 Neil Howe and William Strauss, *Millennials Rising: The Next Great Generation* (2000).

58 *Ibid.*

FOR MORE INFORMATION

Center for Human Resources, The Wharton School of the University of Pennsylvania, 307 Vance Hall, 3733 Spruce St., Philadelphia, Pa 19104-6358; (215) 898-5606; http://www-management.wharton.upenn.edu/chr/. Founded in 1921, the center researches contemporary human-resources issues.

Century Foundation, formerly Twentieth Century Fund, 41 East 70th St., New York, N.Y. 10021; (212) 534-4441; www.tcf.org. A liberal foundation created in 1919 that analyzes political economic and social issues.

Department of Labor, Bureau of Labor Statistics, Postal Square Building, 2 Massachusetts Ave., N.E., Washington, D.C. 20212-0001; (202) 691-5200; www.bls.gov. The government's principal fact-finding agency in labor economics provides projections for occupations, layoffs and unemployment figures and other indicators.

LPA Public Policy Association of Senior Human Resource Executives, 1015 15th St., N.W., Suite 1200, Washington, D.C., 20005-2605; (202) 789- 8670; www.lpa.org. Formerly the Labor Policy Association, this advocacy organization representing 200 major U.S. employers tracks work-related legislation and offers an up-to-date listing of bills considered and approved in Congress.

National Bureau of Economic Research, 1050 Massachusetts Ave., Cambridge, Mass. 02138; (617) 868-3900; www.nber.org. The nonprofit, nonpartisan research organization, founded in 1920, sponsors economic research by leading scholars.

Bibliography

Selected Sources

Books

Capelli, Peter, *The New Deal at Work: Managing the Market-Driven Workforce*, Harvard Business School Press, 1999.

Capelli, management professor and director of the Center for Human Resources at The Wharton School of the University of Pennsylvania, describes how today's market forces, as well as those 100 years ago, leave workers with less security but better leverage in tight employment.

Ellwood, David T. *et al*, *A Working Nation: Workers, Work, and Government in the New Economy*, Russell Sage Foundation, 2000.

Essays by academics describe the winners and losers in the modern job market and offer varying points of view on policy responses.

Herzenberg, Stephen A., John A. Alic and Howard Wial, *New Rules for a New Economy: Employment and Opportunity in Postindustrial America*, Cornell University Press, 1998.

The authors propose strategies for improving job quality in an economy dominated by the service industry, such as more upward career paths for low-skills jobs and multi-employer institutions to aid in training, information exchange and job referrals.

Mishel, Lawrence, Jared Bernstein and John Schmitt, *The State of Working America: 2000/2001*, Cornell University Press, 2001.

This extensive review of data on wages, jobs and poverty offers regional and international comparisons and examines wage growth and inequality, as well as advances in productivity.

Articles

The Associated Press, "Facing Decreased Demand for Coins, Mint Starts Layoffs," *The New York Times*, Nov. 24, 2001.

The report leaves little doubt that the economy is in a major slump, with U.S. Mint workers losing their jobs and major changes in spending patterns.

Goodnough, Abby, "National Science Scores for 12th Graders Slip," *The New York Times*, Nov. 21, 2001, p. A12.

Goodnough reports the latest poor results of national science tests administered in secondary schools and comments on how this weak competency will impact the future job market.

Kalleberg, Arne L., Barbara F. Reskin and Ken Hudson, "Bad Jobs in America: Standard and Nonstandard Employment Relations and Job Quality in the United States," *American Sociological Review*, April 2000, Vol. 65.

The authors offer criteria for judging "bad" jobs versus "good" jobs and suggest that the current service-oriented marketplace generates more contingent and bad jobs.

Whitaker, Barbara, "In the Great Job Desert, Some Hidden Oases," *The New York Times*, Nov. 4, 2001.

Whitaker outlines pockets of job opportunities amid the massive layoffs during the current recession.

Reports and Studies

Bowman, Karlyn, "Attitudes About Work and Leisure in America," American Enterprise Institute for Public Policy Research, Aug. 27, 2001.

This compilation of opinion polls suggests that employee loyalty is still alive, most people like their jobs, but that more workers than in the past now see their jobs as a means of supporting recreation rather than a primary source of identity.

Ellwood, David T., "The Sputtering Labor Force of the 21st Century: Can Social Policy Help?," Working Paper 8321, National Bureau of Economic Research, June 2001.

Ellwood describes the labor market outlook for the next two decades: slow growth, fewer prime-age employees and less-educated workers. He explores the costs and consequences of several potential policy reactions to a problematic work force.

Hecker, Daniel E., "Occupational employment projections to 2010," *Monthly Labor Review*, Bureau of Labor Statistics, November 2001.

This comprehensive review of Bureau of Labor Statistics' projections of job growth and predicted occupation-based composition of the work force in the next decade shows that occupations requiring either a postsecondary vocational award or an academic degree — which accounted for 29 percent of all jobs in 2000 — will account for 42 percent of total job growth between 2000 and 2010.

Patel, David, "Human Resources Management Environmental Scan 2000," Society for Human Resource Management, March 2000.

Patel considers current employee practices and projects future trends, such as increased outsourcing, jobs moved abroad and how technology will affect future jobs.

14 Regulating the New Economy

ADRIEL BETTELHEIM

The collapse of New York's World Trade Center on Sept. 11 subjected the communications infrastructure of one of the most wired cities on Earth to an unprecedented test.

Falling debris severely damaged and disabled a Verizon Communications switching facility with 3.5 million data circuits that served 200,000 of the regional Bell company's voice customers. Wireless phone relay stations were swamped with calls that at moments spiked to 10 times average levels. Computers with dedicated connections to automated equipment in the destroyed towers added to the congestion by continually redialing. For hours, wireless or cellular customers received messages informing them that all circuits were busy. [1]

Internet traffic, on the other hand, hardly slowed down. Thousands used e-mail to check on the safety of friends or loved ones. Others joined online forums to discuss the attacks. A Harris Interactive poll of 4,610 adults conducted in the hours after the catastrophe found 64 percent had used online sources of information to learn more about the attacks by two hijacked airliners. Many observers hailed the continuous flow of information during the calamity as proof of the Internet's versatility and strength.

"Through the darkest week in the nation's history, Americans remained connected," says Harris Miller, president of the Information Technology Association of America.

The resiliency of the Internet back-

From *The CQ Researcher,*
October 19, 2001.

The Sept. 11 terrorist attack on the World Trade Center disabled a major telephone switching facility, here being toured by Federal Communications Commission Chairman Michael K. Powell, second from right. However, the catastrophe barely slowed Internet traffic, which many observers said was proof of the Internet's strength.

Verizon

bone could serve as an apt metaphor for the entire communications sector in the aftermath of Sept. 11. Because communications systems are decentralized and have features to back up each other, the industry emerged from the experience appearing much less vulnerable than airlines, insurers or financial institutions. Phone service in parts of lower Manhattan was restored soon after the attacks, as communications companies trucked in portable systems.

But the attacks are raising new questions about the future of telecommunications and the new economy. America's newly exposed vulnerability — particularly reports that the hijackers purchased tickets and conducted other business online — has intensified calls for expanded surveillance of electronic information on the Internet and wireless phone networks.

A little more than a week after the attacks, Congress began debating whether to give the Department of Justice expanded power to track and intercept e-mails and other Internet activity in order to detect terrorist conspiracies. Law enforcement officials say they need to liberally use available technologies to assess threats before terrorists strike. Civil libertarians and privacy advocates say such surveillance can infringe on the constitutional rights of unsuspecting Americans.

The new focus on eavesdropping is in marked contrast to the tone in the months leading up to the attacks, when Congress appeared poised to pass new standards to protect personal information on the World Wide Web. Lawmakers and high-tech leaders were close to an agreement on some minimal privacy standards, including notification that personal information was being collected on commercial Web sites and establishing "opt out" boxes on sites allowing consumers to block their information from being shared with third parties.

"The new debate over cybersurveillance seems to stem from the fact that technology, while it frees us from physical constraints, does the same for those who wish to do us harm," says Adam Thierer, director of telecommunications studies at the Cato Institute, a Washington think tank. "The balancing act between liberty and security will require a renewed focus on what constitutes an unreasonable search in the world of seamless communications."

The attacks have also triggered greater emphasis on securing corporate and government computer networks, which control everything from financial transactions to operations at

The Growing Voice/Data Market

As telecommunications technology converges, the market in voice and data services is expected to grow to more than $450 billion by 2004, including $36 billion in high-speed broadband services.

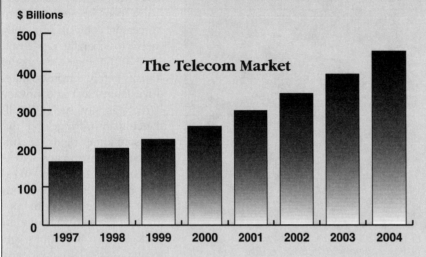

$ Billions

The Telecom Market

Source: "2001 MultiMedia Telecommunications Market Review and Forecast," Telecommunications Industry Association

nuclear power plants and the air-traffic control system. Many government officials and security consultants believe the systems could be tempting targets for future attacks.

Policymakers are considering steps to encourage companies in the electric power, telecommunications, oil and gas, banking, finance and transportation sectors to share security information with the government by guaranteeing them confidentiality. Companies traditionally have been reluctant to share details about their vulnerabilities, fearing disclosure could hurt them competitively. Among the policies being considered to encourage reporting are exempting reports on computer attacks from the Freedom of Information Act and providing some antitrust exemptions for companies that cooperate to fight computer hacking, viruses, worms and other intrusions.

"A cyberattack could potentially impact our national economy, infrastructure, businesses and citizens in very harmful ways," Republican Gov.

James S. Gilmore III of Virginia, chairman of a domestic terrorism task force, told a House Intelligence Committee hearing on Sept. 26.

Response to the Sept. 11 attacks has also — at least temporarily — pushed other key elements of the new-economy agenda to policymakers' back burners. Chief among these are efforts to encourage the deployment of high-speed "broadband" Internet service to poor and outlying areas to narrow the so-called digital divide between Americans who have high-level Internet service and those who don't. Prior to Sept. 11, a furious lobbying war was under way over proposals that would offer regulatory relief to regional Bell companies so they could offer data services outside of their service regions. [2]

Also looming is a debate on whether to extend a moratorium on the taxation of Internet sales that expires on Oct. 21. Policymakers will have to decide whether to let the moratorium lapse, extend it or make it perma-

nent. The decision will come as cash-strapped states are realizing that they cannot afford to lose e-commerce as a possible source of tax revenue. Policymakers will have to weigh those arguments against the political reality of authorizing new tax collections during an economic recession. [3]

Internet companies are anxiously watching the deliberations. The regulation-averse technology sector has long been wary of congressional involvement in its affairs, and enjoyed hands-off treatment for most of the 1990s, when it was creating most of the nation's high-paying jobs. Now companies fear the government could become more involved in setting standards for new technologies, such as forcing them to make equipment that will make it easier for the FBI and other agencies to snoop on communications. The industry also is closely watching the Federal Communications Commission (FCC), the regulatory watchdog agency of the telecommunications sector, which under new chairman Michael K. Powell is realigning its oversight functions and focusing on new incentives to encourage competition.

"We're very concerned about the complexity of new issues being thrown at the industry and the financial burdens that could be placed on carriers at a time when the industry is in a depression," says Grant Seiffert, vice president of governmental relations for the Telecommunications Industry Association, an Internet industry trade group.

However, other observers believe the terrorist disasters will, in some way, insulate the sector from onerous regulations, because its well-being is viewed as vital for the nation's security.

"The experience of Sept. 11 may lead to some relaxation of the rules, because the industry's big players [the Bells and long-distance companies] are viewed as being more valuable, providing stability and generally making things work," says former FCC Commissioner Harold Furchtgott-Roth. "It will help sharpen the debate about regulation, but probably won't tilt it against the industry."

As observers assess the effects of the Sept. 11 attacks on telecommunications and the new economy, here are some questions they are asking:

Should the government be granted expanded surveillance powers over the Internet?

The terrorist attacks not only altered Americans' fundamental perceptions of security but also triggered a thorny policy debate over whether the government should be given expanded powers to track suspects' electronic communications.

The Department of Justice submitted anti-terrorism proposals to Congress eight days after the attacks, calling for expanded wiretapping authority, wider access to electronic information — such as e-mail — and "one-stop shopping" for court orders, allowing authorities to obtain a single warrant for nationwide investigations involving searches and electronic surveillance of a particular suspect. The proposals came as authorities investigated whether the prime suspect, Saudi dissident Osama bin Laden, and his associates used e-mail, embedded computer messages or encryption software — used to scramble electronic messages — to plot their activities. [4]

Advocates for expanded law enforcement authority maintain that such changes are necessary because existing surveillance laws are outdated and did not contemplate today's digitally connected communications systems. The laws also did not envision commercially available encryption software that consumers can use to scramble e-mail or phone conversations.

"This is the time to test whether the American people are willing to go along with expanding the reach of the laws or not," said Sen. Jon Kyl, R-Ariz., a leading advocate of enhanced surveil-

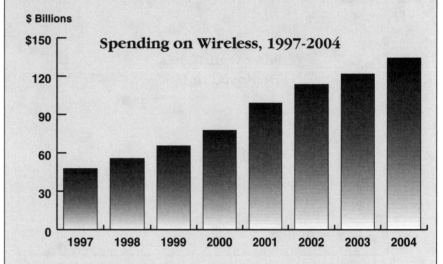

Wireless Communication Spending Surges

U.S. consumers and businesses are expected to spend more than $134 billion on wireless services, including cell phones, pagers and other personal communication devices in 2004. The growth will likely be fueled by more subscribers in the cellular and paging markets.

$ Billions

Spending on Wireless, 1997-2004

Source: "2001 MultiMedia Telecommunications Market Review and Forecast," Telecommunications Industry Association

lance. He noted that under the wiretapping laws in effect at the time of the attacks, authorities had to obtain a search warrant in every jurisdiction through which communications traveled in order to track a suspect's Internet activities — a frustrating and virtually impossible proposition when one considers the ubiquitous nature of the Web.

The Justice Department also sought to allow Internet service providers (ISPs) to voluntarily disclose information about a subscriber if they believe there is imminent danger of death or serious bodily injury. The proposals included numerous other non-technical provisions, the most controversial of which would allow the attorney general to indefinitely detain any non-citizen believed to be a national security risk. [5]

Civil libertarians fear strengthening the government's surveillance powers could infringe on Fourth Amendment rights against illegal searches and seizures. The groups maintain that

telecommunications companies already are required to give law enforcement authorities access to information on their networks. And they note that state and federal courts rarely deny authorities' requests to electronically track suspects, approving some 1,200 orders each year. Electronic tracking requests for international cases are submitted to the Foreign Intelligence Surveillance Court, which meets in secret within the Department of Justice.

"There's not much more the government can ask for because the legal standard is about as low as one can get," says James Dempsey, deputy director of the Center for Democracy and Technology, a civil liberties group. "In moments of crisis and anger, there always are proposals to curtail individual freedoms, but doing that is giving in to the terrorists."

The FBI and other agencies now use technology such as pen registers, which record the numbers dialed on

Miles and Miles of Fiber Optics

An estimated 25 million miles of fiber optic cable will be deployed in the United States by 2004, industry experts predict. The rapid deployment of high-speed lines in the 1990s fueled the digital divide debate.

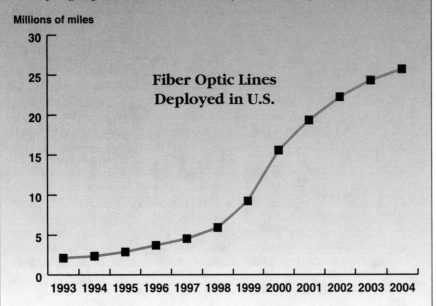

Millions of miles

Fiber Optic Lines Deployed in U.S.

Source: "2001 MultiMedia Telecommunications Market Review and Forecast," Telecommunications Industry Association

over whether to authorize agencies to use surveillance equipment to track e-mail and files accessed from Web sites. Disputes also raged over whether to allow authorities to seize stored voice-mail messages without going through the cumbersome process of seeking a court order for a wiretap.

And it was unclear whether policymakers would allow investigators to obtain more information from Internet service providers, who now are required to hand over only limited information, such as a customer's name and address and how long he has used the service. Some lawmakers expressed misgivings over provisions to make low-level computer intrusion — already a crime under other laws — a federal terrorism offense, which could bring penalties of up to life imprisonment.

The deliberations recalled past debates over online privacy, which often do not break along traditional partisan lines. Anti-terrorism legislation has been held up by an unlikely coalition of staunch conservatives, suspicious of expanded government power, and liberal Democrats concerned about protecting civil liberties.

Following the 1995 Oklahoma City bombing, Rep. Bob Barr, R-Ga., scuttled key provisions in a 1996 anti-terrorism bill that would have allowed authorities to use some illegally obtained wiretap information. Congress eventually expanded wiretapping authority in a 1998 intelligence authorization bill. In order to combat terrorism, it allowed investigators to follow a person from phone to phone without having to prove that he was switching phones to avoid detection.

"If authorities can't conduct proper intelligence-gathering with all of the tools they have, maybe we ought to be looking at the law enforcement and intelligence community and considering how laws are being implemented," Barr said.

a phone line but do not allow investigators to listen to conversations, and trap-and-trace devices, which identify the originating number of a call, similar to Caller ID. Agencies must get a court order to use the technology.

To get permission to use a wiretap and monitor conversations, investigators must provide compelling evidence that there is "probable cause" that a suspect is involved in a criminal activity. The Bush administration and congressional allies would like to allow authorities to extract more substantive information than just telephone numbers from pen registers and trap-and-trace devices, without first having to meet the higher "probable cause" standard.

Such a move would represent a significant expansion of surveillance laws, some of which were established in the 1968 omnibus crime bill, which laid the groundwork for wiretapping

in the electronic age. Among other things, it specified when and how the government could wiretap conventional telephones. In 1986, lawmakers expanded the wiretap statute to cover electronic communications. In 1994, they again expanded the law to address wireless telephones.

In the weeks since Sept. 11, some consensus appeared to be forming around certain Bush administration proposals. Many Republicans and Democrats were receptive to the concept of "roving wiretaps" that allow law enforcement to follow suspects' conversations on any phones they might use instead of a specific line. This would enable law enforcement to track the conversations of a suspect who used multiple wireless phones. But some civil libertarians worried the provision would allow investigators to tap into too many unrelated conversations.

Lawmakers continue to disagree

Nonetheless, many observers believe that a sustained battle against terrorists operating in a clandestine fashion on American soil may require new trade-offs between personal freedom and security. "We haven't been through something like this since Pearl Harbor," said Lance Hoffman, a computer science professor at George Washington University in Washington, D.C. "Incidents of this magnitude always force us to revisit what we want, and where to strike the balance."

Should the government lift some regulations to narrow the "digital divide"?

During the first half of this year, residents of Washington and other selected cities were inundated with television and print advertisements that alternately touted and belittled a congressional bill known as "Tauzin-Dingell." The frequency of the ads, and the opaque nature of their messages about the virtues of high-speed Internet, puzzled even seasoned veterans of Washington's lobbying wars. "Tauzin-Dingell . . . Sounds like some kind of foot condition," chortled Sen. Byron L. Dorgan, D-N.D., at one hearing.

The bill, proposed by House Energy and Commerce Committee Chairman W.J. "Billy" Tauzin, R-La., and ranking Democrat John D. Dingell of Michigan, in fact represented a significant effort to roll back telecommunications regulations in order to address the digital divide. In introducing the most heavily lobbied high-tech bill of the 107th Congress, Tauzin and Dingell proposed lifting restrictions in the 1996 Telecommunications Act and making it easier for regional Bell operating companies to sell high-speed Internet access outside of their service regions.

The bill and the political maneuvering surrounding it came as the Bells — Verizon, BellSouth, SBC Communications and Qwest — continue to fight cable operators for control of

what both expect will become a lucrative market for high-speed broadband service. The Bells maintain the legislation would level the playing field against cable operators, who face considerably less government regulation for their broadband service.

To date, only 6 million American homes receive high-speed Internet service. Cable operators have taken an early lead, serving 75 percent of the market via fiber optic lines and modems attached to consumers' computers. The remaining 25 percent subscribe to digital subscriber lines, or DSL, an alternate technology offered by the Bells that converts their copper phone lines into two-way data conduits.

"If you grant that a cable modem and DSL are virtually identical services operating in the same market, why should we have so many regulatory requirements when they have none?" asks Gary Lytle, president of the U.S. Telecom Association, the trade group representing the Bells.

However, opponents claimed the bill would tilt the competitive balance in favor of the Bells because their phone lines already reach into virtually every home and business. Long-distance companies and other traditional Bell foes insisted the bill also would remove whatever incentive the Bells had to open their local markets to competitors. "We don't need to do special favors for monopolies," said Rep. John Conyers Jr., D-Mich., a vocal opponent of the Tauzin-Dingell bill and ranking Democrat on the House Judiciary Committee. [6]

Tauzin and Dingell specifically would do away with a checklist of requirements that the Bells must meet now to show they have opened their local phone systems to competitors before they can enter the long-distance data market. The Bells insist that the requirements were created to spur competition in phone service, traditionally a regulated market, and did not contemplate the exponential growth

of the high-speed Internet business, which is not regulated.

Still, lawmakers have been slow to embrace the deregulatory push because of the perception that the bill benefits primarily the Bells. The financial demise of several small Bell rivals — known collectively as competitive local exchange carriers, or CLECs — earlier this year intensified criticism that the bill was special-interest legislation and could chill investment in alternative telecommunications companies. House Judiciary Committee Chairman F. James Sensenbrenner Jr., R-Wis., and Conyers insisted on holding hearings on competitive aspects of the legislation and the panel reported the bill unfavorably — a move that riled Tauzin and intensified a growing turf battle between the powerful committee chairmen. (*See sidebar, p. 262.*)

The Sept. 11 terrorist attacks have pushed the matter to the back of Congress' agenda. However, the Tauzin-Dingell bill still could pass the House in 2001 thanks to backing from Republican leaders, who view the Bells as strong political and financial supporters.

Prospects are much slimmer for Senate passage, where there is considerably more anti-Bell sentiment. Tauzin's Senate counterpart, Commerce, Science and Transportation Committee Chairman Ernest F. Hollings, D-S.C., is a leading Bell critic and has said the bill would be "dead on arrival" in the Senate because the Bells would display "monopolistic tendencies" if the measure became law. Hollings was one of the architects of the 1996 Telecommunications Act and believes the law needs more time to open local phone markets.

Hollings is so opposed to giving the Bells regulatory relief that he has drafted his own proposal to divest each of the Bells into separate wholesale and retail companies, which would sell phone service to residential and business customers. Under Hollings'

Shaping the New Economy's Future

K ey decisions about what rules to apply to the new economy will be made by a relatively small cohort of lawmakers and federal regulators. Five who will figure prominently in upcoming debates are:

Rep. W.J. "Billy" Tauzin, R-La. — The alternately charming and tough chairman of the House Energy and Commerce Committee is one of the most aggressive legislators in Congress and a principal decision-maker when it comes to balancing competition and regulation of the new economy. Using his committee's broad jurisdiction, Tauzin, 58, has weighed in on the issue of Internet privacy, pushing a middle-ground proposal to limit online businesses' ability to collect personal information about their customers. He is perhaps best known as cosponsor, with Rep. John D. Dingell, D-Mich., of legislation that would allow regional Bell companies to offer long-distance "broadband" data transmission without first having to prove they opened their local networks to competitors, as stipulated in the 1996 Telecommunications Act. A one-time Democrat, Tauzin retains an activist streak and believes in the value of passing sweeping laws that influence business behavior.

Sen. Ernest F. Hollings, D-S.C. — The blunt-spoken chairman of the Senate Commerce, Science and Transportation Committee supports efforts to develop new technology and set rules for business conduct on the Internet. Hollings, 79, has pushed tough online privacy legislation that would require Internet vendors to get a customer's consent before collecting or sharing

personal information. He also has fought foreign ownership of U.S. telecommunications firms and pushed legislation to limit violent television programming. Hollings is Tauzin's Senate counterpart but is a staunch opponent of Tauzin and Dingell's efforts to give the Bells regulatory relief, arguing the 1996 Telecommunications Act he helped author will gradually bring competition to the long-distance data market. Regarded as something of a maverick, Hollings often takes a heavy-handed approach to telecommunications regulation that can put him at odds with the majority of his own party.

Michael K. Powell, Chairman, FCC — The son of Secretary of State Colin L. Powell is a Republican who is pushing the

Federal Communications Commission to adopt a more market-oriented approach to regulating the telecommunications industry. Elevated from FCC commissioner to chairman in January 2001 by President Bush, Powell, 38, favors relaxing rules that limit the size of broadcast and cable companies and going slow in regulating broadband Internet service. Powell says the

proposal — deemed a legislative longshot — the wholesale unit would have to sell phone switching services to all comers under the same terms it offers its retail affiliate.

If the deregulatory push becomes gridlocked by the competing proposals, observers expect lawmakers to turn to alternatives. Many from rural and inner-city areas are upset that their constituents and Main Street businesses cannot receive high-speed Internet and are gradually falling behind in the

digital world. "There is more pressure than ever for Congress to facilitate deployment of high-speed broadband, but Tauzin-Dingell is not the only game in town," says Cato's Thierer.

One option would impose an "open access" requirement on cable operators, effectively forcing them to allow all Internet service providers to use cable companies' fiber optic lines that run into customers' homes. Currently, customers using cable broadband must sign up with an Internet service provider

affiliated with their cable company. The cable industry strongly opposes such proposals, arguing it would inhibit their ongoing investment in broadband networks and create general uncertainty in telecommunications markets.

Another more politically viable alternative would award tax breaks to any telecommunications vendors that extend high-speed systems to outlying or underserved areas. Legislation proposed by Sen. John D. Rockefeller IV, D-W.Va., and Reps. Phil English, R-Pa., government should work to speed the deployment of fiber optic lines that can simultaneously carry voice, video and data. He also wants to reorganize the FCC so regulatory oversight is determined by the service a company offers — for example broadband Internet — instead of by the technology used to deliver the service. He says this would ensure uniform rules for phone, cable, satellite and wireless companies. Powell enjoys strong support from Republicans and many Democrats in Congress, who contend the FCC imposed excessive regulations on the telecommunications industry during the Clinton administration and did not do enough to foster competition.

Rep. Edward J. Markey, D-Mass. — The ranking Democrat on the House Energy and Commerce Internet and Telecommunications Subcommittee, Markey, 55, is regarded as one of the most conversant lawmakers on the minutia of

telecommunications regulation and helped write the 1996 Telecommunications Act. Like Hollings, he opposes efforts to help the Bells enter the long-distance data market. Markey helped draft the language in telecommunications law requiring the "v-chip" circuitry in new televisions to allow parents to block violent or sexually explicit programming. A humorous, sometimes sarcastic lawmaker, he believes "ruthless Darwinian competition" will bring consumers the most benefits in the new economy.

Sen. John McCain, R-Ariz. — The ranking Republican on the Senate Commerce, Science and Transportation Committee, McCain took a strong stand against any Internet taxes during his

2000 insurgent presidential campaign. He likely will be part of a legislative compromise extending a moratorium on Internet taxes but giving states some taxing power on electronic commerce. A feisty maverick, McCain, 65, worked with Hollings to press entertainment companies to stop marketing violent content to children. But in 1999, over Hollings' objections, he won passage of legislation that limited companies' liability for problems related to the year 2000 computer glitch.

Rep. F. James Sensenbrenner, R-Wis. — Though he has not shown great interest in new-economy issues in the past,

the new chairman of the House Judiciary Committee frequently jousts with Tauzin for jurisdiction over new-economy issues. In the 107th Congress, Sensenbrenner, 58, oversaw efforts to extend the moratorium on Internet taxation and restrict unsolicited e-mail, or "spam." He also figures to be a key player on online privacy legislation and copyright issues affecting digital works, which have to go through his committee.

and Robert T. Matsui, D-Calif., would offer a 10 percent annual tax credit for five years to companies that bring "current generation" broadband to residents and businesses in underserved rural and inner-city areas. Companies that invest in "next generation" broadband services for residential customers would get a 20 percent annual credit for five years. An analysis of a similar proposal in 2000 by the Joint Committee on Taxation estimated that such a credit would cost $1.4 billion over 10 years.

While some lawmakers were willing to consider such tax breaks before Sept. 11, some feel the breaks favor incumbent telecommunications companies that already have extendable networks. Now, the increased cost of military and intelligence spending for the war on terrorism could at least temporarily scuttle additional tax breaks.

"A lot of senators represent a lot of the rural parts of America, and my guess is there would be a lot of interest in it," said Senate Finance Commit-

tee Chairman Max Baucus, D-Mont. "But we all have an upper [spending] limit."

Should states be allowed to collect taxes on Internet sales?

Seldom do behind-the-scenes talks on technology legislation prompt a U.S. senator to post a message on his Web site emphatically denying that any deal has been cut.

But the sensitive question of whether states should be allowed to collect taxes on Internet sales prompted Sen.

Tax on E-Commerce Sales Tempts Localities

E-commerce still comprises a small fraction of total U.S. retail sales, but the issue of Internet taxation looms large because localities believe a congressional moratorium on taxation unnecessarily preempts their taxing authority.*

Period	Retail Sales (in $ millions)		E-commerce as a Percent of Total Sales
	Total	E-commerce	
1999 4th Quarter	$785,869	$5,266	0.67%
2000 1st Quarter	714,425	5,526	0.77
2000 2nd Quarter	777,819	5,982	0.77
2000 3rd Quarter	772,796	6,898	0.89
2000 4th Quarter	817,715	8,881	1.09
2001 1st Quarter	728,662	7,592	1.04
2001 2nd Quarter	807,467	7,458	0.92

* Chart does not reflect business-to-business online transactions.

Source: U.S. Commerce Department

John McCain, R-Ariz., to do just that in June, after word spread among Washington lobbyists that the maverick lawmaker might rethink his long-held opposition to any new Internet taxes.

"Contrary to staff reports, I have not signed on to any proposed legislation on Internet taxes," McCain wrote. "We are currently engaged in discussions." [7]

McCain and colleagues on the Senate Commerce, Science and Transportation Committee were trying to straddle the line between local taxing authorities, who contend electronic commerce is siphoning business away from bricks-and-mortar retailers and slowly eroding their revenue, and the high-tech sector, which says new taxes could quash the Internet economy and help trigger an economic recession.

Anti-tax forces also question how one can even establish where a transaction takes place in the borderless world of cyberspace, where a consumer in one state may connect with a computer server in a second state linked to an e-retailer in a third state or even overseas.

The issue of Internet taxation was shaping up to be the most imminent new economy issue on the fall agenda before the terrorist attacks. A three-year congressional moratorium on taxing Internet access and commerce was due to expire Oct. 21. Lawmakers must decide whether to extend it, as the Bush administration wants, or to work with states to establish and codify a simplified tax code.

Congress was unable to resolve the issue in 1997 and '98, leading to the moratorium that effectively froze some 7,500 state and local taxing jurisdictions from touching the Internet economy. Internet access taxes that were in effect in one-quarter of the states at the time of passage were allowed to continue.

It is not clear how these deliberations actually will affect the economy. E-commerce sales remain a fairly small percentage of all retail sales, according to government data. The Department of Commerce reported e-commerce retail sales totaled $25.8 billion in 2000, representing only 0.8 percent of total retail sales. Moreover, while state revenue has grown significantly, e-commerce has surged; the Nelson A. Rockefeller Institute of Government in Albany, N.Y., found state tax revenues rose 8.7 percent in fiscal 2000, the fastest growth rate in the past decade. But with e-commerce experiencing rapid growth, localities believe it is better to tackle the issue now, believing they could experience significant economic losses.

The current economic downturn has fueled arguments on both sides of the debate. States that have seen income fall with the stock market have more incentive to raise revenue by taxing electronic sales. However, defenders of high tech say that with the Internet economy in extremis even before the terrorist attacks, now is not the time to layer on new taxes.

"The tech sector led the country to prosperity; we need to pay attention to the situation now," said Rep. Zoe Lofgren, D-Calif., whose tech-heavy district includes San Jose.

"Our schools cannot afford to be robbed of this revenue," said Gov. John Engler, R-Mich., chairman of the National Governors' Association. "Fairness requires that remote sellers collect and pay the same taxes that our friends and neighbors on Main Street have to pay."

States cannot collect taxes from e-commerce sellers located outside of their borders. The U.S. Supreme Court, in the 1992 case *Quill Corp. v. North Dakota*, ruled out-of-state mail-order enterprises could not be required to pay use taxes from an out-of-state location. However, the court emphasized that Congress had the final say in the matter and could change the taxing power under the Commerce Clause of the Constitution. The key would be figuring out a way to sim-

Chronology

1930s *Federal and state governments begin interstate and local phone service, in the process establishing monopoly service.*

1934

Congress passes the Communications Act, calling for strict federal regulation of interstate phone service. States simultaneously adopt similar laws to regulate local service. The regulation assures monopolies in both kinds of service are preserved. In exchange, the companies are required to run phone lines to remote and underserved areas.

———•———

1980–1995 *Policymakers begin to establish regulatory frameworks for new kinds of media.*

1984

The Cable Telecommunications Act deregulates the cable television industry, eliminating the authority of state and local governments to regulate the rates cable system owners charge to subscribers.

1986

Congress expands a 1968 federal wiretapping statute to cover electronic communications, conditioned on authorities obtaining a court order.

1992

Congress overrides a veto by President George Bush and reregulates cable until such a time as more competition develops. It marks the most ambitious reregulation of an industry during the Reagan-Bush years.

1993

Ending the traditional practice of awarding electromagnetic spectrum frequencies for free, Congress orders the Federal Communications Commission to start auctioning bandwidths to the highest bidders, with proceeds going to the federal Treasury.

———•———

1996–Present *Congress begins anticipating the convergence of once disparate technologies and adopting some rules for the Internet economy.*

1996

Congress enacts landmark legislation to rewrite the nation's communications laws and create a single marketplace for telecommunications services with evenly matched competitors. Local telephone and cable monopolies are broken up, steps are taken to encourage competition in long-distance phone service, cable price controls are dropped and overall regulation on telecommunications companies is eased.

1998

In a busy year for telecommunications regulation, Congress approves a moratorium on new Internet taxes, updates protections for intellectual property on the Internet, cracks down on Internet sites that allow children to access pornography and passes laws aimed at curbing cell phone fraud. The anti-pornography law is later declared unconstitutional.

1999

Congress gives satellite TV companies the right to deliver local broadcast stations in cities across the country, matching services provided by rival cable TV systems. Policymakers also pass a law limiting companies' liability in connection with the Y2K computer glitch. The Clinton administration eases controls on the export of encryption software designed to scramble communications.

2000

Legislation authorizing the use of electronic signatures to close business deals over the Internet is signed by President Bill Clinton. States gain the power to limit Internet liquor sales, but federal legislation to curb Internet gambling dies. Congress fails to arrive at a consensus to protect privacy of online consumers.

2001

In the aftermath of the Sept. 11 terrorist attacks, the Bush administration requests new powers to expand electronic surveillance on the Internet.

2001

Members of Congress and representatives of the high-tech industry informally agree on baseline standards to protect consumers' personal information on the World Wide Web.

2001

Congress debates ways to narrow the "digital divide" and encourage the deployment of high-speed "broadband" Internet networks, including regulatory relief, tax breaks and open-access mandates.

2001

New Federal Communications Commission Chairman Michael K. Powell initiates a reorganization of the agency with emphasis on developing more uniform rules for cable, satellite, telephone and Internet services.

New Lingo for a New Economy

The new economy has spawned its own lexicon of names and abbreviations denoting the players and services in the rapidly expanding telecommunications market.[1] Following are some commonly used terms that figure into the various debates over regulation:

Broadband — This method of carrying computer data sends multiple transmissions that share a common communications pathway. Used to denote a variety of high-speed Internet services.

Cable Modem — A device that provides high-speed Internet access to homes and businesses over the same fiber-optic cable used to deliver cable television service. The modem in the customer's home or business communicates with a modem at the cable operator's site. New cable modem chips are being developed that can fit into cable TV converter boxes, and they may also be configured as cards within personal computers.

Common Carrier — Any company that offers telecommunications services to the general public, such as telephone companies. They must offer transmission services at non-discriminatory rates to any interested customer, and for regulatory purposes often are treated like gas and electric utilities.

Competitive Local Exchange Carrier (CLEC) — A class of telecommunications resellers that emerged in the mid-1990s. CLECs sell telephone, data services and Internet access to business and residential customers. They deliver the services either over their own fiber-optic lines, over wireless or copper lines they lease from incumbent telecommunications companies such as the Bells, or over a combination. Dozens of CLECs have gone out of business in the past two years. The industry generally blames the Bells for discriminatory pricing that has blocked access to some local networks, but other observers suggest the companies had fundamentally bad business plans.

Compression — The practice of reducing the size of data, images, voice or video files sent over telephone lines, decreasing the capacity of the line needed to transmit the files. Compression is the technology behind convergence.

Convergence — The practice of piggybacking voice, video and computer data on a single network based on Internet cod-

ing. A traditional public phone network is circuit-switched, meaning it saves a path in the network to accommodate a call. Convergent networks use Internet protocols, which send traffic in packages of digital data. Individual packets sent to the same address may be sent over different routes depending on the flow of electronic information. Convergence already is bringing consumers the capability to have phone conversations, download music files or watch videos on their home computers, thus creating quandaries for regulators.

Digital Subscriber Line (DSL) — DSL service sends high-speed Internet service over unused frequencies available on standard telephone wire. The technology was introduced in 1989 as a way of sending television and video signals from a company's central office over copper cable. There are a number of different varieties of DSL service with different transmission speeds. Regional Bell companies see DSL as a competing technology to cable modems but so far have only captured about 25 percent of the broadband market. One advantage of DSL is that it uses existing facilities and does not require building new fiber lines to every customer's home or business.

Local Access Transport Area (LATA) — The service areas set up during the 1984 divestiture of AT&T where regional Bell companies are allowed to sell local phone services. LATAs cover metropolitan statistical areas based on population sizes. Long-distance companies such as AT&T, MCI WorldCom and Sprint may carry calls between LATAs, but Bells can only carry traffic within LATAs. Congress is considering changing those rules with respect to high-speed data transmission.

Local Loop — This is the line that runs from a local phone company's switch to the end user's home or residence. The loop can be made up of optical fiber, copper cable or wireless communications systems. Congress attempted to open the local loop up to competitors by enacting the 1996 Telecommunications Act, but Bell operating companies still control nearly 90 percent of local phone traffic.

---

[1] Annabel Z. Dodd, *The Essential Guide to Telecommunications* (2nd ed., 2000).

---

plify the confusing patchwork of state, city and county taxes.

McCain and other lawmakers had favored a compromise extending the tax moratorium but also would authorize a multistate compact, under which states that passed Internet tax legislation would be able to collect a national online sales tax. In the House, Reps. Ernest Istook, R-Okla., and Conyers have championed a similar proposal.

Compacts are not new ideas. States

historically create such working agreements, then seek Congress' blessing in an effort to restrict interstate commerce to achieve what are deemed national goals. For instance, in 1985 Congress authorized states to form seven regional compacts to develop low-level radioactive-waste disposal sites. And in 1996, lawmakers allowed six New England states to form a dairy compact and raise the minimum prices processors pay for milk.

Nineteen states have passed model legislation developed by the National Governors' Association that would create a simplified system to collect taxes from "remote sellers" located within their borders. Congress may consider authorizing a compact among the states as part of a deal to extend the moratorium on Internet taxation.

National retailers, such as Wal-Mart Stores Inc., have joined commercial real estate owners and groups like the governors' association to seek a compromise allowing such an arrangement. Sen. Hollings, who believes states have a fundamental right to levy taxes, is in their camp. He wants states to be allowed to collect another category of taxes on business activity from technology companies that provide services and send teams of employees into a state, even if they do not maintain a physical presence there.

However, the Bush administration and allies such as Rep. Christopher Cox, R-Calif., favor a straightforward five-year extension of the moratorium. Vice President Dick Cheney in April also called for legislative language permanently banning Internet-specific taxes, such as fees on e-mail and other online services like instant messaging. Tax-reform groups and conservative economists argue that states can make do with what they have now — and may even find it in their best interests to keep taxes low.

"While e-commerce is a minuscule component of consumer spending, its mere existence serves to inhibit excessive taxation," said Cato Institute trade analyst Aaron Lukas. "Politicians fear that if they raise taxes too much, consumers can take advantage of low tax rates elsewhere. Just like shoppers who drive from high- to low-tax states, the Internet will induce state and local governments to keep overall tax rates at a more reasonable level."

Observers predict a close vote if lawmakers must choose between a straightforward extension of the moratorium or a new taxing scheme. The outcome will hinge on whether Congress chooses to heed the concerns of local officials or succumb to fears over imposing new taxes during an economic slowdown. Supporters of an extension may try to avoid a prolonged fight by attaching a tax ban to a fiscal 2002 appropriations bill — a proposal that would reduce the chances of a stalemate.

"We're running out of time," said Rep. Barr, who supports strict curbs on Internet taxes. "We've got to take the lead over here and get something to the Senate, maybe to prod them a little bit." ∎

BACKGROUND

To Regulate or Not

Before the government regulated the new economy, it created its backbone. The Internet was developed in the late 1960s, when the Department of Defense's Advanced Research Products Agency funded computer network research to create an experimental system in which any computer could exchange information with any other. This involved establishing the uniform technical standards for network data and breaking messages up into small packets that could be routed along as many as 20 networks on the way to their final destination — a process that came to be known as packet-switching.

The goal was to decentralize communications, thus avoiding the Cold War prospect of a single military attack destroying the nation's communications infrastructure. The system's design also allowed new networks to be connected to the growing Internet. [8]

The government gradually pulled away from the field in the 1980s as academic researchers and engineers took the lead in devising a series of protocols organizing information into pages of data and linking them via Hypertext Markup Language — codes that describe the structure of each page and its contents. The increased availability of smaller, more powerful computers and the advent of "networking," in which they are linked directly together in local area networks or through telephone lines, greatly enabled consumers to share data, software and memory space — and to communicate with each other through e-mail.

By the mid-1990s, the Internet was surging in popularity; a Department of Commerce report noted that it only took four years to gain 50 million users, compared with the radio, which existed for 38 years before it had 50 million listeners, and the television, which needed 13 years to reach 50 million viewers.

Pressure on the government to develop some rules of the road steadily intensified due to innovation and a growing convergence of once disparate devices such as personal computers, telephones and televisions. The ability to digitalize and move vast amounts of data over high-speed fiber optic lines began to allow people to watch movies, download music files or have phone conversations over their computers. Cable TV franchise operators or local phone companies could package the services and deliver them to consumers over fiber optic or conventional phone lines.

But the advances posed difficult regulatory questions, such as whether to levy tariffs on Internet telephony or bar long-distance phone companies from selling a package of services that used a local phone company's wires. Policymakers separately struggled with issues such as how to regulate devices such as "smart phones" that combine the capabilities of wireless phones, which traditionally have been subject to some government regulation, with palmtop computers, which have not. Complicating their work was a steady stream of high-tech mergers in the late 1990s that further blurred the lines between traditional telecommunications services.

The developments tested official Washington's penchant for avoiding new regulation. Because the information-technology sector created most of the new high-paying jobs in the 1990s, lawmakers in Congress feared burdening it with excessive rules would squelch innovation and halt the engine of economic growth. Internet companies by and large reassured the lawmakers that they could maintain a competitive marketplace and grow their new industry through self-regulation.

One notable exception was the Clinton administration's landmark antitrust case against Microsoft Corp., in which the Department of Justice argued in 1997 that the software giant acted in an anticompetitive fashion by forcing computer makers to bundle its Internet Explorer device for browsing the World Wide Web with their hardware in order to obtain a license for Microsoft's popular Windows 95 operating system. [9]

Action in Congress

Congress in 1996 attempted to address the growing number of legal and regulatory issues that were hindering companies in the Information Age. Lawmakers passed the Telecommunications Act of 1996, which sought to create a single, giant marketplace for telecommunications services with evenly matched competitors. The act broke down legal barriers between industry segments by mixing elements of regulatory relief with new mandates in an effort to balance the competitive powers of regional Bells, long-distance companies, cable TV operators, broad-

In the wake of the attack on the World Trade Center, here shown on Sept. 28, the government may tighten regulation of the telecommunications industry as a matter of national security. One option would be to limit foreign ownership of U.S. telecom firms.

AP Photo/Shawn Baldwin

casters and satellite companies. [10]

The act has played to decidedly mixed reviews, particularly in the area of local phone competition. Both Republicans and Democrats have complained the FCC was slow to implement regulations that would encourage the Bells to allow smaller competitors to interconnect with their local network in exchange for the ability to transmit data outside of their service regions.

Bells in mid-2001 still controlled about 91 percent of local phone lines nationally because rivals mainly targeted business accounts. The act also lifted price controls on cable television services after March 31, 1999, in the hope that phone companies would compete with cable operators and drive down prices. However, the Bells found it difficult to upgrade their systems, and cable companies boosted the cost of their expanded basic tier, containing ESPN, Lifetime and other channels, triggering consumer complaints. The act separately banned the transmission of obscene material over any form of telecommunications, including computer networks — a provision that a federal appeals court and, ultimately, the

Supreme Court found unconstitutional because it hindered free speech. [11]

Since passing the 1996 act, Congress has attempted to craft somewhat more narrowly focused regulations dealing with the Internet and digital works. In 1998, lawmakers updated copyright laws by implementing two international treaties aimed at improving legal protections for digital works, such as computer software and compact discs. They also gave Internet service providers limited liability protection for copyright infringement that takes place on their networks without their knowledge. The 1998 package, known as the Digital Millennium Copyright Act, also banned the use of devices primarily designed to circumvent technology, such as encryption software, used to protect copyrighted works from theft.

While the law began to deal with increasing theft of intellectual property on the Internet, it also illustrated how new technologies quickly can make regulations obsolete. For example, the 1998 act did not envision the advent of file-swapping software, in which individuals can download digital sound or video files from a central computer server, then make sequential copies on their home computers without degradation in quality. This became the source of a major intellectual-property debate in 2000 when major recording labels filed suit in federal court to shut down the Napster music service. [12]

Congress in 2000 authorized the use of electronic signatures to close business deals on the Internet after a lengthy debate that weighed promotion of electronic commerce with the need for

At Issue:

Should Congress lift regulations on Bell operating companies to accelerate the deployment of high-speed Internet service?

THOMAS J. TAUKE
SENIOR VICE PRESIDENT,
VERIZON COMMUNICATIONS

TESTIMONY BEFORE HOUSE JUDICIARY COMMITTEE, JUNE 5, 2001

*a*s recently as 1995, when Congress was rewriting the Communications Act of 1934, revenues generated by the Internet were a mere $5 billion. . . .

But then something unexpected happened. As Alan Greenspan has noted, "until the mid-1990s . . . computers were still being used on a stand-alone basis. The full value of computing power could be realized only after ways had been devised to link computers into large-scale networks." This networking spurred the economic growth of the late 1990s. . . .

But there are limits to the legacy networks and the economic value they can deliver. And these limits were one of the reasons that this economy reached a plateau and, now, is stagnating. . . .

Consumers love buying online, but get frustrated when they have to wait too long for the picture of the dress to download or to complete their transaction. So the customers gave up and did not make the purchase, and the economy suffered. . . .

The problem is that we don't have a national policy that promotes the development of broadband services. Congress established a national policy for voice telephone services in the Communications Act of 1934 and the Telecommunications Act of 1996. It adopted a different policy for video cable services. . . . It has not adopted a policy for broadband. Without a clear national policy, the FCC and the courts have been left to using laws that were enacted for completely different purposes, with predictably confusing results.

Existing law prevents one set of competitors — local telephone companies like Verizon — from competing freely in the Internet marketplace, thus insulating cable companies, such as AT&T, and the largest long-distance companies — again such as AT&T and WorldCom and Sprint — from full competition. It also imposes on telephone company broadband services a host of requirements not imposed on cable. . . .

The FCC cannot solve the problem of regulation that inhibits broadband deployment and skews the competitive marketplace — Congress must do that. The longer the delay . . . the longer the economy will have to wait for the boost that these new services would surely produce. The [proponents of deregulation] want to free the Internet from the . . . constraints that were established for the voice telephone network nearly 20 years ago. They want to remove burdensome regulation that discourages innovation and deployment in data services. And they want to put telephone company broadband providers on a more level competitive playing field with cable. These are all worthy goals. . . .

JAMES K. GLASSMAN
RESIDENT FELLOW,
AMERICAN ENTERPRISE INSTITUTE

TESTIMONY BEFORE HOUSE JUDICIARY COMMITTEE, JUNE 5, 2001

*w*hat is holding up the deployment of broadband? There is a bottleneck at the "last mile" — at the local connection between high-speed, long-distance data lines and the homes and small businesses of America. The Telecommunications Act of 1996 was supposed to loosen that bottleneck and at the same time spread the blessings of consumer choice and competition throughout the telecom system.

The idea behind the act was a sound one: The extensive local networks owned by the Bells had been built over decades and represented billions of dollars in sunk investments, much of which had been subsidized. . . . In the face of an entrenched and uncooperative monopolist, local competition faced barriers to entry that were simply too high, outside of a few major metropolitan areas. Without being able to interconnect to the incumbent's local access facilities on an equivalent, non-discriminatory basis, a CLEC was unable to offer a competitive product to establish itself in the marketplace. So, the Telecom Act of 1996 mandated that the Bells unbundle their networks and provide resale of all retail services at non-discriminatory, cost-based wholesale rates. . . .

Of course, the Bells had a huge incentive to be uncooperative. They didn't want the competition. The act provided a carrot: Open up your local networks to competitors sufficiently and, on a state-by-state basis, you will be . . . allowed into long distance. This was a sensible deal for all parties and a good way to move toward what Congress and the president wanted: deregulation and the benefits — in lower prices, higher quality and broader dissemination — that competition had already provided in long-distance and equipment markets, which the Bell System monopolized before its structural separation in 1984. . . .

The Bells say that if you will relieve them of competitive pressures, they will roll out broadband faster. This is a paternalistic game that might be called, "Trust the Monopolist." Just give us back our monopoly power, and we will work wonders.

Nonsense. Competition, not monopoly, offers a far better guarantee that new technology reaches all Americans. Time and again, Congress and the president — across partisan lines — have trusted competition. And it has been the right course. The order to break up the Bell System in 1984 was an action that trusted competition — and prices fell and quality rose. Again, in 1996, Congress decided to trust competition, and it was right. [The current effort to give Bells regulatory relief] would undo that decision and would instead trust monopolies. That is why it is wrong.

consumer protections. But lawmakers were unable to agree on basic protections to safeguard consumers' personal information in cyberspace. Internet companies said the cost of complying with new privacy notices and other mandates could cost significant sums and set a bad precedent for regulating business conduct in the new digital economy. [13] In the end, lawmakers sided with high-tech companies' demands for self-regulation. ∎

CURRENT SITUATION

Overhauling the FCC

While the post-Sept. 11 political landscape settles, much attention is focusing on the Federal Communications Commission and Chairman Powell's efforts to overhaul the agency. The FCC has oversight over a wide range of new economy issues, from broadcast licenses to radio and television technical standards, telephone rates and charges, cable and pay television rates and data-transmission services.

The commission's power to regulate the telecommunications sector is limited by Congress, but its power to deregulate is relatively broad and discretionary. The 1996 Telecommunications Act, for example, allowed the FCC to stop enforcing any rule that was no longer needed to protect consumers or the public interest. In other words, if a segment of the industry became competitive, in the agency's view, it no longer needed to be subject to regulation.

The FCC drew intense congressional criticism during the Clinton adminis-

tration for sometimes heavy-handed regulation, particularly when reviewing media mergers. Republican Powell has said he wants to cut back on rulemaking and allow market forces to dictate the future shape of the industry. However, the Democratic takeover of the Senate may lead to significant policy clashes with Hollings. The agency is split 3–2 in favor of the political party that holds the presidency. The Senate oversees the agency's budget and works with FCC commissioners on legislation. [14]

One source of friction is media ownership rules. Powell wants to lift a 1975 prohibition on a single company owning a newspaper and television station in the same market. He also has plans to roll back 1996 rules that limit broadcasters and cable companies from owning stations or properties that collectively reach more than 35 percent of the national market. Powell said the rules originated "in a dif-

being appointed chairman. "The convergence of technology tears down those traditional distinctions and makes it evermore difficult to apply those labels to modern communications providers. It makes it more important than ever for us to examine whether those organizational buckets still hold water."

But Hollings and some others are skeptical about continued combinations in the communications industry that have left conglomerates like AOL-Time Warner owning systems that can carry voice, video and high-speed Internet traffic, Internet service providers and programming content. News Corp.'s $5.35 billion bid for Chris-Craft Industries Inc. would have left News Corp., which controls the Fox television network and 23 U.S. TV stations, holding two broadcast stations and a newspaper in New York City, in violation of the current federal rules. The Clinton administration FCC,

---

The FCC drew intense congressional criticism during the Clinton administration for sometimes heavy-handed regulation, particularly when reviewing media mergers. FCC Chairman Powell has said he wants to cut back on rulemaking and allow market forces to dictate the future shape of the industry.

---

ferent media environment" when telecommunications, broadcasting and the Internet were more segregated. Innovations such as computer-to-computer Internet telephony and digital television are forcing the FCC to reevaluate its regulatory approach.

"Communications policy has been written in carefully confined buckets premised on certain types of technology," Powell told the House Commerce Telecommunications and the Internet Subcommittee in March, soon after

under Chairman William E. Kennard, sought to place conditions on the AOL-Time Warner merger to ensure competition in the Internet instant-messaging market.

Hollings in July proposed imposing an 18-month moratorium on FCC efforts to relax media ownership rules, saying the nation faced a choice between "an erosion of diversity in our local markets" and "maintenance of rational ownership restrictions to allow local media outlets to retain some ability to control and disseminate locally relevant news and information." [15]

Hollings' remarks changed the prevailing view in Washington that big media companies would hold sway in the Bush administration and emboldened some lawmakers, who believe the FCC has to prevent a handful of companies from becoming as dominant in their industry as major airlines and banks are in theirs.

"We have to keep in mind the FCC has done a very good job [policing the industry], and a lot of the proceedings and tasks it does that some in Congress view as unnecessary are vitally important," said Rep. Edward J. Markey, D-Mass., a leading House authority on telecommunications who helped draft the 1996 Telecommunications Act.

Powell also wants to reorganize the FCC's regulatory functions to ensure uniform rules apply to telephone, cable, satellite and Internet services, regardless of whether the services travel over copper wire or fiber-optic cable or are beamed through the air.

While he is expected to pursue a generally deregulatory path, Powell also wants Congress to pass legislation giving the FCC the authority to levy significantly higher fines for violations of its rules, such as orders that Bell operating companies let smaller competitors connect to their networks. The FCC collected more than $27 million in fines from SBC Communications Inc., a regional Bell that is the nation's second-largest local phone company, for failing to meet certain standards designed to promote competition in the local phone market.

The FCC currently can levy a maximum fine of $1.2 million to $10 million per incident. Powell believes many of the agency's enforcement tools are viewed as trivial by big telecommunications companies, saying, "if you try to fine a company $75,000 that has net revenues in the millions and bil-

lions, that's just a cost of doing business." [16]

OUTLOOK

Protecting U.S. Security

Telecommunications regulation is lumped with health care, education and other domestic-policy issues that are taking a back seat to defense and intelligence in the aftermath of the Sept. 11 terrorist attacks. However, the government is almost certain to alter regulation of some aspects of the industry as a matter of national security.

One option would be to limit foreign ownership of U.S. telecommunications concerns — or take steps to keep a portion of the electromagnetic radio spectrum in U.S. hands. Ownership bans were enacted during World War I and World War II and were the subject of legislation that Hollings proposed long before the terrorist strikes. Hollings was responding to a bid by Deutsche Telecom to buy VoiceStream Wireless Corp. and argued that such a purchase would violate U.S. law.

Because regulators in recent years have overallocated spectrum for such purposes as digital TV and some next-generation wireless services and created a shortage of bandwidths, there may be a push to reserve bandwidth for military communications systems, which coordinate air-combat targeting, satellite telemetry and other intelligence functions. Already, the wireless industry has shelved a bid to try to use the 1755 to 1850 megahertz band for new Internet services it wants to deliver on hand-held digital devices. The band now is used by government agencies, including

the Pentagon.

Longer term, regulators will focus on how Internet regulation affects the broader economy. Numerous economic studies have documented how by transmitting information quickly, conveniently and inexpensively, the Internet cuts administrative costs and makes record-keeping and bill paying considerably cheaper than the status quo in the world of paper-based records. Brookings Institution economists Robert E. Litan and Alice M. Rivlin have outlined how Web-based technology also can help manufacturers manage supply chains more efficiently and reduce inventory. And it can link companies in joint partnerships irrespective of distances, enabling them to share production schedules and integrate operations. [17]

Observers believe that even if Congress fails to act on myriad new economy issues in 2001, lawmakers will continue to focus on ways to deploy more high-speed telecommunications systems, rationalize taxation of electronic commerce and find ways to legally protect copyrighted works in cyberspace. Such moves could reduce distribution costs and likely increase productivity.

"The economic impact of the Internet will likely not be as insignificant as the pessimists claim, and not as overwhelming as many cyber-enthusiasts suggest," Litan and Rivlin wrote. "[It] should generate a variety of benefits to users, in their capacities as consumers and citizens, that are not easily quantified but nonetheless real." ■

Notes

[1] See "The Markets Rewired," *The Economist*, Sept. 22, 2001, p. 56.
[2] For background, see Kathy Koch, "The Digital Divide," *The CQ Researcher*, Jan. 28, 2000, pp. 41-64.
[3] See "Internet Taxation: Major Issues Loom on the Horizon," *CyberLaw in Focus*, Na-

tional Legal Center for the Public Interest, Vol. 1, No. 3, May 2001.

[4] See Adriel Bettelheim and Elizabeth A. Palmer, "Balancing Liberty and Security," *CQ Weekly*, Sept. 22, 2001, p. 2210.

[5] See Elizabeth A. Palmer, "Committees Taking a Critical Look at Ashcroft's Request for Broad New Powers," *CQ Weekly*, Sept. 29, 2001, p. 2263. For background, see David Masci and Kenneth Jost, "War on Terrorism," *The CQ Researcher*, Oct. 12, 2001, pp. 817-848.

[6] See Yochi J. Dreazen, "Battle Over Bells and Broadband Service Heats Up," *The Wall Street Journal*, May 15, 2001, p. A28.

[7] See Alan K. Ota, "Internet Taxes: No Accord Yet On Moratorium," *CQ Weekly*, June 23, 2001, p. 1521.

[8] See "Computers, Milestones of the 20th Century" (Grolier, 1999), pp. 305-310.

[9] For background, see Kenneth Jost, "Antitrust Policy," *The CQ Researcher*, June 12, 1998, pp. 505-528.

[10] For background, see *Congress and the Nation, Vol. IX, 1993-1996*, Congressional Quarterly, 1998, pp. 387-398.

[11] See Paul Davidson, "Is Telecom Act 'a complete failure?' " *USA Today*, Feb. 8, 2001, p. 3B. See also Adriel Bettelheim, "Digital Commerce," *The CQ Researcher*, Feb. 5, 1999, pp. 89-112, and David Masci, "The Future of Telecommunicaitons," *The CQ Researcher*, April 23, 1999, pp. 329-352.

[12] For background, see Kenneth Jost, "Copyright and the Internet," *The CQ Researcher*, Sept. 29, 2000, pp. 769-792.

[13] For background, see Patrick G. Marshall, "Privacy Under Attack," *The CQ Researcher*, June 15, 2001, pp. 505-528, and David Masci, "Internet Privacy," *The CQ Researcher*, Nov. 6, 1998, pp. 953-976.

[14] See Peter S. Goodman, "Powell Plans Fewer FCC Rules," *The Washington Post*, March 30, 2001, p. E3

[15] See Jube Shiver Jr., "Company Town Showdown Over Media Ownership Rules Is Likely," *Los Angeles Times*, July 19, 2001, p. C6.

[16] See Jube Shiver Jr., "FCC Takes Aim at Regional Bells Regulation," *Los Angeles Times*, May 8, 2001, p. C1.

FOR MORE INFORMATION

American Electronics Association, 601 Pennsylvania Ave, N.W., Washington, D.C. 20004; (202) 682-9110; www.aeanet.org. A large Washington trade group representing software, electronics and telecommunications companies; interested in export controls, technology and privacy issues.

Cato Institute, 1000 Massachusetts Ave., N.W., Washington, D.C. 20001-5403; (202) 842-0200; www.cato.org. A public policy research organization that advocates limited government and individual liberty and encourages voluntary solutions to social and economic policies.

Center for Democracy and Technology, 1634 I St., N.W, Suite 1100, Washington, D.C. 20006; (202) 637-9800; www.cdt.org. A nonprofit group that promotes civil liberties in new computer and communications media and opposes Bush administration efforts to expand electronic surveillance.

Competitive Telecommunications Association, 1900 M St. N.W., Suite 800, Washington, D.C. 20036; (202) 296-6650; www.comptel.org. The trade association representing competitive local exchange carriers trying to compete with the Bells in the local phone market.

Department of Justice, Computer Crime and Intellectual Property Division, 1001 G St., N.W., Suite 200, Washington, D.C. 20001; (202) 514-1026; www.usdoj. gov/criminal/cybercrime. Investigates and litigates criminal and civil cases involving computers and the Internet and also helps coordinate international efforts and formulate policy on computer crime issues.

Federal Communications Commission, 445 12th St., S.W., Washington, D.C. 20554; (202) 418-1000; www.fcc.gov. Oversees most aspects of the telecommunications industry. Its common carrier bureau deals with wireline facilities that furnish interstate communications services. Separate cable services and wireless communications bureaus deal with those industry sectors. The FCC also assesses uses of new wireless technologies, such as e-commerce.

National Governors' Association, 444 N. Capitol St., N.W., Suite 267, Washington, D.C. 20001; (202) 624-5300; www.nga.org. Makes policy recommendations to Congress and the president on a wide range of issues, including telecommunications.

Telecommunications Industry Association, 2500 Wilson Blvd., Suite 300, Arlington, Va. 22201; (703) 907-7700; www.tiaonline.org. A Washington-area trade group of equipment makers, suppliers and distributors involved in the ongoing debate over electronic surveillance and broadband issues.

U.S. Telecom Association, 1401 H St., N.W. Suite 600, Washington, D.C. 20005; (202) 326-7300; www.usta.org. The Washington trade group representing the Bell regional operating companies and their suppliers; it is heavily involved in the debate over high-speed broadband Internet service.

[17] See Robert E. Litan and Alice M. Rivlin, "The Economy and the Internet: What Lies Ahead?" Brookings Institution conference report, December 2000, No. 4.

Bibliography

Selected Sources

Books

Dodd, Annabel Z., *The Essential Guide to Telecommunications*, Prentice Hall, 2000.
A guide to key concepts and technologies in modern telecommunications, with a particularly comprehensive section explaining the Internet and the flow of electronic communications.

Emeritz, Bob, *The Telecommunications Act of 1996: Law and Legislative History*, Pike & Fischer, 1996.
An in-depth legal analysis of this wide-ranging law, including how it changed the federal government's regulatory focus and made sweeping changes to the 1934 Communications Act.

Articles

Bettelheim, Adriel, "Information Technology's Anxious Side," *CQ Weekly*, Oct. 14, 2000, p. 2390.
The Internet economy, the engine that fueled high-paying job growth in the 1990s, will draw increasing regulatory scrutiny in the 107th Congress.

Davidson, Paul, "Is Telecom Act 'a complete failure?' " *USA Today*, Feb. 8, 2001, p. 3B.
Five years after President Bill Clinton signed the far-reaching Telecommunications Act of 1996, Davidson takes a comprehensive look at its impact on phone, digital TV, broadcast, broadband and cable.

Schwartz, John, "Government Is Wary of Tackling Online Privacy," *The New York Times*, Sept. 6, 2001, p. C1.
An overview of concerns hindering legislation to protect personal information in cyberspace, written just before the terrorist attacks.

Schwartz, John, "Securing the Lines Of a Wired Nation," *The New York Times*, Oct. 4, 2001, p. F1.
With the threat of cyberterror no longer abstract, a chain of potential computer disruptions is getting new scrutiny.

Goodman, Peter S., "FCC Sitting Out Telecom War," *The Washington Post*, May 3, 2001, p. E1.
The Federal Communications Commission, under new Chairman Michael K. Powell, is standing aside and allowing market forces to shape the local phone market.

Ota, Alan K., "Chairman Tauzin Charts a Bold Course for Commerce," *CQ Weekly*, Feb. 3, 2001, p. 258.
The elevation of Rep. W.J. "Billy" Tauzin, R-La., to the chairmanship of the powerful House Energy and Commerce Committee could bring dramatic changes to the regulation of the telecommunications market.

Shiver Jr., Jube, "FCC Takes Aim at Regional Bells Regulation," *Los Angeles Times*, May 8, 2001, p. C1.
In his first major legislative initiative since becoming FCC chairman in January, Michael K. Powell has asked lawmakers for more authority to investigate and punish regional Bell companies that stymie federal efforts to promote phone competition. Powell is seeking to boost the current allowable FCC fine from $1.2 million to $10 million per incident.

Reports

"Critical Infrastructure Protection: Significant Challenges in Protecting Federal Systems and Developing Analysis and Warning Capabilities," U.S. General Accounting Office, Sept. 12, 2001, GAO-01-1132T.
An assessment of the government's vulnerability to computer intrusions from terrorists or hostile nations, delivered the day after the Sept. 11 attacks.

"Data Summary on Local Telephone Service Competition," Federal Communications Commission, May 2001.
The latest data on competition in the local telephone market between Bells and smaller rivals show that Bells control about 91 percent of the local telephone lines.

Litan, Robert E., and Rivlin, Alice M., "The Economy and the Internet: What Lies Ahead," Brookings Institution Conference Report, No. 4, December 2000.
Two Brookings Institution economists review economic studies assessing the impact of electronic commerce on the nation's economy, with predictions of future policies.

"Tech Policy 2001," Delaney Policy Group, December 2000.
An overview of the current status of policy debates on 25 issues of interest to technology firms and electronic commerce at the start of the 107th Congress.

Thierer, Adam D., "A 10-Point Agenda for Comprehensive Telecom Reform," Cato Institute Briefing Paper No. 63, May 8, 2001.
An analyst for the libertarian think tank outlines how changing committee chairmanships in Congress and the leadership shakeup at the FCC open a window of opportunity for telecommunications reform.

15 War on Terrorism

DAVID MASCI AND KENNETH JOST

The images of Sept. 11 will be seared into the nation's collective consciousness for generations to come. Two hijacked airplanes, one after the other, smashing into the World Trade Center's twin towers in the heart of New York City's financial district; the two 110-story skyscrapers erupting in flames and then collapsing into a vast cloud of billowing smoke and debris. And in Arlington, Va., an entire section of the massive Pentagon crushed and in flames after being hit by a third plane. *

As the magnitude of the terrorist attacks became clear, Americans reacted with shock and grief. By evening, those emotions had been forged into a sense of national unity, as well as intense anger at the perpetrators of the most devastating terrorist episode in U.S. history. Indeed, the death toll exceeds 3,000, and the economic losses could top $100 billion.

On the night of the attacks, President Bush pledged in brief televised remarks that the government would find the perpetrators, as the first step in a wider "war on terrorism." Although Bush mentioned no suspects, investigators said that the attacks likely were the handiwork of Saudi exile Osama bin Laden and his global terrorist network, Al Qaeda ("the base"). (*See sidebar, p. 280*.) The Islamic fundamentalist rulers of Afghanistan, the Taliban,

---

* A fourth hijacked plane, possibly heading for the White House or Capitol, crashed in western Pennsylvania after passengers overpowered the hijackers.

From *The CQ Researcher,*
October 12, 2001.

Pedestrians run for their lives as one of the twin towers of the World Trade Center collapses, sending billowing smoke and debris throughout lower Manhattan.

AP Photo/Amy Sancetta

who are protecting bin Laden, also quickly drew U.S. attention. [1]

On Sunday, Oct. 7, Bush launched the war he had been promising. At about noon Eastern Time, the White House announced that the United States and Great Britain had attacked military targets in Afghanistan using land- and sea-based planes and missiles, as well as special ground forces.

"These carefully targeted actions are designed to disrupt the use of Afghanistan as a terrorist base of operations and to attack the military capability of the Taliban regime," Bush said in a televised statement from the White House, about a half-hour after the strikes began. The United States had warned the Taliban, he said, to surrender bin Laden, stop supporting terrorism and release foreign aid workers they were holding. "None of these demands were met," Bush said. "And now, the Taliban will pay a price."

The United States has been the oc-

casional target of terrorists, both at home and overseas, for years. [2] But before Sept. 11, the country largely ignored the issue. Suddenly, fighting terrorism — defined in federal law as premeditated, politically motivated violence typically perpetrated against civilians — had become the nation's top priority.

In the weeks following the terrorist attacks, the United States said it had solidified a case against bin Laden, Al Qaeda and, by association, their Taliban supporters. The U.S. military positioned dozens of ships, hundreds of planes and thousands of troops around Afghanistan with the intention of capturing or killing bin Laden, destroying Al Qaeda's infrastructure and weakening or overthrowing the Taliban.

In addition, the U.S. assembled a coalition of European allies — led by British Prime Minister Tony Blair — and moderate Islamic states to support American efforts.

Some analysts argue that the United States cannot just target bin Laden, Al Qaeda and other terrorist groups but also must take military action against those states — like Afghanistan, Iraq and Syria — that support terrorists. The governments of such nations must be overthrown, they say, because they provide the financial and logistical assistance needed to mount complex terrorist operations.

"Without state support, these groups couldn't do the things we saw on Sept. 11," says Jack Spencer, a defense policy analyst at the Heritage Foundation, a conservative think tank. "If we don't deal with state sponsors of terrorism, we're not going to win this fight."

But other experts say that overthrowing governments will cause untold suffering for civilians and disrupt

The Middle East's Ring of Terror

The Afghanistan-based Al Qaeda network is the prime suspect in the Sept. 11 attacks on the United States. Founded in 1987 by Osama bin Laden and Egyptian militants, it bombed the U.S. embassies in Kenya and Tanzania in 1998 and the USS Cole in 2000 and maintains cells in some 60 countries. Several other terrorist organizations operate in and around the Middle East, many with ties to Al Qaeda, and threaten American and Western interests.

Source: U.S. Department of State

those countries for years to come. In addition, they say, action by the United States will probably lead to more terrorism against America and her al-lies. "We're going to end up creating more terrorists because so many people will be outraged by this and want to do something about it," says Dan Smith, chief of research at the Center for Defense Information, a think tank.

Within the United States, the administration launched what Bush and

Attorney General John Ashcroft called the most massive law enforcement investigation in U.S. history. In his televised Sept. 11 address, Bush said he had "directed the full resources of our intelligence and law enforcement communities to find those responsible and to bring them to justice."

Over the course of the next three

Algerian pilot who they said gave flying instructions to four of the hijackers.

The administration also asked Congress to pass a broad anti-terrorism bill that would ease prosecutions, lengthen sentences, expand electronic surveillance and simplify deportation of immigrants. "Our laws fail to make defeating terrorism a national

Bush also has moved to strengthen domestic defenses against terrorism, beefing up security at airports and along the borders. In addition, he announced the creation of an Office of Homeland Security to coordinate and direct anti-terrorism efforts at home. The president tapped Republican Pennsylvania Gov. Tom Ridge to the Cabinet-level job. (*See sidebar, p. 292.*)

While terrorism experts widely support the new office, they caution that Ridge will have little long-term impact unless he has some institutional authority over the 40-plus agencies, from the FBI to the Federal Emergency Management Agency (FEMA), that deal with terrorism. Some analysts, like James Lindsay, a senior fellow at the Brookings Institution, argue that the new office needs power over relevant agency budgets. "Without some sort of lever like that, they're simply not going to listen to him," he says.

Others, like former Sen. Gary Hart, D-Colo., who co-chaired the Commission on National Security in the 21st Century, go further, saying the office should be a new department, with a huge budget and staff.

But some analysts say that another big bureaucracy is not the answer. Instead, they say, Ridge should be charged with setting the direction and goals of anti-terrorism efforts at home and coordinating agencies' efforts to meet those goals. In addition, they say, Ridge will have enough power so long as terrorism is a national priority.

"He'll have the ear and support of the president to back him up," says Rep. Ike Skelton, D-Mo., ranking Democrat on the House Armed Services Committee. "How much more power does he need?"

Despite the intense focus on terrorism, both at home and overseas, administration officials — including Ashcroft — and others have warned that new terrorist attacks against the United States are likely in the near future. "We all know it's going to hap-

---

Major Terrorist Groups

Abu Nidal — Based in Iraq and Lebanon, Abu Nidal, also known as Fatah and Black September, has carried out attacks in 20 countries, including the murders of 11 Israeli athletes at the 1972 Olympic games in Munich and a 1986 Pan Am hijacking in Pakistan that left 22 people dead.

Al-Jihad — Egyptian group works closely with Al Qaeda to replace the Egyptian government with an Islamic state; assassinated Egyptian President Sadat in 1981.

Hamas — Operating in Israel and the Occupied Territories, it has staged many suicide bombings against Israeli targets and seeks to replace Israel with an Islamic Palestinian nation.

Hezbollah — Also known as Islamic Jihad, the radical Shiite Party of God is based in southern Lebanon and allied with Iran. It is suspected in hundreds of attacks against Israel as well as the 1983 bombing of the U.S. Embassy and Marine barracks in Beirut, killing 241 people.

Popular Front for the Liberation of Palestine General Command — Headquartered in Syria, with bases in Lebanon, the PFLP-GC conducts raids against Israel and opposes Yasser Arafat's PLO.

Source: U.S. Department of State

---

weeks, the government identified the 19 hijackers — all men in their 20s and 30s with Middle Eastern names. They had commandeered four flights, steering three to their targets but failing with a fourth; terrorists, passengers and crews all perished. Investigators fanned out across the country. By early October, more than 600 people had been questioned — several were charged with immigration violations but none were linked directly to the terrorist attacks. In Britain, however, the government arrested an

priority," Ashcroft told the House Judiciary Committee on Sept. 24.

Civil liberties advocates sharply criticized some of the proposals, as did some terrorism experts. "The terrorist will have at least a small victory if we change any of our principles just because they've frightened us," says Neal Pollard, founding director of the Terrorism Research Center. Still, Congress seemed likely to pass a bill later this month embodying most of what the administration requested.

pen again," Skelton says.

In particular, terrorism experts worry about chemical, biological or even nuclear attacks. [3] "If we don't get on this now, the likelihood of attack using weapons of mass destruction will grow," Spencer says. "I wouldn't be shocked if something like this happened tomorrow."

But others dismiss such concerns. "When an enemy strikes, there is a tendency to ascribe to that enemy capabilities that they don't possess," says Amy Smithson, a senior associate at the Henry L. Stimson Center, a national security think tank. "These kinds of attacks require an infrastructure and scientific knowledge that groups like Al Qaeda just don't possess."

As government officials and terrorism experts grapple with the prospect of future attacks, here are some of the questions they are asking:

Should the U.S. topple foreign governments that harbor or support terrorists?

On the evening of Sept. 11, with the fires still burning in New York and Washington, President Bush threw down the gauntlet: "We will make no distinction between the terrorists who committed these acts and those who harbor them," he told the nation and the world.

The president's remarks, backed by statements from top national security aides, were intended to put Afghanistan and other states suspected of supporting terrorism on notice that the United States would consider them legitimate military targets.

"We've essentially been at war with states that support terrorism and didn't know it until now," says the Heritage Foundation's Spencer. "President Bush is finally articulating this new reality."

Spencer argues that nations like Iraq, Syria and Iran have used terrorist groups as proxies to make war against the United States. "We have to understand that these states see themselves in a war with us," he says.

Supporters of targeting states in the war against terrorism also say that a strategy that only focuses on groups and individuals is doomed to fail because terrorists depend upon government support. "These groups could never pull off these sophisticated operations if there was no place where they could support their network," Spencer says.

"The fact is, we often think of terrorists as sleeping in caves, like bin Laden in Afghanistan," said Richard Perle, a former assistant secretary of Defense in the Reagan administration. "Terrorists go to office blocks, where they have modern communications technology, where they have the ability to move money around the world, to obtain false documents, the technology of explosives, and the like."

Ultimately, says Dan Goure, a senior fellow at the Lexington Institute, a conservative think tank in Arlington, Va., states that succor terrorists must be overthrown. "To just go after terrorist groups without dealing with the countries that help them is like fighting fleas on a dog one at a time," he says. "You spray the whole dog."

But opponents say that toppling another government would almost certainly inflame tensions throughout the Middle East and create even more terrorism in the long run. "Opposition to the U.S. in the region grows out of a perception that we misuse our power," says the Center for Defense Information's Smith, referring to American military action in the Persian Gulf fighting a decade ago. [4] Large-scale military actions will only contribute to "the sense of powerlessness that already exists among individuals and even countries" and breed more terrorism, he adds.

Moreover, critics say, massive U.S. military action could destabilize or even topple key U.S. allies in the region like Pakistan, Saudi Arabia or even Egypt, making it harder for America to dismantle terrorist groups in the future.

"These states all have large numbers of Islamic fundamentalists who could, in a worst-case scenario, even topple one of these moderate regimes," says Ivan Eland, director of defense policy studies at the CATO Institute, a libertarian think tank. "At the very least, it would mean that we would lose some of our allies in the region as they pulled away [from the U.S.] to avoid upsetting their own internal opposition. So we might find ourselves trying to operate in, say, Afghanistan without having Pakistan to support us, which would make doing that impossible."

In short, Eland says, invading another country is exactly what the terrorists want. "Doing something like that is playing into bin Laden's hands because it will lead to instability and strengthen the hand of the extremists."

"This could get completely out of hand," agrees Anthony Cordesman, a senior analyst at the Center for Strategic and International Studies (CSIS). "You could find yourself at war with the entire Arab world if you're not careful."

Finally, opponents say, U.S. military action, even if successful, usually doesn't solve the problem in the long term. "When the U.S. has toppled governments in the past, they have usually ended up wreaking much more havoc than existed before," says Martha Honey, director of peace and security at the Institute for Policy Studies, a liberal think tank.

Cordesman agrees. "This is a trip that is infinitely easier to start than it is to finish," he says, adding that countries like Afghanistan or Iraq could be broken up into a number of pieces if their regimes are cavalierly overturned.

But supporters of military action argue that creating greater instability or more potential terrorists would be a worthwhile tradeoff if the states that sponsor terrorism were replaced with friendlier regimes.

"If you replace the states that do support terrorism with those that don't, you deny terrorists the kind of support that allows them to mount big operations against us," Goure says. "So even if you have more terrorists, if they can't do anything against us, that's much better."

Will tougher wiretapping and immigration laws help fight terrorism without unduly infringing on civil liberties?

Two days after the Sept. 11 attacks, the Senate approved with little debate a bill significantly expanding the government's power to track suspects' communications on the Internet. The measure — still pending in Congress — was rushed through in the evening hours of Sept. 13 despite questions from Democratic senators about making electronic surveillance easier not only in terrorism cases but also in criminal investigations generally.

When Ashcroft came to Capitol Hill two weeks later with an omnibus anti-terrorism bill, however, skeptics were more insistent. Republican and Democratic lawmakers combined to slow the bill — and eventually force substantial compromises — by complaining that some of the provisions would curtail individual liberties while doing little to prevent future attacks. [5]

The administration's partial retreat followed a buzz saw of criticism from civil liberties organizations on the right and the left. "The civil liberties that we value so much as a society are at stake," said Rachel King, legislative counsel at the American Civil Liberties Union (ACLU). Charles Peña, a defense policy analyst at the Cato Institute, voiced similar caution: "We need to be very careful about rushing to give up some of our liberties in exchange for security," he said.

The Justice Department bill covered a range of topics — including a broader definition of terrorism crimes, maximum life sentences and no time limits for prosecutions. The major controversies, however, centered on provisions to make it easier for the government to engage in electronic surveillance and detain aliens.

Ashcroft told lawmakers the provisions were necessary to deal with the "clear and present danger" of terrorism. "We need to unleash every possible tool against terrorism, and we need to do that promptly," he warned the House Judiciary Committee on Sept. 24.

The immigration provisions called for allowing the attorney general to order the indefinite detention of any non-citizen if he had "reason to believe" the person "may commit, further or facilitate" terrorist acts. The bill also permitted deporting any alien who gave "material support" to a terrorist organization. "The ability of alien terrorists to move freely across our borders and operate within the United Sates is critical to their capacity to inflict damage on our citizens and facilities," Ashcroft said.

Immigrants'-rights advocates sharply criticized the proposed detention power. The bill "would basically allow unilateral detention of anyone on the attorney general's say-so," said David Cole, a Georgetown University law professor who has represented Palestinians in a number of deportation cases. Cole also criticized the "material support" provision, which he described as "guilt by association."

Some conservatives were also critical. "I am against permanent detention without cause," said Todd Gaziano, director of legal studies at the Heritage Foundation.

Some terrorism experts also said the immigration provisions went too far. "There are things that America stands for: land of the free, home of the brave, the melting pot," Pollard of the Terrorism Research Center said. "That's one of the things that has resulted in such strong international support."

The electronic-surveillance section of the administration bill was both broader and more complex. It included provisions for so-called "roving" wiretaps — court orders to wiretap any phone that a suspect might use rather than requiring separate permission for each. Another provision called for allowing the government to obtain a warrant or court order for nationwide electronic surveillance rather than having to obtain authorization in individual judicial districts. And the Justice Department asked for the power to subpoena Internet service providers for the names and e-mail addresses of people in communication with a terrorism suspect.

Ashcroft said that the provisions would help law enforcement powers adapt to new technologies and tactics. "Terrorists are trained to change cell phones frequently, to route e-mail through different Internet computers in order to defeat surveillance," he testified. "We are not asking the law to expand, just to grow as technology grows."

Civil liberties groups said the provisions would reduce judicial protections against privacy-invading surveillance. Nationwide surveillance orders would amount to "a blank check," King said. The Center for Democracy and Technology noted that the government could get a subpoena for Internet contacts with less evidence than would be needed for a search warrant. "The idea that you can go from service provider to service provider without a judge ever actually asking what leads you to believe there's criminal conduct, we said that was too much," said Deputy Director James Dempsey. [6]

The administration appeared to have been surprised by the strength of civil liberties sentiment both from lawmakers and outside groups. In a late-night session on Oct. 1, House Judiciary Committee negotiators reached bipartisan agreement on a bill that modified some of the most controversial provisions in the administration's proposal. In one major change, the new bill would allow detention of immigrants for seven days (not indefinitely) if the attorney general had "reasonable grounds" (rather than "reason to believe") for suspecting terrorist activity.

The House bill, however, retained

Bin Laden's War on America

Americans view him as a murderous religious fanatic, the presumed mastermind of the Sept. 11 attacks on the World Trade Center and Pentagon and other terrorist incidents over the past decade.

Within the Muslim world, however, Osama bin Laden is a hero in some quarters: a man of courage and piety willing to fight outside infidels in the name of their true faith.

The exiled Saudi multimillionaire "articulates the frustrations of people in the Middle East who resent being left behind while the West takes over the world," says David Little, a professor of religion and international affairs at Harvard University. "Their frustration is disorganized and beyond people's control. Bin Laden provides a point of reference and shows that something can be done."

"Bin Laden does not have religious training or recognition within the theological community of any country," explains Suzanne Maloney, a specialist on Persian Gulf politics at the Brookings Institution. Instead, his appeal stems from his proven sincerity, she explains. "He has battle credentials and has been willing to suffer" for his obsession with defending the Muslim world from alleged domination by the United States.

Bin Laden was born in Riyadh, Saudi Arabia, probably in 1957, one of 52 or 53 children of the 10 wives of a prominent construction magnate originally from Yemen.[1] When his father died in the late 1960s, bin Laden may have inherited as much as $300 million — though some authorities estimate the inheritance at much less.

As a teenager living in Beirut, Lebanon, in the early 1970s, he made his mark as a carouser and womanizer. He later studied civil engineering and business administration at King Abdul Aziz University in Jeddah, Saudi Arabia, where he was drawn to radical Islam.

Enraged by the Soviet invasion of predominantly Muslim Afghanistan in 1979, bin Laden began organizing the Afghan resistance alongside U.S.-backed guerrillas, known as *mujaheddin*. Dazzling locals with his wealth, he brought in 9,000 Arab fighters, sent in supplies, helped build arms facilities and recruited

Osama bin Laden, leader of the Al Qaeda terrorist network, has not accepted responsibility for the Sept. 11 attacks on the U.S., but in a speech broadcast on Oct. 7 he thanked God that America was now "full of fear."

AP Photo

Sunni Muslims. The legend of his bravery soon spread, along with reports that he had proposed the Reagan administration's eventual policy of arming the *mujaheddin* with Stinger missiles.

While in Afghanistan, bin Laden came under the influence of the Egyptian Islamic Jihad, the militant group responsible for the assassination of President Anwar el-Sadat in 1981. Working with the Egyptians, in 1987 he founded Al Qaeda — Arabic for "the base" — to serve as the organizational base for a global Islamic crusade.

After the Russian retreat from Afghanistan in 1989, bin Laden ended up back in Saudi Arabia, distributing videotapes extolling his military exploits. In a few years, his likeness had become common in shops and on T-shirts all over the Muslim world.

The Persian Gulf War of 1990-91 sharpened bin Laden's focus on the United States. He deeply resented the Saudi government's willingness to host U.S. troops in the campaign to remove Iraqi forces occupying Kuwait. He viewed his country's cooperation with the United States as an affront to its guardianship of the holy cities of Mecca and Medina.

After the Saudi government expelled bin Laden for anti-government views in 1991, he fled to Sudan, where he ran global businesses in banking, construction and agriculture while allegedly siphoning off funds from Muslim charities. In 1994 he was stripped of his Saudi citizenship for smuggling weapons and spreading terrorist propaganda.

Soon his network was linked — though not conclusively — to co-conspirators responsible for attacks on U.S. soldiers in Somalia, plans to assassinate the pope and President Bill Clinton and bomb U.S. passenger jetliners, the 1993 bombing of New York's World Trade Center and the 1995 bombing of the Khobar Towers, a U.S. military barracks in Saudi Arabia.[2] When U.S. pressure forced him out of Sudan, he moved to Afghanistan again, which was in the midst of a civil war.

In 1996, bin Laden issued his first major *fatwa* — an Islamic religious ruling typically issued by trained or senior clerics — declaring a holy war on "Americans occupying the land of the two holy places." Two years later, he broadened the threat to target not just soldiers but all Americans.

In 1998, he told ABC-TV reporter John Miller that his campaign of violence would "inevitably move . . . to American soil." [3] He also publicly cultivated suicide terrorists, telling followers in a video last summer, "You should love the other world, and you should not be afraid to die." [4]

Al Qaeda serves indirectly as the instrument of bin Laden's war on America. [5] Rather than carrying out attacks itself, bin Laden's group provides financial and other assistance that allows smaller independent organizations to operate.

"Al Qaeda is a Ford Foundation for terrorist groups," says Stephen P. Cohen, a South Asia expert at the Brookings Institution. "They take money that they've raised — from Muslim charitable contributions and other sources — and direct it to specific groups for specific missions."

The organization also provides other terrorist groups with military and other training from bases in Afghanistan. "They train people in camps in Afghanistan and then often send them to serve with the Taliban," Cohen says.

Groups supported by Al Qaeda operate in more than 60 countries, including the United States, Canada and Western Europe. [6] While some are thought to be based in Egypt, Algeria and Saudi Arabia, members include citizens of most Middle Eastern countries as well as militants from Muslim populations in the Philippines and Indonesia, the world's most populous Muslim nation.

Al Qaeda and similar groups represent a change in the nature of terrorism over the last few decades — away from direct state sponsorship and toward non-state terrorism. "If you consider what we were worried about even 15 years ago — Libya, Syria — that's just not the same kind of factor anymore," said Paul R. Pillar, national intelligence officer for the Near East and South Asia for the Central Intelligence Agency (CIA). [7] Today, instead of carrying out the acts of terror themselves, certain states now assist groups like Al Qaeda.

The United States has had bin Laden in its sights since the mid-1990s, but so far to no avail. Sudan made a back-channel offer to arrest bin Laden in 1996 and turn him over to Saudi Arabia. The Saudis declined, and the Clinton administration concluded it had no basis to indict bin Laden in this country. [8]

Carrying a grenade launcher and its ammunition, a Taliban fighter talks on a radio southwest of Afghanistan's capital, Kabul. The alliance has been fighting to over-throw the ruling Taliban for more than five years, but it controls only about

AP Photo/Zaheerudding Abdullah

President Clinton personally authorized a cruise missile attack on suspected training camps in Afghanistan in August 1998 in response to the U.S. embassy bombings earlier in the month. Bin Laden himself was the intended target, but — contrary to the pre-attack intelligence — he had left the site hours earlier. A year later, the CIA trained Pakistani intelligence agents to capture bin Laden, but the plan was abandoned after the Pakistani government fell in a coup Oct. 12, 1999, and the new leader — Gen. Pervez Musharraf — refused to continue the operation. [9]

Within the United States, the government's focus on bin Laden — President Bush declared that he is wanted "dead or alive" — provides a recognizable symbol of the war on terrorism. For bin Laden, the failure of the U.S. initiatives so far only furthers his hopes of reducing the United States from a great power to a humbled, chaotic land.

"We anticipate a black future for America," he told ABC in 1998. "Instead of remaining United States, it shall end up separated states and shall have to carry the bodies of its sons back to America." [10]

— *Charles S. Clark*

[1] For background, see David E. Kaplan and Kevin Whitelaw, "The CEO of Terror, Inc.," *U.S. News & World Report*, Oct. 1, 2001, pp. 18-22; Rob Nordland and Jeffrey Bartholet, "The Mesmerizer," *Newsweek*, Sept. 24, 2001, pp. 44-45; Yossef Bodansky, *Bin Laden: The Man Who Declared War on America* (1999); Simon Reeve, *The New Jackals: Ramzi Yousef, Osama bin Laden and the Future of Terrorism* (1999).

[2] See U.S. Dept. of State, "Patterns of Global Terrorism 2000," 2001 ("Al Qaida" entry in Appendix B) (www.state.gov).

[3] Quoted in Michael Dobbs, "Inside the Mind of Osama bin Laden," *The Washington Post*, Sept. 20, 2001, p. A1.

[4] Michael Powell, "Bin Laden Recruits With Graphic Video," *The Washington Post*, Sept. 27, 2001, p. A19.

[5] For background, see Michael Dobbs, "A Few Loyal Men Direct Bin Laden's Sprawling Network," *The Washington Post*, Sept. 27, 2001, p. A1; Karen De Young and Michael Dobbs, "Bin Laden: Architect of New Global Terrorism," *The Washington Post*, Sept. 16, 2001, p. A8.

[6] See Bob Woodward and Walter Pincus, "Investigators Identify 4 to 5 Groups Linked to Bin Laden Operating in U.S.," *The Washington Post*, Sept. 23, 2001, p. A1.

[7] Quoted in De Young and Dobbs, *op. cit.*

[8] Barton Gellman, "Sudan's Offer to Arrest Militant Fell Through After Saudis Said No," *The Washington Post*, Oct. 3, 2001, p. A1.

[9] Bob Woodward and Thomas E. Ricks, "U.S. Was Foiled Multiple Times in Efforts to Capture Bin Laden or Have Him Killed," *The Washington Post*, Oct. 3, 2001, p. A1.

[10] Quoted in De Young and Dobbs, *op. cit.*

most of the administration's original package, however, leaving civil liberties groups still discontented. "The compromise bill would have a long-term negative impact on basic freedom in America that cannot be justified," said Laura Murphy, head of the ACLU's Washington office.

For its part, the administration said it was encouraged by the bipartisan support for stronger counterterrorism laws, but voiced concern about a "sunset" provision calling for the new provisions to expire at the end of 2003 without congressional reauthorization.

Will the new Office of Homeland Security have the authority it needs to protect the country from terrorists?

On Sept. 20, before a joint session of Congress, President Bush set out the government's strategy for combating terrorism. One of the cornerstones of that plan, the president said, was a new office to direct U.S. counterterrorism efforts. [7]

"Today, dozens of federal departments and agencies, as well as state and local governments, have responsibilities affecting homeland security," Bush said. "These efforts must be coordinated at the highest levels. So tonight I announce the creation of a Cabinet-level position reporting directly to me."

In the week following the speech, the administration fleshed out its plan for the office, likening it to the National Security Council, with relevant department and agency heads — such as the secretaries of Defense and Treasury and the attorney general — working with the new coordinating body.

To underscore the importance of the office, Bush selected the experienced and popular Ridge, a close friend who will certainly have the president's ear. Still, Ridge, who resigned as governor and was sworn in on Oct. 8, faces a daunting task. More than 40 agencies within 20 departments — from the FBI to the Small Business Administration — have some hand in protecting the country from terrorist attack or mitigating any damage done.

Moreover, many analysts say, the fact that Ridge is simply a "counterterrorism czar," someone like the current drug czar who coordinates government agencies in a particular effort, makes it likely that he will play only a small role in shaping policy. These pessimists argue that, at the very least, Ridge needs some authority over the budgets of relevant agencies, which would give him the leverage to influence their policies.

"Unless you give this new office budgetary authority, Ridge will be little more than a cheerleader from the sidelines, because these agency heads and others won't listen to him," says Brookings' Lindsay. "At a place like the Department of Defense, where assistant secretaries can't even get the services to listen to them, do you think this guy from the outside will have even a chance if he doesn't have some control over their money?" he adds.

The most efficient way to bring Ridge into the process, Lindsay says, would be to let him examine agency budgets when they reach the Office of Management and Budget. "The OMB already plays a key role in making all agency budgets, so why not let Ridge help them then."

But some, including Lindsay, argue that budgetary authority alone will probably not be enough to make Ridge effective. According to Cordesman of CSIS, the governor will need specific delineated powers to help departments make major policy decisions. "If Ridge doesn't have the authority to shape programs over the whole structure of federal agencies, then he might as well resign right now," he says.

Some say that the office will not acquire the policy power it needs unless it becomes a full-blown agency. "If you want to get a job done, there's no substitute for having an agency with a budget," said Sen. Joseph I. Lieberman, D-Conn., chairman of the Senate Governmental Affairs Committee. [8]

Indeed, a commission report issued in January by Hart and former Sen. Warren Rudman, R-N.H., recommended the creation of a new federal department to deal with homeland security issues. The commission proposed folding the Coast Guard, Border Patrol, FEMA and Customs Service into the new agency. [9]

"I think anyone who understands how the national government works sees the difference between a czar who seeks to create task forces and working groups among disparate agencies, and the head of an agency who has accountability, statutory responsibility, budget authority and is directly accountable to the president and the people of the United States," Hart said on Fox Television's "Hardball with Chris Matthews" on Sept. 26. "And I think that agency approach which we strongly believe in is the way the president will find he has to go. I simply hope it happens before the next attack occurs."

But those who oppose creating a powerful new entity contend that the focus should be on working better with existing agencies, not trying to create a new one. "This isn't brain surgery," says Missouri Rep. Skelton. "There are so many agencies involved in [combating terrorism] that the right hand doesn't know what the left is doing. We need someone to tie all of these agencies together and direct them."

According to Skelton and others, generating yet another bureaucracy within the federal government is unnecessary and could be counterproductive. "We have trouble enough with bureaucracies that don't talk to each other," says Stephen P. Cohen, a senior fellow at the Brookings Institution. "We don't need to create another bureaucracy — some supra-interior minister — we need someone who could facilitate coordination."

Pollard of the Terrorism Research Center agrees, adding that a new department would just generate unnecessary interagency rivalries. "It should not be a full department, because if it's a new agency, then it will just compete with other agencies that already exist."

Opponents also say that it is unnecessary to give the office authority over other agencies' budgets. Indeed, they warn, conferring budgetary authority could very well hurt other agencies that have many missions — like the Coast Guard — by forcing them to neglect their other duties in order to combat terrorism. "You cannot allow this to cause an agency to change its main mission," Skelton says. "The threat of terrorism is a very real threat, but it's one that has to be handled and coordinated separately."

Moreover, Pollard says, a terrorism czar with the president's ear can have tremendous influence over future spending on terrorism. "I'll tell you already who has budgetary authority — the president," he says. "If [Ridge] makes an analysis, sets a strategy and then says, this is the strategy and this is how all the resources of the federal government should be orchestrated, then he can take his case to the president and I can guarantee to you that the president [can] make those budgetary changes."

And, opponents say, given the magnitude of the Sept. 11 attacks, Ridge will have tremendous political heft. "In the short run, he has all the authority he could ever have," says Sen. Judd Gregg, R-N.H. "The president is standing right beside him, and whatever he wants right now, he's going to get out of the administration." [10] ■

President George W. Bush meets at Camp David on Sept. 15 to discuss responding to the terrorist attacks with (from left), Attorney General John Ashcroft, Vice President Dick Cheney, Secretary of State Colin Powell, Secretary of Defense Donald Rumsfeld and Deputy Secretary of Defense Paul Wolfowitz.

AP Photo/J. Scott Applewhite

BACKGROUND

Ages of Terrorism

Terrorism — motivated variously by religious, nationalist, or political beliefs — has claimed countless thousands of lives through history and caused recurrent public panic and political disruption. Despite its gruesome toll, terrorism has had relatively little lasting impact. It has been "little more than a nuisance," according to Walter Laqueur, a leading historian on the subject. [11]

Nonetheless, the terrorist impulse has proved to be difficult to combat except with sternly repressive measures. And 20th-century technology has created the potential for wider-scale death and destruction, heightening fears of political leaders and citizens in the United States and many other countries.

Religious terrorists date back at least 2,000 years and have contributed to the modern lexicon on the subject. An extreme Jewish faction known as the sicari ("zealots") used terrorist tactics to attack its enemies — mostly other Jews — around the time of the Roman occupation of Palestine. The Order of the Assassins, an 11th-century Islamic sect in northern Persia, targeted Muslims and Christians in Syria and the then-kingdom of Jerusalem.

In recent times, religious and nationalist motivations have sometimes mixed in terrorist movements: witness the Zionist organizations in pre-independence Israel and today the Palestine Liberation Front and the Catholic and Protestant combatants in Northern Ireland.

Nationalist movements have often used terrorist tactics, especially in their early stages. The mixture of legitimate political aspirations with unsavory tactics contributes at times to a sort of moral relativism: One person's terrorist is another person's freedom fighter, it is sometimes said. Some nationalist movements have gone on to achieve their goals — in India, Israel and South Africa, for example — but only after moving beyond terrorism to broader political and diplomatic strategies. Other nationalist movements have less to show for their terror campaigns. The Basque separatist group ETA, for example, has won some concessions from the Spanish government but seems unlikely ever to gain full independence.

Along with the nationalist movements of the colonial and post-colonial era, ideological movements of the left and the right dominated the history of ter-

Chronology: Before Sept. 11

20th century
Religious, nationalist and ideological terrorists leave death and destruction around globe; attacks become more lethal due to technological advances.

———— • ————

1990s *International terrorism on increase; Osama bin Laden forges Al Qaeda terrorist network, blamed for deadly attacks against U.S.*

1991
Bin Laden expelled from Saudi Arabia for anti-government views.

Feb. 23, 1993
World Trade Center bombed; six killed, more than 1,000 injured.

1994
Four Muslim militants sentenced May 24 to 240 years each for convictions in World Trade Center bombing.

1995
Ten militant Muslims convicted Oct. 1 for thwarted conspiracy to bomb United Nations headquarters, other New York City sites.

1996
Bin Laden expelled by Sudan May 18 to Afghanistan; truck bomb explodes June 25 outside Khobar Towers U.S. military barracks in Saudi Arabia, killing 19 servicemembers.

1998
On Aug. 7, bombs damage U.S. embassies in Kenya and Tanzania, killing 224, including 12 Americans; on Aug. 20 U.S. retaliates with cruise missile attack against Al Qaeda training camps in Afghanistan, but fails to kill bin Laden.

———— • ————

2000s *U.S. presses terrorism prosecutions, seeks international support for anti-terrorism moves; domestic preparedness issues on back burner before Sept. 11, 2001, attacks on World Trade Center and the Pentagon.*

2000
National Commission on Terrorism issues report June 5 calling for stepped up security measures, improved intelligence; USS *Cole* severely damaged in explosion Oct. 12 while refueling in Aden, Yemen; 17 seamen killed.

Jan. 31, 2001
Libyan intelligence agent convicted by a Scottish court for 1988 bombing of Pan Am Flight 103; second defendant acquitted.

May 29, 2001
Four men linked to Al Qaeda convicted in 1998 embassy bombings.

June 21, 2001
Thirteen Saudis indicted in Khobar Towers attack; none in U.S. custody.

---

rorism in the 19th and 20th centuries. The mid-19th century Russian-born revolutionary Mikhail A. Bakunin outlined a strategy in his writings of using high-level assassinations to bring about revolution. Anarchists following his model assassinated a Russian czar (1881), the chief British official in Ireland (1882) and two U.S. presidents (James Garfield in 1881 and William McKinley in 1901) — but they failed to produce the hoped for revolutions.

In the 20th century, the Nazis in Germany and the Fascists in Italy used terror tactics as part of their ascensions to power. More recently, left-wing terrorism has burgeoned since the 1960s in such countries as Germany and Italy and in several Latin American nations — where it was often met by government-tolerated paramilitary groups using terrorist tactics themselves.

Terrorism has become more potent in the 20th century, according to Laqueur, at the same that combating it has become more difficult. Ever more lethal firearms and explosives have supplanted the dagger and pistol of earlier eras. Meanwhile, the rise of mass media has increased exponentially the terrorists' ability to instill fear among officials and citizens. Counterterrorism has depended either on infiltration or repression — as in communist Russia or, to some extent, in Northern Ireland. But Laqueur notes that present-day law enforcement agencies in democratic nations have less freedom to maneuver than the police forces of late-19th-century Europe. "By and large," he concludes, "counterefforts against terrorists by democratic states have been only partly effective in recent times." [12]

"Blessed" Missions

The face of terrorism has changed over the past two decades from predominantly political or ideological to predominantly religious. The "religious imperative" has become "the most important defining characteristic of terrorist activity today," writes Bruce Hoffman, a leading terrorism expert

Chronology: After Sept. 11

Sept. 11
Just before and after 9 a.m., two hijacked airliners crash into the World Trade Center in New York; both towers collapse within the hour. Federal Aviation Administration closes the nation's airports. At about 9:43 a.m., a third plane carrying 64 passengers crashes into the Pentagon. Just after 10 a.m. a fourth hijacked plane crashes in rural Pennsylvania, after passengers overpower hijackers. President Bush vows to punish the perpetrators and "those who harbor them."

Sept. 12
North Atlantic Treaty Organization declares an attack against one nation to be an attack against all. Several survivors are pulled from the wreckage in New York. FBI agents begin a massive investigation into the events. Millions of Americans and others around the world line up to donate blood. President Bush visits Pentagon crash site.

Sept. 13
U.S. airports begin reopening.

Sept. 14
A day of mourning declared in the U.S. and other countries. Congress authorizes use of force in response to the attacks and appropriates $40 billion to pay for disaster relief and new military spending. President Bush visits New York disaster site. Pakistan pledges to support U.S. operations against Afghanistan.

Sept. 17
Stock market reopens, suffering big drop. Bush announces that bin Laden is wanted "dead or alive."

Sept. 18
Afghanistan's Taliban regime refuses to hand bin Laden over to the U.S. After intense U.S. and inter-national pressure, leaders of Israel and Palestine agree to a cease-fire.

Sept. 19
Attorney General John Ashcroft proposes anti-terrorism legislation. United and American airlines each eliminate 20,000 jobs due to slowdown in air travel. U.S. warplanes begin deploying in the Persian Gulf.

Sept. 20
President Bush addresses Congress. British Prime Minister Tony Blair meets Bush and offers total support in war against terrorism. Afghani clerics ask bin Laden to leave Afghanistan.

Sept. 21
Congress clears a $15 billion aid package for U.S. airlines. The United Arab Emirates cuts ties with the Taliban regime. Saudi Arabia follows suit three days later.

Sept. 23.
Government grounds crop dusters following reports a hijacker had inquired into buying one of the planes. Bush freezes the assets of 27 organizations and individuals linked to terrorism.

Sept. 24
Ashcroft announces that more than 350 people have been detained in the investigation so far.

Sept. 25
Russia agrees not to object to U.S. use of bases in Tajikistan and Uzbekistan, two former Soviet Republics bordering Afghanistan.

Sept. 26
Saudi Arabia approves the use of its bases for U.S. operations.

Sept. 27
The FBI says "one or more" of the 19 hijackers are linked to bin Laden. Justice Department releases pictures of hijackers. Bush orders National Guardsmen posted at airports.

Sept. 30
Bush administration warns that more terrorism on U.S. soil is likely.

Oct. 1
Blair tells Labor Party conference in Britain that the Taliban must "surrender bin Laden or surrender power." Exiled Afghan king and anti-Taliban leaders agree to convene a Supreme Council in Rome at the end of the month as a first stop toward replacing the Taliban.

Oct. 2
Bush backs the idea of a Palestinian state, indicating shift in U.S. Mideast policy. U.S. officials present evidence of bin Laden's involvement to NATO.

Oct. 3
Bush proposes a $75 billion economic stimulus package.

Oct. 4
Reagan National Airport reopens; intelligence officials tell Congress that additional attacks are likely; U.S. promises an additional $300 million in aid to Afghan people.

Oct. 7
U.S. and Britain launch air strikes against terrorist bases and Taliban air defenses in Afghanistan. Bin Laden urges Muslims everywhere to fight the U.S.

Oct. 8
Former Pennsylvania Gov. Tom Ridge is sworn in as director of the new Office of Homeland Security.

Islam and the Religion of Terrorism

If America attacks our homes, it is necessary for all Muslims, especially for Afghans, to wage a holy war," declared Mullah Mohammed Hasan Akhund, deputy leader of Afghanistan's ruling Taliban, a week after the Sept. 11 terrorist attacks. Though Akhund may claim to speak on behalf of the entire Islamic world, the vast majority of its 1.2 billion Muslims probably found his sentiments extreme, if not altogether alien.

The attacks of Sept. 11 only underscore the profound divide between mainstream Islam and Islam as defined by Osama bin Laden and his associates. Zahid Bukhari, a fellow at Georgetown University's Center for Muslim-Christian Understanding, says the terrorist mastermind's claim that "God has guided a bunch of Muslims to be at the forefront and destroyed America" is "ridiculous." The attacks, Bukhari says, "had nothing to do with Islam."

Neither, other scholars say, does the Taliban's legendary extremism — its draconian restrictions on women's dress and their role in public life, for example, as well as its violent enforcement of those and other rules — originate in Islamic scripture as the Taliban claims. "A lot of the strictness is not necessarily a direct interpretation of the Koran," says Adeeb Khalid, an associate professor of history at Carleton College, in St. Paul, Minn. "What they're really doing is legislating these essentially tribal, social customs, giving them the cachet of Islam."

The Islamic tradition that does inform the Taliban and Osama bin Laden is Wahabism, a puritanical sect that arose in Saudi Arabia in the 18th century and constitutes a tiny slice of the Islamic world.

Both bin Laden's campaign to terrorize Americans and the Taliban's efforts to defend him have been waged, in part, with language. Both cite passages from the Koran in an effort to rally all Muslims, varied as they may be, around the text they all hold sacred. But many Muslims say that their use of Islamic terms like "jihad," "martyr" and "infidel" perverts their original meaning.

"The most abused translation of the word jihad is 'holy war,'" explains Zahid Bukhari, a fellow at Georgetown University's Center for Muslim-Christian Understanding. "That word means to struggle, to strive for. When you struggle to make yourself a good Muslim, that is also jihad. And when you work for your family, your children, a good living, this is also jihad."

In addition to militarizing a term that carries great psychological and spiritual significance to many Muslims, bin Laden and the Taliban fail to acknowledge the Koran's specific injunctions against the killing of innocent people and fellow Muslims.

"You can't have a jihad against women and children," says Jonathan Brockopp, an assistant professor of religion at Bard College, in Annandale, N.Y. "You can't have a jihad in which thousands of Muslims die."

Bin Laden and the Taliban are also selective with their quotations from the Koran. "They often cite a passage that says, 'Fight those who fight you,' and so forth," says Khaled Abou el Fadl, a professor of Islamic law at the University of California at Los Angeles. "But they don't continue the citation. It says, 'Fight them, but don't transgress because God does not love the transgressors.' And 'transgression' means, when you go to war, killing innocent people or non-combatants, such as farmers and hermits."

Even the promise of martyrdom, which some extremists say awaits suicidal terrorists like those who attacked the World Trade Center and Pentagon, is misapplied, experts on Islam say. "Martyrdom is about being an instrument of God's will, not seeking death," explains Brockopp. "In Islam, God is the author of life and death. Death is not something that a human being can have control of, or even see."

Finally, Mullah Akhund's call to arms gives the false impression of a single, unified Islam with shared principles and enemies. In fact, the Islamic world has been divided since the 7th century, after a controversy over Muhammad's successor created two distinct Islamic sects: Sunni and Shi'ite. Subsequent divides continue to roil the Islamic world — between Sunni-dominated Iraq and Afghanistan and Shi'ite Iran, for instance. It is about as meaningful to speak of the world's Muslims as a single people as it is to lump together Roman Catholics, Unitarians and Southern Baptists.

Islam, as practiced by the vast majority of Muslims around the world, fosters humanitarianism and faith, not war. While Sunni, Shi'ite and other Islamic sects may disagree on issues of leadership and Koranic interpretation, they are bound by five basic tenets, or "pillars," which promote social justice and the demonstration of faith, not aggression. According to the Koran, all Muslims must profess their faith in Allah, pray five times a day, act responsibly in their communities, undergo an annual fast, and, if possible, embark on a pilgrimage to Mecca once in a lifetime.

Despite his professed embrace of Islam, bin Laden and his fighters ultimately may do more harm than good to the faith, says UCLA's el Fadl. "Bin Laden defines danger purely in political terms," he says. "I don't see that as a real danger. What is far more dangerous is that Islam becomes associated with inhumanity."

— *Amy Standen*

and director of the Rand Corporation's Washington office. [13]

Islamic groups are both the most diffuse and the most lethal of the religious terrorist movements. But Jewish terrorists have killed in Israel. And homegrown terrorists in the United States have combined millennial Christianity with extreme anti-government views to plot and — once — to carry out the bombing of a federal building.

The rise of religious terrorism — almost half of the 56 known, active international terrorist groups as of 1995 were religiously motivated — represents a deadly trend, according to Hoffman. The religious terrorist views violence as "a sacramental act or divine duty" and, for that reason, is unaffected by "political, moral or practical constraints," he writes. Religious sanction — sometimes explicitly given by a clerical figure who blesses the mission — leads the terrorist to regard large-scale violence and indiscriminate killing not only as justifiable but also as necessary for the attainment of the ultimate goals. (*See box, p. 286.*)

The shift in Islamic-inspired terrorism began with the Iranian revolution of 1979 that ousted the pro-Western shah. Ayatollah Ruhollah Khomeini called on Muslims in other countries to take up his fundamentalist interpretation of Islamic law and join in resisting the tyranny and depravity of non-Muslim powers — primarily, the United States. Fundamentalist movements arose in response to challenge the relatively secular governments of Egypt and Israel. [14]

A newly militant Islamic Resistance Movement — known by its Arabic acronym Hamas — waged a suicide terrorist campaign within Israel that claimed more than 150 lives from 1994 to 1997.

Less prominently, a brand of messianic Jewish terrorism surfaced in Israel and the United States from the 1980s. Rabbi Meir Kahane, while living in the United States in 1980, openly called for Israel to establish an official terrorist group that would "kill Arabs and drive them out of Israel and the Occupied Territories."

The Israeli government spurned the call, but others answered it. Baruch Goldstein, an ultranationalist U.S.-born orthodox Jew, killed 125 Muslims in 1994 when he opened fire on wor-

shippers at the Ibrahim Mosque in Jerusalem. A year later, a young Jewish extremist, Yigal Amir, assassinated Israeli Prime Minister Yitzhak

The Pentagon was damaged and set ablaze on Sept. 11 when terrorists crashed a hijacked American Airlines 757 into the huge building across the Potomac River from Washington, killing 189 people.

Rabin, whom he viewed as a traitor to the Jewish people. (Kahane himself had been assassinated in New York in 1990.)

In the United States, Christian white supremacists fed into an assortment of ostensibly patriotic groups in the 1980s and '90s. Some of the literature quoted scripture; some of the leaders styled themselves as pastors. The government charged leaders of the Aryan Nation in 1987 with having plotted four years earlier to blow up government buildings; a raid on a white supremacist compound in Arkansas in 1984 uncovered gallons of cyanide intended for use in poisoning public reservoirs.

Then in April 1995, domestic terrorism wrought its greatest damage when Timothy McVeigh, a veteran of the Persian Gulf War drawn to the patriot movement, bombed the Alfred P. Murrah federal office building in Oklahoma City, killing 168 people.

The United States suffered most over the past two decades, however, from

religious terrorists linked to the Middle East. One of the groups targeting America was bin Laden's sprawling terrorist organization Al Qaeda. The dissident Saudi had left his native country to help Afghani Muslims resist the Soviet invasion in 1979. When the war ended a decade later, he shifted his focus to fighting the United States — which he said had defiled Islam's holiest places by stationing troops in Saudi Arabia. In February 1998 he issued a *fatwa*, or religious directive, calling on "all Muslims . . . to kill the Americans and their allies."

Rule of Law?

The United States has responded to many of the terrorist attacks of the past two decades by seeking to bring the perpetrators to justice in courts in the United States or in other countries. The legal strategy has drawn increased resources and, despite many obstacles, resulted in some significant convictions. But even before Sept. 11, officials and experts acknowledged that prosecutions and lawsuits could not be a complete answer — some said not the principal answer — to terrorist attacks. [15]

The obstacles to successful prosecutions are, in fact, daunting. For attacks committed overseas, cooperation must be sought from other countries often difficult even when dealing with friendly nations. The United States was not satisfied with Italy's handling of the trials stemming from the 1985 hijacking of the cruise ship *Achille Lauro*, in which an American was killed. The Italian government allowed the reputed leader of the hijackers, Mohammed Abbas of the Palestine Liberation Front, to flee to Yugoslavia; later, 11 of the 15 hijackers were convicted in 1991, but U.S. officials expressed disappointment with the 15-to-30-year sentences meted out.

More recently, the United States has been disappointed with Saudi Arabia's cooperation in investigating the 1998 bombing of the U.S. embassies in Kenya and Tanzania.

Cooperation in terrorism prosecutions is all the more difficult when dealing with adversary nations. The United States had to wage a protracted diplomatic campaign against Libya to force Muammar el-Qadaffi to extradite Libyan intelligence agents accused of bombing Pan Am Flight 103 in 1988 over Lockerbie, Scotland. After more than a decade of economic sanctions imposed by the U.S. and United Nations, Qadaffi allowed the agents to be tried by a Scottish court sitting in the Netherlands. The trial ended on Jan. 31, 2001, with one man convicted and the other acquitted.

Within the United States, successful prosecutions still face many obstacles — especially penetrating secretive groups. Through the 1990s, the government substantially increased law enforcement resources for terrorism investigations. The number of FBI agents assigned to counterterrorism more than doubled from 550 in 1993 to nearly 1,400 in 1992, and the proportion of the FBI budget devoted to counterterrorism rose from 4 percent in 1993 to more than 10 percent in 2000. [16]

The intensified law enforcement efforts helped federal prosecutors win some convictions — but only after lengthy trials. Four Arab men were convicted in 1994 for their roles in the February 1993 bombing of the World Trade Center and sentenced to 240 years each. The next year, 10 militant Muslims were convicted on conspiracy charges stemming from a failed plot to bomb the United Nations headquarters and other targets in New York City. Among those convicted was Sheik Omar Abdel Rahman, a blind cleric from Egypt depict-

ed by the prosecution as the leader of the World Trade Center bombing.

Most recently, four Arabs were convicted on May 29 of plotting to bomb the U.S. embassies in Kenya and Tanzania. Two of the defendants — Khalfan Khjamis Mohamed and Mohamed Rashed Daoud Owhali — were found guilty of conspiracy and murder; two others — Mohammed Saddiq Odeh and Wadih Hage — were convicted of conspiracy. All four were awaiting sentencing at the time of the Sept. 11 attacks.

By the end of the decade, international terrorism was viewed as an increasing threat that required broader and stronger responses from the government. The National Commission on Terrorism, in its June 2000 report, called law enforcement "often invaluable in the investigation and apprehension of terrorists." But the bulk of the report was devoted to diplomatic and military responses to terrorist incidents and improved intelligence gathering and preparedness to prevent attacks.

America Attacked

In lower Manhattan, Sept. 11 began as a beautiful late summer day, the sun shining in a clear blue sky. But the beauty was shattered at 8:45 a.m., when an American Airlines 767 out of Boston crashed into the north tower of the World Trade Center. Within seconds, black smoke was belching from gaping holes about four-fifths of the way up the tower.

At first, people thought it was an accident. But at 9:03 a.m., a second plane, a United Airlines 767 also out of Boston, hit the south tower. News crews, already on the scene, captured the incident, and millions of Americans watched it live. Just before 10 a.m., both towers collapsed, killing thousands of office workers and rescue personnel.

After a brief statement condemning the attacks, President Bush cut short

his visit to an elementary school in Sarasota, Fla., to return to Washington. But before Air Force One was airborne, another jumbo jet — an American Airlines 757 — smashed into the Pentagon, collapsing a huge slice of one its five sides and setting much of the surrounding area on fire. A fourth commandeered plane, apparently headed for Washington, crashed in the western Pennsylvania countryside after passengers overwhelmed the hijackers.

After unscheduled stops at military bases in Louisiana and North Dakota — for security reasons — Bush returned to Washington in the late afternoon to meet with national security advisers. That evening, the president addressed the nation, promising to find the perpetrators.

The nation's airports had been closed soon after the attacks and all airplanes ordered to land at the nearest available airport; they would not reopen for three days.

In the days following the attacks, much of the focus was on rescue efforts. In New York, where most of the casualties occurred, thousands of firefighters, emergency workers and volunteers scoured the rubble for survivors. But only a few people were pulled from the wreckage. By the following week, rescue operations shifted to removing the more than 1 million tons of debris.

Meanwhile, the government detailed 4,000 FBI agents to look for evidence. By week's end, hundreds of people — mostly of Middle Eastern origin — had been detained for questioning.

The investigation quickly revealed that some of the 19 hijackers — all from Saudi Arabia and other Middle Eastern countries — had lived quietly in the United States for years, often on expired visas. Some had begun learning to fly airplanes at American flight training schools as early as 1996.

But even before the search for clues had really gotten under way, U.S. lawenforcement authorities had fingered Saudi millionaire bin Laden and his Al

Fears of Chemical, Biological Attacks Growing

Before Sept. 11, experts generally assumed that most non-state-sponsored terrorist groups did not have the resources or expertise to successfully deploy weapons of mass destruction. But the sophistication of the New York and Washington attacks leads some to reconsider.

"Osama bin Laden has a lot of money and a lot of resources," says Luciana Borin, an anti-terrorism specialist at the Johns Hopkins University Center for Civilian Biodefense Studies in Baltimore. "I believe bin Laden's Al Qaeda network has all that it takes."

Others, however, remain unconvinced. "I don't think we need to be worried about this threat right now," says Jessica Stern, a lecturer on terrorism at Harvard University's John F. Kennedy School of Government. [1]

Experts are perhaps most concerned about the potential for biological or chemical attacks. Indeed, only minutes after the trade center towers were hit, a special team arrived at the scene to test for traces of such non-conventional weapons.

Nothing was detected, but experts say little could have been done if deadly agents had been discovered. In addition, recent simulations of biological or chemical attacks conducted by government and academic groups have not been encouraging. After one simulation last year in Denver, Tara O'Toole, deputy director of the Johns Hopkins center, concluded that the United States is "totally unprepared" to deal with such situations. [2]

In another exercise — at Andrews Air Force Base near Washington last June — "terrorists" supposedly unleashed the smallpox virus on Oklahoma City. Code-named Dark Winter, the simulation ended after the "virus" had spread to 25 states and killed several million people. "We stopped the game because there was no real end," says Susan Reingold, a fellow at the Center for Strategic and International Studies (CSIS).

Organizers chose smallpox because it is considered one of the most likely terrorist bioweapons and one the government has devoted significant resources to defend against. Yet the nation's vaccine stockpile is woefully inadequate. "We only have at most 12 million doses," Reingold says.

The dismal results of such exercises were echoed in a General Accounting Office report last month, which said the government's bioterrorism strategy was so disjointed that federal agencies disagree on which agents pose the biggest threat. [3] The Centers for Disease Control and Prevention, for example, considers smallpox a major risk, but the virus isn't even on the FBI's top 10 bioweapons risk list. [4]

Terrorists have never carried out a successful attack with biological agents, according to historian Walter Laqueur, a leading terrorism expert now at CSIS. Laqueur acknowledges, however, "a successful small-scale attack" by former members of a religious cult in Oregon in 1984 that contaminated salad bars with the salmonella bacterium and sickened at least 750 people. [5]

Nevertheless, the FBI this week was investigating two cases of inhaled anthrax in South Florida. Officials said having two cases occur so close together indicated intentional contamination, but Attorney General John Ashcroft warned on Oct. 8 it was too soon to blame terrorists.

The largest incident of chemical terrorism occurred in 1995, when Japanese cult members released sarin nerve gas into the Tokyo subway at rush hour. Thousands of passengers were exposed, and 12 died.

The limited success of the Tokyo incident shows that the fears of thousands of casualties are exaggerated, say many experts. "Despite spending tens of millions of dollars on research and technology, [the cult] couldn't figure out how to scale up production [of the gas] enough to do extensive damage," notes Amy Smithson, a senior associate at the Henry L. Stimson Center, a national security think tank.

But others say the Sept. 11 attacks signal that more sophisticated acts are likely. "It's clear there are people who won't stop at anything to harm the United States," Reingold says.

Others worry that terrorists could acquire nuclear weapons. "They're sophisticated enough to acquire the fissile material and turn it into a World War II, first-generation bomb," warns Paul Leventhal, president of the Nuclear Control Institute. "The prudent assumption is that they are nuclear capable and we have to work on interdiction. It's a very worrisome situation."

Both conventional weapons and nuclear materials repeatedly have been stolen from Russian military bases, usually with the aid of poorly paid employees. Russia has the world's largest stockpile of chemical weapons — 40,000 tons — often stored in flimsy, poorly guarded sheds. [6]

Many also worry that Pakistan's 30 to 50 nuclear weapons could be stolen by bin Laden supporters in the Pakistani military, or that the weapons could fall into Muslim extremists' hands if the shaky regime crumbles.

Finally, officials worry that terrorists here could hijack a large jet and target one of America's 103 nuclear power plants, causing widespread fallout and thousands of casualties. Leventhal's group wants anti-aircraft batteries placed at nuclear power plants.

"The first plane that hit the World Trade Center passed directly over Indian Point, a nuclear plant just north of New York City," Leventhal notes. "We're really lucky that wasn't their mission."

— Patrick Marshall

[1] See Walter Laqueur, *The New Terrorism: Fanaticism and the Arms of Mass Destruction* (1999), pp. 49-78. For opposing views, see Richard A. Falkenrath, *et al.*, *America's Achilles' Heel: Nuclear, Biological, and Chemical Terrorism and Covert Attack* (1998); Jessica Stern, *The Ultimate Terrorists* (1999).

[2] Quoted in *The Economist*, Nov. 16, 2000.

[3] General Accounting Office, "Combating Terrorism: Selected Challenges and Related Recommendations," Sept. 20, 2001.

[4] Sheryl Gay Stolberg, "The Biological Threat: Some See U.S. As Vulnerable in Germ Attack," *The New York Times*, Sept. 30, 2001.

[5] For a longer description, see Judith Miller, Stephen Engleberg and William J. Broad, *Germs: Biological Weapons and America's Secret War* (2001).

[6] Amelia Gentleman, "Russia lacks money to get rid of its nerve gas: Deadly cache stays as US freezes aid that could bail out Kremlin," *The Guardian*, June 11, 2001.

Qaeda group as the probable masterminds behind the attack. Within days, the administration began demanding that Afghanistan's ruling Taliban regime, which gives sanctuary to bin Laden, hand him and his followers over to U.S. authorities.

At the same time, Bush and Secretary of State Colin Powell began assembling a coalition to support what they repeatedly described as a "war" against terrorism. By Sept. 12, the U.S. had secured the assistance of Pakistan, which promised to allow American overflights and to provide other support when needed. Other states that border Afghanistan — notably Uzbekistan and Tajikistan — pledged to allow American forces to use their territory.

Meanwhile, the Pentagon began moving U.S. forces into place for military action against Afghanistan. Three aircraft carriers in the Eastern Mediterranean and Southwest Asian regions — with more 200 fighter planes and 33 support ships and submarines — were positioned to strike at the landlocked country. [17] Another carrier task force left Japanese waters to join them. In addition, the U.S. has called up more than 30,000 reservists and moved hundreds of fighters and bombers into the Persian Gulf region. ■

CURRENT SITUATION

Forging a Coalition

After the terrorist attacks, nations around the globe rallied to show support for the victims and the people of the United States. American flags were flown and the "Star Spangled Banner" was sung in cities everywhere. Vigils and official memorial services were held in London, Paris, Berlin and other world capitals.

Meanwhile, governments rushed to pledge support — even strategic competitors like Russia and China. [18]

But several weeks into the crisis, the mood around the world has calmed somewhat. "While there is still tremendous support for the U.S., countries aren't just going to be cheerleaders while we do whatever we want," says James B. Steinberg, director of the Foreign Policy Studies Program at Brookings.

During this period, the United States has worked to court two crucial sets of countries as it forges a coalition against terrorism. Not surprisingly, America has gathered its traditional allies — those countries mostly in Western Europe and Asia that share U.S. goals. The United States also has formed alliances in the Middle East, first with countries that border those states that might be targeted by America and second with the so-called moderate Arab countries that have supported the United States in the past.

Among the traditional allies, the United States has received strong support. A day after the attack, the North Atlantic Treaty Organization (NATO) — a U.S.-led transAtlantic military alliance that includes most of Western and Central Europe — invoked Article 5 of its charter saying that an attack against one member state is an attack against all. It was the first such declaration in NATO's 52-year history. [19]

Following the declaration, European support for the United States solidified, buoyed by polls showing that substantial majorities of Western Europeans favored joining in American military strikes. At a European Union summit meeting on Sept. 20, members expressed "total solidarity" with the United States. [20]

The United Kingdom — traditionally America's staunchest ally — led the roster of European backers, pledging all possible assistance in the fight against terrorism, including military help. Prime Minister Blair visited New York and Washington to show his country's sol-idarity with the American people and to honor the more than 300 Brits who died in the attacks. British submarines joined in the first bomb and missile attacks on Afghanistan, and elite British troops known as the Special Air Service (SAS) are operating alongside American Special Forces in the country.

French President Jacques Chirac also flew to the United States to pledge French help and has since offered military assistance, including ground forces, for upcoming campaigns. Other traditional allies, including Germany, Australia, and Canada have also pledged military assistance, up to and including ground forces.

While Russia has ruled out joining any military coalition, it has signaled that it will not object to American forces basing out of Tajikistan and Uzbekistan, two former Soviet republics that border Afghanistan. Moreover, Russian President Vladimir Putin said the military strikes against Afghanistan were justified retaliation for the Sept. 11 attacks. "Such a colossal loss cannot pass unnoticed or go without an adequate response," he said in remarks broadcast on Russian television. [21]

America's other great strategic competitor, China, has been less helpful, but for now has shown no inclination to interfere or even object to American military action in Afghanistan.

Support is more wobbly in the Middle East, where the United States needs backing from countries neighboring Afghanistan as well as moderate Arab states. So far, the U.S. has received surprisingly strong support from Pakistan, which shares a long border with Afghanistan and helped bring the Taliban to power. Indeed, Pakistan is one of only three countries — along with Saudi Arabia and the United Arab Emirates (UAE) — that accepted the legitimacy of Taliban rule before the attacks. Saudi Arabia and the UAE have since broken off diplomatic relations with the Taliban.

In the days following the attacks,

the Bush administration successfully pressured Gen. Pervez Musharraf, Pakistan's president, to close the border with Afghanistan, cut off support for the Taliban and allow the United States to use his country as a military staging area. And on Oct. 3, Pakistan described the evidence linking bin Laden to the attacks as credible and convincing.

But arm-twisting Muslim Pakistan into cooperating carries significant risk for both countries. A substantial number of Pakistan's 140 million people are fundamentalists, many of whom support bin Laden and the Taliban to one degree or another. Strong protests in the wake of American and British air strikes have increased worries that fundamentalists could destabilize and even topple the current government.

If Gen. Musharraf were deposed, Pakistan could find itself with an Islamic fundamentalist government not dissimilar to Iran's, or even the Taliban. In a nation that has exploded nuclear devices and is thought to have 30 to 50 nuclear-tipped warheads, such a change could be disastrous for the United States.

Among America's traditional Arab allies, support for the U.S. has often been cautious. Egypt, Jordan and Saudi Arabia have large numbers of Islamic fundamentalists and, like Pakistan, they fear that too much of a pro-American line might foment political instability.

Saudi Arabia, a key U.S. ally during the gulf war and past target of Al Qaeda attacks, initially balked at an American request to use air bases and a U.S.-built state-of-the-art command center. Only after the U.S. and Europe applied pressure did the Saudis agree to allow attacks against Afghanistan to originate from their soil. [22]

Finally, the crisis has strained relations between the U.S. and its strongest ally in the region, Israel. In an effort to appeal to Arab public opinion, President Bush has shown greater sympathy for Palestinian aspirations, stating on Oct. 1 that he had always been in favor of Palestinian statehood. Bush's remarks prompted Israeli Prime Minister Ariel Sharon to accuse him of "appeasement." Sharon's statement prompted a rare public rebuke from the administration,

Virginia Gov. James Gilmore (c), with (l) Maj. Gen. Claude Williams, Maj. Scott Flannery, and Col. Carl Shuey, walk through Ronald Reagan Washington National Airport on Oct. 10. The governor toured the facility and reviewed the National Guard troops that are guarding the airport.

which called his remarks "unacceptable." [23] Sharon later apologized.

Military Options

On Oct. 7, the United States and Great Britain began what both countries say will be a protracted military offensive against terrorist camps and military targets in Afghanistan. While the attacks — involving 40 aircraft and 50 sea-launched Cruise missiles — came from the air, Secretary of Defense Donald Rumsfeld stated

that some of the operations would be "covert," implying that ground forces could be involved. [24]

One purpose of the strikes, which continued in the days that followed, was to destroy training camps known to be used by bin Laden's Al Qaeda terrorist network. These targets — mostly in eastern Afghanistan — were hit by huge B-1 and B-52 bombers using old style "iron" bombs, designed to do great damage. [25]

Also targeted were Taliban military bases throughout the country. In particular, the allies hoped to incapacitate the regime's airfields, air defenses and communications facilities in order to take unfettered control of the skies. These targets were hit with laser-guided bombs designed to prevent widespread collateral damage and civilian casualties.

While bombers and missiles were flying, the United States also was conducting humanitarian flights, dropping large quantities of food and medical supplies to Afghan refugees in the southern part of country, near the border with Pakistan. Rumors of U.S. military strikes had caused a flood of refugees from Kabul and other Afghan cities in the weeks before Oct. 7. Prior to the Sept. 11 crisis, the United Nations had estimated that 5 million Afghans were in danger of starving to death due to a three-year-old drought and neglectful Taliban policies. The current crisis is expected to raise that number to 7.5 million, the U.N. says. [26]

The military and humanitarian missions were deliberately handled simultaneously to show that the United States wasn't trying to bring further hardship to the Afghan people. In his speech to the nation on the Sunday the attacks commenced, Bush said that while terrorists and their Taliban supporters would suffer, "the oppressed

Beefing Up Security at Home

The president announces that smallpox has been reported in Oklahoma City. Terrorists are suspected. Within two weeks, the disease spreads to 25 states. Faced with a shortage of vaccine, officials must decide who should be protected. Within a few months, 1 million Americans are dead.

Last summer, after playing this smallpox war game codenamed "Dark Winter," government officials discovered the nation is woefully unprepared to combat a biological attack. In fact, they learned, the Centers for Disease Control and Prevention (CDC) only stockpiles about 12 million doses of smallpox vaccine — far too little to prevent an epidemic. [1]

The dilemma is whether to beef up security for hundreds of potential attacks — only to be hit where one wasn't anticipated. [2] In almost every area where security was tightened following the Sept. 11 attacks, experts found gaping loopholes. The new challenge will be thinking outside the traditional pigeonholes of agency turf and past terrorist tactics, experts say.

After the attacks, security was intensified at the most obvious places, such as bridges, water supplies, chemical plants, theme parks and landmark buildings. [3] Freight shipments were delayed for hours at the Canadian border. Trucks carrying potentially hazardous chemicals on highways were stopped. [4]

President Bush announced several airport security proposals, including stationing National Guard troops at airport metal detectors and increasing the number of armed marshals on planes. [5] National Security Council staff, in anticipation of the military strikes in Afghanistan, had coordinated a largely secret effort to increase security at major transportation hubs, nuclear power plants, drinking water supplies and other vulnerable points. [6]

Bush also tapped Republican Gov. Tom Ridge of Pennsylvania to head a new Office of Homeland Security to coordinate anti-terrorism activities among some 46 often-warring departments and agencies.

The success of the new office will hinge largely on whether Ridge has the power to issue orders to headstrong, competing agencies like the FBI and the CIA. "Is Ridge going to be like a drug czar? I hope not," says Randall Larsen, director of the Anser Institute for Homeland Security, in Arlington, Va. Larsen says lack of budget authority meant past drug czars couldn't even get senators to return their phone calls.

Noting that previous efforts have failed to get agencies like the FBI and the CIA to share information, James Adams, a senior fellow at the Center for Strategic and International Studies (CSIS), says, "They won't do this willingly. They'll have to be forced."

Raymond W. Kelly, former commissioner of the U.S. Customs Service, experienced the frustration of federal agencies refusing to share information, even when it could have helped track terrorists. "At Customs, I needed more information about what was coming across our borders, and it was very difficult to get intelligence-gathering sources to do that," says Kelly, now security chief at Bear, Stearns & Co.

Major challenges for Ridge will be tightening U.S. borders and monitoring the immigrants already here. Customs officers inspect less than 2 percent of the 340,000 vehicles and 58,000 cargo shipments crossing U.S. borders daily, according to a federal commission led by former Sens. Gary Hart, D-Colo., and Warren B. Rudman, R-N.H. [7]

"We don't have any ability to filter bad from good at our border" says Stephen Flynn, a senior fellow at the Council on Foreign Relations and an expert in border control. Flynn says U.S. ports "leak like a sieve." Even with stepped-up checking of trucks, he says, "there is still no credible inspection" at the Canadian border beyond checking licenses and manifests and "some dogs roaming around."

The lax surveillance reflects two economic realities — funding for inspections has not kept pace with increases in global trade, and no one wants to slow it down, Flynn says.

The Immigration Flood

Several suspected terrorists linked to the World Trade Center attack remained in the country with expired visas without attracting notice. That's because the government does not track aliens' whereabouts once they enter the country, says Peter Andreas, author of the 2000 book *Border Games* and an assistant professor of political science at Brown University.

But, he cautions, the lax policy grows out of the public's historical reluctance to have the kind of Big Brother surveillance common in other countries. "The concern is that in our eagerness to do something big in stopping terrorism," he says, "we will undermine our open society."

In the case of suspected terrorists who legally entered the country, the border wasn't the problem, Andreas adds: "Giving them visas in the first place and having no mechanism to track expired visas was the weak point."

At Los Angeles International and other airports, the Immigration and Naturalization service offers an identity card that scans an individual's unique eye iris, as well as fingerprints. So far, the system is voluntary. Flynn suggests that electronic IDs could prevent the fraudulent use of passports, as was reported among some of the suspected terrorists.

A task force reporting to Transportation Secretary Norman Y. Mineta has examined a national computerized identification system that would store individuals' face prints and fingerprints in a database. [8] Airline check-in counters could access the database and check a facial ID of a passenger against pictures of terrorist suspects.

Civil liberties groups worry that ID cards could be an invasion of privacy and lead to a violation of civil liberties. Retorts Schiavo, "You don't have a constitutional right to fly."

Recent polls suggest that the public may be willing to sacrifice some privacy for security. In a poll conducted on Sept. 13 and 14, 56 percent favored national electronic ID cards. [9]

Aviation Security — Still Flawed

Major security gaps in aviation remained untouched by Bush's Sept. 28 speech aimed at reassuring the flying public, some aviation experts say.

"Nothing" in Bush's announcement "gave us a big increase in security," says Mary Schiavo, former inspector general of the Federal Aviation Administration (FAA). It will take years to put armed air marshals on each of the 30,000 daily flights as promised by Bush, Schiavo says.

For foolproof security, Schiavo says, "We have to look at every bag, every carry-on, every food cart." But that will only happen if the nation funds upgraded detection equipment and better-paid baggage screeners, she says.

"I don't want to trust my life and the life of my loved ones to people we can't screen making $8.50 an hour," says Neil C. Livingstone, CEO of GlobalOptions, a terrorism consulting firm. Employees of catering and cleaning companies who fill food carts and clean planes are often illegal immigrants subject to no security checks, he adds.

Israel's approach to airport security, which relies heavily on personal interrogations and profiles suspicious passengers, has produced a near-perfect record against bombings and hijackings, some experts maintain. [10]

"Ethnic profiling is very important," Livingstone argues, acknowledging that civil libertarians will be offended. The FAA's random searches miss the target, he insists. "If we're looking for Arabs or Islamists, we shouldn't waste time looking for little old ladies."

Bioterrorism — Thinking the Unthinkable

"Biological weapons are a real threat. In any exercise, the U.S. response has been a shambles," says security expert Adams.

Although smallpox exists officially only in two labs in the U.S. and Russia, experts believe rogue states or terrorists may have it.

According to the CDC, smallpox is only one of six highly infectious diseases that terrorists could use. [11] For some, like anthrax — a potentially deadly bacteria — the CDC is stockpiling antibiotics. In fact, the FBI said on Oct. 8 it was investigating possible terrorist links to two definite cases of anthrax and a suspected third case in South Florida.

Some experts say the nation should beef up its human intelligence to know if would-be terrorists are infiltrating laboratories. "We need to know who's learning to do what in our labs just like we need to know who's learning to fly," comments a former senior Health and Human Service Department official. "What are they doing after they leave the labs?"

Other experts say it is virtually impossible to keep a deadly pathogen out of the country and that the United States should concentrate on training hospitals and public health systems to recognize and stop unusual diseases. Larsen of the Anser Institute says he has breezed into senators' offices and

even the White House with a test tube containing bacteria similar to anthrax.

"There's no detection system in the world to know that I had a test tube in my pocket. You're not going to prevent it coming into the country," he says.

Sen. Edward Kennedy, D-Mass., and Sen. Bill Frist, R-Tenn., are proposing $1.6 billion to fund an array of public health programs including increasing stockpiles of anti-bioterrorism vaccines and training public health professionals. [12]

Theoretically, biological agents could be sprayed from a crop duster plane, released in powdered form through ventilation systems or sneaked into water supplies. However, huge quantities of any agent would be needed to contaminate a typical city's water supply, experts say. [13] Sending a terrorist infected with smallpox to the United States is a plausible scenario, according to Asha George, biological program officer at the Nuclear Threat Initiative. By contrast, it would require specialized knowledge to transform a pathogen like anthrax into particles small enough to be inhaled.

The Japanese cult that put nerve gas in Tokyo subways in 1995 failed when it tried to spread anthrax in 1993. "Aum Shinrikyo had enormous financial resources and Ph.D. scientists, yet they never mastered anthrax," says Christopher F. Chyba, co-director of Stanford University's Center for International Security and Cooperation. "That suggests it's not as easy to master as it is sometimes depicted."

— Sarah Glazer

[1] See www.homelandsecurity.org for full script and lessons learned from "Dark Winter," June 22-23, 2001.

[2] See Malcolm Gladwell, "Safety in the Skies," *The New Yorker*, Oct. 1, 2001, p. 50.

[3] See "State of the Union: America the Vulnerable?" *The Wall Street Journal*, Sept. 28, 2001, p. B1.

[4] Daniel Machalara and Rick Brooks, "After Terror Attacks, Shipping Goods Takes Longer and Cost More," *The Wall Street Journal*, Sept. 27, 2001, p. A1, and "States are Checking Trucks Hauling Hazardous Matter," p. A8.

[5] Elisabeth Bumiller, "Bush to Increase Federal Role in Security at Airports," *The New York Times*, Sept. 28, 2001, p. A1.

[6] Robert Pear and Judith Miller, "Entire Nation on High Alert as Security is Stepped Up," *The New York Times*, Oct. 6, 2001, p. B1.

[7] See Eric Pianin *et al.*, "Across U.S., A Security Scramble," *The Washington Post*, Sept. 23, 2001.

[8] Facial recognition systems were under consideration by the transportation task force that reported to President Bush. See Robert O'Harrow, Jr., "Facial Recognition System Considered for U.S. Airports," *The Washington Post*, Sept. 24, 2001.

[9] Lisa Guernsey, "Living Under the Electronic Eye," *The New York Times*, Sept. 27, 2001, p. G1.

[10] Gladwell, *op. cit.*

[11] The other diseases are anthrax, botulism, plague, tularemia and viral hemorrhagic fever. See www.bt.cdc.gov.

[12] See Laurie McKinley, "Suddenly, Public Health Administration is Seen as Top Priority," *The Wall Street Journal*, Sept. 28, 2001, p. A16. Also see, Sheryl Gay Stolbert, "Some Experts Say U.S. is Vulnerable to a Germ Attack," *The New York Times*, Sept. 30, 2001, p. A1.

[13] See Gregg Winter and William J. Broad, "Added Security for Dams, Reservoirs and Aqueducts," *The New York Times*, Sept. 26, 2001.

people of Afghanistan will know the generosity of America and her allies."

Many defense experts have applauded the administration's initial steps, arguing that targeted air strikes and the humanitarian campaign designed to win over the Afghan people should help weaken the Taliban. "With their initial strikes . . . the United States and United Kingdom are off to a good military start in the struggle against global terrorism," wrote Brookings senior fellow Michael O'Hanlon on the day of the first attacks. [27]

Still, they caution, bombing will not be enough unseat bin Laden or the Taliban, in part because there are few permanent strategic targets. "This is a very mobile enemy, and so things worth striking from the air are going to be hard to find," says the Center for Defense Information's Smith.

Instead, analysts say, America and its close allies are likely to use elite commando units that enter and exit the country quickly to destroy Taliban and terrorist targets. "The only sort of military unit that makes sense for a foreign army is the four-man team primed to perform one task and then get out quickly," said Richard Cleghorn-Brown, a communications expert who served with Afghan resistance forces against the Soviets in the 1980s. [28]

According to newspaper reports, American and British units have been conducting reconnaissance missions in the country for weeks, looking for bin Laden and scouting the terrain for future action. [29] These units are likely to now be employed selectively for special operations

Air strikes are likely to be used in conjunction with these small units. "When they find something too large to take care of themselves, they'll call in air power," Smith says.

Many defense experts say that almost any military strategy will revolve around the Northern Alliance, the remnant of Afghanistan's government before the Tal-

iban came to power and its only major opposition. The alliance controls less than 10 percent of the country and has only 10,000 to 12,000 soldiers, compared with the Taliban's 40,000 men under arms. Still, its strongholds in northeast Afghanistan could give the U.S. an ideal staging area for special-forces raids into Taliban-controlled territory.

The alliance also will probably serve as the nucleus of any U.S.-inspired attempts to remove the Taliban. America has already promised the alliance financial and military assistance in the hope of bolstering its ability to fight the Taliban and begin retaking territory. In addition, American planes have struck Taliban forces near the Northern Alliance, and an offensive by the opposition group is expected.

But some analysts wonder whether the alliance is capable of toppling the Taliban, even with massive U.S. assistance, in part because of the recent assassination of its legendary leader, Ahmed Shah Massoud, who helped drive the Soviets out. "Since the death of Massoud, we really don't know if they are still a cohesive fighting force," Smith says.

Even if they are, says CSIS's Cordesman, it is unlikely the alliance could take and hold much of the country without at least some of the nation's largest ethnic group, the Taliban-allied Pashtun, joining the opposition. "The Pashtun make up 40 percent of the population and have to be part of any force that replaces the Taliban," he says. "So, first, the alliance will have to lure some of these people away from the Taliban before they can hope to unseat [the regime]."

"You have to hope that this snowballs, that as [the alliance] becomes stronger other tribes and groups will want to join up," agrees O'Hanlon.

Such a scenario is possible, O'Hanlon and others say, as Afghanistan is a tribal nation of competing ethnic groups, and even the Taliban is made up of a host of factions, many of which could defect under the right cir-

cumstances. Already, there are reports that Abdul Haq — a respected former leader of the anti-Soviet resistance — and other Afghan exiles are trying to convince Taliban commanders to defect. [30] And the country's former monarch, King Zahir Shah (now living in Rome) has expressed an interest in trying to help the country establish a post-Taliban government. [31]

Still, O'Hanlon believes that it will be many months before the Northern Alliance — even with outside help and allies in Afghanistan — can oust the Taliban. In the meantime, he says, "We have to convey the resolve that the U.S. wants to help, that we're not just in this for a few months."

Another potential military target often mentioned is Iraq, which the United States forced out of Kuwait in the Persian Gulf War. Since then, Iraqi President Saddam Hussein has thwarted international efforts to eliminate his ability to produce biological and chemical weapons. There also is some evidence linking Iraq to past terrorist attacks and, possibly, the Sept. 11 catastrophe.

The fact that a U.S.-led coalition shattered Iraq's military in a matter of days has led many analysts to call for another offensive against Hussein, this time with the intention of toppling the regime.

But Cordesman says such action is unlikely. "First, you'd need solid evidence that they were really involved in [the Sept. 11] attack, solid enough to convince the Saudis, the Turks, the Kuwaitis and the Jordanians, all of whom don't want the uncertainty such an attack would bring."

The greatest uncertainty, Cordesman and others say, involves what would happen if Saddam's regime were to be dismantled. Since Iraq has three sizable minorities — the Kurds in the North, Sunni Muslim Arabs in the Center and Shia Muslims in the South — the country could fragment into several unstable states if Saddam was replaced by a weak central authority.

Finally, Cordesman says, even if the

At Issue:

MARK KRIKORIAN
EXECUTIVE DIRECTOR,
CENTER FOR IMMIGRATION STUDIES

WRITTEN FOR THE CQ RESEARCHER, OCT. 8, 2001

*i*n the wake of the Sept. 11 atrocities, there has been much discussion of the need for increased border control. But the actual number of people we admit across our borders also needs to be reduced.

The Immigration and Naturalization Service (INS) simply cannot undertake the reforms and expansion necessary for homeland defense if it is also forced to process hundreds of thousands of new immigrants, foreign students and workers each year.

The General Accounting Office reported in May that the receipt of new applications (green cards, citizenship, temporary workers, etc.) has increased 50 percent over the past six years and the backlog of unresolved applications has quadrupled to nearly 4 million. The number of citizenship applications filed in the 1990s was about 6.9 million, triple the level of the 1980s; temporary admissions nearly doubled in the 1990s to more than 30 million; and the number of (very labor-intensive) applications for asylum in the 1990s was nearly 1 million, more than double the level of the 1980s.

Now, one might argue that the INS could indeed tackle security issues without cutting immigration if it was given more money. This is exactly what Congress and the administration have in mind — the agency may end up with a fiscal 2002 budget up 10 percent from 2001, to more than $5.6 billion. And more will be on the way.

Some have also proposed reorganizing the INS, by splitting the service and enforcement functions into either two agencies or two separate INS chains of command. Some kind of administrative reorganization now seems very likely.

But more money and better organization won't be enough on their own. The only way to give the INS the breathing room it needs to put its house in order and to deal with homeland security is to reduce its workload wherever possible.

Some demands upon the service can't be reduced — tourists will keep coming, legal immigrants will keep applying for citizenship. But the admission of new immigrant, foreign students and workers is not a given. Cutting legal immigration back to the spouses and minor children of American citizens, plus a handful of genuine Einsteins and authentic refugees, and reducing the current caps on various student and worker visas is essential if INS — and the State Department's Consular Affairs Bureau — are to fulfill their homeland defense roles.

DANIEL T. GRISWOLD
ASSOCIATE DIRECTOR,
CENTER FOR TRADE POLICY STUDIES,
CATO INSTITUTE

WRITTEN FOR THE CQ RESEARCHER, OCT. 8, 2001

*w*e can stop terrorists from entering the United States without closing our borders or even reducing the number of hardworking, peaceful immigrants who settle here. Obviously, the U.S. government should "control its borders" to keep out anyone who intends to commit terrorist acts. The problem is not that we are letting too many people into the United States but that the government is not effectively keeping out the wrong people.

We must do what is necessary to stop potentially dangerous people at the border. Law enforcement and intelligence agencies must work closely with the State Department, the Immigration and Naturalization Service and U.S. Customs to share information about potential terrorists. Computer systems must be upgraded and new technologies adopted to screen out the bad guys without causing intolerable delays at the border.

More agents need to be posted at ports of entry to more thoroughly screen for high-risk travelers. In the wake of Sept. 11, long-time critics of immigration have tried to exploit legitimate concerns about security to argue for drastic cuts in immigration. But immigrants are only a small subset of the total number of foreigners who enter the United States every year. Only about 1 out of every 20 foreign nationals who enter the United States come here to immigrate. The rest are tourists, business travelers, students, and Mexican and Canadians who cross the border for a weekend to shop or visit family and then return home with no intention of immigrating.

The 19 terrorists who attacked America did not apply to the INS to immigrate or to become U.S. citizens. Like most aliens who enter the United States, they were here on temporary tourist and student visas. Oddly, Mark Krikorian does not suggest we reduce the number of temporary visas even though that is the most likely channel for terrorists to enter the country. We could reduce the number of immigrants to zero and still not stop terrorists from slipping into the country on non-immigrant visas.

It would be a national shame if, in the name of security, we were to close the door to immigrants who come here to work and save and build a better life for themselves and their families. Immigrants come here to live the American dream; terrorists come to destroy it. We must do more to keep dangerous people out, but we must not allow America's tradition of welcoming immigrants to become yet another casualty of Sept. 11.

U.S. Studied Terrorist Threat for Years

Scores of studies have probed America's vulnerability to terrorist attack. Many were by congressional panels and federal agencies — like the State Department's annual "Patterns of Terrorism" report. In January, a bipartisan commission of former legislators and military leaders predicted a catastrophic attack in the next 25 years.

Before Sept. 11, the reports largely were ignored. "Our political leadership didn't hear us, the military leaders didn't hear us and the media didn't listen," said former U.S. Sen. Gary Hart, D-Colo., co-chairman of the bipartisan panel.

Hart's commission, echoing nearly every panel that has studied the problem, noted that more than 40 federal agencies and dozens more at state and local levels with responsibility for America's safety do not effectively work with one another.

Key studies and their recommendations include:

"Combating Terrorism: Selected Challenges and Related Recommendations," General Accounting Office (GAO), September 2001.* The just-published report notes considerable duplication of federal, state and local anti-terrorism efforts and calls for a central authority to coordinate all anti-terrorism activities. The report also recommends:

- Assessing the terrorist threat from nuclear, chemical and biological weapons.
- Delaying the creation of new National Guard teams until their missions are fully coordinated.
- Clarifying strategy for combating cyber-terrorism.

(* For 107 other GAO reports on terrorism, plus 35 studies on airport security, go to www.gao.gov.)

"Road Map for National Security: Imperative for Change: The Phase III Report of the U.S. Commission on National Security/21st Century," United States Commission on National Security/21st Century, February 2001 — Co-chaired by Hart and former Sen. Warren Rudman, R- N.H., the panel concluded that significant changes must be made in U.S. national security or the country could lose its global influence and leadership. The report also recommended:

- Establishing a National Homeland Security Agency.
- Reorganizing Congress' role in national-security affairs and establishing a select committee for homeland security.

"The Second Annual Report of the Advisory Panel to Assess Domestic Response Capabilities for Terrorism Involving Weapons of Mass Destruction," December 2000 — Headed by Gov. James S. Gilmore III, R-Va., the commission said federal programs were uncoordinated and that the federal government has not adequately assessed state and local programs. The commission said all levels of government should coordinate their efforts against terrorism — including cyber, radiological and nuclear. It recommended:

- Creating a National Office for Combating Terrorism to oversee preparation of the federal response to an attack, with special emphasis on preserving civil liberties.
- Consolidating congressional oversight over domestic preparedness and creating a special committee for combating terrorism.
- Strengthening intelligence gathering, information sharing, planning, training and equipment of all who must respond to terrorism.

"The Changing Threat of International Terrorism," National Commission on Terrorism, June 2000 — This third congressionally mandated report concluded that although U.S. anti-terrorism policies are on the right track, significant aspects of implementation are "seriously deficient." Chaired by L. Paul Bremer III, former ambassador-at-large for counterterrorism, the panel said the United States must use all legal avenues to disrupt terrorist activities, convince other nations to stop supporting terrorists and ensure that federal, state and local officials are better prepared for attacks. The report recommended:

- Intelligence and law enforcement authorities use the full scope of their authority to collect intelligence, including extensive electronic surveillance
- CIA guidelines restricting recruitment of "unsavory sources" do not apply to counterterrorism contacts.
- Strict U.S. sanctions on countries supporting terrorists.
- Disruption of financial support for terrorists.
- Increased preparation for biological, chemical, nuclear or radiological attacks.
- Creation by the president and Congress of a comprehensive plan for reviewing and funding counterterrorism.

"Patterns of Global Terrorism — 2000," Department of State, April 2001 — This report on international terrorism in 2000 highlights Afghanistan as a chief area for concern. The report says the State Department will base its cooperation with international partners on four tenets:

- No deals with terrorists.
- Terrorists will be brought to justice for their crimes.
- Isolation and pressure will be applied to states that sponsor terrorism.
- The U.S. will bolster the counter-terrorism capabilities of countries that work with the U.S.

"30 Years of Terrorism: Terrorism in the United States: 1999," Department of Justice/Federal Bureau of Investigation. The report outlines FBI policies on terrorism and provides background information on active terrorist organizations and emerging threats. The report's conclusions include:

- The threat from unconventional weapons, including radiological, cyber and radio frequency, is growing.
- State sponsors of terrorism and terrorist organizations represent significant threats to the U.S.
- International terrorism has shifted from numerous direct attacks to fewer high-impact attacks.
- The motivation for terrorism has evolved from a "means to an end" to an end itself.

— Scott Kuzner

U.S. were to allay the concerns of its regional allies, it would need to deploy at least three to four heavy divisions and "over a thousand" planes — a six-month undertaking. "During that time, Saddam would prepare to deploy his chemical and biological weapons against you, which would be a huge problem."

Tangled Trails

Investigators began piecing together the details of the Sept. 11 attacks — including the identities of the hijackers — within days. Four weeks later, FBI Director Robert Mueller says the government has some 200,000 leads to follow. But the government has yet to disclose hard evidence linking accomplices within the United States to the plot. [32]

Airline passenger manifests readily established the stated identities of the hijackers, but at least six names later turned out to be aliases. Two of the hijackers, it was learned, had been flagged earlier by the Central Intelligence Agency as potential terrorists, but they eluded FBI efforts to find them.

Most attention focused on the apparent leader of the hijackers, Mohamed Atta — who apparently piloted the first plane into the World Trade Center. An Egyptian in his early 30s, Atta belonged to Islamic fundamentalist groups while a student in Germany. He had first visited the United States in 1999 and returned several times over the next two years.

The hijackers' trail was quickly traced back overseas. Atta and two of the other hijackers identified as team leaders had lived in Hamburg, a magnet to many Muslims and some suspected terrorist cells. German authorities said they were seeking two fugitives thought to have provided logistical support to the hijackers. By month's end, however, the only person arrested overseas was the Algerian pilot charged in London with having overseen flight instruction for the hijacker pilots. U.S. authorities initiated extradition proceedings, but those could take years, observers warned.

In the early days after the attacks, law enforcement sources depicted "most" of the hijackers as linked to bin Laden and Al Qaeda. Solid evidence was slow to emerge, however. In a Sept. 27 press briefing, Mueller confirmed only that "one or more" of the hijackers had "contacts" with Al Qaeda.

A week later, though, British Prime Minister Blair released — with White House approval — some details of the evidence against bin Laden. In an 11-page report posted on the prime minister's official Web site, Blair said the British government was "confident" that bin Laden and Al Qaeda "planned and carried out the atrocities of 11 September 2001." At least three of the hijackers have been "positively identified" with Al Qaeda, Blair said, and "one of bin Laden's closest and most senior associates was responsible for the detailed planning of the attacks." [33]

Four weeks into the investigation, the government has detained or questioned more than 600 people and is said to be seeking several hundred others. Investigators had strong suspicions about three men with Middle Eastern surnames who had received flight training: One had reportedly asked for instructions on steering a jetliner but not on takeoff or landing; the other two were found with large amounts of cash and box-cutter knives like those used in the hijackings. As of early October, however, only one person had actually been charged: a Virginia man who allegedly aided the hijackers — unwittingly — by helping several of them obtain fraudulent driver's licenses.

Investigators had succeeded in tracing about $500,000 in funds the hijackers received from overseas that they used to finance their operations. As part of the counterterrorism fight, Bush and other administration officials vowed to seize terrorists' assets and deny terrorist groups access to banking systems in the U.S. and abroad. In early October, the government said it had frozen some $100 million of suspected terrorists' assets in the United States. Overseas, 19 countries agreed to freeze the assets of bin Laden and his associates. Notably, such important Middle Eastern financial centers as Saudi Arabia, Kuwait, Qatar, Egypt and Jordan did not join in the financial seizures.

Whatever progress the investigators were making behind the scenes, much of the news focused on false leads and dead ends. Early on, Mueller conceded that innocent people were likely to be caught up in the dragnet. A Saudi doctor in Texas who came under suspicion was held by the FBI for more than two weeks before being cleared and released. Nine people were arrested in Pennsylvania for fraudulently obtaining licenses to transport hazardous materials, but no connection to a possible terrorist chemical weapons attack was found.

Disquietingly, the attacks appeared to be prompting scattered incidents against Arab, Muslim or Sikh Americans. In the worst episode, an Arizona man allegedly went on a shooting spree Sept. 15, killing a turban-wearing Sikh American and firing shots into buildings occupied by an Afghani and a Lebanese-American.

Meanwhile, the administration was nearing agreement with Congress on the details of anti-terrorism legislation, with prospects for passage in both the House and the Senate shortly after the Columbus Day recess. [34]

Late on Oct. 3, the House Judiciary Committee approved a compromise bill, 36–0. Shortly afterward, Senate Judiciary Committee Chairman Patrick J. Leahy, D-Vt., announced that negotiators had reached a bipartisan agreement with the administration after resolving several sticking points. Among the major changes Senate negotiators wrested was a provision to limit the sharing of wiretap and grand jury information to officials with an explicit need for the information.

Even with the broadened law enforcement powers, Ashcroft was making no promises that terrorist incidents would not recur. "There is absolutely no guarantee that these safeguards would have avoided the Sept. 11 occurrence," Ashcroft told the House panel on Sept. 24. ■

OUTLOOK

More to Come?

Among many terrorism and defense experts, there is a sense of inevitability about the possibility of future attacks against the United States. "I don't think it's going to get much better for a while, no matter what we do," says CATO's Eland. "There will probably be another catastrophic event, and sooner rather than later."

Spencer of the Heritage Foundation agrees. "No one should be surprised if something terrible happens again," he says. "At the very least, we will have to deal with smaller terrorist strikes, car bombs and the like."

One reason for concern, says Attorney General Ashcroft, is that some of the associates of the hijackers are probably still in the U.S. "It's very unlikely that all of those associated with the attacks of Sept. 11 are now detained or have been detected," he told CNN on Sept. 30. [35] Ashcroft added the risk of attack would probably rise after the U.S. began military retaliation.

Another reason future attacks seem likely, terrorism analysts say, stems from the competitive nature of terrorist organizations. "My thought is that some groups other than bin Laden's may escalate the attack against the U.S. in an effort to get the same sort of notoriety that he has," Eland says. "That means that they'll likely be going after targets that will lead to mass casualties."

Pessimists also predict more attacks because the devastation on Sept. 11 shattered the illusion of American impregnability and probably emboldened many terrorist groups. "We've been proven to be vulnerable, and that means that more people are going to start seriously thinking about ways to get us," says Cordesman of CSIS.

If new attacks come, analysts say, they will probably be carried out in a very different way. "There's a conscious effort to vary tactics as a way of trying to overcome defenses," the CIA's Pillar said. "For that very reason, the next big attack, even if it's by the same organization, might use a whole different modus operandi."

Many worry that new attacks will involve chemical or biological agents. "I'm not trying to be alarmist, but we know that these terrorist organizations . . . have probably found the means to use biological or chemical warfare, and that's bad for the world," said Andrew H. Card Jr., President Bush's chief of staff. [36]

But in the view of Jessica Stern, a lecturer in terrorism at the John F. Kennedy School of Government at Harvard University, "There's just no indication that Al Qaeda or the others have really gotten that far with weapons of mass destruction."

The Stimson Center's Smithson agrees. "This isn't something a group of people moving from cave to cave in Afghanistan would be able to do," she says.

In addition, Stern says, the nation's dramatically heightened state of alert should give it a much better chance of preventing terrorist attacks, at least in the near future. "In the wake of the Sept. 11 attack, we should be better able to thwart big efforts," she says. "My concern is that we won't be able to sustain this attention on [terrorism] in the years ahead — and what may happen after that." ■

Notes

[1] For background, see David Masci, "Islamic Fundamentalism," *The CQ Researcher*, March 24, 2000, pp. 241-264, and Ahmed Rashid, *Taliban: Militant Islam, Oil and Fundamentalism in Central Asia* (2000).

[2] For background, see Mary H. Cooper, "Combating Terrorism," *The CQ Researcher*, July 21, 1995, pp. 633-656.

[3] For background, see Mary H. Cooper, "Missile Defense," *The CQ Researcher*, Sept. 8, 2000, pp. 689-712, and Mary H. Cooper, "Chemical and Biological Weapons," *The CQ Researcher*, Jan. 31, 1997, pp. 73-96.

[4] For background, see David Masci, "Middle East Conflict," *The CQ Researcher*, April 6, 2001, pp. 273-296, and Patrick G. Marshall, "Calculating the Costs of the Gulf War," *The CQ Researcher*, March 15, 1991, pp. 145-168

[5] For coverage, see Adriel Bettelheim and Elizabeth A. Palmer, "Balancing Liberty and Security," *CQ Weekly*, Sept. 22, 2001, pp. 2210-2214; Elizabeth A. Palmer, "Committees Taking a Critical Look at Ashcroft's Request for Broad New Powers," *CQ Weekly*, Sept. 29, 2001, pp. 2263-2265.

[6] Quoted in Alison Mitchel and Todd S. Purdum, "Ashcroft Seeking Broad Powers, Says Congress Must Act Quickly," *The New York Times*, Oct. 1, 2001, p. A1.

[7] For background, see Kenneth Jost, "Bush Presidency," *The CQ Researcher*, Feb. 2, 2001, pp. 65-88.

[8] Quoted in Karen Tumulty, "Looking Out for Next Time," *Time*, Oct. 1, 2001.

[9] U.S. Commission on National Security/21st Century, "Roadmap for National Security, Feb. 1, 2001.

[10] Quoted in Chuck McCutcheon, "Defining Homeland Security," *CQ Weekly*, Sept. 29, 2001, pp. 2252-2254.

[11] Walter Laqueur, *The New Terrorism: Fanaticism and the Arms of Mass Destruction* (1999), p. 3. Other background drawn from Laqueur's opening chapter, "Terrorism and History," pp. 3-48.

[12] *Ibid.*, p. 46.

[13] Bruce Hoffman, *Inside Terrorism* (1998), p. 87. Other background drawn from pp. 87-129. See also Laqueur, *op. cit.*, pp. 127-155.

[14] For background, see David Masci, "Israel

at 50," *The CQ Researcher*, March 6, 1998, pp. 193-216, and Mary H. Cooper, "Muslims in America," *The CQ Researcher*, April 30, 1993, pp. 361-384.

[15] For background, see Philip Heymann, *Terrorism and America: A Commonsense Strategy for a Democratic Society* (1998), pp. 105-127; Paul R. Pillar, *Terrorism and U.S. Foreign Policy* (2001), pp. 79-92.

[16] Cited in *ibid.*, p. 80.

[17] Cited in "An Alliance of Old and New," *The Economist*, Sept. 29, 2001.

[18] For background, see David Masci, "China Today," *The CQ Researcher*, Aug. 4, 2000, pp. 633-656, and David Masci, "U.S.-Russia Relations," *The CQ Researcher*, May 22, 1998, pp. 457-480.

[19] For background, see Mary H. Cooper, "Expanding NATO," *The CQ Researcher*, May 16, 1997, pp. 433-456.

[20] John Vinocur, "EU Solidarity Declaration Gives Both Sides a Victory," *The International Herald Tribune*, Sept. 24, 2001.

[21] Dan Balz, U.S. Strikes Again at Afghan Targets," *The Washington Post*, Oct. 9, 2001.

[22] Howard Schneider, "Ending Doubts, Saudis to Allow U.S. to Use Base," *The Washington Post*, Sept. 28, 2001.

[23] Jane Perlez and Katherine Seelye, "U.S. Strongly Rebukes Sharon for Criticism of Bush," *The New York Times*, Oct. 6, 2001.

[24] Thomas Ricks and Vernon Loeb, "Initial Aim is Hitting Taliban's Defenses," *The Washington Post*, Oct. 8, 2001.

[25] *Ibid.*

[26] Karen DeYoung and Alan Sipress, "Dual Strategy of Assault, Reward," *The Washington Post*, Oct. 8, 2001.

[27] Michael O'Hanlon, "Next, the Hard Part," *The Washington Post*, Oct. 8, 2001.

[28] Quoted in *The Economist, op. cit.*

[29] Jack Kelley, "Special Forces Hunt Bin Laden," *USA Today*, Sept. 28, 2001.

[30] Steve LeVine, Danny Pearl and Hugh Pope, "For All Its Ferocity, Taliban Could Prove An Easy Foe to Oust," *The Wall Street Journal*, Oct. 1, 2001.

FOR MORE INFORMATION

American Civil Liberties Union, 122 Maryland Ave., N.E., Washington, D.C. 20002; (202) 544-1681; www.aclu.org. The ACLU lobbies to protect civil liberties and litigates to guarantee constitutional rights.

The Brookings Institution, 1775 Massachusetts Ave., N.W., Washington, D.C. 20036; (202) 797-6400; www.brook.edu. A think tank that conducts research on a host of public-policy issues, including foreign and defense policy.

Cato Institute, 1000 Massachusetts Ave., N.W., Washington, D.C. 20001; (202) 842-0200; www.cato.org. A public-policy research organization that advocates limited government and individual liberty.

Center for Democracy and Technology, 1634 Eye St. N.W., Suite 1100, Washington, D.C. 20006; (202) 637-9800; www.cdt.org. Promotes civil liberties such as privacy and free speech in new computer and communications media.

Center for Strategic and International Studies, 1800 K St., N.W. Suite 400, Washington, D.C. 20006; (202) 887-0200; www.csis.org. An independent research institute that studies international and domestic policy issues including terrorism, national security and the Middle East.

The Henry L. Stimson Center, 11 Dupont Circle, N.W., Ninth Floor, Washington, D.C. 20036; (202) 223-5956; www.stimson.com. Conducts research on national security issues.

The Heritage Foundation, 214 Massachusetts Ave., N.E., Washington, D.C. 20002; (202) 546-4400; www.heritage.org. A public-policy research organization that advocates a strong national defense and forceful foreign policy.

Washington Institute for Near East Policy, 1828 L St., N.W., Suite 1050, Washington, D.C. 20036; (202) 452-0650; www.washingtoninstitute.com. Conducts research on the Middle East with the aim of promoting debate and improving the effectiveness of U.S. policy in the region.

[31] Melinda Henneberger, "Ex-King and Rebels to Hold Special Counsel," *The New York Times*, Oct. 2, 2001.

[32] For a detailed reconstruction of the hijackers' known activities in the months leading up to the attacks, see Amy Goldstein, "Hijackers Led by Core Group," *The Washington Post*, Sept. 30, 2001, p. A1, and accompanying chart, p. A28.

[33] "Responsibility for the Terrorist Atrocities in the United States, 11 September 2001" (www.number-10.uk/gov).

[34] Elizabeth A. Palmer, "Anti-Terrorism Bill Heads to Floor But Tough Negotiations Lie Ahead," *CQ Weekly*, Oct. 6, 2001, p. 2327.

[35] Quoted in Dana Milbank, "More Terrorism Likely, U.S. Warns," *The Washington Post*, Oct. 1, 2001.

[36] Quoted in *Ibid.*

Bibliography

Selected Sources

Books

Bodansky, Yossef, *Bin Laden: The Man Who Declared War on America*, Forum, 1999.

The book traces Osama bin Laden's life from his early years in Saudi Arabia through his leadership of Al Qaeda and purported role in the attacks on the U.S. embassies in Kenya and Tanzania in 1998. Bodansky is director of the Congressional Task Force on Terrorism and Unconventional Warfare and author of eight books on terrorism.

Falkenrath, Richard A., Robert D. Newman, and Bradley A. Thayer, *America's Achilles' Heel: Nuclear, Biological, and Chemical Terrorism and Covert Attack*, MIT Press, 1998.

The authors contend that the United States is highly vulnerable to attack by nuclear, biological or chemical weapons and recommend ways to guard against the danger. Falkenrath, the lead author, is an assistant professor of public policy at Harvard University's John F. Kennedy School of Government. For a less apprehensive assessment, see Jessica Stern, *The Ultimate Terrorists* (Harvard University Press, 1999). Stern is a lecturer at the Kennedy School.

Heymann, Philip, *Terrorism and America: A Commonsense Strategy for a Democratic Society*, MIT Press, 1998.

Heymann, a Harvard law professor and former deputy U.S. attorney general, argues that an effective strategy against terrorism can deal with threats to security while still preserving "our liberties and our unity."

Hoffman, Bruce, *Inside Terrorism*, Victor Gollancz, 1998.

Hoffman, a leading expert on terrorism and now director of the Rand Corporation's Washington office, provides a contemporary overview of terrorism focused on a handful of major themes, including religion and terrorism and the internationalization of terrorism. He predicts a "bloodier and more destructive era of violence ahead." The book includes reference notes and a 31-page bibliography.

Laqueur, Walter, *The New Terrorism: Fanaticism and the Arms of Mass Destruction*, Oxford University Press, 1999.

Laqueur, a leading historian on terrorism now at the Center for Strategic and International Studies, provides an historical and contemporary overview of terrorism. He sees a trend away from nationalist or radical movements with political aims toward smaller, more fanatical groups seeking vengeance and destruction. The book includes a 17-page bibliographic essay. Laqueur's other books include *The History of Terrorism* (Transaction, August 2001) and *The Age of Terrorism* (Little, Brown, 1987).

Pillar, Paul R., *Terrorism and U.S. Foreign Policy*, Brookings Institution, 2001.

A CIA counterterrorism expert argues in this book published before the Sept. 11 attacks that the United States has prevented some terrorist attacks and brought terrorists to justice, but has failed to fully integrate counterterrorism into U.S. foreign policy. The book includes detailed chapter notes.

Reeve, Simon, *The New Jackals: Ramzi Yousef, Osama bin Laden and the Future of Terrorism*, Northeastern University Press, 1999.

Reeve, an investigative journalist, traces the life of Yousef, the British-educated Islamic extremist convicted of masterminding the 1993 bombing of the World Trade Center, and his links to Osama bin Laden. The book ends with a warning that the West can do little to prevent future terrorist attacks. The text of bin Laden's 1998 *fatwa* urging a jihad against the United States is included.

Reports and Studies

U.S. Department of Justice, Federal Bureau of Investigation, *Terrorism in the United States 1999: Thirty Years of Terrorism, A Special Retrospective Edition*, 2000.

The FBI's most recent report on terrorism provides a three-decade retrospective as well as a detailed review of events in 1999.

U.S. Department of State, *Patterns of Global Terrorism 2000*, April 2001.

The department's most recent annual report said that global terrorism "continues to pose a clear and present danger" but that strengthened international cooperation had contributed to a decline in state-sponsored terrorism.

Useful Web Sites

For an extensive terrorism bibliography, see the Web site of the private Terrorism Research Center: www.terrorism.com

Government sites: The White House (www.whitehouse.gov); U.S. Department of State (www.state.gov); U.S. Department of Defense (www.defenselink.mil); Federal Bureau of Investigation (www.fbi.gov); North Atlantic Treaty Organization (www.nato.int); 10 Downing Street (office of British prime minister) (www.number-10.gov.uk).

News media: Cable News Network (www.cnn.com); PBS NewsHour (www.pbs.org/newshour); The New York Times (www.nyt.com); The Washington Post (www.washingtonpost.com); CQ Press (www.cqpress.com).

16 Globalization Backlash

BRIAN HANSEN

A cold rain was falling as dawn broke over Seattle, Wash., on Nov. 30, 1999. It was typical weather for the city on Puget Sound, but there was nothing typical about the events about to unfold.

Seattle was hosting a summit meeting of the World Trade Organization (WTO), which encourages countries to remove tariffs, subsidies and import quotas. Microsoft Chairman Bill Gates and other business leaders had welcomed the WTO's 135 member governments to the summit, billed as a festival of "free trade," the catchphrase of so-called neocapitalists. [1]

It didn't quite work out that way. Some 50,000 mostly young protesters packed downtown to oppose WTO policies that they say engender environmental damage and hurt the world's poorest people. Most had permits for legally sanctioned protests. Several thousand used non-violent civil disobedience to try to shut down the four-day meeting. And a cadre of black-garbed anarchists — the so-called Black Bloc — smashed store windows, started bonfires and hurled debris at police.

With then-President Bill Clinton flying toward Seattle on Air Force One, federal officials ordered the streets cleared. Moving block by block, riot police fired tear gas, rubber bullets and concussion grenades at anyone in their path, including neighborhood residents who were rousted out of their beds by the commotion. Washington Gov. Gary Locke called out the National Guard, and Seattle Mayor Paul Schell outlawed

From *The CQ Researcher,*
September 28, 2001.

A protester battles a 310 police officer in Washington, D.C., during the demonstrations against the International Monetary Fund

all forms of political expression in a 50-square-block area around the heavily guarded convention center.

More than 500 people were arrested or detained, but the charges were dropped against most. The city resembled a war zone, with armored vehicles patrolling the streets and police helicopters hovering overhead. Downtown businesses sustained more than $2.5 million in property damage, plus $10 million in lost holiday sales. The damage to Seattle's reputation as a laid-back city is incalculable.

And the new trade round that had been expected to emerge from the summit? That was trashed, too, just like the Nike Town store and other hated symbols of global capitalism. At the end of the week, the WTO meeting collapsed — delegates left without even issuing a final communiqué. Technically, the

talks bogged down over a U.S.-led demand that European countries stop subsidizing their farm exports. But many WTO delegates said the protesters had played a significant role in scuttling the meeting. [2]

Former U.S. Rep. Don Bonker, D-Wash., who represented a nonprofit interest group at the meeting, said the protests had a "powerful influence" on the nervous delegates inside the convention center. [3]

The protesters jammed a monkey wrench into the workings of the WTO, one of the key cogs of the modern global economy. But the "Battle of Seattle," as it became known, was just the beginning. Since then, a passionate but free-form "movement" has ascended the international stage.

Activists in the burgeoning movement are focusing much of their attention on three key drivers of economic globalization: the WTO; the World Bank, which finances development projects in Third World countries; and the International Monetary Fund (IMF), which loans money to countries with balance-of-payment problems. [4]

The three institutions were established by the United States and other industrialized countries nearly 60 years ago to bolster living standards and economic stability in the developing world. According to numerous studies, nations that have embraced the tenets of globalization — open trade and investment policies — have seen per capita income rise and poverty decrease. [5]

But critics say the three institutions have done far more harm than good, engendering widespread poverty, inequality and environmental degradation throughout the Third World. [6] The primary beneficiaries of World Bank, IMF and WTO policies, critics charge, have

Loan Payments vs. Aid for Citizens

Many poor countries spend more on servicing their foreign debt than on health care and other basic needs. Brazil, for example, spends three-quarters of its revenue on interest payments and less than half that amount on social services. The problem arose in the 1980s when lenders required poor countries to cut spending on social services to increase the chances they would be repaid.

Government Spending in Poor Countries, 1995

Debt interest payments as % of government revenue*		Social services as % of government expenditure**
75.6%	Brazil	34.5%
41.2	Bulgaria	35.0
23.0	Cameroon	29.0
57.8	Guatemala	38.4
33.6	India	11.9
31.7	Kenya	27.1
59.9	Madagascar	34.6

* Totals may exceed 100 percent because expenditures may exceed revenues.
** Includes health, education, social security, welfare and community services.

Source: World Bank, "World Development Report, 1998–99"

been multinational corporations, private-sector financiers and corrupt government officials. Anti-globalization protesters have targeted virtually every major economic summit and high-level political gathering since the ill-fated WTO conference. Most recently, as many as 150,000 protesters last July besieged the economic summit in Genoa, Italy, where leaders of the most industrialized nations had gathered.

The protesters promise more of the same. Indeed, all summer they had been planning to protest the IMF/World Bank annual meeting slated for Washington, D.C., at the end of this month. *

No one knows what will come of the backlash against corporate-led economic globalization, but one thing is clear: For good or for ill, the protesters

---

* The bank and IMF canceled the meetings following the terrorist attacks on the World Trade Center and Pentagon on Sept. 11, although one IMF financial committee may meet in late October or early November.

who found their footing on the rain-slicked streets of Seattle sparked a grass-roots movement that world leaders and multinational corporations have been unable to ignore.

"This movement is unstoppable," said French sheep farmer Jose Bove, who became a movement icon in 1999 when he used his tractor to demolish a McDonald's restaurant under construction in Millau, France. "We have seen nothing yet." [7]

But many free-trade advocates say that Bove and other activists don't understand the complexities — or the benefits — of economic globalization.

"The cause espoused by the anti-globalists, while right in some of the particulars, is wrong in the aggregate," said Edward M. Graham, a senior fellow at the Institute for International Economics, a Washington, D.C., think tank. "Precisely those people whom the anti-globalists purport to represent — the world's poorest people, especially

those in developing countries and also in the lower-income classes here in the United States — would be most adversely affected by the reversal of globalization." [8]

Globalization critics share a number of common concerns, such as economic inequality between the richest and poorest nations, environmental degradation and the growing influence of transnational corporations. But the movement is also a hodgepodge of different actors fighting for different causes. The foot soldiers include students opposed to sweatshops, environmentalists working to save rainforests and labor union members striving to keep their jobs in the United States from moving overseas. [9] Other goals include debt cancellation for poor nations, protection for endangered sea turtles and the elimination of genetically engineered foods. [10]

Movement loyalists also harbor divergent views regarding tactics. Most want to work within the law; others embrace non-violent civil disobedience; and a small number of militants say violence is an acceptable way to effect change. Similarly, some activists maintain that the contemporary global economic system can be reformed, while others advocate abolishing it altogether.

Some observers find the protesters' myriad objectives bewildering. Trevor Manuel, South Africa's finance minister, said he was baffled last September when an IMF/World Bank meeting in Prague, Czech Republic, was besieged by 8,000 demonstrators.

"I know what they're against but have no sense of what they're for," Manuel said. [11]

Movement organizers concede that they have a multifaceted message, but they say it's not exceedingly complicated.

"I think people make our agenda so much more complex than it needs to be, and we do it to ourselves — we let ourselves be categorized as this giant movement that wants this panacea-like vision that's a mile wide and an inch deep," says John Sellers, director of the Ruckus Society, a Berkeley, Calif., group that teaches non-violent civil disobedience tactics to environmental and human rights organizations.

"We want better living conditions, more democracy and more justice. We want better treatment of human beings, and we want better treatment of the planet. That's what it comes down to."

As the battle over globalization continues, here are the key issues being debated:

Does globalization hurt people in developing countries?

By several measures, corporate-led globalization arguably has sparked the most fundamental restructuring of the world's economic and political systems since the Industrial Revolution.

In the trade sector, for example, world merchandise exports now top $5 trillion annually — an 18-fold increase over the 1948 level. [12] Corporate investment in foreign countries, or FDI (foreign direct investment), swelled from $200 billion in 1990 to $884 billion in 1999 — more than quadrupling in only nine years. [13] And capital market flows, or the computer-assisted shifting of financial assets back and forth between foreign currency markets, now exceeds a staggering $2 trillion per day. [14]

Proponents of globalization argue that poor people, especially in Third World countries, benefit from such economic initiatives — that a rising tide raises all boats, as economists say. Indeed, countries that have most succeeded in opening their economies to the world — such as Chile, Mexico, China and South Korea — have enjoyed the greatest increases in per capita income in recent years, according to numerous studies. By contrast, poverty rates continue to climb and wages continue to drop where trade and investment barriers remain the most impermeable, such as South Asia, the Middle East and

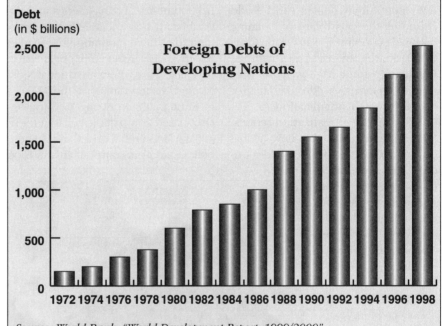

Poor Nations' Debt Mountain

Developing countries owe more than $2 trillion, and the amount is still growing, according to the World Bank. The total debt is over $400 for every man, woman and child in the developing world — where the average income is less than $1 a day in the poorest countries.

Foreign Debts of Developing Nations

Debt (in $ billions)

Source: World Bank, "World Development Report, 1999/2000"

Sub-Saharan Africa, studies show. [15]

"The more closed the economy, the greater the likelihood that very large numbers of citizens suffer from poverty and are deprived of access to the flow of communications, commerce, visitors and ideas that enhance human liberty and creativity," says Robert D. Hormats, vice chairman of Goldman Sachs International, a New York-based global investment banking and securities firm. "Truly progressive minds sincerely committed to the advancement of poor people in developing countries should be converted into firm allies, not enemies, of globalization." [16]

U.S. companies often provide the cleanest and best working conditions in poor countries, says Murray Weidenbaum, chairman of the Center for the Study of American Business at Washington University, in St. Louis. By calling for stricter regulation of multina-

tional corporations, Weidenbaum says, globalization critics are undermining their own goal of alleviating poverty.

"The often-maligned multinational corporation has been in the vanguard in terms of delivering rising living standards and improved working conditions at home and abroad," Weidenbaum says. "American companies operating overseas have . . . frequently been the leaders in offering higher wages and setting more enlightened business standards."

But critics of globalization note that despite the abolition of trade and investment barriers and the flood of capital into foreign markets, some 1.2 billion people — 23 percent of the population of the developing world — still live on less than $1 per day. [17] Another 2.8 billion — 56 percent of the developing world — have less than $2 daily. And even under the World Bank's most optimistic forecast, at least 2.3 billion people will be living on $2 per day or less by 2015, they note with alarm.

"The restructuring of the world economy under the guidance of the Washington-based financial institutions [i.e., the World Bank and the IMF] increasingly denies Third World countries the possibility of building national economies," says Maria Clara Couto Soares, an economist with the Brazilian Institute for Social and Economic Analyses, a Rio de Janeiro-based research organization.

Like many globalization critics, Soares argues that the new global economy propelled Third World countries into a morass of unmanageable debt. According to this oft-cited critique, the IMF and World Bank precipitated the problem by loaning Third World governments billions of dollars for ill-conceived development projects. Many countries then had to borrow more money from the IMF to service their massive debts.

The IMF loans usually required debtor nations to implement austerity measures known as structural adjustment programs (SAP), which typically called for cutting government spending, reducing wages and improving tax-collection programs. Moreover, to make debtor countries more attractive to foreign investors, SAPs often required them to raise interest rates; privatize state-run enterprises; cut tariffs, quotas and other restrictions on imports; and remove restrictions on foreign investment in local industries, banks and other financial services.

Anti-globalization protesters claim that SAPs make Third World countries de facto colonies of rich nations and multinational corporations, hurting poor people in the process.

"When one looks at the realities that are experienced by Africans, as well as the peoples in other regions of the Global South [Asia, Latin America and the Caribbean], it is undeniable that structural adjustment programs, free-market reforms, debt relief and privatization have failed," says Kenyan national Njoki Njoroge Njeheu, director of the 50 Years is Enough network, a Washington, D.C.-based group dedicated to reforming the IMF and World Bank. "These policies and programs — cuts in food subsidies, cuts in credit to farmers, non-food cash-crop farming, user fees for health and education and water privatization — condemn millions to hunger, malnutrition, poverty and death." [18]

But Thomas C. Dawson, director of the IMF's External Relations Department, defends structural adjustment as "simply a matter of life adjusting to change. The idea that the fund or the bank go into countries and slash social spending is simply not the case. Our belief is that countries with [SAPS] show

increases — not decreases — in social spending." [19]

Should the anti-globalization movement revise its tactics?

From the moment the first storefront window was smashed at the WTO protest in Seattle, a debate has raged within the movement: Should it utilize or condone tactics involving property destruction or violence?

Many oppose violence simply because it attracts too much media attention on tactics. The media's zeal for shattered windows and violent protester/police confrontations, they say, is obscuring and cheapening their substantive critique of the global economic system.

"I've had candid conversations with a number of reporters who have told me that they can't turn on their cameras until the tear gas and pepper spray starts flying, because they're not there to report on the issues," says Sellers of the Ruckus Society. "For the television media, obviously, it's a very provocative and titillating kind of coverage to show windows being smashed and scrapping in the streets. We've been made to look very scary, and we've been stripped of our political message."

The most combative — and visible — protesters are linked to the Black Bloc, named after a German anti-fascist movement of the 1980s. Black Bloc anarchists took part in the Seattle protest and every large anti-globalization action since. In Seattle, about 50 individuals wearing black balaclavas used hammers and crowbars to attack business establishments such as Nike Town and McDonald's, which they condemn

French farmers near Marseilles push grocery carts filled with apples to protest the impact of globalization and U.S. trade policies on agriculture.

AP Photo/Claude Paris

as evil manifestations of corporate hegemony.

For John Zerzan, 57, a self-described anarchist writer from Eugene, Ore., the confrontation in Seattle was a much-needed change from the "boring, ritualized demonstrations that haven't been effective" in the past.

"I was extremely heartened," Zerzan says. "At my age, after the decades of nothingness, the decades of consumerism and the rising levels of emptiness — when people stand up to [corporate greed] and speak out against it and move against it, it's just thrilling."

Zerzan says he respects the peaceful protesters who were willing to be tear-gassed, pepper-sprayed and arrested in Seattle. But those who chanted "no violence" and physically tried to prevent anarchists from smashing windows sickened him.

"They're just accomplices to the system, playing the same old game that the system wants them to play," Zerzan says. "The 'peace cops' are still around, and they're still working to preserve the fiction that peaceful demonstrations are effective."

Since Seattle, Black Bloc anarchists and other violent protesters have become more aggressive. In April 2000, at a protest against the World Bank and IMF in Washington, D.C., anarchists charged police lines with a Dumpster and a section of chain-link fence. That August, at the Democratic National Convention in Los Angeles, black-garbed youth and other protesters pelted police with sticks, bottles and chunks of concrete. The next month, at the IMF/World Bank meeting in Prague, a handful of aggressive protesters attacked police with firebombs and cobblestones. In April of this year, at a free-trade summit in Quebec City, protesters pelted police with rocks, hockey pucks, billiard balls and Molotov cocktails.

Last July, anti-globalization violence reached a crescendo. At the G-8 summit in Genoa, at least 100,000 people took to the streets to call for Third World

debt relief, environmentally friendly trade policies and other objectives. Most of the protesters behaved peacefully, but in a now-familiar pattern, a small minority — about 5,000 people — destroyed property and attacked police. Carlo Giuliani, a 23-year-old protester from Genoa, was shot and killed by police as he prepared to hurl a fire extinguisher at officers inside a law-enforcement vehicle.

Giuliani's death created a schism within the anti-globalization movement. Militants hailed Giuliani as a martyr, with some vowing to exact revenge for what they viewed as state-sanctioned murder. But many moderate groups sought to distance themselves from the violence. Christian Aid, Friends of the Earth and the Catholic Agency for Overseas Development all canceled their participation in weekend rallies in support of debt relief, poverty reduction and environmental causes. Pop music superstar Bono, a spokesman for Drop the Debt, an international campaign to cancel the debts of the world's poorest countries, lamented that the campaign had been "making headway" before Genoa exploded in violence.

"Violence is never right, but anger is understandable, especially faced with the obscenity of the ever-widening gap between the haves and the have-nots," Bono said. "It is right to bang your fist on the table, but not in the face of your opponent — whether police or protester." [20]

"We must be peaceful," agrees Carol Welch, deputy director for international programs for Friends of the Earth, "because violence only gives our opponents an excuse to dismiss our very valid concerns."

In the aftermath of Genoa, anti-globalization groups are re-evaluating their plans to protest at future economic and political summits. Still, they say they don't want to be held hostage by the threat of violence.

"We definitely don't want to retreat," Welch says. "Being out on the

streets is an important way of getting your message out. No movement has been able to get its agenda through without turning out masses of people in the streets to push for major change."

Are police overreacting to the anti-globalization movement?

In the wake of the WTO summit in Seattle, national governments and police agencies have tried to counteract movement violence at future meetings by restricting protesters in various ways, most of which have been challenged in court. They include:

- Erecting towering security fences to keep protesters blocks away.
- Establishing "No Protest Zones."
- Launching pre-emptive police raids on protesters' headquarters.
- Arresting protest organizers on "conspiracy" charges.
- Requesting extraordinarily high bails for jailed protest organizers.
- Outlawing gas masks for anyone except police officers.
- Detaining suspected protesters at international borders.
- Using undercover police officers to infiltrate protesters' meetings.

Movement organizers also charge that police have inserted undercover "provocateurs" into crowds to incite peaceful protesters to violence. In addition, some protesters who have been arrested allege that they were denied food, water and medical attention while in police custody. Others say they were subjected to physical and psychological abuse.

Activists say these measures, at the least, infringe on their First Amendment rights to protest. Movement organizers say U.S. law-enforcement agencies — not anti-globalization activists — engendered the stifling, paramilitary security culture that now characterizes international economic summits and high-level political gatherings.

"The atmosphere at all of these big summits [since Seattle] was created by the authorities screwing things up in

"We Owned Downtown Seattle"

Mike Dolan recoils at the suggestion that he's the architect behind the anti-globalization movement. The man described by *The Washington Post* as a "cross between Lenin and Woody Allen" says he's simply a trade-policy "wonk" who happens to be a good grassroots organizer.

Very good indeed. In 1999, Dolan, 45, played a key role in orchestrating the massive protests that derailed the Seattle meeting of the World Trade Organization (WTO), an event viewed by many as the birth of the anti-globalization movement. Dolan spent seven months organizing the WTO protests while serving as deputy director of Global Trade Watch, a Washington, D.C.-based group founded by consumer advocate Ralph Nader. Affable, intelligent and intense, Dolan forged a remarkable coalition that united both labor unions and environmental groups against the WTO. "Hardhats and hippies together at last," was an oft-heard aphorism in the streets of Seattle.

Dolan now heads Global Trade Watch's West Coast office in Oakland, Calif., where he is taking aim at the so-called fast-track trade-negotiating initiative currently pending on Capitol Hill.

In a wide-ranging interview recently, he waxed philosophical about the WTO protests and the future of the anti-globalization movement:

On organizing the WTO protests:

"Even before they chose Seattle, I was gearing up. When I heard that President Clinton had tendered the invitation that the ministerial should be launched from U.S. soil, I was on the edge of my seat waiting to hear which city they would choose. The final three were Honolulu, San Diego and Seattle. I was ready if it was San Diego. I was ready if it was Seattle. And I was crossing my fingers that it wouldn't be Honolulu, because that kind of mobilization would have been very difficult.

When the decision was made in January 1999, I immediately got on the phone with activists I'd been working with for years, since NAFTA, the mother of all trade fights. I called some people in Seattle and said, 'OK, it's you — let's get ready; I'll be right out.' I hit the ground in Seattle and started preparing the infrastructure.

I was [traveling] back and forth to Seattle, and I had my team in D.C. taking responsibility for regions of the country.

That summer, the secretary of Commerce, Bill Daley, went out on a 'free-trade bus tour,' trying to extol and proclaim the benefits of free trade. He'd go to a town and go to a factory and do these standup events around the benefits of free trade. I was always there a couple of days in advance, and I'd organize the protests of those events, which allowed me to both dog Daley and at the same time do crowd building for Seattle."

On the Events of Nov. 30, 1999:

"We owned downtown Seattle. We owned it. It was ours. I see [1960s anti-war activist] Tom Hayden standing on a street corner. I said, 'How's this compare to Chicago in '68?' And he said, 'The difference, Mike, is that you're winning.' That's what I felt like — that we were totally winning something.

And the biggest serendipity was this: The Direct Action Network decided sometime back in August that Tuesday, Nov. 30, was going to be the day of the principal direct action.

The labor movement, meanwhile, decided that Tuesday the 30th was going to be the day of their big march. Neither was talking to the other, but they were both talking to me.

So the day reached its climax, in my mind, when the labor movement marched into downtown Seattle and saw what was going on. The marshals started to turn the march around and back to the Seattle Center. Many of the unionists did turn around, but many peeled off and joined us downtown on the streets. The alchemy of that moment — labor joining direct action in the streets — was exactly what needed to happen."

On tactics

"The whole issue of tactics is so thorny. I don't think that vandalism is an effective aspect of this movement. I am against this notion that we can destroy capitalism one window at a time. I don't think we win if we continue to go this direction with vandalism and fighting the police. And when the Black Bloc joins an already-arranged peaceful demonstration against an institution like the WTO, the media focus is suddenly directed, laserlike, on them and their tactics. There is the perpetual threat of our critique getting lost in the mainstream media because of the tactics of a small minority of people."

Seattle, not by the masses of people that the movement has put in the streets," says Randall Hayes, founder and president of the Rainforest Action Network, a San Francisco-based environmental group. "The behavior of the police comes back to the behavior of the police, and not so much to the movement."

Ronald M. McCarthy, a nationally recognized expert on crowd control and civil disturbances, strongly disputes Hayes' eyewitness account of what transpired in the streets of Seattle. McCarthy, a former Los Angeles police officer, now heads a law-enforcement consulting firm in San Clemente, Calif. The city of Seattle hired McCarthy to review the city's handling of the WTO conference

and the associated protests. The $98,000 report concludes that police displayed "exceptional restraint" in attempting to restore order. The ultimate responsibility for the chaos and property damage, the report states, rests with the protesters who came to Seattle to "shut down Seattle and the World Trade Organization by any means necessary." [21]

On media coverage:

"There are two questions about the media coverage. The first is whether our critique is getting out more. I think the mainstream print media are starting to look more closely at why we're out in the streets. *The Washington Post* and *New York Times* ran stories about [the G-8 protests in] Genoa that weren't derogatory, so it's improving in the context of the critique. However, I do not think that the media coverage is improving on the question of tactics. The media continue to talk about Seattle as though the protesters created a violent situation. That's not true. I was there — I know who initiated the violence, and it was the police. The Seattle Police Department launched this movement, from that perspective.

And the mainstream media continue to get it wrong, wrong, wrong, about how the so-called violence and mayhem of this movement got started. It started on the morning of Nov. 30, 1999, in downtown Seattle, when the police, overwhelmed by the numbers, unable to go about the choreography of arresting peaceful demonstrators, responded with non-lethal crowd-control measures.

And the story now should be, 'Why did the Italian police carry live ammunition on the streets of Genoa?' And why did they order 200 body bags? Where are those stories?"

On protesting at future economic summits:

"I think it's more likely that the meetings are going to stay away from us. The WTO going to Qatar for its next ministerial is all about getting away from places where protest is easy or freedom of speech is respected. The [now canceled] IMF/World Bank meetings in D.C. will probably be the last time these institutions meet with fanfare publicly in a place where freedom of assembly is respected. But irrespective of the debate on tactics, I think we're going to see more of a divergence within the movement. I think summit-stalking will be replaced by more work at the community and grass-roots levels, such

Grass-roots organizer Michael Dolan

AP Photo/Dave Martin

as targeting individual members of Congress and specific corporations."

On reforming the economic system:

"It will have to be radically reformed. I'm not an abolitionist in the sense that I'm opposed to a rules-based international system of commerce. The question for me is, 'Who writes the rules?' Are they to be written at the behest of the transnational corporations that profit from them? We want to change the way the rules of the global economy are made and democratize that process. That isn't a revolutionary position."

On using the Internet:

"I don't consider the Internet to be a particularly good organizing tool. It's really good at transferring information and data from autonomous data points, but it's not necessarily all that good for getting commitments. You just can't rely on commitments made digitally. Nevertheless, we totally wired it."

On the future of anti-globalization:

"Just look at the current 'fast-track' fight to see how far we've moved the ball down the field. Now there won't be a fast track that doesn't include labor rights, environmental standards and consumer protections written into the core text of trade agreements. The Jordan [trade] agreement is a baby-step forward, but it wouldn't have been possible without this movement being what it is.

Even the WTO and some of these other institutions are trying to increase their transparency levels; they're sucking up to the NGOs [non-governmental organizations] now. There is a greater public consciousness about the true costs of corporate globalization. We have a Republican president and a Republican House of Representatives who are still resisting what we consider to be an historical imperative to recognize and address the true costs of globalization. It hasn't been smooth sailing all along. But at the end of the day, the positives outweigh the negatives. So yes, we're totally winning."

"It took an event like the WTO in Seattle to show the rest of the country it's a whole new era of protest," McCarthy says. "We're seeing a level of violence [by protesters] that we haven't seen in the past."

McCarthy identified only two instances of improper police behavior: when an officer pepper-sprayed two people inside a car, and an officer who fired a non-lethal projectile point-blank into the chest of a retreating protester, then kicked him in the groin.

"That's all we saw on thousands of hours of videotape," McCarthy says. "If there was mass police misconduct, we would have seen it."

Nevertheless, people who spent time at protests say they've seen all kinds of police misconduct. James Lafferty, executive director of the Los Angeles chapter of the National Lawyers Guild, said LAPD officers "almost started a riot" in August when they stormed into about 9,000 people at an officially sanctioned protest concert outside the Democratic National Convention.

After about 60 black-garbed youths began hurling bottles and chunks of concrete over the security fence erected around the Staples Center, the site of the convention, police told the protesters they had 15 minutes to leave or they would be arrested. Minutes later, as they were exiting the fenced-in "protest pit," mounted officers charged into the crowd. They fired rubber bullets at the retreating protesters, who were stampeding toward the one exit that had not been sealed off. Truncheon-wielding police officers bludgeoned a number of protesters who were scrambling toward the bottlenecked exit.

"It was a huge overreaction," Lafferty said. "It was the most outrageous thing I have ever seen." [22]

Police Chief Bernard Parks said the crackdown was justified. "We feel very good about the way we handled it," Parks said. "We gave full warning early on that we were not going to tolerate people throwing objects either at demonstrators or at police." [23]

One of the most controversial police actions occurred in the early morning on July 22, at a school in Genoa. Ninety-three people were sleeping in the school after taking part in the massive protests at the G-8 summit. Without warning, about 70 Italian police officers smashed through the front door, dragged the activists from their beds and beat them brutally. Others were thrown down stairs, kicked in the teeth, and dragged around by their hair. Witnesses said the protesters were crouching on their hands and knees during the attack, their fingers raised in the universal sign of peace.

"The blows rained down one after another; all you could hear were the screams and the sick thuds of flesh being battered," said Sherman Sparks, a 23-year-old protester from Salem, Ore. "I saw no one put up resistance." [24]

Television images filmed a few hours after the raid showed pools of blood on the floor, blood-spattered walls and several teeth strewn about.

All of the protesters were arrested after they were beaten. Thirty-two were taken to jail, where many said they were abused further. Sixty-one were hospitalized, some with serious injuries. Roberto Papparo, head of the emergency department at Genoa's biggest hospital, said some of the protesters "wouldn't be alive anymore" if they had not received medical attention. [25]

Italian authorities initially justified the bloody raid by claiming that the school was harboring members of the Black Bloc. They later said they had been mistaken and conceded that most of the people in the school were non-violent demonstrators.

Miriam Heigl, a 25-year-old political science student from Munich, Germany, who was arrested but not injured in the mayhem, believes the crackdown was designed to send a message to the anti-globalization movement.

"We had this feeling that everything was completely arbitrary and that [the police] had lost their minds," Heigl said. "But now I see it was all done extremely professionally. They wanted to disorient and break us, as though they were dealing with a gang of hardened terrorists." [26] ■

BACKGROUND

Rise of IMF, World Bank

Today's globalization debate grew out of decisions made in the final months of World War II at a New Hampshire mountain resort called Bretton Woods. Representatives of 44 countries met to craft a plan for rebuilding the war-ravaged global economy. They created three new institutions that would exert great influ-

ence over international economic activity: the World Bank, IMF and General Agreement on Tariffs and Trade (GATT), which later evolved into the World Trade Organization.

Under what became known as the Bretton Woods plan, the World Bank would issue loans to bolster economic development in developing countries; the IMF would regulate and stabilize currency exchange rates; and GATT would establish ground rules governing international trade. In the 1970s, the IMF expanded its role and began extending short-term loans to countries with balance-of-payment problems. [27]

The loan programs supported major development projects throughout the Third World. But the loans — and the projects they funded — also ensnared many developing nations in financial quagmires that plague them to this day. Borrowing nations fell into financial troubles for a number of reasons. Corruption ran rampant in the first few decades of the bank and the fund: Frequently, loan funds were diverted from projects and kicked back to local officials. [28] Money was skimmed off to purchase luxury items for local elites.

But many Third-World governments simply made poor investment decisions. Frequently, they were pressured into investing in large-scale infrastructure items such as hydroelectric dams, which often cost borrowing nations more money than they earned. The civil unrest that resulted from infrastructure projects that forcibly relocated people from their land, for example, required many cash-strapped governments to bolster their military spending. [29]

Countries that fell behind on their loans often borrowed more money to tide them over. By the mid-1970s, many Third World governments were carrying enormous debts that they had no realistic hope of repaying. Beginning in the 1980s, the IMF and World Bank offered to renegotiate the terms of these debts if the debtor nations agreed to implement structural adjustment pro-

Chronology

1940s–1950s
After World War II, industrialized countries rebuild the international financial system.

July 1944
Delegates from 44 countries meet in Bretton Woods, N.H., to create World Bank, International Monetary Fund (IMF) and General Agreement on Tariffs and Trade, later the World Trade Organization (WTO).

1952
Belgium receives first IMF loan.

1980s *IMF and World Bank impose stricter conditions on loans to developing nations.*

March 25, 1980
World Bank approves its first structural adjustment program (SAP) loan to Turkey.

August 1982
IMF implements major structural adjustment programs in Mexico and several other countries that cannot service their foreign debts.

1990s *Global economy expands rapidly; Zapatista uprising in southern Mexico foreshadows rise of anti-globalization movement.*

Jan. 1, 1994
North American Free Trade Agreement (NAFTA) goes into effect, prompting Zapatista rebels in Chiapas to take up arms.

Jan. 1, 1995
WTO replaces GATT.

Nov. 29-Dec. 3, 1999
About 50,000 people protest WTO meeting in Seattle, energizing anti-globalization movement.

2000–Present
Anti-globalization protests erupt at international economic and political gatherings.

April 15–17, 2000
Some 20,000 demonstrators target the IMF and World Bank spring meetings in Washington, D.C.

July 31–Aug. 4, 2000
More than 5,000 people protest against economic globalization and other issues at Republican National Convention in Philadelphia.

Aug. 14–17, 2000
Demonstrators at Democratic National Convention in Los Angeles protest economic globalization.

Aug. 23, 2000
In answer to critics, IMF provides information about its activities.

Sept. 19–28, 2000
As many as 15,000 protesters besiege IMF/World Bank meeting in Prague, Czech Republic.

Jan. 20, 2001
Thousands protest the inauguration of President George W. Bush, a free-trade advocate.

March 7, 2001
IMF announces a review of its structural adjustment programs.

April 20–22, 2001
As many as 60,000 protesters descend on Quebec City, Canada, where world leaders are discussing the Free Trade Area of the Americas.

June 7, 2001
Thousands of teachers, state workers and students in Bogota, Colombia, protest IMF-mandated budget reforms.

June 14–16, 2001
About 25,000 anti-globalization protesters target European Union summit in Göteborg, Sweden.

June 24, 2001
As many as 50,000 people demonstrate against the World Bank in Barcelona, Spain, even though the meeting is canceled.

July 20–22, 2001
As many as 200,000 protest the Group of Eight meeting of leading industrialized countries in Genoa, Italy; police kill a 23-year-old protester.

Sept. 29–30, 2001
World Bank/IMF meetings planned for Washington, D.C., are postponed after terrorist attacks on World Trade Center and Pentagon. Up to 100,000 anti-globalization protesters had been expected.

Nov. 9–13, 2001
Protesters vow to target a WTO meeting to be held in Doha, Qatar, a country with little tolerance for political dissent.

June 26–28, 2002
Protesters vow to target the Group of Eight meeting to be held in Kananaskis, Alberta, a remote community in the Canadian Rockies.

grams. SAPs typically compelled debtor nations to implement sweeping changes in their economic and social policies so that they could make prompt and regular interest payments on their debts. SAPs also pressured debtor nations to reduce wages and subsidies and cut government spending in education, health care and other social programs. SAPs also forced debtor nations to develop export-oriented economies so that they were better able to service their debts.

In response, many debtor nations sold off their natural resources and agricultural commodities to global markets, which increased their dependency on imported goods and services. At the same time, at the recommendation of the bank and the fund, they privatized their public assets, lowered corporate taxes and removed foreign investment restrictions.

These initiatives greatly benefited multinational corporations, many of which took advantage of IMF/ World Bank policies and set up shop in debtor nations, where they quickly supplanted local businesses. Multinationals that put down roots in indebted nations also benefited from readily available supplies of cheap labor and, often, lax environmental standards. [30]

Anti-globalization activists, though, are not at all happy with the socioeconomic picture that's been created by the World Bank and IMF.

"These institutions have had over 50 years to prove themselves, and they've failed," says Kevin Danaher, co-founder and public education director of Global Exchange, a San Francisco human rights group. "There's more inequality and envi-

ronmental destruction now than there was when they started. They're helping multinational corporations and hurting people."

World Bank President James D. Wolfensohn, in a speech in the Czech Republic last September, conceded that the world is "scarred by inequality." But, he said, the World Bank and its sister organizations are fighting to ameliorate that condition.

"If we are serious about fighting inequity, we must . . . help poor people build their assets, including education,

Subcommander Marcos led the Zapatista National Liberation Army in opposing Mexico's support of the North American Free Trade Agreement (NAFTA) and its policies toward land reform.

Reuters/Henry Romero

health, and land," Wolfensohn said. "We have learned that economic growth is the most powerful force for sustained poverty reduction." [31]

Zapatistas vs. NAFTA

In 1993, six years before anti-globalization activists besieged the WTO in Seattle, lawmakers and lobby-

ists were wrangling over a controversial "free trade" proposal in the halls of Congress. The battle was over the North American Free Trade Agreement (NAFTA), which proposed to eliminate all tariffs and most other trade barriers between the United States, Canada and Mexico. NAFTA grew out of a 1988 free-trade agreement between the United States and Canada, two of the world's most advanced industrialized nations. [32]

Bringing Mexico into the deal was extremely controversial. As a developing country beset with widespread poverty, Mexico exercised little control over worker safety, product quality or environmental protection. Nevertheless, free-trade advocates argued that NAFTA would hasten Mexico's economic development and create American jobs, under the theory that demand for U.S. products would rise with Mexican consumers' disposable income.

Critics said that NAFTA would prompt U.S.-based businesses to shut down their factories and move south to Mexico, where they could take advantage of cheap, nonunionized labor and lax environmental regulations.

After heated debate, NAFTA supporters won. On Nov. 17, 1993, the House passed the measure, 234-200. Three days later, it cleared the Senate, 61-38. President Clinton signed the measure on Dec. 8; NAFTA went into effect a few weeks later, on Jan. 1, 1994.

In Washington, the NAFTA fight was over. But in the southern Mexican state of Chiapas, the battle — a real one — was just beginning. Hours after NAFTA went into effect, about 1,000 Chiapans took up arms against the Mexican government. The rebels seized four villages and attacked government soldiers with pistols, shotguns and automatic weap-

The Black Bloc Strikes Again

Anti-globalization protesters are largely non-violent, but they do have militant factions — including the high-profile radicals known as the "Black Bloc."

The loosely knit alliance of self-described anarchists, noted for their black baggy clothing and masks, evolved from the 1980s Autonomen movement in Germany, which squatted in abandoned buildings to protest for increased individual rights.

The Black Bloc first made headlines in the United States in 1991, when a cadre smashed windows at the World Bank in Washington, D.C., to protest the Persian Gulf War. After dropping out of sight for several years, the bloc returned to national headlines in the late 1990s on the coattails of the burgeoning anti-globalization movement.

Clusters of Black Bloc anarchists have taken part in every large anti-globalization protest since the 1999 World Trade Organization (WTO) conference in Seattle. About 50 black-garbed protesters used crowbars and sledgehammers to ransack Seattle businesses they viewed as symbols of global capitalism. The marauders infuriated many mainstream anti-globalization protesters, who felt that their substantive message — a critique of WTO policies — was being lost in the maelstrom of bonfires and broken glass.

Indeed, as the mayhem continued, many mainstream anti-globalization groups condemned violence and property destruction.

A day after the WTO conference ended, one Black Bloc faction justified its controversial tactics in a communiqué posted to the Internet. "We contend that property destruction is not a violent activity unless it destroys lives or causes pain in the process," the group known as the ACME Collective said. "By this definition, private property — especially corporate private property — is itself infinitely more violent than any action taken against it." [1]

The collective said it vandalized the Fidelity Investments building in downtown Seattle because the firm is a "major investor in Occidental Petroleum, the bane of the U'wa tribe in Colombia." Likewise, Old Navy, Banana Republic and

GAP outlets were sacked because they are "rapers of Northwest forest lands and sweatshop laborers," the group wrote. A McDonald's restaurant was hit, the group said, because the global burger baron is a "slave-wage fast-food peddler responsible for the destruction of tropical rainforests for grazing land and slaughter of animals." And Planet Hollywood was trashed "for being Planet Hollywood."

Black Bloc anarchists and mainstream anti-globalization protesters agree that multinational corporations have too much control over people's lives. But unlike the non-violent mainstream, Black Bloc loyalists maintain that capitalism is intrinsically repressive and that its negative effects cannot be mitigated.

John Zerzan, 57, a self-described anarchist writer from Eugene, Ore., became the public face of anarchism after the 1999 WTO protests. Zerzan faults the mainstream anti-globalization movement for simply "focusing on the latest policy wrinkle" while ignoring the systemic depravity of the modern capitalist system.

"[Mainstream anti-globalization activists] can fight the latest symptoms forever and not begin to scratch the surface of what's generating all of this horrible, pathological destruction that's taking place in every sphere and life zone on the planet," Zerzan says.

Zerzan considers property destruction as a legitimate tactic for bringing about social change. Indeed, he maintains that violence has played a requisite role in all successful revolutions and social movements — including those led by Mahatma Gandhi for independence in India and Martin Luther King Jr. for civil rights in the United States. [2] Still, Zerzan says that under ideal circumstances, the need for violence will be minimal.

"If enough people get involved, the police apparatus will become irrelevant," he says. "The state's powers of coercion are really very fragile."

Protesters block Pennsylvania Avenue, in Washington, D.C., during demonstrations in April 2000 designed to disrupt the annual meetings of the World Bank and International Monetary Fund.

AP Photo/Rick Bowmer

---

[1] The ACME Collective, "N30 Black Bloc Communiqué," Dec. 4, 1999.

[2] For a more detailed explanation of this theory, see, for example, Ward Churchill with Mike Ryan, *Pacifism as Pathology: Reflections on the Role of Armed Struggle in North America*, 1998.

ons. The Mexican government moved quickly to crush the uprising with thousands of soldiers backed by tanks and helicopter gunships.

More than 100 Indians, soldiers and local villagers were killed in the first few weeks of the insurrection. But the rebel movement managed to survive the government's initial counterattack. The rebels fled to the jungle highlands, where for the next seven years they waged a media-savvy campaign for indigenous rights.

The Indian rebels called themselves the Ejercito Zapatista de Liberacion Nacional, or the EZLN. The English-speaking media dubbed them the Zapatista National Liberation Army, or simply the "Zapatistas." The group was named after Emiliano Zapata, a popular hero of the 1910-1917 Mexican Revolution who defended peasants' rights to land seized from wealthy landowners. The EZLN rebels said they rose up in 1994 because NAFTA had gutted a key ideal of that revolution: communal land rights for Mexico's indigenous people.

"The Free Trade Agreement is the death certificate for the Indian people of Mexico, who are dispensable to the government of [then-Mexican President] Carlos Salinas de Gortari," the EZLN declared in a Jan. 1, 1994, statement faxed to the news media. "Today we rise up in arms against this death sentence."

The catalyst of the EZLN uprising was an amendment that Salinas and his legislative allies had made to the Mexican Constitution. The amendment was mandated by the NAFTA package that free-trade advocates had pushed through the U.S. Congress. It allowed Mexican peasants to sell commonly held farmland and to privatize collective holdings. The amendment essentially did away with the land-reform policy implemented after the Mexican Revolution, which gave all peasants the right to a piece of land. [33]

Free-trade advocates said the amendment was necessary to bring capitalism to the Mexican countryside. That it did. Poverty-strapped Indians invariably sold their small plots of land to agricultural conglomerates, which began planting corn, coffee and other crops on huge tracts of land, as cash-crop agriculture supplanted subsistence farming.

But the constitutional changes ushered in by NAFTA did little to benefit the thousands of Indians who were displaced from their lands. They identified strongly with the EZLN rebels, as did millions of sympathizers and globalization critics around the world. The rebels were led by the charismatic Subcom-mander Marcos. With their bandoleers of bullets and black ski masks, they were a huge hit with the media and took every opportunity to decry the scrapping of the nation's communal land-holdings policy.

Militarily, the Zapatistas were no match for the Mexican army. But cracking down on the rebels would have almost certainly damaged the image of the new, modern Mexico. Still, international investors hoping to take advantage of NAFTA wanted political stability — not armed rebels.

In 1996, a Mexican congressional committee drafted a bill that allowed indigenous groups to govern themselves at the local level. The accord also granted Mexico's 10 million Indians collective ownership of land and natural resources. But Ernesto Zedillo, who had succeeded Salinas as Mexico's president in August 1994, shelved the bill. Claiming they had been betrayed, the rebels halted all peace talks. Zedillo sent some 70,000 troops into Chiapas, where the atmosphere remained volatile for years.

In July 2000, Vicente Fox was elected president of Mexico. On Dec. 1, in his first official act, Fox submitted the original Indian-rights bill to the Mexican Congress, a gesture that thrilled the EZLN rebels. On Feb. 25, 2001, a delegation of 24 Zapatistas laid down their weapons and embarked on an 1,800-mile caravan to Mexico City, where they hoped to press government leaders to support the bill. On March 28, clad in colorful tribal dress, military fatigues and their trademark black ski masks, the outlaw rebels addressed the Mexican Congress. They decried centuries of ill treatment of the nation's indigenous peoples, who suffer disproportionately high levels of illiteracy, unemployment and malnutrition. And, notably, the rebels told the lawmakers that their military mission was over.

"Our warriors have done their job," said a Zapatista woman known as Commander Esther. "The person speaking to you is not the military leader of a rebel army, but the political leadership of a legitimate movement." [34]

But the EZLN rebels changed their tune after the Mexican Congress finished with the Indian rights bill, which went into effect on Aug. 15. The measure does institute a sweeping ban on discrimination, and it guarantees specific indigenous rights. But lawmakers stripped the bill of many of its original provisions, including those pertaining to Indian autonomy over land and natural resources. In a statement faxed to the media, the EZLN denounced the measure as "illegitimate, reactionary, and anti-democratic," adding that it could open the door to new violence.

Others argued that the original bill would have compromised Mexican sovereignty and unity.

"It was a recipe for the Balkani-zation of the country," said George Grayson, a foreign affairs expert at the College of William and Mary in Williamsburg, Va. [35]

CURRENT SITUATION

New Demands

T hroughout the summer, the anti-globalization movement geared

Reality According to www.indymedia.org

The anti-globalization revolution will be televised — but not just from the usual vantage point of corporate-owned media conglomerates. That's the idea behind the Independent Media Center (IMC), a volunteer network of newsgathering outlets dedicated to counteracting the mainstream media's allegedly "distorted" coverage of the movement and other progressive causes.

The first IMC was established in 1999 in Seattle by several alternative media organizations and a small cadre of technologically talented political activists. Operating out of a rented storefront equipped with two-dozen borrowed computers, the center generated alternative news coverage of the protests against the World Trade Organization (WTO).

Some 400 volunteers worked out of the Seattle IMC, posting up-to-the-minute reports, photographs and video footage of the WTO protests on the center's Web site. IMC "tech geeks" culled the best clips from each day's video footage to produce segments that were uplinked to satellites for use by public-access television stations across the U.S. In addition, the center produced its own Web-based newspaper, the *Blind Spot*.

Using their own video cameras, IMC reporters captured startling images of the police/protester clashes that erupted throughout downtown Seattle. But the volunteer journalists also filed numerous stories explaining the protesters' reasons for being in the streets in the first place. Eric Galatas, a Denver resident who played a key role in establishing the Seattle IMC, says the corporate-owned mass media could not be trusted to convey that message.

"We knew that the critics of corporate globalization would get very little information through the corporate-owned media filters that would be present in Seattle, and we felt that our job was to help those voices be heard," Galatas says.

Anyone with a story to tell can publish it on the IMC's Web-based "news wire." The IMC operates on an "open publishing" principle, which allows contributors to post text files, photographs, audio segments and video footage to the news wire without editing. While designed to be an open forum, the newswire is monitored by IMC volunteers, who occasionally remove items deemed to be "inappropriate" or "obviously false or libelous."

Galatas acknowledges that the IMC supports the causes espoused by anti-globalization protesters and other social activists. But that shouldn't diminish the value of the information IMC disseminates, he says.

"We encourage people to challenge everything — question what we say, question what the corporate media says, because everybody has an angle," Galatas says. "We don't believe that there is any such thing as true objectivity. Everybody reports from a point of view — we're just pretty up front about what that point of view is."

The public should question the impartiality of the IMC's coverage, says Peter Hart, an analyst with Fairness & Accuracy in Reporting (FAIR), a left-leaning media watchdog group based in New York City. But the mainstream media should be subjected to that same level of scrutiny, Hart says.

"Sometimes the [IMC's] content can be less accurate," Hart says. "But keep in mind that there are stories floated in the mainstream media that are totally bogus. There are going to be mistakes made everywhere."

Hart says the IMC has added "a new dimension to journalism," giving the public a chance to view the anti-globalization movement from a "different perspective."

The IMC has come a long way since its humble beginnings in Seattle two years ago. IMCs are now operating in more than 50 locations around the world, including Washington, D.C., London, Prague, Mexico City and Montreal. Galatas estimates that the IMC's coverage of the Democratic and Republican conventions last summer reached at least 30 million households.

Adam Stenftenagel, a freelance Web developer who provides technical support for the IMC in Boulder, Colo., expects that the IMC phenomenon will continue to grow.

"We've gone from one little IMC to over 50 in less than two years," Stenftenagel says. "Eventually we'll be competing on a real level with the mass media."

---

up for another massive protest against the IMF and World Bank during their scheduled annual meetings in Washington, D.C., in September. The Mobilization for Global Justice, which was helping to plan the demonstrations, in August submitted four demands to the two financial institutions. The group demanded that the bank and the IMF open all meetings to the media and the public; cancel all debts owed by impoverished nations; end all structural adjustment programs that they say hinder people's access to food, health care and education; and stop funding socially and environmentally destructive projects, such as oil, gas and mining initiatives.

The anti-globalization coalition 50 Years is Enough went even further. It called for the two institutions to pay reparations to people allegedly harmed by SAPs and large infrastructure projects that have damaged communities and the environment, such as large dams.

The bank and the fund say the groups' demands mischaracterize the work done by their institutions. IMF spokesman William Murray notes that the fund provides billions in debt relief to poor countries and allows credentialed journalists and representatives of NGOs to attend some of its meetings. Moreover, the IMF has never taken a stand against countries spending money on health care and other social services, Murray added.

"I don't think it's in any way correct to characterize our policies as anti-poor," says Caroline Anstey, director of media relations for the World Bank, adding that the bank is willing to enter into a dialogue with its critics — but only those who renounce violent tactics.

Nevertheless, Adam Eidinger, a movement organizer from Washington, D.C., denies that violence had been planned for the capital. "We're preparing for a peaceful protest," he says. "The police are preparing for a violent protest."

The protesters describe President Bush as "the face of corporate globalization" on Beatbackbush.org. a Web site that circulates information about the IMF/World Bank protest in Washington. The demonstrators had planned to surround the White House on Sept. 29 and then to hold a massive downtown rally the next day.

D.C. police were bracing for up to 100,000 protesters — a turnout that would rival the demonstrations that shook the nation's capital during the Vietnam War. Washington Mayor Anthony A. Williams outlined that scenario in an Aug. 6 letter to President Bush seeking funding to handle the protests.

"Intelligence information indicates that the protests and demonstrations surrounding this IMF/World Bank meeting will be of an intensity, scope and magnitude that we have never seen in this city," Williams wrote. "If the [financial] resources cannot be identified in very short order, the [law enforcement] agencies will not be able to protect our city and insure the integrity of these meetings." [36]

D.C. officials asked Bush for $29 million for security. The administration offered $16 million. The IMF and World Bank balked at the District's request to cover all or part of the $13 million shortfall.

"We've always taken the position that it's the responsibility of the host gov-

Police tactics were criticized by protesters as too heavy-handed at the anti-globalization demonstrations at the World Trade Organization meeting in Seattle, Wash., in November 1999. More than 500 people were arrested or detained, but the charges were dropped against most. Downtown businesses sustained more than $2.5 million in property damage.

AP Photo/Beth A. Keiser

ernment to provide a secure working environment," said the IMF's Murray. [37]

D.C. Police Chief Charles Ramsey had planned to bring in some 3,600 officers from other cities, doubling the size of the D.C. police force. In addition, about 1,000 federal law-enforcement personnel from the FBI, Secret Service and other groups were to be deployed.

The $29 million security budget did not include a $2 million outlay for a controversial, nine-foot-high hurricane fence that would have cordoned off 220 acres of downtown Washington. The fence was to stretch for two-and-a-half miles around the IMF, World Bank and the White House. It would have also corraled parts of nearby George Washington University (GWU), four apartment buildings, a church and dozens of stores, restaurants and offices. [38]

On Aug. 20, lawyers for anti-global-ization groups and individuals asked a federal court to block the fence, arguing that that walling off a large section of the city would infringe on protesters' First Amendment rights.

"The police are violating our rights when they function as the armed protectors of the IMF, the World Bank and the right-wing Bush administration," says Larry Holmes, co-director of the New York City–based International Action Center, a protest group. "It is illegal to turn vast parts of Washington into the private property of the IMF and World Bank delegates."

In another controversial move, D.C. police pressured GWU to close its Foggy Bottom campus during the protests. Even though the meetings were canceled, the university still plans to force nearly 5,400 students to move out of university residence halls for several days.

"[Students] continue to have a right to be involved in activities around the World Bank," said Terrance W. Gainer, executive assistant police chief. "They just won't be able to do it from the university." [39]

Protests in Colombia

Massive protests erupted in Colombia and Argentina last summer when the two Latin American nations agreed to implement austerity programs recommended by the IMF. Like many anti-globalization activists, Kevin Danaher of Global Exchange was not surprised by the backlash.

"The IMF is basically telling [Colombia and Argentina] to sacrifice

Main Street for Wall Street," he says. "That's great for the elites who live in gated mansions and ride around in limos, but for the majority of the people, [the austerity programs] will make things worse."

In Colombia, beginning in May, more than 300,000 unionized teachers and at least 125,000 health-care workers went on strike or participated in work slow-downs to protest an IMF-mandated austerity plan that caps federal outlays to states and municipalities. The strikers said the plan would inevitably lead to cutbacks for schools and hospitals, because it leaves spending priorities up to the states. Tens of thousands of Colombians took to the streets in protest when the plan was enacted in June. The government responded by deploying riot police and armored vehicles with water cannon to Bogota and other cities. [40]

A similar story played out in Argentina, which agreed to implement an IMF-backed austerity measure in July so that it would not default on its existing IMF loans. The plan, which mandates deep cuts in workers' salaries and retirees' pensions, sparked strikes and large protests. Angry government workers clashed with police in several cities. On July 31, a protester was killed and several were injured in skirmishes in the interior cities of Rosario and Cordoba.

Many economists described the austerity program as a vital step in restoring investor confidence in Argentina, which is in a deep recession.

"Argentina now is in the right balance," said Frances Freisinger, a specialist on Latin America at Merrill Lynch. "The government is taking some tough measures, but you need a powerful and positive confidence shock to turn this [economic crisis] around." [41]

China to Enter WTO

A nti-globalization activists suffered a setback on Sept. 17, when negotiators agreed to allow China into the WTO. Its entry had been stalled since 1986 because of concerns about the country's human-rights record and fears that China would use its vast labor pool to undercut competitors.

In exchange for WTO membership, China committed to opening and liberalizing its regime, including agreeing not to use price controls to protect its domestic industries or service providers. It will also allow foreign corporations to establish venture-capital enterprises in certain cities. In return, the agreement gives China more chances than it has ever had to capture foreign markets.

U.S. Trade Representative Robert B. Zoellick hailed China's entry into the WTO, saying, "China has made a firm commitment to the rest of the world to open its markets and adhere to international, market-based rules, which will help American workers, consumers, farmers and exporters."

Critics of globalization denounced the China/WTO deal. "We have a lot of concerns about China's human-rights and worker's-rights policies, and we feel that China's membership in the WTO will not address those very real concerns," says Thea Lee, chief international economist at the AFL-CIO, which represents 13 million American workers. "They haven't really made any commitments to human rights or worker's rights as a part of this deal."

The WTO will formally adopt the 1,000-page China agreement at its meeting in Doha, Qatar, in November. China's own legislature will then have to approve the deal. ■

OUTLOOK

New Strategy

T he anti-globalization movement soon may have to give up its massive protests at international economic summits. Even before the Sept. 11 terrorist attacks in New York and Washington, D.C., global financial institutions had begun to schedule their meetings in out-of-the-way venues not conducive to large-scale demonstrations. The WTO, for example, is slated to hold its next ministerial conference in Qatar, an Islamic monarchy in the Persian Gulf that has exhibited little tolerance for dissent. But even that meeting may be postponed or canceled due to post-attack security concerns.

Faced with logistical challenges, anti-globalization groups are turning their attention from summit-hopping to legislative battles on Capitol Hill. This fall, many movement organizers plan to take on a globalization-friendly measure known as trade promotion authority (TPA). Also known as "fast track," TPA requires Congress to vote on trade agreements negotiated by the executive branch within a specified number of days, with limited debate, and with no amendments allowed. Free-trade advocates say fast track is needed to effectively negotiate trade agreements, because other nations are frequently reluctant to sign pacts that could be significantly altered by Congress.

"It is not in our interest to have complicated negotiations with a [potential trading partner] and then have to follow it up with 535 negotiations at home," said William M. Daley, secretary of Commerce during the Clinton administration, referring to the number of House and Senate members. [42]

U.S. presidents have not had fast-track authority since 1994. Since then, the United States' ability to negotiate trade pacts has decreased significantly. The Clinton administration and free-trade advocates in Congress tried to bring fast track back in 1997 and 1998, but failed. Those efforts were blocked by critics — mostly Democrats — who wanted future trade agreements to have built-in protections for labor rights and the environment.

A similar battle is now under way in Washington. President Bush wants fast-track authority to negotiate a trade agreement known as Free Trade Area of the Americas (FTAA), which would liberalize trade in 34 countries throughout the Western Hemisphere. Enacting fast track also would help to launch a new round of trade talks at the upcoming WTO summit in Qatar, say administration officials and free-trade advocates in Congress.

"President Bush needs the authority to negotiate trade deals on America's behalf — to get us back into the trade arena," says Rep. Bill Thomas, R-Calif., chairman of the House Ways and Means Committee. "We're committed to giving him that authority." [43]

That may not be easy. House Republicans postponed a vote on fast track in August because they did not have enough Democratic votes to pass the measure. Rep. Sander Levin, D-Mich., says that Republicans are "headed for a dead end" on fast track unless they put guarantees for workers' rights and the environment into their legislation.

"You can't have expanded trade without dealing with the expanding issues of trade," Levin said. [44]

House Republicans are drafting a compromise bill that they hope several dozen Democrats will support. A vote could come this fall.

"The minute we have the votes we'll be on the floor," said Rep. Dick Armey, R-Texas, the House majority leader. [45]

Mike Dolan, an organizer with Public Citizen's Global Trade Watch, concedes that Congress is likely to enact a fast-track measure before year's end, but he predicts that free-trade supporters will not get everything they want.

"No fast track will pass that doesn't include labor and environmental standards," Dolan says. "The current fast-track fight shows how far we've

moved the ball down the field."

Indeed, Dolan says, the movement also has pushed the WTO, the World bank and the IMF to institute significant reforms, though he says they still have a long way to go. In early September, for example, the bank ended the secrecy surrounding some of its key decisions and operations. Under a new policy, the bank will publish drafts of its "poverty-reduction strategy papers," which outline plans to promote economic growth in developing countries.

Likewise, the IMF is reviewing the conditions — or the structural adjustment programs — that it attaches to its loans. Moreover, for the first time, the IMF has agreed to consider outsiders' views when devising economic-austerity programs.

Among the most significant bank reforms is the Heavily Indebted Poor Countries Initiative — HIPC. Launched in 1996 in response to pressure from anti-globalization groups, HIPC provides debt relief to 23 of the world's poorest, most indebted countries — projected to amount to $34 billion over time. According to bank officials, the HIPC initiative, along with other debt-relief programs, will cut the external debt in these countries by more than 60 percent and enable them to devote more of their resources to education, health and social-welfare programs.

Critics say the HIPC initiative doesn't go far enough. Most favor 100 percent debt cancellation — something the bank has thus far been unwilling to do. Critics also want the initiative to be decoupled from the economic-austerity programs forced on poor countries by the IMF. Until such programs are terminated, critics say poor countries will continue to be de facto colonies of rich nations.

With such changes being made, Dolan has no doubts that the movement is "winning" the fight it picked with global capitalism.

"There is a greater public consciousness about the true costs of corporate globalization now, Dolan

says. "We have moved the goalposts, and the debate on globalization has been forever changed." ∎

Notes

[1] For background, see Mary H. Cooper, "World Trade," *The CQ Researcher*, June 9, 2000, pp. 497-520.

[2] For background, see Mary H. Cooper, "U.S. Trade Policy," *The CQ Researcher*, Jan. 29, 1993, pp. 73-96.

[3] Stephen Dunphy, "Talks Collapse; Meeting Ends — Group Will Leave Here Without an Agreement," *The Seattle Times*, Dec. 4, 1999.

[4] For background, see Mary H. Cooper, "International Monetary Fund," *The CQ Researcher*, Jan. 29, 1999, pp. 65-88.

[5] See, for example, David Dollar and Aart Kraay, "Trade, Growth and Poverty," World Bank Working Paper No. 2615, June 2001.

[6] For background, see Brian Hansen, "Children in Crisis," *The CQ Researcher*, Aug. 31, 2001.

[7] John Vidal, "This Movement is Unstoppable," *The Guardian*, July 23, 2001.

[8] Graham spoke at a debate on globalization at the Council on Foreign Relations, Washington, D.C., Feb. 13, 2001.

[9] For background, see Kenneth Jost, "Labor Movement's Future," *The CQ Researcher*, June 28, 1996, pp. 553-576.

[10] For background, see Charles S. Clark, "Child Labor and Sweatshops," *The CQ Researcher*, Aug. 16, 1996, pp. 721-744, David Hosansky, "Saving the Rain Forests," *The CQ Researcher*, June 11, 1999, pp. 512-535, and Mary H. Cooper, "Setting Environmental Priorities," *The CQ Researcher*, May 21, 1999, pp. 432-455.

[11] William Drozdiak and Steven Pearlstein, "Protesters Block IMF, World Bank Meeting in Prague," *The Washington Post*, Sept. 27, 2000.

[12] World Trade Organization, "Seattle: What's at Stake," 1999.

[13] World Bank, "Assessing Globalization," briefing paper, April 2000.

[14] Richard Barnet and John Cavanagh, "Electronic Money and the Casino Economy," in Jerry Mander and Edward Goldsmith, eds., The Case Against the Global Economy (1996), pp. 360-373.

[15] Dollar and Kraay, *op. cit.*

[16] Testimony before Senate Committee on Finance, Feb. 27, 2001.

[17] Statistics in this section from World Bank, "World Development Indicators 2001," April 2001.

At Issue:

Should the IMF and World Bank cancel all the debts of poor countries?

WORLD DEVELOPMENT MOVEMENT
WWW.WDM.ORG.UK

FROM "DEBT RELIEF: FROM FANFARE TO FATIGUE: ARE ALL THE G8 LEADERS TURNING THEIR BACKS ON DEBT RELIEF?" SEPTEMBER 2001

*d*ebt relief is a vital component in achieving poverty reduction for the world's poorest countries. The human cost in terms of insufficient and delayed debt relief is huge, with crucial resources still being diverted from health and education. Some African countries are repaying debts of $1.4 billion a year — money they desperately need for basic prevention and care to tackle HIV and AIDS.

The amounts of debt that have already been written off are limited, and are clearly not enough if the cost of poverty reduction is taken into account. The Highly Indebted Poor Countries (HIPC) Initiative has so far delivered less relief than expected, and certainly falls far short of offering a real exit from the debt crisis. On average, the 23 HIPCs have only had their debt-service payments reduced by 27 per cent. These countries still spend an average of 5.9 per cent of their gross national product on debt servicing, which is, on average, more than they spend on health and education combined.

Meanwhile, debt relief is still conditional on harsh economic reforms, which have been shown to do little to alleviate poverty and which may worsen it in some cases. A World Bank report shows that between 1981 and 1997, human well being decreased in 28 countries implementing IMF prescriptions. In over half of these countries, people experienced income stagnation, rising poverty and/or falling life expectancy.

Throughout the lifetime of the HIPC Initiative, donors have focused on how much debt relief they can afford to give, rather than how much the poorest countries need. In this context, it is worth remembering that the financial assets of the industrialized countries of the [Organization for Economic Cooperation and Development] are estimated at around $53 trillion. The United States budget surplus in 2001 is projected to be around $265 billion. Meanwhile, the entire debt of the 52 countries most in need could be wiped out for only $71 billion.

It is not the lack of resources that is the problem. Ultimately, eradicating poverty comes down to political will. Calls to extend debt relief to include 100 per cent cancellation of debt owed by HIPCs to the World Bank and IMF have been met with stonewalling explanations of the cost. Yet an independent report has shown just how affordable such a scheme would be.

INTERNATIONAL MONETARY FUND AND WORLD BANK

FROM A JOINT POLICY STATEMENT, JULY 2001

*i*n 1999, we committed ourselves to "deeper, broader and faster" debt relief to every eligible country that could translate the resources into better prospects for its poor. By the end of June 2001, relief was flowing to 23 countries, 19 of them in Africa, for debt-service relief amounting to some $34 billion. And we are committed to helping the remaining [heavily indebted poor countries, or HIPICs] access debt relief under the HIPIC Initiative.

Some argue that the further reduction of debt service obligations would allow HIPICs to make more poverty-related investments. But the HIPC Initiative is already changing the picture. So far, after debt relief, social expenditures in the 23 HIPCs are projected to rise by an average of $1.7 billion per year during 2001-2002. Most of these resources will be directed toward health, education, HIV/AIDS programs, basic infrastructure and governance reform. And contrary to the statements of some debt campaigners, HIPCs will spend on average much more — not less — on priority social investments than on debt service.

The debt reduction under the HIPC Initiative should be seen as a one-time action, the first step toward enabling the HIPCs to stand on their own feet. . . .

Of course, good results from borrowing were not seen everywhere. Some countries, for many different reasons, have not experienced significant gains. In HIPCs, unsustainable debt is a result. The international community has a collective obligation to address this problem. The HIPC Initiative is doing this. But we must also be there to support the future development needs for all countries. That is why the Initiative is focused specifically on the most highly indebted poor countries. Total debt cancellation for those countries alone would come at the expense of other borrowing countries. Those who call for 100 percent cancellation for the HIPCs alone must recognize that this would be inequitable for other poor countries.

Supporters of 100 percent debt cancellation must be honest about the costs. The total public external debt for low-income countries stands at some $460 billion. HIPCs and other poor countries will rely on external financing for their development needs long into the future. A growing portion of this need is being met by bilateral and multilateral agencies on concessional terms. Total cancellation could imperil these funds. It would also undermine the confidence of investors whose funds are vital for the long-term development of the low-income countries.

[18] Testimony before House Subcommittee on Domestic and International Monetary Policy, April 25, 2001.

[19] Press briefing, IMF headquarters, Washington, D.C., Aug. 30, 2001.

[20] Press conference, Genoa, Italy, July 27, 2001.

[21] R.M. McCarthy & Associates, "An Independent Review of the World Trade Organization Conference Disruptions in Seattle, Washington, Nov. 29-Dec. 3, 1999," July 2000.

[22] Arthur Spiegelman, "L.A. Police Defend Swift Crackdown on Protest," Reuters, Aug. 15, 2000.

[23] Ibid.

[24] Alice Tallmadge, "Protesters Give Account of Police Raid at G-8 Summit," *The Portland Oregonian*, July 31, 2001.

[25] Yaroslav Trofimov and Ian Johnson, "G-8 Protesters Describe Police Attack on Group in a School," *The Wall Street Journal*, Aug. 6, 2001.

[26] Ibid.

[27] Cooper, "International Monetary Fund" *op. cit.*

[28] See, for example, Graham Hancock, *Lords of Poverty: The Power, Prestige, and Corruption of the International Aid Business* (1989).

[29] For background, see, for example, Milton J. Esman and Ronald J. Herring, eds., *Carrots, Sticks, and Ethnic Conflict: Rethinking Development Assistance* (2001).

[30] For background, see, for example, Walden Bello, in Mander and Goldsmith, *op. cit.*

[31] Address to IMF/World Bank Group Board of Governors, Prague, Czech Republic, Sept. 26, 2000.

[32] For background, see Mary H. Cooper, "Rethinking NAFTA," *The CQ Researcher*, June 7, 1996, pp. 481-504.

[33] For background, see, for example, George Collier, *Basta! Land and the Zapatista Rebellion in Chiapa* (1994).

[34] Niko Price, "Zapatista Rebels Speak in Mexico's Congress," The Associated Press, March 29, 2001.

[35] Traci Carl, "Indian Rights Law Takes Effect in Mexico, Despite Opposition," The Associated Press, Aug. 15, 2001.

[36] Cited by Arthur Santana, "D.C. Police Brace for Next Month's IMF Protests," *The Washington Post*, Aug. 17, 2001.

FOR MORE INFORMATION

Bretton Woods Committee, 1990 M St., N.W., Suite 450, Washington, D.C. 20036; (202) 331-1616; www.brettonwoods.org. A bipartisan group dedicated to increasing public understanding of international financial and development issues and the role of the World Bank, IMF and WTO. Members include industry and financial leaders, economists, university leaders and former government officials.

50 Years is Enough Network, 3628 12th St., N.E. Washington, D.C. 20017; (202) 463-2265; www.50years.org. Founded on the 50th anniversary of the World Bank and International Monetary Fund, the coalition of more than 200 anti-globalization groups is dedicated to reforming the policies and practices of the two international financial institutions.

Global Exchange, 2017 Mission St., Suite 303, San Francisco, Calif. 94110; (415) 255-7296; www.globalexchange.org. A central pillar of the anti-globalization movement, Global Exchange is dedicated to promoting environmental, political and social justice around the world.

Global Trade Watch, 215 Pennsylvania Ave., S.E., Washington, D.C. 20003; (202) 546-4996. www.tradewatch.org. A division of Public Citizen, GTW was instrumental in derailing the "fast-track" trade negotiating initiative in the 1990s and in orchestrating the protests in Seattle.

Institute for International Economics, 1750 Massachusetts Ave., N.W., Washington, D.C. 20036; (202) 328-9000; www.iie.com. A pro-globalization research institution devoted to the study of global macroeconomic issues, investment and trade. IIE has contributed to the development of the WTO, NAFTA and other initiatives.

International Forum on Globalization, 1009 General Kennedy Ave., Suite 2, San Francisco, Calif. 94129; (415) 561-7650; www.ifg.org. A coalition of non-governmental organizations that educates activists, policymakers and the media about the effects of economic globalization.

Ruckus Society, 4131 Shafter Ave., Suite 9, Oakland, Calif. 94609; (510) 595-3442; www.ruckus.org. Teaches non-violent, civil-disobedience skills to environmental and human rights organizations and helps other groups carry out "direct-action" protests.

[37] Spencer S. Hsu and Manny Fernandez, "D.C. to Ask World Bank and IMF to Share Costs," *The Washington Post*, Aug. 21, 2001.

[38] For more about fences at anti-globalization protests, see David Montgomery, "Global Economy's New Guardian," *The Washington Post*, Aug. 30, 2001.

[39] Amy Argetsinger, "GW to Shut Down During IMF Protests," *The Washington Post*, Sept. 7, 2001.

[40] The Associated Press, "Colombia Hit by Huge Protests," June 8, 2001.

[41] Thomas Catan, "Protests Greet Argentine Austerity Bill," *The Financial Times*, Aug. 1, 2001.

[42] Testimony before Senate Finance Committee, Feb. 27, 2001.

[43] Press release, June 13, 2001.

[44] Jim Abrams, "House Republicans Moving Ahead on Trade Bill," The Associated Press, June 13, 2001.

[45] Ibid.

Bibliography

Selected Sources Used

Books

Burtless, Gary, Robert Z. Lawrence, Robert E. Litan and Robert J. Shapiro, *Globaphobia: Confronting Fears About Open Trade*, Brookings Institution, Progressive Policy Institute and Twentieth Century Fund, 1998.

The authors conclude that liberalized trade and investment policies offer more benefits than costs over the long run.

Collier, George, *Basta! Land and the Zapatista Rebellion in Chiapas*, Institute for Food and Development Policy, 1994.

Collier examines why indigenous people in southern Mexico took up arms against the government after enactment of the North American Free Trade Agreement.

Friedman, Thomas L., *The Lexus and the Olive Tree: Understanding Globalization*, Farrar Straus Giroux, 1999.

The foreign-affairs columnist for *The New York Times*, is an unabashed supporter of the new global economy, symbolized by the Lexus. He also recognizes how globalization threatens local communities and culture — the olive tree.

Greider, William, *One World, Ready or Not: The Manic Logic of Global Capitalism*, Touchstone Books, 1998.

Greider argues that a number of reforms are needed to head off an international economic and social crisis.

Korten, David, *When Corporations Rule the World*, Kumarian Press, 1995.

A former Harvard Business School professor documents the devastating human and environmental consequences resulting from corporations' quest for short-term financial gain.

Mander, Jerry, and Edward Goldsmith (eds), *The Case Against the Global Economy: And For a Turn Toward the Local*, Sierra Club Books, 1996.

Essays by critics of globalization including Vandana Shiva, Ralph Nader and Herman E. Daly suggest possibilities for creating a more just and democratic future.

Wallach, Lori, and Michelle Sforza, *Whose Trade Organization? Corporate Globalization and the Erosion of Democracy*, Public Citizen, 1999.

This critique of the World Trade Organization (WTO) examines its negative impact on the environment, labor rights and economic development in the Third World.

Articles

Anderson, Sarah, "Revelry in Quebec," *The Progressive*, June 1, 2001.

A firsthand account of the protests at the third Summit of the Americas.

Cooper, Mary H., "World Trade," *The CQ Researcher*, June 9, 2000, pp. 497-520.

Analyzes the effects of globalization on labor rights and the environment following the Seattle protests.

Dickey, Christopher, Rod Nordland and Martha Brant, "First Blood: Death and Violence in Genoa May Mark a Permanent Split in the Ranks of the Anti-Globalization Movement," *Newsweek International*, July 30, 2001.

Analyzes how a protester's death at the Summit of Eight (G-8) meeting in Genoa, Italy, may affect the cohesiveness of the anti-globalization movement.

Patterson, Wendy, "Masked Rebels Grab Spotlight in Mexico's Congress," *The Christian Science Monitor*, March 30, 2001.

An overview of the Zapatista rebel group, which made an historic appearance before the Mexican Congress to plead for the passage of an Indian-rights bill.

Stiglitz, Joseph, "What I Learned at the World Economic Crisis," *The New Republic*, April 17, 2000.

A former World Bank economist says globalization protesters are largely correct in their criticism of the IMF.

Reports and Studies

American Civil Liberties Union, "Out of Control: Seattle's Flawed Response to Protests Against the World Trade Organization," July 2000.

The ACLU concludes that Seattle police committed "outright assaults" on citizens.

Dollar, David, and Aart Kraay, "Trade, Growth and Poverty," World Bank Working Paper No. 2615, June 2001.

The authors conclude that globalization leads to faster growth and poverty reduction in poor countries.

Friends of the Earth, "The IMF: Selling the Environment Short," March 2000.

This report criticizes IMF policies for accelerating environmental damage in borrowing countries.

R. M. McCarthy & Associates, "An Independent Review of the World Trade Organization Conference Disruptions in Seattle, Washington," July 2000.

A former Los Angeles Police Department officer concludes that police acted properly in quelling the 1999 WTO protests.